Early Childhood
Education
Rediscovered

Readings

Early Childhood Education Rediscovered

Readings

Edited by **JOE L. FROST**

The University of Texas at Austin

HOLT, RINEHART and WINSTON, INC.
New York Chicago San Francisco Atlanta Dallas
Montreal Toronto London

To my Mother and Father

VERMONT COLLEGE
MONTPELIER, VERMONT

Preface

The rediscovery of early childhood education has roughly paralleled recent developments arising from massive federal support to the nation's schools. A great deal of this support continues to be directed toward compensatory programming for the disadvantaged child. And it is precisely this focus—the comprehensive reexamination of the teaching-learning process for disadvantaged children—that has resulted in the recognition of certain research and experimental efforts which point to early childhood as a period of critical importance in the development of humans toward intellectual self-sufficiency.

Educators, psychologists, and others involved in federally sponsored programs have consistently found that the effects of early deprivation are relatively permanent; that educational programming for the child at the elementary school level is often too late; that by age six the harm has been done. Although enriched elementary school programs have produced significant gains for disadvantaged children, to date no large-scale, interventional elementary school project has produced wide-range, systematic success in achieving academic equality for disadvantaged children.

As a result, the following alternatives appear in order. We can (1) start earlier, (2) focus upon innovative sets of educative assumptions for the disadvantaged, or (3) set aside the goal of "catching up" academically.

The first and second alternatives may prove to be essential; few are seriously considering the third alternative. Unquestionably, the task of "catching up" at age five or six is extremely complicated. For progress during the elementary school years must be approximately one-third to one-half greater than for "average" children (disadvantaged children are one to three years behind when they arrive at school). The intellectual gap between the advantaged and the disadvantaged broadens with each passing year. "Catching up" appears to require some kind of acceleration. Acceleration may result in undesirable emotional and social consequences, though the possibility exists that rapid intellectual growth accompanied by the development of literacy may create its own rewards in social and emotional development. For the cognitively restricted four- or five-year-old we seem to have no reasonable alternative but to proceed to experiment with imaginative programs for cognitive stimulation. No thinking educator is willing to sacrifice the child's personality structure to cognitive goals. Both are mutually related: one without the other is indefensible.

Preschools are *nice* for all children but *essential* for the disadvantaged.

Although evidence supporting preschools for all children is largely speculative and controversial in nature, most educators and child development specialists tend to agree that few three-, four-, and five-year-olds gain the essential ingredients for optimum development from the home environment alone. The cumulative evidence supporting preschools for the disadvantaged is largely unequivocal. Examination of such evidence suggests programming elements for *all* children.

The same factors that have provided the framework for research efforts in the rediscovery of early childhood education form the rationale for the development of this book. Content can be attributed in part to several factors that have heralded the rediscovery:

1. Research with animals and humans demonstrating pronounced effects of environmental stimulation during infancy and early childhood on development and school achievement.

2. Longitudinal growth studies identifying the early years as the period of most rapid growth in human characteristics and the most susceptible period for learning or nonlearning through experiential stimulation or deprivation.

3. The movement from a stimulus-response, innately fixed, view of intelligence to a perceptual, transactional theory of learning viewing potential and intelligence as modifiable by experience.

4. The alleged success of the Montessori approach in effecting cognitive development in young children.

5. The developmental studies of young children by the Swiss psychologist, Jean Piaget.

6. The establishment of Operation Head Start as the most promising approach of the antipoverty war.

7. The heartening experience of educators, child development specialists, parents, and others in on-going programs of early childhood education.

The challenge of imaginative curricula development has intensified with the renewed interest in early childhood education. Development of innovative approaches drawing upon experimental evidence is changing time-honored views of the educative process for our young. Extreme positions would appear to revolve around social versus cognitive foci. Actually, no such dichotomy exists in practice. The movement from a "socially oriented" toward a "cognitively oriented" approach has been, except in rare cases, evolutionary, not revolutionary. Here again, the current obsession to bring disadvantaged children alongside their more cognitively oriented peers has added fuel to the evolution.

At the present time, radical curricula changes are being contemplated. For example, programmed instruction and machine teaching for reading, numeration, and so on, is moving into early childhood curricula. Many teachers, especially those trained for elementary school work, are relying increasingly on the use of established routines and printed materials to, presumably, help children learn more, faster, and earlier. Yet others continue to insist that programs retain the essential features of ordered flexibility and social orientation that have characterized nursery schools and kindergartens for many years.

With the advent of state legislative action for public support of kindergartens, teacher training and public school programs are being revised to accommodate the rapidly growing demands for facilities and well-trained personnel. During such revisionistic periods direction is often vague. The material in this book has been selected and organized to assist the pre-service teacher, in-service teacher, administrator, college educator, and others in placing the evidence and issues in proper perspective.

From the initial concern of Part 1—"Do Young Children Need Preschools?"—to the positions of Part 8—"What Should Be Taught in the Preschool?"—no conscious attempt has been made to produce conformity of thinking about the positions presented. Yet it is expected that the evidence and points of view will lead careful readers to logical conclusions about the nature of good programs for young children.

The prevailing controversy about the worth of the Montessori approach is explored in Part 2. The positions are argumentative in nature and largely speculative, but they do have the common strength of concern from experience. Suggestive programming elements may arise from a synthesis of the positions presented.

Equally relevant, but more theoretically based, are the discussions of Piaget's child in Part 3. Undoubtedly the most famous, and perhaps the most controversial developmental psychologist of this decade, Piaget's extensive studies about the development of young children have produced voluminous information about the development of children. As with Montessori's work, practical application has been relatively dormant, but recent curricula revisions are reflecting Piaget's work with growing frequency. No alert early childhood educator is likely to dismiss these studies before careful examination for curricula implications.

Changing beliefs about cognitive development, instrumental in the revived interest in young children, are presented in Part 4. Emerging from these selections is the realization that careful examination of the effects of extreme rearing practices is a valuable technique for gaining deeper understanding about the potential role of environmental manipulation in the educative process for *all* children.

The predominantly positive results from Head Start programs in every geographical area of the country give practical support to the extensive studies by Bloom, Hunt, and others that displace "fixed intelligence" with "environmentally modifiable" views and point to early childhood as the optimum period for intellectual development. These changing views have added strength to the drive for universal downward extension of schools. Accounts of the success of Head Start, such as those presented in Part 5, have prompted President Johnson to continue Operation Head Start on a year-round basis.

The current movement from rigid scheduling toward a sequentially structured learning scheme, the common misunderstanding of "school readiness," and research on "learning set" has led to focus on young children "learning to learn," as illustrated in Part 6. Viewing early learning from this perspective may indeed help to replace the characteristic lock-step pattern of many kindergartens and most primary classrooms with true non-gradedness and individualization of teacher-pupil-media encounters.

The information explosion is changing views, and subsequently, the operational behavior of early childhood educators. The task of keeping abreast of developments is complicated for these people and even more difficult for others. Presently, many people with little or no formal training in early childhood education are faced with the task of planning programs for four- and five-year-olds. Parts 7, 8, and 9 are designed to assist these people with that task.

The question, "What Should Be Taught?" is crucial, for it is essentially teacher devised encounters that make school different from random experiences the child may construct for himself in other contexts. The creation of a facilitating physical environment is one important segment of the teaching responsibility that will have its effects upon the development of children.

I wish to express my sincere gratitude to the authors and publishers who graciously consented to the reprinting of their materials in this book. A special thanks to the authors of invited papers—Dr. Edward Earl Gotts, Dr. John Pierce-Jones, and Dr. Thomas Rowland of New York University, Miss Carole Honstead, Oregon State University, for taking time from busy schedules to share their wisdom with others. And finally, my appreciation to Dr. Ira Gordon, Univ. of Fla., for helpful suggestions during the planning stages of this book.

J.L.F.

Austin, Texas
April 1968

Contents

1 *Do Young Children Need Preschools?*

A growing educational concern is whether all four- and five-year-olds should have the opportunity to attend preschools. Few, indeed, deny the necessity of preschool intervention for the disadvantaged. The evidence arising from Operation Head Start, long-range experimental programs, and certain other studies builds a strong case for continuity and expansion of compensatory programs for these young children. Benjamin Bloom's classic study, *Stability and Change in Human Characteristics*, adds additional strength to the proposition of the Educational Policies Commission that universal compensatory education begin at age four for economically and socially deprived children.

Though our course of action for the disadvantaged appears quite clear, the question of whether *all* children should begin school at age four remains speculative. Mabel Mitchell and Andrew Mitchell present an opposing case, suggesting that such action would lead to further degeneration of family life; that many parents are quite capable of providing the kind of early training essential for their young charges.

The value of early schooling for some children is indeed speculative, but Jean Spaulding and others believe that the great bulk of four- and five-year-olds would benefit from early schooling. It is the rare family that can provide for the variety and depth of experiences available in a carefully planned early school program.

Ira Gordon aptly reviews forces contributing to the rediscovery of early childhood and reinforces the need for early training with research evidence from psychology, sociology, and medicine. Fully cognizant of the role of mothers in early childhood development, Gordon developed the Florida Parent Education Project wherein mothers are instructed in stimulation exercises for their children. Such instruction is designed to (a) enhance the

1

development of infants and children and (b) increase the mother's competence and sense of personal worth. The failure of later childhood compensatory programs to fully compensate for early deprivation suggests that infant programming may be quite desirable, or perhaps essential, for children living under severely restricting circumstances.

Consistent with the character of education and the nature of human beings, attempts to prescribe for all children results in failure to accommodate for individuality. Should *all* children begin school at three? or four? or five? or should this be delayed to age six? What difference does family experience make toward readiness for school? What kind of schools should children have? These and other fundamental questions should affect our decisions about the formal training of young children.

The kindergarten class, an arena of games and frills to the unskilled observer, builds a foundation for successful achievement in the primary grades. E. L. Widmer recognizes that the good kindergarten program broadens social contacts with others, cultivates the foundation for literacy through the expansion of language as a communicative form and broadens the child's understanding of the social and scientific world. Such important factors as esthetic taste, sense of responsibility, and thinking behavior are not innate; they have to be learned, and early childhood is an optimum period for learning.

Learning continuity, characteristic of children in varying degrees, is largely dependent upon corresponding extension of experiences to accommodate the growing child's exploratory behavior. Rose Mukerji focuses upon fundamental bases for continuous learning. She recognizes that very little supportive data for early school experience is to be found. Yet she believes that the early childhood years are particularly fruitful for several reasons: These are the root years (three, four and five) for learning about self in relation to others; for concept formation; for language; and for creativity. These *are* the root years. Yet the logic of continuous learning and its implications for individuality must be clearly understood and properly accommodated.

The dilemma of discontinuity is nowhere more obvious than in the futile attempts of schools during past generations to compensate for the effects of restricted environmental conditions by remedial rather than preventative methods. Alteration of existing curricula has systematically failed to reach the lower-class child and the intellectual gap between the middle class and the poor has widened with the passage of time. Only recently have educators clearly recognized that this is "locking the door after the horse is stolen" behavior. J. W. Getzels directs attention to this dilemma, suggesting that the essential learning differences have their basis in early childhood experiences. It is during this period that the child literally *learns to learn*, acquiring the tools for school tasks. Failure to do so, characteristic of lower-class children, results in learning discontinuity. He continues to raise pertinent questions about the effects of environment on learning to learn; the timing of experience; the educational consequences of discontinuity between experience and school expectations; and the nature of compensatory preschool programs. Should compensatory preschool education be expanded? How can we afford it? Getzels states that "when one measures the present waste and pain against the vision of what might be, the more telling question is: How can we not afford it?"

While some are continuing to debate the advisability of universal preschools for four- and five-year-olds, others like Bettye M. Caldwell are examining evidence about the effects of differential patterns of early care upon child development. Such evidence suggests that learning difficulties in childhood may be circumvented through programming of infant environments. This is, of course, particularly relevant for children reared in deficient environments. General acceptance of the view that maximum effectiveness of compensatory programming is dependent upon beginning during the very early years of life may hinge, not only upon the success of experimentation with infants, but also upon the systematic failure of programs for disadvantaged four- and five-year-olds to *erase* the effects of early environmental restriction.

On the basis of available evidence the following conclusion appears to be appropriate. Preschools are *nice* for all children but they are *essential* for the disadvantaged. Consequently, those concerned with the development of public school kindergartens in those states not presently providing them, and others who are involved in planning programs for younger children, should carefully consider lest those for whom preschools *must* be provided—the disadvantaged—are lost in the shuffle. Some priorities are in order.

1   Universal Opportunity
for Early Childhood Education*

EDUCATIONAL POLICIES COMMISSION OF THE NEA
AND THE AMERICAN ASSOCIATION OF SCHOOL ADMINISTRATORS

In May of 1966, the following statement (here slightly abridged) was issued by the EPC as another of its contributions to thinking on a major educational issue. In July, a resolution prompted by this statement was presented to the NEA Representative Assembly. Mabel M. Mitchell, an Assembly delegate, urged that the proposed resolution be amended to include only disadvantaged children rather than all four-year-olds.

The resolution was then amended in accordance with her proposal and passed by the Representative Assembly; it is official policy for this 1966 school year. Here (in part) is the resolution:

The NEA affirms the principle that the home and family are the basic unit in our free society and that parents have prime responsibility for the character development of their children.

It also believes that the general system of universal public education should be expanded. To these ends the Association recommends that opportunity for compensatory education begin at the age of four for those children who, through economic or social deprivation, may be seriously impeded in their progress through public schools and consequently in their participation in a democratic society. . . .

All children should have the opportunity to go to school at public expense beginning at the age of four.

Research shows clearly that the first four or five years of a child's life are the period of most rapid growth in physical and mental characteristics and of greatest susceptibility to environmental influences. Consequently, it is in the early years that deprivations are most disastrous in their effects. They can be compensated for only with great difficulty in later years, and then probably not in full. Furthermore, it appears that it is harder to modify harmful learnings than to acquire new ones. Finally, experience indicates that exposure to a wide variety of activities and of social and mental interactions with children and adults greatly enhances a child's ability to learn. . . .

Family life and family love are among the most cherished of American values. In addition, they are important to the healthy development of the individual physically and spiritually, and they are basic to his

* *NEA Journal*, November 1966, vol. 55, no. 8. Reprinted by permission.

happiness. They are regarded as a birthright of every child and parent. Moreover, except in extreme cases of neglect and mistreatment at home, it is hard to conceive of an institutional alternative to the home and family that could do as well.

Therefore, although early schooling is needed, family life must be strengthened, not replaced. The need is for a complement, not an alternative, to family life. But the need is compelling. . . .

Early education is advisable for all children, not merely because of the need to offset any disadvantages in their background, but also because they are ready by the age of four for a planned fostering of their development and because educators know some of the ways to foster it through school programs. Early education has long been available to the well-to-do, and it is commendable that governments are now acting on the need to make it available to some of the poor. But the large middle group should have the same opportunities. . . .

In proposing that school extend downward to the age of four, the Educational Policies Commission does not intend a simple downward extension of, or preparation for, the program now offered in most first grades. We envision a program uniquely adapted to children of ages four and five; the program for six-year-olds would be altered to take into account the earlier schooling of the children, rather than vice versa. The program suitable for four- and five-year-olds differs in basic ways from the traditional first grade, for it is not focused on reading, writing, and arithmetic and it need not be an all-day program.

What is here advocated is not preschooling but an integral and a vitally important part of schooling. Education in this two-year period can affect the character of the child and all his future life more deeply than his education at any later period. . . .

To be entrusted with such a responsibility and to discharge it successfully, the teacher needs to have an understanding of children and a knowledge of methods which she can get only from study and experience. Little children tend to be so active physically and mentally that no preset pattern of experience can turn to maximum advantage the many opportunities for development that present themselves. A teacher needs the almost total flexibility required to make the necessary decisions from moment to moment and the considerable competence required to make the best decisions.

The objectives of instruction in these years lie in four major areas—intellectual, emotional, social, and physical. The intellectual goals include the promotion of curiosity, growth of language, and generation of readiness for the intellectual activities that will come in later years. They also include the development of the ability to handle concepts, to perceive and meet problems, and to observe and listen. . . .

One of the main contributions which early education can make to a child's intellectual development is the enlargement of his span of experience. Under skilled guidance, a child's new contacts with the world become new learnings and open new possibilities. There are new worlds to discover in virtually every situation—the world of nature, the world of play, the economic world, the world of oneself, the world of one's relations with others. Before entering school all children have some experience of some of these worlds and can benefit from more; some children have surprisingly scanty experience of anything and learn surprisingly little from such exposure as they have. . . .

The emotional goals of early education include promotion of children's sense of security and self-respect; there are no more important prerequisites to learning, happiness, or mental health. To this end, a child must find school a congenial place. He must frequently have a sense of accomplishment, a sense that he is able to learn by himself and to help others. He must feel respected and valued.

Relations between school and home are particularly vital at the nursery level. A little child adjusts most naturally to a new environment if his parents are often there. It should be common practice for mothers to accompany children to school and become involved in school experiences. Both parent and teacher can also profit from association with each other. The teacher profits from the parent's knowledge of each child, and parents can learn ways in which they might help further the goals of early education. It is highly desirable that the parents recognize what early education is trying to do for their children.

Early schooling should be part of the excitement of childhood. The curiosity, inventiveness, and spontaneous energy of young children are sources from which a lifetime of learning can develop. A school program for these children should therefore offer experiences designed to enhance these qualities.

The third major area in which early education seeks development is that of a child's relations with other children and adults. A young child tends to see himself as the center of the world. If a child is to lead a happy and responsible life, however, he must balance his egocentricity with a concern for and responsibility toward others. He must learn that other children, too, are "me's." On the other hand, if he never asserts himself or if he has been taught to obey others blindly, he must learn that he, too, can contribute and that he, too, has rights that are to be respected. . . .

Finally, early education must devote considerable attention to the child's physical well-being and development. . . .

The objectives and program here suggested have long characterized the practice of many nursery school educators. If such education were universalized, most children would reach six years of age with a level of development strikingly different from that which they bring to school today. More of them would probably resemble in general development and learning ability the children who come to school today from the most-favored homes. These are not necessarily the wealthiest homes. Rather they are those in which parents take the most responsible, rational, and appropriate roles in the rearing of their children. They are homes which give love, inspiration, challenge, support, and experience. . . .

The children who came from such homes have an appetite for learning and great readiness for it and for the school. Many first grades in their present form could not meet the needs of children so capable and so eager to learn. With universal early childhood education, almost every child would have a higher starting point in knowledge and developed ability. . . .

We therefore think it important that the program for six-year-olds be based on the program for four- and five-year-olds. The need for this close association does not necessarily imply any one administrative structure. . . . However, the importance of continuity in the program suggests that it might be unwise to set off the first two years as a separate entity.

There are 8,400,000 four- and five-year-olds in the present population. Five million of them are not now in school. It is difficult to estimate the cost of providing educational opportunities for all these children, but it is well within the nation's capacity to pay.

The Educational Policies Commission recommends that the federal government provide general support to the schooling of four- and five-year-olds. But all levels of government must cooperate in seeking the funds, and early childhood education should be financed and administered as an integral part of public education. The money would bring many returns. The number of children requiring costly, slow, and sometimes fruitless remedial services at the elementary or secondary level would probably decline drastically. The return to the nation in enhanced capabilities of the population would be immense. The return to children in a more joyful, creative, and productive childhood would be immeasurable.

Universal Education for Four-Year-Olds?

> "I OPPOSE IT," *says Mabel M. Mitchell, chairman, English Department, Boulder City (Nevada) High School (with Andrew J. Mitchell, principal, Boulder City Elementary School).*

As educators, we frequently find ourselves agreeing with a proposal because our attention is focused on one aspect of it rather than on its total significance. In the case of the EPC proposal, I believe that the clear need for some sort of compensatory education for disadvantaged four-year-olds made many of us overlook the fact that it may not be a good idea for every four-year-old.

Before we determine a course of action for all children of this age, let us consider what it is that we are all working for. Is not our main goal to help boys and girls grow into responsible, law-abiding, productive citizens? If so, how do we go about it?

In my opinion, we cannot go about it by any proposal that would lessen the importance of the family, for the child who has a stable, loving home is likely to be the child receptive to education, susceptible to good ideas, acceptable to his fellowmen, and able to withstand the slings and arrows of misfortune.

We have somehow gotten our social machinery in reverse. We are passing laws, creating new government agencies, pouring out billions of dollars from the public treasury, and frantically pursuing every panacea imaginable in an effort to correct our social ills on a massive, total-society basis.

No society, I believe, can ever purify itself by artificial, superimposed endeavors. We must begin with the individual, and the best place to train individuals in the virtues so lacking in our society is the home.

To those who say, "But the home has failed; the school must take over," I submit that the home, too, is a product of our schools. Rather than encourage the further disintegration of family life, the educational program of the school should be directing young people toward some belief, tradition, and practice in the proper establishment of home life and in the proper rearing of children.

Furthermore, is our memory so dim that we've forgotten the sterile, debilitating effect of national, regimented education and control of youth in Hitler's Germany? I am not implying that those who are in favor of universal public education for four-year-olds are engaged in a conspiracy to foster governmental control of four-year-olds' minds. What I am saying is that providing early childhood training is a parent's privilege and responsibility.

In conclusion, let me mention briefly two other factors that we need to consider:

1. There is woefully insubstantial evidence concerning the value and effectiveness of early school experiences. Indeed, a growing number of educators are beginning to suspect that the pressures of competition in learning to read, for example, may be contributing to the increase in youthful mental patients as well as delinquents.

2. Educators disagree about the age at which children should enter school. We do agree, however, that all children are not ready for school

at the same age and that some would be better off if their schooling were delayed beyond the usual entrance age.

> "I FAVOR IT," *says Jean Spaulding, general consultant, preschool, primary specialist, State Department of Education, Salem, Oregon; a former teacher of kindergarten and primary school.*

Universal opportunity for early childhood education? Of course!

Research has demonstrated that guided experiences developed around the interests and abilities of a young child enrich his understanding of himself and the world in which he lives. In this lies the greatest significance of early childhood education. A four- or five-year-old is happier as a four- or five-year-old because of this understanding. What happens as he develops this understanding, moreover, may affect all the years a child will live, for under the right circumstances, four- and five-year-olds can cultivate attitudes and develop skills which will help them throughout life.

Despite private schools available to the affluent and the new programs and projects of the Head Start variety available to the poor, the great bulk of four- and five-year-olds do not have the opportunity to get maximum benefit from the years when they are four and five. Almost every child is best equipped to offer. Important as family life is, few families can at this age needs to have certain experiences that an organized program give a child formal and informal group experiences that have the wide variety and depth of those offered by a well-developed early school program.

All children need to relate to others—both children and adults— who are outside the regular pattern of family life. In a school setting, a girl who dawdles at home will learn to speed up her work tempo so that the others won't have to wait; an only child will learn about the need to take turns in playing with an intriguing new fire truck. These children will be learning to work with others. This social skill and others like it are needed in every facet of life.

The moment to nurture creative thinking and to stimulate curiosity comes early in a child's life. One day a little girl notices a rainbow where the sun strikes the fishbowl. "What makes the rainbow?" she wonders. The teacher points to the glass wind chimes, where more color sparkles. The girl ponders. Soon she notices the same colors in soap bubbles when she washes her hands. "Why?" Now she is ready for the teacher to read from the book that will help answer her questions.

The child doesn't know that she is learning simple research skills, using inquiry techniques, or studying general science, but she is. She is developing the kind of curiosity that she will need as she pursues education all through her life.

When children in a class examine a new rock or a strange flower added to their collections—or when they have an experience like pressing the buttons on an adding machine that really works—they develop observation skill and the ability to look for detail.

Education for all our fours and fives will take us a step toward the educational goal of promoting each child's development to the fullest potential. When parents and teachers work together as a team, early childhood education can add breadth of understanding to children and parents alike. The child gains, the family gains, and society gains.

2 The Young Child: A New Look*

IRA GORDON, *Institute for Development of Human Resources, University of Florida*

During the 1960s we have rediscovered infancy and early childhood and have taken a new look at the young child. As I tried to think of what the "new look" means several questions occurred to me. Why has this rediscovery taken place in the 1960s? What is there about 1963 or 1965 that has brought about the rediscovery of early childhood? What led up to it? It seems to me that we have had a juxtaposition of three kinds of forces.

First, we have had a political change in that we have rediscovered the poor. Those of us who are sometime biblical scholars know that the poor have always been with us, but certainly in the past few years we have rediscovered them in terms of devoting considerable energy, money, and intellect to the problems of the poor. As one looks at poverty, it becomes increasingly important to recognize that the roots of it stem back into the family, back into the kinds of beginnings in the home that the child has. So, political forces have forced us to look at infancy and the young child.

Second, the psychologists have rediscovered infancy and the young child. We are particularly indebted not to an American, but to a Swiss, Jean Piaget, who toiled in the vineyards, unrecognized, unappreciated, and scoffed at because he did not fit our statistical analysis techniques

* A speech delivered at the conference on *The Young Child: Florida's Future* at the University of Florida, June 16, 1967.

for at least thirty years. With the recent rebirth of interest in his work, Piaget's ideas and his research have once again forced us to say, "What are the origins of intellect? Where does intelligence begin?"

Third, there has been a rediscovery in sociology that language learning begins in the home. The work of Basil Bernstein in England has indicated to us that social class has played a predominant role in the kind of language, and therefore in the kind of thought, that one can use as he grows.

Thus, political pressures and psychological and sociological understandings have combined to bring about a rediscovery of the young child.

I would like particularly to discuss the present research in psychology because I really know very little about politics or sociology and because I feel more comfortable in psychology. The best way to illustrate the change that has taken place, it seems to me, is to compare 1950 to 1967. The research of the 1950s, particularly the psychoanalytical literature, such as the work of Margaret Ribble and some of the earlier work of René Spitz, presents the infant as a rather disorganized bundle. In the early learning studies of Carmichael, the idea that the infant may be very capable isn't given much thought at all. He is perceived as coming into the world disorganized, not able to hear, to see, and little able to sense. He is incompetent and disorganized. Our view of the infant today is just the opposite. The Russian and American research in learning and the changing research by Spitz in psychoanalysis now paint a picture of the infant as a competent organism. We know he is able to see and that he sees with a good deal of sharpness within a few days of life. We know he is able to hear, not just loud noises banging in back of him, but that he can distinguish, very early in the game, levels of sound and tone. We know we can condition him to different levels of sound and tone. We know certainly he can sense. (Mothers have known this all along but psychologists are probably fifty years behind mothers and the schools are another fifty years behind them, so that we are probably where the mothers were in 1867 at this point.)

When one begins to look at infants as able to learn, as able to take in information about what is going on around them, a shift of immense import has occurred. Americans being what they are—Piaget calls this "the American question"—once we think we can teach somebody something or that a capacity for learning is demonstrated, we invest all of our energies in finding out just what can be learned. We want to know how much and how early we can pour "knowledge" into the infant. We have a real shift. Now that we think he's capable, we're going to try and make him as capable as he can be. Ten or fifteen years ago we didn't think he was capable so we thought, why fuss with him at all? Just let him lie in the crib and if he disturbs you, feed him some phenobarb or paregoric:

Put him to sleep and get him out of the way. This attitude represents part of the shift.

Second, we used to behave as though all infants were pretty much alike. Mothers know different; they know very well that they are not, and some fathers also know this. But we had a notion, particularly growing out of a learning theory that ignored whatever genetic base there might be, which ignored individuality. J. B. Watson in the 1930s said that if you gave him an infant and he had control of him, he could make out of him whatever he wanted. All children were seen as pretty much alike. Now in the 1960s our emphasis, even though we don't quite understand it and don't know quite what to do with it, is on the tremendous range of individual uniqueness, not only of adults but also of infants as early as the first five days of life. The work of Kessen, for example, who took motion pictures of infants lying in cribs, shows that you can very rapidly distinguish activity level, the number of times the infant puts his thumb in his mouth, all kinds of measures that accumulate to point out how stable youngsters become in their individuality right from the very beginning. This, coupled with competency, has raised a host of questions. How do you make children even more individual and competent if this is what we are dedicated to do in our society?

The third major change is in our view of infants and young children as reactive, simply respondents to stimuli. We had the view that children were reactive and not active in their own right. Further, we had a notion of motivation that the most satisfying state for the infant, or for anybody, was really the passive state. We have continually talked about drive reduction, about getting back to equilibrium as though equilibrium was the desirable state. To some degree mothers believed as the old psychologists did. If you were to ask a mother if her baby is a good baby, she would say "yes, he's sleeping 20 hours a day." This was good, in the sense that it freed the mother to do all the other things she wanted to do around the house. Her definition of a good baby was the passive, reactive baby. But from the current psychological point of view, the definition of a good baby or a normal baby is the active, curious, inquiring, poking, seeking, and exploring kind of baby. When babies reach two or three, families have noticed this. They know the problems of dealing with the "whys" of the toddler who follows Mom around all the time with "why," "how," "tell me this," "tell me that," to the point where the mother would almost cheerfully put him back into the passive, reactive state, or put him to sleep if she could. But we now realize that this curiosity, this inquiry, this seeking, this competence motivation does not simply emerge at the age of two, but that it is probably part of the orginal biological make-up of the human infant.

The last major change is the elimination of the old argument of heredity versus environment. Although there are still people who place most of their belief in the genetic end of the scale, and some who place most of their belief in the environmental end of the scale, many of us realize that these two forces cannot be separated. We talk now in terms of a transactional type of orientation rather than simply of a genetic unfolding orientation. We realize now that whatever a youngster may become is very much a function of the interplay between that body which he brings with him, which is already competent, which is already active, which is already curious, which is already individual, and the nature of the life circumstances which we provide for him. Since by and large we are in the business of educating, it is the second factor—that of environment—upon which we can really work. That doesn't mean that we ignore genetics, but our problem is: If intelligence is built out of transactions, then what is the optimum experience? What is it we ought to be doing in the early years to give this baby the best start? Let us focus on the business of transaction, since we, as a group, are well aware of activity.

Probably the best way to look at it is to say that we used to talk about structure and function as though structure led to function. You had to have the anatomy in order to do something. You had to arrive at a certain point in maturation in order to learn something. We can picture that notion as a one-way street in which you have structure with a one-headed arrow pointing at function. This was the old view, and with it we would concern ourselves with measuring maturation, with measuring readiness, and with measuring whatever the genetic contribution was that we thought measurable. On the basis of that measurement, we would say, "Ah ha! This child is not ready for first grade," or "This child is not ready for kindergarten." To some degree the work of Ilg and Ames still stresses the orientation that a youngster should not be exposed to certain kinds of experiences because he isn't ready for them. A transactional psychologist would say that it is experience which contributes to readiness. Readiness will not occur, maturation will not occur, learning will not occur, and intelligence will not develop if we simply sit back and wait for structure.

We now put another arrowhead on structure ←→ function, in which function plays a role in determining and creating structure.

In 1962 I had what I thought at that time was a fascinating hypothesis. We knew that a child's level and rate of physical maturity influenced his self-concept. We had very good California studies to support this notion. My hypothesis was: "If the evidence shows systematic uniqueness, and there is a relationship between one's developmental status and his self-concept, could the self-concept be a factor in affecting growth? This would require a new type of longitudinal study, but would certainly be well worth the effort. Why should not the self affect growth patterns as well as growth patterns affect the self?" I checked this with some physiologists and other people who were far more knowledgeable than I. They told me it was an absolutely absurd and ridiculous notion that psychological feelings could effect the rate of maturation. After all, the rate of maturation was the independent variable and the way the child felt about it was the dependent variable. Now I would like to refer you to the June 8, 1967 issue of the *New England Journal of Medicine* in which evidence is reported that a child's growth can be severely stunted by his own emotional state and the marital discord of his parents. Powell *et al.* (1967) studied thirteen children at Johns Hopkins. They stated that, "During the past six years we have observed and evaluated 13 children, most of whom initially were believed to have growth failure on the basis of idiopathic hypopituitarism. However, a number of unusual features were noted in the histories that suggested emotional disturbances in the children and abnormal home environments. These were not common to the histories of patients with idiopathic hypopituitarism. When these patients were placed in a convalescent hospital, they demonstrated remarkable growth acceleration without receiving growth hormone or agents" (p. 1271). This is the beginning of data about transaction the other way. There are other data about nutrition and growth failure, but that is easier to accept. It seems, however, that the emotional situations at home, which we have always known can affect personality development, might even be affecting physical growth, which we thought to be constant. Similarly, Sayegh and Dennis studied environmentally retarded orphans in Lebanon and discovered they were intellectually retarded. They tried to do something about it, and they reported in *Child Development* in 1965 that the results of their studies supported the hypothesis that appropriate supplementary experiences can result in rapid increases in behavioral development on the part of environmentally retarded infants. What did they do with these infants? They took ten infants between 7 and 12 months of age, none of whom could maintain a sitting position when placed in that posture on a flat surface (yet all the norms say a 7-month-old ought to be able to do this). They added another three who were 1 year of age but who could not sit unaided, and they then divided them into an experimental and a control group. How did they bring about change? They sat a subject in a chair and ". . . attempted to keep before him, on the tray of his chair, objects which he might observe or manipulate. When a subject was on a foam-rubber pad, he was sometimes too high and sometimes too prone, and when he had learned to sit, he was placed in a sitting position. On the pad as in the chair he was provided with objects for inspection and manipulation. The experimenters attempted to provide each child with objects which interested him and to present new objects as soon as interest in the old ones was lost. Among the objects that were most often successful in eliciting interest and stimulating manipulation were an aluminum ash tray with an iridescent surface, a red plastic ash tray, a number of plastic medicine bottles, a set of multiple colored discs with perforated centers, aluminum jelly molds, cardboard boxes, paper bags, fly swatters, all the kind of stuff you would have around your house to some degree. Each of the objects was light in weight, manipulative, and harmless. Many were brightly colored and reflected images. None were identical with material used in test items. No test materials were presented during the training session" (p. 33). The results indicated that they brought these children back into the more normal developmental pattern that we would expect from middle-class youngsters. These studies deal with overcoming retardation, with getting back on a normal track. They don't force us really to change our theory about the role of genetics and experience, because it has been long understood that environment plays a role in whether a trait will be developed even if there appears to be a very strong genetic base for it. What the children did simply was to overcome something that got in the way. The results, however, still don't emphasize that intelligence is creatable or that behavior can be modified beyond what we thought it might become.

Let us take a look at intelligence from this view. J. McVicker Hunt (1966) of Illinois, who has been foremost in synthesizing the research, says in his book, *Intelligence and Experience*, "The assumption that intelligence is fixed and that its development is predetermined by the genes is no longer tenable" (p. 342). He supports this with longitudinal studies, twin studies, and a variety of experimental work.

We have concentrated on measuring children in terms of what is, as though this were equal to what might be if we were to change the circumstances. It seems that the field of early childhood education is more concerned with changing circumstances projecting what might be rather than dealing with what is. As valuable as Ben Bloom's work has been in pointing up and synthesizing longitudinal studies, it may cause us to make the same error all over again. In this book, *Stability and Change in Human Characteristics*, Bloom describes what is. I do not know how many of you are familiar with the misinterpretations that have come out of it about the relative size of intelligence in the first four years of life as compared to after age 17. Bloom says that half the *variance* in IQ measurement at age 17, half of *what accounts for the difference* among seventeen-year-olds, is already present at age 4. But he is dealing with survey and correlational statistics; not in experimentation, not in intervention. We have to ask ourselves a different question, "What might intelligence be?" Further, people have highlighted Bloom's notion that half of one's intelligence at age 17 is already present at age 4. It should be noted that the data he uses to support the statement that half of what accounts for the variability among children at age 17 can be accounted for by the measurement of intelligence at age 4. There is really quite a difference in these two statements. If we provided different experiences before age 4, if we approached the early childhood years differently, and if we continued to modify our procedures throughout the school years, would Bloom's findings remain the same? It doesn't strike me that they will necessarily do so, if we change conditions.

I would like to share with you a Japanese experiment discussed by Hunt. Suzuki developed a program, which consists of several well-defined steps modeled on his conception of children's spontaneous language learning, for teaching the violin to young children. Beginning in the latter part of their first year of life, and continuing through the second year, the youngsters heard recordings of an expert violinist playing very simple themes. Suzuki then taught the mother how to play some of these simple themes so that she could provide a model for the child, just as she provides a model for behavior in the general socialization of the child. The expectation that the children would try to imitate their mothers was borne out. After the child had asked repeatedly to be allowed to play his mother's violin, he was given a small violin of his own. While the child was enjoying his new "toy," he was also given some coaching on how to use his left hand to get different tones and how to use his right hand to bow. The results of this program have been that thousands of preschool children have learned to play the violin with a very high quality of performance. Paul Roland, president of the Strings Teachers Association in America, reported to Hunt that four- and five-year-olds obtained as fine a quality of sound on their little half-violins as do all but the best high-school age violinists in America. Should controlled experimental analysis confirm Suzuki's work, it would show that auditory images based on listening to expert violinists can serve as standards which will help to guide the child's motor development in playing the violin.

It has generally been believed that modeling such as is done by painters, pianists, and even professional football players can be done efficiently only if one is already skilled in the activity to be learned. The evidence from Suzuki and from Omar Kyam Moore and his talking typewriter suggest that standards can be built that will later shape the motor actions required for the performance of skills. Although the criteria by which the child judges his performance are based on the expert violinist's recordings, the child's behavior is a direct function of his interpersonal relationship with his mother. Hunt ends by saying "Whether or not my earlier suggestion that all modification of representational central processes may be forced by inputs discrepant with those already in the storage be true, these various considerations indicate a much greater role for the input side in learning, even in the learning of the very young, than recent theories have given it." Now it seems to me that he is saying, if youngsters are provided with models of behavior, and if youngsters are provided with perceptual experiences, these models and perceptual experiences influence motor activity. Our classical notions of learning always assumed that the motor was where you began. To learn a pattern of behavior you had to engage in the pattern of behavior. If you wanted to learn how to ride a bike, you had to get on the bike and ride. To some degree the research indicates that one way to learn to ride a bike is to first watch other people ride it, see what they are doing, and then try and copy their behavior. You still can't get away from motor activity; such activity is still very basic. However, the children were modeling their activity on the mothers'. I think one of the most important ideas in Hunt's discussion is that the child's desire to imitate, to copy, to relate to the mother is a real key to early learning.

This is where we are. If Hunt is right, then we are responsible for the inputs we control as parents and educators. If Piaget, Art Combs, Bloom and others are right, the earlier the inputs, the greater the gain.

I would like to introduce one other term that relates Piaget's use of accommodation. The term is "discrepancy," as Hunt uses it. Kessen writes about what he labels the "significant stimulus." Some people have said, for example, about Harlem children, or about any children growing up in the big city, whether in a slum or not, that they are surrounded by stimuli. If they are surrounded by stimuli and if these stimuli are inputs, what is the problem? Why aren't they making the kinds of progress we would expect? If we thought that deprivation was just the absence of stimuli, as it was in the orphanage, then how do we understand that in a slum a child is overwhelmed with stimuli but doesn't seem to be able to take advantage of it, to grow and develop in terms of intellectual progress? Kessen's notion of the significant stimulus seems to be of importance here. What stimuli matter to the child? We talk of stimulation as if it were all of a piece, but what is stimulating to one may be noise to another. We must fall back on our concepts of individuality both in terms of the ability to take in inputs and in the ability to tolerate inputs. What is stimulation to one may be noise to another, or it may be simply background that isn't heard. I watch my own adolescents, for example, who listen to the radio. They can be on the telephone, be watching television, doing their homework, all with the radio on full blast, all at the same time. I am overwhelmed by the stimuli, but they don't hear 98 percent of it; it is background to them. If I sneak into the room and turn off the radio, that's the significant stimulus. Something is absent that they expect to be there. This is discrepant to them, this is the significant stimulus, this is what makes the difference. The problem we have with children is to figure out what is of discrepant value. If we give them the same diet all the time it gets boring. We know we have to separate the discrepant from the noise. This is where we still have a long way to go, because we don't really know what counts to very young children. We can get some notion from Sayegh and Dennis that shapes and glitters count. We have some notion from Friedlander at Western Reserve that a combination of sound and glitter counts. But we also know that if you place something in front of the young child that continues to glitter, eventually he doesn't respond to it anymore. You have to turn it off for a while and come back to it.

This is one area in which the theories are somewhat ahead of what we know. We know that stimulation is important, we go around saying you should have Head Start, you should have nursery programs, you should have lots of things, but we are really not quite clear as to what stimuli have value. In addition, the notion of transaction requires that we look at a different side of the coin, the effect of the child on the mother. Here we also have a long way to go. We understand intuitively, especially those of us who are parents, how children change us. But we have little research on the phenomenon. We know that nursing does not simply provide nutrients for the infant, but also creates psychological and physiological responses in the mother. It seems to play a role in restoring the uterus back to normal, it has elements of an orgasm attached to it so that it is an extremely satisfying experience if everything else is going well. Nursing is not simply an effect of the mother on the child, but has rewards for the mother as well. But once we move past nursing we don't really know (Mr. Anderson in Miami is faced to some degree with this problem) what playing with the child, what teaching the child, what modeling with children does for the mother or the teacher. Those of us who have been teachers in classrooms know what classes do to us. We don't really understand it from a research orientation. We don't understand it enough to control the sequences, to set it up, to manage it. So I suspect this is going to be an important area of work. We have some leads from Peabody that in their early child project the mother finds what she sees in the preschool so satisfying for her child that she spreads the gospel in the neighborhood. We have some indications from our Florida Parent Education Project that there are rewards to the mother in the way she deals with the infant. Again there may be some diffusion of this in the neighborhood. But we need clearly to explore how the child's behavior is the stimulus to the mother and how it leads the mother to relate to the child in certain ways. When we have this behind us a little bit, we then need to learn how to inject this into our preschool programs and how to make more effective use of the influence of the child on the mother in the curriculum of the school.

We have used mothers in parent cooperative nursery schools or in Head Start programs as aides. But by and large we continue to think in terms of what this is going to do for the child. We need also to say that if it changes the mother, then it is going to have an impact on her future children, as well as on her continued relationship with her child. One of our hopes, for example, in the Florida Parent Education Project is that the mother will find her experience with her child so satisfying to her that she will continue to seek her own ways of relating to the infant past the point we would normally expect. As we understand her culture, she would begin to ignore the child as it becomes a crawler, a toddler who sets out on his own. Traditionally, from our understandings at least, she diminishes her relationship to the child as it grows. We hope, if we can get a good thing going in the first year, she will feel so good about it that she will continue her relationship with this child and find her own ways to do it. The experience with the child shapes the mother just as much as the experience shapes the child. We really need to look at this area intensively.

It seems to me we face a whole area of challenge. Our old norms are shaken. Our old theories no longer hold up. If we want the child to make the most of whatever it is that he has, or if we believe that we can create potential, our present theory of the child as competent, as active, as individual, as engaged in transaction requires that we intervene, that we do something during this period. But it requires that we intervene when we do not yet know when or how to intervene, or what the effects will be on other family members. We do know that the future belongs to this young child. We have the task of helping him to develop. We cannot sit idly by and let him flower, because he will not. We have to find and define the optimum environment, and then we have to convince our public that it needs to provide it for him.

3   In Kindergarten*

E. L. WIDMER, *University of Miami*

When was the last time you watched a five-year-old? Really looked at him while he played or worked?

A five-year-old is a symphony of movement and sound—unless he has heard too many stern warnings to be quiet, to behave, to "act his age" and not be "a baby." This is his age.

* Reprinted from *Elementary School Journal* by E. L. Widmer by permission of The University of Chicago Press. Copyright 1967 by The University of Chicago Press.

What happens to this lively being in kindergarten?

Kindergarten is a great adventure for a child. It is usually his first experience away from home. It is his first experience with a large group of children for a whole day or a half-day on a regular basis. It is his first experience, on a large scale, in being accepted by others, not because he is part of a fond family, but because of who he is and what he does. Kindergarten is his first experience in learning away from home.

The baby is growing up visibly now.

What about this place where he spends so many of his waking hours? What is a kindergarten?

Let's consider that question carefully. A kindergarten is a strategic portion of the elementary-school years devoted to the five-year-old child. In kindergarten he is guided by a professionally trained teacher. He is surrounded by equipment and materials, indoor and outdoor space geared to his needs at this fifth year of life. The program encompasses all the traditional subject matter such as reading, writing, arithmetic, science, but in its own unique way, based on what we know of the child at this stage of life. The program also encompasses other areas such as social studies, the language arts, recreation, health, physical education, the humanities, which are also important for the child's development.

Doesn't the kindergartner just play all day? He may seem to be playing, for he certainly is not rooted to a chair and a desk for any length of time. He sits sometimes—during work period when he is busy with a project, or at story time when he is enthralled with a book that has colorful pictures and a fascinating plot, or at concert time when he listens to music, especially music with words that tell a story. He sits when he draws and works with clay, puzzles, scissors and paste, and construction paper. But, even when he sits, he sits actively. Everything seems to move, even though he stays in one spot or approximately in one spot.

But he has lots of company. Five-year-olds are wrigglers. They find it difficult to stay in one spot for long. That is one reason why you will find a lot of activity going on in the good kindergarten.

At certain times during the kindergarten day the child circulates freely and joins in block-building activities, in painting at the easel, in dramatic play in the housekeeping corner, in play at the sandbox, in construction with wood and tools, in experimenting with science equipment and materials.

Outdoors he plays vigorously in games with the teacher and the group. He joins other kindergarten children at the much favored jungle gym, the sandbox, and swings. He enjoys using boxes, boards, wagons, tricycles, kegs, wheelbarrows, the seesaw, and the sliding board.

The restless energy of five-year-olds, then, is one reason for all that bustling activity.

Another reason why you will find lots of activity going on in the good kindergarten is that learning is not a passive process. It is an active process. The good kindergarten program recognizes this fact by allowing for creative activity, play, dramatization, first-hand observation, experimentation, and use of the child's five senses. Children's universal interest in doing, in exploring, is an ally of education. The good kindergarten program recognizes and uses this fact.

What else does the good kindergarten program do? What is its role?

1. *The kindergarten program helps promote and maintain the child's health and physical development.* In a good kindergarten program the child is able to use his large muscles in active play outdoors in the fresh air, as well as indoors with special equipment and materials. When he is tired, he rests on mats or cots. Activity alternates with quiet work and play, to lessen the danger of overtiredness. To guard further against this danger, the periods are kept relatively short, and there is little stress on small-muscle activity and close work. Good nutrition and good eating habits are discussed, and they are also practiced at snack time or midmorning lunch.

2. *The kindergarten program gives a child the opportunity to broaden his social contacts with other children and adults.* His circle of acquaintances has widened from a few playmates living nearby to a schoolroom filled with children of similar age, his teacher or teachers, other teachers in the building, the school nurse, the principal, the custodian, the bus driver. He is one among many. He must learn to share, to co-operate, to wait his turn. These are important learnings. At five he is readier than last year or the year before to undertake these learnings in a small group, in larger groups, and in activities the day holds. The teacher's guidance and supervision help him.

3. *The kindergarten program provides a rich environment for living, thinking, and learning.* The richer and the more stimulating a child's school environment, the more certain it is that he will learn the three R's better when the right time comes.

A rich environment includes an abundance of first-hand experiences and a wide variety of equipment and materials suited to the child's needs at this period of his life. A rich and stimulating environment also includes the necessary space, freedom, and time to explore, test, experiment, see, hear, feel, taste, and smell.

But the raw materials, important as they are, cannot come to life without an atmosphere in the schoolroom that not only allows questions and wonderings, but welcomes them. A friendly, relaxed, accepting environment is inviting to growth. But a child who is upset and unhappy because of demands that are too big for him is not free to wonder. He is too full of worry to follow his curiosity in search of answers.

4. *The foundation for the three R's is cultivated in kindergarten.* The foundation for reading, writing, and arithmetic is cultivated through the readiness program. Readiness is another way of saying that the stage is set, the curtain raised, and the show ready to begin. Before this grand opening, or "teachable moment," much behind-the-scenes effort has been going on. The kindergarten readiness program is a behind-the-scenes effort to prepare the child for the "teachable moment," or the grand opening of the show. This grand opening may take place sometime during the kindergarten year, but the results may not be evident till later.

The readiness program in the three R's is not merely a preparation for the development of future skills, however. The program is preparation, but the kind that needs full living right now and is concerned with what a child is able to do right now, at this particular point in his development.

The program includes first-hand experiences to form a background for the symbols he will bump into throughout his life. Words are symbols. Numbers are symbols, too. A symbol is nothing until it means something to somebody. A symbol is dead and lifeless until somebody recognizes it. Experiences are the keys that help unlock the meanings behind symbols.

In kindergarten, the child learns about symbols in the way that has most meaning for him—by living the symbols. He lives the words *zoo, train, circus, pet, friend, play, happy, trip, store, farm, animals, bus, picnic, ride* when he experiences them first-hand. Words come alive because he and the other children have had an exciting trip to the nearby train station, and they are all eager to tell what they have seen and heard. They make up a story about their trip. While they tell the story, the teacher writes it on chart paper. The words come alive because they were part of an adventure that really happened to each child. The children "read" the story together. Maybe afterward one or two children will ask to have individual words repeated or will even recognize a word or several words by themselves.

Words come alive when a child hears a favorite story read about children just like himself or about animals or pets or trains or fire engines. Words come alive when he sees them under a big, colorful picture or an illustration of a beloved story. Words come alive when a child's drawing or painting is labeled with a sentence of his own choosing. He may recognize the words *paint, crayons, scissors, table, chair, book, paste, window, door* because these are things he uses and sees, and the teacher has put little signs on them. He may recognize his name because his teacher pasted it above his cubby or his locker or his shelf where he keeps his things. He may learn to print his name because he can hold a pencil quite well for a short while and he is eager to label his own work.

The child lives the number symbols *one, two, three, four, five, six, seven, eight, nine, ten* when he counts straws, when he counts napkins, when he counts noses, when he counts crackers, when he counts out construction paper and discovers he needs another sheet for Jane and more for Billy and John. He lives the number symbols when he compares size, when he shares equally what he has, when he matches one to one, when he measures milk for cookie recipes, when he solves the problem of how many children can paint at the available easels and how many brushes they will need so that each color has its own brush. He understands the word and the number symbols because he uses them in concrete ways and because he lives them.

5. *The kindergarten program provides opportunities for the child to expand language as a means of communication and expression.* Originality in the expression of a child's own thoughts is the goal in language, whether this expression is by means of words, pictures, or dramatization. The child has many opportunities to express himself to other children, to small groups, to teachers, to the whole group. He expresses himself at conversation time when he shares his experiences and sometimes a favorite toy from home. He expresses himself in dramatic play in the housekeeping corner and in play with puppets. He likes to repeat rhymes and jingles and poetry introduced by the teacher. He communicates when he exchanges ideas, when he plans with the teacher and the group, when he solves problems, when he discusses, questions, remarks, chants. He has opportunities to communicate and express himself, and he has opportunities to listen to others in audience situations. He listens to the teacher when it is her turn and waits his turn to speak. He listens during story time, and he tells stories himself about the pictures in books.

All these experiences and opportunities help him develop the ability to collect and express his thoughts. These experiences help develop his vocabulary, his sentence structure, and his poise. These experiences and opportunities help him develop the ability to listen, to hear, and to follow simple directions.

6. *Kindergarten broadens the child's understanding of the social world.* You have noticed how interested a child is in his world. He asks questions, endlessly it seems to you. But there is a difference now. Earlier he asked questions, too. He hardly waited for the answer, though, and lost interest when the explanation was too long or too complicated or too dull. Now he really wants to know and pesters until he has an answer that is satisfying to him. Or he rummages about in his world until he finds an answer that is satisfying for the time being.

The good kindergarten program recognizes a child's urge to find out. It recognizes that he most wants to find out about his immediate environment, or living space. He brings impressions with him from his four or five years of living. These previous impressions as well as new impressions, both simple and complex, need sorting out and interpretation. The good kindergarten program realizes that a child's world is broadened by this sorting-out, finding-out, and putting-together process. This process takes time, requires help and opportunities for many real experiences. Also needed are understanding and skilled guidance.

The child's social world is broadened by direct contact with the school personnel and with the school plant itself. His social world is broadened by many experiences outside the school, such as trips to points of interest in the community. His social world is broadened by hearing stories about children of other lands and how they live, by discussing the child's and his classmates' homes and families, and how we are all inter-dependent. To foster further understanding of the world around him, a child has the opportunity to live, play, and work with children who have a different skin color as well as different capacities, different backgrounds, and diverse experiences. All this is part of his learning. It takes time, it needs help, it requires skilled guidance. It takes plenty of the right kind of opportunities to investigate and to grow in his five-year-old way.

7. *Kindergarten broadens the child's understanding of the scientific world.* The child brings with him the most important ally of further understanding and further growth: curiosity. This curiosity, or wanting-to-know, is very real. It causes a child to want-to-do. It is the trigger that starts the finding-out, sorting-out, and putting-together process. This curiosity, then, is the biggest ally of education. The process of finding out, or discovery, sorting out, or analysis, and putting-together, or synthesis, is not completed in the kindergarten year. It can continue all through life. The word *can* is used advisedly, for the process can continue only if curiosity remains alive, and is not smothered by too much pressure or too much tension.

Kindergarten programs give a child the time and the opportunity to express his curiosity in questioning, in exploring, in experimenting. Many of the answers about the scientific world will necessarily be partial ones. But even partial answers can ultimately lead to the whole answer. And a child's appreciation is heightened with exposure to a variety of topics.

In the child's study of nature, his powers of observation are being cultivated during his important early years, when he is highly curious. He is taught to think of plants and animals as friends and helpers whose ways can be learned by observation. He is helped to see domestic animals as helpers who deserve care and consideration. It is not likely that a cow will be found in the child's kindergarten room, but a wide variety of other animals will be. Domestic animals, pets, fish, frogs, and insects are as much a part of kindergarten as light fixtures and window shades. The plant world has its representatives in kindergarten also, in the form of an outdoor garden, a window box, potted plants, and a terrarium. The representatives of the plant and the animal kingdom are as varied as the fertile minds of the children and the teacher, and as numerous as the size of the room will allow. The emphasis is where it rightly belongs: on care and observation and function rather than on structure.

8. *The kindergarten program provides satisfying esthetic experiences for the child.* It recognizes that the movement and sound in a five-year-old need outlets and rich experiences. Music and rhythmic and art experiences in the kindergarten program are designed to help a child express his creativity. He sings and chants songs of his own making. He draws, models, paints, constructs, and weaves products that meet his child standards. He dances, and he uses rhythmic instruments in ways that mean something to him.

These esthetic experiences in music and art are also designed to introduce the rich cultural heritage from our land and other lands. The child listens to and learns to sing songs he can enjoy. He listens to music he can learn to love. He learns new ways of using rhythmic instruments to make new sounds to increase his enjoyment, to find new outlets for his expressions. He learns the feel of new media in art, and he experiments with familiar media.

Even though he is not yet concerned with the artistic standards of the adult world, nor should he be, he is helped and encouraged to express his ideas artistically. He is helped and encouraged by having a wealth of stimulating experiences, time for creation, varied and suitable equipment and materials. He is also helped with technique. The emphasis here is not on how the child could or should do something to produce an acceptable product in adult eyes. The emphasis is on how he can achieve a certain end he has in mind, with the help of simple technique. The emphasis is on his impressions of his world, rather than on adult impressions of what he should see.

The kindergarten provides for further satisfying esthetic experiences by providing a bright, cheerful, eye-appealing room scaled to child size. He sees and enjoys the carefully selected framed pictures on the walls. He enjoys and contributes to the collection of colorful cards, photographs, pictures on the bulletin board. He enjoys the objects tastefully arranged in the room. These may be vases, dolls, puppets in costumes, figures of animals, and other artifacts brought from the teacher's own home or borrowed from a children's museum. He enjoys the picture books with their illustrations, drawn from imaginary and real experiences in his world.

9. *The kindergarten program provides opportunities for the child to develop his sense of responsibility.* The five-year-old loves to be a helper. If he is given tasks that are not too big or too demanding for him, he can complete them. He can experience the glow that comes from a finished job, perhaps not well done by adult standards, but well done by child standards. There are jobs that need to be done daily as a part of the routine

of the room. The coat closet and the separate cubby need to be kept neat. A coat or a jacket or a sweater is not tossed in the corner but hung up as are cap and scarf. Boots and rubbers are placed neatly so that they can dry and be ready for wear. The resting mat or blanket is folded before it is put away in the cubby. There are plants to be watered. There are pets to be fed and watered. There are materials and equipment that need to be put away at clean-up time. At work time, materials are used economically, and the job is done. Usually enough time is allotted to finish a job in one session. If the project is not completed, it can be carefully put away for the next work period. There are utensils and refreshments to be passed out and then cleared away at midmorning lunch time. There are visitors to be greeted and made comfortable.

The child gets to school on time in the morning. Preferably, he walks to school by himself or rides on the school bus with the other children. And he gets home in the afternoon, preferably by himself.

Small accomplishments, these, by adult standards. But giant steps in the direction of growth by kindergarten child standards.

This is the crux: The good kindergarten program is an open invitation to the fives.

An invitation to growth.

4 Roots in Early Childhood for Continuous Learning*

ROSE MUKERJI, *Brooklyn College*

If we believe that the early childhood years are the foundation years, we must accept the principle of continuity of learning. Do we believe in differing tempos of learning, that we can help children "catch up," that young children need abundant individual attention? Are we nurturing the roots of later development?

Early childhood education is "in." Those of us who work in the field as teachers, administrators, or researchers are suddenly very much in fashion. We even made the 1964 Democratic Party Platform, which said,

* Reprinted with permission from *Young Children*, September 1965, vol. 20, no. 6. Copyright © 1965, National Association for the Education of Young Children. Permission also granted by *Childhood Education*, September 1965, vol. 42, no. 1. Copyright © 1965, The Association for Childhood Education International.

". . . more educational resources must be directed to pre-school training."
Also, in his State of the Union message to Congress on January 5 of this
year, President Johnson, as part of his goal to improve the quality of
American life through a $1.5 billion educational program said, "For the
pre-school years we will help needy children become aware of the excitement of learning" (*New York Times*, 1965).

There is a certain logic in the new emphasis on early childhood.
Some problems in our society have become terribly urgent. School drop-
outs are not only unemployed but, in most cases, they are unemployable
in the changing labor market. Democratic values are being challenged on
many fronts. The effects of living in depressed urban or rural areas, in
poverty, in segregated ghettos, are being shown in widespread personal
tragedy and waste that our conscience cannot allow.

Because we are concerned, we are now witnessing a coming together
of many forces in concerted efforts to develop programs that will tackle
the global nature of these problems. We are seeing a groundswell of
opinion which says that to be effective any program must begin with
young children—younger than we thought. Sociologists, economists, political leaders, community leaders, and labor and business leaders are now
joining the educators and other social scientists in this new trend. The
focal point has moved steadily downward—from adolescence to childhood and now to early childhood, which extends from primary grades
down through kindergarten to children of three and four.

The image of a clean slate for each child at the beginning of the
administrative calendar year applies only to the chalkboard, not to the
child. Even if the ubiquitous cumulative files were inadvertently inciner-
ated, the stream of a child's learning would continue to flow—maybe in
turbulence or in almost stagnant pools—but continuous nevertheless. Because this is the nature of a child's development, new learning can be
rooted only in previous learning, and earlier learning affects that which
follows. The idea of continuous learning is, therefore, inevitable. The
logic of utilizing the educational potential of the early childhood years is,
I believe, self-evident.

Although it is obvious that no single agency or institution can, by
itself, solve the problems already mentioned, it is also obvious that the
schools as an institution have a special responsibility for tackling the
problems that face our children. I do want to make it clear that I'm not
talking about only the special problems faced by our disadvantaged
children. I'm talking about the problems every child faces as he struggles
to make his way in our complex society, to grow up, to become civilized,
if you will, to become a person with a zest for living and learning, for
becoming independent, for becoming socially responsible, for feeling
good about himself as a person. And so it is that, at a time when many

forces in our society are becoming increasingly, and sometimes dramatically, aware of the importance and potential power of early childhood education, the schools themselves are becoming more and more involved in how to utilize these early years in nourishing the later school experiences of our children through continuous learning patterns.

Some Questions

In this connection, we should ask ourselves some pointed questions. We should ask whether our programs for young children take into account the research and empirical findings that are the basis of early childhood educational practice. We should also ask whether we have fallen into some comfortable ruts of familiarity. We should ask about high pressure, Madison Avenue gimmicks that are purported to solve any and every problem. We should ask questions that are 1965 questions. We should continue to ask basic questions that were already 2,000 years old in Plato's time. We should ask what early childhood education *can* do and what it *cannot* be expected to do. Let's not fall into the trap of expecting preschool and early childhood education to do the impossible. But let us ask in what particular and significant ways early childhood education can serve to improve the continuous learning of all our children.

About Compensatory Programs

Putting all three- or four-year-olds from depressed areas into school will not, in itself, inevitably reverse the downward pull of failure which is too often their life story. We need to ask what kind of compensatory programs will make a difference. Is it enough to provide a verbally rich environment when the content has no relevance to children's lives and problems? Does the very way in which compensatory programs are organized tend to extend, rather than to reduce, segregation in education? What do we lose by ignoring the special impact of peer models on children's learning when we limit early childhood classes to those from a single socioeconomic class?

About Individualizing Instruction

Fortunately we know quite a bit about the general developmental patterns through which children grow and the general sequence of levels through which they mature. We also have a substantial amount of knowledge about the wide range within each level and within any age group. This foundation saves us from getting trapped in the "numbers game." According to the numbers game, if *one* three-year-old can do a certain thing, whether it be to skip with alternating feet or to read a few words, then *every* three-year-old can do so, and it is the obligation of a teacher to apply enough skillful pressure to make every three-year-old accomplish these tasks.

Because of the wide developmental range of children within any chronological year, it is impossible to draw a blueprint of a good program for every three-year-old group, for every five-year-old group, or for every seven-year-old group. Even in this age of superstandardization, no amount of pressure from teachers, or administrators, or parents can standardize children's tempos in learning. Consequently, we are obliged to temper and adapt our teaching not only to the generalized developmental levels of growth and learning but also to the specific styles and tempos of individual children. Doesn't our very conception of the term "early childhood education" imply that these years from three to seven or eight should be considered as a single organic unit in which learning is not only continuous but also proceeds at different tempos for different children? I believe it does.

About Money and Numbers

In thinking about individualizing instruction in a group setting, shouldn't we ask, "What ratio between teachers and young children makes the teaching-learning encounter really productive?" Some of the newer compensatory programs are following earlier, excellent programs by setting up classes of fifteen youngsters with one teacher for five-year-olds. For four-year-olds, the ratio is seven to one; and for three-year-olds, the ratio is five to one. Does that sound expensive? If so, then we might consider the actual current cost, which requires increased special school personnel to cope with children's failure. Just think of the present demand for remedial teachers, tutoring services, auxiliary teachers, consultants, helping teachers, and, the latest designation, "other teaching personnel." And what of the frustration and fragmentation that results from having to mesh the schedules of all these people?

One young first-grade teacher once told me, "I'm exhausted trying to keep up with all the so-called help I'm getting. Sometimes I feel I'm teaching for the clock and the auxiliary teachers instead of my children. Just give me twenty children and shut my door. I think I can do a pretty good job on the rest." Maybe the more effective way will turn out to be the most economical way in financial as well as in human terms.

About Time and Scope

Out of concern for the education of our children, suggestions are being made to lengthen the school day for young children. Yes, we should ask questions about how long the school day should be for specific children. But even more, we should take a careful look at what happens to children during the extended day. Aside from the amount, what is the *quality* of one-to-one interaction between teacher and child? Important as this is for all children, it is of critical importance to our large population of disadvantaged young children, whose learning deficits, to some degree, stem directly from the lack of individual contact with an adult who is encouraging, supportive, and enriching.

We need to ask the questions that loom larger and larger on the horizon. How can we build bridges between the school and the home? How can we build bridges among the children, the parents, and the teachers? How can we implement the multidimensional approach that includes social services, health services, community agencies, and educational agencies in the service of children who are, first and foremost, members of a primary family group? Is not the conception underlying Project Head Start of the Economic Opportunity program a move toward helping communities build such bridges?

Potential Power of Early Childhood Education

The new emphasis on three- and four-year-old school experience somehow implies that, by starting earlier, children can get to a certain point faster or that they can go further along the educational road. There are, as yet, very little data to substantiate this. Why, then, do so many people now place so much hope on extending downward and strengthening the earliest years of children's school experience? Why do they agree that these early years may be the most fruitful in meeting the challenge of educating our children effectively? I, for one, believe that the early childhood years are particularly fruitful and have great potential power for improving education, for four reasons.

Psychosocial Roots

In the first place, these are the root years during which children meet the challenge of knowing who they are in relation to people outside the unique confines of the family. These are the key years in which children learn how others accept them and their demands. They work through problems of getting along with others. They build their strategies of rejection, of acceptance, of domination, of submission, of abstention, of leading, of following, of compromising, of gradually putting themselves in another's shoes and learning empathy for the human experience.

In the early school years, a child may learn to be self-confident, to strengthen inner controls and disciplines, to see in the mirror of other children and adults that he is a worthy human being. A child may also learn that he is a failure; that he is inferior for reasons he cannot control; that somehow his family is wrong; that he can't understand the dialect of school talk; that teachers can't understand his home dialect; that he is not worthy of respect or of being cared for.

I do not mean to imply an either-or self-concept in children. I only sketch the opposite poles and leave you to fill in the continuum and complexity of feelings that more accurately describe the psychosocial experience of young children during their early school years. The implications of the continuous learning idea rest on the fact that a young child's view of himself has a profound and pervasive effect on how he functions during his elementary and later school years. The school, therefore, must give him many opportunities to build on his strengths and to taste frequently the sweetness and encouragement of success in privately significant and socially important events. A program is needed that builds not on those strengths which fit neatly within the blinders of our conventional concepts but on those reality-based strengths that permit a child to cope with the demands of his life, however torturous they may sometimes be.

Roots of Concept Formation

In the second place, the early childhood years are the root years in concept formation. In fact, according to Hunt (1964), "It now looks as though early experience may be even more important for the perceptual, cognitive, and intellectual functions than it is for the emotional and temperamental functions."

These are the years when curiosity impels a child to reach out into his environment, to touch, to squeeze, to taste, to ask the interminable "why"—to try to know. His primary strategy for intellectual growth is active, manipulative, and sensory. He utilizes concrete material and active intercourse to build his conceptual scheme of the world.

What are young children curious about? They are intensely curious about people and their relationships, about ages, about marriage, and about parenthood. To illustrate, student teachers recorded the following one morning:

Three-year-old: How come you have a mommy if you're a lady?
Four-year-old: (to student teacher) Do you have any children?
Student T: No, Andy, I don't.
Four-year-old: But aren't you a teacher?
Student T: Yes.
Four-year-old: Aren't all teachers mommies?
Three-year-old: Girls don't marry girls—do they?

In this way children try to fit a new element into a previously determined category, and find that it doesn't quite fit. However, as they meet an element of dissonance, the teacher can help them formulate a more precise category and a more accurate concept.

Young children are also trying to figure out certain quantitative measures. As one three-year-old said to another student teacher:

You must be the oldest teacher in the room because you have the biggest feet!

Or, as one five-year-old figured:

David: When are we going home?
Student T: We'll be going soon.
David: Look at your watch and tell me.
Student T: In an hour.
David: (thinks for a moment) Oh, you mean two programs from now.

Or, as one four-year-old complained:

Beverly: I don't see why Anne is bigger than I am but she's only three and I'm four.
Beverly: Yes, Anne is taller, but you are older.
Teacher: Oh, I know. Anne is bigger than I am but I was here for more time.

Listening to the questions and comments of an individual child points up how uneven his conceptual map is at a given time. Iver, a little boy of three, verbalized these thoughts in a five minute period:

A subway is a little house for a train and tracks are a sidewalk for a train.
Do animals grow to be people?
(When his mother wanted him to go back to sleep because it was too early for her) The lightning is mixing with the darkning and it's almost daytime.

There is no question that a single experience, no matter how successful, is not enough to build a reliable concept. A child must make many approaches from many angles over a period of time before a concept has some measure of stability. The work of Piaget, Bruner, Jersild, and others support the proposition that children cannot move toward abstract structure and reasoning without a broad base of direct encounters from which to abstract and generalize. Early childhood programs are now, and must continue to be, rich and diversified in concrete, manipulative, and sensory learning experiences. In such a setting, children will gradually develop a strategy for collating relevant data and encompassing an element of dissonance that leads them to refine previous concepts and make them more precise. In other words, the way in which conceptual growth takes place, building previous encounters into manageable sets and abstractions, underscores the absolute necessity of a continuous learning framework within the school.

Roots of Language

In the third place, the early childhood years are the root years for language development. Although there can be thought without language, many kinds of thought are intimately linked with, and dependent upon, language. Concepts are often coded linguistically. Language becomes a highly efficient way to store information, to recover information, and to solve problems. It is a tool for organizing and structuring data according to identity, similarity, difference, according to space and time, and according to cause and effect relationships.

Whenever comparisons are drawn between middle-class and lower-class children, a point is made of the marked differences in the way that language is used by the children. Labeling disadvantaged children as nonverbal, is, I am glad to say, a cliché not substantiated by careful study. In their self-structured play situations many of these children are highly verbal. They may use Spanish or other languages, and they may use forms other than the standard English dialect, but one could hardly call them nonverbal. These same children may *appear* to be nonverbal when they feel inadequate and, therefore, they may resist making verbal responses to teacher-initiated and controlled discussions.

It is, however, true that the quality of verbalization between the two classes is different. Disadvantaged children have vocabulary disabilities. The length and complexity of their sentences, their articulation and sound discrimination do not match those of the more favored group. But when it comes to the expressiveness of language, the distinctions are less clear. It would be difficult to improve on the power of this exclamation about a five-year-old girl, "Man, she gotta wallop, knock you cross de moon!"

In analyzing the causes of differences in language development between children of different classes, many researchers point out that middle-class children are flooded with words in their environment and that they have many opportunities to talk with adults. Disadvantaged children, on the other hand, lack this extensive verbal stimulation. In fact, most of their conversation is with other children who are similarly lacking in verbal skills.

The implications for teacher intervention in helping children to build a stronger base are many. They point to the necessity for teachers to talk with children about what interests children in a one-to-one, or a small-group, setting. They also point to the necessity of providing opportunities to build meaningful vocabulary through interesting stimuli and involvement. Teachers can consciously introduce words and synonyms related to children's play, provide opportunities for children to recall these words during structured meetings when children report on their activities, make tape recordings of children's interesting experiences and provide sets of earphones for groups of children to listen to these tapes independently. The measure of success in enhancing children's language can be found in the degree to which the extended language becomes part of children's communication during their play.

Artificial word drill in a vacuum will hardly accomplish the same results. It may *seem* to take less time, but since the purpose is mainly to please the teacher (and some children readily respond to this kind of pressure) the new words and ways of speaking do not become the children's own within their play. Since reading, even in our literacy-oriented society, does not replace verbal language communication but is built on it, and, since language is so intimately connected with conceptualization and thinking, it is evident that a continuity of teaching is necessary to develop language ability from nursery school through kindergarten, through primary grades and beyond.

Roots of Creativity

In the fourth place, the early childhood years are the root years for creativity. Torrance (1963), who has done considerable research in creativity, says, "From the research evidence available so far and from the observation of many investigators, creative imagination during early childhood reaches a peak between four and four-and-a-half years and is followed by a drop at about age five when the child enters school for the first time. . . . There are now indications that the drop in five-year-olds is a man-made or culture-made phenomenon rather than a natural one."

If this is so, I would call it not a man-made phenomenon but a man-made tragedy. In a society that needs all the creativity it can foster to save itself from destruction and decay, we certainly can't afford to stifle the first seeds of creativity in our young children.

There may be some room for semantic differences as to the creativity of young children. However, there is no question that a young child's free exploration and manipulation of materials and ideas is very closely akin to the first improvisational and free-wheeling stage of the most sophisticated and mature efforts toward creativity of any kind. The child's play, which is an ever-recurring creative act for him, is his fountainhead of creative experience. He not only tests himself and his ideas through play, he not only discovers relationships and truths through play, he not only practices and drills himself intensely through play, he also sustains the creative process through which he learns.

It has been found that, as the young child continues in school, not only is his highly creative behavior unrewarded, but it is not looked on favorably by his teachers or his peers (Eisner, 1963). Getzels and Jackson have found that teachers prefer high IQ students to highly creative students. But if we wish to encourage creativity in our children, we must value it. We must develop a curriculum that has many opportunities for original work, for self-selected work, for real problem-solving situations, and for the practice of discovery techniques as ways of learning. If we really value creativity, we will understand that the supportive and psychologically safe atmosphere in our classrooms must continue throughout the child's school career. The creative spirit is too sensitive to be chopped off during the primary years, and then be expected to reappear later. Continuous learning is indispensable to the nurturing of creativity.

Because the early childhood years are the root years for beginning self concepts in a world of people, for beginning intellectual concepts, for a foundation of oral language, and for creativity, it is no wonder that thoughtful and concerned people in education and related spheres of our society, consider early childhood education to be an excitingly unique arena for improving the educational experience of our nation's learners, providing, of course, that the children are seen as continuously growing, in the center of a multi-dimensional life.

References

Eisner, Elliot W. April 1963. Research in creativity: some findings and conceptions. *Childhood Educ.*, p. 373.

Hunt, J. McV. 1964. The psychological basis for using pre-school enrichment as an antidote for cultural deprivation. *Merrill-Palmer Quart.*, **10**, 3.

New York Times. January 5, 1965, p. 16, col. 4.

Torrance, Paul. April 1963. Creativity—what research says to the teacher. *Nat. Educ. J.*, **28**, 10.

5   Pre-school Education*

J. W. GETZELS, *University of Chicago*

Let me say at once that I have not myself worked with pre-school children in the educational setting. But this is not without some advantage in a paper whose primary intent is to raise issues rather than to settle them, for I am not already so committed to a particular theoretic or pedagogic point of view that any other is immediately unacceptable, if not altogether inconceivable.

That there is a crucial need for change in the educational provisions for the lower class or culturally deprived child hardly bears argument. We need not belabor the point here. Nor is the need an entirely new one, although the wonder and tragedy is that we have just got around to doing anything about it in a concerted way. *Middletown* (Lynd and Lynd, 1929) in the late twenties, *Who Shall Be Educated* (Warner *et al.*, 1944) in the early forties, *Social Class Influences upon Learning* (Davis, 1948) in the late forties all dealt with this issue. Indeed, more than a generation ago the Lynds showed that at least in Middletown by the time a child entered school he was already typed intellectually by economic status. Although only 13.4 percent of the Business Class children in the first grade were below 90 in IQ, fully 42.5 percent of the Working Class children were below this level in the same grade. The Lynds raised the question then in essentially the terms we are doing to-day: To what extent was this observed difference in intelligence a reflection of the "modification of native endowment by varying environmental conditions"?

Nor were proposals for doing something special for the lower class child in school lacking. Among the proposed lines of attack were: the curriculum should be altered to take into account the experience of these children, education should be differentiated according to their abilities, the existing curriculum should be enriched to enable the lower class child to catch up with the middle class child, and so on. But what all these

* *Teachers College Record*, December 1966, vol. 68, no. 3. Reprinted by permission. This is a version of a paper presented by Professor Getzels at the 1965 White House Conference on Education. In his text, he sums up with unusual clarity the research done with respect to deprivation in the pre-school years; he provides an overview of programs, and he identifies what he believes to be the chief issues confronting us in this field. Most significantly, perhaps, he raises some questions about the standards which are to govern the "transformation" of deprived children into fully functioning members of society. Is it simply the children who are to be transformed? What of the schools themselves?

proposals had in common was that they attempted to work within the prevailing organization of the schools. Their fundamental intent was remedial rather than preventive—to do something *after* the child was in school rather than *before*.

The Dilemma of Discontinuity

It is precisely for this reason that these proposals seemed only to pose the dilemma rather than to provide a solution. For they neglected to face up fully to two unavoidable issues. First is the claim for the preeminent impact of early experience, that it is during the early period that the child not only acquires a characteristic set of values, language, and fund of information, but he literally *learns to learn*. He acquires the tools, so to speak, for meeting the problems he will face in school. Second is the claim that the values, language, information, and methods of learning acquired by the middle class child is *continuous* with what will be required of him in school; the values, language, information, and method of learning acquired by the lower class child are *discontinuous* with what will be required of him in school. It is as if the one group obtained a set of tools applicable to the school situation, and the other a set of tools *not* applicable to the school situation, but the school expected the two groups to perform as if they had equally applicable tools and resources.

It is in these terms—the problem of learning to learn and the relationship between pre-school experience and educational expectations—that we may raise the following questions:

1. What is the effect of environment on the development of school-related abilities?
2. How early must the opportunity for school-related experiences be available in the environment?
3. What are the differences in the continuity or discontinuity of pre-school experiences and school expectations between culturally-deprived and non-deprived children?
4. What is the nature of compensatory pre-school education, and what are some of the current procedural issues?
5. What are some of the long-range underlying issues?

I need hardly say that I shall not be able in the pages at my disposal to deal with these questions in any depth. But I have taken my charge seriously: in view of the goals of the White House Conference, it is more important for the paper to open for exploration a wide range of issues than to provide conclusions, recommendations, or attempt to settle any one issue definitively.

Effects of Environment

We may begin with what seems to be the fundamental question underlying the entire problem of cultural deprivation and pre-school education: What is the effect of environment on learning to learn?

We have already cited the study of a generation ago by the Lynds showing a cognitive deficit in lower over upper class children. Studies along this line have steadily increased in number, rigor, and specificity of demonstrated relationship. To mention only a sampling: Irwin (1948) found a systematic relationship between mastery of speech sounds in infants 1 to 30 months of age and the occupational status of the family; Milner (1951) found a significant relationship between the reading readiness of first grade children and the "verbal environment" at home; Montague (1964) found a similar relationship between the arithmetic concepts of kindergarten children and the socio-economic status of their families; and, in a notable series of studies, Deutsch and his colleagues (1964) have gone a step further in specificity and shown that not only are there differences in cognitive performance between social-class and race groups but within the groups, a "particular level of cognitive performance reflects certain specific environmental characteristics"; Hess (1964) has shown the same relationship for the acquisition of language and the nature of the mother-child interaction. In short, numerous studies attest to the view that the development of both general and specific cognitive abilities—the abilities required for success in school—is determined in many critical ways by the availability of relevant experiences in the pre-school environment.

The Timing of Experience

We may turn to the second question that seems to be crucial: How *early* must the opportunity for the relevant experience be available? Is, for example, the present school age—the magic number six—time enough? We know very little about this for any specific ability nor, of course, in view of different rates of maturation, for any given individual. Nonetheless, an increasing number of studies are showing that it is the lack of *early* experience that may be most damaging, not only to such psychological abilities as learning but even to such presumably physiological abilities as vision.

The most direct evidence on what we may call the "timing" of experience comes from experiments with animals—experiments that cannot be done with humans. For example, Austin Riesen (1947) some years ago deprived animals of light at various stages during their growth. He found that it was deprivation during the early period that resulted in the most serious perceptual deficit. There is, however, relevant if less direct evidence for humans as well. For example, Bloom (1964) estimated that the long-term over-all effect of living in a "culturally deprived" as against a "culturally abundant" environment to be 20 IQ points, and hypothesized that this effect was spaced developmentally as follows: from birth to 4 years, 10 IQ units; from 4 to 8 years, 6 IQ units; from 8 to 17 years, 4 IQ units. The rank-order correlation between the hypothesized effects and empirical data from a number of studies was .95, the absolute amount of the observed effects being substantially greater even than the estimates.

But the evidence that is perhaps most dramatically instructive for humans is from the "natural experiments" provided by individuals who were congenitally blind and given sight by surgical operation as adults. As Hebb (1949) points out, Senden studied the perceptual behavior of numerous such individuals, and much to his surprise and most people's disbelief, found that these patients literally had to *learn to see*. There was a period when, despite no structural defect in sensory apparatus, these persons could not distinguish between a square and a triangle, a sphere and a cube. They had to stop and count the corners one after another just as a young child does. To perceive these objects as whole figures, with distinctive features immediately evident, was not possible for a long time, not because they could not see—note, they could see and count the corners—but because they had not had the necessary *experience in generalizing* from vision.

It is entirely possible that the normal child goes through a similar process of literally learning to perceive, and that as adults we are able to "see" a square or a triangle at a glance as a result of the imperceptible but complex learning we did as children. Much of what may appear as somehow arising "innately"—perception, language, value, what has been called the child's characteristic "learning set" or what I should like to call his "codes for future learning"—is in large measure acquired through the mediation of appropriate multiple and early experiences. The question is not whether there are individual differences that are innate. The point rather is that given the same potentiality for learning at birth, the availability and timing of experience appear to facilitate or inhibit the expression of the potentiality. And as we have already indicated, there are significant differences in this respect: the relevant experiences tend to be available for some children and not for others. Indeed, the term culturally deprived may be taken to mean lack of availability of such experiences at the appropriate time.

Learning the Codes

This brings us to the third question: What are the differences in the continuity or discontinuity of pre-school experiences and school expectations between culturally deprived and non-deprived children, or more specifically, what is the nature of the differences in the "learning sets" or "codes for future learning" acquired by the two groups?

We have already remarked on such specific differences as are measured by vocabulary, arithmetic, reading-readiness tests and such general perceptual and cognitive differences as are measured by intelligence tests. Two other salient differences must also be considered in this connection.

There are two general "codes" a child learns through his early contacts with the environment: one is a *language code*, the other a *value code*. The language code gives him the categories for structuring and communicating his experiences. The value code tells him what in his experience is important—worth attending to. In a sense, language becomes the window through which he perceives experience, and values determine what in his experience he will cherish or reject. And it is argued that it is precisely with respect to the character of these crucial codes—the value code and the language code—that the disadvantaged child differs most sharply from the advantaged child and from school requirements.

Explicitly or implicitly, the school requires an *achievement* ethic, with consequent high valuation of the future, deferred gratification, and symbolic commitment. It takes for granted that every child has had an opportunity to experience beliefs that anyone can get to the top, and if he tries he too can get to the top. The future, not the present, is what counts, and one must use the present to prepare for the future. Time therefore must not be wasted—note the vernacular "time is money." It is expected that the child will be able to defer immediate gratification for later gratification through symbolic commitment to "success." Not only are these the values of the school, but they are the values of the environment in which most middle class children are brought up.

In contrast to this, it is pointed out, the lower class child has experienced only a *survival* or *subsistence* ethic (not an achievement ethic) with consequent high evaluation on the *present* (not the future) on *immediate gratification* (not deferred gratification) and *concrete commitment* (not symbolic commitment). Where the lower class child lives hardly anyone ever gets to the top—often one can hardly move across the street. And time is not important or potentially valuable if there is not going to be anything to do with it anyway. The commitment is to immediate and concrete gratification—to the satisfactions of here and now—for what does an appeal to symbolic success mean where success is measured only by subsistence or survival? In short, the lower class in contrast to the middle class child may face a severe discontinuity in values upon coming to school—a discontinuity that may have a profound effect on his behavior toward school, and no less an effect on the school's behavior toward him.

What we have said about value is also applicable to language. The work to which I shall refer is by Basil Bernstein (1964), which is consonant with other studies in this area. He argues that different social strata generate different speech systems or linguistic codes, regulating the selection an individual makes from what is available in the language as a whole. These linguistic codes, which develop early and are stabilized through time, come to play an important role in the intellectual, social, and affective life of the child. There are two language codes: one "elaborated," the other "restricted." In the restricted code, the vocabulary and syntactic structure are drawn from a *narrow* range of possibilities, the organizing elements of the speech are *simple*, and there is *considerable dependence on extra-verbal channels of communication* like gestures. In the elaborated code, the vocabulary and syntactic structure are drawn from a *wide* range of possibilities, the organizing elements of the speech are *complex*, and there is *little reliance on extra-verbal channels of communication:* the message must be given and sought in the verbal material itself.

As may already have been anticipated, a middle class child is likely to experience and acquire an elaborated language code; a lower class child a restricted language code. But the school is of course predominantly concerned with elaborated language codes. Accordingly, in language as in values, for one child school is *continuous* with his early experience, for the other child school is *discontinuous* with his early experience.

The Pains of Failure

It is often said that the lower class child fails in school because he is apathetic or aggressive. Without denying this, some would turn it around and raise the further question whether he is not also increasingly apathetic and aggressive in school because he fails. For what can be more tormenting than to be faced day upon day with a situation you cannot handle and yet may not leave on pain of severe punishment? Insofar as the pre-school experiences of the lower class child have not prepared him for school, school can only be a source of frustration: he is neither ready to do what is required nor can he escape. The reaction to this type of frustration is hopelessness and rage. In school, the hopelessness is manifested in apathy, i.e., psychological withdrawal from the source of frustration, and the rage in aggression, i.e., physical attack upon the source of frustration. Ultimately, not only does this failure lead to dropping-out with consequent unemployability, but the patterns of apathy and aggression maintained over the compulsory school years often become stabilized into deep-seated maladjustment and delinquency. From this point of view, compensatory pre-school education may be seen as an effort to bring the experience of the lower class child into greater continuity with the expectations of the school—expectations that presuppose middle class value and language codes for its children—not only in order to increase learning but to avoid the frustrating consequences of the discontinuities between the home and the school.

Manifold Programs

We may turn now to the fourth question we posed: What is the nature of the current programs in compensatory pre-school education?

The number and diversity of compensatory pre-school projects are growing so rapidly that it is hazardous to say anything about *the* nature of the programs without risk of over-simplifying and being out of date almost at once. It is more instructive to speak of *alternatives* in the current undertakings. For example, within walking distance of the University of Chicago are several separate programs. One is in a long established predominantly middle-class nursery. The proposed curriculum includes free play, group games, show and tell, and neighborhood trips—activities which do not differ from what is done regularly in this nursery. Another is in the local public school, which has never dealt with nursery or pre-kindergarten children—middle or lower class. Among the stated aims are to give the children experience with the tools of learning—pencils, crayons, books, etc.—and to develop their readiness for regular school activities. A third program, which grew out of a volunteer college student project, was designed specifically for culturally-deprived children. The staff was selected on the basis of experience in pre-school education with such children, and there is heavy emphasis on auditory and visual discrimination, rhythmics, and self-expression. A fourth program is in a local Montessori School, and will presumably be influenced by its philosophy and methods. From among the Montessori activities are included " 'practical life' projects (e.g., buttoning, tying, cleaning dishes, polishing copper, peeling carrots)" and there is emphasis on the ability "to look at, *see*, and handle materials." Only one of the programs was in existence a year ago.

The diversity and recency that we have seen here in miniature are representative of current pre-school programs at large. An inventory of compensatory education programs—exclusive of Project Head Start—shows pre-schools in operation in some 70 cities (Hess, 1965). Over half of these have been established within the past year or two. There is diversity in every aspect of the programs: the auspices may be as various as the public school system itself, a national welfare agency, or the local junior league; and, the personnel may range from two teachers, a social worker, two psychologists and a nurse for 32 children to six teachers and 36 teacher-aides for 240 children. The purpose of one program is said to be "to give the children of the poor the *same* experiences that are provided routinely to children of middle and upper-income families: vocabulary, verbal expression, cultural experience, and appreciation of learning"; but, in another the focus is on very different and more primitive activities: "development of listening skills and visual discrimination; provision of activities which engage touch, taste, and smell; and teachers will work with parents in orienting them toward the program and having them assist the development of the child."

Despite the variability in specific activities, the programs may be classified at least for analytic purposes into three broad categories. Explicitly or implicitly, in one the predominant assumption is that the observed deficiencies of the culturally deprived child are more superficial than fundamental—the differences are in quantity rather than in kind—and the pre-school experiences that are needed are *supplementary*; from this point of view, if a nursery or pre-school activity is good for the middle class child it is good also (if perhaps at some simpler level) for the lower class child. In the second, the assumption is that the significant deficiencies reside in the lack of familiarity with school-related objects and activities—say, pencils, books, the use of crayons, following directions—and the pre-school experiences the culturally deprived child needs are predominantly *academic-preparatory*. In the third, the assumption is that because of powerful environmental effects, the culturally deprived child becomes fundamentally different in self-concept, language, value, and perceptual process; from this point of view neither the supplementary nor the preparatory activities in themselves are sufficient: what is required are *specialized programs* that will *compensate for*, in the sense of *counteract*, the deleterious environmental effects (Bloom *et al.*, 1965; Deutsch, 1964). This diversity raises an obvious and serious issue: Which of the alternatives is likely to be more fruitful than another? It is not that a categorical answer can be forthcoming at once, but dealing with the issue systematically may lead to criteria for selecting activities and evaluating outcomes rather than proceeding by hit or miss.

Comparisons Needed

In view of the theoretical and procedural differences, it might be expected that observations to guide our choice would be abundant. This is unfortunately not so. There are no systematic comparisons of the relative effectiveness, say, of what we have called the supplementary and academic-preparatory procedures. There are no systematic comparisons of the relative effectiveness of different points of intervention within what we have called the specialized programs. Two relevant observations from the research that is available so far, however, can be made. One is that pre-school programs do tend to be effective in raising intelligence test scores, vocabulary level, expressive ability, arithmetical reasoning, and reading readiness. Independent reports by Bereiter *et al.* (1965), Gray and Klaus (1963), the Ypsilanti Public Schools (Weikart *et al.*, 1964), and the Racine studies (Larson and Olson, 1965) all point to one or more of these effects. This is enormously encouraging, even though they used different procedures and it is impossible to say what it is specifically in the pre-schools that accounts for the positive effects. The second observation is less encouraging. Although Deutsch (1962) has reported differences in the fifth grade favoring children who attended pre-school over those who did not, two recent experimental studies that have followed their pre-school and control children through kindergarten and first grade report that the initial differences tended *not* to be maintained in the regular school situation. The Racine study states bluntly:

> Potentially, the most useful conclusion which can be drawn from these data is that "one shot" compensatory programs would seem to be a waste of time and money. The fact that differences between groups disappeared and that in several areas the rate of growth of both groups regressed during the traditional first grade year supports this contention.
> If these implications are supported by future research it would seem that curricular revision over the entire twelve year school curriculum is a necessary part of any lasting solution to the basic problem of urban public school education.

It must be emphasized that this is but one study done with only a handful of subjects at the kindergarten rather than earlier period. Nonetheless, the issues raised by the data, tentative as they are, must be taken seriously: Assuming that compensatory pre-school education is effective during the pre-school period, what provisions need to be made in the regular school and in the home to maintain the effectiveness?

The most extensive pre-school undertaking is of course Project Head Start. It represents the awakening of the American conscience to the nation's most serious problem, and we can take pride that a generation hence no one will be able to say as we were about a generation ago that although the problem was recognized nothing courageous to solve it was attempted. But the very significance and massiveness of Head Start raises in urgent form all the issues implicit in the preceding discussion: What, for example, are the criteria for selecting activities from the available alternatives? On what basis will the effectiveness of what is being done be evaluated? Granted, it is difficult to see how any educational harm can come to the children, and there may be residual gains in medical care. But this too needs to be considered: May not long-term mischief be done to the idea of compensatory pre-school education if the possible lack of positive educational effects from this type of "one shot" program are immediately attributed to what some like to think is the inevitable failure of lower-class parents to cooperate, the immutability of the abilities of the children, or to the conception of compensatory education itself, rather than to possible shortcomings in the operation of the specific programs? To pose such a question is not to derogate what is being undertaken, but it does raise the issue as to whether a greater base in conceptualization, long-term planning, and evaluative research than is presently the case is not indicated for the future.

The Problem of Transformation

We turn finally and briefly to the last question: What are some of the broad underlying issues in the field?

We have been dealing with such procedural problems as the choice of alternate programs, the manner of evaluating outcomes, the selection of teachers and activities. These represent issues of means assuming the ends—the ends being, to put it most sharply, to transform the pre-school lower-class child in accordance with the requirements of the prevailing school. But there are at least two troublesome issues with respect to this that need examination. The first is concerned with the nature of the transformation we are prepared to impose on the culturally deprived child, and the second with the character of the school that will presumably serve as the standard for the transformation.

We must go back to the definition of "culturally deprived." The concept of cultural deprivation assumes that there is a normative or dominant middle-class culture, and that some children are deprived of experience with *this* culture (not *all* culture). From this point of view, the middle class child is also culturally-deprived—deprived in relation to the values and experiences of *another* culture, say intimacy and cooperativeness as against aloofness and competiveness. It is a *relational* not a quantitative concept, and cultural deprivation in the present context means only deprived of middle-class values, not necessarily good or plentiful values, and more especially of the values and experiences needed to get along in the school as it is currently constituted. It does not mean that the culturally deprived child necessarily has fewer values, nor that he may not have other values and experiences that are *assets*.

And this raises the first issue. Assume with Frank Riessman (1962) among others that the lower class child *does* have certain assets in the way of values and experiences which are not only functional in his environment but are of intrinsic worth: "the cooperativeness and mutual aid that mark the extended family; avoidance of the strain accompanying competitiveness and individualism; equalitarianism, informality, and warm humor; freedom from self-blame and parental over-protection; the children's enjoyment of each other's company, and lessened sibling rivalry; the security found in the extended family and in traditional outlook." What will be the effect of imposing contrary middle-class attitudes such as achievement-anxiety on these assets and the child's functioning in his environment, especially if his environment remains as it is? Can a program of compensatory education for the disadvantaged even at its best be salutary in any ultimate way without altering the disadvantaged environment giving rise to the disadvantaged child? Will the ravages of poverty and discrimination on the child's conception of life and of himself disappear if Appalachia and Harlem are permitted to remain as they are?

The second issue is not unrelated to the first. Compensatory early education is predicated on the criterion of success in school as the measure of fruitful socialization; the children are to be raised according to the modes of behavior and thought rewarded in the classroom. But there are those who would say that the demands of the present elementary school are themselves contradictory: on the one hand, the school rewards complacency, conformity, and docility, and on the other, it implies later success through ingenuity, daring, and competitiveness. And more, it is defective educationally: it can hardly serve as a model. Thus, to mention only three or four observers reporting from different points of vantage, Bruno Bettelheim (1961) suggests that "learning inhibitions can come from a child's desire for honesty and truth, and from trying to succeed in terms of his own life experience and of clear-cut desires and values"— do Sally, Tom, and Puff represent "honesty and truth in the light of his own experience" for the Negro child or for that matter for any child; Jules Henry (1957) shows how relentlessly honest feeling and originality are stamped out in the elementary school by the prevailing rivalry which is at once stimulated and feared by the teacher herself; Patricia Sexton

(1965) points out how the femininity of the school, to use her term, "emasculates" the boys not only affectively but cognitively; and Edgar Friedenberg (1959) and Robert Hutchins (1953) from their very separate framework raise the same issue: is the middle-class social and intellectual way of life as reflected in the school really a Given of the Natural Order, so to speak? In the face of this, one must ask: Can the standards of today's school be taken safely as the model for the transformation of the culturally-deprived child? Is this what we want for our children, or should not some thought be given as well, even in the present context, to the transformation of the school itself?

Summary

Let me summarize what I have tried to do, and add a comment by way of conclusion. I have attempted to indicate something of the history of cultural deprivation and education, and pointed out that it is by no means a new problem. What was not realized so much before was the crucial significance of the early experiences of the child. I sketched some of the empirical evidence for the effect of early experience on learning to learn and the educational consequences of the discontinuity between the experiences of the lower class child and the expectations of the school. I described the diversity of current compensatory pre-school programs and outlined some of the pertinent research. I then raised two types of issues: first, issues concerned with immediate operational problems like the selection of activities, teachers, and the evaluation of outcomes, and second, issues concerned with long-term underlying problems like the consequences of letting the objectives and values of the present school determine the criteria for the socialization of our children.

In raising these issues my intent was of course not to restrain our efforts in compensatory pre-school education. On the contrary, the intent rather was to encourage the kind of dialogue that will be equal to the seriousness and magnitude of the task. To consider alternatives of method and to recognize the possibility of unintended consequences now when programs are still in process of formation may avoid irrevocable commitments to be regretted later. In view of the magnitude of the task and complexity of the social, economic, and educational issues, there is no doubt that pre-school education will be costly in time, effort, and funds, and the question is often asked: How can we afford it? It seems to me this is the one question that needs no answer, for when one measures the present waste and pain in humankind against the vision of what might be, the more telling question is: "How can we *not* afford it?

References

Bereiter, C., J. Osborn *et al.* February 1965. *An academically oriented pre-school for culturally deprived children.* A paper delivered at American Educational Research Association.

Bernstein, Basil. March 1964. *Elaborated and restricted codes: their origin and some consequences.* A paper delivered at the University of Chicago.

Bettelheim, Bruno. Winter 1961. The decision to fail. *School Rev.,* **69**, pp. 377–412.

Bloom, Benjamin S. 1964. *Stability and change in human characteristics* (New York: John Wiley & Sons, Inc.).

———, A. Davis, and R. Hess. 1965. *Compensatory education for cultural deprivation* (New York: Holt, Rinehart and Winston, Inc.).

Brown, B. R., and Martin Deutsch. March 1964. *Some effects of social class and race on children's language and intellectual abilities: a new look at an old problem.* A paper read to the Society for Research in Child Development.

Davis, Allison. 1948. *Social class influences upon learning.* (Cambridge, Mass.: Harvard University Press).

Deutsch, Martin. July 1964. Facilitating development in the pre-school child: social and psychological perspectives. *Merrill-Palmer Quart.,* **10**, pp. 249–263.

———. December 1962. *The influence of early social environment on school adaptation.* A paper presented at the Symposium on School Drop-outs, Washington, D.C.

Friedenberg, Edgar Z. 1959. *The vanishing adolescent* (Boston: The Beacon Press).

Gray, S. W., and R. A. Klaus. November 1963. *Early training project: interim report* (Nashville, Tenn.: George Peabody College for Teachers). Mimeographed.

Hebb, D. O. 1949. *The organization of behavior* (New York: John Wiley & Sons, Inc.).

Henry, Jules. January 1957. Attitude organization in elementary classrooms. *Amer. J. Orthopsychiat.,* **28**, pp. 117–133.

Hess, Robert D. 1965. *Inventory of compensatory education projects* (Chicago, Ill.: School of Education, University of Chicago). Mimeographed.

———. November 1964. Education and rehabilitation: the future of the welfare class. *J. Marriage and the Family*, **26**, pp. 422–429.

Hutchins, Robert M. 1953. *The conflict of education in a democratic society* (New York: Harper & Row).

Irwin, O. C. 1948. Infant speech: the effect of family occupational status and of age on use of sound types. *J. Sp. H. Disord.*, **13**, pp. 224–226.

Larson, R. G., and J. L. Olson. April 1965. *Final report: a pilot project for culturally deprived kindergarten children* (Racine, Wisc.: Unified School District #1). Mimeographed draft.

Lynd, Robert S., and Helen M. Lynd. 1929. *Middletown* (New York: Harcourt, Brace & World, Inc.).

Milner, Esther. 1951. A study of the relationship between reading readiness in grade one school children and patterns of parent-child interactions. *Child Develpm.*, **22**, pp. 95–122.

Montague, D. O. 1964. Arithmetic concepts of kindergarten children in contrasting socio-economic areas. *Elem. Sch. J.*, **64**, pp. 393–397.

Riesen, Austin. 1947. The development of visual perception in man and chimpanzee. *Science*, **106**, pp. 107–108.

Riessman, Frank. 1962. *The culturally deprived child* (New York: Harper & Row).

Sexton, Patricia C. June 1965. Schools are emasculating our boys. *Sat. Rev.*, **68**, p. 57.

Warner, W. Lloyd, Robert J. Havighurst, and M. B. Loeb. 1944. *Who shall be educated* (New York: Harper & Row).

Weikart, D. P., C. K. Kamii, and N. L. Radin. June 1964. *Perry pre-school project progress report* (Ypsilanti, Mich.: Ypsilanti Public Schools). Mimeographed.

6   What is the Optimal Learning Environment for the Young Child?*

BETTYE M. CALDWELL, *Syracuse University*

A truism in the field of child development is that the milieu in which development occurs influences that development. As a means of validating the principle, considerable scientific effort has gone into the Linnaean task of describing and classifying milieus and examining developmental

* *American Journal of Orthopsychiatry*, January 1967, vol. 37, no. 1. Copyright, the American Orthopsychiatric Association, Inc. Reproduced by permission. Presented at the 1965 annual meeting of the American Orthopsychiatric Association, New York City. The author's work is supported by Grant Nos. MH-07649 and MH-08542, NIMH, U.S. Public Health Service, and by Grant No. D-156(R), Children's Bureau, Social Security Administration, Department of Health, Education, and Welfare.

consequences associated with different types. Thus we know something about what it is like to come of age in New Guinea (Mead, 1953) in a small Midwestern town (Barker and Wright, 1955), in villages and cities in Mexico (Lewis, 1959) in families of different social-class level in Chicago (Davis and Havighurst, 1946) or Boston (Maccoby and Gibbs, 1954; Pavenstedt, 1965), in a New York slum (Wortis *et al.*, 1963), in Russian collectives (Bronfenbrenner, 1962), in Israeli Kibbutzim (Irvine, 1952; Rabin, 1957; Spiro, 1958), in the eastern part of the United States (Provence and Lipton, 1962), and in a Republican community in Central New York (Caldwell *et al.*, 1963). Most of these milieu descriptions have placed great stress on the fact that they were just that and nothing more, i.e., they have expressed the customary scientific viewpoint that to describe is not to judge or criticize. However, in some of the more recent milieu descriptions which have contrasted middle- and lower-class family environments or highlighted conditions in extreme lower-class settings (Pavenstedt, 1965; Wortis *et al.*, 1963), often more than a slight suggestion has crept in that things could be better for the young child from the deprived segment of the culture. Even so, there remains a justifiable wariness about recommending or arranging any environment for the very young child other than the type regarded as its natural habitat, viz., within its own family.

Of course, optimizing environments are arranged all the time under one guise or another. For example, for disturbed children whose family environments seem effectively to reinforce rather than extinguish psychopathology, drastic alterations of milieu often are attempted. This may take the form of psychotherapy for one or both parents as well as the disturbed child, or it may involve total removal of the child from the offending environment with temporary or prolonged placement of the child in a milieu presumably more conducive to normal development. Then there is the massive milieu arrangement formalized and legalized as "education" which profoundly affects the lives of all children once they reach the age of five or six. This type of arrangement is not only tolerated but fervently endorsed by our culture as a whole. In fact, any subculture (such as the Amish) which resists the universalization of this pattern of milieu arrangement is regarded as unacceptably deviant and as justifying legal action to enforce conformity.

For very young children, however, there has been a great deal of timidity about conscious and planned arrangement of the developmental milieu, as though the implicit assumption has been made that any environment which sustains life is adequate during this period. This is analogous to suggesting that the intrauterine environment during the period of maximal cellular proliferation is less important than it is later, a suggestion that patently disregards evidence from epidemiology and experimental embryology. The rate of proliferation of new behavioral skills during the first three years of life and the increasing accumulation of data pointing to the relative permanence of deficit acquired when the environment is inadequate during this period make it mandatory that careful attention be given to the preparation of the developmental environment during the first three years of life.

Conclusions from Inadequate Environments

It is, of course, an exaggeration to imply that no one has given attention to the type of environment which can nourish early and sustained growth and development. For a good three decades now infants who are developing in different milieus have been observed and examined, and data relating to their development have made it possible to identify certain strengths and deficiencies of the different types of environments. Of all types described, the one most consistently indicted by the data is the institution. A number of years ago Goldfarb (1949) published an excellent series of studies contrasting patterns of intellectual functioning shown by a group of adopted adolescents who had been reared in institutions up to age three and then transferred to foster homes or else placed shortly after birth in foster homes. The development of the group that had spent time in the institution was deficient in many ways compared to the group that had gone directly into foster homes. Provence and Lipton (1962) recently published a revealing description of the early social and intellectual development of infants in institutions, contrasting their development with that of home-reared children. On almost every measured variable the institutional infants were found wanting—less socially alert and outgoing, less curious, less responsive, less interested in objects, and generally less advanced. The findings of this study are almost prototypic of the literature in the field, as pointed out in excellent reviews by Yarrow (1961) and Ainsworth (1962).

Although there are many attributes in combination that comprise the institutional environment, the two most obvious elements are (1) absence of a mother and (2) the presence of a group. These basic characteristics have thus been identified as the major carriers of the institutional influence and have been generalized into an explicit principle guiding our recommendations for optimal environments—learning or otherwise—for young children whenever any type of milieu arrangement is necessary. This principle may be stated simply as: the optimal environment for the young child is one in which the child is cared for in his own home in the context of a warm, continuous emotional relationship with his own mother under conditions of varied sensory input. Implicit in this principle is the conviction that the child's mother is the person best qualified to provide a stable and warm interpersonal relationship as well as the necessary pattern of sensory stimulation. Implicit also is the assumption that socio-emotional development has priority during the first three years and that if this occurs normally, cognitive development, which is of minor importance during this period anyway, will take care of itself. At a still deeper level lurks the assumption that attempts to foster cognitive development will interfere with socio-emotional development. Advocacy of the principle also implies endorsement of the idea that most homes are adequate during this early period and that no formal training (other than possibly some occasional supervisory support) for mothering is necessary. Such an operating principle places quite an onus on mothers and assumes that they will possess or quickly acquire all the talents necessary to create an optimal learning environment. And this author, at least, is convinced that a majority of mothers have such talents or proclivities and that they are willing to try to do all they can to create for their children the proper developmental milieu.

But there are always large numbers of children for whom family resources are not available and for whom some type of substitute milieu arrangement must be made. On the whole, such attempts have followed the entirely logical and perhaps evolutionary approach to milieu development—they have sought to create substitute families. The same is usually true when parents themselves seek to work out an alternate child-care arrangement because of less drastic conditions, such as maternal employment. The most typical maneuver is to try to obtain a motherly person who will "substitute" for her (not supplement her) during her hours away from her young child.

Our nation has become self-consciously concerned with social evolution, and in the past decade a serious attempt has been made to assimilate valid data from the behavioral and social sciences into planning for social action. In this context it would be meaningful to examine and question some of the hidden assumptions upon which our operating principle about the optimal environment for the young child rests.

Examining the Hidden Assumptions

1. *Do intermittent, short-term separations of the child from the mother impair the mother-child relationship or the development of the child?* Once having become sensitized to the consequences of institutionalization, and suspicious that the chief missing ingredient was the continued presence of the mother, the scientific and professional community went on the *qui vive* to the possibly deleterious consequences of any type

of separation of an infant from its mother. Accordingly, a number of studies (Caldwell *et al.*, 1963; Gardner *et al.*, 1961; Hoffman, 1961; Radke, 1961; Siegel and Hass, 1963) investigated the consequences of short-term intermittent separation and were unable to demonstrate in the children the classical syndrome of the "institutional child." In reviewing the literature, Yarrow (1961) stressed the point that available data do not support the tendency to assume that maternal deprivation, such as exists in the institutional environment, and maternal separation are the same thing. Apparently short cyclic interruptions culminated by reunions do not have the same effect as prolonged interruptions, even though quantitatively at the end of a designated period the amount of time spent in a mother-absent situation might be equal for the two experiences. Also in this context it is well to be reminded that in the institutional situation there is likely to be no stable mother-child relationship to interrupt. These are often never-mothered rather than ever-mothered children, a fact which must be kept in mind in generalizing from data on institutional groups. Thus until we have data to indicate that such intermittent separation-reunion cycles have similar effects on young children as prolonged separations, we are probably unjustified in assuming that an "uninterrupted" relationship is an essential ingredient of the optimal environment.

2. *Is group upbringing invariably damaging?* In studies done in West European and American settings, social and cognitive deficits associated with continuous group care during infancy have been frequently demonstrated. Enough exceptions have been reported, however, to warrant an intensification of the search for the "true" ingredient in the group situation associated with the observed deficits. For example, Freud and Dann (1951) described the adjustment of a group of six children reared in a concentration camp orphanage for approximately three years, where they were cared for by overworked and impersonal inmates of the camp, and then transported to a residence for children in England. The children, who had never known their own mothers but who had been together as a group for approximately three years, were intensely attached to one another. Although their adjustment to their new environment was slow and differed from the pattern one would expect from home-reared children, it was significant that they eventually did make a reasonably good adjustment. That the children were able to learn a new language while making this emotional transition was offered as evidence that many of the basic cognitive and personality attributes remained unimpaired in spite of the pattern of group upbringing. The accumulation of data showing that Kibbutz-reared children (Rabin, 1957) do not have cognitive deficits also reinforces the premise that it is not necessarily group care *per se* that produces the frequently reported deficit and that it is possible to retain the

advantages of group care while systematically eliminating its negative features. Grounds for reasonable optimism also have been found in retrospective studies by Maas (1963) and Beres and Obers (1960) although in both cases the authors found evidence of pathology in some members of the follow-up sample. Similarly Dennis and Najarian (1957) concluded from their data that the magnitude of the deficit varied as a function of the type of instrument used to measure deficit, and Dennis (1960) showed that in institutions featuring better adult-child ratios and a conscious effort to meet the psychological needs of the infants the development of the children was much less retarded than was the case in a group of children residing in institutions with limited and unsophisticated staff. It is not appropriate to go into details of limitations of methodology in any of these studies; however, from the standpoint of an examination of the validity of a principle, it is important to take note of any exceptions to the generality of that principle.

In this context it is worth considering a point made by Gula (1965). He recently has suggested that some of the apparent consistency in studies comparing institutionalized infants with those cared for in their own homes and in foster homes might disappear if it were possible to equate the comparison groups on the variable of environmental adequacy. That is, one could classify all three types of environments as good, marginal, or inadequate on a number of dimensions. Most of the studies have compared children from palpably "inadequate" institutions with children from "good" foster and own homes. He suggests that, merely because most institutions studied have been inadequate in terms of such variables as adult-child ratio, staff turnover, and personal characteristics of some of the caretakers, etc., one is not justified in concluding *ipso facto* that group care is invariably inferior or damaging.

3. *Is healthy socio-emotional development the most important task of the first three years? Do attempts to foster cognitive growth interfere with social and emotional development?* These paired assumptions, which one finds stated in one variety or another in many pamphlets and books dealing with early child development, represent acceptance of a closed system model of human development. They seem to conceptualize development as compartmentalized and with a finite limit. If the child progresses too much in one area he automatically restricts the amount of development that can occur in another area. Thus one often encounters such expressions as "cognitive development at the *expense* of socio-emotional development." It is perhaps of interest to reflect that, until our children reach somewhere around high school age, we seldom seem to worry that the reverse might occur. But, of course, life is an open system, and on the whole it is accurate to suggest that development feeds upon develop-

ment. Cognitive and socio-emotional advances tend on the whole to be positively, not negatively, correlated.

The definition of intelligence as *adaptivity* has not been adequately stressed by modern authors. It is, of course, the essence of Piaget's definition (1952) as it was earlier of Binet (Binet and Simon, 1916). Unfortunately, however, for the last generation or so in America we have been more concerned with how to measure intelligent behavior than how to interpret and understand it. Acceptance of the premise that intelligent behavior is adaptive behavior should help to break the set of many persons in the field of early child development that to encourage cognitive advance is to discourage healthy socio-emotional development. Ample data are available to suggest that quite the reverse is true either for intellectually advanced persons (Terman *et al.*, 1925; Terman and Oden, 1947) or an unselected sample. In a large sample of young adults from an urban area in Minnesota, Anderson and associates (1959) found that the best single predictor of post-high school adjustment contained in a large assessment battery was a humble little group intelligence test. Prediction based on intelligence plus teacher's ratings did somewhat better, but nothing exceeded the intelligence test for single measure efficiency.

It is relevant here to mention White's (1959) concept of competence or effectance as a major stabilizing force in personality development. The emotional reinforcement accompanying the old "I can do it myself" declaration should not be undervalued. In Murphy's report (1962) of the coping behavior of preschool children one sees evidence of the adjustive supports gained through cognitive advances. In his excellent review of cognitive stimulation in infancy and early childhood, Fowler (1962) raises the question of whether there is any justification for the modern anxiety (and, to be sure, it is a modern phenomenon) over whether cognitive stimulation may damage personality development. He suggests that in the past severe and harmful methods may have been the culprits whenever there was damage and that the generalizations have confused methods of stimulation with the process of stimulation *per se*.

4. *Do cognitive experiences of the first few months and years leave no significant residual?* Any assumption that the learnings of infancy are evanescent appears to be a fairly modern idea. In his *Emile*, first published in 1762, Rousseau (1950) stressed the point that education should begin while the child is still in the cradle. Perhaps any generalization to the contrary received its major modern impetus from a rather unlikely place— from longitudinal studies of development covering the span from infancy to adulthood. From findings of poor prediction of subsequent intellectual status (Bayley, 1949) one can legitimately infer that the infant tests measure behavior that is somewhat irrelevant to later intellectual performance. Even though these behaviors predictive of later cognitive behavior

elude most investigators, one cannot infer that the early months and years are unimportant for cognitive development.

Some support for this assumption has come from experimental studies in which an attempt has been made to produce a durable effect in human subjects by one or another type of intervention offered during infancy. One cogent example is the work of Rheingold (1956), in which she provided additional social and personal stimulation to a small group of approximately six-month-old, institutionalized infants for a total of eight weeks. At the end of the experimental period, differences in social responsiveness between her stimulated group and a control group composed of other babies in the institution could be observed. There were also slight but nonsignificant advances in postural and motor behavior on a test of infant development. However, when the babies were followed up approximately a year later, by which time all but one were in either adoptive or boarding homes or in their own natural homes, the increased social responsiveness formerly shown by the stimulated babies was no longer observed. Nor were there differences in level of intellectual functioning. Rheingold and Bayley (1959) concluded that the extra mothering provided during the experimental period was enough to produce an effect at the time but not enough to sustain this effect after such a time as the two groups were no longer differentially stimulated. However, in spite of their conservative conclusion, it is worth noting that the experimentally stimulated babies were found to vocalize more during the follow-up assessments than the control babies. Thus there may have been enough of an effect to sustain a developmental advance in at least this one extremely important area.

Some very impressive recent unpublished data obtained by Skeels, offer a profound challenge to the assumption of the unimportance of the first three years for cognitive growth. This investigator has followed up after approximately 25 years most of the subjects described in a paper by Skeels and Dye (1939). Thirteen infants had been transferred from an orphanage because of evidence of mental retardation and placed in an institution for the retarded under the care of adolescent retardates who gave them a great deal of loving care and as much cognitive stimulation as they could. The 13 subjects showed a marked acceleration in development after this transfer. In contrast a group of reasonably well matched infants left on the wards of the orphanage continued to develop poorly. In a recent follow-up of these cases, Skeels discovered that the gains made by the transferred infants were sustained into their adult years, whereas all but one of the control subjects developed the classic syndrome of mental retardation.

The fact that development and experience are cumulative makes it difficult ever to isolate any one antecedent period and assert that its influence was or was not influential in a subsequent developmental period. Thus even though it might be difficult to demonstrate an effect of some experience in an adjacent time period, delayed effects may well be of even greater developmental consequence. In a recent review of data from a number of longitudinal studies, Bloom (1964) has concluded that during the first three to four years (the noncognitive years, if you will) approximately 50 per cent of the development of intelligence that is ever to occur in the life cycle takes place. During this period a particular environment may be either abundant or deprived in terms of the ingredients essential for providing opportunities for the development of intelligence and problem solving. Bloom states:

> The effects of the environments, especially of the extreme environments, appear to be greatest in the early (and more rapid) periods of intelligence development and least in the later (and less rapid) periods of development. Although there is relatively little evidence of the effects of changing the environment on the changes in intelligence, the evidence so far available suggests that marked changes in the environment in the early years can produce greater changes in intelligence than will equally marked changes in the environment at later periods of development. (pp. 88–89)

5. *Can one expect that, without formal planning, all the necessary learning experiences will occur?* There is an old legend that if you put six chimpanzees in front of six typewriters and leave them there long enough they eventually will produce all the works in the British Museum. One could paraphrase this for early childhood by suggesting that six children with good eyes and ears and hands and brains would, if left alone in nature, arrive at a number system, discover the laws of conservation of matter and energy, comprehend gravity and the motions of the planets, and perhaps arrive at the theory of relativity. All the "facts" necessary to discern these relationships are readily available. Perhaps a more realistic example would be to suggest that, if we surround a group of young children with a carefully selected set of play materials, they would eventually discover for themselves the laws of color mixture, of form and contour, of perspective, of formal rhythm and tonal relationships, and biological growth. And, to be sure, all this *could* occur. But whether this will necessarily occur with any frequency is quite another matter. We also assume that at a still earlier period a child will learn body control, eye-hand coordination, the rudiments of language, and styles of problem solving in an entirely incidental and unplanned way. In an article in a recent issue of a popular woman's magazine, an author (Holt, 1965) fervently urges parents to stop trying to teach their young children in order that the children may learn. And, to be sure, there is always something to be said

for this caution; it is all too easy to have planned learning experiences become didactic and regimented rather than subtle and opportunistic.

As more people gain experience in operating nursery school programs for children with an early history deficient in many categories of experience, the conviction appears to be gaining momentum that such children often are not able to avail themselves of the educational opportunities and must be guided into meaningful learning encounters. In a recent paper dealing with the pre-school behavior of a group of 21 children from multiproblem families, Malone (1966) describes the inability of the children to carry out self-directed exploratory maneuvers with the toys and equipment as follows:

> When the children first came to nursery school they lacked interest in learning the names and properties of objects. Colors, numbers, sizes, shapes, locations, all seemed interchangeable. Nothing in the room seemed to have meaning for a child apart from the fact that another child had approached or handled it or that the teacher's attention was turned toward it. Even brief play depended on the teacher's involvement and support. (p. 5)

When one reflects on the number of carefully arranged reinforcement contingencies necessary to help a young child learn to decode the simple message, "No," it is difficult to support the position that in early learning, as in anything else, nature should just take its course.

6. *Is formal training for child-care during the first three years unnecessary?* This assumption is obviously quite ridiculous, and yet it is one logical derivative of the hypothesis that the only adequate place for a young child is with his mother or a permanent mother substitute. There is, perhaps unfortunately, no literacy test for motherhood. This again is one of our interesting scientific paradoxes. That is, proclaiming in one breath that mothering is essential for the healthy development of a child, we have in the very next breath implied that just any mothering will do. It is interesting in this connection that from the elementary school level forward we have rigid certification statutes in most states that regulate the training requirements for persons who would qualify as teachers of our children. (The same degree of control over the qualifications and training of a nursery school teacher has not prevailed in the past, but we are moving into an era when it will.) So again, our pattern of social action appears to support the emplicit belief in the lack of importance of the first three years of life.

In 1928, John B. Watson wrote a controversial little trade book called *The Psychological Care of Infant and Child.* He included one chapter heretically entitled, "The Dangers of Too Much Mother Love." In this chapter he suggested that child training was too important to be left in

the hands of mothers, apparently not because he felt them intellectually
inadequate but because of their sentimentality. In his typical "nondirec-
tive" style Watson wrote:

> Six months' training in the actual handling of children from two to
> six under the eye of competent instructors should make a fairly satis-
> factory child's nurse. To keep them we should let the position of nurse
> or governess in the home be a respected one. Where the mother herself
> must be the nurse—which is the case in the vast majority of American
> homes—she must look upon herself while performing the functions of
> a nurse as a professional woman and not as a sentimentalist masquerading
> under the name of "Mother." (p. 149)

At present in this country a number of training programs are currently being formulated which would attempt to give this kind of professional training called for by Watson and many others. It is perhaps not
possible to advance on all fronts at the same time, and the pressing health
needs of the young child demanded and received top priority in earlier
decades. Perhaps it will now be possible to extend our efforts at social
intervention to encompass a broader range of health, education, and
welfare activities.

7. *Are most homes and most parents adequate for at least the first
three years?* Enough has been presented in discussing other implicit
assumptions to make it unnecessary to amplify this point at length. The
clinical literature, and much of the research literature of the last decade
dealing with social-class differences, has made abundantly clear that all
parents are not qualified to provide even the basic essentials of physical
and psychological care to their children. Such reports as those describing
the incidence of battered children (Elmer, 1963; Kempe *et al.*, 1962)
capture our attention, but reports concerned with subtler and yet perhaps
more long-standing patterns of parental deficit also fill the literature. In
her description of the child-rearing environments provided by low lower-
class families, Pavenstedt (1965) has described them as impulse determined
with very little evidence of clear planfulness for activities that would
benefit either parent or child. Similarly, Wortis and associates (1963)
have described the extent to which the problems of the low-income
mother so overwhelm her with reactions of depression and inadequacy
that behavior toward the child is largely determined by the needs of the
moment rather than by any clear plan about how to bring up children
and how to train them to engage in the kind of behavior that the parents
regard as acceptable or desirable. No social class and no cultural or ethnic
group has exclusive rights to the domain of inadequate parentage; all
conscientious parents must strive constantly for improvement on this
score. However, relatively little attention has been paid to the possibly
deleterious consequences of inadequacies during the first three years of

life. Parents have been blamed for so many problems of their children in later age periods that a moderate reaction formation appears to have set in. But again, judging by the type of social action taken by the responsible professional community, parental inadequacy during the first three years is seldom considered as a major menace. Perhaps, when the various alternatives are weighed, it appears by comparison to be the least of multiple evils; but parental behavior of the first three years should not be regarded as any more sacrosanct or beyond the domain of social concern than that of the later years.

Planning Alternatives

At this point the exposition of this paper must come to an abrupt halt, for insufficient data about possible alternative models are available to warrant recommendation of any major pattern of change. At present there are no completed research projects that have developed and evaluated alternative approximations of optimal learning environments for young children in our culture. One apparent limitation on ideas for alternative models appears to be the tendency to think in terms of binary choices. That is, we speak of individual care *versus* group care, foster home *versus* institution, foster home *versus* own home, and so on. But environments for the very young child do not need to be any more mutually exclusive than they are for the older children. After all, what is our public education system but a coordination of the efforts of home plus an institution? Most of us probably would agree that the optimal learning environment for the older child is neither of these alone but rather a combination of both. Some of this same pattern of combined effort also may represent the optimal arrangement for the very young child.

A number of programs suggesting alternatives possibly worth considering are currently in the early field trial stage. One such program is the one described by Caldwell and Richmond (1964). This program offers educationally oriented day care for culturally deprived children between six months and three years of age. The children spend the better part of five days a week in a group care setting (with an adult-child ratio never lower than 1:4) but return home each evening and maintain primary emotional relationships with their own families. Well child care, social and psychological services, and parent education activities are available for participating families. The educational program is carefully planned to try to help the child develop the personal-social and cognitive attributes conducive to learning and to provide experiences which can partially compensate for inadequacies which may have existed in the home environment. The strategy involved in offering the enrichment experience to children in this very young age group is to maximize their potential and hopefully prevent the deceleration in rate of development which seems to occur in many deprived children around the age of two to three years. It is thus an exercise in circumvention rather than remediation. Effectiveness of the endeavor is being determined by a comparison of the participating children with a control group of children from similar backgrounds who are not enrolled in the enrichment program. Unfortunately at this juncture it is too early for such projects to do more than suggest alternatives. The degree of confidence which comes only from research evidence plus replicated experience will have to wait a little longer.

Effective social action, however, can seldom await definitive data. And in the area of child care the most clamorous demand for innovative action appears to be coming from a rather unlikely source—not from any of the professional groups, not particularly from social planners who try to incorporate research data into plans for social action, but from *mothers*. From mothers themselves is coming the demand that professionals in the field look at some of the alternatives. We need not be reminded here that in America at the present time there are more than three million working mothers with children under six years of age (*American Women*, 1963). And these mothers are looking for professional leadership to design and provide child-care facilities that help prepare their children for today's achievement-oriented culture. The challenge which has been offered is inevitable. After almost two decades of bombarding women with the importance of their mothering role, we might have predicted the weakening of their defenses and their waving the flag of truce as though to say, "I am not good enough to do all that you are saying I must do."

It is a characteristic of social evolution that an increased recognition of the importance of any role leads to the professionalization of that role, and there can be no doubt but that we are currently witnessing the early stages of professionalization of the mother-substitute role—or, as I would prefer to say, the mother-supplement. It is interesting to note that no one has as yet provided a satisfactory label for this role. The term "baby-sitter" is odious, reminding us of just about all some of the "less well trained" professionals do—sit with babies. If English were a masculine-feminine language, there is little doubt that the word would be used in the feminine gender, for we always speak of this person as a "she" (while emphasizing that young children need more contact with males). We cannot borrow any of the terms from already professionalized roles, such as "nurse" or "teacher," although such persons must be to a great extent both nurse and teacher. Awkward designations such as "child-care worker," or hybridized terms such as "nurse-teacher" do not quite seem to fill the bill; and there appears to be some reluctance to accept an untranslated foreign word like the Hebrew "metapelet" or the Russian "Nyanya." When such a word does appear, let us hope that it rhymes well and has a strong trochaic rhythm, for it will have to sustain a whole new era of poetry and song. (This author is convinced that the proper verb is *nurture*. It carries the desired connotations, but even to one who is not averse to neologisms such nominative forms as "nurturist," "nurturer," and "nurturizer" sound alien and inadequate.)*

Another basis for planning alternatives is becoming available from a less direct but potentially more persuasive source—from increasing knowledge about the process of development. The accumulation of data suggesting that the first few years of life are crucial for the priming of cognitive development call for vigorous and imaginative action programs for those early years. To say that it is premature to try to plan optimal environments because we do not fully understand how learning occurs is unacceptable. Perhaps only by the development of carefully arranged environments will we attain a complete understanding of the learning process. Already a great deal is known which enables us to specify some of the essential ingredients of a growth-fostering milieu. Such an environment must contain warm and responsive people who by their own interests invest objects with value. It must be supportive and as free of disease and pathogenic agents as possibly can be arranged. It also must trace a clear path from where the child is to where he is to go developmentally; objects and events must be similar enough to what the child has experienced to be assimilated by the child and yet novel enough to stimulate and attract. Such an environment must be exquisitely responsive, as a more consistent pattern of response is required to foster the acquisition of new forms of behavior than is required to maintain such behavior once it appears in the child's repertoire. The timing of experiences also must be carefully programmed. The time table for the scheduling of early postnatal events may well be every bit as demanding as that which obtains during the embryological period. For children whose early experiences are known to be deficient and depriving, attempts to program such environments seem mandatory if subsequent learning difficulties are to be circumvented.

Summary

Interpretations of research data and accumulated clinical experience have led over the years to a consensual approximation of an answer to

* In a letter to the author written shortly after the meeting at which this paper was presented, Miss Rena Corman of New York City suggested that the proper term should be "nurcher," a compound of the words, "nurse" and "teacher." To be sure, a "nurcher" sounds nurturant.

the question: what is the optimal learning environment for the young child? As judged from our scientific and lay literature and from practices in health and welfare agencies, one might infer that the optimal learning environment for the young child is that which exists when (a) a young child is cared for in his own home (b) in the context of a warm and nurturant emotional relationship (c) with his mother (or a reasonable facsimile thereof) under conditions of (d) varied sensory and cognitive input. Undoubtedly until a better hypothesis comes along, this is the best one available. This paper has attempted to generate constructive thinking about whether we are justified in overly vigorous support of (a) when (b), (c) or (d), or any combination thereof, might not obtain. Support for the main hypothesis comes primarily from other hypotheses (implicit assumptions) rather than from research or experimental data. When these assumptions are carefully examined they are found to be difficult if not impossible to verify with existing data.

The conservatism inherent in our present avoidance of carefully designed social action programs for the very young child needs to be re-examined. Such a re-examination conducted in the light of research evidence available about the effects of different patterns of care forces consideration of whether formalized intervention programs should not receive more attention than they have in the past and whether attention should be given to a professional training sequence for child-care workers. The careful preparation of the learning environment calls for a degree of training and commitment and personal control not always to be found in natural caretakers and a degree of richness of experience by no means always available in natural environments.

References

Ainsworth, Mary. 1962. Reversible and irreversible effects of maternal deprivation on intellectual development. *Child Welfare League of America*, pp. 42–62.

American Women. 1963. A report of the President's Commission on the Status of Women (Washington, D.C.: Superintendent of Documents).

Anderson, J. E., *et al.* 1959. *A survey of children's adjustment over time* (Minneapolis, Minn.: University of Minnesota).

Barker, R. G., and H. F. Wright. 1955. *Midwest and its children: the psychological ecology of an American town* (New York: Harper & Row).

Bayley, Nancy. 1949. Consistency and variability in the growth of intelligence from birth to eighteen years. *J. genet. Psychol.*, **75**, pp. 165–196.

Beres, D., and S. Obers. 1950. The effects of extreme deprivation in infancy on psychic structure in adolescence. *Psychoanal. Stud. of the Child*, **5**, pp. 121–140.

Binet, A., and T. Simon. 1916. *The development of intelligence in children.* Translated by Elizabeth S. Kite (Baltimore, Md.: The Williams & Wilkins Company).

Bloom, B. S. 1964. *Stability and change in human characteristics* (New York: John Wiley & Sons, Inc.).

Bronfenbrenner, Urie. 1962. Soviet studies of personality development and socialization. In American Psychological Association, Inc., *Some views on Soviet psychology*, pp. 63–85.

Caldwell, Bettye M., *et al.* 1963. Mother-infant interaction in monomatric and polymatric families. *Amer. J. Orthopsychiat.*, **33**, pp. 653–664.

——, and J. B. Richmond. 1964. Programmed day care for the very young child—a preliminary report. *J. Marriage and the Family*, **26**, pp. 481–488.

Davis, A., and R. J. Havighurst. 1946. Social class and color differences in child-rearing. *Amer. Sociol. Rev.*, **11**, pp. 698–710.

Dennis, W. 1960. Causes of retardation among institutional children. *J. genet. Psychol.*, **96**, pp. 47–59.

——, and P. Najarian. 1957. Infant development under environmental handicap. *Psychol. Monogr.*, **71**, 7, Whole No. 536.

Elmer, Elizabeth. 1963. Identification of abused children. *Children*, **10**, pp. 180–184.

Fowler, W. 1962. Cognitive learning in infancy and early childhood. *Psychol. Bull.*, **59**, pp. 116–152.

Freud, Anna, and Sophie Dann. 1951. An experiment in group upbringing. *Psychoanal. Stud. of the Child*, **6**, pp. 127–168.

Gardner, D. B., G. R. Hawkes, and L. G. Burchinal. 1961. Noncontinuous mothering in infancy and development in later childhood. *Child Develpm.*, **32**, pp. 225–234.

Goldfarb, W. 1949. Rorschach test differences between family-reared, institution-reared and schizophrenic children. *Amer. J. Orthopsychiat.*, **19**, pp. 624–633.

Gula, M. January 1965. *New concepts for group care.* A paper given at the conference on Group Care for Infants and Young Children (Washington, D.C.: Children's Bureau, Department of Health, Education, and Welfare).

Hoffman, Lois Wladis. 1961. Effects of maternal employment on the child. *Child Develpm.*, **32**, pp. 187–197.

Holt, J. 1965. How to help babies learn—without teaching them. *Redbook*, **126**(1), pp. 54–55; 134–137.

Irvine, Elizabeth E. 1952. Observations on the aims and methods of child-rearing in communal settlements in Israel. *Human Relat.*, **5**, pp. 247–275.

Kempe, C. H., *et al.* 1962. The battered-child syndrome. *J. Amer. Med. Assn.*, **181**, pp. 17–24.

Lewis, O. 1959. *Five families* (New York: Basic Books, Inc.).

Maas, H. 1963. Long-term effects of early childhood separation and group care. *Vita Humana*, **6**, pp. 34–56.

Maccoby, Eleanor, and Patricia K. Gibbs. 1954. Methods of child-rearing in two social classes. In W. E. Martin and Celia B. Stendler (eds.), *Readings in child development* (New York: Harcourt, Brace & World, Inc.), pp. 380–396.

Malone, C. A. 1966. Safety first: comments on the influence of external danger in the lives of children of disorganized families. *Amer. J. Orthopsychiat.*, **36**, pp. 3–12.

Mead, Margaret. 1953. *Growing up in New Guinea* (New York: New American Library of World Literature, Inc.).

Murphy, Lois B., *et al.* 1962. *The widening world of childhood* (New York: Basic Books, Inc.).

Pavenstedt, E. 1965. A comparison of the child-rearing environment of upper-lower and very low-lower class families. *Amer. J. Orthopsychiat.*, **35**, pp. 89–98.

Piaget, J. 1952. *The origins of intelligence in children*. Translated by Margaret Cook (New York: International Universities Press, Inc.).

Provence, Sally, and Rose C. Lipton. 1962. *Infants in institutions* (New York: International Universities Press, Inc.).

Rabin, A. I. 1957. Personality maturity of Kibbutz and non-Kibbutz children as reflected in Rorschach findings. *J. proj. Tech.*, pp. 148–153.

Rheingold, Harriet. 1956. The modification of social responsiveness in institutional babies. *Monogr. Soc. Res. Child Develpm.*, **21**, p. 63.

———, and Nancy Bayley. 1959. The later effects of an experimental modification of mothering. *Child Develpm.*, **30**, pp. 363–372.

Rousseau, J. J. 1950. *Emile (1762)* (Woodbury, N.Y.: Barron's Educational Series, Inc.).

Siegel, Alberta E., and Miriam B. Hass. 1963. The working mother: a review of research. *Child Develpm.*, **34**, pp. 513–542.

Skeels, H., and H. Dye. 1939. A study of the effects of differential stimulation on mentally retarded children. *Proc. Amer. Assn. on ment. Defic.*, **44**, pp. 114–136.

Spiro, M. 1958. *Children of the Kibbutz* (Cambridge, Mass.: Harvard University Press).

Terman, L. M., *et al.* 1925. Genetic studies or genius: Vol. 1. *Mental and physical traits of a thousand gifted children* (Stanford, Calif.: Stanford University Press).

————, and Melita H. Oden. 1947. *The gifted child grows up: twenty-five years' follow-up of a superior group* (Stanford, Calif.: Stanford University Press).

Watson, J. B. 1928. *Psychological care of infant and child* (London: George Allen & Unwin Ltd.).

White, R. W. 1959. Motivation reconsidered: the concept of competence. *Psychol. Rev.*, **66**, pp. 297–333.

Wortis, H., *et al.* 1963. Child-rearing practice in a low socio-economic group. *Pediatrics*, **32**, pp. 298–307.

Yarrow, L. J. 1961. Maternal deprivation: toward an empirical and conceptual re-evaluation. *Psychol. Bull.*, **58**, pp. 459–490.

Yarrow, Marian Radke. 1961. Maternal employment and child rearing. *Children*, **8**, pp. 223–228.

PART **2** *The Rediscovery of Montessori*

Among the reasons for the current revival of interest in the writings and methods of Dr. Maria Montessori one may find hope or discontent. Hope that her methods may help to overcome the devastating effects of impoverished living upon young children. Discontent that symptoms of pushing children through childhood are manifested in the structured nature of many Montessori schools.

This compendium of writings places Montessori in historical perspective, presents discussions of her philosophy and methods and critically examines both features. The writers appropriately represent medicine, psychology, child development, and education. The usual views about controversial subjects are well represented—"more research needed," "wait and see," "remarkable contributions," "little to contribute."

Benjamin Spock and Mildred L. Hathaway are primarily concerned with describing differences between a high-quality Montessori school and a high-quality American school. They consider similarities and differences in philosophy and methods but suggest that the differences are largely quantitative. The tendency for both groups to borrow from each other is viewed as a wholesome tendency.

Psychologists are becoming increasingly aware of the alleged contributions of Montessori to our understanding of child training. Riley W. Gardner believes that promising links between Montessori's contributions and contemporary theories are yet to be explored. It appears particularly likely that the recent research emphasis on cognitive processes will result in reexamining certain features of the Montessori program. The significance of Dr. Montessori's insight may well be realized through integration with the more elaborate work of Jean Piaget. Gardner continues provocatively to the conclusion that putting convictions of educators to the test may force the modification of some cherished conceptions and result in implications profitable to both educators and psychologists.

Less enthusiastic about the promise of Montessori's contributions, Evelyn G. Pitcher believes Montessori purists "evidence more enthusiasm than sound psychology." She is quite accurate in drawing attention to the fact that systematic studies demonstrating the superiority of Montessori classrooms over other schools have not materialized. Of additional concern is the apparent tendency of "pushy" parents and technique-oriented teachers to impose learning on children. Pitcher does not accept the view that academically oriented preschools for the disadvantaged produce better results than conventional preschools. "Children who have a lot to learn can learn it rapidly in a number of different ways."

An analysis of the psychology implicit in the Montessori method is presented by Robert Travers. Selected quotes from Montessori's book, *The Montessori Method*, are critically examined in the context of modern psychology. Travers found that certain Montessori propositions appear to have their roots in psychology dating back to Aristotle, some have obscure origins or represent speculation, while others may represent novel contributions.

In his usual lucid style, J. McVicker Hunt explains reasons for the long-term decline of interest in the Montessori system near the beginning of World War I and the resurgence of interest since World War II. Montessori conceptions tended to run counter to emerging psychological theory and educational philosophy during this period of decline. Dissonant conceptions included the belief that the importance of preschool training is minimal, that intelligence is fixed at birth, development is predetermined, behavior is motivated by instincts or painful stimuli, and the response side of the reflex arc is the essential one in education. The emergence of a body of evidence repudiating each of these conceptions and supporting opposite points of view has vitalized the sudden explosion of interest. Yet Hunt suggests caution for those who would view Montessori as sacrosanct. Numerous reservations about its appropriateness for disadvantaged children *or* upper-middle-class children are obvious.

Despite the serious objections of some and the wholehearted approval of others, Montessori's contributions appear to be destined for the conventional fate of so many innovations—integration into the scheme of educational things. It is through such searching and examining, experimenting and selecting that hope is sustained for improving educational programs.

7   Montessori and Traditional American Nursery Schools— How They Are Different, How They Are Alike*

BENJAMIN SPOCK, M. D.

MILDRED L. HATHAWAY, *East Cleveland Schools*

In recent years American parents have become much concerned about the quality of their children's schooling in general and about the relative merits of specific methods of teaching. One reason has been the increasing competition for admission to good colleges as the result of the "baby boom" during and after World War II and of the conviction of an ever-increasing percentage of parents and children that a college education is worth pursuing at all costs.

Another factor was the success of the Russians in launching their two Sputniks well ahead of our spacecraft. This shook profoundly our belief that we are first in all fields. A number of the people who had always believed that modern American education was too permissive, too concerned with the emotions and life adjustment, jumped to the conclusion—quite unjustified, the present authors believe—that this was the main cause of our backwardness in launching spacecraft. They demanded more emphasis on academic fundamentals, more science, more academic speed, on the assumption—unproved, we think—that children who learn to read and write and figure earlier than their peers will remain ahead thereafter.

The heightened concern of parents and educators has extended down into the nursery-school years. It has been focused, in the case of many parents, on the relative merits of traditional American nursery schools and of Montessori schools, reintroduced into America from Europe a few years ago, when they aroused a great deal of interest. Both the authors have frequently been asked the question, "Which is the better school?" We can't answer this unanswerable question. Every parent has different ideas about what kind of person he wants his child to turn out to be and what methods seem best for getting him there. The Montessori approach will appeal to some parents, the American to others, which is as it should

* From the March 1967 issue of *Redbook*. Copyright © by McCall Corporation, 1967.

be. The aim of this article is only to point out some differences between a high-quality Montessori school and a high-quality American school.

We think that even parents who live in communities where there are no Montessori schools will be interested in this discussion, because it brings out some of the underlying principles of the best modern American schools that may not be apparent on the surface.

It will be evident that the present authors have been trained and have worked in the traditions of modern American education and of dynamic psychology. But they have been greatly interested in the contributions of the Montessori method.

Maria Montessori, born in 1870, the first Italian woman to earn an M.D. degree, became first a specialist in the training of mentally defective children, then an experimenter and theorist in education for all young children. Other innovators before her, rebelling against the traditional reliance on rote memory and drill, had stressed the importance of sensory experience in learning. Montessori felt education should be based not only on the great responsiveness of children's senses but also on their own desire to master real skills. Beginning in 1907, schools using her methods sprang up all over the world. By 1916 there were nearly 200 authorized schools in the United States, and countless others using her name.

Montessori emphasized that the child is deeply interested in work that the adult thinks of as play. Success or failure in work has an enduring effect on his character. Children soon tire of toys that have only one function but they seek out, continue to work with and keep returning to materials that let them see their errors and correct them, that aid their understanding of the physical world and that develop their intellect. Montessori materials were designed so that when used in the proper sequence they gradually lead children, over a period of several years, into an understanding of abstract ideas with a minimum of adult explanation and interference. After the teacher has introduced them to the child one by one, she can retire into the background while he teaches himself.

The initial program, starting usually at three years, consists of "exercises in daily living" such as sweeping, polishing and pouring.

Usually the next phase of the program provides exercises in sensory discrimination. The child works in a prescribed sequence, using a variety of materials one at a time. Some of the simplest ones are, for example, rods for visual perception of length, geometric solids for touching, 64 spools of different colors and shades for color discrimination, a set of musical bells for distinguishing sounds, tablets of wood of the same size but of different weights.

In the third phase, visual and auditory discrimination is eventually developed into reading; the sense a child gains of certain relationships between a number of objects leads him into mathematical and physical concepts; and the child's manual dexterity is developed by gradual steps into writing. By the age of five or six many children are reading, writing and performing mathematical exercises.

Materials are not used before the teacher recognizes the child's readiness and demonstrates each item's use to him. Sometimes the procedure is learned by one child's happening to observe another, an accepted practice. After this the child selects an item from the shelf whenever he wants to use it, works with it as long as he wishes, then returns it to the shelf. Since there is only one set of materials for 20 to 30 children, respect for another's rights and performance is learned. When a child masters one activity he is shown another. He may choose to begin another activity or continue with the one he has just mastered. He sets his own pace. In the conventional sense the child is not rewarded or praised. His achievement may be acknowledged by the teacher, but his inward satisfaction is expected to be the strongest motive in carrying him along.

During the initial stage of their school adjustment, the teacher interacts freely with the children in much the same way an ordinary preschool teacher does; she is likely to divert activities, interrupt and suggest others as she sees fit. After that, however, much of her success as a teacher depends on her success as an observer. Rather than encourage children to be dependent on her, she helps them to help themselves. She doesn't point out what others are doing. A child who is bothering others or being destructive is stopped or diverted, but not scolded or punished by her. She is supposed to be cheerful, calm and self-effacing. Nevertheless, she is keeping a sharp eye on every child in her group, noting what use he is making of the materials, and to what level of mastery he has advanced, anticipating his readiness for the next sequential step.

You can see that Montessori was particularly concerned that children learn for themselves, and also that they not be squelched by disapproval.

The Montessori movement had disappeared from the American scene by the mid-1920s because of the strong appeal of the tenets of "progressive education," or "child-centered education," which were being developed by Francis Parker, John Dewey and William Kilpatrick. It was reintroduced into America in 1959, has spread quite rapidly and has aroused a lot of attention and some controversy. Among the groups that had been slow to show enthusiasm for the American type of nursery education were the Catholic clergy and Catholic laymen. Some of them feared that nursery education might weaken family and religious ties by encouraging mothers to turn over the rearing of their children to secular educators at a spiritually tender and impressionable age and to feel free then to go to work. Also the American teacher's aim to develop self-control in the child, rather than always to exert a strong authoritative control herself, and the rather casual atmosphere in the classroom gave the impression to some that discipline was not being maintained. By contrast, the emphasis in Montessori education on a planned sequence of activities, designed to lead up quite specifically to academic work, had an understandable appeal. In any case, a large proportion of Montessori schools in America have been established by groups of Catholic parents, though it is reported that the majority now are nondenominational.

Montessori herself extended her methods to apply to the elementary grades, but as a rule Montessori schools in the United States carry children only to the age of five or six. (Most American nursery schools take children up to the age of five.)

Now let's consider the similarities in philosophy between Montessori and American nursery education. Both have great belief in the child's own potentialities, in his drive to learn and develop according to an inborn pattern; they see their responsibility in providing a suitably stimulating environment. Both see the long-term goal as helping the child on his way to a well-adjusted adulthood in which he will feel comfortable with his work, with other people and with himself, will think intelligently, will be creative and will take responsibility. Both respect the individual and believe that the earliest years are of crucial importance. Both believe that what the child learns that will be valuable to him, he learns by first taking in impressions, then doing something active himself in response. Both see the child as eager to master projects correctly and as willing to make corrections and keep trying while he sees hope of success.

Now for some differences. In the Montessori school the standard pieces of equipment are to be used by the child in the way intended by Montessori, after he has shown the teacher he is capable; the American school has some of the same equipment and the child is expected to use it similarly, but he also is encouraged to use it to experiment, to dramatize, to improvise, to create.

There also are brought into the American school all kinds of objects from the outside worlds of nature and civilization (or the children are taken out on excursions), to enlarge horizons, arouse questions and provide answers—guinea pigs to be cared for, seeds to be planted, mud to mold, cookies to make, a stethoscope to play doctor with. The Montessori teacher also takes her class on trips and encourages the observation of natural phenomena; but she attempts to be more systematic and structured in their presentation because she aims to bring to the child's awareness the inherent order and structure in nature.

In the Montessori school the learning of a domestic skill such as washing a table or washing the hands is divided into a set sequence of steps, and when a child has mastered the whole sequence he often keeps repeating it. The outsider watching this might conclude that the achievement consisted mainly of getting the sequence in the right order. The Montessori teacher would explain that the sequence is used only as a means to an end and the sequence itself is relied on only as long as it is necessary to achieve the task. In an American school a child washes a table because he has dirtied it or thinks it should be clean for the next group activity or because the teacher asks him to do it for either of these reasons. Or he may just think that washing it would be fun. He is shown the materials but otherwise the task is unstructured. He is usually left to work out his own way of doing it as long as he appears able to accomplish the task and is not making trouble.

In the American school there are always at hand creative materials such as easels and paints, clay, scissors and colored paper. Story reading and storytelling are regularly utilized methods for widening vistas, enriching and mastering the emotions.

In regard to children's feelings, there is no absolute difference in the two philosophies but considerable quantitative difference in emphasis. The Montessori teacher recognizes the fact that the emotions play a part in learning. In the best training of American teachers there is a major focus on the guidance of the child's feelings—of anger or fear or jealousy, for instance—as much as on the guidance of his intellect. The teacher not only believes that any emotional or social maladjustment may interfere seriously with a child's ability to learn much, or perhaps even to stay in the group. She also expects to do all that she can as a teacher to help him get or stay on the right emotional track to a happy future. She knows that young children need help in understanding their own feelings and in managing them. Feelings are not to be denied, but their appropriate expression must be learned. At one time the teacher encourages their expression and at another time controls them through diversion and other means. (She doesn't believe, as some think, that the child should be allowed to take out all his feelings on people or on the furnishings, nor does she believe that he should never be frustrated.)

The American teacher believes, for example, that young children, no matter how much they look forward to entering school, have feelings of anxiety and sadness and sometimes anger about leaving their mother's side. Some children can work these out for themselves. Others need help not only to master the negative feelings but also just to recognize them, as the first step toward mastery. So one job for the teacher, which most adults would not think of, is to put names to the child's feelings for him, so that he can talk about them instead of having to act them out in disruptive behavior. Children need to learn also that other people have feelings—of anger, for instance, if their projects are interfered with.

The teacher in the American nursery school provides dress-up costumes, a housekeeping corner, dolls, blocks and cars, because children love to play out all kinds of human dramas with them, because children in this way develop their imagination and creativity and because this is how children begin to learn to feel and act like men and women. Also this is an effective way of mastering fears and angers and jealousies that are too overwhelming to acknowledge directly but that, if desired entirely, may interfere with wholesome emotional development.

The principal feeling that is clearly recognized in the Montessori school and for which satisfaction is deliberately sought is the joy of achievement. (The American teacher usually counts on this gratification too.)

The American nursery school gives social adjustment a high priority. Children are encouraged to cooperate in marching, music, dramatic and domestic play, block-building, sharing tricycles and seesaws. (Of course, most children who are sociable can also work alone, and prefer to do so at times.) The child who is too shy or too aggressive receives a lot of individual help and object lessons in how to get the fun of shared work and friendship.

Children in a Montessori school have opportunities for companionship and cooperation in games, and around the edges, you might say, of the formal learning exercises. Also they do observe and teach one another. Some activities offer more opportunity for working together than others. But for the most part a child in a Montessori school is expected to work alone.

Whereas the Montessori teacher attempts to efface herself, except at the time of children's first admission, and to avoid letting them become dependent on her, physically or for approval, the American nursery-school teacher assumes that the majority of younger children will want to make a dependent relationship at first, as a bridge from their closeness to their mothers, and that there is no disadvantage in this provided they gradually lessen it as she helps them to make friends with one another and to become absorbed in the activities. She continues to be their warm friend while things go well and their comforter when they hurt themselves or get into scrapes. She assumes each child is learning to be more grown up in feelings and interests by identifying with her in much the same way that he matures by identifying with his parents at home. A satisfactory identification depends on the adult's warmth, approval and capacity to share pleasures. A child especially needs support during periods of regression and loss of control. It is by learning that there are many people who can give him affection and support that a child is prepared to become an adult who cares about many people.

A warmhearted Montessori teacher couldn't help but provide some of this inspiration and support, we believe, but she would not consider it a matter of major emphasis.

There has been a wholesome tendency in recent years for both groups to become less defensive and to borrow a little from each other. And within each group there has been increasing experimentation to determine which methods are actually more successful not only for children from economically comfortable homes but also for those who have been deprived.

8   A Psychologist Looks
               at Montessori*

RILEY W. GARDNER, *The Menninger Foundation, Topeka, Kansas*

Psychologists are, at long last, becoming more aware of the remarkable contributions that Maria Montessori made to our understanding of child training and the broader problems of child development. Her contributions are of signal importance in their own right, and their implications for developmental theory have too long been ignored.

The potential of her contributions for certain types of research in child development is still largely unexplored. The links between her contributions and some contemporary theories, and the potential links between her contributions and some growing bodies of empirical knowledge, are also still largely unexplored. The recent upsurge of interest among psychologists in cognitive processes, in individual differences in structural arrangements of cognitive processes, and in the intimately related area of the development of specific cognitive skills—all contribute to a current *Zeitgeist* in psychology in which a closer look at the Montessori method is especially pertinent.†

The current national concern for culturally deprived children makes it more important than ever that psychologists consider every method of education that may deepen, strengthen, and accelerate early cognitive development. Culturally deprived children have generally arrived at our

* Reprinted from *Elementary School Journal* by Riley W. Gardner by permission of The University of Chicago Press. Copyright 1966 by The University of Chicago Press.

† Based on an address to the annual meeting of the American Montessori Society, New York City, June 19, 1965. The work on individual differences by Gardner and colleagues has been supported by the Menninger Foundation and the United States Public Health Service. The current research described is supported by Research Grant MH-05517 and research career program award K3-MH-21-936 from the National Institutes of Health.

public schools without the sensory-motor and other cognitive skills required for effective learning in that setting. These children have experienced defeat after defeat in the public schools—defeats largely attributable to inadequate preparation, rather than to inadequate cognitive potential.

Maria Montessori's great empathy with the young child and her keen observations of his special modes of processing information led her to emphasize sensory-motor learning. Her approach was far in advance of the general psychological understanding of her time. The significance of her insight into the appropriateness of intellectual training through sensory-motor modalities at ages three to six is still too little realized.

One psychological theorist, however, arrived at an elaborate explication of the sensory-motor nature of the very young child's intelligence that is highly relevant to the Montessori method. That theorist is Jean Piaget, who is generally considered to be our leading child psychologist.

Beginnings of Growth

Piaget speaks of sensory-motor intelligence as the first stage or period of intellectual development (Flavell, 1963; Piaget, 1950, 1951, 1952, 1962). In his view, this form of intelligence predominates during the first two years or so. The ground floor of the intellectual structures that form later is a sensory-motor one. As Piaget (1962) puts it: "Sensory-motor intelligence rests mainly on actions, on movements and perceptions without language, but these actions are coordinated in a relatively stable way. They are coordinated under what we may call schemata of action. These schemata can be generalized in actions and are applicable to new situations. For example, pulling a carpet to bring an object within reach constitutes a schema which can be generalized to other situations when another object rests on a support. In other words, a schema supposes an incorporation of new situations into the previous schemata, a sort of continuous assimilation of new objects or new situations to the actions already schematized" (pp. 121–122).

This passage gives us a shorthand version of Piaget's critically important concept of structuralized schemata and of his notion of assimilation. Assimilation of new experiences with previously formed schemata and accommodation of behavior to external conditions are, in his view, the two major over-all modes of interaction with the environment.

In my discussions with Piaget in 1961, it became clear that he views the very young child's dreams also as primarily sensory-motor in quality (Gardner, 1962). A very young child's dreams may consist primarily of the replication of previously experienced sensory-kinesthetic patterns, rather than thought patterns involving visual images.

Learning from Children

For both Montessori and Piaget, understanding of the sensory-motor nature of the young child's intelligence stemmed from unusually astute observations of young children. Montessori sensed the unique nature of early intelligence, employed it in her methods with young children, and understood that only by using methods appropriate to the age level (or the level of retardation) could maximum acceleration of cognitive development be achieved.

Piaget called the period at which Montessori training usually begins the "preoperational" period. The appearance of symbolic functions distinguishes the preoperational stage from the earlier sensory-motor stage. Up to this point, intelligence primarily involves egocentrically organized actions and perceptions locked to the immediate space that surrounds the child.

Passage to the preoperational stage involves an important change in the child's perception. Perceptual distortion brought about by simple centration (the concentration of attention on the most obvious, single aspect of the stimulus field) yields to more effective perception based on decentration (the deployment of attention to various adaptively relevant aspects of the stimulus field). This more advanced form of attention deployment implies somewhat greater cognitive independence of the immediate situation.

Symbols

This major change is brought about in part by the use of symbols. In the preoperational stage, the use of symbols is still primitive, however, and unlike the more adequate uses of symbolism that characterize the subsequent stages of concrete and formal operations. In fact, according to Piaget, the child at the preoperational stage is ready only to begin a long series of steps toward the ultimate mastery of interrelationships among symbols required for formal operations. But—and here is one of the remarkable similarities between Montessori and Piaget—he points out that, at the preoperational stage, the child is capable of manipulating transformations and other mental operations "only when he manipulates the object concretely" (1962, p. 125).

Montessori intuitively hit on this formulation, which is a cornerstone of Piaget's concept of the preoperational stage. Montessori developed this idea in a way that long preceded effective formulation by psychologists. Piaget himself has been all but unique among psychologists, for it is only in his theory that one finds full recognition of the sensory-motor period as the base on which subsequent stages of intellectual development are built. Most other theories of intelligence have emphasized verbal development and the manipulation of visual images and ideas almost exclusively.

In retrospect, it would seem that many could not appreciate Montessori's emphasis on the learning potential of the young child partly because they evaluated the child's potential against the standard of the concrete and formal operations used by adults.

Childhood—A Special World

In a classic paper, "On Memory and Childhood Amnesia," Ernst Schachtel (1947) describes how the accretion of idea structures during development prevents the adult from experiencing as freshly as he did when a child. To extend Schachtel's thinking, adults are incapable not only of regaining the vividness of childhood experience, but also of recreating the structural world in which they lived as children. Hunt (1964) has noted other reasons for the negative reactions that the Montessori approach inspired when it was introduced in this country. The insights into the child's mind provided by Montessori and later by Piaget were achieved, not by what Piaget calls "adultomorphic" thinking, but by unbiased, astute, direct observations of the child.

Piaget (1952) has emphasized, as Rapaport (1958) and others did, that the formation of later schemata and the effective maintenance of schemata depend in part on external stimulation. The extensive recent work on stimulus deprivation is relevant to one portion of this formulation. Piaget also emphasizes the importance of richly varied early experience. Only such experience provides an ample array of preliminary schemata with which new experiences effectively assimilate.

Here we may be confronted with a limitation of the original Montessori method, which, in spite of its ingenious use of certain specialized kinds of materials, is not primarily designed to broaden the range of objects the child comes in contact with, or the range of sensory-motor interactions with the environment. But no set of educational devices, however cleverly constructed, can be expected to provide all the requirements of optimal cognitive growth (which involves effective over-all equilibration of the forces and structures within the child, including a broad range of affective and motivational factors).

Lessons from Others

It is not possible to deal with Piaget's extremely complex theory in more detail here, but it should be noted that his theoretical constructs include elaborate conceptions of the development of the capacity to abstract and the capacity to perform the operations involved in mathematical thinking. His general emphasis—in his papers on educational methods (Flavell, 1963)—on the necessity of active interaction between the learner and the environment is highly compatible with the Montessori approach. His emphasis on interactions with peers as the principal means of overcoming the child's egocentrism in learning is analogous, in part at least, to some of the later stages of Montessori training.

It should be noted here that Piaget's theory provides a theoretical context for the conceptualization of research on the Montessori method and its variations. It would be extremely interesting to determine whether the sensory-motor approach of early Montessori training affects the ages at which children move from one stage of development to another, as Piaget formulated these stages. It would also be interesting to know whether the attentional controls developed with Montessori training accelerate the gradual process of decentration that makes the child's perception progressively more accurate.

The Montessori method seems to encourage accommodation to external reality, rather than assimilation to the personalized motives and fantasies of the child (such as are expressed in spontaneous play). Therefore, a study of the effects of her method on the balance of assimilation and accommodation would also be worthy of the complex research that would be required. Other subjects worthy of extensive exploration are the generality of effects of Montessori training on various aspects of cognitive performance and the permanence of the effects of training.

What Is Needed for Growth?

This discussion of some overlapping features of formulations by Montessori and Piaget leads naturally to a consideration of major conditions for optimal cognitive growth.

Among these conditions is the creation of learning situations that involve particular kinds and qualities of autonomy. Several writers have commented on the concept of autonomy that Montessori used. I shall focus here on the nature of this autonomy and note some analogies between the kind of autonomy provided by the Montessori school and the kind of autonomy that may ordinarily be optimal for the different kind of learning involved in psychotherapy.

When we say that the child is allowed to learn autonomously in the Montessori school, we mean this in a very special sense. His primary autonomy is from the adult teacher, who—in contrast to the teacher who uses a traditional didactic approach—intrudes into the child's world of discovery in a non-evaluative way, and that only when it seems necessary. The child is, of course, not completely autonomous in the situation. His autonomy is limited by the self-correcting didactic materials he uses. The Montessori method seems to put the child into effective co-ordination with certain features of external reality in such a way that he becomes the instigator of his learning.

The Teacher and the Therapist

A common axiom about learning seems to guide this approach and the approach often involved in effective psychotherapy. In psychotherapy, the patient is placed in a situation in which he may come into more effective communication with his ideas and feelings. The therapist, like the Montessori teacher, may intrude in a non-evaluative way, and then only when he deems it necessary. The essential didactic material is the therapist's conception of reality, of psychological health, and of the most efficient routes to such health. The patient learns that certain kinds of expressions on his part produce corrective communications from the therapist.

The implicit or explicit axiom about learning common to these techniques could be stated in the following terms: both the therapist and the Montessori teacher assume that optimal learning involves a special kind of personal change. This kind of self-instigated change has more permanent effects, and is experienced as more real, than any change one might attempt to impose from without. All effective learning involves personal change, and the most effective kinds of learning seem to be those in which the learner is the initiator of the change and involves himself in active commerce with the learning materials.

It is important to be clear about the special kind of autonomy that seems to be most effective for cognitive development *per se* and for the different kind of cognitive-affective development that can occur in psychotherapy.

How Much Control at Home?

Some children whose families are on the lowest rungs of our socio-economic ladder suffer from harmful excesses of autonomy. That is, they are required to develop all too little control in their early development, and they develop this control without the self-correcting experiences necessary for cognitive and affective differentiation.

In our middle class, many children seem to suffer from rather severe limitations of autonomy that are in part a class-related feature of parent-child interaction. Recent studies seem to indicate that the middle-class mother is remarkably more involved and intrusively participant in her children's behavior than the lower-class mother. Sessions with middle-class children and mothers have been recorded in such studies. The amount of intervention, criticism, correction, and other participation in the child's activities by middle-class mothers was a bit awe-inspiring. It is well known that middle-class parents try to shape their children's personalities and belief systems in detail, while lower-class parents more often respond to their children's overt behavior. Witkin and his colleagues have made fascinating studies (Dyk and Witkin, 1965; Witkin *et al.*, 1962) of the limiting effects of growth-inhibiting mothers on the child's capacity for certain kinds of psychological differentiation. The findings indicate gross individual differences among parents. In general, however, the middle-class parent seems to find it difficult to leave his child alone.

A Haven

It could be that the Montessori method provides a valuable island of autonomy for such children—an island on which they can realize their intellectual potential unhampered by the kind of adult participation they experience at home. It would indeed be interesting to learn whether the extensive work on perceptual sensitivity and discrimination included in early Montessori training increases the aspects of differentiation that Witkin and his associates explored.

Among the other requirements for effective cognitive growth may be a psychological climate in which the child is free to spend at least some of his time exploring his world with complete autonomy. Inhibition of the freedom to explore comes from a variety of sources and has a variety of forms. Nunberg (1961), among others, has noted that every human being is intensely curious about the world around him. It is, in fact, difficult to conceive of the successful evolution of the human species without this kind of curiosity. It is truly remarkable, however, how thoroughly the capacity to be curious can be masked or blunted. Members of our research group recently made an extensive study of the personality organizations, including the cognitive organizations, of a group of preadolescent children ranging in age from nine to thirteen years (Gardner and

Moriarity, 1967). In general, we were negatively impressed with the degree to which intellectual and other forms of curiosity seem to be inhibited at this age in the midwestern subculture.

Curbs on Curiosity

As we analyzed the results, we found ourselves becoming vividly aware of one of the many sources of this inhibition: the imposition upon the child, by authoritarian means, of highly structured beliefs and other conceptions held by the parents. In some families, such preformed views are imposed on the child's budding conception of reality in ways that make it inappropriate for him to ask certain kinds of questions or to attempt to answer them for himself. In fact, the child may become unable to experience certain obvious kinds of questions about his world. Here, in extreme cases, is a massive, blanket-like source of curiosity-inhibition that I fear we all, as parents, are susceptible to in some degree.

As my colleagues and I in the Cognition Project at the Menninger Foundation have pointed out, all of us tend to promote not only our belief systems, but also our cognitive styles—that is, our modes of approach to reality (Gardner, 1964; Gardner *et al.*, 1959).

Active Child—Passive Child

Another important dimension of cognitive development is that of activity *versus* passivity with respect to the child's interaction with the external world. When we interfere with a child's play, when we influence his modes of behavior, when we impose our beliefs upon him, we may be performing a service, but we may also be unaware of the harm we are doing. In the home and in the school, the child is all too frequently forced to assume a purely passive position in which he is required to register and later reproduce material that has been imposed upon him, and which—fortunately or unfortunately—the human being is uniquely prepared to resist.

To me, one of the most valuable aspects of the Montessori method and the psychotherapeutic methods I alluded to is the latitude they provide for active coping behavior. David Rapaport (1961) has explored active and passive ego stances and their implications for personality organization. A host of other observations, including the research findings of Witkin and his colleagues, are pertinent to this general idea. The American child is too often inhibited by situations in which his spontaneous activity can be held to a minimum.

Some recent developments in psychoanalytic theory also have implications for Montessori's method. These have been called developments in "ego psychology."

Early Theory

Contrary to popular understanding, psychoanalysis has always been an intensely cognitive theory. Since psychoanalysis originated primarily in the clinic, its early formulations were devoted to the realm of the unconscious, the apparently instinctive forces at work in the personality, and the resolution of conflicts between instincts. From the beginnings of psychoanalytic theorizing in the 1890's, the formulations of defense mechanisms against unconscious conflicts were stated in cognitive terms. It is, in fact, from the concept of *defense* that we have obtained the general notion of cognitive structures that is used in some of our current research. For many years, academic psychology largely ignored the cognitive structures that intervene between stimulus and response. Some of us, including Witkin and his colleagues and myself, have recently devoted extensive research programs to further explication of various aspects of such cognitive structure formation and the development of such cognitive structures.

Beginning with a classic monograph by Hartmann (1958), psychoanalysis has moved into a more thoroughgoing consideration of the ego structures that intervene between drives and intentions on the one hand and external reality conditions on the other. This attempt to broaden the scope of psychoanalytic theory, with its emphasis on adaptive mechanisms, has led to an intensified exploration of various aspects of cognitive structuring. This work has led to the development by Klein (1954) and others of a concept of non-defensive "cognitive control" structures that emerge in the course of development as enduring arrangements of cognitive processes and that are components of over-all "cognitive style."

Explorations of Individuality

We have spoken of principles of cognitive control in describing the results of our studies of individual differences in cognitive functions. In my own laboratory, we have devoted our attention to a half-dozen or so relatively independent dimensions of cognitive organization and have spent considerable time exploring relationships among these dimensions, intellectual abilities, and defense mechanisms (Gardner, 1959, 1964; Gardner *et al.*, 1959; Gardner and Schoen, 1962). Among the areas of individuality we have explored are those apparent in the categorizing of persons and events, in the capacity to attend selectively, in certain aspects of memory formation, in modes of scanning the internal and the external world, in tolerance for unrealistic experiences, and in the capacity to inhibit irrelevant motoric responses during the performance of cognitive tasks.

I would like to summarize briefly some general observations from this group of studies. We have found that adults are, indeed, characterized by a number of enduring, individually different, cognitive strategies in the execution of intentions under particular classes of environmental conditions. We have found that these dimensions of individual difference are, for the most part, not reducible to intellectual abilities or defense structures. We have found that the developmental changes characterizing these varied aspects of cognitive organization are remarkably different. We have found that the cognitive structures apparent in preadolescent children are remarkably similar in some ways to the cognitive structures apparent in adults, even though the qualitative manifestations of the operation of these structures are different.

Studies of Twins

We are now engaged in further explorations of cognitive control principles, intellectual abilities, defense mechanisms, and a wide variety of other aspects of personality organization, including modes of structuring perceptions of other persons and physiological responses to external stimulation. We are doing this study with a large group of twins and their parents (Gardner, 1964; Gardner *et al.*, 1960).

We are interested in the importance of heredity to the enduring individual differences we have found. We are interested in the role of the parent as an imitative model, and in the effects of parental attitudes and child-rearing strategies on the emergence of different patterns of cognitive organization. We are also interested in familial similarity of personality organization and in a variety of related issues.

Our studies have been carried out during the past fifteen years. New as these studies are on the psychological horizon, they are potentially relevant to educational processes. Let us note here a few of the possible areas of overlap and then touch briefly on some of the many possibilities for research.

The Imprint of Memory

Our studies of individual differences in certain aspects of memory formation have centered on the fact that the perception of new experiences tends to be shaped by memories of earlier experience. Individuals differ greatly in the degree to which this shaping occurs. In one test we use to measure this dimension of individual differences, the subject is asked to judge the sizes of squares. We present one square at a time and allow the subject sufficient time to judge its size. We begin with a series of small squares and gradually add slightly larger sizes. In the course of a rather lengthy test, we progress from a square that is one inch in size to a square that is more than thirteen inches in size. At the end of this procedure, some normal adults (and children) judge the final 13.7-inch squares to be as small as 5 inches. This is a remarkable degree of perceptual distortion induced by the perception of smaller squares earlier. Other individuals are largely unaffected by the order in which they perceive the squares. Since the performance of the first subjects may seem unusual, I might note that our perceptions of new acquaintances are often colored by perceptions of other individuals we have known. In a recent study, we found that this tendency to "homogenize" the present and the past, which is in one sense maladaptive, is associated with ego weakness in preadolescent children (Gardner and Moriarity, 1967). That is, it seems to be one component of poor reality contact.

On Montessori Method

A recent visit to a Montessori school impressed us with the discovery that the children, in their work with weights and sizes, were being trained to make sequential discriminations of the kind our subjects make in the squares test. One thing the child must do in these situations is to judge each stimulus independent of the others he has lifted, seen, or felt. It appeared that he might be receiving training in the kind of veridical sequential perception we have called *sharpening*—that is, the experiencing of new stimuli in their own right, independent of what has happened before. It would be interesting to test children taught by Montessori methods to see whether they later show consistent superiority in this area of memory formation and to determine whether Montessori training generalizes to other aspects of memory formation.

On observing the children in this school, one other aspect of our work on individual differences immediately came to mind. We were impressed with the variety of ways in which the Montessori method develops effective inhibition of irrelevant motoric activity, while, at the same time, developing both focal attention and concentration on sequences of operations involved in complex tasks. This observation interested us particularly because we have long been impressed with the notion that specific forms of selective attention—to say nothing of the longer-range forms of selective attention involved in the planned execution of complex activities—are among the most valuable and uniquely human of our evolutionary gifts.

Human development has been described as the development of effective inhibitions of irrelevant responses. This definition seems incomplete. In a recent paper, I described human development as the emergence of control mechanisms that involve both inhibition and facilitation (Gardner, 1967). The Montessori method may accelerate certain aspects of both kinds of controls. It would be of great interest to know whether the Montessori method accelerates the development of such complex control structures.

Avenues of Research

There are other possibilities for research on relations between recent studies of individual differences and the work of Montessori teachers. The results would be important to the development of an adequate concept of the emergence of cognitive structures.

Anyone who works in the area of individual differences is soon and lastingly impressed with the extreme range of differences among normal children in almost every major cognitive function. These differences are as evident in the aspects of cognitive style that seem to involve something like preference as they are in aspects of cognitive style more easily conceptualized as skill or ability variables. The evidence has been so impressive that we hesitate to accept, without qualification, any view of child development that does not include recognition of this degree of individuality.

We are interested in the outcome of studies yet to be done that may tell us something of individual differences in rates of achievement of the stages described by Piaget. We would also be most interested in research on the question of whether the sequence of methods suggested by Montessori is ideally the same for all children. Montessori teachers may already be experimenting with variations of the original sequence, or such variations may have been made intuitively in work with individual children.

We have not dealt here with some of the other psychological issues raised by the Montessori method. For example, we have not considered the current controversy over the relationship between the development of creativity and sensory-motor skills, language skills, and mathematical skills. We have not dealt with the relationship between what might be called affective development and cognitive development. This subject would take us into a broader arena and would include some of the major pillars of the child's personality.

The possibilities for research on the Montessori method are extensive. To elicit the interest of psychologists in such endeavors and to elicit their cooperation in explorations of child development will expose the educator to the anxieties of putting convictions to the test and of being forced to modify some cherished conceptions. To do so, however, may clarify the psychological implications of educational methods in a way profitable to psychologists as well as educators.

References

Dyk, Ruth B., and H. A. Witkin. March 1965. Family experiences related to the development of differentiation in children. *Child Develpm.*, **36**, pp. 21–56.

Flavell, J. H. 1963. *The developmental psychology of Jean Piaget* (Princeton, N.J.: D. Van Nostrand Company, Inc.).

Gardner, R. W. 1967. Organismic equilibration and the energy-structure duality in psychoanalytic theory: an attempt at theoretical refinement. *J. Amer. Psychoanal. Assn.*

————. 1964. The development of cognitive structures. In Constance Scheerer (ed.), *Cognition: theory, research, promise* (New York: Harper & Row), pp. 147–171.

————. September 1964. *Cognitive control and person perception.* A paper presented at the annual meeting of the American Psychological Association, Los Angeles, California.

————. September 1964. *The Menninger Foundation study of twins and their parents.* A paper presented at the annual meeting of the American Psychological Association, Los Angeles, California.

————. 1962. Cognitive controls in adaptation: research and measurement. In S. Messick and J. Ross (eds.), *Measurement in personality and cognition* (New York: John Wiley & Sons, Inc.), pp. 183–198.

————. May 1962. Four discussions with Professor Piaget. *Bull. of the Menninger Clinic*, **26**, pp. 117–119.

————. November 1959. Cognitive control principles and perceptual behavior. *Bull. of the Menninger Clinic*, **23**, pp. 241–248.

————, and Alice Moriarity. 1967. *Personality development at preadolescence: an exploratory study of structure formation.*

————, and R. A. Schoen. 1962. Differentiation and abstraction in concept formation. *Psychol. Monogr.*, **71**, No. 41, Whole No. 560.

————. May 1962. Control, defence, and centration effect: a study of scanning behaviour. *Brit. J. Psychol*, **53**, pp. 129–140.

————, and R. I. Long. November 1962. Cognitive controls of attention and inhibition: a study of individual consistencies. *Brit. J. Psychol.*, **53**, pp. 381–388.

————, D. N. Jackson, and S. J. Messick. 1960. Personality organization in cognitive controls and intellectual abilities. *Psychol. Issues*, **2**, No. 4, Whole No. 8.

————, P. S. Holzman, G. S. Klein, Harriet B. Linton, and D. P. Spence. 1959. Cognitive control: a study of individual consistencies in cognitive behavior. *Psychol. Issues*, **1**, No. 4, Whole No. 4.

Hartmann, H. 1958. *Ego psychology and the problem of adaptation* (1939). Translated by D. Rapaport (New York: International Universities Press, Inc.).

Hunt, J. McVicker. 1964. Introduction. Revisiting Montessori. In Maria Montessori, *The Montessori method* (New York: Schocken Books), pp. xi–xxxv.

Klein, G. S. 1954. Need and regulation. In M. R. Jones (ed.), *Nebraska symposium on motivation* (Lincoln, Nebr.: University of Nebraska Press), pp. 224–274.

Nunberg, H. 1961. *Curiosity* (New York: International Universities Press, Inc.).

Piaget, J. May 1962. The stages of the intellectual development of the child. *Bull. of the Menninger Clinic*, **26**, pp. 120–128.

————. 1952. *The origins of intelligence in children* (New York: International Universities Press, Inc.).

————. 1951. *Play, dreams and imitation in childhood* (New York: W. W. Norton & Company, Inc.).

————. 1950. *The psychology of intelligence* (New York: Harcourt, Brace & World, Inc.).

Rapaport, D. 1961. Some metapsychological considerations concerning activity and passivity. *Archivos de Criminología Neuropsiquiatría y Disciplinas Conexas*, **9**, (Quito, Equador), pp. 391–449.

————. January 1958. The theory of ego autonomy: a generalization. *Bull. of the Menninger Clinic*, **22**, pp. 13–35.

Schachtel, E. February 1947. On memory and childhood amnesia. *Psychiatry*, **10**, pp. 1–26.

Witkin, H. A., R. B. Dyk, H. F. Faterson, D. R. Goodenough, and S. A. Karp. 1962. *Psychological differentiation* (New York: John Wiley & Sons, Inc.).

9   An Evaluation of the Montessori Method in Schools for Young Children*

EVELYN G. PITCHER, *Eliot-Pearson Department of Child Study, Tufts University*

Our nation now seems ready to believe that the preschool child is ready to learn and that learning, to be optimal, must take place at optimal times.

Maria Montessori devoted her professional life to this belief some years ago and promoted materials, theories and training schools to support her convictions. Her once revolutionary ideas have been absorbed into contemporary thinking and are already at work in behalf of early childhood education. Now, with the rediscovery of the crucial importance of early learning, the Montessori method, first useful with slow-learning children and then adapted to children in Italian slums, has been reintroduced in various ways in this country.

Variety of Montessori Schools

We have in America a variety of Montessori schools. They range from ultra-orthodox to moderate approaches. The purists (divided by confusing schisms) evince more enthusiasm than sound psychology, setting forth rigid techniques and materials as a catechism of True Faith.

Those with more moderate approaches utilize basic Montessori materials and theories (many of which in one form or another are already evident in American nursery schools) but feel free to add other materials or include other methods of teaching. A critical question arises: what is a *true* Montessori school? What is the advantage of using the name if there is deviation from orthodox method or mystique? Does the use of the name have sales value for parents who are looking for unusual *academic* opportunities for their children? The question naturally arises as one reads much of the literature sent out by the Montessori-type schools, such as the following testimonial from a prominent one in California:

> Five-year-olds are able to read, write, analyze parts of speech, square numbers, add and subtract fractions, multiply, divide, while being successfully introduced to elementary history, geography, science, art, music, and the study of three languages simultaneously.

* *Childhood Education*, April 1966, vol. 42, no. 8. Reprinted by permission of The Association for Childhood Education International.

A recent newspaper release describing a Montessori school directed by Nancy Rambush in Mount Vernon, New York, tells, "By eliminating juice-and-cracker breaks, unneeded rest periods, bathroom trips, and wrap struggling, the essential teaching aspects of a nursery-school program could be concentrated into an hour-a-day program. . . . Generally the one-hour nursery-mat program is based on Montessori educational techniques, with the youngsters free to learn as they choose in a 'prepared environment.' Eight children attend the nursery-mat at a time, in one-hour shifts, and three teachers are available to work with them. The nursery-mat also contains Edison Responsive Environment Equipment, the electric 'typewriter' device developed by O. K. Moore with which a preschooler can teach himself to read and type."

The article goes on to describe the phenomenal advances disadvantaged children have made in reading readiness—one, indeed, has progressed to such an extent that he has been advised to skip kindergarten!

This last article reflects a real confusion of thought between compensatory education for disadvantaged children which might bring them to "normal" levels of operation and speeded-up academic accomplishments that merit skipping a year of life. Whether intentional or not, announcements from Montessori schools have tended to foster the latter belief, particularly in suburban hotbeds of "pushy" parents where eager scouts sometimes spend time ferreting scholastic talent out of the sandbox.

Studies Measuring Compensatory Early Education

Several provocative studies have attempted to measure the effects of compensatory education on young children. Two were reported at recent conferences. Fred Strodbeck of the University of Chicago at the Wheelock College Institute, Boston, November 1964, told about setting up three different types of nursery school programs: one a "reading-readiness" nursery; another a highly permissive "therapeutic type" school with teachers acting as surrogate mothers; and the third a "conventional" nursery, described as a place where a teacher prevented aggression and risk-taking, demonstrated materials, gave a maximum of warmth, food and creature comforts. In all three schools there were gains, as measured by the Peabody Vocabulary and Stanford Binet, but the highest gain came in the "conventional school," the least gain in the "therapeutic" kind of school.

Carl Bereiter, from the University of Illinois, at a meeting of the New England Psychological Association in Boston last November talked about the results of an academically oriented preschool for disadvantaged children which he and Siegfried Engelman organized in Urbana.

In a program lasting only two hours a day, children had separate teachers for each subject, emphasizing language, reading and arithmetic. Children were mobilized in twenty-minute sessions of intensive instruction, sandwiched between less structured activities such as singing, coloring, listening to stories. Language involved a patterned drill such as in teaching a foreign language; arithmetic at first involved simple counting operations with no attempt to relate the subject to the external world. The straight-forward reading program emphasized phonics. Bereiter likened this program to a sort of athletic drill session, where there was a great deal of praise for trying hard, improving, thinking. Scores from ITPA (Illinois Test of Psycholinguistic Abilities) and Binet show striking gains in a school year. Language scores of four-year-old children, selected from the bottom of the opportunity scale, moved forward something like two years at ITPA-age in six months.

The writer also did a study last year in a day care center in Boston testing disadvantaged children before and after a six-month experience in a "conventional" full-time day care nursery school, where parents had intensive help from social workers and teachers. The children were matched with a control group who had no day care services. The children in school developed remarkably in language and adaptive areas beyond the control group, making gains of from eighteen to twenty-one months in the six-month interval as tested by Gesell Developmental Evaluations.

These studies, utilizing quite different methods, represent work with disadvantaged children which helped them overcome their deficiencies and brought them closer to "normal." Evidence seems incontestable that school programs, even of short duration, can mobilize children to develop crucial, testable learnings. Mme. Montessori also demonstrated that the Montessori method accomplished dramatic compensatory education with disadvantaged children. Children who have a lot to learn can learn it rapidly in a number of different ways.

Other Questions

The focus of this article directs us now to other questions. Is the true or modified Montessori method the *best* way to work with disadvantaged children? Is it the best way to work with average or superior children? *There have been no systematic studies that demonstrate the superiority of the Montessori classroom over schools not thus labeled.*

While awaiting results from such studies, our concern is with a program whose popular appeal rests on speed in acquiring academic skills.

We are acquainted with a four-year-old girl who learned to read by means of the Doman Reading Exposure materials at two and a half. Despite her extraordinary ability to read, sound out and compose words phonetically, a recent developmental evaluation revealed her to be still very much a four-year-old with childlike understandings of herself and the world. "What is wet? Who am I? What is a girl?" are important and baffling questions for her. She has relatively poor fine motor skills and a rather surprising lack of zeal for activities other than reading. Clearly it would be a great disservice to this child to have her skip kindergarten.

Learning is in danger of being seen as the shortest distance between two points, and the techniques of compensatory education are often attractive to people who do not need them. Education actually is more devious, takes more time, involves more subtleties; there must be room for idleness and talk, for the accidental and informal. We want to have children get to know everyday phenomena in many firsthand, sensory ways, to question thoughtfully and think for themselves. They need to enjoy the satisfactions of problem solving and learning skills, lest they stop seeking. They also need to express their feelings and sense of self through dramatic play, dance, graphic art, literature. We want to help children to begin to symbolize ideas with pictures and signs as well as with spoken words. We want to cultivate in them a delight in language used playfully and imaginatively, in ways other than just labeling or demanding. We want them to have fun as they play, since play is a young child's natural way of working.

Also, we believe *the teacher is the single most important factor in early group experiences for young children.* The education of young children cannot be carried on without finding better ways to foster teachers of talent and real humanity. In them content and method are inextricably interwoven. They must understand developmental sequences and expectancies and the subtle techniques that promote sound mental health. They must have knowledge and zeal and standards of excellence in basic learnings in arts and sciences, and man's relationships to man, and the ability to interpret these to children in *many* ways. They must be genuinely loving, tolerant, gracious, intellectually curious and in harmony with life, since the values they incorporate will be the values they teach. A dull, warped teacher may indeed hold a child away from his world; a teacher who emphasizes rote learning tends to mechanize learning and promote unfavorable attitudes toward authority figures.

Finally, since young children are extremely dependent on home and family, *it is unrealistic to think of their education apart from their parents*, who are compelling models to be imitated in sex roles, values, language, personal idiosyncrasies, beliefs. We must find more and better ways to promote that infinite patience, love, concern and understanding parents need.

Unless we have been in an arid wasteland for the past fifty years, we have made progress in implementing all these goals, but have done so through unlabeled programs based more on questions and wonderings and the use of many points of view than on rigid formulas, drill in rote learnings and answers that close off inquiry. Learning and teaching are still highly complex, highly individualized problems, and we are not yet ready to produce the blueprint that charts the way for everyone.

10 Analysis of the Characteristics of Children Implicit in the Montessori Method*

ROBERT TRAVERS, *Western Michigan University*

On the following pages, the italicized statements refer to characteristics of children stressed by Maria Montessori in her book *The Montessori Method* (Schocken Paperback Edition 1964). Following each statement of a characteristic are found references to the pages or passages on which the statement is based.

1. *Children show extensive individual differences.*
   "To one whose attitude is right, little children soon reveal *profound individual differences.*" (p. 231)

   Comment: This proposition reflects the interest shown by Montessori's contemporaries in individual differences, but there is little implied in her writing concerning the effects that individual differences should have on teaching. She also has nothing to say about the nature of the dimensions of individual differences.

2. *A stage in development is reached in which the child seeks out new experiences—an activity which becomes rewarding in itself.*

   "In dealing with normal children, we must await this spontaneous investigation of the surroundings, or, as I like to call it, the *voluntary*

* A paper prepared originally for the Association for Supervision and Curriculum Developments' Commission on Instructional Theory, Ira Gordon, Chairman.

explosion of the exploring spirit. In such cases, the children experience a joy at each fresh discovery. They are conscious of sense of dignity and satisfaction which encourages them to seek for new sensations from their environment and to make themselves spontaneous observers." (p. 227)

Comment: This statement could have been made by a contemporary educator. It is also found in many places in the writings of Piaget.

3. *Objects and their names become associated together by being presented together; that is to say learning can take place through contiguity of stimuli.*

"Touching the rough and smooth cards in the first tactile exercise she should say, 'This is smooth, This is rough.' repeating the words." (p. 255) This is the theme of much of Chapter XVII.

Comment: This is Aristotle's association by contiguity which still finds a place in modern psychology.

4. *Learning proceeds first by perceiving objects and then by undertaking motor activities in relation to the objects.*

"We have always started from ideas, and have proceeded thence to motor activities." (p. 218)

Comment: The derivation of this concept is obscure. It is not in keeping with the writings of most 19th century psychologists. It also could not find support in contemporary psychology.

5. *Simple sensory learning transfers to complex perceptual tasks.*

This is the theme of much of Chapter XIV.

Comment: This position foreshadows the development of the concept of early and late learning as evolved by Hebb.

6. *Effective use of the senses require that they be educated. The education of the senses precedes the learning of the names of sensory attributes.*

"For normal children however there exists a period . . . which contains the real sense education. This is the acquisition of a fineness of differential perception." (p. 178)

"One should proceed from a few stimuli contrasting, to many stimuli in gradual differentiation always more fine and imperceptible." (p. 184)

Comment: In Montessori's day nothing was known about the feasibility of sensory education, but today the evidence suggests that sensory sensitivity can be increased with practice.

7. *The child educates himself.*

"The child educates himself." (p. 173)

"With my methods, the teacher teaches little and observes much." (p. 173)

Comment: This proposition does not anticipate some of the current speculation concerning the nature of the learning process but merely reflects the fact that Madame Montessori believed that most teachers interfered too much with the child during learning.

8. *Children reflect in their development the cultural evolution of man.*

"In short, such education makes the evolution of the individual correspond with that of humanity . . . The same path must be traversed by the child who is destined to become a civilized man." (p. 160)

Comment: This position reflects speculation current at the end of the last century. Psychologists had advanced the notion that the play of children represented a recapitulation of the history of the race. Jung had advanced the notion of a memory which somehow reflected the past history of man. The proposition, though acceptable in the days of Montessori, would no longer be acceptable.

9. *Much of the motor behavior of the young child results from his particular physical proportions.*

"The baby loves to walk on all fours because like the quadruped animals, his limbs are short in comparison with his body." (p. 140)

"The tendency of the child to stretch out on his back and kick his legs in the air is an expression of physical needs related to the proportions of his body." (p. 140)

Comment: This notion is reflected in many current general textbooks on educational psychology but probably represents one of Montessori's novel contributions.

10. *Young children cannot learn readily from complex situations and, hence, teaching by demonstration requires that very simple situations be used.*

"The lesson must be presented in such a way that the personality of the teacher shall disappear. There shall remain in evidence only the object to which she wishes to call attention." (p. 108)

"Another characteristic quality of the lesson in the 'Children's House' is simplicity." (p. 108)

Comment: Moving from the simple to the complex had long been accepted as a sound educational principle before Montessori. Undoubtedly she must have been familiar with the educational writings of Herbart who accepted this approach to the presentation of subject matter. Today there would be considerable controversy with respect to this issue.

11. *Children will show some behaviors which annoy others or are dangerous. These must be suppressed. Children have no natural basis for discriminating right from wrong.*

"The liberty of the child should have as its limit the collective interest . . . We must, therefore, check in the child whatever offends or annoys others." (p. 87)

"It is, of course, understood, that here we do not speak of dangerous acts, for these must be *suppressed, destroyed.*" (p. 88)

". . . then I had to intervene to show with what absolute rigour it is necessary to hinder, and little by little suppress, all those things which we must not do, so that the child may come to discern clearly between good and evil." (p. 93)

Comment: This appears to reflect a rejection of some of the notions of J. J. Rousseau which were held by some educational reformers of Montessori's day.

12. *Under appropriate conditions, the child learns to regulate conduct from inside himself.*

"We call an individual disciplined when he is master of himself, and can, therefore, regulate his own conduct." (p. 86)

Comment: At the time when the above statement was written, it would probably have reflected a well-established doctrine. Even the highly-disciplined private schools of the age claimed to have designed their program on the basis of the belief that education must lead to self-regulated behavior, except that they followed the doctrine that self regulation was learned through external regulation. Montessori, in contrast, proposed that self regulation should begin at an early age.

13. *Freedom of movement and activity is important for education for it permits the child to create situations from which he can learn.*

"The fundamental principle of scientific pedagogy must be, indeed, the liberty of the pupil;—such liberty as shall permit a development of individual, spontaneous manifestations of the child's nature." (p. 28)

"And this freedom is not only an external sign of liberty, but a means of education. If by an awkward movement a child upsets a chair, which falls noisily on the floor, he will have evident proof of his own incapacity . . . Thus the child has some means by which he can correct himself." (p. 84)

"The ability to move which he acquires here will be of use to him all of his life. While he is still a child, he becomes capable of conducting himself correctly, and yet, with perfect freedom." (p. 84)

"Since the child learns to move rather than to sit still, he prepares himself not for school, but for life." (pp. 86–87)

Comment: This proposition was novel in its day. It suggests that much education proceeds by what we would call today a feedback loop involving *situation–response–new situation*.

14. *Young children learn by being exposed to displays which they cannot yet understand.*

"Above the blackboards are hung attractive pictures, chosen carefully, representing simple scenes in which children would naturally be interested. Among the pictures in our 'Children's Houses' in Rome we have hung a copy of Raphael's 'Madonna della Seggiola' and this picture we have chosen as the emblem of the 'Children's Houses.'" (p. 82)

"The children cannot, of course, comprehend the symbolic significance of the 'Madonna of the Chair,' but they will see something more beautiful than that which they feel in more ordinary pictures, in which they see mother, father, and children. And the constant companionship with this picture will awaken in their heart a religious impression." (p. 83)

Comment: This raises issues which are still as controversial as they were near the turn of the century. Recent developments in perceptual learning suggest that some learning through mere exposure to an environment may occur, but probably not the complex learnings which Montessori suggests.

15. *The young child has both limited power to coordinate his muscles and to use his sense organs. Perpetuation of these limitations through lack of education constitute the basis of many later defects.*

    (See pp. 44–45 for supporting statements)

    Comment: This is central to the core of Montessori's educational theory. Mental retardation was considered to be due largely to lack of proper education and to restrictions imposed by the environment.

16. *Men are good for reasons other than that they fear punishment.*

    "The enormous majority of citizens are honest without any regard whatever to the threats of the law." (p. 26)

    "Men, when they are punished, are punished by internal sources, rather than external forces." (p. 26)

    "The real punishment of normal man is the loss of the consciousness of that individual power and greatness which are the sources of his inner life." (p. 27)

    Comment: This conception of human nature probably stems from Montessori's deeply religious orientation to life in which a simple philosophy of hedonism would find no place.

17. *The highest reward for a child is that of knowing he has achieved.*

    "God forbid that poems should ever be born of the desire to be crowned in the Capitol . . . The true reward lies in the revelation through the poem of his own triumphant inner force." (pp. 24–25)

    Comment: This looks like achievement motivation in terms of our present-day language.

11   Revisiting Montessori*

J. MCVICKER HUNT, *University of Illinois*

The enlightened self-interest that provided the first *Casa dei Bambini* in
the slum tenements of Rome will find a responsive note today. Modern
administrators and educators are faced with vandalism and aimless violence
among economically and culturally deprived children who reject and are
rejected by the traditional school system. In offering Dr. Montessori space
for the new enterprise, the director of the Roman Association for Good
Building and the owners of the buildings in the San Lorenzo district were
motivated in large part by the hope that keeping the unruly young children, usually left alone during the day by their working parents, in
something like a school would prevent vandalism and save damage to their
property.

It is 70 years since Montessori became interested, while yet a medical
student serving as an intern in the psychiatric clinic of Rome, in the "idiot
children" then housed in the insane asylums. It is 66 years since she began
the work with mentally deficient children that led her to examine Jean
Itard's (1801) attempts at educating the "wild boy of Aveyron" and to
utilize the materials and methods devised by Edouard Séguin (1844, 1866)
for educating the mentally deficient children. It is 57 years since she
extended her modified Séguin-approach in education of retarded children
to the education of normal young children in the first *Casa dei Bambini*,
or "Homes of Children" as Dorothy Canfield Fisher translated the term.

According to the reports (Fisher 1912, Stevens 1913), Montessori's
success far surpassed her sponsors' fondest hopes, if not also hers. Not
only was vandalism prevented, but these children, three to seven years old,
became avid pupils. Not only did they learn "cleanliness," "manners,"
"some grace in action," and "something about proper diet," but they
became acquainted with animals and plants and with the manual arts. They
got both sensory and motor training with the didactic apparatus and even
learned the basic symbolic skills of counting, reading, and writing, often

* Reprinted by permission of Schocken Books, Inc. from *The Montessori
Method* by Maria Montessori. Copyright © 1964 by Schocken Books, Inc. This
paper was originally published as the introduction to the republication of *The
Montessori Method*, as translated from the Italian by Anne E. George for the
first publication in English in 1912, by Schocken Books, 67 Park Avenue, New
York City 10016, in 1964. Dr. Hunt is professor of psychology and education
at the University of Illinois, and is also Director of the Coordination Center
for the National Laboratory for Early Childhood Education. The paper re-
published here was prepared with the support of USPHS Grant MH K6-18567.

before they were five years old. People were impressed. When, in 1909, Montessori published her *Scientific Pedagogy as Applied to Child Education in the Children's Houses*, people from all over the world beat Emersonian paths to her door and pressed her to communicate her methods to others.

Americans were among the first to become interested, and their interest rapidly exploded into a social movement. Perhaps the explosion of interest and its waning is best illustrated by rates of publication about Montessori's work. Jenny Merrill first described Montessori's work in the December, 1909, and March, 1910, issues of the *Kindergarten Primary Magazine*. The year 1911 brought six reports of Montessori's work. The number rose to 54 in 1912, and then jumped to a maximum of 76 in 1913. Then the explosion appears to have rapidly subsided: in 1914 the number of publications declined to 55; they dwindled to 15 in 1915, to eight in 1917, and amounted to less than five a year thereafter.

Why this sudden explosion of interest? Why the equally sudden fall? Why revisit today what may appear from such evidence to have been a mere fad in American education? What concerns does such a revisit arouse? These are the issues I would like to discuss in introducing this new edition of *The Montessori Method*.

Why the Explosion of Interest?

A definitive accounting for this explosion of interest in Montessori's work is hardly possible, but certain factors help to explain it. Americans had been primed to hope for progress with all kinds of problems. Winning the West had encouraged such hope. The "muck-rakers" had been uncovering, in article after article on "the shame of the cities" in *McClure's Magazine*, the seamy side of the human urban condition. American excitement about reform, recently fostered by the progressive Republicanism of Theodore Roosevelt, was still high. Many people, moreover, had become accustomed to see in children the chief hope of fundamental reform. This hope had been fostered by a half-century of activity of the Froebel Society, by nearly a quarter-century of G. Stanley Hall's child-study movement, and by John Dewey's (1900, 1902) attempts—inspired chiefly by the "reform Darwinism" of Lester F. Ward and Albion Small (Cremin, 1962)—to make that age-old institution the school an instrument of progress and social reform.

Reports of Montessori's success in the "Houses of Children" made her pedagogic methods look to many of the most progressive-minded like the way to a new day, or like the most rapid route yet uncovered to fundamental reform. Many of these progressive-minded people who visited

Montessori or became interested in her work had, like Alexander Graham Bell, tremendous prestige; some of them, like McClure, controlled major sources of mass communication; others, like Dorothy Canfield Fisher (1912) and Ellen Yale Stevens (1913), had facile pens. They got the news out fast, and they spread it wide. These factors help explain the explosion of interest.

But why did the interest subside almost as rapidly as it exploded? Perhaps it failed, at least in part, because the Dottoressa rejected McClure's offer in 1913 to build her an institution in America. On the other hand, her rejection may merely have saved her a painful defeat.

Conceptions of nature and of how to deal with any problem may fail either because they run counter to the facts of empirical observation or because they run counter to other conceptions which are somehow better anchored in the beliefs of men at a given time, or because of some combination of these two. On the side of empirical observation, the impressions of Montessori's great educational success reported by American writers lent support to the validity of her conceptions. Some of these people should have been good observers; they included, for instance, such psychologists as Dorothy Canfield Fisher (who is better known for her novels), Arnold and Beatrice Gesell, Joseph Peterson, Howard C. Warren, and Lightner Witmer (see Donahue, 1962, for their publications). However, various conceptions of Montessori ran into almost head-on dissonance with conceptions which, from a variety of communicative influences, were becoming dominant in the minds of those Americans who became most influential. Most of Montessori's support had come from the elite of the political and educational progressives and through popular magazines; it had not come from those formulating the new psychological theories nor from those formulating the philosophy of education. Although Montessori got support from Howard C. Warren (1912), then president of the American Psychological Association, and from Lightner Witmer (1914), founder of the first Psychological Clinic at the University of Pennsylvania, she failed to get support from those psychologists of the functional school or of the emerging behavioristic school whose conceptions were shortly to become dominant. With such emerging theories, with the conceptions of the intelligence-testing movement, and with the psychoanalytic theory of psychosexual development, then just beginning to get a foothold in America following Freud's visit of 1909 at the invitation of G. Stanley Hall, Montessori's notions were too dissonant to hold their own.

Conceptions Dissonant with Montessori's

These dissonant conceptions need to be stated because it is in them that we have been seeing radical changes since World War II. Some of them were still relatively inexplicit at the time; they did not figure in the published criticisms of Montessori's pedagogy. Others were explicit; they did figure in the criticisms.

First, the notion that school experience for three- and four-year-olds could be significantly important for later development was deprecated. For those who thought behavior controlled by conscious intentions, the fact that such early experiences could seldom be recalled seemed to mean that they could have no influence. For those who followed the conservative Darwinism of Herbert Spencer and William Graham Sumner, the development of the individual organism was supposed to be predetermined by heredity. I shall return to give this belief special attention. For those giving credence to the new psychoanalytic theory of psychosexual development, it was the fate of the instinctual modes of pleasure-striving that was supposed to matter, not cognitive development. Moreover, for taxpayers the notion of extending the age for schooling down to three years looked like a highly unnecessary addition to the burden of school taxes. Worse, it looked to some like an infringement on the functions and rights of the family.

Second, the belief in fixed intelligence, later a basic assumption of the intelligence-testing movement, was among those little noted at the time. This notion has roots in Darwin's theory of evolution by natural selection (see Hunt, 1961, pp. 10ff). Americans had absorbed the notion of natural selection about a decade after the Civil War from John Fiske's *Outlines of Cosmic Philosophy* and from Herbert Spencer's *Synthetic Philosophy*. Although this conception of evolution was optimistic about progress, the characteristics of an individual organism or person were seen as fixed by his heredity. The assumption of fixed intelligence is but a special case of this more general view. This assumption came into American psychological thought via J. McKeen Cattell, who was a student of Darwin's younger cousin, Francis Galton, and via G. Stanley Hall, whose students at Clark University established the mental-testing movement. The notion was widely disseminated among educators as "the constant I.Q." (see Hunt, 1961, ch. 2). Montessori's conception of mental retardation as a defect calling for pedagogical treatment was basically dissonant with this notion. Thus, with her intellectual roots in the work of Itard and Séguin, she was definitely out of step with one of the central notions rapidly becoming dominant in the educational psychology of America.

Third, the belief in predetermined development. This also figured but slightly in the published criticisms of Montessori's method. This belief, like the belief in fixed intelligence, has roots in Darwin's theory of evolution by natural selection. It was also implicit in the notion that "ontogeny recapitulates phylogeny," that is, that each individual in its development goes through the same stages that the species goes through in its evolution.

Belief in recapitulation was at the heart of G. Stanley Hall's developmental psychology. He apparently communicated it to all of his students but John Dewey, and these included such important figures in the testing movement as Goddard, Kuhlmann, and Terman, as well as Arnold Gesell, who gave the developmental psychology of the 1920's and 1930's its normative character. Just as Montessori was making her first trip to America, the earliest studies showing the evanescence of the effects of practice were coming out. They appeared to imply that teaching children reading, writing, and counting before they were about eight years old was, at best, a waste of time and, as Kilpatrick (1914) noted, might possibly be harmful. Here again, Montessori was out of step with the conceptual movements in psychology.

Fourth, the belief that *all* behavior is motivated by instincts or by painful stimuli, homeostatic needs, and sex, or by acquired drives based on these. When Montessori was opening the Houses of Children, William McDougall (1908) was writing the *Social Psychology* that disseminated in America the English vogue of attributing behavior to inborn instincts. It rapidly became popular, and many educational psychologists advocated that teachers arrange to associate the content of each lesson with one of the instincts listed by McDougall. At very nearly the same time, the students of animal learning, following C. Lloyd Morgan (1894) in Britain and Edward L. Thorndike (1898) in the United States, were discovering that to elicit specified activities from animal subjects, it was helpful, if not necessary, to induce these activities with painful stimulation or such homeostatic needs as hunger or thirst. The animal then acted to eliminate these distressing drive-stimuli. In Austria, during the same period, Freud (1900) was developing his drive theory and popularizing the statement that "all behavior is motivated." In this statement, Freud commonly left implicit: "by wishes originating in physiological stimuli or homeostatic needs or pain" (see Freud, 1915). According to this doctrine, the aim of all behavior is to reduce or to eliminate excitement from such sources, and implicit in it is the point that animals and children will become quiescent in the absence of such motivation (see Hunt, 1963a). These conceptions of motivation were just emerging as the dominant view when popular interest in Montessori's work exploded. To those who held any version of such a view of motivation, Montessori's notion of basing her method of education upon "children's spontaneous interest in learning" must have appeared to be as nonsensical as perpetual motion. Moreover, for these people Montessori's claim that her materials were intrinsically interesting to children must have seemed too obviously false to be worth empirical investigation.

Fifth, the belief that the response side of the reflex arc is the one essential in education. This notion had roots in the psychological theorizing of the past. G. Stanley Hall had popularized his aphorism that, "the mind of man is hand-made." In Britain, C. Lloyd Morgan (1894) had almost eliminated mind as a concept by showing how loose was the analogical reasoning in imputing to animal subjects the same conscious processes human beings can report. Morgan's work, which is a part of a stream of European mechanistic thought about living organisms that can be traced back to Descartes, set the stage for E. L. Thorndike's (1898) studies of problem-solving in animals. Thorndike's interpretation replaced *mind* with connections between stimuli and responses. The stream flowed on into the behavioristic revolt, led by John B. Watson (1914), which replaced *consciousness* with *behavior* as the subject-matter of psychology. Methodologically, of course, the observables *are limited to* the situation and the organism's activities. These were dubbed stimuli and responses. Stimulus-response theory, however, went further to limit the function of the brain to essentially static connections between stimuli and responses after an analogy with that dramatic new invention, the telephone switchboard. Moreover, it was the response side which supplied the evidence of learning. As a consequence, interest in perception and central processes suffered. With such a view emerging into dominance, it is hardly surprising that Montessori's emphasis on sensory training met all too often with contempt. It is not surprising that Montessori was characterized by Kilpatrick (1914), her most articulate critic, as representing theory more than half-a-century behind the times. Furthermore, Montessori described her "education of the senses" with the graded "didactic materials" as having, "as its aim, the refinement of differential perception of stimuli." This is the language of the faculty psychology which Thorndike and Woodworth (1901) had discredited by their epochal experiments on the transfer of training. Here again, Montessori was out of step with the *Zeitgeist*.

Sixth—and this is not a theoretical conception—there is the traditional desire of teachers for an orderly classroom and for control of the educational process. The influence of Rousseau, Pestalozzi, and Froebel had already helped to call into question this traditional desire for control. Pestalozzi had compared children to plants unfolding from within and requiring only a favorable and cultivated environment for their growth. Froebel wrote in similar fashion. In Froebel's kindergartens, however, the teacher continued to be at the center of the stage (see Fisher, 1912). In the Houses of Children, on the other hand, the lock-step of education was almost completely broken. Each individual child had a stage of his own where the didactic materials were at the center of his attention. The role of the teacher was limited to that of observer-helper of the children in their spontaneous efforts to cope with the didactic materials. One gleans that this demotion was irritating to many teachers with other than Montessori training and indoctrination, and I believe this irritation persists among teachers today.

Perhaps Montessori was unfortunate to have as her chief critic William Heard Kilpatrick (1914). Kilpatrick was an eloquent lecturer at Teachers College, where he was known as the "million-dollar professor." In 1913, at the height of the enthusiasm for Montessori's work, it was Kilpatrick who appeared before the annual meeting of the International Kindergarten Union to point out that, except for her Houses of Children, Montessori's ideas about education were not new. Further, he considered her to belong in the Rousseau-Pestalozzi-Froebel tradition with beliefs in the educational process as an unfolding of what was present at birth, and in liberty as a necessary condition for this unfolding in faculties of the mind and in sense-training. Since these beliefs had to be "strictly revised to square with modern conceptions," he felt "compelled to say that in the content of her doctrine, she belongs to the mid-nineteenth century, some fifty years behind the present development of educational theory" (Kilpatrick, 1914, pp. 62–63).

Kilpatrick also compared Montessori with his guiding light, John Dewey. He wrote: "The two have many things in common. Both have organized experimental schools; both have emphasized the freedom, self-activity, and self-education of the child; both have made large use of 'practical life' activities. . . . There are however wide differences. For the earliest education, Madame Montessori provides a set of mechanically simple devices. These in large measure do the teaching. A simple procedure embodied in definite, tangible apparatus is a powerful incentive to popular interest. Professor Dewey could not secure the education which he sought in so simple a fashion. Madame Montessori was able to do so only because she had a much narrower conception of education, and because she could hold to an untenable theory as to the value of formal and systematic sense-training. Madame Montessori centered much of her effort upon devising more satisfactory methods of teaching reading and writing, utilizing thereto in masterly fashion the phonetic character of the Italian language. Professor Dewey, while recognizing the duty of the school to teach these arts, feels that early emphasis should rather be placed upon activities more vital to child-life which should at the same time lead toward the mastery of our complex social environment. . . . Madame Montessori hoped to remake pedagogy; but her idea of pedagogy is much narrower than is Professor Dewey's idea of education. His conception of the nature of the thinking process, together with his doctrines of interest and of education as life—not simply a preparation for life—include all that is valid in Madame Montessori's doctrines of liberty and sense-training, afford the criteria for correcting her errors, and besides, go vastly further in the construction of the educational method" (Kilpatrick, 1914, pp. 63–66).

One can make this comparison in another way. Montessori was reforming pedagogy and basing her innovations on her own clinical observations of children, first those mentally retarded and then those culturally deprived who participated in the Houses of Children. Dewey (1897), on the other hand, was attempting to foster social reform in the schools, and he based his attempt, as already noted, on the reformed Darwinism of Lester F. Ward and Albion Small, to be contrasted with the conservative Darwinism of Herbert Spencer and Herbert Graham Sumner. Dewey's approach was part of that progressive movement in post-Civil War America that reached its peak during the 1890's. Kilpatrick's comparison was effective. His little book circulated widely among teachers and educators. It was a wet blanket on the fire of enthusiasm for Montessori's work.

Why Revisit Montessori Today?

All this was a half-century ago, when the beliefs of Stimulus-response theory, the intelligence testers, and psychoanalysis were becoming dominant. They remained dominant for the period between the two World Wars and through World War II. Stimulus-response methodology was highly productive of observational evidence. Ironically, it is this evidence from S-R methodology which has been the undoing of the beliefs dominant in psychological theory, even some of those central to S-R theory. Moreover, it is this evidence from S-R methodologies which suggests that Montessori built pedagogically better than her critics knew, even though the language of her constructs may seem even more quaint today than Kilpatrick found it in 1912. Consider in turn the various beliefs synopsized.

Belief in the Unimportance of Early Experience

It was Freud's (1905) observation that the free associations of his patients led back to infancy, and his imaginative interpretation in the theory of psychosexual development, that began to lend force to the notion that very early experience, even preverbal experience, might be important for the development of adult characteristics. Freud's theory, however, put the emphasis on the fate of instinctive modes of infantile pleasure-striving, *i.e.*, sucking, elimination, and genitality. To a substantial degree, objective studies of the effects of these factors explicitly concerned in early psychosexual development have generally tended to depreciate their

importance (see Child, 1954; Hunt, 1945; Orlansky, 1949; Sears, 1943).*
On the other hand, studies of the effects of various kinds of early infantile
experience in animal subjects have left very little room for doubt that
early experience is a factor in behavioral development. Ready-made infantile responses, like the sucking of the calf—as any farmer knows—or of
the human infant (Sears and Wise, 1950), the pecking response in chicks
(Padilla, 1935), or the flying response of young birds (Spalding, 1873),
will wane if these patterns go unused for too long a time. Similarly, such
presumably instinctive patterns as mothering fail to develop in female
rats that have been deprived of licking themselves by means of Elizabethan
collars worn from weaning to adulthood (Birch, 1956). Even certain
aspects of the anatomical maturation itself appear to depend upon experience. Chimpanzees (Riesen, 1958), kittens (Weiskrantz, 1958), rabbits
(Brattgård, 1952), and rats (Liberman, 1962) that are reared in darkness
develop anomalous retinae which are deficient in Müller fibers and show
deficient RNA production in the retinal ganglion cells (Brattgård, 1952;
Liberman, 1962; Rasch, Swift, Riesen, and Chow, 1961). Moreover, rats
deprived of vision for the 10 days immediately after the eyes open are not
as quickly responsive to visual cues in adulthood as are litter-mates which
were deprived of hearing for 10 days after their ears opened, and vice
versa (Wolf, 1943; Gauron and Becker, 1959). (That is, the rats deprived
of hearing are not as quickly responsive to aural cues as are rats deprived
of vision.) Although there is still much confusion concerning this issue,
rats petted, shook, or submitted to electric shock and to marked drops in
temperature have shown repeatedly, as adults, a reduction in the tendency
to defecate and urinate in a strange open field, increased readiness to enter
strange places, and more rapid learning to avoid shock than controls left
unmolested in the maternal nest (see Denenberg, 1962; Levine, 1961).
These are but a sample of the various kinds of effects of infantile experience on the adult behavior of animal subjects (see also Beach and Jaynes,
1954). Still others will be noted in connection with other beliefs. Clearly,
Montessori's concern with the experience of three- and four-year-olds
need be no will-o'-the-wisp.

Belief in Fixed Intelligence

The belief in fixed intelligence was based in considerable part upon
the notion that the genes which carry the heredity of the individual fix
his intellectual capacity. It is probably true that the genes determine an

---

* I must except here a growing variety of factors in parent-child relationships which are being shown to be quite important (see Becker, 1962). These
studies stem in large part from the psychoanalytic conception of the Oedipal
relationship as that conception has been elaborated in the learning theory of
Dollard and Miller (1950).

individual's potential to develop intellectual capacity, but they do not guarantee that the individual will achieve his potential capacity. Elsewhere (Hunt, 1961), I have summarized the evidence (a) that scores from tests administered in the preschool years predict very poorly scores for tests administered at adolescence, (b) that substantial differences in the I.Q. have been found for identical twins reared apart and that the degree of difference of I.Q. is related to the degree of difference between the sets of circumstances under which the twins have developed, and (c) that the commonly predicted drop in intelligence to be expected from the fact that the majority of each new generation comes from the lower half of the population intellectually has failed to occur and that, instead, rather substantial increases have been found.

It is especially interesting to note that Harold Skeels has recently followed up those individuals in the study by Skeels and Dye (1939). In this study, a group of 13 infants with a mean I.Q. of 64.3 and a range between 36 and 89 and with chronological ages ranging from seven to 30 months, was transferred from an orphanage to a school for the mentally retarded. There they were placed on a ward where the older and brighter girls became very much attached to them and would play with them during most of the infants' waking hours. After being on this ward for periods ranging between six months, for the seven-month-old youngster, and 52 months, for the 30-month-old youngster, they were retested. Each of the 13 showed a gain in I.Q.: the minimum gain was seven points, the maximum was 58 points, and all but four showed gains of more than 20 points. In the same study, for purposes of contrast, were 12 other orphanage inmates, this group having a mean I.Q. of 87, an I.Q. range from 50 to 103, and an age range from 12 to 22 months. These infants were left in the orphanage. When they were retested after periods varying from 21 to 43 months, they all showed a decrease in I.Q. One decrease was only eight points, but for the remaining 11 children, the decreases varied between 18 and 45 points, with five exceeding 35 points. In the follow-up study, all of these cases were located after a lapse of 21 years. The findings are startling. Of the 13 in the group transferred from the orphanage to the school for the mentally retarded: all are self-supporting; none is a ward of any institution, public or private; 11 of the 13 are married, and nine of these have had children. On the other hand, of the 12 children, originally higher in I.Q., who were kept in the orphanage: one died in adolescence following continuous residence in a state institution for the mentally retarded; five are still wards of state institutions, one in a mental hospital and the other four in institutions for the mentally retarded; of the six no longer wards of state institutions, only two have been married and one of these is divorced. In education, the disparity between the two groups is similarly great. For the 13 transferred from the orphanage to the school for the mentally retarded, the median grade completed is the twelfth (*i.e.*, graduation from high school); four have gone on for one or more years of college work, with one of the boys having received a bachelor's degree from a big state university. Occupationally, the range is from professional and semi-professional to semi-skilled laborers or domestics. For the 12 who remained in the orphanage, half failed to complete the third grade, and none got to high school. Only three of the six not now in state institutions are now employed (Skeels, personal communication, 1964). Clearly there is a difference here that counts. The superiority of the foster home, where the child receives a variety of experience and stimulation, over the old orphanage is relevant here (see Goldfarb, 1963).

Evidence that early experience influences adult problem-solving capacity comes also from studies with animal subjects. This work stems from the neuropsychological theorizing of Donald Hebb (1949). Hebb was concerned with the facts of attention and thought. For him, the switchboard conception of brain-function could not be true, for these facts imply that semi-autonomous processes must be operating within the brain. He also found evidence for these in neurophysiology, and he termed them *cell assemblies*, based upon early learning involving perceptual experiences, and *phase sequences*, based upon the sequential organizations of later learning. The electronic computer has replaced the telephone switchboard as the mechanical model of brain function. On the assumption that problem-solving would be a function of the richness of these semi-autonomous central processes, Hebb (1947) compared the problem-solving ability of rats reared in cages in the laboratory with that of rats reared as pets in his home. The problem-solving ability was measured by the Hebb-Williams (1946) test of animal intelligence. The pet-reared animals were superior to their cage-reared litter-mates. Thompson and Heron (1954), also at McGill, have done a similar experiment with dogs as subjects. Some were reared under isolation in laboratory cages from weaning to eight months of age. Their litter-mates were reared for this same period in homes as pets. The cage-reared and the pet-reared dogs were put together in a dog-pasture for 10 months; then, at 18 months of age, their problem-solving ability was assessed in the Hebb-Williams mazes. The pet-reared dogs were superior to their cage-reared litter-mates. In fact, the superiority of the pet-reared dogs over the cage-reared dogs appears to have been even more marked than the superiority of the pet-reared rats over the cage-reared rats. This suggests that the degree of effect of infantile experience on adult problem-solving capacity may well be a function of the proportion of the brain not directly connected with either receptor inputs or motor outputs. This proportion, termed the A/S ratio by Hebb (1949) increases up the phylogenetic scale.

There is a good possibility that the cultural deprivation involved in being reared under slum conditions may be somewhat analogous to cage-rearing while being reared in a family of the educated middle class most resembles pet-rearing. This possibility suggests that an enrichment of early experience during the preschool years might well serve as an antidote for this cultural deprivation, if it comes early enough (see Hunt, 1964). It might thereby give those children whose lot it has been to be born to parents living in slums a more nearly even opportunity to hold their own in the competitive culture of the public school once they get there. The "Houses of Children" established by Montessori in the San Lorenzo district of Rome and the methods of teaching that she developed there provide a splendid beginning precisely adapted for this purpose of counteracting cultural deprivation.

Belief in Predetermined Development

The notions that psychological development is predetermined by the genes and that the response repertoire emerges automatically as a function of anatomic maturation are no longer tenable. The early evidence appearing to support such a conception of development was either based on investigations with such lowly organisms as Amblystoma and frogs (see Hunt, 1961, pp. 49ff), or it was based upon the effects of practicing a given kind of skill. Such lower organisms as these amphibia used as subjects by Carmichael (1926) and Coghill (1929) differ from mammals, and especially from human beings in two very fundamental ways. They have substantially greater regenerative capacity, and this fact suggests that biochemical determiners may well be considerably more prepotent in determining their development than such factors are in determining the development of mammals. They also have a much lower proportion of the brain not directly connected with receptor inputs or motor outputs (in Hebb's terms, a lower A/S ratio). This fact suggests that semi-autonomous central processes deriving from experience must have a much smaller role in determining their behavior than it has in mammals, and especially in man. Moreover, the evidence concerning the effects of very early experience both on the anatomical development of the retinae and on adult behavior in animal subjects is clearly dissonant with this notion of predetermined development.

Those studies showing that practice has but evanescent effects on such early abilities as tower-building, ladder-climbing, buttoning, and cutting with scissors (see Gesell and Thompson, 1929; Hilgard, 1932) missed the point that abilities appear to be hierarchically organized, that the experiences governing the age at which such abilities appear do not constitute exercise in those abilities themselves. Rather, they constitute encounters with quite different circumstances important in establishing abilities lower in the hierarchy. At the level of school subjects, this can be illustrated by noting how useless practice in long division is if the child has not learned to add and subtract. More to the point, however, is such evidence from animal studies as Birch's (1956) finding that female rats do not mother their young properly if they have been deprived of licking themselves by means of Elizabethan collars. Still more to the point, at the level of human beings, is that dramatic finding of Dennis (1960) that children being reared in a Teheran orphanage where visual and auditory inputs are relatively homogeneous are markedly delayed in their *locomotor* development. Of these children, 60% were still not sitting up alone at two years of age, and 85% were still not walking at four years of age. Variations of visual and auditory input would appear in terms of our conceptions of practice to have little to do with locomotor skills. Thus, while the genotype does set limits on an individual's potential, it does not guarantee that this potential in capacity will be reached. The achievement of genotypic potential appears to be a function of a continuous interaction between the organism and its environment. It has long been obvious that there must be a biochemical interaction manifested in the processes of food and water intake and elimination, but it now appears that psychological development is also highly dependent upon what one may characterize as the organism's informational interaction with the environment.

One more factor relevant to the role of early experience in psychological development. During the earliest phases, the longer a developing organism is deprived of a given sort of experience, or, to put it another way, the longer an organism is deprived of a given kind of informational interaction with the environment, the more likely is the effect of that deprivation to become permanent. For instance, in the work of Cruze (1935, 1938) chicks reared in darkness for only five days quickly developed their expected accuracy in pecking, but chicks allowed only some 15 minutes out of darkness for pecking each day for 20 days not only failed to improve but also appeared to be permanently deficient in pecking accuracy. Moreover, when Padilla (1935) kept newly-hatched chicks from pecking for eight consecutive days or longer, the chicks lost completely their inclination or capacity to peck. Such relationships are still inadequately understood, but they have a clear implication for childhood education. They imply that the longer cultural deprivation lasts, the greater and the more permanent will be its effects. Such considerations make it important to consider ways to enrich preschool experience as an antidote for such cultural deprivation, and the earlier the better (see Hunt, 1964). Moreover, from the observations of Americans who visited Montessori's Houses of Children, one gathers they were successful at precisely this business of counteracting the effects of cultural deprivation on those symbolic skills required for success in school and in an increasingly technological culture. Here, having based her pedagogy on earlier attempts to educate the mentally retarded was probably a highly pertinent advantage.

Belief that "All Behavior is Motivated"

The proposition that all behavior is motivated by painful stimulation, homeostatic needs, or sex, or by acquired drives based upon these, has run into an accumulation of dissonant evidence. One of the most obvious implications of this commonly-believed proposition is that organisms will become quiescent in the absence of such motivation. They do not. For instance, play in animals is most likely to occur in the absence of such motivating conditions (Buhler, 1928; Beach, 1945). Similarly, manipulative behavior in chimpanzees (Harlow, Harlow and Meyer, 1950), spatial exploration in rats (Berlyne, 1960; Nissen, 1930), spontaneous alternation in rats (Montgomery, 1953, 1955), and visual and auditory exploration in monkeys (Butler, 1953, 1958) have all been found to occur repeatedly in the absence of such motivation (see Hunt, 1963a).

Such evidence has recently been given theoretical recognition in the postulation of a variety of new drives and needs. Such drives and needs, however, are no more than descriptions of the behavior they propose to explain. Moreover, in motive-naming we are merely revisiting the instinct-naming popularized by McDougall (1908) early in this century and rejected immediately after World War I. We should know better. This evidence has also been unfortunately recognized in motives named in terms of their telic significance, such as the "urge of mastery" of Ives Hendrick (1943) and the "competence motivation" of White (1959), and in terms of spontaneous activity by such people as Hunt (1960). I say unfortunately recognized because such conceptual approaches provide no means of developing hypotheses about testable antecedent-consequent relationships.

Elsewhere I have proposed a mechanism for motivation inherent in information processing and action (Hunt, 1963a) or, if you will, within the organism's informational interaction with the environment. The nature of this mechanism has been suggested by the recent radical change in our conception of the functional unit of the nervous system from that of reflex arc to that of feedback loop. From the standpoint of the feedback loop, activity is instigated, not merely by the onset of some kind of stimulation, but by the occurrence of a discrepancy between the input of the moment and some standard existing within the organism. This discrepancy I have termed, following the lead of Miller, Galanter, and Pribram (1960), *incongruity*. As I see it, some standards, like those for homeostatic needs, are built into the organism, but some standards are established through experience as coded residues of encounters with the environment which are stored within the nervous system. In the language of common sense, they are expectations. Probably these residues are stored within those intrinsic portions of the brain not directly connected with receptor inputs and motor outlets. Incongruity is typically accompanied by emotional arousal, but emotional arousal does not appear to be, by itself, a sufficient determiner of whether the organism will approach or withdraw from a source of stimulation (see Haywood and Hunt, 1963). The determiners of approach and withdrawal, presumably associated with the hedonic value of the source of input, appear to inhere within the organism's informational interaction with circumstances. If there is too little incongruity, the organism approaches sources of incongruity, but if there is too much incongruity, the organism withdraws from sources of incongruous inputs (see Hebb, 1949). The former condition is illustrated in the study of Bexton, Heron, and Scott (1954). There, McGill students refused to remain within a situation where variation in receptor inputs was minimized even though they were paid $20 a day. On the other hand, withdrawal from too much incongruity is illustrated in Hebb's (1946) studies of fear. There, chimpanzees encountering various familiar situations in an unfamiliar guise retreated with distressed vocalizing and pupils wide open. Such withdrawal appeared in a young pet chimpanzee when the highly-familiar and much-loved experimenter appeared in a halloween mask or even merely in the coat of the animal keeper. These facts appear to mean that there is an optimum incongruity which is continually sought (Hunt, 1963a). It is a basis for continuous cognitive growth with joy. It also justifies the older notions that children have a spontaneous interest in learning. In basing her pedagogy on such motivation, I now believe Montessori was on solid ground.

The notion of an optimum of incongruity, coupled with the notion that the standard upon which incongruity is based derives from experience, gives rise to what I have termed "the problem of the match" (Hunt, 1961, pp. 267ff). This "problem of the match" implies that if the circumstances encountered are to be attractive and interesting and are yet to be challenging enough to call forth those accommodative changes, within the structure of central processes, that presumably constitute learning, they must be properly matched to those "standards" which the child has already developed in the course of his past experience. The status of our knowledge about these matters is entirely inadequate for us to arrange such matches entirely from the outside. It would appear that the child must have some opportunity to follow his own bent. Thus, we come to the importance of that liberty emphasized by the Rousseau-Pestalozzi-Froebel tradition and by Montessori.

It was this "problem of the match" that prompted my interest in Montessori's work. When I wrote *Intelligence and Experience*, this problem of the match loomed as a large obstacle in the way of maximizing intellectual potential. I deserve no credit for discovery, however, because as recently as two years ago, the name of Montessori would have meant to me only one of those educational "faddists" who came along shortly after the turn of the century. It was after a day-long discussion of such matters with Lee Cronbach and Jan Smedslund at Boulder in the summer of 1962, that Jan Smedslund asked me if I knew of Montessori and her work. When I claimed no such knowledge, he advised me to look her up, because, and I quote his words as I remember them, "she has a solution to your problem of the match—not a theoretical solution, but a practical one." I believe Smedslund is correct, for in arranging a variety of materials in graded fashion, in putting together children ranging in age from three to seven, and in breaking the lock-step in infant education, Montessori went a long way toward a practical solution. Grading the materials permits the child to grow as his interests lead him from one level of complexity to another. Having children aged from three to seven years together should permit the younger children a graded series of models for imitation and the older ones an opportunity to learn by teaching. Breaking the lock-step provides that opportunity for the child to make his own selection of materials and models. In the present state of our knowledge about the match, I believe only the child can make an appropriate selection. Thus, I believe there is an important psychological basis for Montessori's practice.

Belief in the Relative Importance of Motor Response and Receptor Input

The belief that it is the motor response that is all-important in learning is less tenable than it was half a century ago. Although the issue is still far from settled, recent evidence appears to indicate that the role of the eyes and the ears, and perhaps the tactile organs, may be much more important in the organism's on-going informational interaction with the environment than are the motor outlets. In this connection, it is exceedingly interesting to recall that Hopi children reared on cradleboards walked as soon as did Hopi children reared with the free use of their arms and legs. Tying of the arms and legs to the cradleboard inhibits movement almost completely during the waking hours. Dennis and Dennis (1940) found that the distributions of ages of walking for the cradleboard-reared Hopi children and those allowed free movement could be superimposed, one on the other. The average age for both conditions of rearing was about 15 months. Consider, in this same connection, the finding by Dennis (1960) that 60% of the Teheran-orphanage children are not yet sitting up alone at two years of age and that 85% are not walking at four years of age. The children in this orphanage have free use of their arms and legs, but the variety of visual and auditory inputs encountered is highly restricted. Note too that those Hopi children reared on cradle-boards were often carried about on their mothers' backs. Thus, while their arms and legs might be restricted, their eyes and ears could feast upon a rich variety of inputs. From such considerations and from the evidence assembled by Fiske and Maddi (1961), it would appear that variations in the circumstances with which an infant has informational interaction is an exceedingly important determiner of his rate of early development and of his achieving his genotypic potential in ability.

Still another line of suggestive evidence comes from the work of O. K. Moore. This concerns what he calls "responsive environments." In teaching nursery-school children to read, he has them strike the keys of an electric typewriter so arranged that, as each key is struck, the child sees the letter struck and hears the name of the letter. Nursery-school children are introduced to the apparatus by a child who explains that "we take turns." Each day a child is asked if he wishes his turn. Given this opportunity, each child nearly always does. After a period of free explora-tion of the keyboard, the speaker in the apparatus can be used to tell the child what letter to strike. By keeping all keys but the named one fixed, the child can gradually be taught the keyboard. By means of further programmed changes in the experience, children can fairly rapidly be led to the point where they are typing from dictation. While this program concerns reading, it minimizes the motor side and is based on visual and auditory responses from the typing on the apparatus. When children with several months of such experience are provided with a blackboard, Moore reports that after noting that some of their marks resemble the letters they have learned on the typewriter, they quickly explore making all those letters with chalk. Moreover, the motor dexterity and the control of these four- and five-year-olds, as it appears in their writing, has been judged by experts to be like that typical of seven- and eight-year-olds (Moore, personal communication). Such observations suggest that motor control may be less a matter of educating the child's muscles than it is of his having clear images of what he is trying to make with his hands. On the basis of such evidence, perhaps Montessori's pedagogical emphasis on "sensory learning," based as it was on careful clinical observation of the learning of mentally retarded children was closer to reality than the theories of those who held such emphasis in contempt. Her theoretical attribution of the effects of "sensory learning" to increased power of a discriminative faculty may have been logically circular, but it was no more wrong than the emphasis on the response side.

In view of the various lines of recent evidence that I have been synopsizing, Montessori's pedagogy appears to fall into step with what may well be a new *Zeitgeist*. Moreover, developments in technology are putting a new premium on the ability to solve problems in linguistic and mathematical terms. Those lacking these skills are finding less and less opportunity to participate in the culture, even to the degree that they can make a living. Furthermore, those children born to parents without these skills suffer that cultural deprivation associated with poverty and slums which makes them retarded in the underlying capacities required to succeed in the public schools. It would appear from the evidence cited that enrichment of preschool experience would be a promising antidote to such cultural deprivation. Montessori's Houses of Children in the San Lorenzo district of Rome supply an apt model with which to start. Thus, these changing beliefs about child development and the problem of coping with cultural deprivation in a culture where technology is playing an increasingly important role are reasons sufficient for revisiting Montessori's approach to child pedagogy.

Words of Caution

On the other hand, there are dangers in revisiting Montessori's approach. While her practice is no longer out of step with the conceptions emerging from recent evidence, her theory was never the kind that supplies a good guide to the observation and investigation required to settle the various issues that are still highly problematical. Those who turn to Montessori's approach to pedagogy should simultaneously examine the changes in the conception of psychological development now being formulated. One hopes that these changes are more than another one of those swings in the pendulum of opinion that have so commonly characterized our notions of education and child-rearing. But, like the new conceptions of half a century ago, these of today may be wrong in substantial part, and it is highly important to confront them with evidence that will correct them.

In revisiting Montessori's pedagogical practice, there may be the danger of developing a cult which will restrict innovation and evaluation. Let me be concrete. Interesting and valuable as the didactic apparatus assembled and invented by Montessori is, there should be nothing sacrosanct about it. What has become the standard assembly of didactic materials may be too rich for a start with children who are severely deprived culturally. This may be true even though the children in the original San Lorenzo houses were indeed culturally deprived. From conversations with teachers, I have gathered that some of these culturally deprived children become uncontrollably excited when confronted with this standard assembly. These children remind one of the cage-reared dogs of Thompson and Heron (1954) when they are first released from their cages into a laboratory room filled with objects. On the other hand, with children of upper-middle-class families, the standard assembly may already be "old stuff." Of the same order is the dissatisfaction with kindergarten commonly shown by children who have already been in nursery school for a year or two (see Simmons, 1960). This dissatisfaction can be attributed to boredom. It may be seen as a consequence of too little variation in the match between the circumstances available to such children and the information and skills they have already assimilated (see Hunt, 1961, 1963*a*). Children of the middle class who have encountered a rich variety of situations and things become "I-do-myself-ers" very early. They may become avidly interested, even at only three years of age, in learning to read, to write, to count, and to experience quantity in its various aspects. Unless someone is making approval and affection contingent upon a child's show of such interest, no one need fear for over-stimulation. Gratifying their interest in acquiring such skills can be a source of exhilaration. Gratifying their interest in reading may be facilitated by means of new kinds of didactic apparatus. Electronics make feasible what O. K. Moore calls "responsive environments." These were outside the ken of Montessori. Even now no one can anticipate their full pedagogical potential. The point is that the standard assembly should be viewed only as a starting point, and those revisiting Montessori should imitate her resourcefulness in inventing pedagogical apparatus and in adapting it to the use of individual children.

There may be another aspect to this danger of cultishness. This is the danger of standardizing the ways in which each child is supposed to utilize the various didactic materials. In response to my recommendation that Montessori's pedagogy be reexamined, various people have complained about Montessori teachers who insist that each child must pass through each of a set of prescribed steps of work with each kind of material. Such insistence obviously misses the meaning of what I call the "problem of the match" and ruins the practical solution of it that Jan Smedslund found in Montessori pedagogy. It loses the basic advantage of breaking the lock-step of having all children doing the same thing at the same time by demanding that all children do the same series of things with each kind of didactic material. Either way, the basic pedagogical implication of individual differences is missed, and children lose the growth-fostering pleasure of following their own predilections in their informational interaction with the environment.

In revisiting Montessori's pedagogy, there may also be dangers of underemphasis, first, on the role and importance of interpersonal relationships, and, second, on the importance of the affective and aesthetic aspects of life concerned with art and music. In recent years, emphasis on social and emotional adjustment has tended to over-stress social and affective matters at the expense of cognitive development, but this does not justify an over-correction and neglect of these matters. Even though the traditional three "R"s are important channels for the enrichment of a child's future informational interaction with the environment, and even though learning them is fun under proper circumstances, they are not all of life. Montessori teacher-training might well borrow some of the social and disciplinary skills so much emphasized recently in the education of nursery-school teachers. Moreover, Montessori schools might well increase the variety of sensory materials; they might well supply opportunities for children to encounter more in the way of art and music, to make music, and to learn musical technique.

Perhaps one of the most important things to be gained by revisiting Montessori's pedagogy is her willingness and ability to observe children working with the didactic apparatus, and from observation to invent, on the spot, modifications of the situation that will foster a child's psychological development. She referred to this variously as "scientific pedagogy," as "pedagogical anthropology," and even as "experimental psychology." When she considered Itard's work with the "wild boy of Aveyron" as "practically the first of attempts at experimental psychology" (Montessori, 1909, p. 34), however, she confused experimentation with clinical observation, as indicated by the fact that she notes further, that "Itard was perhaps the first educator to practice the observation of the pupil in the way in which the sick are observed in hospitals" (1909, p. 34). Careful clinical observation is needed in pedagogy, but it is not easy to teach this to teachers. Those who have attempted to do so have commonly fallen back upon metaphors and similes for their communication. I would now guess that the cutting edge of psychological development resides chiefly in the individual's attention and intention or plan. If a teacher can discern what a child is trying to do in his informational interaction with the environment, and if that teacher can have on hand materials relevant to that intention, if he can impose a relevant challenge with which the child can cope, supply a relevant model for imitation, or pose a relevant question that the child can answer, that teacher can call forth the kind of accommodative change that constitutes psychological development or growth. This sort of thing was apparently the genius of Maria Montessori.

Another of the most important things to be gained from revisiting Montessori's pedagogy is a scheme of preschool education nicely adapted by its origins to contribute toward the solution of one of the major educational challenges of our day. Children from the homes of many parents of the lower class come to the first grade, and even to kindergarten, unprepared to profit from regular school experience. In the light of the evidence which has become available largely since World War II, we can no longer rest upon the assumption that their lack of preparation is predetermined by the genes received from their parents of lower-class status. Regular schooling, moreover, may come too late. We must try to help these children overcome their handicap by enriching their experience during their preschool years. Montessori has provided a model. According to the impressionistic reports of observers, her "Houses of Children" worked quite well. We can well emulate Montessori's model, but we should not stop with it. Moreover, in the future those who become concerned with the question of the effectiveness of Montessori's model, and of revisions to come, should have more than the impressionistic reports of observers to go on. They should have demonstrations employing the experimental method and the best techniques available for educational and psychological assessment.

References

Beach, F. A. 1945. Current concepts of play in animals. *Amer. Naturalist*, **79**, pp. 523–541.

————, and J. Jaynes. 1954. Effects of early experience upon the behavior of animals. *Psychol. Bull.*, **51**, pp. 239–263.

Becker, W. C. 1962. Developmental psychology. *Annu. Rev. Psychol.*, **13**, pp. 1–34.

Berlyne, D. E. 1960. *Conflict, arousal, and curiosity* (New York: McGraw-Hill, Inc.).

Bexton, W. H., W. Heron, and T. H. Scott. 1954. Effects of decreased variation in the sensory environment. *Canad. J. Psychol.*, **8**, pp. 70–76.

Birch, H. G. 1956. Sources of order in maternal behavior of animals. *Amer. J. Orthopsychiat.*, **26**, pp. 279–284.

Brattgård, S. 1952. The importance of adequate stimulation for the chemical composition of retinal ganglion cells during early post-natal development. *Acta Radiology*, Suppl. 96.

Buhler, K. 1928. Displeasure and pleasure in relation to activity. In M. L. Reymert (ed.), *Feelings and emotions: the Wittenberg symposium* (Worcester, Mass.: Clark University Press), chap. 14.

Butler, R. A. 1958. The differential effect of visual and auditory incentives on the performance of monkeys. *Amer. J. Psychol.*, **71**, pp. 591–593.

————. 1953. Discrimination learning by rhesus monkeys to visual exploration motivation. *J. comp. physiol. Psychol.*, **46**, pp. 95–98.

Carmichael, L. 1926. The development of behavior in vertebrates experimentally removed from influence of external stimulation. *Psychol. Rev.*, **34**, pp. 253–260.

Child, I. L. 1954. Socialization. In G. Lindzey (ed.), *Handbook of social psychology* (Reading, Mass.: Addison-Wesley Publishing Company, Inc.), chap. 18.

Coghill, G. E. 1929. *Anatomy and the problem of behavior* (Cambridge, Mass.: Cambridge University Press).

Cremin, L. A. 1962. *The transformation of the school: progressivism in American education, 1870–1957* (New York: Alfred A. Knopf).

Cruze, W. W. 1938. Maturation and learning ability. *Psychol. Monogr.*, **50**, No. 5.

————. 1935. Maturation and learning in chicks. *J. comp. Psychol.*, **20**, pp. 371–409.

Denenberg, V. H. 1962. The effects of early experience. In E. S. E. Hafez (ed.), *The behavior of domestic animals* (London: Baillière, Tindall & Cox, Ltd.), chap. 6.

Dennis, W. 1960. Causes of retardation among institutional children. *J. genet. Psychol.*, **96**, pp. 47–59.

————, and Marsena G. Dennis. 1940. The effect of cradling practice upon the onset of walking in Hopi children. *J. genet. Psychol.*, **56**, pp. 77–86.

Dewey, J. 1902. *The child and the curriculum* (Chicago, Ill.: University of Chicago Press, Phoenix Books P3, 1960).

————. 1900. *The school and society* (Chicago, Ill.: University of Chicago Press, Phoenix Books P3, 1960).

————. 1897. *My pedagogic creed* (Washington, D.C.: Progressive Education Association of America).

Dollard, J., and N. E. Miller. 1950. *Personality and psychotherapy* (New York: McGraw-Hill, Inc.).

Donahue, G. E. 1962. Dr. Maria Montessori and the Montessori movement: a general bibliography of materials in the English language, 1909–1961. In Nancy M. Rambusch, *Learning how to learn* (Baltimore, Md.: Helicon Press, Inc.).

Fisher, Dorothy Canfield. 1912. *A Montessori mother* (New York: Holt, Rinehart and Winston, Inc.).

Fiske, D. W., and S. R. Maddi. 1961. *Functions of varied experience* (Homewood, Ill.: Dorsey Press).

Fiske, J. 1869. *Outlines of cosmic philosophy* (New York: Appleton-Century-Crofts).

Freud, S. 1915. Instincts and their vicissitudes. *Collected papers*. Paper no. 4 in vol. 4 (London: Hogarth Press, Ltd).

————. 1905. Three contributions to the theory of sex. In A. A. Brill (trans. and ed.), *The basic writings of Sigmund Freud* (New York: Modern Library, 1938).

————. 1900. The interpretation of dreams. In A. A. Brill (trans. and ed.), *The basic writings of Sigmund Freud* (New York: Modern Library, 1938).

Gauron, E. F., and W. C. Becker. 1959. The effects of early sensory deprivation on adult rat behavior under competition stress: An attempt at replication of a study by Alexander Wolf. *J. comp. physiol. Psychol.*, 52, pp. 689–693.

Gesell, A., and Helen Thompson. 1929. Learning and growth in identical twin infants. *Genet. Psychol. Monogr.*, 6, pp. 1–124.

Goldfarb, W. 1953. The effects of early institutional care on adolescent personality. *J. exp. Educ.*, 12, pp. 106–129.

Harlow, H. F., M. K. Harlow, and D. R. Meyer. 1950. Learning motivated by a manipulation drive. *J. exp. Psychol.*, 40, pp. 228–234.

Haywood, H. C., and J. McV. Hunt. 1963. Effects of epinephrine upon novelty preference and arousal. *J. abnorm. soc. Psychol.*, 67, pp. 206–213.

Hebb, D. O. 1949. *The organization of behavior* (New York: John Wiley & Sons, Inc.).

————. 1947. The effects of early experience on problem-solving at maturity. *Amer. Psychol.*, 2, pp. 306–307.

————. 1946. On the nature of fear. *Psychol. Rev.*, 53, pp. 259–276.

————, and K. Williams. 1946. A method of rating animal intelligence. *J. genet. Psychol.*, 34, pp. 59–65.

Hendrick, I. 1943. The discussion of the "instinct to master." *Psychoanal. Quart.*, 12, pp. 561–565.

Hilgard, Josephine R. 1932. Learning and maturation in preschool children. *J. genet. Psychol.*, 41, pp. 36–56.

Holmes, H. W. 1912. Introduction. *The Montessori Method*, as translated from the first Italian edition of *Scientific pedagogy as applied to child education in "the children's houses"* (Philadelphia, Pa.: Frederick A. Stokes Company).

Hunt, J. McV. 1964. How children develop intellectually. *Children*, 11, No. 3, pp. 83–91.

————. 1963a. Motivation inherent in information processing and action. In O. J. Harvey (ed.), *Motivation and social interaction: cognitive determinants* (New York: The Ronald Press Company), chap. 3.

————. 1963b. Piaget's observations as a source of hypotheses concerning motivation. *Merrill-Palmer Quart.*, 9, pp. 263–275.

————. 1961. *Intelligence and experience* (New York: The Ronald Press Company).

———. 1960. Experience and the development of motivation: some re-interpretations. *Child Develpm.*, **31**, pp. 489–504.

———. 1945. Experimental psychoanalysis. In P. L. Harriman (ed.), *Encyclopedia of psychology* (New York: Philosophical Library, Inc.), pp. 140–156.

Itard, J. M. G. 1801. *The wild boy of Aveyron.* Translated by George and Muriel Humphrey (New York: Appleton-Century-Crofts, 1932).

Kilpatrick, W. H. 1914. *The Montessori system examined* (Boston: Houghton Mifflin Company).

Levine, S. 1961. Psychophysiological effects of early stimulation. In E. Bliss (ed.), *Roots of behavior* (New York: Paul B. Hoeber, Inc.).

Liberman, R. 1962. Retinal cholinesterase and glycolysis in rats raised in darkness. *Science*, **135**, pp. 372–373.

McDougall, W. 1908. *An introduction to social psychology* (Boston: Luce).

Merrill, Jenny B. 1909. New method in kindergarten education. *Kndgrtn. Prim. Mag.*, **22**, pp. 106–107, 142–144, 211–212, 297–298.

Miller, G. A., E. Galanter, and K. H. Pribram. 1960. *Plans and the structure of behavior* (New York: Holt, Rinehart and Winston, Inc.).

Montessori, Maria. 1929. The discovery of the child. Translated from the third Italian edition of *The method of scientific pedagogy applied to child education in "the children's houses"* (Madras, India: Kalakshetra Publications; sold by The Theosophical Press, Wheaton, Ill., 1962).

———. 1909. *The Montessori method: Scientific pedagogy as applied to child education in "the children's houses": with additions and revisions.* Translated by Anne E. George; introduction by H. W. Holmes (Philadelphia, Pa.: Frederick A. Stokes Company, 1912).

Montgomery, K. C. 1955. The relation between fear induced by novel stimulation and exploratory behavior. *J. comp. physiol. Psychol.*, **48**, pp. 254–260.

———. 1953. Exploratory behavior as a function of "similarity" of stimulus situations. *J. comp. physiol. Psychol.*, **46**, pp. 129–133.

Moore, O. K. 1960. *Automated responsive environments* (Hamden, Conn.: Basic Education, Inc.). A film.

Morgan, C. L. 1894. *An introduction to comparative psychology.* Second ed., 1909 (London: Scott).

Nissen, H. W. 1930. A study of exploratory behavior in white rat by means of the obstruction method. *J. genet. Psychol.*, **37**, pp. 361–376.

Orlansky, H. 1949. Infant care and personality. *Psychol. Bull.*, **46**, pp. 1–48.

Padilla, S. G. 1935. Further studies on the delayed pecking of chicks. *J. comp. Psychol.*, **20**, pp. 413–433.

Rasch, E., H. Swift, A. H. Riesen, and K. L. Chow. Altered structure and composition of retinal cells in dark-reared mammals. *Exp. Cell Res.*, **25**, pp. 348–363.

Riesen, A. J. 1958. Plasticity of behavior: psychological aspects. In H. F. Harlow and C. N. Woolsey (eds.), *Biological and biochemical bases of behavior*, pp. 425–450.

Riess, B. F. 1954. The effect of altered environment and of age on mother-young relationships among animals. *Annals N.Y. Acad. Sci.*, **51**, 6, pp. 1093–1103.

Sears, R. R. 1943. Survey of objective studies of psychoanalytic concepts. *Bull. Soc. Sci. Res. Coun.*, No. 51.

———, and G. W. Wise. 1950. Relation of cup feeding in infancy to thumb-sucking and oral drive. *Amer. J. Orthopsychiat.*, **20**, pp. 123–138.

Séguin, E. 1866. *Idiocy: and its treatment by the physiological method.* (Albany, N.Y.: Columbia University Teachers College Educational Reprints, 1907).

———. 1846. *Traitement moral, hygiène et education des idiots* (Paris: Bibliotheque d'education speciale, 1906).

Simmons, Virginia C. 1960. Why waste our five-year-olds? *Harper's Mag.*, **220**, No. 1319, 71ff.

Skeels, H. M., and H. B. Dye. 1939. A study of the effects of differential stimulation of mentally retarded children. *Proc. Amer. Assn. ment. Defic.*, **44**, pp. 114–136.

Spalding, D. A. 1873. Instinct. *Macmillan's Mag.*, **27**, pp. 282–293.

Stevens, Ellen Yale. 1913. *A guide to the Montessori method* (New York: Frederick A. Stokes).

Thompson, W. R., and W. Heron. 1954. The effects of restricting early experience on the problem-solving capacity of dogs. *Canad. J. Psychol.*, **8**, pp. 17–31.

Thorndike, E. L. 1898. Animal intelligence. *Psychol. Rev. Monogr. Suppl.*, **2**, No. 8.

———, and R. S. Woodworth. 1901. The influence of improvement in one mental function upon the efficiency of other functions. *Psychol. Rev.*, **8**, pp. 247–261, 384–395, 553–564.

Warren, H. C. 1912. The "house of childhood": a new primary system. *J. educ. Psychol.*, **3**, pp. 121–132.

Watson, J. B. 1914. *Behavior, an introduction to comparative psychology* (New York: Holt, Rinehart and Winston, Inc.).

Weiskrantz, L. 1958. Sensory deprivation and the cat's optic nervous system. *Nature*, **181**, pp. 1047–1050.

White, R. W. 1959. Motivation reconsidered: the concept of competence. *Psychol. Rev.*, **66**, pp. 297–333.

Witmer, L. 1914. The Montessori method. *Psychol. Clin.*, **8**, pp. 1–5.

Wolf, A. 1943. The dynamics of the selective inhibition of specific functions in neuroses. *Psychosom. Med.*, **5**, pp. 27–38.

For several decades Jean Piaget has been busily engaged in studying children. Initial studies of his own children led to more detailed investigations of many children at the University of Geneva, where he has remained. Though his work has been labeled "unscientific" by some, the significance of his contributions has literally had the effect of a bomb in educational and psychological circles during very recent times. Hardly a major curriculum development project has failed to draw upon his ideas. Many currently popular educational writers are indebted to Piaget for their most profound statements. It is his work, more than any other, that promises to form the basis for an eventually workable theory of instruction. The importance of Piagetian theory to understanding early childhood development and to constructing appropriate programs for the very young is evident from the selections in this section.

Carole Honstead presents an overview of Piaget's major ideas, emphasizing implications for early childhood enrichment. She relates Piaget's work to current conceptions of intellectual development held by other authorities and explains much of the terminology associated with Piaget's writing. Increasingly, the results of replication and application research are broadening our understanding of Piaget. Certain of these studies are reviewed by Honstead, who then concludes by drawing further implications for the educative process.

The existence of cognitive stages and the constancy of sequence is widely accepted. But Thomas Rowland and Carson McGuire believe that the American tendency to attribute *time per se* to the status of a significant variable is a misinterpretation. Such misinterpretation is consonant with the invalid notion of fixed intelligence and predetermined development that is effectively condemned by J. McVicker Hunt elsewhere in this volume. The teacher should grasp the concept of sequence without the chains of time boundaries. Neither stages of development nor readiness factors should be linked to time per se. Rowland and McGuire appropriately detect that the order in which stages succeed one another *usually* is constant, withholding final judgment until crosscultural research lends validation. It is probable that extreme deprivation *can* affect the sequence of stage attainment or even determine whether a particular stage will be reached. Wayne Dennis (1960) found that children in a Teheran orphanage, deprived of stimulation constancy, were severely limited in locomotor ability. Eighty-five percent of the four-year-olds could not walk alone and sixty percent of the two-year-olds could not sit alone.

Rowland and McGuire discuss some of the relevant concepts of Piaget, keeping the classroom educator in mind. The changing mood toward intellectual development promises that the next educational revolution may reach into the crib. The thinking of adults may also develop in time-free stages and, these authors believe, the ability to adapt effectively to new and complex situations—convergent thinking, divergent thinking, symbol aptitude, and pattern recognition—may become areas of inquiry into intelligence.

Whenever education reaches the "overboard" stage in regard to a current fancy or trend, individuals bring issues into proper perspective through their penetrating analyses. Shirley Cohen expresses the appreciation and uneasiness aroused by Piaget's view of the child. His work

> . . . introduces me to a world of children which I have seldom seen—to a view of the child as a cognitive creature moving inexorably towards higher and higher levels of maturity as he adapts to the world of reality . . . I am initially attracted by his "assimilating," "accommodating" children when I read him; but then I turn away, somehow disappointed, unconvinced, repelled somehow by the events in his world.

If Piaget's theory is to be a complete theory of child development it must deal not only with "cold blooded" cognition but also with "warm blooded" cognition—social-interpersonal interactions. And how do fear and anxiety, long-range goal striving, extrinsic motivation, and individual adapting styles affect Piaget's intrinsically motivated, basically satisfied, child?

The terminology of the cognitive psychologist is

used by J. Frances Huey to illustrate processes of early learning basically consistent with Piaget's early cognitive stages. Perception, association, abstraction, conceptualization, and symbolization are described as mental activities that can be acquired by children age six and under. Practical implications for teachers are listed.

A more detailed step-by-step approach for facilitating transition from sensori-motor to conceptual intelligence is discussed by Hanne D. Sonquist and Constance K. Kamii (Kamii spent the 1966–1967 school year studying under Piaget, Inhelder, and others at the University of Geneva. Minor revisions were made in this paper as a result). Sonquist and Kamii applied a framework for a preschool curriculum for disadvantaged children, derived from Piaget's concepts, to a practical teaching situation. Although statistical evaluation is not presented, the observations of the writers suggest that the operation was "fruitful." The carefully designed sequence of levels and types of representation, with accompanying practical techniques for teaching, suggest numerous applications for future experimentation. Such an approach, though making great demands on teachers, promises to approximate the goal of meeting the unique cognitive needs of young disadvantaged children. Similar promising adaptations of Piagetian theory will undoubtedly find their way into preschools before this print is widely available, some seven months hence.

Reference

Dennis, Wayne. 1960. Causes of retardation among institutional children: Iran. *J. genet. Psychol.*, **96**.

12   The Developmental Theory of Jean Piaget*

CAROLE HONSTEAD, *Oregon State University*

Nearly fifty years ago, a Swiss psychologist named Jean Piaget began talking about the growth of intelligence. Contrary to the then common idea that intelligence was affected only by heredity, Piaget emphasized the fact that intelligence is also deeply affected by the total environment. Moreover, he developed a theory about the actual process of thinking and the growth of logical thought from birth to maturity. This theory, though eclipsed in importance during the 1930's and 1940's by other psychological innovations, has been rediscovered since that momentous day when Sputnik was launched.

Sputnik shocked teachers, parents, and psychologists into an awareness that the quality of education was not rich enough in intellectual stimulation. In the search for ideas to improve the educational system, new light fell on Piaget's emphasis on enriched experiences in early childhood as being important to later intellectual attainment. In a nutshell, Piaget's reasoning is this: "Ideas grow on ideas, and they are the start of learning" (National School Public Relations Association, 1966, p. 5). Early childhood is the time when ideas basic to all learning are formed.

The emphasis on enriched experiences in the early years of life has resulted in governmental programs such as Operation Head Start and other educational efforts for young disadvantaged children, and a general increase of interest in intellectual activities in preschools and elementary schools. Piagetian theory, the primary impetus to all this action, will be of special interest to educators of young children.

Piaget's Background

Jean Piaget was born on August 9, 1896, in Neuchatel, Switzerland. He was an extremely intelligent child and published a one-page paper on a partly albino sparrow at the age of ten. His interest in biology continued; he received his doctor's degree in biology from the University of Neuchatel in 1918. His doctoral dissertation concerned mollusks found in a local lake—rather a far cry from his later work in psychology! However, he read widely in the fields of philosophy, religion, sociology,

---

* A paper prepared especially for this book of readings.

132

biology, and psychology. He soon became interested in the relationship of biology in learning and settled on developmental psychology as his major interest.

Piaget received valuable training from Alfred Binet and other well-known psychologists of the time. In 1921, he was offered the position of Director of Studies at the Institut J. J. Rousseau in Geneva. He has stayed at that institution ever since, and most of his research has been conducted there.

Piaget's own three children furnished him many opportunities to study the development of intelligence in infancy. During the 1920's he watched them closely and made detailed notes on their behavior. He also conducted many experiments to test their intellectual capacities. These investigations also helped Piaget cement his ideas on the foundations of intellectual development and on the relationship of those foundations to more advanced intellectual functioning.

Since those days spent with his children in the 1920's, Piaget's theory has continued to broaden. His careful clinical studies and prolific writings have given psychologists and educators all over the world clearer ideas about the development of intelligence. Studies by other researchers repeating and applying Piaget's theories have also further clarified Piaget's ideas.

Changing Concepts of Intellectual Development

Piaget began expressing his developmental theory at a time when heredity was considered to be the only factor determining intellectual level. His thinking has contributed much to the progress of modern concepts about intellectual growth.

Since it was thought until rather recent years that a person born with a certain level of intelligence was destined to stay at that level all of his life, his heredity was the all-important factor in establishing his intellectual ability. Life experiences were not seen to have any effect on him. This concept of fixed, or predetermined, intellectual development came mainly from experiments performed on frogs, salamanders, and other animals with primitive brains. Early investigators thus assumed that human brains functioned like those of the lower animals. Inherited traits could be utilized or unutilized, but could not be changed.

With this concept of fixed intelligence in mind, psychologists developed ways of measuring it. The basing of intelligence tests on the I.Q., or intelligence quotient, became popular and widely used. It became easy for teachers and parents to classify children into categories based on one or two test scores. The children were then given work to do that was appropriate for the degree of intelligence the tests showed they had. It was assumed that nothing could be done to raise the I.Q.; if a child had a low I.Q., sympathy, but very little constructive help, could be given.

In modern theory of intelligence, the quality of experience is seen to have a profound impact on intellectual growth. The brain can be pictured somewhat like an electronic computer. That is, each experience is "programmed" into the intrinsic portion of the cerebrum, that part of the brain that is sensitive to incoming experiences. These experiences then build upon ones already stored in the cerebrum, resulting in more and more complex learning and problem-solving. ". . . Intellectual capacity at any given time may be conceived as a function of the nature and quality of this programming" (Hunt, 1961, p. 85). It is now believed that intelligence is deeply affected by experience.

Research has verified the importance of experience, especially early experience, to the intellectual functioning of animals. These studies are summarized in Hunt's book, *Intelligence and Experience.* The importance of enriched early experiences in humans is illustrated vividly by the research of Wayne Dennis (Gordon, 1966), who studied babies from an orphanage and from a well-baby clinic in a Lebanese community. The infants in the orphanage were given very little individual attention. On the other hand, the infants at the well-baby clinic came from families where they received much individual attention. Dennis found that the intelligence level of the orphanage babies, measured by the Cattell infant scale, was significantly lower than the clinic babies.

Piaget's theory and research have contributed strong evidence to support the idea of experience influencing intelligence. Yet, Piaget sees experience as only one of four factors affecting intellectual growth. These four influences, as well as other basic points of his theory, will be examined in the next section.

Basic Concepts in Piagetian Theory

There are two components of Piaget's theory. The first, called the *stage-independent* theory, is concerned with the framework of concepts and terms which forms the foundation for the second, or *stage-dependent*, part of the theory. The stage-dependent component depicts the actual stages of intellectual growth from birth to maturity.

The stage-independent and the stage-dependent parts of Piaget's theory are interrelated, but are distinct enough to be discussed separately. The former component will be examined first. Later, the latter component, that of the developmental stages, will be explained.

Stage-Independent Theory

Piaget sees intelligence as the building of experiences on each other, forming ever more complex structures or *schemas*. However, he views *experience* as only one of four factors influencing intellectual growth. The other three factors are *maturation, social transmission*, and *equilibration*.

Maturation is the process of neural and physical growth. Social transmission is the passing on of information from person to person. None of these factors, while important to growth, is a complete explanation of the progress of logical thought. Some growth occurs as a logical necessity, independent of the role of experience. Maturation cannot take place apart from experience. Social transmission may result in false concepts, or deformed knowledge, as Piaget explains it.

Equilibration, for Piaget, is the most fundamental of all the factors. It is the process of achieving equilibrium, of finding a balance between those things that were previously understood and those that are yet to be understood. A child, encountering something new to him, actively works at relating it to something he knows. As the new object in its turn becomes familiar to him, he reaches a new level of equilibrium. He has thus gone through the process of equilibration—of self-regulation.

The growth of intelligence could be pictured as a flight of stairs. Each step is a balanced equilibrium. A person, as he mentally mounts these stairs, is continually interpreting stimuli in his environment from the standpoint of his previous experience, and is also constantly changing his ideas to fit the view from the step he is on. Piaget calls the process of seeing stimuli in the light of familiarity, *assimilation. Accommodation* is the process of changing ideas to fit the new situation. Assimilation and accommodation thus work together to form successive stages of equilibrium. The goal at the top of the stairs is mature thought, that is, the ability to perform logical operations. *Adaptation* is the term used to explain this simultaneous assimilation-accommodation process.

Suppose Peter, a preschool child, goes to the park to play. He sees a fence with horizontal boards and decides to climb it. He tries to put his foot between the boards, as he would in climbing a ladder, but the space is not large enough. He tries to reach to the top of the fence to pull himself up, but he is neither tall enough or strong enough. He looks around for help, and sees a log nearby. After thinking a moment, he pulls the log over to the fence, climbs up on it, reaches for the top of the fence, and swings himself over to the other side.

Seen from Piaget's point of view, what has really happened in Peter's mind? The searching for alternatives and the solution to Peter's problem can be labeled *operations*. The actual subject matter, the problem of climbing the fence, is called a *schema*. Peter's unsuccessful ideas about climbing the fence can also be called a schema. He had been successful in past situations with these climbing ideas. Consequently, he *assimilated* the present problem into his previous experiences. However, his past experiences did not give him enough help. Therefore, he has had to *accommodate* himself to the new situation by finding a new solution: the use of the log as a footstool. Peter has thus *adapted* himself to the situation. He has reached a slightly higher stage of *equilibrium*. He has completed only one of a countless number of equilibration processes on the stairway to mature, logical thought.

The reader may ask, "What prevents an individual from learning all there is to know in one fell swoop?" The answer is that one "can assimilate only those things which past assimilations have prepared him to assimilate" (Flavell, 1963, p. 50). There can never be a large gap between the new and the old. Accommodation to a new schema that has no basis in past experience cannot happen. In the example above, Peter had previous climbing experiences to rely on as he accommodated himself to his new problem. If he had done no climbing at all before trying to scale the fence, he would have been unable to see a solution. It is this necessary backlog of assimilated experiences "which insures both the gradualness and continuity of intellectual development" (Flavell, p. 50).

> Self-activity is crucial in the adaptive process; for Piaget, "Penser, c'est operer." If equilibrium is to be achieved at a higher level, then the child must be mentally active; *he* must transform the data. The elements to be incorporated may be present in an experience or the child may be *told* of the error in his thinking, but unless his mind is actively engaged in wrestling with data, no accommodation occurs. Children, like adults, are not convinced by being told they are wrong, nor by merely seeing evidence that contradicts their thinking. They have to act upon the data and transform them, and in so doing, make their own discoveries (Stendler, 1965, p. 330).

The concept of *conservation* is an essential part of Piaget's theory. Some aspect of it appears during every stage of development. To be able to conserve means that the child can see that certain properties of an object stay the same when the appearance of the object is changed.

> A simple example of conservation would be that of an apple resting on a table. It will still be an apple when placed on a chair (conservation in the face of spatial displacement). A round ball of clay weighing 50 grams will still weigh 50 grams when it is rolled into the shape of a sausage (conservation of weight) (Frost and Honstead, 1966, p. 5).

The concept of conservation covers a wide range of cognitive areas, such as number, time, volume, and length. The gradual discovery of conservation aids the child in understanding the constant properties of objects. Classification of these objects thus becomes much easier.

Stage-Dependent Theory

The stage-dependent part of Piagetian theory is concerned with intellectual growth from birth through adolescence. Piaget defines three major stages, or periods, of growth. These are in turn divided into sections. Approximate ages for the boundaries of the periods and sections have been set by Piaget. However, these chronological ages are affected by such things as inherited intelligence, previous experiences, and culture. It is much more important to understand *how* development takes place than exactly *when* it can be expected to occur. Nevertheless, age estimates are given here as rough guidelines to the developmental process.

The *sensori-motor period* begins at birth and lasts until the average child is 18 months or two years of age. The period of preparation for and organization of *concrete operations* holds sway from 18 months or 2 years to 11 or 12 years. Finally, the gaining of *formal operations* ranges from 11 or 12 years to 15 or 16 years.

SENSORI-MOTOR INTELLIGENCE. This period of development, though occurring before the child acquires language, is one of the most important periods in the whole sequence of development. The human being changes from an organism capable only of reflex actions to an individual capable of internalized thoughts.

> The infant comes into the world with two kinds of reflexes: those like the knee jerk that are not altered by experience, and others like grasping and sucking that are modified as the infant exercises them. The modification occurs through assimilation and accommodation. The infant, for example, accommodates the grasping reflex to the shape of the object to be grasped, curving the fingers in one way for a long, narrow object, and in a different way for a plastic play ring. Later, looking and grasping become coordinated; the infant can put out his hand and grasp that which he sees. Each newly discovered experience brings with it a need to repeat the experience; activity begets activity. And as the infant operates upon the physical world with his sensori-motor system, he acquires notions of objects, space, time, and causality. Ask a ten-month-old baby, "Where's Mommy?" and he looks toward the door through which Mommy has just disappeared; he "thinks" about the concepts of time and objects with his motor system, *i.e.*, Mommy was here but is not now. However, she still exists. Objects have a permanence and do not cease to exist when out of sight (Stendler, p. 332).

With the beginnings of language and the internalization of sensori-motor schemata, the sensori-motor stage is completed. The child passes to the first phase of the period of concrete operations.

THE CONSTRUCTION OF CONCRETE OPERATIONS. The learning of language shows that the child is beginning to acquire symbolic thought. He begins to understand that all meaning consists of a relationship between some aspect of reality and the symbol for that aspect. For example, a child sees a furry animal with four legs, a tail, ears, whiskers, and a "meow" sound. He calls that animal a "cat." The animal is the reality; the word "cat" is the symbol.

There are three phases leading to the attainment of concrete operations. The first phase of this period, that of *preconceptual thought*, covers an approximate age span of 1½ to 4 years. Perceptions dominate the child's thinking. He makes judgments in terms of how things *look* to him, not how they actually are. For instance, he is shown two balls of clay, equal in size and weight. One ball is then squeezed into a sausage shape. The child is asked if there is as much clay in the sausage as in the ball. He will say no, because the sausage looks longer, and therefore bigger to him. He sees only one property of the clay, that of increased length.

The child has difficulty in realizing that an object can possess more than one property. The operation of combining parts to form a whole, and then seeing one of the parts in relation to the whole, has not yet been developed. A five-year-old boy, riding on a train, asked his mother, "Which car is the streamliner?" His mother explained that "streamliner" was the special name for the whole train. "No," the little boy insisted, "there's the coach, the dome car, the dining car, and the streamliner." He could not understand the concept of the whole, or the streamliner, being made up of the sum of its parts, or the various cars.

During this phase, a child is not capable of deductive reasoning, because he cannot see a relationship between the general and the particular. Instead, he engages in preconceptual reasoning, which proceeds from the particular to the particular.

The reader may well ask what the child *can* do during this time.

> We see, for example, the rudiments of classification; the child can make collections of things on the basis of some criterion. He can also shift that criterion. Thus, if we present a kindergarten child with a collection of pink and blue squares and circles, some large and some small, and ask him to sort them into two piles with those in each pile being alike in some way, he can usually make two different collections on the basis of color and shape (a few children discover the third criterion of size). Such an ability, of course, is essential to the formation of classes and eventually to the notion of hierarchy of classes.
>
> The child is also beginning to arrange things in a series. He can compare two members of a set within a series when they are in consecutive order; he knows that Tuesday comes after Monday. But since Friday comes after Tuesday, which is after Monday, does Friday also come after Monday? This operation, involving seeing logical relations between things or events that are arranged in a series, is not yet possible to the preoperational child, but experiences with seriation are preparatory to the development of such operations (Stendler, pp. 332–333).

The phase of *intuitive thought* extends over the ages of four to seven or eight years. It is a continuation of preconceptual thought and leads to the attainment of concrete operations. Conservation is understood in some instances but not others. Equilibrium between assimilation and accommodation is lacking. The child still makes judgments on the basis of how things look to him.

When the child reaches the ages of approximately nine to twelve, he moves from intuitive thought into the final phase, that of the *attainment of concrete operations.* His formerly rigid, preconceptual way of reasoning suddenly gives way to flexibility, a sort of "thawing out" process (Piaget, 1950, p. 139). He can understand, easily and naturally, the concept of conservation. "Grouping" of ideas thus comes about; logical, deductive reasoning is possible. However, concrete operations are limited in that they are capable of operational groupings only with concrete objects, such as blocks, sticks, clay, liquids, and marbles. Logical thought does not yet extend to verbal stimuli.

Piaget defines four properties of logical thought which develop during the attainment of concrete operations. They are explained by Ragan and Stendler (1966).

> *Additive Composition:* It is possible for the child to think of a whole as being made up of the sum of its parts, and to put parts together to form a class. He can build a concept, for example, of animals as composed not just of mammals (his earlier, perceptual notion), but also of all living things other than plants, including insects, snakes, birds, and so on. He comes to see that Cleveland is in Ohio and that Ohio is but one of 50 states. He can form classes and superclasses in a hierarchical arrangement and see that the whole is greater than any one of the parts—that the set of animals is larger than the set of ducks, because ducks are animals.

> *Reversibility:* A second property of logical thought is that it is reversible. In fact, every cognitive action can be reversed. The child can combine subclasses of animals into a supraclass and he can reverse the process, separating them into the original groups. If he is asked, "Suppose all the animals in the world were dead, would there be any birds left," he can quickly put mammals, birds, insects, fishes, and so on, together to form the supraclass of animals (additive composition) and then reverse the combining process to see that all subclasses of animals would have to be dead if all animals were.

> *Associativity:* Thought is flexible at this stage of cognitive development; the child can put together in various ways to solve a problem. Shown a long stick and a series of segments that add up to the same length, he is sure that the segments together will equal the long stick regardless of whether they are arranged in zigzag fashion. There are different ways of putting parts together or of thinking about the same problem, and a result obtained in two different ways remains the same in both cases.

Identity: When comparing two classes of objects or events, the child can establish identity by making a one-to-one correspondence between the elements in each class. Suppose the teacher asks of his sixth-grade pupils, "Would you say that the bat is a bird?" To answer the question, pupils must think of the characteristics of bats and those of birds and then do a one-to-one correspondence between the two. If the elements can be said to be identical, and all the elements are used, then the two sets are identical. Whenever pupils are asked to compare or contrast, they make use of such an identity operation (pp. 54–56).

The child may use more than one of these properties in solving a particular problem.

FORMAL OPERATIONS. The period of formal operations, beginning at 11 or 12 years of age, accomplishes the final development of the operational groupings. Hinrichs describes the characteristics of an individual who has entered the period of formal operations: ". . . He is able to examine consequences of various combinations of factors in a systematic and orderly fashion. His thinking is then no longer bound to the immediate task. . . . Rather he is able to think of possible variables and even deduce potential relationships . . . state them verbally and then test them in actual experience" (Hinrichs, 1964, p. 209).

Thus, the individual, hopefully, reaches the goal of reflective intelligence. However, full logical development in adults is spotty, as students in Geneva discovered when they tried the Piaget tests on husband, wives, or other adults. There will also be a great variation in intellectual ability among children of any age group.

Research on Piagetian Theory

Replication Research

In recent years, much research has been carried out on Piagetian theory. Investigators have been curious about the validity of Piaget's ideas and have repeated some of his tests.

David Elkind (1961) was one of the first investigators to carry out systematic replications of Piaget's studies. He agreed with Piaget's findings of three, age-related, developmental stages. Elkind also found, as did Piaget, that children acquire conservation of mass before conservation of weight, and conservation of weight before conservation of volume. This latter result was further confirmed by Uzgiris (1964).

Piaget's theories of the development of number and geometrical concepts have been broadly confirmed by Dodwell (1960, 1961, and 1962) and Lovell, Healey, and Rowland (1962). Other pieces of research also agree with his results.

Application Research

The studies in this category are primarily concerned with exploring and clarifying the processes by which conservation is acquired. Of interest to educators is the work of Jan Smedslund (1961). The main question he considered was that of the ways in which experience influences cognitive development. He found that external reinforcement, such as practice or training on various tasks, was not effective in bringing about conservation in those children who had not previously acquired it. Wohlwill and Lowe (1962) also came to this conclusion.

Smedslund concluded that *cognitive conflict*, or an upset of the balance between assimilation and accommodation of a particular concept, may be the effective factor in the acquisition of conservation.

Other studies suggest that the most effective way of helping children gain the concept of conservation is to encourage self-teaching.

Wallach and Sprott (1964) showed evidence that recognition of reversibility may account for the normal development of number conservation, and also of some other conservations such as amount. They emphasized that informal exploratory experience with the reversible properties of concrete objects may speed up intellectual development.

An exploratory study by Sigel, Roeper, and Hooper (1966) suggests that teaching children the essential concepts leading up to the acquisition of conservation may be wise. They conducted special training on multiple classification, multiple relations, and reversibility in a small group setting. Tests of conservation given after the training showed significant improvement over pre-tests.

Braine (1959) mentioned that the importance of vocabulary, *i.e.*, knowledge of words such as "long," "length," "amount," "more," and "same," should not be underestimated when analyzing the results of Piagetian experiments. If children do not fully understand instructions and explanations, they cannot perform to the best of their ability.

Studies by Wohlwill and Lowe (1962), Almy (1964), Dodwell (1961), and Honstead (1966), testing children of various socio-economic levels on Piaget-type tasks, suggest that the enriched environment of the middle-class child causes him to acquire conservation concepts sooner than the lower-class child.

Implications for Education

A major goal of education is to guide children toward higher levels of learning. Crucial learnings take place during the first six to eight years of life. Enriched educational experiences result in intellectual growth—

new accommodations in Piaget's terms. The accommodations become assimilated; the individual is thus ready for more difficult accommodations.

In order to build ideas on ideas, then, the teacher must start at the child's present level of thinking, not where he would be if he were "average." The teacher must "tune in" to each child in her class. Part of this interaction process could be the informal administering of Piaget-type tasks, to determine where the child is in Piaget's developmental sequence.

It is important for young children to be exposed to a wide variety of objects, pictures, places of interest, and sensory experiences. In addition, they need opportunities for social approval, opportunities to have their questions answered, and opportunities to imitate appropriate models of behavior. Experiences such as these give children a backlog of images which help them to learn language skills and to grasp new concepts.

However, Hess and Shipman (1965) carry the requirements for an enriched program one step further. These experiences must have a pattern of sequential meaning. Field trips, pictures, and activities must relate to each other and to what the child already knows in order to be meaningful to him.

Sonquist and Kamii (1967) state that the Piagetian framework for early education is to aid the transition from sensori-motor to conceptual intelligence and to build a solid foundation for future growth. They stress that every item and every activity in the classroom be directed toward this aim. For example, a daily schedule emphasizes the ordering of time: after play time comes outdoor play, and then juice time arrives.

Juice time itself can be used to teach order by stressing the sequence of events. "Children learn that when everyone is sitting down, the cookies will be passed, and when each child takes a cookie, the basket will be empty" (Sonquist and Kamii, p. 240). Juice time also presents opportunities to teach conservation, *i.e.*, a cookie broken into two pieces is still a cookie.*

Piaget sees the self-teaching of the child as essential to the learning process. The teacher can help the child play an active part in his own learning by furnishing him materials he can handle, such as blocks for counting and size comparisons, transparent color cards for mixing colors, and Montessori materials which are self-correcting. She can allow him to make mistakes. Trial and error learning is part of the self-teaching process.

Emphasis is also placed, in Piaget's theory, on interaction of child with child and child with teacher. Learning takes place when people stimu-

* **For other concrete suggestions for incorporating Piagetian concepts in teaching disadvantaged children, see Sonquist and Kamii (1967). *Ed. note:* See selection 16 by Sonquist and Kamii and selection 47 by Stendler.**

late each other. Perhaps the teacher can incorporate some small-group work with concrete objects. In this informal atmosphere, free discussion can take place, questions can be answered, and individuals can be recognized.

Teachers need to work closely with parents, communicating the learning that is taking place in the classroom. Parents thus may be able to see ways in which they can build on the child's school experiences at home. In this way, enrichment of the child's total environment may take place.

Finally, Millie Almy stresses that Piaget's theory applies best in "those instances in which the developing child's basic needs for emotional security are being adequately met" (Cohen, 1966, p. 217). If anxiety is produced by too much pressure for progress, learning may be slowed down. The child may regress in all areas of development. In other words, not all learners engage happily in "cold-blooded cognition" (Cohen, p. 217).

The theories of Piaget can be utilized in many educational areas. Teachers of young children have an especially important role to play. As the fields of child development, psychology, and education become more aware of the implications of Piaget's theories, other applications will become apparent.

References

Almy, Millie C. 1964. Young children's thinking and the teaching of reading. *Bulletin* **19** (Washington, D.C.: Office of Education, U.S. Department of Health, Education, and Welfare), pp. 97–102.

Braine, Martin D. S. 1959. The ontogeny of certain logical operations: Piaget's formulation examined by nonverbal methods. *Psychol. Monogr.: gen. and appl.*, **73**, No. 5, pp. 1–43.

Cohen, Shirley. 1966. The problem with Piaget's child. *Teach. Coll. Rec.*, **68**, pp. 211–218.

Dodwell, P. C. 1962. Relations between the understanding of the logic of classes and of cardinal number in children. *Canad. J. Psychol.*, **16**, pp. 152–160.

———. 1961. Children's understanding of number concepts: characteristics of an individual and of a group test. *Canad. J. Psychol.*, **15**, pp. 29–36.

———. 1960. Children's understanding of number and related concepts. *Canad. J. Psychol.*, **14**, pp. 191–205.

Elkind, David. 1961. The development of quantitative thinking: a systematic replication of Piaget's studies. *J. genet. Psychol.*, **98**, pp. 37–46.

Flavell, John H. 1963. *The developmental psychology of Jean Piaget* (Princeton, N.J.: D. Van Nostrand Company, Inc.).

Frost, Joe L., and Carole A. Honstead. Summer 1966. *The developmental theory of Jean Piaget.* Prepared for the Minnesota Mathematics and Science Teaching Project.

Gordon, Ira J. 1966. New conceptions of children's learning and development. *Assn. Supervis. Curric. Develpm. Yrbk., 1966*, pp. 49–73.

Hess, Robert D., and Virginia Shipman. 1965. Early blocks to children's learning. *Children*, **12**, pp. 189–194.

Hinrichs, Grace B. 1964. Psychology of learning. In *Methods manual for teaching science in elementary schools: trial version* (Minneapolis, Minn.: Minnemast Project, University of Minnesota).

Honstead, Carole A. 1966. *Relationships between socioeconomic level, intelligence, and Piagetian concept attainment in kindergarten children* (Ames, Iowa: Iowa State University). Unpublished master's thesis.

Hunt, J. McV. 1961. *Intelligence and experience* (New York: The Ronald Press Company).

Lovell, K., D. Healey, and A. D. Rowland. 1962. Growth of some geometrical concepts. *Child Develpm.*, **33**, pp. 751–767.

National School Public Relations Association. 1966. *The first big step* (Washington, D.C.: The Association).

Piaget, Jean. 1950. *The psychology of intelligence* (New York: Harcourt, Brace & World, Inc.).

Ragan, William B., and Celia B. Stendler. 1966. *Modern elementary curriculum* (New York: Holt, Rinehart and Winston, Inc.).

Sigel, Irving E., Annemarie Roeper, and Frank H. Hooper. 1966. A training procedure for acquisition of Piaget's conservation of quantity: a pilot study and its replication. *Brit. J. educ. Psychol.*, **36**, pp. 301–311.

Smedslund, Jan. 1961. The acquisition of conservation of substance and weight in children, I: introduction. *Scand. J. Psychol.*, **2**, pp. 11–20.

———. 1961. The acquisition of conservation of substance and weight in children, II: external reinforcement of conservation of weight and of the operations of addition and subtraction. *Scand. J. Psychol.*, **2**, pp. 71–84.

———. 1961. The acquisition of conservation of substance and weight in children, III: extinction of conservation of weight acquired "normally" and by means of empirical controls on a balance. *Scand. J. Psychol.*, **2**, pp. 85–87.

————. 1961. The acquisition of conservation of substance and weight in children, IV: attempt at extinction of the visual components of the weight concept. *Scand. J. Psychol.*, **2**, pp. 153–155.

————. 1961. The acquisition of conservation of substance and weight in children, V: practice in conflict situation without external reinforcement. *Scand. J. Psychol.*, **2**, pp. 56–160.

————. 1961. The acquisition of conservation of substance and weight in children, VI: practice on continuous vs. discontinuous material in problem situations without external reinforcement. *Scand. J. Psychol.*, **2**, pp. 203–210.

————. 1963. The acquisition of conservation of substance and weight in children, VII: conservation of discontinuous quantity and the operations of adding and taking away. *Scand. J. Psychol.*, **3**, pp. 69–77.

Sonquist, Hanne D., and Constance K. Kamii. 1967. Applying some Piagetian concepts in the classroom for the disadvantaged. *Young Children*, **22**, pp. 231–246.

Stendler, Celia B. 1965. Aspects of Piaget's theory that have implications for teacher education. *J. Teach. Educ.*, **16**, pp. 330–335.

Uzgiris, Ina C. 1964. Situational generality of conservation. *Child Develpm.*, **35**, pp. 831–841.

Wallach, Lise, and Richard L. Sprott. 1964. Inducing number conservation in children. *Child Develpm.*, **35**, pp. 1057–1071.

Wohlwill, Joachim F., and Roland C. Lowe. 1962. Experimental analysis of the development of the conservation of number. *Child Develpm.*, **33**, pp. 153–167.

13   Development of Intelligent Behavior I: Jean Piaget*

THOMAS ROWLAND, *The University of Texas*
CARSON MC GUIRE, *The University of Texas*

For many years, Piaget's work was almost unknown to American psychologists, primarily it seems because of the lack of adequate translations into English of his elegant but difficult French. D. E. Berlyne was one of the earliest to recognize this inadequacy and to take positive action. Berlyne with Piercy (1950) translated Piaget's *Psychology of Intelligence*. Later, he spent the year 1958–59 with Piaget in Geneva. Berlyne's book,

* *Psychology in the Schools*, January 1968, vol. 5, no. 1. Reprinted by permission.

Structure and Direction in Thinking (1965) introduces a system of neo-behavioristic concepts to permit an integrative conceptualization of thinking. In this recent volume, Berlyne discusses, curiosity as a motive and learning through discovery, as well as the Geneva research and recent developments in Russian psychology.

As a result of such work as Berlyne's and others, the current influence of Piaget's research and writing can be discerned in the ideas of a host of important psychologists, including such diverse figures as D. P. Ausubel (1963) and J. S. Bruner (1965). Today most of his works are available to students, many in inexpensive paperback editions. One such edition, *Psychology of Intelligence* has been reviewed by Carson McGuire (1967). The review is a highly condensed form of much of the essence of Piaget's work, written in technical terms. This paper, however, further amplifies what is said below:

> Piaget views intelligence as a mental *adaptation* to new circumstances, both *"accommodation"* to stimuli from the environment and modification of the environment by imposing upon it a structure of its own, i.e., *"assimilation."* Thus intelligence as adaptation involves an *equilibrium* toward which the cognitive processes tend (the act of "equilibration"). The equilibration is between the action of the organism on the environment and vice versa. Remember that language is a partial substitute for action. Symbols, particularly those of mathematics (which are free of the deception of imagery), refer to an action which could be realized. When such symbols take the form of internalized actions they may be interpreted as operations of thought; i.e., an internal action translatable into behavior. Piaget relates affect and cognition—all behavior "implies an energizer or an 'economy' forming its affective aspect." The interaction with the environment which behavior instigates requires a form or structure to determine the possible circuits between subject and object—the cognitive of behavior (schemata). *Similarly, a perception . . . , sensory-motor learning (i.e. habit . . .), insight and judgment all amount, in one way or another to a structuring of the relations between the environment and the organism.*

Hunt (1961) identifies five main themes which he says dominate Piaget's theoretical formulations, namely: (a) the continual and progressive change in the structure of behavior and thought in the developing child; (b) the fixed nature of the order of the stages; (c) the invariant functions of *accommodation* (adaptive change to outer circumstances) and of *assimilation* (incorporation of the external into the inner organization with transfer or generalization to new circumstances) that operate in the child's continuous interaction with the environment; (d) the relation of thought to action; and (e) the logical properties of thought processes.

Roger Brown (1965) attributes to Piaget some 25 books and 160 articles, identifying the goal of the Geneva program as the discovery of *the successive stages* in the development of intelligence. Much current American research, such as that at the University of Chicago, reported by Fowler (1966) and Kohlberg (1966), lends strong support to the goals of Piaget's approach to the development of intelligence, while making an important clarification with their insistence that while the stages of Piaget are real and the sequence is constant, the "American misinterpretation" which attributes to *time per se* the status of a significant variable is to be denied. The prospective teacher should grasp this concept of sequence without the chains of time boundaries, especially in view of the long-standing force in American psychology: the Gesellian interpretation of stages with firm upper and lower time limits. *This maturationist view of fixed intelligence and predetermined development is no longer considered valid.* Stages, as identified by Piaget, appear to occur in a constant, invariant sequence, but there are no time boundaries. To support this viewpoint, Smedslund (1961) and Wallach (1963) independently designed a program with the specific intention of accelerating a child's development. Both discovered that acceleration appeared to be successful only if the child was approaching readiness at the time of intensive intervention; otherwise it had no significant effect. Piaget (1953) indicated that this would be the case, saying: "When adults try to impose mathematical concepts on a child prematurely, his learning is merely verbal; true understanding of them comes only with his mental growth." Because many of the conceptions studied by Piaget seem resistant to change by training, there would seem to be a substantial readiness factor involved. Probably readiness is sensory stimulation at least partially a matter of varied stimulation (Bruner, 1959) and/or (Brown, 1965). Readiness, like "stage," should not be linked to time per se.†

Piaget has hypothesized four distinct but chronologically *successive* models of intelligence, namely: (a) sensory motor, (b) preoperational, (c) concretely operational, and (d) formally operational. Imaginal thought, Piaget (1947, trans. 1950) believes, begins at the end of sensory motor and facilitates a transition into the preoperational stage. Bruner (1964), in what seems to be a related concept concerning the development of intelligence, identifies three stages in cognitive representation of experience; namely: (a) enactive, (b) iconic, and (c) symbolic.

The Geneva research begins with some aspect of common *adult* knowledge. The method of inquiry is to ask questions; and data are the responses of the children. An example of this first method of research is

† At the University of Texas we prefer to use the term "development" instead of "growth" which is felt to be redundant. Development is understood to include: (a) increase in mass; (b) differentiation of parts; and (c) coordination of parts. Rosenzweig (1966) in his research with brains of rats suggests that feedback from learning experiences influences development.

reported in many of Piaget's early works such as *Judgment and Reasoning in the Child* (1924). A different approach was used primarily with his own children, when Piaget employed as the starting point a *set of performances*. His method was *naturalistic observation of infant behavior with experimental interventions*. This second approach is demonstrated most effectively in *The Origins of Intelligence in Children* (1936).

Later Geneva studies began with *systematic adult knowledge*, asked questions and provided materials for manipulation. The resultant data included the *manipulations* and *verbal responses* of the children. In America there is an increasing tendency to set up contrived experiences which parallel Piaget's research. For example Bruner and his associates (Bruner, Oliver, Greenfield, Hornsby, Kenney, Maccaby, Modiano, Mosher, Olson, Potter, Reich & Sonstroem, 1966) in their book, dedicated to Piaget, report many experiences designed for children which are directly related to the Geneva program, such as Olson's (Bruner, et al., 1966, 135–153) experiment on the development of conceptual strategies with ninety-five children. Of striking similarity is the experiment on multiple ordering conducted by Bruner and Kenney (Bruner et al., 1966, 154–167).

An important understanding brought out in the research and writings of Piaget and others (Kohlberg, 1966; Fowler, 1966; and Brown, 1965) is that typically the child's intelligence turns out to be qualitatively different from adult intelligence. As a result the child simply does not see nor understand things as an adult would.

Answers of children, which appear to be "incorrect" from an adult point of view are not viewed as ignorance. They are regarded as imperfect understandings of various intellectual matters. Much importance is attached to the observation that the imperfect responses often are alike across a sample of children. Nevertheless, the *order* in which the stages succeed one another usually is *constant*. The word "usually" should be stressed since a range of crosscultural research has not yet been carried out. A beginning has been made by Goodnow (1962) who worked with children in Hong Kong. She began her research with the stated intention of determining if children from other milieus would produce results similar to those obtained by Piaget and his associates in Geneva. Combinatorial reasoning, conservation of space, weight and volume tasks of the Geneva program were administered to approximately 500 European and Chinese boys between the ages of 10–13. Ravens Progressive Matrices also were administered. Chinese boys had almost no formal education. Goodnow summarizes:

> Similarities across milieus were more striking than differences: there was an odd difference between the combinatorial task . . . and the conservation tasks . . . ; replication of the Geneva results was fair to good;

the differences accruing suggest a need for a closer look at the concept "stability of reasoning" and at the expected interrelationships among various tasks. (p. 1)

Piaget believes the child in the period of sensory-motor intelligence does not have internal representations of the world, even though he acts and perceives. With the development of *imagery*, the most primitive form of *central representation* (the beginning of the second stage), the sensory-motor period ends.

For the adult, an object has an identity which is preserved through various transformations by perceptual constancies, namely: size constancy, shape constancy, and color constancy. Other aspects of the object's invariant identity, regardless of changes of appearance, are dependent on knowledge of certain reversible operations, e.g. the adult does not suppose that a car is a different car because the rear does not have the appearance of the front. For adults, disappearance from sight does not imply the cessation of existence, and objects are continuous in time and space. To an adult, an object retains its identity through changes of position and illumination, and exists outside the domain of personal experience, as Viet Nam exists even though we may not have been there.

Piaget holds that the adult's aspects of identity and perceptual constancies are learned, e.g. one of the most difficult things to understand about the infant's conception of an object is that he does not realize that it exists independently of himself. For example, during the period of sensory-motor intelligence, where the child is governed by his perceptions (what he touches, hears, particularly what he traces), he begins to develop the fundamental categories of experience and a conception of causality begins.

The first signs of imagery are a particular kind of imitation and play. *Deferred imitation* is imitation of an absent model, and Piaget postulates the existence of a *central representation* that guides the performance of the child. *Imagery* is also suggested by representational play; and it is imagery, according to Piaget, which makes the development of highly symbolic language possible.

Preoperational and concretely operational levels of intelligence are essentially two levels of response to a common array of tasks; the preoperational being (from an adult point of view) less adequate. Though the preoperational child uses language to identify things, ask questions, issue commands, and assert propositions, he does not distinguish between mental, physical, and social reality. He may believe that anything that moves is alive, such as a cloud, and will likely believe that a plant will feel a pin prick. He may expect to command the inanimate and have it obey. To the preoperational child everything is originally made or created—all things are *artifacts*. The parents, as sources for everything, may serve as *models* who make and create things. Close-tied parental figures also may become models for the child's spontaneous conception of a deity. He sees the parents as infinitely knowing and powerful as well as eternal. The preoperational child is enslaved to his own viewpoint, completely unaware of other perspectives and thereby unaware of himself as a viewer. Things are just the way they are. They are unquestioned. This *egocentrism* is reflected in the child's difficulty in explaining verbally anything to another person. The egocentric child assumes his listener understands everything in advance. It appears that the egocentric child is moving out of his egocentrism in the later developments of the preoperational stage. As the onset of imagery begins this period, so the movement from egocentrism seems to end the preoperational and child begins to function intellectually in the concretely operational stage.

The intelligence of the older child, who has accumulated learning experiences, is more adult-like in its separation of the mental and physical world. He grasps the points-of-view of others as well as relational concepts which tie objects and ideas together. The preoperational child has begun to develop the constancies (space, time, size, shape, color) necessary for survival. For example, the child who cannot tell the difference perceptually between an oncoming auto a block away and one ten feet away is not likely to survive. To survive in a world of moving vehicles, he has to learn to understand some of the underlying invariance behind the world of shifting appearances. Yet, to a large degree, he is still controlled by perception. Piaget believes that the preoperational child, despite his limitations from an adult viewpoint, operates with an intelligence that is of a different order from that of the concretely operational child, who depends less on perception. This dependence on perception often leads the preoperational child to focus upon a single dimension of a problem. He is unable to *decenter*, i.e. he is able to recognize a view which he has just experienced, but not able to pick out views he might experience from different positions. The preoperational child cannot treat relations as left or right, before or behind. Compared to his elders, he is lacking in operations—the central events which do not imitate perception as does the image. Piaget believes that *operations are derived from overt operations—* interaction between the organism and environments (see McGuire review, Piaget, 1967). Piaget is convinced that *intelligence develops out of motor activity*, not just out of passive observation—the wider the range of the activity, the more diversified will be the intellectual operations of the developing child.

The *concretely operational* child can deal to a degree with potentiality as well as actuality to which the preoperational child is limited. The *formally operational* child approaches what is to Piaget the highest level of intelligence: the ability to represent, in advance of the actual problem, a full set of possibilities. The consequences of formally operational intelligence are identified as "characteristics of adolescence" by Brown (1965), who attributes to Piaget and Inhelder the belief that the reformism of the adolescent is a temporary return to egocentrism. Inhelder and Piaget and Brown (1965, p. 236) (1958), identify as "cultural variation" the phenomenon of primitive societies in which *no one attains formally operational intelligence.*

Piaget finds evidence for his theories in the study of the games and the rules for games as children play them, since the understanding of rules appears to reflect the level of intelligence. The child who plays egocentrically holds the rules to be inviolable, and may feel that they have always existed. In a transitional stage (late concrete operations) boys begin to play elaborately articulated social games. His observations of this stage caused Piaget to poke fun at educators who think children of this age are not capable of learning abstract subject matter. For this level of intelligence, a rule can be changed if consensus of the participants is obtained.

Another aspect of the Geneva studies (Piaget, 1948), the *development of moral conceptions*, begins with the understanding that adults judge naughtiness or wickedness on a *basis of intentions*, and can make independent judgments of seriousness as opposed or related to wickedness. In the preoperational child, however, most often naughtiness was judged in terms of perceived *objective damage*; on the other hand, older children judged naughtiness by the intentions of the offender. Similarly, studies of the child's conception of a lie seem to reflect the level of intellectual development. Young children said a lie was "naughty words" while older children believed a lie to be a statement not in accord with fact, for them reprehensibility is proportional to the variance between the falsehood and truth. Too great a departure became a joke instead of a lie, because no one would believe it. Much older children simply saw a lie as an untruth with the intent to deceive. Piaget asserts that in these developmental sequences a child's morality becomes increasingly inward, a process which Brown calls "enculturation" (1965, p. 241).

References

Ausubel, D. P. 1963. A teaching strategy for culturally deprived pupils: cognitive and motivational considerations. *Sch. Rev.*, **71**, pp. 454–463.

Berlyne, D. E. 1965. *Structure and direction of thinking* (New York: John Wiley & Sons, Inc.).

Brown, R. 1965. *Social psychology* (New York: The Free Press).

Bruner, J. S. 1966. *Toward a theory of instruction* (Cambridge, Mass.: Belknap Press).

————. 1965. *The growth of mind.* The president's address to the Seventy-third Annual Convention of the American Psychological Association, Chicago.

————. 1964. The course of cognitive growth. *Amer. Psychol.*, **1**, pp. 1–15.

————, Rose R. Oliver, Patricia M. Greenfield, Joan R. Hornsby, Helen J. Kenney, M. Maccoby, Nancy Modiano, F. A. Mosher, D. R. Olson, Mary C. Potter, L. C. Reich, and Anne McK. Sonstroem. 1966. *Studies in cognitive growth* (New York: John Wiley & Sons, Inc.).

————, Jacqueline J. Goodnow, and G. A. Austin. 1959. *A study of thinking* (New York: John Wiley & Sons, Inc.).

Fowler, W. 1966. Dimensions and directions in the development of affecto-cognitive systems. *Human Develpm.*, **9**, pp. 18–29.

Goodnow, Jacqueline J. 1962. A test of milieu effects with some of Piaget's tasks. *Psychol. Monogr.*, **76**, No. 36, Whole No. 555.

Hunt, J. McV. 1961. *Intelligence and experience* (New York: The Ronald Press Company).

Inhelder, B., and J. Piaget. 1958. *The growth of logical thinking* (New York: Basic Books, Inc.).

Kohlberg, L. 1966. Cognitive stages and preschool education. *Human Develpm.*, **9**, pp. 18–29.

McGuire, C. 1967. *Behavioral science memorandum #13* (Austin, Tex.: Research and Development Center for Teacher Education, University of Texas). Mimeographed.

————. 1965. Commentaries. In Mary Jane Aschner and C. E. Bish (eds.), *Productive thinking in education, part II: motivation, personality, productive thinking* (Washington, D.C.: National Education Association), pp. 180–190.

Piaget, J. 1966. *Psychology of intelligence* (Paris: Alcan, 1947; translated by M. Piercy and D. E. Berlyne, Routledge & Kegan Paul Ltd., London, 1950; Totowa, N.J.: Littlefield, Adams).

————. 1965. How children form mathematical concepts. *Sci. Amer.*, November 1953. In P. H. Mussen, J. J. Conger, and J. Kagan, *Readings in child development and personality* (New York: Harper & Row).

————. 1952. *Judgment and reasoning in the child.* First ed., 1924 (New York: Humanities Press, Inc.).

————. 1952. *The origins of intelligence in children.* First ed., 1936 (New York: International Universities Press, Inc.).

————. 1948. *The moral judgment of the child.* First ed., 1932 (New York: The Free Press).

Rosenzweiz, M. R. 1966. Environmental complexity, cerebral change and behavior. *Amer. Psychol.*, **21**, pp. 321–332.

Smedslund, J. 1966. The acquisition of conservation of substance and weight in children, III: extinction of conservation of weight acquired "normally" and by means of empirical controls on a balance scale. *Scand. J. Psychol.*, 1961, **2**, pp. 85–87. In R. C. Anderson and D. P. Ausubel (eds.), *Readings in the psychology of cognition* (New York: Holt, Rinehart and Winston, Inc.), pp. 602–605.

Wallach, M. A. 1963. Research on children's thinking. In the 62nd Yrbk. Nat. Soc. Study Educ., *Child psychology* (Chicago: University of Chicago Press).

14 The Problem with Piaget's Child*

SHIRLEY COHEN, *New York City Schools*

In recent years Jean Piaget's theories of cognitive development have become a major stimulant for new ideas about curriculum planning for young children. One can scarcely pick up a current book on early childhood or elementary education without finding a reference to his work. In the light of his strong influence, it seems important to examine Piaget's conception of the young child and compare it with what other researchers and practitioners have found. This paper is an attempt at an examination of Piaget's theory as it relates to motivation. It is also an expression of the appreciation and the slight uneasiness aroused in me by Piaget's view of the child.

His work has a certain fascination, and I have often tried to become involved in it. It introduces me to a world of children which I have seldom seen—to a view of the child as a cognitive creature moving inexorably towards higher and higher levels of maturity as he adapts to the world of reality. Piaget shows us the nature of the logical system in

* *Teacher's College Record*, December 1966, vol. 68, no. 3. Reprinted by permission. Shirley Cohen, an educational psychologist now working with the New York City Board of Education, here considers Piaget's model from both her professional vantage points. She finds something troubling and unrecognizable, she writes, about the child described as perpetually well-motivated, always curious, easily launched on a course of conceptual learning. Summing up the relevant inquiries of some contemporary psychologists, she envisages an eventual rapprochement with Piaget; but she hopes to see attention paid to the insecure child and an approach not so exclusively "cognitive" and "cold."

which the child operates. He makes more comprehensible the apparent irrationalities in young children's behavior which once seemed puzzling or humorous to us. I am initially attracted to his "assimilating," "accommodating" children when I read him; but then I turn away, somehow disappointed, unconvinced, repelled somehow by the events in his world. Even when they show interest, experience function-pleasure, play, imitate, achieve mastery, the children seem so prosaic to me, so unlike the children I have known.

Impacts of Innovation

I have tried to examine my reaction and discover what prevents me from fully appreciating the work of such an important man, an innovator who may be of the stature of Freud. Is it the difficulty of adapting to his language and system? That may be part of it, since Piaget has made so few accommodatory gestures towards contemporary psychology, and his writings seem so foreign, even in translation.

Do I find burdensome the consequences of his picture of the child? I think of the shock caused Freud's early audience by his portrait of the child as a storehouse of libidinal energies. No, I conclude, there is nothing burdensome about Piaget's view. It is optimistic; it pleases teachers and parents as well. The world of reality was inherently threatening to the expression of basic drives in Freud's child. The environment treats Piaget's child far more kindly, providing opportunities for the intrinsic needs to function, interact, learn, and grow. We can manipulate Piaget's cognitive organism to positive ends far more readily than we could manipulate Freud's little sexual animal. Is the child lethargic, dull, withdrawn? Most likely, we feel that he is a victim of sensory deprivation in infancy. All we need to do is set up pre-school centers rich enough in stimuli to compensate for unfortunate beginnings. All we need to do is stock the foundling homes and other child-caring institutions with toys to manipulate, sights and sounds to experience.

Mothers need no longer feel guilty about producing lasting damage through seductive relationships with their sons. Parents, teachers, and society at large need not be fearful about inhibiting the expression of sexual and aggressive impulses, just so long as the cognitive counterparts are left intact. Pre-school and primary grade teachers are free to focus on language development, classifying, sorting and labeling, science, arithmetic, and other activities more attractive to their sensibilities than messing with the fingerpaints, waterpaints, and clay thought so essential in earlier times. They need no longer be so concerned with the elusive concept of identi-

fication, for the children seen through Piaget's eyes are inherently motivated to experience, learn, and expand their cognitive structures.

Nevertheless, there is something about Piaget's children which gnaws
at me. Something is missing. They are not like real children I have
known. They are flat, unidimensional, not whole.

The Question of Motivation

Piaget paid little attention to the question of motivation while he
conducted his studies of cognitive development; but it was in the area of
motivation that a minor revolution was taking place at the same time. This
revolution would one day make possible a rapprochement of Piaget's work
with the main body of psychology.

To the Swiss investigator, the joyful, repetitive, exploratory, experimental, imitative behavior he observed in his infant subjects was clearly
self-reinforcing. The motivation for such responses to the environment
was to be found in the functioning itself. To have a schema, thought
Piaget, is enough reason for its use; and the exercise of functions must be
conceived to be inherently satisfying and self-reinforcing (Flavell, 1963).
He said that "the essential impetus for cognitive activity lies within the
cognitive apparatus itself." He pointed out that "in the young child, the
principal needs are of a functional category. The functioning of the
organs engenders, through its very existence, a psychic need *sui generis.*"
Also:

> How can we explain why the individual, on however high a level of
> behavior, tries to reproduce every experience he has lived? The thing
> is only comprehensible if the behavior which is repeated presents a func-
> tional meaning, that is to say, assumes a value for the subject himself!
> But whence comes this value? From functioning itself (Piaget, 1962).

The Motifs of Piaget

To clarify this notion of inherent functional motivation, it is necessary
to present some of Piaget's fundamental concepts. "Life," he writes, "is
a continuous creation of increasingly complex forms and a progressive
balancing of these forms with the environment," while intelligence is one
instance of *adaptation* to the environment.

Cognitive adaptation involves the creation of mental structures (or
schemata) which can be used in dealing with the environment. Schemata
are created through the invariant functions of *assimilation* and *accommodation*. Assimilation is the process of incorporating the data of experience

into the organism's mental structures, the process of forming schemata or attaching new data to structures already formed. Accommodation is the process of trying out newly-formed internalizations for fit with the data of reality, with modifications made when necessary. Infants' accommodation is a motor act; later, it can be achieved through thought. Intelligent adaptation is an equilibrium or balance of assimilation and accommodation.

The answer to the question of motivation is, then, imbedded in the nature of Piaget's system itself. The child interacts because to live is to interact, to assimilate *aliments* from the environment. The repetition which is notable in children's behavior represents adaptation-in-the-making, or the process of assimilation and accommodation coming into balance with the outside world. This exercise of newly-formed schemata is associated by Piaget with K. Buhler's concept of "function-pleasure," (the inherent pleasure in exercise of newly acquired functions) which is seen particularly in children's play. Reinforcement comes in the growing acquisition of mastery, in the growing process itself. Interest falls off once mastery or equilibrium are achieved.

We can present a more dynamic view of Piaget's system by talking about the infant trying out procedures "to make interesting spectacles last" and getting "pleasure at being the cause." An example is given below:

> Observation 94.—At 0; 3 (5) Lucienne shakes her bassinet by moving her legs violently . . . which makes the cloth dolls swing from the hood. Lucienne looks at them smiling, and recommences at once. . . . At 0; 3 (16) as soon as I suspend the dolls, she immediately shakes them. . . . Lucienne, at 0; 4 (27) is lying in her bassinet. I hang a doll over her feet which immediately sets in motion the schema of shakes. . . . But her feet reach the doll right away and give it a violent movement which Lucienne surveys with delight. Afterwards she looks at her motionless foot for a second, then recommences (Piaget, 1962).

Here we see an infant repeating a schema of action which has produced an interesting event. She comes to anticipate this event, the reproduction of which becomes an end, while her own action is the means. This is the beginning of intention and goal-directed behavior.

Drive-Reduction: Pro and Con

While Piaget was conceptualizing the function-motivated cognitive child, most psychologists were struggling with a conception of man as driven and molded by organic tensions.

To Freud, for instance, the source of all activity was somatic tensions, particularly the rumblings of the libido. The goal of behavior was to reduce these tensions, thereby returning the organism to a condition of homeostasis. The primary mechanism which Freud used to explain how the everyday behaviors of work and play were related to these organic tension states was sublimation, i.e., the adoption of new, socially approved aims which allowed for a certain amount of discharge of libidinous strivings. Cognitive activities, for example, were traced back to sexual curiosity and the desire to see sexually stimulating sights.

Learning theorists like Hull and his followers explained the seemingly nonorganically-rooted behavior of men on the basis of secondary reinforcement: the gaining-of-value of some act or object or place associated with a primary reinforcement. This value could be negative as well as positive, as when a particular place arouses anxiety because of pain previously experienced there. Dissatisfaction with the drive-reduction approach, however, mounted rapidly when evidence against it as a complete theory of motivation began coming from animal studies, observations of children (Piaget's in particular), and observations of adult interests taken to be distinctively human.

Animal studies revealed tendencies to explore even when satiated, as in the case of Butler's monkeys who solved a discrimination problem when the sole incentive was a half-minute's view of the laboratory (Berlyne, 1960), and of Montgomery's rats who, when satiated, chose the longer arm of a Y maze which led them into territory for additional exploration (White, 1959). Such studies also revealed that manipulation tasks could be repeated in the absence of reward. Harlow, for example, found that monkeys would perform repeatedly the action of removing a hook and pin to raise a hasp (Berlyne, 1960). Finally, they revealed a response alternation, which Berlyne interprets as a shunning of monotony or a seeking of novelty. ("one of the most consistently reported observations about rats is that they will alternate responses on successive trials, if both are equally rewarded. This tendency . . . has been noted in human beings and in animals of other species. . . .")

Drive-reduction models, similarly, could not explain the curiosity, explorativeness, and pleasure-in-functioning of well-cared-for infants who were not sublimating and whose basic needs had been met. Nor could they explain the distinctive variety, the long-term devotions, and the sustained productiveness of adult human behavior. There were too many assumptions and questionable links in the chain leading from primary drives to man's interests in construction, invention, art, and mathematics. Moreover, instances of behavior which seemed to lead to increased stimulation rather than tension reduction could not be readily handled by the tension-reduction model.

The Model Modified

Various modifications of the model began to be offered. Allport proposed the "functional autonomy" of motives, indicating that a behavior may become an end value in itself even when originally serving to satisfy an organic need. Maslow postulated a "hierarchy of needs," proceeding from the organic through the social-personal to the cognitive and aesthetic (Hall and Lindzey, 1957). Psychoanalysts began talking of desexualized energies. The achievements of the ego, e.g., language, motility, perception, operating relatively independently of instincts in a "conflict-free sphere," were more widely accepted. Learning theorists, such as Berlyne, tried to postulate an additional primary drive for exploration, making its own contribution to bodily well-being.

White has brought together many strands of evidence pointing to a motive outside the realm of orthodox drive-reduction theory. He has coined the terms "effectance" and "competence" to describe some of the important things left out by a drive reduction theory; behavior motivation independent of instinctual drives (White, 1963). Effectance motivation has to do with the process of producing effects in the environment through activity. The specific consequences are not as important as the "joy in being the cause." Competence refers to the organism's capacity to interact effectively with the environment; it is effectance motivation which has met with good results. In view of the directedness and persistence needed to achieve competence in the human environment, White feels that a motivational component must be evoked.

That "something left out by drive-reduction models" has been given a variety of other labels. It has been called an exploratory motive; curiosity; a need for activity; a manipulative drive; a mastery drive; a behavior-primacy theory. It is related also in some sense to Rogers' self-actualization theory, and to Maslow's growth motivation.

Woodworth's "behavior-primacy theory" seems to have gone even further away from a drive-reduction point of view than most of the other theories, including White's. He writes: ". . . the inclusive drive is the tendency to deal with the environment. . . ." (Woodworth, 1958).

Rogers (1963) describes the congruence of his motivational model with that of White by saying: "Much of the material summarized by White . . . adds up to the point I too have been making, namely, that the organism is an active initiator and exhibits a directional tendency." But Rogers carries the idea further than White. Self-actualization is the single goal for Rogers; it is a constructive, self-enhancing motive. Unlike Woodworth and even White, this approach to motivation is primarily concerned with the organism, not so much with interactions between organism and environment.

Growth and Style

Maslow posits two kinds of motivation: growth motivation and deficiency motivation. Deficiency motivation operates via reduction of tension and restoration of equilibrium; but deficiency motivation relates only to short-term episodes. Growth motivation has nothing to do with achieving homeostasis. It has no consummation, no end state; gratification of growth needs breeds increased rather than decreased motivation. It is a long-term movement towards becoming and being distinctly human. Maslow adds another dimension to the motivational model when he differentiates people who are predominantly growth motivated and people who are predominantly motivated by deficiencies. This is the concept of personal *style* of interaction. The self-actualizing person (growth oriented) is characterized by relative autonomy in relation to the environment; they are not only reactors, they are self-directed initiators. What leads to these differences in style of living? Maslow theorizes that the child is naturally growth-oriented. He cites observations like those of Piaget, of exploring, absorbed, delighted children, moving on to new experiences of their own accord. What interferes with this growth is the "fixative and regressive power of ungratified deficiency needs, of the attractions of safety and security, of the functions of defense and protection against pain, fear, loss, and threat. . . ." (Miller, 1963). If moving towards growth endangers safety, if each step towards growth meets with disapproval or failure, then the child will choose safety.

Building Bridges

Piaget's model of development grew over the years in relative isolation from other systematic positions; and the bridge-building task left to others is now being attempted by psychologists. I will set down some of the points of congruence between Piaget's formulations and those of "effectance" theory and related positions.

1. *The need to adapt to the environment is intrinsic to living.* Intelligence is one instance of the biological adaptation which suits the organism to live in the environment. This idea is very similar to Woodworth's primary drive to deal with the environment and White's effectance behavior: Effectance behavior is viewed as "a major aspect of the adaptive process."

2. *Cognitive behavior is functionally motivated and self-reinforcing.* It is not a derivative of organic drives. This view is also held by White and fits in with Hebb's idea that a major share of motivation and reinforcement is intrinsic to the storing and processing of receptor impulses and motor outlets (Hunt, 1961).

3. *Cognitive behavior functions optimally when primary drives are in abeyance.* Wolff points out that Piaget noted fluctuations in level of performance caused by the state of the organism and hypothesizes that Piaget obtained optimal levels of performance by observing during periods when organic tensions were satisfied (Wolff, 1960). Likewise, animal studies show that the organism explores and manipulates when in a state of satiation, and that a primary avoidance drive such as fear interferes with exploratory behavior.

4. *Action is characteristic of cognitive behavior.* As pointed out by Flavell (p. 82), even operations are interiorized actions. Similarly the animals studied by Berlyne and Harlow and the organism described by White are active ones. They wander about and seek stimulus variety.

5. *Wide sensory experiences in infancy are important in cognitive development.* The more new things the infant experiences and adapts to, the more he will be interested in. Studies of apathetic, dull institutionalized children, which once seemed to highlight the destructive effects of maternal deprivation, are now being interpreted as reflecting the effects of early deprivation of sensory stimulation and opportunities to explore and manipulate.

6. *Interest is determined by what has already been adapted to.* That which is too distant from experience is not interesting. Likewise, once a stable adaptation to an object or event has been achieved, the child loses interest in its repetition. Novelty therefore plays a part in determining interest and in maintaining curious manipulative behavior.

Cold-Blooded Cognition

As Flavell points out, Piaget concerns himself only with the "cold-blooded aspects of cognition, i.e., thought and perception of a relatively passionless, nonneed-oriented variety," leaving out the realms of "feeling and affect, of affectively toned 'warm-blooded' cognitions, of social-interpersonal interactions and the like." If Piaget's theory is to be a complete theory of child development, it must deal with this omnibus area. We may even question whether his view of the "cold-blooded aspects of cognition" can be accurate and complete, if he structures his observation situations in such a way as to keep out the affective aspects so often involved in thought and perception. Is it enough to integrate Piaget's formulations with Freud's or White's? Can a real integration be achieved in this way? What aspects of Piaget's system need to be filled out, and how can this be best done?

Flavell suggests three ways of relating Piaget's work to other theories so as to give it greater comprehensiveness: 1) Using Piaget's insights into the nature of the child's cognitive structure at different ages to enrich the understanding of social and affective interactions. 2) Using Piaget's notions and methods in examining events of a more sanguine nature. 3) Relating Piagetian phenomena to non-cognitive antecedents or conditions.

Flavell's suggestions are interesting and provocative. Work along these lines might prove quite fruitful. But, in light of the nature of Piaget's system in which cognitive structuring is always primary, one might question whether Piaget could allow for Flavell's third suggestion. Piaget has made several comments on the relationship between affect and cognition. Both intelligence and affect, he says, are involved in adaptive actions. Feelings express the value given to actions for which intelligence provides the structures. Alongside the growth of cognitive structure relating to the inanimate world are growing intellectual structures which relate to people. These affective schemes are limited by the limitations of the cognitive constructions. The child acts on information derived from interpersonal situations involving emotions in much the same way as he handles information from impersonal sources (Piaget, 1962). We can see that, although Piaget talks of the interaction of feelings and cognition, it is always the feelings which are affected by the mental structures; never the other way around. How does this relate to the work in perception which seems to show that it is affected by needs? How does it relate to educators' experiences with "underachievers," i.e., bright children with learning difficulties?

The Insecure Child

Millie Almy (1964) tells us that Piaget's theory applies best in "those instances in which the developing child's basic needs for emotional security are being adequately met." The vagueness of the criteria would make it difficult to say how many children this description would exclude from consideration; doubtless, a good many. I begin to wonder whether exceptions to Piaget's formulations must be made under special conditions, even with the basically satisfied children. What happens to these children when they are frightened, anxious? Piaget doesn't explore this question. He gives his children unthreatening tasks to perform in familiar, secure settings. But learning experiments have shown the profound effect of anxiety on complex problem solving. Piaget does briefly note that under the impact of newness, transitions not yet solidified may be marked by regression to an earlier stage. How long does this regression last? How extensive an effect can it have? These are some of the questions which I think have to be asked in regard to Piaget's system. Experimentation along these lines might be one good way of filling it out.

Another way in which I think Piaget's system can be filled out is by the study of individual differences in styles of adapting. If the two types of children described by Maslow exist, then what is the difference in the cognitive behavior of the two groups? Lois Murphy (1962) points to important differences in styles of coping among a group of normal three-year-olds. She finds that adaptation is often not an easy, automatic process. While some of her children act very much like Piaget's happy explorers, other children fear to experience and seem to suspect the worst in every new situation. Coping does not always mean a direct path towards higher and more mature levels of functioning. There are detours, arrests, regressions. This mastery is a tale of rocking backwards and forwards, seeking shelter and then venturing tentatively out. Piaget shows us the child in situations which he structures for them. Is this the same child as the one who is left to structure for himself, to set his own even short-term goals?

Emotions and Ideas

Bruner (1966) finds that school learning successes and failures can't be explained completely on the basis of "intrinsic learning," a concept akin to Piaget's pleasure in cognitive functioning. He sees powerful and intractable linkages between emotions and concepts and ideas, which mold both the level and the nature of cognitive functioning. He finds that a different form of cognitive organization takes place under an environment which places high importance on external rewards and punishments, in which primitive needs are kept active, and in which steps at mastery are met with negative response; and an environment in which function-pleasure and interest are the learning guides. Children with learning problems most often come from environments where extrinsic motivation is the rule. As a result these children's adaptation comes to have a defensive character. Mastery is no longer the aim. The energies that normally go towards this end are put into a defensive kind of assimilation which scans the environment for "things that will hurt me," and a defensive kind of accommodation which is essentially escape. In Bruner's exposition we again find evidence for the need to fill out Piaget's system, and perhaps the idea of filling it out more by studying the learning behavior of children with learning difficulties.

Piaget gives me the impression of being himself a person who perceives the environment as inviting and accepting. His children likewise react as if they trusted the world, as if the environment were waiting to welcome them. But what he misses is what happens when the world of reality seems to be a threatening, demanding, punishing one. We have seen that some children perceive the world in just this way. Will they still follow the rules of Piaget's system? This is a big question to me because I have been working with just such children for the last few years. My own observations leave me to think that the answer to this question may not be an unqualified yes.

One more important question needs to be asked. What is the relation of need-to-function motivation to long-term goals and strivings in people? It seems to me that Piaget's organism might go on forever in short-range adaptations to novelty in the environment. How can it explain, for example, why an adolescent will spend hours each day, month after month, practicing a musical instrument, to the end of becoming a concert artist, when during that same period of time this adolescent could have explored and adapted to hundreds of novel situations? As Bruner (1959) has stated: Piaget's theory will not be complete until he incorporates into it the goals for which man strives.

References

Almy, Millie. 1964. New views on intellectual development in early childhood education. In A. H. Passow and R. Leeper (eds.), *Intellectual development* (Washington, D.C.: Association for Supervision and Curriculum Development).

Berlyne, D. E. 1960. *Conflict, arousal, and curiosity* (New York: McGraw-Hill, Inc.).

Bruner, J. S. 1966. *Towards a theory of instruction* (Cambridge, Mass.: Belknap Press).

————. 1959. Inhelder's and Piaget's the growth of logical thinking: a psychologist's viewpoint. *Brit. J. Psychol.*, **50**, pp. 363–370.

Flavell, J. H. 1963. *The developmental psychology of Jean Piaget* (Princeton, N.J.: D. Van Nostrand Company, Inc.).

Hall, C. S., and G. Lindzey. 1957. *Theories of personality* (New York: John Wiley & Sons, Inc.).

Hunt, J. McV. 1961. *Intelligence and experience* (New York: The Ronald Press Company).

Miller, N. E. 1963. Some reflections on the law of effect produce a new alternative to drive reduction. In M. R. Jones (ed.). *Nebraska symposium on motivation* (Lincoln, Nebr.: University of Nebraska Press).

Murphy, Lois. 1962. *The widening world of childhood* (New York: Basic Books, Inc.).

Piaget, Jean. 1962. *Play, dreams, and imitation in childhood.* Translated by C. Gattegno and F. M. Hodgson (New York: W. W. Norton & Company, Inc.).

———. 1962. *The origins of intelligence in children.* Translated by Margaret Cook (New York: W. W. Norton & Company, Inc.).

Rogers, Carl R. 1963. Actualizing tendency in relation to "motives" and to consciousness. In M. R. Jones (ed.), *Nebraska symposium on motivation* (Lincoln, Nebr.: University of Nebraska Press).

White, R. W. 1963. Ego and reality in psychoanalytic theory. *Psychol. Issues*, **3**, No. 3, Monogr. 2.

———. 1959. Motivation reconsidered: the concept of competence. *Psychol. Rev.*, **66**, pp. 297–333.

Wolff, P. H. 1960. The developmental psychologies of Jean Piaget and psychoanalysis. *Psychol. Issues*, **2**, No. 1, Monogr. 5.

Woodworth, R. S. 1958. *Dynamics of behavior* (New York: Holt, Rinehart and Winston, Inc.).

15   Learning Potential of the Young Child*

J. FRANCES HUEY, *Northern Illinois University, DeKalb, Illinois*

Conspicuous in the current flush of interest in the learning potential of young children is discussion of Piaget's studies of intellectual development. Much attention and research are focused on his stages of intuitive reasoning and of concrete operations. This analysis dramatizes the difficulty that children under about age seven have in learning and thinking about relationships of such concepts as volume, quantity, number, space and shape.

This paper focuses on the kinds of learnings that *can* be acquired by children age six and under, that is, in the period covering the approximate ages Piaget gives for his first three stages of intellectual development: (a) sensori-motor intelligence, (b) preconceptual intelligence, and (c) intuitive reasoning.

* *Educational Leadership*, November 1965, vol. 23. Reprinted with permission of the Association for Supervision and Curriculum Development and J. Frances Huey. Copyright © 1965 by the Association for Supervision and Curriculum Development.

The beginnings of cognitive development are presented here in terms of the mental activities that provide continuity of process and experience throughout these and later stages. Although basically consistent with Piaget's philosophy, the terminology is essentially that of the cognitive psychologist. It should be recognized that the very beginnings of cognitive development must be inferred and that any brief treatment risks oversimplification.

Beginning Cognition

As maturation of the associative areas of the brain permits, the infant begins to *make* sense out of his world. From the beginning, he must *construct* from his sensory experiences the meanings that he acquires. The business of learning is a "do-it-yourself" enterprise.

The child's first developmental task related to learning probably is to make gross *discriminations* between sensory patterns that capture his attention. As traces of *memory* begin to emerge, he develops a primitive sense of "same" and "different." The sense of sameness that gradually permits him to recognize a recurring pattern is perhaps the basis of his first *generalization*. Discrimination learning in all sensory areas continues to be important to intellectual development. By the time the child is age six, our society expects him to have developed sufficient powers of audio-discrimination to be able to speak his native language reasonably well, and sufficient visual discrimination to achieve beginning success in the mastery of written symbols. Powers of making finer and more accurate discriminations increase well into adulthood.

As two or more sensory patterns recur for the infant in close succession and as gradually developing memory permits him to recognize and later recall them, these sensory patterns are likely to be stored together as memory images. He has made an *association.* Thereafter, as long as the bond remains unaltered, whenever the first sensory pattern appears, he is likely to expect the second. The second pattern thereby gives *meaning* to the first. The process of recognizing or interpreting any sensory experience at hand using the memory of previously associated experiences is *perception.*

Although the process of perception is apparently a simple mental process, it is basic to all learning. It mediates the meaning of all incoming sensory data in terms of the individual's past experiences, thus assuring that the new meanings he acquires will be integrated into the whole of his store of knowledge, his *cognitive structure* (or Piaget's "schemata").

The more abundant the child's sensory experiences and past associations, the richer his perceptions and the greater his learning potential will be. These early experiences of the preverbal period, formerly believed to be primarily significant for affective development, are now regarded as particularly significant in providing the foundation of intellectual development.

While the number of associations that a young child makes is enormous, the number of simple associations that he can hold in mind without interrelating and classifying them has been a matter of question and conjecture. Suggested limitations lead to the assumption that primitive mental processing of associations begins early. The associative area of the cerebrum, sometimes referred to as the *intrinsic* area of the brain as distinct from the *extrinsic* or sensorimotor area, is believed to be the area that organizes such sensory data.

Probably the earliest organization may be thought of as a network or matrix of interrelated associations. From the study of cybernetics comes the insight that later logical processing in the brain is similar in some respects to the logical programming of a modern electronic computer. Concepts, which are essentially sets of clasified ideas, are the key products of this mental organization.

Concept Formation

Concept formation requires the ability to recognize a particular common factor or set of factors in a group of complex experiences. This is the process of *abstraction*, actually a form of perception. Classification is not complete without the generalization that *all* members of this set meet the test of the specific criterion. Babies between the ages of 12 and 24 months when presented with concrete objects that repeated more than one form tended to group these objects on the basis of like forms in the course of their spontaneous play.

Concepts develop slowly during this early deductive process of discovering classes, accumulating positive instances, and rejecting negative ones. Piaget emphasizes the primitive quality of early concepts when he discusses "object concepts." Such nonverbalized concepts, valuable to a child in directing his own activity, are of limited use because they cannot be communicated.

A concept to be communicable must be represented by a *symbol* that is understood by others to carry the same meaning that the child intends. This symbol is usually a word. Symbols are aids to thinking that enable the individual to reflect upon objects or situations which are not actually present. In dramatic play the young child uses sounds, actions, toys and improvised structures as symbols for aspects of his experiences. *Symbolization* increases for the individual as language is acquired, as written symbols are mastered, and as thought patterns reach higher levels of abstraction.

While children often make up their own words as symbols for their concepts, it is obvious that for concepts to be educationally adequate someone must supply the proper word as he needs it. Concept formation and language development are mutually interdependent processes, for virtually every word other than proper nouns represents a concept. Words also help in conceptualizing experiences. The "what's that" stage of language development signals a particularly active stage of early concept discovery. In discussing "intuitive" thought, however, Piaget emphasizes that not before about age seven are concepts sufficiently firm and inter-related to permit logical reasoning in concrete situations.

As a child's fund of concepts learned from direct experiences increases, he can begin to develop and extend concepts from vicarious experiences, especially from stories, pictures and direct conversation. Television has considerable potential in this respect. Children may also pick out unfamiliar words that they hear in various situations and inquire about their meaning. When concept learning starts with the *term* and proceeds with definition and illustrations it is learned *inductively*, more in the fashion of many later concepts met in school. The skill of teaching a concept in this fashion is in utilizing the child's concepts that are well formed and vivid for him to help him construct mental images of representative members of the new class or concept.

Implications for the Teacher

While young children cannot learn concepts and generalizations at a high level of abstraction, the teacher can do much to help them learn within the framework of their cognitive activities as already described. The following implications are pertinent:

1. Set the stage for abundant sensory experiences varied so as to promote discrimination learnings and abundant associations.

2. Provide abundant opportunities for self-selected learning activities especially of the manipulative and experiential types.

3. Provide many opportunities for children to observe work activities of adults so that they will have experiences to think about.

4. Encourage children with toys, other play accessories, conversations and art materials to symbolize their experiences through play, art and language.

5. Direct children's attention to learning opportunities they may miss, to opportunities to use their previous associations, and to opportunities for abstracting common elements (e.g., "all blue things").

6. Provide an environment of simple language that helps clothe each child's experience with language *while* he is absorbing the experience.

7. Encourage each child to use the language that he has to clothe his own experiences in his own language.

8. Plan opportunities for experiences that will help children discover new concepts and redefine concepts already met, including differentiation of concepts.

9. Provide opportunities for vicarious experiences through stories, pictures and conversation that relate to recent direct experiences.

10. Pace learning opportunities, not too many at one time, for the group and/or for the individual child, so that clear images are possible, new learnings are reinforced to the point of usefulness, and the hazard of overstimulation is avoided.

Be aware that the learning potential of the young child is increased by every opportunity he has to learn in *his* way.

References

Carroll, J. B. Spring 1964. Words, meanings and concepts. *Harv. educ. Rev.*, **34**, pp. 190–193.

Flavell, J. H. 1963. *The developmental psychology of Jean Piaget* (Princeton, N.J.: D. Van Nostrand Company).

Getzels, J. W., and K. Elkins. December 1964. Perception and cognitive development. *Educ. Res.*, **34**, pp. 559–563.

Hunt, J. McV. July 1964. The psychological basis for using preschool enrichment as an antidote for cultural deprivation. *Merrill-Palmer Quart.*, **10**, pp. 209–248.

Huttenlocher, Janellen. April 1965. Children's intellectual development. *Rev. educ. Res.*, **35**, 2, pp. 114–121.

Piaget, Jean. 1950. *The psychology of intelligence* (London: Routledge & Kegan Paul Ltd.).

Russell, David H. 1962. Class lectures.

———. 1956. *Children's thinking* (Boston: Ginn & Company).

16   Applying Some Piagetian Concepts in the Classroom for the Disadvantaged*

HANNE D. SONQUIST, *Perry Preschool Project, Ypsilanti, Michigan*
CONSTANCE K. KAMII, *Ypsilanti Public Schools*

With many programs such as Head Start in operation throughout the country, the need for compensatory preschool education is now widely accepted. The question is no longer whether or not to operate preschools, but what to teach disadvantaged children once they are in preschool. Traditional nursery school techniques have been successful in helping middle-class children to attain the goals that are held for them. For disadvantaged children, who have unique cognitive deficits, however, traditional techniques have been found to be of limited effectiveness (John, 1964; Kamii et al., 1966). It appears that a curriculum for these youngsters must stress cognitive growth in addition to social and emotional development.

The theory that seemed to the authors to offer the most insight into the development of intelligence was that of Jean Piaget. His theory states, fundamentally, that each step in cognitive growth makes the next step possible. His developmental stages suggested ways of building a curriculum which would follow the sequence he described. A framework for a preschool curriculum for disadvantaged children was derived from his concepts (Kamii and Radin, 1967), and the present paper applies this framework to the practical teaching process.[1] It describes an approach tried during the past year at the Perry Preschool and found to be a fruitful endeavor even in this brief period.

* Reprinted with permission from *Young Children*, March 1967, vol. 22, no. 4. Copyright © 1967, National Association for the Education of Young Children.

[1] This paper was written in connection with the Perry Preschool Project, David P. Weikart, Director. The Project is supported in part by the U.S. Office of Education, Cooperative Research Project No. 2494. The views expressed in this paper are not necessarily those of the many individuals who assisted in the formulation of the concepts described. The authors wish especially to acknowledge the contributions of Louise Derman, Norma Radin, Colby Hart, Carol Huth Emmer, Donna McClelland, and Helga Orbach of the Perry Preschool Project, Irving E. Sigel of the Merrill-Palmer Institute, and Marianne Denis and Hermine Sinclair of the Institute of Sciences of Education, University of Geneva.

The basic function of preschool, according to this framework, is facilitating the transition from sensory-motor intelligence to conceptual intelligence and building a solid foundation for future growth. Two specific dimensions along which preschools need to work to effect this transition were delineated as symbolization and the mastery of elementary types of relationships. The former helps the child to move from concrete, sensory-motor intelligence to representational intelligence, and the latter enables him to coordinate the relationships among things and events. Although the two dimensions must be closely integrated in actual teaching, they will be illustrated separately. Activities which integrate both goals will be described in the final section.

Before proceeding to teaching activities, it may be useful to state how the program described in this paper differs from that used in traditional nursery schools. The following distinctions can be made:

1. The materials and activities used are basically the same as in a traditional nursery school, but they are used in different ways and for different purposes.

2. The teaching goals of a preschool for disadvantaged children are not *primarily* to extend children's experience quantitatively, but to enable them to integrate and elaborate it for the development of intelligence.

3. Since preschools have disadvantaged children for a very limited amount of time each day, and so much learning must be done, every item in the room and every activity during the day should be especially selected for their contribution to the learning process.

4. Since time is limited and the cognitive deficits are numerous, careful programming is essential so as not to skip important intermediate steps.

Symbolization

As can be seen in Table I, Piaget has designated three levels of symbolization, the "index," the "symbol" and the "sign."[2] The "index" and "symbol" are at preverbal levels and serve to strengthen the symbolic process. This symbolic process must be thoroughly developed at preverbal levels in preschool, so that, eventually, the "sign" (words) will evoke vivid and meaningful mental images.

The most fundamental principle to be emphasized with regard to representation is that, if the child is to have vivid mental images, he must first gain a thorough familiarity with objects themselves. One of the most important functions of preschool, then, is to provide many opportunities for the child to use and manipulate a variety of real objects. Repeated

[2] See Kamii and Radin, 1967, for a fuller explanation.

TABLE I
Levels and Types of Representation

Level	Type	Example
Sign	Words	The word "duck"
	Clay models and drawings (the making of models and drawings)	Making clay figure of duck
	Pictures (the recognition of pictures)	Recognizing picture of duck
Symbol	*Onomatopoeia* (the uttering and recognition of characteristic sounds)	"Quack, quack"
	Make-believe (the use of objects to represent other objects)	Box to stand for duck
	Imitation (the use of the body to represent objects)	Squatting walk
Index	*Part* of object	Head of duck
	Marks casually related to object	Footprints in mud
	Real objects, actions, and events	Real duck

manipulation of the object in many contexts enables him to "construct" it in his mind.

Piaget states that even directly perceived objects must be "constructed" by intelligence. For example, a duck seen from the front looks very different from one observed from its side, and the object perceived from a particular angle must be "constructed" by the child in his mind. This ability to construct three-dimensional objects eventually develops into the ability to represent them meaningfully in memory.

Representation at the "Index" Level

The child gradually becomes capable of "constructing" whole objects even when he perceives only fragmentary parts. For example, he becomes able to "construct" a duck when he sees only its head, and he becomes able to "construct" a telephone when he hears only the ringing of a

[3] Sigel's work (1965) on the classificatory ability of lower- and middle-class Negro preschoolers revealed that, for lower-class Negro children, objects and their pictorial representations do not have the same meaning, or amount of information. While middle-class children could classify equally well real objects and pictures of the same objects, those from the lower class could classify much better with objects than pictures.

telephone. The part which represents the object is an example of what Piaget terms the "index."

Representation at the index level can be taught by means of the mystery-bag game. In this game, the teacher puts an object in the bag and asks the child to identify it by feeling it with his hand. The teacher can also make the noise of a drum behind a screen and ask the children to guess what the hidden object is. Having children guess what an object is by smell is also a way of encouraging them to "construct" the whole on the basis of limited sensory information.

It seems desirable, before asking children to "construct" objects from their parts, to ask them to remember whole objects. The easiest game is one in which the teacher shows an object to the child before hiding it, and, after a brief wait, asks the child to pick out of an array of items the one like the one which was hidden. Both the remembering of whole objects and the "constructing" of objects from indices can be made progressively harder by increasing the number of items in the array, or by lengthening the interval before the child is asked to respond. Another dimension for programming is to move the child from motoric to verbal responses. In asking for a verbal answer, the teacher asks for the name of the object after the child has picked it out of the array.

Representation at the "Symbol" Level

As can be seen from Table I, the "symbol" includes five types of nonverbal representation which have in common the evocation of mental images. The five types are the use of the body to represent objects (imitation); the use of objects to represent other objects (make-believe); the use of utterances to characterize objects (onomatopoeia); the recognition of pictures as representing real objects, and the making of representations in two and three dimensions. These five types are discussed below.

THE USE OF THE BODY TO REPRESENT OBJECTS (IMITATION). Piaget points out that the child's first spontaneous attempts at representation consist of moving his body to imitate other people and objects. This use of the body is also seen in the child's motoric manner of communication. The teacher can extend this ability to communicate motorically by showing him an object, such as a drum, and asking him to make body movements to demonstrate how to use the object. The child will thus be required to translate his mental image into motoric representation of the object. The game of charades can readily be adapted to the preschoolers' abilities, so that a stirring motion represents a spoon, a squatting walk represents a duck, and a pounding motion represents a hammer.

Traditional nursery school activities such as music and story reading can be used to encourage motoric representation. If music and stories are to be used for this purpose, the content of these activities must be selected to elicit motor encoding, e.g., "This Is the Way We Wash Our Clothes." While it is the mental image which initially makes motor encoding possible, it is equally true that motor encoding makes the mental image more vivid.

THE USE OF OBJECTS TO REPRESENT OTHER OBJECTS (MAKE-BELIEVE). Piaget observed that children spontaneously use objects to symbolize other objects. The pre-school environment can be structured to provide maximum opportunities to encourage this form of representation. The teacher can create an environment so that the child will use a block as a "car," line up chairs to make a "train" or pretend that sand is "food."

To this end, for example, games that use cars going in a circle can be played, and the cars can later be removed so that blocks will be used as substitutes for cars. As an intermediate step to make the block resemble a car, wheels may at first be attached to the block. The wheels can later be removed, when the teacher is sure that the child is able to pretend that the block is a car. The child will thus be enabled gradually to impose his mental image on the block, thereby exercising the symbolic process with objects that bear some resemblance to the real object.

THE USE OF UTTERANCES WHICH CHARACTERIZE OBJECTS (ONOMATO-POEIA). Onomatopoeia is a vocal form of representation, but it is considered a "symbol" (rather than a "sign") inasmuch as it does not involve words, and it still bears a resemblance to real objects. The teaching implication of this vocal form of representation is that children can be asked to make animal sounds and other sounds, and to identify utterances such as "quack, quack," "ding-ding," "choo-choo." When they can identify the objects represented by these utterances, the children can be said to be able to "construct" mental images from the sounds.

THE RECOGNITION OF OBJECTS IN PICTURES. Every preschool program encourages children to recognize objects in pictures. What needs to be emphasized is the loss of meaning to lower-class children when they are moved from the level of real objects to the pictorial level of representation (Sigel and Anderson, 1965). The matching of real objects to their pictures is probably not enough to facilitate this transition. It seems necessary to juxtapose children's interactions with objects and with pictures. If children are involved in an activity such as doll play or block building, showing them a picture of other children engrossed in the same activity gives them a meaningful experience in recognizing the idea of "doll play" or "block building." Juxtaposing motor encoding from objects and from pictures is another way of facilitating the child's entrance into the symbolic world. It also appears desirable to teach elementary relationships (described in the next section) simultaneously at the concrete and pictorial levels.

THE MAKING OF REPRESENTATIONS IN TWO AND THREE DIMENSIONS. Art activities are excellent for the development of mental images. Clay may be molded into round shapes to represent balls or fruits. Shapes can be pasted together to represent people and animals. A variety of shapes may also be used for sponge printing, again in such a way that the children will combine shapes to represent objects (e.g., circles combined to make snowmen).

Representation at the "Sign" (Word) Level

All the foregoing activities at preverbal levels of symbolization are intended for the strengthening of the symbolic process so as to build a foundation for representation at the verbal level. Therefore, language must accompany all teaching. The child who has had a variety of preverbal symbolic experiences will be able to create a mental image when he hears the teacher's words. The word "ball" alone will enable him to visualize it and recall that it is round, bounces, can be thrown, etc. He no longer needs to hold the object, pretend to bounce or throw it, or see its picture to have a mental image of a ball.

The child needs language not only to understand concepts but also to retrieve and express them. To express himself, he needs to know the form with which to communicate his knowledge, desires and feelings. Every informal opportunity must, therefore, be used by the teacher to teach these language forms, or patterns, but since language training is beyond the scope of this paper, it will not be discussed here.

Elementary Types of Relationships

Relationships are difficult for children to learn because they require the abstraction of connections among objects and events. Two kinds of elementary relationships have been outlined in Table II: logico-mathematical and spatio-temporal relationships. The former includes grouping (pre-classification) and ordering (pre-seriation), and the latter includes spatial relationships and temporal ones, such as sequence and cause-and-effect.

Logico-mathematical Relationship

GROUPING (PRE-CLASSIFICATION). A successful way to begin the teaching of grouping appears to be with the concepts of "same" and "different." From the beginning of the school year, the children can have the opportunity at clean-up time to group together things that are the same (e.g., unit blocks, hollow blocks, plates, cars and trucks).

A more formal task might be to require dichotomization by attributes, e.g., the separation of saucers from the same size plates, long

TABLE II
Elementary Types of Relationship

A. *Logico-mathematical relationships*

1. Grouping (pre-classification)
   a. Same   (perceptual criteria)
   b. Similar   (perceptual and conceptual criteria)
   c. Go together   (conceptual criteria)

2. Ordering (pre-seriation)
   a. Sizes   (e.g., "big" and "little")
   b. Quantities   (e.g., "many" and "few")
   c. Qualities   (e.g., "hard" and "soft")

B. *Spatio-temporal relationships*
1. Spatial reasoning   (e.g., "here" and "there," "on," and "under")
2. Temporal reasoning   (e.g., "before" and "after," "first" and "second,"
                          "if-then," and "because")

---

brushes from short ones, and long unit blocks from square ones. When a new basis for grouping is introduced, it appears best to begin with dichotomies of objects that are identical in every way except for one precise difference.

Motor encoding can be used to teach classification. If the child cannot construct the group of "food," for example, pretending to put certain edible things in his mouth may be helpful in separating the class of "food" from "non-food."

To move children further in their ability to classify, the program must also include opportunities to deal with concepts such as "some" and "all." *All* the plates belong in the cupboard, *some* of the plates, here, and *some*, there. *All* the brushes go in jars, *some* are big, *some*, small. Class inclusion might later be introduced so that children will eventually become capable of dealing quantitatively with a category within a more inclusive category (e.g., if there are dogs and cats in front of the child, there are more animals than dogs). The quantification of class inclusion is a very advanced stage in the development of classificatory ability, according to Inhelder and Piaget (1964), and it seems to the authors that children should at least be exposed only to some preparatory activities, e.g., finding out whether or not there will be any animals left if all the dogs are taken away.

As the children's classificatory ability increases, it becomes possible to move up in level of symbolization from the grouping of real objects to the grouping of pictures. It seems important, whenever possible, to juxtapose tasks involving real objects with those involving pictures of the same objects (Sigel and Anderson, 1965). Classification with pictures, too, must be programmed to move from dichotomies of grossly different categories (e.g., watches and vehicles) to finer discriminations (e.g., men's watches and women's watches), with language always accompanying all teaching activities.

ORDERING (PRE-SERIATION). Seriation in the present context refers to the sequential ordering of items from the one containing the greatest amount of some variable to that containing the least amount.[4] The simplest seriation task involves sizes, e.g., "big," "bigger" and the "biggest."

A prerequisite for seriation according to size is the ability to discriminate different sizes. To teach this skill, it is again necessary to begin at the simplest level, in this case dichotomies of two grossly different sizes. When children have been exposed to an environment containing only a few objects, all of two sizes, they will soon become able to manipulate, order and verbally express relations of two sizes, "big and little" and "large and small." When two sizes are mastered, the environment can be enriched in such a way that children will order objects of three or more sizes.

For example, in the doll corner, the children will be able to arrange the small and large pot, small and large spoon, etc. During the first weeks of school, the block and truck areas should have shelves with only two sizes of blocks, cars, trucks, and figures of animals and people. As the year progresses, the environment can be enriched by adding more categories of items in more than two sizes so that children will become able to follow instructions such as "Put *all* the little blocks in the *biggest* truck."

Pre-seriation tasks should be built into the program to permeate the entire day. In art activities, for example, two sizes of brushes and paper may be used at first. By the time Christmas bells and Valentine hearts are made, the children will be able to order them in three or four different sizes. It seems important that children thus not only are talked *at* about these concepts, but also are given meaningful opportunities to use them so that, again, words will have meaning. Juice time, too, can be used as an opportunity to discriminate and order different sizes of cups, cookies, and containers. On the playground, children can take big and little steps, make long and short shadows and climb on high and low swings.

Seriation may be applied to other qualities and quantities, e.g., hardness and numbers. As concepts of qualities are more abstract than visible concepts of sizes, the children will need more language to clarify them. The programming must move carefully and slowly so that the children will compare the salient aspects of various objects and generalize from

[4] See Kamii and Radin, 1967, for a fuller explanation.

them (e.g., arriving at the concept of "hard" and "soft" by comparing a raw apple with a cooked one and a block with a piece of foam rubber of the same shape, size, and color).

Spatio-temporal Relationships

SPATIAL RELATIONSHIPS. The child's past experience of moving his body can be used to start the systematic teaching of spatial relationships. Putting a cup *on* the table and pushing a car *under* a block structure are examples of learning object-to-object spatial relationships in a motoric way. Jumping *over* things and crawling *under* them are examples of the child's motoric experiences with object-to-self relationships.

The next level of spatial understanding is the recognition of the position of objects without actual manipulation, e.g., recognizing a cookie as being *on* the table. Finally, children can be asked to recognize positions in space from pictures and to verbalize the spatial relationship. They will then be expected to say, for example, that a rooster is *on top of* the barn.

TEMPORAL RELATIONSHIPS. Relationships of time must be emphasized throughout the school day. The daily schedule reinforces the concept of temporal order. After play-time, for example, comes outdoor time, and then refreshment. Juice time can be used to teach order by stressing the sequence of events. Children learn that when everyone is sitting down, the cookies will be passed, and when each child takes a cookie, the basket will be empty. Every opportunity should be used throughout the day to make children aware of the sequence of school activities, and to discuss which activities have taken place, and what comes next.

Cause-and-effect relationships can also be taught at juice time. Children experience the fact that when they push a cup with too much vigor, the juice spills, and when a cookie is dropped, it usually breaks. Juice time is also an opportunity to prepare children for conservation, i.e., the notion that the quantity remains the same despite altered appearance (Kamii and Radin, 1967). For example, a cookie broken into two pieces still has the same quantity.

Sequence and causality can be pointed out in many other ways during the course of the day. The children learn that if they hang up their coats, they can find them, that if a block building is pushed, it will fall down. The teacher has the opportunity to stress, for example, that when children put on their coats, they can go outside, and that certain kinds of behavior will cause a consistent and predictable response on the part of the teachers.

Integration of Symbolization and Elementary Types of Relationships

The teaching of cognitive content can be planned on any one of the following three levels: the manipulation of the environment to induce the child to "discover" the desired learning; the manipulation of the environment to make "discovery" inevitable, and direct teaching. An example of the first level is to provide the child with measuring spoons in the hope that he might notice size differences. In this case, the teacher does not intervene even if the child does not notice size. The environment can also be manipulated to make "discovery" inevitable. For example, when measuring spoons are to be hung up on their outlines on a pegboard, clean-up time, which involves returning spoons to their appropriate places, makes size discrimination a necessary part of living at school. Direct teaching for the same learning might occur when the activity is baking. At this time, measuring spoons are compared in size and capacity as children measure ingredients. Preschools must use all three levels of teaching either in a sequenced order or simultaneously. It appears best to begin with a period of free exploration and manipulation before direct teaching is attempted.

Symbolization and the mastery of elementary relationships are so interrelated that in almost all situations the two become integrated. In structured group activities, as well as in informal situations in the housekeeping, block and art areas, both dimensions permeate all aspects of the child's school experience. An activity which clearly demonstrates the two dimensions and offers an opportunity for all three levels of teaching is socio-dramatic play.[5] In the doll corner, as has been pointed out, the outlines of utensils on a pegboard can lead the child to learn both symbolization and pre-seriation. The doll corner equipment can be programmed not only to encourage socio-dramatic play but also to provide opportunities to classify dishes as to size and function, to put spoons in the silverware tray where they belong, to put all of one kind of thing in one place, to pair shoes, to put purses and hats into designated places, and to sort doll clothes according to size. In addition to serving as props for role play, dress-up clothes provide experiences in manipulating large and small buttons, long and short skirts, big and little hats or shoes.

Socio-dramatic play can also be used to teach representation at the index level. If things are "bought" at the store and put into a bag, the teacher can ask the child, when he returns to the doll corner, to reach into the bag (without looking into it) and to name each item before taking it out. Things to be delivered may also be put in trucks and covered. When the child arrives at the delivery place, he can be asked to recall the contents. If the child can recall his purchases and knows that the items remain unchanged after being covered and moved, he can be said to have a basic foundation for representational thinking.

[5] **"Socio-dramatic play"** refers to interaction among children which may include role play, e.g., playing "house," with parents' and children's roles enacted.

Playing store lends itself to the learning of quantities. Children "shopping" with bottle caps as symbols of money learn one-to-one correspondence by buying one item for one bottle cap. Here, too, the programming must be planned to move slowly from one-to-one correspondence to the point where a child can see whether he has *more* or *less* money than another child. Size concepts and seriation can later be taught by providing both differently sized play money and food items. To buy the largest size, the child will need the largest play money. He learns about sequence by going to the store, choosing his purchase, "paying" for it and then putting it into a bag to "take home." He learns about cause and effect by finding that to buy an item, he needs money.

Socio-dramatic play can be used to obtain diagnostic information about the child's level of symbolization and his level of mastery of elementary relationships. In playing "tea party," for example, if a child gets out a pitcher, goes to the sink for water, sits at the table, and pours the "tea," he can be said to have followed the proper sequence. If he stops pouring before the water overflows, the teacher can conclude that the child not only understands cause and effect in this context but also is able to anticipate future happenings. When the pitcher is empty and the child pretends to refill it rather than actually refilling it, it can be concluded that the child has progressed considerably in his symbolic process. The art and block areas can also provide opportunities for similar diagnostic observations.

In conclusion, there appears little doubt that the traditional nursery school program, which is effective with middle-class children, can be adapted to the needs of disadvantaged children if there is continuous awareness that the program must begin at the sensory-motor level and move slowly into symbolization and the teaching of relationships. As each new step is mastered, the child will have a firmer foundation on which to build future learning.

The approach described in this paper makes enormous demands on the teacher, but it appears that the only way to prepare hard-to-educate children for later learning is by insuring the mastery of prerequisites. It is hoped that skillful and creative teaching techniques will combine this cognitive framework with the many other goals of nursery education for the deprived, i.e., socio-emotional growth, language development and parental involvement. The merging of all these endeavors holds the promise that compensatory education can help the disadvantaged child to succeed in school, fulfill himself and find a meaningful place in our society.

References

Flavell, J. J. 1963. *The developmental psychology of Jean Piaget* (Princeton, N.J.: D. Van Nostrand Company).

Hunt, J. McV. 1961. *Intelligence and experience* (New York: The Ronald Press Company).

Inhelder, Barbel, and J. Piaget. 1964. *The early growth of logic in the child* (New York: Harper & Row).

John, Vera P. August 1964. *A brief survey of research on the characteristics of children from low-income backgrounds.* Prepared for the U.S. Commissioner of Education (New York: Institute for Developmental Studies, New York Medical College). Mimeographed.

Kamii, Constance K., and Norma L. Radin. 1967. *A framework for a preschool curriculum based on some Piagetian concepts* (Ypsilanti, Mich.: Michigan Public Schools). *J. of creative Behavior.*

———, and D. P. Weikart. September 1966. *A two-year preschool program for culturally disadvantaged children: findings from the first three years.* A paper read at the American Psychological Association, New York.

Piaget, J. 1962. *Play, dreams and imitation in childhood* (New York: W. W. Norton & Company, Inc.).

———. 1954. *The construction of reality in the child* (New York: Basic Books, Inc.).

Sigel, I. E., and L. M. Anderson. March 1965. *Categorization behavior of lower- and middle-class Negro preschool children: differences in dealing with representation of familiar objects.* Revision of paper read at The Society of Research in Child Development, Minneapolis. Mimeographed at the Merrill-Palmer Institute, Detroit.

PART 4

Cognitive Development in Young Children

Changing views of how children develop cognitively have contributed significantly to the rediscovery of early childhood education. Unprecedented interest in cognition by both psychologists and educators is stimulating research interest. As this interest gains force and insights emerge, educational implications naturally follow. Almost invariably these implications tend to fix infancy and early childhood as optimum periods for rapid cognitive development.

The notion of innately fixed intelligence is effectively buried by J. McVicker Hunt. He presents a documented case for the flexibility of intelligence and the importance of experience in effecting developmental change. Hunt continues to explore changing conceptions of motivation and the role of preverbal experience. His book, *Intelligence and Experience*, should not be overlooked by early childhood educators.

William Fowler elaborates a conceptual schema for early concept learning that has had extensive application in the University of Chicago Nursery School and other projects. He views development as "a process of acquiring increasingly complex mental structures and modes of functioning through the cumulative interaction of the growing child with his environment." He attempts to program concept learning systematically and to devise techniques for the teacher. The work of Piaget is used extensively in these attempts. For illustration Fowler applies his approach to concepts in community structure.

Piaget's concepts of cognitive stages are refined into tasks by Lawrence Kohlberg in an effort to establish the reality of such stages. Having previously reproduced age differential responses to tasks which Piaget observed, Kohlberg believes that such responses imply more than the mere existence of cognitive stages: (1) Young children's responses represent a spontaneous manner of thinking about the world that is qualitatively different from the way adults think. (2) Different developmental structures of thought imply consistency of level of response from task to task. (3) Development follows an invariant sequence. Two tasks are used to illustrate the empirical meaning of these statements. Finally, Kohlberg examines problems that stages pose in the education of young children. Cognitive stages appear to exist; they are not established by heredity but result from interaction between organism and environment. This implies the need for differentiation between teaching specific skills and the development of general cognitive structures. Preschool cognitive development programs, then, would be defined in terms of the child's concepts, which are to be developed, rather than in terms of adult concepts, which are to be taught.

A large body of evidence confirms that deprivation of stimulating experiences results in intellectual underachievement and cognitive disadvantage. Robert L. Green, Louis J. Hofmann, and Robert F. Morgan review some of this research. Harold M. Skeels lends support with his provocative study of the effects of adoption on children from institutions. Collectively, these studies imply that preventative education is vastly superior, financially and humanely, to curative education.

Yet, we remain insecure about determining significant stimuli. What is stimulating to one child may be mere noise to another. And we remain unenlightened about the nature of cognitively stimulating child-rearing practices, though there is little doubt that the mother plays a significant role. The roots of cognitive disadvantage rely more heavily on what she *does* after the child is born than on what she *was* before he was born.

Norman E. Freeberg and Donald T. Payne summarize literature dealing with child-rearing practices that influence cognitive development. Despite increasing interest in the enhancement of cognitive skills in very young children, systematic research on the effects of rearing practices on specific cognitive skills is limited. Furthermore,

> The infant we have rediscovered requires that we intervene when we don't know how or when or what effect it will have on the rest of the family. This is one

area in which theory is way ahead of what we know (Gordon, 1967).

Cognition is defined by Ada Schermann as "a generic term for any process whereby an organism becomes aware of or obtains knowledge of an object." The cognitive domain . . . "includes those objectives which deal with the recall or recognition of knowledge and the development of intellectual abilities and skills." The implications for nursery schools are dual; the provision of information and the extension of the child's ability to acquire and process information for himself. Schermann directs her thinking toward the latter implication.

Reference

Gordon, Ira. June 1967. Rediscovering the young. A conference on *The young child: Florida's future*, University of Florida.

The Implications of Changing Ideas on How Children Develop Intellectually*

J. MCVICKER HUNT, *University of Illinois*

The task of maximizing the intellectual potential of our children has acquired new urgency. Two of the top challenges of our day lie behind this urgency. First, the rapidly expanding role of technology, now taking the form of automation, decreases opportunity for persons of limited competence and skills while it increases opportunity for those competent in the use of written language, in mathematics, and in problem solving. Second, the challenge of eliminating racial discrimination requires not only equality of employment opportunity and social recognition for persons of equal competence, but also an equalization of the opportunity to develop that intellectual capacity and skill upon which competence is based.

During most of the past century anyone who entertained the idea of increasing the intellectual capacity of human beings was regarded as an unrealistic "do-gooder." Individuals, classes, and races were considered to be what they were because either God or their inheritance had made them that way; any attempt to raise the intelligence quotient (IQ) through experience met with contempt. Man's nature has not changed since World War II, but some of our conceptions of his nature have been changing rapidly. These changes make sensible the hope that, with improved understanding of early experience, we might counteract some of the worst effects of cultural deprivation and raise substantially the average level of intellectual capacity. This paper will attempt to show how and why these conceptions are changing, and will indicate the implications of these changes for experiments designed to provide corrective early experiences to children and to feed back information on ways of counteracting cultural deprivation.

* Reprinted with permission of J. McVicker Hunt and *Children*, May-June 1964, U.S. Department of Health, Education, and Welfare, Welfare Administration, Children's Bureau. The work on which this article is based has been supported by the Russell Sage Foundation, the Carnegie Foundation, and the Commonwealth Fund; and its writing by a grant (MH K6-18567) from the U.S. Public Health Service.

Changing Beliefs

Fixed Intelligence

The notion of fixed intelligence has roots in Darwin's theory that evolution takes place through the variations in strains and species which enable them to survive to reproduce themselves. Finding in this the implicit assumption that adult characteristics are determined by heredity, Francis Galton, Darwin's younger cousin, reasoned that the improvement of man lies not in education, or euthenics, but in the selection of superior parents for the next generation—in other words, through eugenics. To this end, he founded an anthropometric laboratory to give simple sensory and motor tests (which failed, incidentally, to correlate with the qualities in which he was interested), established a eugenics society, and imparted his beliefs to his student, J. McKeen Cattell, who brought the tests to America.

About the same time G. Stanley Hall, an American who without knowing Darwin became an ardent evolutionist, imparted a similar faith in fixed intelligence to his students, among them such future leaders of the intelligence testing movement as H. H. Goddard, F. Kuhlmann, and Lewis Terman. This faith included a belief in the constant intelligence quotient. The IQ, originally conceived by the German psychologist Wilhelm Stern, assumes that the rate of intellectual development can be specified by dividing the average age value of the tests passed (mental age) by the chronological age of the child.

The considerable debate over the constancy of the IQ might have been avoided if the work of the Danish geneticist Johannsen had been as well known in America as that of Gregor Mendel, who discovered the laws of hereditary transmission. Johannsen distinguished the genotype, which can be known only from the ancestry or progeny of an individual, from the phenotype, which can be directly observed and measured. Although the IQ was commonly treated as if it were a genotype (innate capacity), it is in fact a phenotype and, like all phenotypes (height, weight, language spoken), is a product of the genotype and the circumstances with which it has interacted (Hunt, 1961).

Johannsen's distinction makes possible the understanding of evidence dissonant with the notion of fixed intelligence. For instance, identical twins (with the same genotype) have been found to show differences in IQ of as much as 24 points when reared apart, and the degree of difference appears to be related to the degree of dissimilarity of the circumstances in which they were reared. Also, several investigators have reported finding substantial improvement in IQ after enrichment of experience, but their critics have attributed this to defects in experimental control.

When results of various longitudinal studies available after World War II showed very low correlation between the preschool IQ and IQ at age 18, the critics responded by questioning the validity of the infant tests, even though Nancy Bayley (1940) had actually found high correlations among tests given close together in time. Blaming the tests tended to hide the distinction that should have been made between cross-sectional validity and predictive validity: What a child does in the testing situation correlates substantially with what he will do in other situations, but attempting to predict what an IQ will be at age 18 from tests given at ages from birth to 4 years, before the schools have provided at least some standardization of circumstances, is like trying to predict how fast a feather will fall in a hurricane.

Predetermined Development

Three views of embryological and psychological development have held sway in the history of thought: preformationism, predeterminism, and interactionism (Hunt, 1961). As men gave up preformationism, the view that the organs and features of adulthood are preformed in the seed, they turned to predeterminism, the view that the organs and features of adulthood are hereditarily determined. G. Stanley Hall in emphasizing the concept of recapitulation—that the development of the individual summarizes the evolution of his species—drew the predeterministic moral that each behavior pattern manifest in a child is a natural stage with which no one should interfere. The lifework of Arnold Gesell exemplifies the resulting concern with the typical or average that has shaped child psychology during the past half century.

The theory of predetermined development got support from Coghill's finding that frogs and salamanders develop behaviorally as they mature anatomically, from head-end tailward and from inside out, and from Carmichael's finding that the swimming patterns of frogs and salamanders develop equally well whether inhibited by chloretone in the water or stimulated by vibration. Such findings appeared to generalize to children: The acquisition of such skills as walking, stair climbing, and buttoning cannot be speeded by training or exercise; Hopi children reared on cradleboards learn to walk at the same age as Hopi children reared with arms and legs free (Dennis and Dennis, 1940).

Again, however, there was dissonant evidence. Although Cruze found that chicks kept in the dark decreased their pecking errors during the first 5 days after hatching—a result consonant with predeterminism—he also found that chicks kept in the dark for 20 days failed to improve their pecking. Moreover, studies of rats and dogs, based on the theorizing of Donald Hebb, suggest that the importance of infantile experience increases up the phylogenetic scale (Hebb, 1949).

Evidence that such findings may apply to human beings comes from studies by Goldfarb (1953) which indicate that institutional rearing (where the environment is relatively restricted and unresponsive) results in lower intelligence, less ability to sustain a task, and more problems in interpersonal relations than foster-home rearing (where the environment provides more varied experiences and responsiveness). Wayne Dennis (1960) has found that in a Teheran orphanage, where changes in ongoing stimulation were minimal, 60 percent of the 2-year-olds could not sit alone and 85 percent of the 4-year-olds could not walk alone. Such a finding dramatizes the great effect preverbal experience can have on even the rate of locomotor development. Presumably the effect on intellectual functions would be even greater.

Static Brain Function

In 1900, when C. Lloyd Morgan and E. L. Thorndike were attempting to explain learning in terms of stimulus-response bonds, they used the newly invented telephone as a mechanical model of the brain's operation. Thus they envisioned the brain as a static switchboard through which each stimulus could be connected with a variety of responses, which in turn could become the stimuli for still other responses.

Soon objective stimulus-response methodology produced evidence dissonant with this switchboard model theory, implying some kind of active processes going on between the ears. But it took the programing of electronic computers to clarify the general nature of the requirements for solving logical problems. Newell, Shaw, and Simon (1958) describe three major components of these requirements: (1) memories, or information, coded and stored; (2) operations of a logical sort which can act upon the memories; and (3) hierarchically arranged programs of these operations for various purposes. Pribram (1960) found a likely place for the brain's equivalents of such components within the intrinsic portions of the cerebrum which have no direct connections with either incoming fibers from the receptors of experience or outgoing fibers to the muscles and glands.

So, the electronic computer supplies a more nearly adequate mechanical model for brain functioning. Thus, experience may be regarded as programing the intrinsic portions of the cerebrum for learning and problem solving, and intellectual capacity at any given time may be conceived as a function of the nature and quality of this programing (Hunt, 1961; Hunt, 1963).

As Hebb has pointed out, the portion of the brain directly connected with neither incoming nor outgoing fibers is very small in animals such as frogs and salamanders, whence came most of the evidence supporting the belief in predetermined development. The increasing proportion of the intrinsic portion of the brain in higher animals suggests an anatomic basis for the increasing role of infantile experience in development, as evidenced by the greater effect of rearing on problem solving ability in dogs than in rats (Hunt, 1963). Frogs and salamanders have a relatively higher capacity for regeneration than do mammals. This suggests that the chemical factors in the genes may have more complete control in these lower forms than they have further up the phylogenic scale.

Motivation by Need, Pain, and Sex

Our conception of motivation is also undergoing change. Although it has long been said that man does not live by bread alone, most behavioral scientists and physiologists have based their theorizing on the assumption that he does. Freud popularized the statement that "all behavior is motivated." He meant motivated by painful stimulation, homeostatic need, and sexual appetite or by acquired motives based on these; and this concept has generally been shared by physiologists and academic behavioral theorists.

Undoubtedly, painful stimulation and homeostatic need motivate all organisms, as sex motivates all mammalian organisms, but the assertion that all behavior is so motivated implies that organisms become quiescent in the absence of painful stimulation, homeostatic need, and sexual stimulation. Observation stubbornly indicates that they do not: Young animals and children are most likely to play in the absence of such motivation; young rats, cats, dogs, monkeys, chimpanzees, and humans work for nothing more substantial than the opportunity to perceive, manipulate, or explore novel circumstances. This evidence implies that there must be some additional basis for motivation.

Reflex vs. Feedback

A change in our conception of the functional unit of the nervous system from the reflex arc to the feedback loop helps to suggest the nature of this other motivating mechanism. The conception of the reflex arc has its anatomical foundations in the Bell-Magendie law, based on Bell's discovery of separate ventral and dorsal roots of the spinal nerves and on Magendie's discovery that the dorsal roots have sensory or "input" functions while the ventral roots have motor or "output" functions. But the Bell-Magendie law was an overgeneralization, for motor fibers have been discovered within the presumably sensory dorsal roots, and sensory fibers have been discovered within the presumably motor ventral roots.

The most important argument against the reflex as the functional unit of the nervous system comes from the direct evidence of feedback in both sensory input and motor output. The neural activity that results when cats are exposed to a tone is markedly reduced when they are exposed to the sight of mice or the smell of fish, thus dramatizing feedback in sensory input. Feedback in motor output is dramatized by evidence that sensory input from the muscle spindles modulates the rate of motor firing to the muscles, thereby controlling the strength of contraction (Hunt, 1963).

Incongruity as Motivation

The feedback loop which constitutes a new conceptual unit of neural function supplies the basis for a new mechanism of motivation. Miller, Galanter, and Pribram (1960) have called the feedback loop the Test-Operate-Test-Exit (TOTE) unit. Such a TOTE unit is, in principle, not unlike the room thermostat. The temperature at which the thermostat is set supplies a standard against which the temperature of the room is continually being tested. If the room temperature falls below this standard, the test yields an *incongruity* which starts the furnace to "operate," and it continues to operate until the room temperature has reached this standard. When the test yields *congruity*, the furnace stops operating and the system makes its exit. Similarly, a living organism is free to be otherwise motivated once such a system has made its exit.

Several classes of similarly operating standards can be identified for human beings. One might be described as the "comfort standard" in which incongruity is equivalent to pain. Another consists of those homeostatic standards for hunger (a low of glycogen in the bloodstream) and for thirst (a high level of hydrogen ion concentration within the blood and interstitial fluids). A third class, which stretches the concept of incongruity somewhat, is related to sex.

Other standards derive from the organism's informational interaction with the environment. Thus, a fourth class appears to consist of ongoing inputs, and, just as "one never hears the clock until it has stopped," any change in these ongoing inputs brings attention and excitement. Repeated encounters with such changes of input lead to expectations, which constitute a fifth class of standards. A sixth class consists of plans quite independent of painful stimulation, homeostatic need, or sex. Ideals constitute a seventh class.

There is evidence that incongruity with such standards will instigate action and produce excitement (Hunt, 1963). There is also evidence that an optimum of such incongruity exists. Too little produces boredom as it did among McGill students who would remain lying quietly in a room no more than 3 days, although they were paid $20 a day to do so. Too much produces fearful emotional stress, as when a baby chimpanzee sees his keeper in a Halloween mask (Hebb, 1946), a human infant encounters strangers, or primitive men see an eclipse.

While this optimum of incongruity is still not well understood, it seems to involve the matching of incoming information with standards based on information already coded and stored within the cerebrum (Hunt, 1963). Probably only the individual himself can choose a source of input which provides him with an optimum of incongruity. His search for this optimum, however, explains that "growth motivation" which Froebel, the founder of the kindergarten movement, postulated and which John Dewey borrowed; and it may be the basic motivation underlying intellectual growth and the search for knowledge. Such motivation may be characterized as "intrinsic" because it inheres in the organism's informational interaction with the environment.

Emotional vs. Cognitive Experience

Another fundamental change is in the importance attributed to early— and especially very early—preverbal experience. Traditionally, very little significance had been attached to preverbal experience. When consciousness was believed to control conduct, infantile experience, typically not remembered, was regarded as having hardly any effect on adult behavior. Moreover, when development was conceived to be predetermined, infantile experience could have little importance. While Freud (1938) believed that preverbal experiences were important, he argued that their importance derived from the instinctive impulses arising from painful stimulation, homeostatic need, and especially pleasure striving, which he saw as sexual in nature.

Freud's work spread the belief that early emotional experiences are important while early cognitive experiences are not. It now appears that the opposite may possibly be more nearly true. Objective studies furnish little evidence that the factors important according to Freud's theory of psychosexual development are significant (Hunt, 1946; Orlansky, 1949). Even the belief that infants are sensitive organisms readily traumatized by painful stimulation or intense homeostatic need have been questioned as the result of studies involving the shocking of nursling rats.

Rats shocked before weaning are found to be less likely than rats left unmolested in the maternal nest to urinate and defecate in, or to hesitate entering, unfamiliar territory, and more likely to be active there. Moreover, as adults, rats shocked before weaning often require stronger shocks to instigate escape activity than do rats left unmolested; they also show less fixative effect from being shocked at the choice-point in a T-maze (Salama and Hunt, 1964). Evidence that children from low socioeconomic and educational classes, who have frequently known painful stimulation, are less likely to be fearful than middle-class children, who have seldom known painful stimulation, suggests that the findings of these rat studies may apply to human beings (Holmes, 1935).

While such observations have contradicted the common conception of the importance of early emotional experience, the experiments stemming from Hebb's theorizing (1949) have repeatedly demonstrated the importance of early perceptual and cognitive experience. At earlier phases of development, the variety of circumstances encountered appears to be most important; somewhat later, the responsiveness of the environment to the infant's activities appears to be central; and at a still later phase, the opportunity to understand the causation of mechanical and social relationships seems most significant.

In this connection, a study by Baldwin, Kalhorn, and Breese (1945) found that the IQ's of 4- to 7-year-old children tend to increase with time if parental discipline consists of responsive and realistic explanations, but tend to fall if parental discipline consists of nonchalant unresponsiveness or of demands for obedience for its own sake, with painful stimulation as the alternative.

Motor Response and Receptor Input

One more important traditional belief about psychological development which may have to be changed concerns the relative importance of motor response and receptor input for the development of the autonomous central processes which mediate intellectual capacity. A century ago, the "apperceptive mass" conceived by Herbart, a German educational psychologist, was regarded as the product of previous perceptual input; and Froebel and Montessori both stressed sensory training. However, after World War I, the focus of laboratory learning-studies on response, coupled with the notion of brain function as a static switchboard, gradually shifted the emphasis from the perceptual input to the response output. It is hard to make the great importance attributed to the response side jibe with the following findings:

1. Hopi infants reared on cradleboards, where the movements of arms and legs are inhibited during waking hours, learn to walk at the same age as Hopi infants reared with arms and legs free (Dennis and Dennis, 1940).

2. Eighty-five percent of the 4-year-olds in a Teheran orphanage, where variations in auditory and visual input were extremely limited, did not walk alone (Dennis, 1960).

Such observations and those of Piaget (1936 and 1945) suggest that the repeated correction of expectations deriving from perceptual impressions and from cognitive accommodations gradually create the central processes mediating the logical operations of thought. Wohlwill (1960) and Flavell (1963) have assembled evidence which relates the inferential processes of thought to experience and have given this evidence some formal theoretical organization.

Counteracting Cultural Deprivation

The intellectual inferiority apparent among so many children of parents of low educational and socioeconomic status, regardless of race, is already evident by the time they begin kindergarten or first grade at age 5 or 6 (Kennedy *et al.*, 1963). Such children are apt to have various linguistic liabilities: limited vocabularies, poor articulation, and syntactical deficiencies that are revealed in the tendency to rely on unusually short sentences with faulty grammar (John, 1964). They also show perceptual deficiencies in the sense that they recognize fewer objects and situations than do most middle-class children. And perhaps more important, they usually have fewer interests than do the middle-class children who are the pace setters in the schools. Moreover, the objects recognized by and the interests of children typical of the lower class differ from those of children of the middle class. These deficiencies give such children the poor start which so commonly handicaps them ever after in scholastic competition.

So long as it was assumed that intelligence is fixed and development is predetermined, the intellectual inferiority of children from families of low educational and socioeconomic status had to be considered an unalterable consequence of their genes. With the changes in our conception of man's intellectual development, outlined in the foregoing pages, there emerges a hope of combating such inferiority by altering, for part of their waking hours, the conditions under which such children develop. The question is "how?"

Clues From Intrinsic Motivation

A tentative answer, worthy at least of investigative demonstration, is suggested by the existence of a change during the preschool years in the nature of what I have called "intrinsic motivation." An approximation of the character of this change has been supplied by the observations which Piaget made on the development of his three children (Hunt, 1963; Piaget, 1936 and 1945). At least three stages in the development of intrinsic motivation appear. These may be characteristic of an organism's progressive relationship with any new set of circumstances and seem to be stages in infant development only because the child is encountering so many new sets of circumstances during his first 2 or 3 years.

In the first stage the infant is essentially responsive. He is motivated, of course, by painful stimulation, homeostatic need, and, in Freud's sense, by sex. Russian investigators have shown that the orienting response is ready-made at birth in all mammals, including human beings (Razran, 1961). Thus, any changes in the ongoing perceptual input will attract attention and excite the infant. During this phase each of the ready-made sensorimotor organizations—sucking, looking, listening, vocalizing, grasping, and wiggling—changes, by something like Pavlov's conditioning process, to become coordinated with the others. Thus, something heard becomes something to look at, something to look at becomes something to grasp, and something to grasp become something to suck. This phase ends with a "landmark of transition" in which the infant, having repeatedly encountered certain patterns of stimulus change, tries actively to retain or regain them (Hunt, 1963).

During the second stage the infant manifests interest in, and efforts to retain, something newly recognized as familiar—a repeatedly encountered pattern of change in perceptual input. The infant's intentional effort is familiar to anyone who has jounced a child on his knee and then stopped his jouncing only to find the child making a comparable motion, as if to invite the jouncing adult to continue. Regaining the newly recognized activity commonly brings forth such signs of delight as the smile and the laugh, and continued loss brings signs of distress. The effort to retain the newly recognized may well account for the long hours of hand watching and babbling commonly observed during the child's third, fourth, and fifth months. This second stage ends when, with these repeated encounters, the child becomes bored with the familiar and turns his interest to whatever is novel in familiar situations (Hunt, 1963).

The third stage begins with this interest in the novel within a familiar context, which typically becomes noticeable during the last few months of the first year of life. Piaget (1936) describes its beginnings with the appearance of throwing, but it probably can be found earlier. While he throws the child intentionally shifts his attention from the act of throwing to the trajectory of the object that he has thrown.

Interest in the novel is also revealed in the infant's increasing development of new plans through an active, creative process of groping, characterized by C. Lloyd Morgan as "trial-and-error." It also shows in the child's increasing attempts to imitate new vocal patterns and gestures (Hunt, 1963; Piaget, 1945).

Interest in the new is the infant's basis for "growth motivation." It has also been found in animals, particularly in an experiment in which rats in a figure-eight maze regularly changed their preference to the more complex loop.

Thus Piaget's (1936) aphorism, "the more a child has seen and heard, the more he wants to see and hear," may be explained. The more different visual and auditory changes the child encounters during the first stage, the more of these will he recognize with interest during the second stage. The more he recognizes during the second stage, the more of these will provide novel features to attract him during the third stage.

Effects of Social Environment

Such development prepares the child to go on developing. But continuing development appears to demand a relationship with adults who enable the infant to pursue his locomotor and manipulative intentions and who answer his endless questions of "what's that?", "is it a 'this' or a 'that'?", and "why is it a 'this' or a 'that'?." Without these supports during the second, third, and fourth years of life, a child cannot continue to profit no matter how favorable his circumstances during his first year.

Although we still know far too little about intellectual development to say anything with great confidence, it is unlikely that most infants in families of low socioeconomic status suffer great deprivation during their first year. Since one distinguishing feature of poverty is crowding, it is conceivable that an infant may actually encounter a wider variety of visual and auditory inputs in conditions of poverty than in most middle- or upper-class homes. This should facilitate the intellectual development of the infant during his first year.

During the second year, however, crowded living conditions would probably hamper development. As an infant begins to move under his own power, to manipulate things, and to throw things, he is likely to get in the way of adults who are apt already to be ill-tempered from their own discomforts and frustrations. Such situations are dramatized in Lewis's "The Children of Sanchez," an anthropological study of life in poverty (1961). In such an atmosphere, a child's opportunity to carry out the activities required for his locomotor and manipulative development must almost inevitably be sharply curbed.

Moreover, late in his second or early in his third year, after he has developed a number of pseudo-words and achieved the "learning set" that "things have names," the child in a crowded, poverty-stricken family probably meets another obstacle: His questions too seldom bring suitable answers, and too often bring punishment that inhibits further questioning. Moreover, the conditions that originally provided a rich variety of input for the very young infant now supply a paucity of suitable playthings and models for imitation.

The effects of a lower-class environment on a child's development may become even more serious during his fourth and fifth years. Furthermore, the longer these conditions continue, the more likely the effects are to be lasting. Evidence from animal studies supports this: Tadpoles immobilized with chloretone for 8 days are not greatly hampered in the development of their swimming patterns, but immobilization for 13 days leaves their swimming patterns permanently impaired; chicks kept in darkness for as many as 5 days show no apparent defects in their pecking responses, but keeping them in darkness for 8 or more days results in chicks which never learn to peck at all (Hunt, 1961).

Possible Counteracting Measures

Such observations suggest that if nursery schools or day-care centers were arranged for culturally deprived children from age 4—or preferably from age 3—until time for school at 5 or 6 some of the worst effects of their rearing might be substantially reduced.

Counteracting cultural deprivation at this stage of development might best be accomplished by giving the child the opportunity to encounter a wide variety of objects, pictures, and appropriate behavioral models, and by giving him social approval for appropriate behavior. The setting should encourage him to indulge his inclinations to scrutinize and manipulate the new objects as long as he is interested and should provide him with appropriate answers to his questions. Such varied experiences would foster the development of representative imagery which could then be the referents for spoken words and later for written language.

Children aged 3 and 4 should have the opportunity to hear people speak who provide syntactical models of standard grammar. The behavioral models would lead gradually to interest in pictures, written words, and books. The objects provided and appropriate answers to the "why" questions would lead to interest in understanding the workings of things and the consequences of social conduct. Thus, the child might gradually overcome most of the typical handicaps of his lower-class rearing by the time he enters grade school.

There is a danger, however, in attempting to prescribe a remedy for cultural deprivation at this stage of knowledge. Any specific prescription of objects, pictures, behavioral models, and forms of social reinforcement may fail to provide that attractive degree of incongruity with the impressions which the toddler of the lower class has already coded and stored in the course of his experience. Moreover, what seem to be appropriate behavioral models may merely produce conflict. Therefore, it may be wise to reexamine the educational contributions of Maria Montessori (Montessori, 1907; Rambusch, 1962). These have been largely forgotten in America, perhaps because they were until recently too dissonant with the dominant notions of motivation and the importance attributed to motor responses in development.

Montessori's contributions are especially interesting, despite some of the rigid orthodoxy that has crept into present-day Montessori practice, because she based her teaching methods on children's spontaneous interest in learning, that is, on "intrinsic motivation." Moreover, she stressed the importance of teachers' observing children to discover what things would most interest them and most foster their growth. Further, she stressed the need to train the perceptual processes, or what we would today call the information processes. The coded information stored in culturally deprived children from lower-class backgrounds differs from that stored in children with middle-class backgrounds. This difference makes it dangerous for middle-class teachers to prescribe intuitively on the basis of their own experiences or of their experiences in teaching middle-class youngsters.

Montessori also broke the lockstep in the education of young children. She made no effort to keep them doing the same thing at the same time. Rather, each child was free to examine and work with whatever happened to interest him, for as long as he liked. It is commonly believed that the activity of preschoolers must be changed every 10 or 15 minutes or the children become bored. But Dorothy Canfield Fisher (1912), the novelist, who spent the winter of 1910–11 at Montessori's Casa de Bambini in Rome, observed that 3-year-olds there commonly remained engrossed in such mundane activities as buttoning and unbuttoning for 2 hours or more at a time. In such a setting the child has an opportunity to find those particular circumstances which match his own particular phase of development and which provide the proper degree of incongruity for intrinsic motivation. This may well have the corollary advantage of making learning fun and the school setting interesting and attractive.

Montessori also included children from 3 to 6 years old in the same group. In view of the changes that occur in intellectual development, this has the advantage of providing younger children with a variety of novel models for imitation while supplying older children with an opportunity to teach, an activity which provides many of its own rewards.

Conclusions

At this stage of history and knowledge, no one can blueprint a program of preschool enrichment that will with certainty be an effective antidote for the cultural deprivation of children. On the other hand, the revolutionary changes taking place in the traditional beliefs about the development of human capacity and motivation make it sensible to hope that a program of preschool enrichment may ultimately be made effective. The task calls for creative innovations and careful evaluative studies of their effectiveness.

Discoveries of effective innovations will contribute also to the general theory of intellectual development and become significant for the rearing and education of all children. Effective innovations will also help to minimize those racial differences in school achievement which derive from cultural deprivation and so help to remove one stubborn obstacle in the way of racial integration.

Although it is likely that no society has ever made the most of the intellectual potential of its members, the increasing role of technology in our culture demands that we do better than others ever have. To do so we must become more concerned with intellectual development during the preschool years and especially with the effects of cultural deprivation.

References

Baldwin, A. L., J. Kalhorn, and F. H. Breese. 1945. Patterns of parent behavior. *Psychol. Monogr.*, **58**.

Bayley, Nancy. 1940. Mental growth in young children. In the *39th Yrbk. Nat. Soc. Study Educ.* (Bloomington, Ill.: Public School Publishing Co.).

Dennis, W. 1960. Causes of retardation among institutional children: Iran. *J. genet. Psychol.*, **96**.

——, and Marsena G. Dennis. 1940. The effect of cradling practice upon the onset of walking in Hopi children, *J. genet. Psychol.*, **56**.

Fisher, Dorothy Canfield. 1912. *A Montessori mother* (New York: Holt, Rinehart and Winston, Inc.).

Flavell, J. H. 1963. *The developmental psychology of Jean Piaget* (Princeton, N.J.: D. Van Nostrand Company, Inc.).

Freud, S. 1938. Three contributions to the theory of sex. In A. A. Brill (ed.), *The basic writings of Sigmund Freud* (New York: Modern Library, Inc.).

Goldfarb, W. 1953. The effects of early institutional care on adolescent personality. *J. exp. Educ.*, **12**.

Hebb, D. O. 1949. *The organization of behavior* (New York: John Wiley & Sons, Inc.).

——. 1946. On the nature of fear. *Psychol. Rev.*, **53**.

Holmes, F. B. 1935. An experimental study of the fears of young children. In A. T. Jersild and F. B. Holmes (eds.), *Children's fears*, Child Development Monographs, No. 20 (New York: Teachers College, Columbia University).

Hunt, J. McV. 1963. Motivation inherent in information processing and action. In O. J. Harvey (ed.), *Motivation and social interaction: cognitive determinants* (New York: The Ronald Press Company).

——. 1963. Piaget's observations as a source of hypotheses concerning motivation. *Merrill-Palmer Quart.*, **9**.

——. 1961. *Intelligence and experience* (New York: The Ronald Press Company).

——. 1946. Experimental psychoanalysis. In P. L. Harriman (ed.), *The encyclopedia of psychology* (New York: Philosophical Library, Inc.).

John, Vera P. 1964. The intellectual development of slum children. *Merrill-Palmer Quart.*, **10**.

Kennedy, W. A., *et al.* 1963. A normative sample of intelligence and achievement of Negro elementary school children in the Southeastern United States. *Monogr. Soc. Res. Child Develpm.*, Serial No. 90, **28**.

Lewis, O. 1961. *The children of Sanchez* (New York: Random House, Inc.).

Miller, G. A., E. Galanter, and K. H. Pribram. 1960. *Plans and the structure of behavior* (New York: Holt, Rinehart and Winston, Inc.).

Montessori, Maria. 1912. *The Montessori method* (1907) (Philadelphia, Pa.: J. B. Lippincott Company).

Newell, A., J. Shaw, and H. A. Simon. 1958. Elements of a theory of human problem-solving. *Psychol. Rev.*, **65**.

Orlansky, H. 1949. Infant care and personality. *Psychol. Bull.*, **46**.

Piaget, J. 1952. *The origins of intelligence in children.* First ed., 1936. Translated by Margaret Cook (New York: International Universities Press, Inc.).

––––––. 1951. *Play, dreams, and imitation in childhood.* First ed., 1945. Translated by C. Gattegno and F. M. Hodgson (New York: W. W. Norton & Company, Inc.).

Pribram, K. H. 1960. A review of theory in physiological psychology. *Annu. Rev. Psychol.*, **11**.

Rambusch, Nancy McC. 1962. *Learning how to learn: an American approach to Montessori* (Baltimore, Md.: Helicon Press, Inc.).

Razran, G. 1961. The observable unconscious and the inferable conscious in current Soviet psychophysiology: interoceptive conditioning, semantic conditioning, and the orienting reflex. *Psychol. Rev.*, **68**.

Salama, A. A., and J. McV. Hunt. 1964. "Fixation" in the rat as a function of infantile shocking, handling, and gentling. *J. genet. Psychol.*, **100**.

Wohlwill, J. F. Developmental studies of perception. *Psychol. Bull.*, **57**.

18   Concept Learning in Early Childhood*

WILLIAM FOWLER, *University of Chicago*

Today we seem to be witness to an explosion of interest in cognitive processes and their origins in early development that was hardly foreseeable a few years ago. There is a growing awareness of the possible importance of the early years as a foundation, if not critical, period for the establishment of basic learning sets and cognitive styles. There is also a widening of interest in the long-term, emergent and developmental character of complex thought processes.

Much of the impetus for the scientific popularity of these new foci has paralleled, if it cannot be entirely attributed to, the national and even international political sociology of our era. The race from Sputnik and the bottomless demands for education of underdeveloped world populations have seemingly contributed to the discovery that our own country is also inhabited by large populations of intellectually underprivileged people. With this discovery we have come to believe that poverty may be related to cultural deprivation and that social deprivation may be partly founded on certain root perceptual and conceptual deprivations, traceable to the earliest years of childhood.

Under such crash circumstances, it is hardly surprising to find that much of the research on problems of early cognitive development, deprivation and stimulation are in the nature of crash, field projects aimed at developing viable educational settings for preschool, culturally disadvantaged children. More basic efforts to formulate and study the experiential-developmental course of concept formation in the beginning phases may be found in the writings of investigators like Deutsch and his colleagues (1964), Hunt (1961), Hess (1963), myself (e.g., 1962, 1965) and others.

Two Historical Frameworks

Notwithstanding this exponential growth of activity on these problems, much current research thinking on the emergence of cognitive

---

* Reprinted with permission from *Young Children*, November 1965, vol. 21, no. 2. Copyright © 1965, National Association for the Education of Young Children. Paper presented at the annual meeting of the American Educational Research Association, Chicago, Illinois, February 12, 1965.

processes remains encapsulated in either of two limiting frameworks. Both frameworks fail to concern themselves adequately with the etiology of concept development. Of these widely prevalent viewpoints, one tends merely to *characterize* and the other simply to *measure* intellectual processes at various ages, relating them, respectively, either to long-term, descriptive developmental theories or to short-term, general behavior theory models. In neither model is there much attempt to *explain* or *control* the course of development over time. On the one hand, the newer orientations which follow the molar, structural concepts of Piaget tend to be mired in ideal type, age-stage comparisons rather than tracing the specific, antecedent conditions and mechanisms which *produce* development. On the other hand, much of experimental child psychology, following the classical S-R model, while not uninfluenced by the structural concepts of Piaget, continues to ignore the developmental history and life's circumstances of the subjects under study. In short, there is, as yet, little experimental effort to undertake basic research on long-range *educational* problems of cognitive development.

A Conceptual Model

In the course of attempting to grapple with some of these divergent orientations and explanatory gaps, I have evolved something of a model of developmental learning processes in the early years. The schema is aimed at pulling together a variety of poorly related concepts from the fields of learning and cognitive development for consideration in the little developed area of systematic education and long-term programing of concept learning in early childhood.

Preliminary descriptions of the model have been derived in the main from my work on early reading (Fowler, 1962, 1965). More recently, I have been formulating the same type of conceptual organization in terms of broader subject areas of knowledge, formulations which I should like to present herein. As a means of general orientation, I shall furnish a brief overall picture of the schema. I shall then probe some of the central concepts in greater detail, illustrating their utility as we have been applying them at the Laboratory Nursery School and in projects with culturally disadvantaged preschoolers. At various points, I will also endeavor to relate them to some of the developmental issues and problems of (early) cognitive development.

Following the notion that development is a process of acquiring increasingly complex mental structures and modes of functioning through the cumulative interaction of the growing child with his environment, our approach is one of attempting (1) to program systematically concept learning and (2) to devise the most effective techniques and role for the teacher. To accomplish the first point, we can identify relatively focal structures in the social and physical world and set up learning programs which will enable a young child to learn specific features and relations of and between structures as well as lead him to the foundation of general concepts. To insure cumulative success for each child, we define functional units of analysis along continua of complexity.

Under the second main proposition, we establish a learning situation and style of relations to facilitate cue-guided stimulation. The general framework is founded on a discovery-problem-solving approach but is liberally immersed in dramatic and play-oriented activities. Much of the activity entails physical manipulation of miniature or pictured objects by children in small group settings.

The Concept of Structure

Proceeding from this very brief summary to some elaboration, the concept of structure as used here applies both to the patterning of the external world and the organization of the child's mental processes in schemata, as Piaget calls them (1952). It is assumed that it is the lawful ordering of reality in patterned and operating systems which makes possible the emergence of adaptive structures in the child's mind and patterned, interrelated systems of action. Meaning, in other words, has its basis in terms of the close and ordered relations of mental structures to reality structures.

At the beginning, in infancy, reality structures, as represented in the mind, are presumably grossly incomplete, immediate, and little generalized. Piaget makes much of this kind of distinction and the long developmental distance between what he defines as the early perception of infralogical structures and the only gradual and later emergence of classificatory mental structures (Flavell, 1963). By the former he means the direct perception of single objects and their components and the corresponding part-whole relations, spacio-temporal contiguity and physical continuity involved. Classificatory structures, on the other hand, are essentially constructions of the mind, although based on similarities and regularities among objects which are abstracted to form type structures. Physical proximity and continuity are not conditions for the formation of abstract or logical structures, according to Piaget.

In my organization of a schema for beginning conceptual learning, I consider it important to concentrate upon both single, object structures (and their internal organization) and abstract classificatory structures. Direct, perceptual-motor manipulations of simple structures may well

predominate in the intellectual modes of the infant and preschool child.
From an educational point of view, however, the problem appears to be
one of facilitating the developmental transformation of the child's intellectual operations from the level of these infralogical structures to more
complex and abstract forms of logical functioning. According to Piaget
and some evidence, the latter, complex structures typically evolve during
the four- to seven-year-age span (Flavell, 1963; White, 1965). But virtually all of the evidence for Piaget's theories and the so-called "norms"
of mental development have been gathered with little regard to prior
experience, let alone the child's total life history (Fowler, 1962). In other
words, there has been scarcely any assessment at all of the critical and
cumulative role that learning plays in the development of concepts.

Planning and the Cumulative
Nature of Learning

The importance of planning and guiding stimulation from the beginning and throughout the ontogenetic span of development is inherent in
the cumulative nature of discrimination-generalization processes. The
terms discrimination and generalization themselves imply processes of
choosing among dimensions of reality to form concepts about it. They also
imply the possibility of alternate paths along which a child can develop.
The first discriminations and generalizations acquired become foundation
concepts upon which subsequent discriminations and generalizations must
be erected. All ensuing concepts formed serve as cumulative constraints
determining which higher order paths to abstraction and which set of
representations of reality we come to comprehend—or even whether we
attain any at all. A central assumption, then, upon which my early
concept learning model is founded is that we should concern ourselves
with guiding and systematically programing a child's cognitive development from the earliest periods of life.

The first step in setting up a stimulation program is the selection of
a particular subject area of reality, for example, modes of transportation,
community structure, zoology, reading, foreign languages, or almost any
domain of reality which can be defined and presented in a form sufficiently simplified for a child to learn as Bruner has suggested (Bruner,
1960). Availability of materials and ease of obtaining pictures are likely
to be important determinants of choice. Closeness of relation to the preschool child's interest, dominant in the culture, is secondary under the
assumption that teaching techniques utilized are adequate to arouse and
sustain interest in unfamiliar material, although this may influence learning gradients established.

Analytic-Synthesizing Approach

The act of selecting a specific area of reality for a learning program is *per se* a demonstration of one principle upon which the conceptual model is built, namely, the utility of an analytic, simplifying approach to studying the world. Having decided upon some area considered appropriate as a content area of value for children to learn, extension of this principle leads to an analysis of the structure into primary elements and infrastructural relationships as well as to charting a program according to levels of difficulty.

The approach is not one of merely studying elements as simplified and isolated bits, however. It is rather concentrating upon parts—both elements and simple relationships—to sharpen perceptual focus but also to study them as components subordinate to some supra-ordinate system or larger infralogical structure. The aims here are to simplify the intricacies of a structure through selecting out key dimensions while ignoring others. This, in turn, is assumed not only to facilitate learning about particular infralogical structures but to orient learning toward the development of abstracting processes.

A key principle represented here is the importance of steering between the extremes of molecular (S-R) versus molar (gestalt) styles of learning, an unproductive polarization of alternatives which has long plagued theories of learning and education. By presenting material in a shifting but interrelated focus of attention on simplified parts and wholes, through a process of analysis and synthesis, the child is enabled to acquire a better conceptual grasp of both the forest and trees. Alternating analytic-synthesizing approaches toward stimulation facilitates learning simply because reality *is* organized in ways that parts bear some relation to one another and to a total structure, through the use they serve in the construction and operation of a structure. It is, in fact, the apparent organization and working of reality domains according to structural-functional mechanisms and relations which forms an important basis for this conceptual model of the stimulation process.

Learning Sequences

In our current experimentation there are a variety of alternate schemes for establishing sequential levels of difficulty which we have been exploring. The organization of levels which we have found more or less useful are, roughly: first, the gross perception of objects and their functions; second, focus upon salient features of objects, their functions and relations to the whole; third, ecological relations of the given structure and its components to other structures and aspects of the environmental context generally; fourth, classificatory activities, which involve sorting and grouping of objects according to abstracted structures and functions of objects and in relation to the organization of larger supraordinate systems.

In general, while we may define certain kinds of organizational foci and related tasks in terms of "levels," much of this is a matter of convenience in outlining perspectives and guides for teachers. There is in actual practice considerable overlap among the levels in keeping with our analytic-synthetic approach, as well as in order to capitalize upon a child's curiosity to explore the various internal features and functions of objects and their relations to the ecological fabric. In some ways we are dealing as much with directions of analysis as we are with levels of difficulty.

There are, nevertheless, at least two ways in which gradients are followed. Aside from the presumably greater demands for conceptualizing and abstracting processes which the classificatory tasks impose, within each of the major levels or directions of structural analyses, certain definite gradients of difficulty are established and more or less followed. Among the criteria for setting up these gradients are degree of familiarity or cultural commonness of objects; the complexity of a specific object structure, its parts and mechanisms; and the number of attributes, parts and objects and interrelations which are concentrated upon in a given event sequence or operation of a system or subsystem. There is the additional factor of ordering symbolic mediation in amount and kind of difficulty. This is more easily included in our description of the instructional techniques and situation.

An Illustration: The Structure of a Community

Having outlined our approach to defining the dimensions of a schema, it may be useful to illustrate their applicability to a domain such as the structure of a community. By community, here, I mean roughly some local unit of socio-economic organization which embraces clusters of residential, manufacturing, agricultural and distributive units of activity and the network of relations among them.

With respect to our own contemporary scene, therefore, some of the obvious conceptual units with which to start a program are a home, school, store, factory, farm, or community electrical circuits. Each of these concepts can be conveniently represented in concrete form—which draws in another major pillar of the model. Early stimulation programs are heavily built around the manipulation of real objects—usually in miniature or in pictures—in keeping with the low power abstracting abilities of early development.

Starting with pictures and toy models and occasional excursions to stores, houses, factories, garages, parks and people, at the first level, we explore a child's familiarity with the major dimensions of a community structure. The type of cognitively oriented and developed child of middleclass professional parents who attends the Laboratory Nursery School is already familiar with most of the objects and many of their component features. One is likely, therefore, to find oneself almost at once launched somewhere on at least a second level series of discovering and discriminating such particulars as cash registers, greasing cars in a gas station, or money and checking accounts in a bank. But wherever one begins, gradients of complexity are selected and pursued on the basis of ordering in their number and complexity the typical structural-functional components of each community distribution unit, e.g., of a garage—pumps for serving gasoline, rack for servicing a car, and so on. The mechanisms for operating a gasoline pump are presumably more complicated than the process of gasoline flowing into an automobile's gas tank.

From these examples, it may be apparent that centering attention upon the internal structure of a community subordinate structure like a garage, as opposed to its external relations with the community, is a fairly arbitrary approach. It is here that the overlapping of units and relationships among structural levels becomes most evident. For instance, tools are standard components of a hardware store at one level of structural analysis; but tools also relate to and are synthesizable in terms of other categories, e.g., houses and home repair, and broader community concepts of maintenance, comfort and shelter. Structures at one level constitute the units at another level of analysis. The principle here, in sum, is merely to simplify the study of structural systems by momentarily isolating components from the network of internal-external relations of systems and subsystems. Components are sorted out, concentrated on and synthesized in one set of relations and directions, a step or so at a time.

In this maze of guided learning, further complexity is attained along two main arteries. One of these, again, involves the kind and number of relations toward which the child's understanding of the total community organization, operations and multilateral pattern of relationships is led. Ultimately, it is possible to conceive of sketching in for a child a still highly simplified but relatively complete picture of a community which embraces such concepts as the basic functions of money, the division of labor, socio-economic class and the like. To realize this goal, however, we must also traverse the second major arterial sequence, namely, classificatory concepts, or our fourth level of structural analysis.

Learning Classificatory Concepts

From one point of view, classificatory or generalizing activities, as with the three other directions of analysis, are not something entirely deferrable to a more advanced stage of the stimulation program. The moment we lead a child to distinguish a hardware store from a store in general, as a generic, we are introducing generality, or membership in a category. We thus overlook the fact that a hardware store sells tools and a grocery store, food, identifying only attributes they have in common, especially that of selling goods. When we do this, of course, we are introducing abstracting processes. Thus the supposedly simple labeling of individual stores—hardware, grocery, shoestore—in a community is in fact ranging across examples of a type concept. These roots of the language abstracting process through words begin very early according to Vygotsky (1962).

Notwithstanding, abstracting activities are treated in this structural model as a separate more complex type of activity. In a sense, word labeling and object discrimination activities probably do involve abstracting and generalizing. Yet, it is presumably a much simpler process to discriminate a single object from among a cluster of objects, to which a word label is associated, on the basis of gross configurations, than it is to sort objects—even those immediately perceivable—into groups on the basis of selected attributes which some but not all objects have in common. It is also evident that second and higher levels of hierarchical classification (e.g., a given individual works at a waitress type of job, which, in turn, is a class of semi-skilled work within a still larger framework of working-class occupations) are even further removed from simple object discrimination, labeling type tasks. How far a child can progress through these levels remains to be determined since Welch (1940) and this writer (1961) found almost no second level hierarchy concepts available to three- and four-year-olds even following relatively long-term programs of stimulation continuing over several months or more. It is hoped that present attempts to analyze and program along the specific structural lines of the current model, however, may prove more successful than earlier crude attempts.

Teaching Techniques

The techniques employed for cognitive stimulation in the early years of child development may be described in terms of a situational setting and a few principles of interest arousal based on positive attitudes and styles in teaching relations, competence motivation (White, 1959) and incidental learning. It is productive to organize a stimulation program within the framework of a project unit of work for which the sequential guides and materials we have illustrated are prepared. The project is presented to a specific group of children over a period of several months on some regular basis, preferably no more than a few minutes or so per day. Brevity, frequency and flexibility are important considerations in dealing with the brief attention and short recall spans and quasi-stable learning styles characteristic of the younger developmental periods. Small groups of four to eight children in a small area, visually and aurally separated from the valence of competing activities and attractions, is useful. The interest of groups of this size in insulated settings can be more easily corralled and group games managed. At the same time, the size permits individual tailoring and a loose framework of guidance for promoting productive self- and paired direction of small projects.

The teaching approach itself rests on two types of techniques, one of these an atmosphere of play-game activities, the other a problem-solving orientation. The individual stimulus units—pictures and small objects (when available)—are presented to the children, singly and in small clusters (as more are learned), and spread out on a flat surface (table or floor) around which the children are seated. The basic forms of the learning tasks consist of three kinds of processes: discrimination-identification, matching-constructing and sorting-grouping activities. Pictures or objects are discriminated from others in a set and/or identified (verbally labeled) at the teacher's request. Pictures are matched with other identical or similar pictures or put together with a pattern of other pictures to construct (synthesize) a larger structural scene. And pictures are sorted and arranged in groups according to criteria defined by the teacher for the abstract classificatory processes. All three types of activities are viewed as still rooted in the basic dimensions of discrimination-identification processes. The more complicated forms are merely extensions and elaborations which encompass multilateral relations, inter-relations or parts to wholes, and discrimination of classes of objects and *classes* of ecological settings upon the basis of selected cues identifying type functions and structures.

There is a model question to be employed by a teacher which guides a child's attention effectively in the discrimination-generalization activities, while setting up for him a search task and an active role involving physical manipulation of concrete "things." The basic question or instruction follows some variant of the basic form, "Where is the bank?" or "Find all the pictures which show people working in factories." It may be seen that this question is readily adaptable to involving a child in specific tasks whose success is contingent upon performing higher level cognitive operations of a classificatory type. Thus, "Put the pictures of professional workers in this pile and the pictures of skilled workers in this pile."

Play orientations consist of "seek and find" and various targeting types of games, and other similar, competence challenging, means-end problem-solving tasks. In this category are included the finding of correct choice pictures hidden under one of a series of boxes or large cards; dropping a picture in a box after discriminating it correctly from among a cluster on a table; or pinning a discriminated picture at a correct position in an ecological mural painted on a broad expanse of paper on the wall. Open-ended ecological settings may be constructed from materials and pictures provided, or cut-up pictures may be assembled in a picture-puzzle and used in synthesizing and matching tasks.

A second category of incentive technique used consists of a teacher narrating tales around the objects and scenes while she manipulates the stimuli in dramatic role play. The child is invited to participate along with the teacher in the course of the story development, which exposes him—incidentally—to further reinforcement experiences.

In every stimulation task, correction of "wrong" responses is avoided and liberal use of praise addressed to the child's effort is recommended. In this dramatic framework original and imaginative constructions can thus be encouraged. Yet, learning can also easily be channelized in definite directions of sequence and organization. The teacher simply has to re-demonstrate a model associational task or to re-ask for a desired discrimination from time to time. Through varying widely the forms of the play activity in which the basic discrimination-sorting tasks are immersed, a large number of repetitions can easily be provided without the usual avoidance learning consequences of drill. Reinforcement is also multiplied in the small group setting, where each child observes the responses of the other children.

Gradient of Symbolic Mediation

While all play-instructional sessions are organized around discrimination-generalizing task activities, there is a further gradient of difficulty built into the program, namely the degree of symbolic mediation deriving from the arrangement of the tasks themselves. Initially, all new objects and relationships are labeled and defined for the child, as each is introduced. Immediately following this demonstration by the teacher, the next task or step in order of difficulty requires the child to discriminate the same item in response to an instruction which also provides a verbal label.

His task at this beginning level is thus to associate this orally furnished label with the visual stimulus pattern placed immediately in front of him. Even at this stage, memory and, hence, mediation are involved in this perceptual-associative act. There is necessarily some time-lapse, however brief, between the model associative act performed by the teacher and the cognitive linkage between word and act performed by the child.

In subsequent stages, the gradient for the amount of symbolic mediation may be steepened through extending in time and space the distance between a teacher's demonstration model and a child's performance. Thus, at later stages of the program, a child might be asked (in review) to perform associational tasks which neither a teacher nor himself (self-reinforcement) had performed for some weeks.

Mediation also increases in proportion as the distance between the visual stimuli and the emission of a verbal concept is increased. Displacing a picture from a table at which a child is sitting to a blackboard may be one step. Bringing a picture from home, where the search cannot even be initiated until some hours after the verbalization is stated by a teacher at school, requires considerably longer memory storage. Similarly, in other ways, more complex mediation is demanded by removal of ecological context cues or by inserting objects in varied ecological scenes. In the same manner we may show other pictures of similar type objects whose structure or function may be similar but whose components, organization of structure, or mechanisms may vary. One may also increase the number, variety and spread of parts and relations which must be scanned and conceptualized, and so on. Again, each of these kinds of variations are introduced carefully, step-by-step, graded in terms of their degree of similarity, closeness and complexity in comparison with the original stimulus patterns and task requirements. We may also simply ask a child to identify a presented stimulus or set of relations, the teacher furnishing no verbal cues; the child must then rely entirely on his own internal mediation in response to the query, "What is ——?" This last form of task tends to *test* rather than *teach* a child and is generally minimized except in measurement sessions.

Positive Motivation, Flexible Sequences and Inquiry Orientations

The important factor is to insure success at each step of the program, that is to link each step in size and distance to the prior sequence of steps, always presenting bites of a size a child can chew. This is considered critical in order to minimize failure experiences, foster achievement motivation and a *sense* of intellectual mastery and autonomy, and produce progress in complexity of cognitive functioning and the extent of specific and general concepts absorbed.

Any of these sequences along a continuum—or in stages—of complexity need not be rigidly adhered to in the actual learning situation. Indeed over-concern with simplicity is likely to stultify teaching style and inhibit curiosity and exploration of structure, thus defeating a major educational goal. In addition to the active, physically manipulative search role which is continually set up for the child, an inquiry orientation is embedded into the nature of the guiding, stimulating process. Any given series of analytic construction and classification tasks requested of a child includes alternate and sometimes overlapping means and classificatory structures for conceptualizing. These shifts of foci are intended to convey to the child the idea of alternate pathways of inquiry about the world, while preserving the utility of guidance along and among particular paths and systems.

Within this kind of flexible framework, some rough approximation to a course graded according to levels of complexity is considered essential in setting instructional priorities if rates and degree of mastery are to be maximized. A balance between encouraging wider inquiry and insuring continuing progress through grading material to each child's level and style is attempted. The implications for producing a thoughtful citizenry are inherent in the developing of attitudes of inquiry. On the other hand, the value of programing lies in the fact that unless stimuli are ordered sequentially, it is difficult to regulate the flow of stimulation to conform to each child's rate, style and level of acquisition. In the absence of the opportunity to pace and tune the presentation of stimulus patterns in close approximation to each child's evolving levels of comprehension, we offer less than ideal conditions to promote the operation of mechanisms for advancing cognitive development and mastery.

Problems of Disadvantaged Children

In closing, deficiencies in the grading and tuning process loom with the largest prominence in educational settings for culturally disadvantaged children, or any children who have experienced massive doses of sensory-cognitive deprivation or distortion. The difficulty of tuning into the non-productive and sometimes rigidly concrete psycho-cognitive styles of these types of children, even at the three-year level, has recently been most graphically displayd to this investigator (Fowler, 1961, 1965). Efforts to stimulate cognitive development in two such Negro children among a small group of identical twins and triplets over an eight-months' span in an experimental nursery school failed almost completely. There were no significant changes in cognitive functioning despite stress placed upon personal warmth, small group learning situations and the use of play-activity techniques. While all of the latter techniques may conceivably have been improved, the known lack of systematic programing has influenced my present efforts to proceed in this direction in projects on compensatory education.

Emphasis upon careful sequencing should not minimize the importance of emotionally supportive teaching attitudes and flexible teacher styles or the value of dramatic play activities and games. The curious fact, however, is that while these children often manifestly enjoyed the relations and the activity situations, they nevertheless made no real headway in learning. One question to which I am presently addressing myself is: to what degree can the introduction of systematic programing—while retaining the motivating techniques—reorient these essentially non-cognitive learning styles and sets already apparently so ingrained by the age of three?

References

Bruner, J. S. 1960. *The process of education* (Cambridge, Mass.: Harvard University Press).

Deutsch, M. 1964. Facilitating development in the pre-school child: social and psychological perspective. *Merrill-Palmer Quart.*, **10**, 3, pp. 249–263.

Flavell, J. H. 1963. *The developmental psychology of Jean Piaget* (Princeton, N.J.: D. Van Nostrand Company, Inc.).

Fowler, W. 1965. A study of process and learning in three-year-old twins and triplets learning to read. *Genet. Psychol. Monogr.*, **72**, pp. 3–89.

———. 1962. Cognitive learning in infancy and early childhood. *Psychol. Bull.*, **59**, 2, pp. 116–152.

———. 1961. Cognitive stimulation, IQ changes, and cognitive learning in three-year-old identical twins and triplets. *Amer. Psychol.*, **16**, 373 (abstract).

Hess, R. D., and Virginia Shipman. 1963. *Cognitive environments of urban pre-school children.* Progress report (Chicago, Ill.: Urban Child Center, University of Chicago).

Hunt, J. McV. 1961. *Intelligence and experience* (New York: The Ronald Press Company).

Piaget, J. 1952. *The origins of intelligence in children* (New York: International Universities Press, Inc.).

Vygotsky, L. S. 1962. *Thought and language* (New York: John Wiley
    & Sons, Inc.).
Welch, L. 1940. A preliminary investigation of some aspects of the hier-
    archical development of concepts. *J. genet. psychol.*, **22**, pp. 359–378.
White, R. W. 1959. Motivation reconsidered: the concept of competence.
    Psychol. Rev., **66**, pp. 297–333.

19   Cognitive Stages and Preschool Education*

LAWRENCE KOHLBERG, *University of Chicago*

In most sophisticated discussion of stages, they are viewed as more or less useful theoretical fictions. We have stages described by Freud, by Erikson, by Gesell, by Piaget. All these stages may be more or less useful abstractions from developmental process; they certainly cannot all be true or real, and perhaps it is useless to expect any to be. Flying in the face of such logical sophistication, I have nevertheless been engaged for the last five years in a program of research designed to show that cognitive stages are real structures to be found in development.

To do this, I have attempted to refine Piaget's concepts and measures of cognitive stages into about twenty tests or tasks; administered these tasks semi-longitudinally to children aged four to eight; and compared children's performance on these tasks to their performance on a battery of the usual psychometric tests of general and special intellectual abilities.

How can such a study show that cognitive stages are real? Needless to say we have been able to reproduce the age differential responses to our tasks which Piaget observes and calls stages, though at slightly earlier ages than Piaget reports. To say that these responses represent cognitive stages, however, implies more than this.

(1) It implies first, that young children's responses represent not mere ignorance or error, but rather a spontaneous manner of thinking about the world that is qualitatively different from the way we adults think, and yet has a structure or logic of its own.

(2) Second, the notion of different developmental structures of thought implies consistency of level of response from task to task. If a

* *Human Development*, 1966, vol. 9, nos. 1–2. Reprinted with permission
of the publisher and S. Karger, Basel/New York.

child's response represents a general structure rather than a specific learning, then the child should demonstrate the same relative structural levels in a variety of tasks.

(3) Third, the concept of stage implies an invariance of sequence in development, a regularity of stepwise progression regardless of cultural teaching or circumstance. Cultural teaching and experience can speed up or slow down development but it cannot change its order or sequence.

I shall try to show what these criteria mean empirically for two of the tasks we have used to get at the child's orientation to reality. Then I shall examine some of the problems reality stages pose for early education.

Our first task assesses children's conceptions of their own dreams. All children have dreams, and the content of these dreams has been much studied. But how does the child experience the dream? What sort of experience does it appear to him to be, when he wakes up and thinks about it? We all know that young children can be quite disturbed by nightmares. According to Piaget this is because the young child thinks of the dream as a set of real events, rather than as a mental imagining.

As an example, in my own study I asked children if they had had a bad dream and if they were frightened when they woke up from their bad dream. *Susie*, aged 4, told us she dreamt about a giant and answered, "Yes, I was scared, my tummy was shaking and I cried and told my mommy about the giant."

Then I asked, "Was it a real giant or was it just pretend? Did the giant just seem to be there, or was it really there?" "It was really there but it left when I woke up. I saw its footprint on the floor."

According to Piaget, *Susie's* response is not to be dismissed as the product of a wild imagination, but represents the young child's general failure to differentiate subjective from objective components of his experience. He calls this failure "realism." One aspect of realism is the confusion of thoughts with things, and of symbols with that which symbols stand for. Children between the ages of two and three often seem to react to pictures and toys of animals or objects as if they really were the animal they represent. On his third birthday, my eldest son was delighted by his bunny birthday cake until it was time to cut it, when he burst into tears at the bunny's destruction.

Often children's tendency to treat the image as real has a more playful quality. As an example, when I showed a picture book to *Pam*, aged 2½, she said, "Ohh, there's a bee. Will the bee sting me?"

I answered no, "It can't sting you, it's only a picture of a bee."

Pam continued, "The bee will sting me" and moved away from the book to the other side of the room. Her tone of voice was half-distress, half-playful.

TABLE I
Sequence in Development of Dream Concept in
American and Atayal Children

Step	Scale Pattern Types						
	0	1	2	3	4	5	6
(1) *Not real*—Recognizes that objects or actions in the dream are not real or are not really there in the room.	—	+	+	+	+	+	+
(2) *Invisible*—Recognizes that other people cannot see his dream.	—	—	+	+	+	+	+
(3) *Internal Origin*—Recognizes that the dream *comes from* inside him.	—	—	—	+	+	+	+
(4) *Internal Location*—Recognizes that the dream *goes on* inside him.	—	—	—	—	+	+	+
(5) *Immaterial*—Recognizes that the dream is not a material substance but is a thought.	—	—	—	—	—	+	+
(6) *Self-caused*—Recognizes that dreams are not caused by God or other agencies but are caused by the self's thought processes.	—	—	—	—	—	—	+
Number of American children in each pattern.	8	10	2	4	16	14	18
Total in scale patterns = 72. Other patterns = 18.							
Average (median) age of American children in given pattern or stage.			4,10	5,0	5,4	6,4	6,5	7,10
Number of Atayal in each pattern.	1	1	3	3	2	2	0
Average age of Atayal of given pattern.	8	8	10	20	12	11	

For quite a while beyond the age that children treat toys and pictures as unreal, they continue to think that dreams are real, however. Table I shows the actual steps of development I have found in children's beliefs about dreams. The first step, achieved before five by most American middle class children, is the recognition that dreams are not real events. The next step, achieved soon thereafter, is that dreams cannot be seen by others. By age six children are clearly aware that dreams take place inside them, and by seven, they are clearly aware that dreams are thoughts caused by themselves.

Case Record of Dream Concept at Two Ages
(4½ and one year later)

Stevie's Dream Concept, Age 4½

(Do you know what a dream is? Do you dream sometimes during the night?)
"Yes. I dreamed I put peanut butter all over the floor and a robber came in to steal and he slipped on the floor and fell down and ran away."
(Were you scared?)
"No."
(What have you had a bad dream about?)
"I've dreamed about a truck running over me."
(Were you scared?)
"I woke up and I was scared. I wake up in the night sometimes and I rock. Then if I rock I won't dream of that."

(1) — Does not recognize dream is not real
{
(When you dreamed about the truck was it a real truck?)
"Yes."
(Was it just that the truck seemed to be there, as if it was there, or was it really there?)
"It was really there."
(Was it the same as when you see a truck during the day?)
"Yes."
}

(See this [a boy doll]? It's a boy, isn't it? Is it a real boy?)
"No, it's just a toy."
(Why did you dream about that truck? What made you have that dream?)

"I have to rock to get a dream. Then if I rock I can dream of something I like. I'll dream I'm flying up to the moon."

(3) + Dreams have an internal origin

(6) — Dreams not self-caused

(Where does the dream come from? Where are dreams made, where do they come from?)
"I don't know."
(Do they come from within you or from outside of you?)
"From inside your eyeball."
(Who makes the dreams come forth? Is it you or somebody else?)
"Your sister."
(While you are dreaming, where is your dream, where does it go or what place is it in?)
"It's in your eyeball. Then it comes out."

(4) — Does not recognize dream goes on inside him

(Is it inside of you or in your room?)
"It stays in your room forever."
(Is it only that it seems to be in the room, as if it is, or is it really in your room?)
"It's really in the room but then you don't see any dream, just air."
(When you dream, are your eyes closed or open?)
"Sometimes closed, sometimes open."
(Then is there something in front of you when you are dreaming?)
"My eyes, the dream."

(2) + Dream is invisible to others

(If your mother is in the room, can she also see your dream?)
"No, she'd need magic to do that. If she had magic, she could turn to something in the dream."
(What about me? If I were in your room, could I see your dream?)
"If you had magic."

(5) — Dream is material (air)

(What is a dream made of?)
"Air."
(Can we touch dreams?)
"No. Your finger would go right through it. You can only touch paper and things you can see. You can only see the dream when you're sleeping."

THE DREAM

Stevie's Dream, Age 5½

Instructions: Ask the child each one of the following questions, always making sure he understands it well. When necessary, change the wording of the questions using terms with which the child is more familiar, but be very careful never to suggest any meaning not included in the instructions.

(1) *Introduction:*
"Do you know what a dream is? Do you dream sometimes during the night?"
(If he says he does not, go on to 3.)

(2) *If he says he dreams, ask:*
"What did you dream about last time, can you tell me a dream you had?"
"A bear got sick and then my mother caught the sickness and I took a stick and hankie and put my clothes in and ran away."
"What have you had a bad dream about?" (If previous dream not a nightmare.)
"What happened after the dream was over? What did you think and do?" (After a bad dream.)
    "I went under the covers."
"Were you scared?"   *Yes*   No
"Were you scared when you woke up?"   Yes   *No*
"Why were(n't) you scared when you woke up?"
    "I forgot about it. I was thinking about other dreams."

(1) + Recognizes that dream events are not real (though some question)
    { "Was it just that the bear *seemed to be there*, or was it really there?"
    { "Was it the same as when you see a bear during the day?"
        "Yes."

(6) + Recognizes dreams are self-caused
    { "Why did you dream about that, what made you have that dream?"
        "I was thinking about skeletons and I popped into that dream."
"Then do you know why we dream, why there are dreams?"
    "Because it's fun to dream."

(3) *The origin of the dream:*

(3) + Recognizes dreams come from within

"Tell me, where does a dream come from?"
"Where are dreams made, from where do they come?"
    "Your mind."
"Do they come from *within you* or from outside of you?"
"Who makes the dreams come forth?"
"Is it *you* or is it somebody else?"
    "Don't know."

(4) *Location of the dream:*

(4) + Recognizes dreams take place inside

"While you are dreaming, where is your dream, where does it go or in what place is it?"
    "It's in my head."
"Is it *inside of you* or in your room?"

(5) *If the dream is in the head, in the thoughts, etc.,*
    (thus internal and not external) say:

"If we could open your head while you are dreaming, if we could look into your head, could we see your dream?"
    "Maybe—no, I don't think so, because there's bones in the head."
"(If not) Why do you say that we could not see your dreams?"

(6) *If the dream is in the room, on the wall, close to his eyes, under the bed, etc.,* say:

"Is it only that the dream seems to be in your room or is it really in your room?"
(If not really in room): "Where is the dream then?"

(2) + Dreams invisible to others

"If your mother is in the room, can she also see your dream?"
    "No."

(7) *Substance of the dream:*

(5) + Dream is immaterial (some-what questionable)

"What is a dream made of?"
    "Thin air."
"Is it made of paper?"
"Then, what is it made of?"
"Can we touch dreams?"
    "No."
"Is a dream a *thought* or is it a thing?"
    "A thought."

The method by which these steps are judged is illustrated in this case record of *Stevie*, at age 4½ and then again at age 5½.

One technical question of great importance about this or any aspect of cognitive development is the question of whether these steps form an invariant order or sequence of development. Table I shows a series of patterns of pluses or minuses called scale types. These patterns indicate that the steps we have mentioned form an invariant order or sequence in development. If there is an invariant order in development, children who have passed a more difficult step in the sequence, indicated by a plus, should also have passed all the easier steps in the sequence and get pluses on all the easier items. This means that all children should fit one of the patterns in Table I. For instance, all children who pass or get a plus on Step 3, recognizing the dream's internal origin, should also pass Step 2 and Step 1. The fact that only 18 out of 90 children do not fit one of these patterns is acceptable evidence for the existence of invariant sequence in the development of the dream concept.

TABLE II
Scale Scores of S from Age Four to Age Five

Age 4	Stevie's Dream	Age 5
—	(1) Actions or objects of the dream are not really there.	±
+	(2) Dreams are not visible to others.	+
+	(3) Dreams do not originate in the external physical world.	+
—	(4) Thinks dreams may take place inside.	+
—	(5) Sure dreams take place inside.	+
—	(6) Dreams are not material things.	?
	(7) Dreams are caused in a purely subjective	
—	or immaterial fashion by the child himself.	+

The importance of this issue of sequence becomes apparent when we ask, "How does the child move from a view of dreams as real to a view of dreams as subjective or mental?" The simplest answer to this question is that the older child has learned the cultural definition of words like "dream" and "real". The child is frequently told by parents that his dreams are not real, that he shouldn't be upset by them, that dreams are in his mind. In the ordinary view, this verbal teaching eventually leads the child from ignorance to knowledge of the culture's definition of the dream. It is a little hard for this verbal learning view to account for invariant sequence in the development of the dream concept since it seems unlikely that children are taught Step 3 later than Step 2 or Step 1. The difficulty in explaining invariant sequence on the basis of adult teaching is pointed up by some cross-cultural data I collected. While I was studying moral development among the Atayal, a Malaysian aboriginal group in Formosa, I found that, like many preliterate tribes, the Atayal believed in the reality of dreams. An example is provided by an informal interview I had with the seventy-year-old village medicine woman. I went to her because I had a bad cold and asked her to treat me. In the course of her diagnostic interviewing I told her I had dreamt of a snake the night before. She told me, "Maybe you're sick because of what you dreamed last night and the snake made you sick."

I asked, "Was it a real snake?"

"No, it was a ghost using a snake's form—if you do some bad thing in the daytime the ghosts punish you at night—your body stayed in bed but your soul went to the mountains with the ghost."

She eventually determined that my ghosts were mad at me because I'd tried to leave them behind, to come to Formosa. Having made the diagnosis, she went on to treatment by a variety of spells. Like good medical people in this country, she refused to guarantee the results of treatment because she wasn't sure how effective her spells were for American ghosts.

In any case, the medicine woman, like most adult Atayal I talked to, equated the soul, the dream, and ghosts. Dreams like ghosts, are neither thoughts nor things, dreams are caused by ghosts and during the dream the soul left the body and experienced things in far places.

When I interviewed Atayal boys and young men of various ages I found a very interesting pattern in the age development of their dream concepts. The youngest Atayal boys were much like the youngest American boys in their response. Until the age of eleven, the Atayal boys seemed to develop toward a subjective conception of the dream through much the same steps as American children, though more slowly. I say they develop through the same steps, because (as Table I shows) the Atayal boys' answers fell into the same sequential scale pattern as the American boys. In other words, the Atayal children tend to develop naturally toward a subjective concept of the dream up to age eleven, even though their elders do not believe dreams are subjective and, hence, are giving them no teaching to this effect. Both the youngest children's conceptions of the dream as real and the school age children's view of the dream as subjective are their own; they are products of the general state of the child's cognitive development, rather than the learning of adult teachings.

If Atayal children develop naturally toward a subjective conception of the dream, how is it that the adults accept a view of dreams as external? At around age eleven something very different seems to happen to the Atayal dream concepts than to American dream concepts.

The boys and young men over eleven score lower on the scale than do the younger children. At around age eleven they first seem to learn the adult culture's view of the dream. But this learning is also in many ways regression to their own earliest modes of belief, since the adults and young child's beliefs are similar in many ways.

In spite of what I have said so far, I'm sure that most of you are *not* yet convinced that young children have a different experience of reality from our own. You may feel, as I often have, that what children say in interviews about dreams as real or about picture book bees that sting them, are mere matters of words. You may feel that while children say all sorts of strange and wonderful things they don't "really" mean them.

What then, in the way of action do notions of the real and of the unreal correspond to? Obviously, this cannot be answered by considering dream concepts, but requires a more concrete situation. In constructing such a situation we have been guided by a notion of Piaget's related to the appearance—reality or subjective—objective distinction. It is apparent that one of the major results of the differentiation of subjective and objective is the construction of a world of permanent, unchanging, objects. The infant under ten months does not have a conception of a permanent object. If, when he is reaching toward a bright toy, it is covered with a handkerchief, he stops reaching; the toy no longer exists to him. By 18 months he knows objects permanently exist though he cannot see them, but it is not until he is about six years old that he views their physical dimensions and identity as unchangeable. Things that change in appearance change in reality.

It is, of course, part of the charm of young childhood that objects can change their identity and that the young child can play at being, and feel he really is, a variety of persons and creatures. Sometimes this fluidity in the identity of things is a source of anxiety, sometimes of delight. As an example, last Halloween we bought my boy, just turned three, a dog costume.

We put it on him in front of the mirror and he said, "I'm a doggie" and laughed delightedly. I asked him, "Are you a doggie or are you really a boy?" "I'm a doggie, real doggie" and he ran to the kitchen, took a dog biscuit and half-pretended, half-tried to eat it.

Because children vary too much in their reactions to people in costume and masks, and because such stimuli are too closely related to self, we have chosen another situation for systematic study of children's constancy reactions. Instead of putting a mask on a human, we put a mask of a small fierce dog on a live and well-trained cat named *Maynard*. Children of three and four, when asked what the animal is, tend to say it is now a dog, and feed it dog food when given a choice.

Children of six tend to be firmly aware of what is going on, as do many of the five-year-olds. Of most interest are the reactions of the five-year-olds who can't make up their mind what is going on.

As an example, *Janice* pets the cat with warmth before the mask is put on. She withdraws sharply after the mask is put on, but looks closely at the animal. When asked, she says the animal is a dog but adds, "If I put my finger near his mouth, he really won't bit me, will he?" She doesn't try the experiment. When pressed, she says the cat turned into a dog, but when pressed further, says it's not a real dog, it just has on a dog face. Finally, she agrees to pet it and does so very gingerly. Again, she is asked whether it is a real dog and she answers, "That's the problem, is it a cat or a dog? I think it's a dog. I'll feel his ears. It is a dog . . . but still it has cat's eyes so how can it be a dog? I think it's a dog."

Janice has a true scientific open-minded and exploratory attitude toward the animal's identity, which she will soon lose for a closed-minded view that cats are cats and dogs are dogs and cats can't be dogs no matter what.

In general, what the children say about the animal corresponds with how they act toward him. Only the children who say he is a real dog, refuse to pet the animal and are generally fearful. We are now trying to determine whether the fear is due to the change or to the appearance of the dog as such, so we are now turning Maynard into Harvey, our rabbit. In any case we expect to continue to find consistency in children's verbal and action orientations.

In addition to sequence, we find consistency in children's responses to various tasks involving reality-appearance differentiation. This consistency is indicated by the second factor in Table III. It suggests that the child's level of reality orientation corresponds to a general mental-cognitive structure rather than to momentary or situational wishes or fears.

Given such evidence of the reality of stages, what are its implications for education.

In the United States, the doctrine of stages was assumed for sometime to mean that children's behavior unfolded through a series of age-specific patterns, and that these patterns and their order was wired into the organism. This indeed was the view of Gesell, and Americans misunderstood European stage theorists as maintaining the same thing. The implications of the Gesellian theory for early education were clear; early teaching and stimulation would do no good since we must wait for the unfolding of the behavior, or at least the unfolding of the readiness to learn it.

TABLE III
Loadings of Piaget Reality-Constancy Tasks
on First Centroid Factor at Two Ages*

	Younger subjects First		Older subjects First	
	Factor	M.A.	Factor	M.A.
Cat constancy	78	22	43	31
Sex constancy	63	56	60	39
Conservation of substance	53	30	22	59
Dream	44	47	16	56
Magic	20	71	48	58
Concept	05	55	52	20
Inclusion	(all Ss failed)		43	60

* This factor was extracted from the covariance matrix remaining when the indicated product moment correlations of each task with Stanford Binet mental age had been partialled out.

In contrast, Piaget used the existence of stages to argue that basic cognitive structures are not wired in, but are general forms of equilibrium resulting from the interaction between organism and environment. If children have their own logic, adult logic or mental structure cannot be derived from innate neurological patterning because such patterning should hold also in childhood. It is hardly plausible to view a succession of spaces, times and logics as an evolutionary and functional program of innate wiring.

At the same time, however, as Dr. Fowler has suggested, Piaget argued that stages indicate that mental structure is not merely a reflection of external physical realities or social concepts of different complexities. The structure of the child's concepts in Piaget's view is not only less complex than the adult's—it is different.

In relation to early teaching, this implies the need for a clear awareness of the difference between teaching specific skills and concepts and attempting to develop general cognitive structures.

The programs for early teaching of reading used by William Fowler or Omar K. Moore clearly show that the Gesellian view is wrong. The teaching of reading, however, does not involve the development of cognitive structure. Development of cognitive structure occurs in the process of developing spoken language, the translation of spoken language into visual signs is mainly the acquisition of sensory motor skills. Development of number concepts involves much more in the way of cognitive-structural change, but is still relatively specific. When we come to orientations to reality we face a much more general issue.

Progressive educations have tended to nurture the child's lack of differentiation of appearance and play from reality as a source of creativity, imagination and self-expression. The imaginative freedom of preschool thought and art, they feel, all too soon becomes suppressed by the elementary school child's desire to rigidly copy reality, apply rules and find the right and true answer.

Perhaps I can dramatize the limitations of this approach by describing an exchange in a first grade science program. A potted cactus stood before the class and the children were asked to discuss whether it was a plant or animal and how they could tell. Eventually all the children but one agreed it was a plant and that plants didn't move, didn't ingest food, etc. One boy held out, however, and said he still thought it was an animal disguised as a plant. One could never tell, however, he said, because everytime the animal saw someone coming it would instantly turn back into a plant. The teacher, in the progressive spirit, accepted and examined this foolproof hypothesis with open-minded equanimity. The boy involved had answered our Piaget questions two years earlier in a similar spirit, though without the self-enclosed systematization. The adults in his home had consciously tried hard to enter into his own child's world with him, and so, perhaps together with progressive teachers had protected this mode of thought.

If this interchange illustrates the limitations of the progressive approach to preschooler's reality sense or creativity, it indicates the limitations of conservative approaches, as well. Obviously, the mode of thought illustrated by this child is quite resistant to efforts to impose adult cultural realities and adult skills upon the child. Neither social suppression, nor the elaborate teaching of a science curriculum, would appear to succeed in bringing about the developmental transformation of this mode of thought to a more mature pattern. What seems required is a new approach which would take into account the fact that the preschooler's orientation to reality is a developmental stage which should be integrated into later stages of development. To put off "reality" until elementary school is only to divorce the child's preschool world of the subjective from the elementary school world of the objective. What seems required is an approach which would not suppress the cognitive energies employed in preschool thought structures but would encourage their gradual transformation into more adult forms. This requires that the preschool cognitive stimulation programs be defined in terms of the child's concepts which are to develop rather than in terms of adult concepts of science or of number or of language which are to be taught.

20   Some Effects of Deprivation
            on Intelligence, Achievement,
            and Cognitive Growth*

ROBERT L. GREEN, *Michigan State University*
LOUIS J. HOFMANN, *Yeshiva University*
ROBERT F. MORGAN, *Hawaii State Hospital*

Many assumptions have been made concerning the probable effects of extended periods of non-schooling. A typical assumption is that basic learning such as the attainment of verbal concepts, reading comprehension, and arithmetic reasoning can be acquired more readily in a formal school setting with a teacher trained in educational methodology. However, a review of the literature indicates that the above assumption, so often taken for granted, rarely has been empirically assessed. This lack of psychological research on the effects of non-schooling stems from the national trend of universal school attendance.

There is, however, a body of research focusing on such factors as the impact of the environment on school achievement with varying individual and measurement characteristics. There are a few studies touching on selected aspects of the cognitively deprived child. What studies there are can be organized into the areas of (1) intelligence, (2) achievement, and (3) cognitive growth.

Intelligence Disadvantage

Examination of the research to date shows that an individual's intelligence in the school context is not independent of many aspects of that context, nor of several personal characteristics brought to the schooling situation, nor of certain aspects of the tests used to measure intelligence while in the educational context. Specifically, the variables can be schematized as follows: (1) *Personal Characteristics*—(age, sex, race, motivation); (2) *Context Characteristics*—Immediate (socio-economic class, parental education and marital status, number of siblings, radio in the home, grade level, and amount of prior education), General—

* *The Journal of Negro Education*, Winter 1967, vol. 36, no. 1. Reprinted by permission. This article is based on research supported by cooperative research project #2321, U.S. Office of Education.

(national stress [war versus peace], population density [urban versus rural], caste limits [degree of segregation], and cognitive deprivation); (3) *Measurement Characteristics* (time emphasis [speeded versus non-speeded items], examiner [color and attitude], and language emphasis [verbal versus non-verbal items]).

Personal Characteristics

The individual represents a composite of the fixed factors of his heredity, and these factors provide a basis for the molding influence of the environment. The limits of a general intelligence or an adaptational aptitude may well be spelled out by individual heredity. However, the two fixed characteristics which past research has indicated as highly relevant to intelligence and schooling are sex and race.

Arlitt (1922) found that Negro girls aged 5 and 6 intellectually excelled the Negro boys of the same ages in Philadelphia and New Orleans. Anastasi and D'Angelo (1952) found that, in Northern mixed and unmixed neighborhoods, five-year-old white girls surpassed white boys in intelligence while Negro boys surpassed Negro girls of the same age levels. The difference was more pronounced in racially unmixed neighborhoods. Thus, at an age where white and Negro intelligence is equatable, the general trend is that girls outperform the boys, but as the degree of caste limitation is increased, the relationship may reverse itself. Unfortunately, Arlitt's pooling of Negro children from segregated New Orleans and unsegregated Philadelphia precludes confirmation of Anastasi's findings.

Just as the influence of sex on intelligence typically tends to favor one sex over the other but may reverse with certain caste limitations, race as an influence on intelligence typically tends to favor one race over another (whites over Negroes in the United States). This influence may also fluctuate according to the severity of caste limitations.

Of the literature cited here, four studies used white and Negro comparison groups of school children. (Only groups actually tested by the author in question are being considered as "comparison groups".) In three of the four studies (Anastasi and D'Angelo, 1952; Clarke, 1941; Higgins and Sivers, 1958), children drawn from Northern integrated schools and areas were tested. In all three, no significant I.Q. differences were found between races. One did find Negroes to be significantly lower on the Colored Raven Progressive Matrices (CRPM) I.Q., but they attributed this to deficiency in a special skill since no significant difference was found on the Stanford-Binet I.Q. On the other hand, in the fourth study (24) in which the sample was drawn from a segregated community, Negroes were found to have significantly lower Binet or

Otis I.Q.'s than whites. These data suggest race, in itself, has no effect on general aptitude except in the context of severe caste limitation.

Five studies (Arlitt, 1922; Higgins and Sivers, 1958; Kennedy *et al.*, 1961; Tomlinson, 1944; Young and Bright, 1954) testing intelligence at different ages all found the I.Q. of Negro children to decrease with age. Higgins and Sivers also found the I.Q.'s of white children (from the lower socio-economic class) to decrease with age. Tomlinson found the biggest jump to be between ages 4 and 5 suggesting either a critical period, a traumatic effect from introduction into a school situation, or both. In all cases, white and Negro intelligence were comparable when tested from ages 4 to 6. The apparent negative effect of schooling context over time on the intelligence of lower-class white and Negro children is certainly contrary to what is normally expected of the education process.

The motivation to perform well on an intelligence test can influence the resultant I.Q. This variable fits better under the rubric of individual characteristics rather than with the measurement variables since three studies show motivation may often, regarding Negroes, be a permanently depressed personal characteristic independent of the testing context. Miner (1957) suggests that this depressed motivation definitely lowers the measured I.Q.'s of many Negroes. Roen (1960) agrees and links the depressed motivation to a lack of self-confidence, and Davidson *et al.*, (1950) attributes it to a lack of social goals in the face of limited opportunity. Thus, the attitudes reinforced in a Negro by his educational context will shape the motivational level which, in turn, determines how open the child's intelligence will be to growth in that same educational context.

Context Characteristics

Among the factors in a child's immediate context studied as germane to its intellectual growth are socio-economic class, parental education and marital status, number of siblings, the presence of a radio in the home, the amount of prior education, and grade level. Five studies (Arlitt, 1922; Blanks, 1955; Horton and Crump, 1962; John, 1962; Kennedy *et al.*, 1961) show intelligence to increase with increasing socio-economic status of the individual or his family. A sixth study (Jenkins, 1943) points out that, of sixteen Negro children with an I.Q. over 160, none had parents in lower than middle-class socio-economic status. The lowest educational level among the parents was high school graduation. Horton and Crump (1962) also found, in the comparison of three-year-old Negro children of high and low intelligence, that the mothers' education, the number of siblings, and the number of married parents differentiated the groups. Intelligence increased with decreasing number of siblings and decreasing frequency of unmarried parents. Robinson and Meenes (1947), in testing Negro third graders on I.Q., did not find that any of the above factors correlated significantly with intelligence, but they did find that having a radio in the home did. Lorge (1945) tested intelligence before and after a twenty-year interval and found change to depend greatly on the education received in between. Thus, intelligence is not only related to schooling, but also may be contingent to an extent on its continuation.

Recently, a group of investigators reported a study in depth of children in a Southern county whose schools had been closed for several years to prevent integration (Green *et al.*, 1964). The predominantly low educational level of the parents offered little alternate instruction at home. Intelligence, achievement, social, and demographic data were collected for approximately 1700 children aged 5 to 22. The sample was divided into those having had no schooling whatsoever (*No Education* group) and those receiving at least some out-of-county education (*Education* group). The mean I.Q. score of the *Education* group (still victims of *some* non-schooling) was approximately 80. Up to the age of 8, this was also the mean I.Q. for the *No Education* group; after age 8, the overall mean I.Q. of children without any formal schooling averaged 65. I.Q. for both groups appeared to be lower, the older the age group tested. Thus, in an actual sample of children undergoing the non-schooling treatment, measured intelligence level appeared to be dependent upon formal instruction at all ages.

One final factor occasionally linked to the intelligence of a child is the grade in which he happens to be. Lacy (1926), for example, found the I.Q.'s of Negro children to decrease with increasing grade, finally leveling off between sixth and twelfth grade. Lorge (1945), however, emphasized that years of school attendance and the highest grade completed are not always the same thing: i.e., grade level is not synonymous with the time exposed to education nor is it synonymous with age. In the South especially, children of quite advanced age are found in the early grades since promotion is contingent on a fixed level of achievement. Another study suggests that grade level in itself influences intelligence only as it correlates with age; e.g., Kennedy *et al.* (1961), studying Southern Negro children (where age and grade are not as highly correlated as elsewhere in the United States), found no significant difference in I.Q. by grade level but found a very significant difference by age.

In terms of the general context, national stress was reported to have depressed I.Q. in Holland's schools during World War II (deGroot, 1948). Based on that study, increasing population density appears to lead to increased intelligence. Coppinger and Ammons (1952) found the

I.Q.'s of Louisiana Negroes to be higher in urban than rural areas. Kennedy *et al.* (1961), in their survey of five Southern states, found no significant difference between rural and urban Negro I.Q.'s but did find a significant higher urban I.Q. than either one of the latter two. All of Jenkins' (1943) Negro children who earned I.Q.'s of 160 or higher came from major cities. He suggests that only the cities have the recognition methods and necessary facilities to nourish exceptionally intelligent Negro children.

The effects of caste limits on intelligence have been discussed throughout this section, especially under the topic of race and sex. Low socio-economic status, as applied to all races, and segregation and discrimination against minorities (predominantly the Negroes) provide a general context against which the intelligence (and achievement) of the minorities involved is far from independent.

Measurement Characteristics

As previously mentioned, a low caste group may have typically depressed achievement motivation to carry into an intelligence testing situation. Items depending heavily upon high motivation will therefore present more difficulty for a group of this nature than would items not as heavily motivation-weighted. Davidson *et al.* (1950), in comparing the intelligence test results of white and Negro psychoneurotics, definitely found the Negroes performing better at passive (unspeeded) attention problems than at active (speeded) attention problems. Bean's (1942) administration of a verbal and non-verbal I.Q. test to Louisiana Negro eighth graders and his conclusion (that since both elicited low scores, cultural opportunity—verbal test—alone is an insufficient explanation for low Negro I.Q.) is suspect because both tests were speeded.

Pasamanick and Knobloch (1955) found Negro children at age 2 (in their third I.Q. test session) showing sudden decline in verbal responsiveness to a white examiner. This illustrates that attitude, empathy, color, all the things an examiner's manner and appearance convey to the subject, may be relevant variables even at the tender age of two years.

An attempt has often been made to differentiate the intelligence of different groups on the basis of verbal versus non-verbal (or performance) intelligence tests. Occasionally, non-verbal measures are labeled "culture-free." However, the high correlation usually seen between verbal and non-verbal I.Q. tests suggests that they have a lot in common. Predictably then, "verbal" and "non-verbal" differences will be contradictory in different studies depending mostly on sampling error. For example, in testing the I.Q. of Southern Negro children both Bean (1942) and Kennedy *et al.* (1961) found verbal items to elicit lower I.Q.'s while Hammer (1954) and Newland and Lawrence (1953) found non-verbal items to elicit lower I.Q.'s. Clarke (1941), in a Northern comparison between white and Negro children, found the Negroes superior on verbal items. In general, past opinion has been that Negroes are at a disadvantage with the verbal items and at an advantage with non-verbal since the latter are supposedly more free from the effects of cultural deprivation. However, the research does not consistently support this notion.

As previously mentioned, Higgins and Sivers (1958) found Negroes to fall below whites on the Colored Raven Progressive Matrices (CRPM), a "culture-free" I.Q., although the Stanford-Binet showed no significant differences for the same groups. Levinson (1961) demonstrated that Jewish children, initially scoring equally well on verbal and non-verbal items, showed higher verbal than non-verbal I.Q.'s after two years in a Yeshiva Day School that emphasized verbal facility. Thus, intelligence tests, influenced to an extent by the presence or absence of verbal training, are also influenced by training and acculturation in general. Neither the intelligence tests nor the children who take them are ever "culture-free."

Achievement Disadvantage

Although, as the preceding section has demonstrated, intelligence is no longer considered to be a single general factor invariable for the individual, it still can be treated as a relatively stable set of aptitude limits. Between these limits fall the achievement levels elicited by specific tasks. Logically then, achievement should be sensitive to the same variables as intelligence and, in addition, fluctuate with factors of its own. Past research shows this to be the case. Of the research to be cited in this section, some refer to the same factors as the preceding section while others focus in unexpected directions. The variables to be presented can be schematized as follows: (1) *Personal Characteristics* (motivation, health, attention span, verbal ability, and imagination); (2) *Context Characteristics*—Immediate (socio-economic class, home conditions [number of parents, number of siblings, parents' education, parents' emphasis on self-responsibility, degree of physical punishment, verbal environment], school conditions [verbal facilities, remedial programs]), General (caste limits [degree of segregation] and cognitive deprivation); and (3) *Measurement Characteristics* (time emphasis, examiner, language emphasis).

Personal Characteristics

Schultz (1958), when testing the achievement of Florida ninth graders, found high achievement to be inversely correlated with the number of days absent from school. This might be due to ill health causing reduced exposure to educational content. Ransom (1939) found good health to correlate with good achievement. He also found attention span as well as health to be relevant to achievement for Atlanta first graders. Scott (1963), after testing Oregon fifth and sixth graders, decided reading ability is the key to ability in other areas such as arithmetic and social studies. It was noted in the preceding section that all intelligence tests correlate somewhat with verbal ability (even the "nonverbal"). It would seem, then, that the development of verbal ability is a crucial factor in both intelligence and achievement. Finally, Milner (1951) suggests that imagination may be a relevant variable as low scorers on a mental maturity test had relatively less of it than the high scorers.

Context Characteristics

Among the immediate contextual variables, once again socio-economic class and certain home conditions apply. Curry (1962) found that scores of Southwestern white sixth graders on a standardized achievement test increased with socio-economic class rise with the exception of the highest scoring group which seemed to be independent of class level. Another finding was that parents' occupation levels correlated with a child's achievement.

Schultz also found achievement relating to number of parents, number of siblings, and parental education level—all in the expected direction. Milner confirmed the importance of parental education in her study and added the observed significant effects of a warm emotional and highly verbal family environment (correlated with high achievement) and high incidence of physical punishment (correlated with low achievement). Ransom also stressed the relevance of home conditions in general.

Willis (1939), in his study, found differential progress in a remedial reading program varying with the amount of verbal facilities (number of books in the library) the school had to offer. A group of white ninth graders in Nashville showed greater improvement than an equally intelligent group of Negro ninth graders. The enrichment program itself facilitated reading ability in both groups. Brazziel and Gordon (1963) also reported facilitating effects when a special program (Higher Horizons) was transplanted from New York to a Southern segregated Negro seventh grade. By stressing self-concepts, self-expression, imagination, and better parent-teacher relations, reading and arithmetic performance showed improvement.

Green *et al.* (1964), in their study of educationally deprived children found the *Education* group to attain higher mean grade equivalent scores than the *No Education* group on all subtests of the Stanford Achievement

Tests at all age levels. Both groups achieved at lower levels than a comparison group from a neighboring (similarly rural) county. Schooling made the greatest difference for spelling and language at early ages and for arithmetic at older ages; paragraph meaning and paragraph comprehension showed relatively uniform differences at all age levels investigated. Educationally deprived children as old as 17 demonstrated imperfect time-telling ability on a time-telling test. The 14- through 18-year-olds did not tell time significantly better than the neighboring county's schooled third and fourth graders. Thus, the overall effect of the absence of local schools was a depression of readiness skills at all age levels, even for children who had been exposed to a little formal education.

Among the general contextual characteristics, caste limitations again appear to be important. Hansen (1963) presents statistics to show that the integration of Washington, D. C., led to higher Negro achievement without depressing the achievement level of the white children. This was attributed to the more efficient pooling of resources although it is probable that the cessation of separate education involves cognitive effects as well as resource-using efficiency. Recently integrated areas offer excellent research situations for relating the cognitive variables to achievement. An additional finding in this area by McQueen and Churn (1960) is that, on the whole, elementary school students in a long integrated western community do not significantly differ in achievement according to race.

Cognitive deprivation, whether of educational, social, or cultural nature relates to both intelligence and achievement in the school situation. It, therefore, has been included in the preceding variables schema without discussion since the next section will present the handful of pertinent articles in some detail.

Cognitive Disadvantage

The published papers touching on cognitive deprivation, while few in number, compensate for their low frequency with a richness in ideational quality. These contributions may be schematized as follows: (1) *Personal Characteristics* (emotional atmosphere, lack of teacher interest, social deprivation and restrictions); (2) *Critical Age Period* (I.Q. spread, educational facilities for deprived children); and (3) *Perceptual Deprivation Experiments in the Laboratory* (lack of cognitive deprivation, importance of cognitive deprivation).

Personal Characteristics

The enrichment programs mentioned in the preceding section showed relative success in raising the achievement level of the school children exposed to such programs. Deprivation forms the other side of the coin and is, the literature suggests, the more important side. Brazziel and Terrell (1962), for example, reported a first grade class receiving abundant interest and encouragement to reach the fiftieth percentile of an intelligence test after seven months while three control classes receiving apparently lukewarm attention and interest fell between the thirteenth and sixteenth percentiles. Thus, an enriched emotional atmosphere secured average performance while slight deprivation of teacher interest tremendously depressed the measured intelligence.

This emotional deprivation on the teacher's part, with its apparently devastating effects, has been observed to be more frequent with selected groups of children. Deutsch (1960) noted that the teachers of Negro children often reinforce negative self-images in their students by their verbal behavior.

The social deprivation and restriction inherent in most institutions may also hamper a child's intellectual development. Green and Zigler (1962) reported retarded performance on monotonous tasks to occur with institutionalized retarded children but not with non-institutionalized retarded children and normals.

Green *et al.* (1964) found several pronounced cognitive effects of non-schooling in their sample. For both deprived groups, the predominant admired model was one or the other parent. Peers, teachers and professional figures were rarely chosen. Occupational aspirations, positively related in the sample to educational aspiration, were found to be higher in the *Education* group. However, the realism of the vocational choices was not significantly related to the amount of non-schooling. The average self-concept of ability for both groups of educationally deprived children did *not* differ significantly from the neighboring county's children or from a large sample of Northern children. This was attributed to either an unintentionally biased sample, an unexpected independence of self-concept from schooling, or to the nation-wide interest and attention (and testing) the deprived children were receiving.

Critical Age Period

There also seems to be evidence for a critical age period during which the effects of deprivation may be maximized. Jackson (1958) puts this time period between nine months and kindegarten age as judged by the jump in I.Q. spread. Levine (1962) suggests that the crucial time for developing the capacity of environmental interpretation, symbolism, and language is between the ages of 2 and 4. He recommends educational facilities for lower socio-economic class children who might otherwise be deprived of adequate stimulation from their surroundings during these critical years. Milner (1951) (discussed in the preceding section) also advocated pre-school training programs for emotionally deprived children.

Perceptual Deprivation Experiments in the Laboratory

Bruner (1961) takes the deprivation problem out of the necessary past monopoly of field experiments by connecting perceptual deprivation experiments performed under the close control of the laboratory with the cognitive deprivation occurring daily in the lives of thousands of children. Lack of cognitive deprivation, Bruner maintains, is prerequisite to a child's capacity for adaptive inference in dealing with his environment. Deutsch (1960), Brazziel and Terrell (1962), and Green and Zigler (1962) have pointed to the importance of cognitive deprivation via a child's teacher or his institutional surroundings.

The effects of social and cultural deprivation have then been sifted for years. Educational deprivation's effects have been touched upon only recently. Research must move quickly to catch up with the flood of the *suggested* disadvantage of inferior or aborted education on intelligence, achievement, and the many facets of cognitive growth. To what extent and in what ways are the formalized means of cultural transmission central to adaptation to the environment? It has taken psychology a long time to formulate the question in testable terms. The answers are only just beginning to emerge.

References

Anastasi, Anne, and Rita Y. D'Angelo. 1952. A comparison of Negro and white preschool children in language development and Goodenough draw-a-man I.Q. *J. genet. Psychol.*, **81**, pp. 147–165.

Arlitt, Ada Hart. 1922. The relation of intelligence to age in Negro children. *J. appl. Psychol.*, **6**, pp. 378–384.

Bean, L. 1942. Negro responses to verbal and non-verbal test materials. *J. Psychol.*, **13**, pp. 343–350.

Blanks, A. C. 1955. A comparative study of mentally bright and mentally dull Negro high school seniors (with reference to personality, background, school achievement, interest, ambition, and school marks). *Dissert. Abstr.*, **15**, pp. 1200–1201.

Brazziel, W. F., and Margaret Gordon. 1963. Replications of some aspects of the higher horizons program in a southern junior high school. *J. Negro Educ.*, **33**, pp. 107–113.

————, and Mary Terrell. 1962. An experiment in the development of readiness in a culturally disadvantaged group of first grade children. *J. Negro Educ.*, **31**, pp. 4–7.

Bruner, J. S. 1961. *The cognitive consequences of early sensory deprivation* (Cambridge, Mass.: Harvard University Press).

Clarke, D. P. 1941. Stanford-Binet scale "L" response patterns in matched racial groups. *J. Negro Educ.*, **10**, pp. 230–238.

Coppinger, N. W., and R. B. Ammons. 1952. The full-range picture vocabulary test: VIII. A normative study of Negro children. *J. clin. Psychol.*, **8**, pp. 136–140.

Curry, R. L. 1962. The effects of socio-economic status on the scholastic achievement of sixth grade children. *Brit. J. educ. Psychol.*

Davidson, K. S., *et al.* 1950. A preliminary study of Negro and white differences on form I on the Wechsler-Bellevue scale. *J. consult. Psychol.*, **14**, pp. 489–492.

deGroot, A. D. 1948. War and the intelligence of youth. *J. abnorm. soc. Psychol.*, **43**, pp. 596–597.

Deutsch, M. 1960. Minority group and class status as related to social and personality factors in scholastic achievement. *Soc. appl. Anthrop.*, Monograph No. 2, pp. 1–32.

Green, C., and E. Zigler. 1962. Social deprivation and the performance of retarded and normal children on a satiation type test. *Child Develpm.*, **33**, pp. 499–508.

Green, R. L., *et al.* 1964. *The educational status of children in a district without public schools.* Cooperative Research Project No. 2321 (Washington, D.C.: U.S. Office of Education, Department of Health, Education, and Welfare).

Hammer, E. F. 1954. Comparison of the performances of Negro children and adolescents on two tests of intelligence, one as an emergency scale. *J. genet. Psychol.*, **84**, pp. 85–93.

Hansen, C. F. 1963. The scholastic performances of Negro and white pupils in the integrated public schools of the District of Columbia. *J. educ. Soc.*, **36**, pp. 287–291.

Higgins, C., and Cathryne H. Sivers. 1958. A comparison of Stanford-Binet and colored raven progressive matrices I.Q.'s for children with low socio-economic status. *J. consult. Psychol.*, **20**, pp. 265–268.

Horton, C. P., and E. P. Crump. 1962. Growth and development XI: descriptive analysis of the backgrounds of 76 Negro children whose scores are above or below average on the Merrill-Palmer scale of mental tests at three years of age. *J. genet. Psychol.*, **100**, pp. 255–265.

Jackson, E. Grant. 1958. The impact of environment on racial achievement. *J. Human Relat.*, **6**, pp. 47–63.

Jenkins, M. D. 1943. Case studies of Negro children of Binet I.Q. 160 and above. *J. Negro Educ.*, **12**, pp. 159–166.

John, Vera P. 1962. The intellectual development of slum children: some preliminary findings. *Panel: Programs for the socially deprived, urban child.*

Kennedy, W. A., V. Van De Riet, and J. C. White, Jr. 1961. *The standardization of the 1960 revision of the Stanford-Binet intelligence scale on Negro elementary school children in the Southeastern United States.* Cooperative Research Project No. 954 (Washington, D.C.: U.S. Office of Education, Department of Health, Education and Welfare).

Lacy, L. D. March 1926. Relative intelligence of white and colored children. *Elem. Sch. J.*, pp. 542–546.

Levine, D. U. 1962. City schools today: too late with too little? *Phi Delta Kappan*, **44**, pp. 80–83.

Levinson, B. 1961. Subcultural values and I.Q. stability. *J. genet. Psychol.*, **98**, pp. 69–82.

Lorge, I. 1945. Schooling makes a difference. *Teach. Coll. Rec.*, **46**, pp. 483–492.

McQueen, R., and B. Churn. September 1960. The intelligence and educational achievement of a matched sample of white and Negro students. *Sch. and Soc.*, **88**, pp. 327–329.

Milner, Esther. June 1951. A study of the relationship between reading readiness in grade one school children and patterns of parent-child interaction. *Child Develpm.*, **22**, pp. 95–112.

J. B. Miner. 1957. *Intelligence in the United States* (New York: Springer Publishing Co., Inc.).

Newland, T. E., and W. C. Lawrence. 1953. Chicago non-verbal examination results of an East Tennessee Negro population. *J. clin. Psychol.*, **9**, pp. 44–46.

Pasamanick, B., and Hild Knobloch. 1955. Early language behavior in Negro children and the testing of intelligence. *J. abnorm. soc. Psychol.*, **50**, pp. 401–402.

Ransom, Katharine A. 1939. A study of reading readiness. *Peabody J. Educ.*, **16**, pp. 276–284.

Robinson, Mary Louise, and M. Meenes. 1947. The relationship between test I intelligence of third grade Negro children and the occupations of their parents. *J. Negro Educ.*, **16**, pp. 136–141.

Roen, S. 1960. Personality and Negro-white intelligence. *J. abnorm. soc. Psychol.*, **61**, pp. 148–150.

Schultz, R. E. 1958. A comparison of Negro pupils ranking high with those ranking low in educational achievement. *J. educ. Sociol.*, **31**, pp. 265–270.

Scott, Carrie M. 1963. The relationship between intelligence quotients and gain in reading achievement with arithmetic reasoning, social studies, and science. *J. educ. Res.*, **56**, pp. 322–326.

Tomlinson, Helen. 1944. Differences between pre-school Negro children and their older siblings on the Stanford-Binet scale. *J. Negro Educ.*, **12**, pp. 474–479.

Willis, L. J. November 1939. A comparative study of the reading achievements of white and Negro children. *Peabody J. Educ.*, **17**, pp. 166–171.

Young, Florence M., and H. A. Bright. 1954. Results of testing 81 Negro rural juveniles with the Wechsler intelligence scale for children. *J. soc. Psychol.*, **39**, pp. 219–226.

21   Effects of Adoption on Children from Institutions*

HAROLD M. SKEELS, *National Institute of Mental Health*

The National Institute of Mental Health is presently carrying on three followup studies of adults who were reared away from their own parents. The purpose is to determine the adult status of children previously studied by the Iowa Child Welfare Research Station, State University of Iowa, in cooperation with the Children's Division, Iowa Board of Control of State Institutions, which initiated modes of intervention in infancy or early childhood. These include followup studies of—

  I. A longitudinal study of 100 adopted children (Skodak and Skeels, 1949). The followup of this study is being carried on by the original investigators.

  II. A study of the effects of differential stimulation on mentally retarded children (Skeels and Dye, 1938). The followup of this study is also being carried on by the original investigator.

  III. A study of the mental development in adoptive homes of children whose biological mothers were mentally retarded (Skeels and Harms, 1948). The followup of this study is being carried on by Lowell W. Schenke, psychologist, Iowa Board of Control of State Institutions, with one of the original investigators (the writer) serving as consultant.

* Reprinted with permission of Harold M. Skeels and *Children*, January–February 1965, U.S. Department of Health, Education, and Welfare, Welfare Administration, Children's Bureau.

In all three of these studies, the children selected for study were considered to be biologically sound and without demonstrable abnormality as determined through diagnostic evaluation by competent pediatricians. With the inclusion of the present followup studies, they cover a life span of 30 years, the present ages of the subjects being within a range of 25 to 35 years.

Adopted Children

In regard to the followup of Study I, all adoptive parents and adopted children have been located after a lapse of 16 years since the last contacts of the earlier study. Interviews with adoptive parents and their adult adopted children are nearing completion. Analysis of the data will start in the near future.

Preliminary indications are that these adoptive children as adults are achieving at levels consistently higher than would have been predicted from the intellectual, educational, or socio-economic level of the biological parents, and equal to the expectancy for children living in the homes of natural parents capable of providing environmental impacts similar to those which have been provided by the adoptive parents.

Mentally Retarded Children

In regard to followup of Study II, all subjects have been located after a lapse of 21 years, all interviews completed, with the data presently being processed.

Preliminary findings of this followup study are particularly startling. In the original study, 13 children in an experimental group, all mentally retarded at the beginning of the study, were at an early age transferred from one institution to another which provided a much higher degree of one-to-one emotional relationship between mother-surrogates and the children. Later, 11 of these children were placed in adoptive homes.

A contrast group of 12 children, initially at a higher level of intelligence than those in the experimental group, remained in a relatively non-stimulating institutional environment over a prolonged period of time. In the initial study, the children in the experimental group showed a decided increase in rate of mental growth, whereas the children in the contrast group showed progressive mental retardation.

In the adult followup study, the two groups continued to be remarkably divergent. All 13 children in the experimental group are self-supporting, and none is a ward of any institution, public or private. Eleven of the 13 children are married, and 9 of these have children.

Of the 12 children in the contrast group, 1 died in adolescence following continued residence in a State institution for the mentally retarded; 4 are still wards of institutions—1 of these is in a mental hospital, and 3 are in institutions for the mentally retarded. Among those no longer wards of institutions, only two have married, and one of these is divorced. Two of the four females in the contrast group were sterilized in late adolescence to preclude the possibility of procreation if later placed out to work.

In education, disparity between the two groups is great. In the experimental group, the median grade completed is the 12th; in the contrast group, the 3d. Four subjects in the experimental group have had one year or more of college work, one of the boys having received a B.A. degree. Occupationally, the experimental group ranges from professional and semiprofessional positions to semiskilled labor or domestic work. In the contrast group, 50 percent of the subjects are unemployed, and those that are employed are, with the exception of one person, unskilled laborers.

One girl in the experimental group who initially had an IQ of 35 has subsequently graduated from high school and taken one semester of work at a college. She is married and has two boys. These boys have been given intelligence tests and have achieved IQ scores of 128 and 107.

If this girl had had the continuing experience characteristic of those in the contrast group, she would have remained all these years on a custodial ward in an institution for the mentally retarded, or have been sterilized in late adolescence or early adulthood and subsequently placed out on a nonskilled labor type of domestic employment.

In fact, "but for the grace of God," any one of the cases in the experimental group might have experienced the impact of deprivation of those in the contrast group, and vice versa.

Cost to the State

We are also studying the cost to the State of each subject in the experimental group and the contrast group of Study II—based on information as to per capita cost for institutional care per month or year for each of the years from 1932 to 1963. Preliminary indications are shocking.

In the experimental group the median total cost is less than $1,000, whereas in the contrast group it is 10 times that, with a range from $7,000 to $24,000. One case in the contrast group can be cited of a person who has been a ward of the State institution for over 30 years. The total cost to the State in this instance has been $24,113.

In the 1930's, the monthly per capita cost at State children's institutions and at mental hospitals ranged around $17 per month. This has progressively increased over the years until the present figure is considerably more than $200 per month. We can speculatively extrapolate on the cost to the State of the subjects in Study II had our comparisons started in 1963 instead of 1932. Assuming that costs were constant from 1963 to 1993, the case in the example cited would have cost the State $100,000.

Mentally Retarded Parents

As already mentioned, Study III involved children whose biological mothers were considered to be mentally retarded. The children had been separated from their natural mothers in early infancy, either by voluntary release or by court commitment, and had been placed in adoptive homes before they were 2 years old. The study included a total of 87 cases. IQ scores were obtained on each of the mothers, none of whom achieved higher than 75. The range extended down to an IQ of 32.

After a time interval of 21 years, efforts are under way to locate the adoptive parents and children of this study, and indications are that all or most of them will be found. Several interviews have already been completed.

In the followup, in addition to securing information on the adult status of the children, intelligence tests are being administered to the second generation—the grandchildren of the mentally retarded, biological grandmothers.

Preliminary findings in this followup study suggest that the first generation (the children of the original study) compares favorably in occupational status as adults with the Iowa population of comparable ages according to 1960 census figures. The second-generation children are scoring average and above on intelligence tests.

Some Implications

Since the preliminary findings of these three followup studies are substantiated by reports of many supporting studies published in the past 20 years, it would seem that we have adequate knowledge for designing programs of intervention to counteract the devastating effects of poverty, socio-cultural deprivation, maternal deprivation, or a combination of these ills. This means making expenditures for prevention, rather than waiting for the tremendous costs of a curative nature. It does not, of course, preclude further research and exploratory studies to determine the optimum modes of intervention and the most appropriate ages for initiating such procedures.

References

Skeels, Harold M., and Harold B. Dye. 1938. A study of the effects of differential stimulation on mentally retarded children. (Proceedings and addresses of the American Association on Mental Deficiency.) *J. Psycho-asthenics*, **44**, 1.

Skodak, Marie, and Harold M. Skeels. September 1949. A final follow-up study of one hundred adopted children. *J. genet. Psychol.*, **75**, 1.

———, and Irene Harms. June 1948. Children with inferior social histories; their mental development in adoptive homes. *J. genet. Psychol.*, **72**, 2.

22 Parental Influence on Cognitive Development in Early Childhood: A Review*

NORMAN E. FREEBERG, *Educational Testing Service*
DONALD T. PAYNE, *Educational Testing Service*

Despite the extent of child development research on intellectual skills and learning, the answer to a parent who asks specifically "What can I do during my child's preschool years to improve his learning ability or intelligence?" would have to be couched in fairly broad and guarded generalizations. If the question were pressed further by our hypothetical parent and an optimum sequence of training techniques was requested, the child specialist might feel that his recommendations were even further removed from a body of relevant literature. Perhaps little more than a generalization to provide "maximum environmental enrichment" could, at present, be supported with confidence. But it appears that evidence for an outline of more substantial proportions is beginning to emerge. The present review will attempt to deal with the extent and applicability of available literature to the question posed and those aspects of the research effort that remain to be undertaken if a more satisfactory answer is to be given.

* *Child Development*, March 1967, vol. 38, no. 1. Reprinted with permission of The Society for Research in Child Development, Inc. Copyright 1967 by The Society for Research in Child Development, Inc. This work was supported in part under a contract with the Institute for Educational Development, New York.

Significance of Early Learning

It has been no small task to arrive at a point where one could speak with assurance of even as general a concept as the enhancing of human cognitive development through an early environment "rich in experience." To do so has required marshaling evidence for the effects of experience upon intellectual growth and against the two long-entrenched assumptions of fixed intelligence, and a maturational hypothesis that prescribes the unfolding of cognitive abilities in a predetermined relation to anatomic development. Hunt (1961) has dealt with the task incisively. With Hebb's (1949) work on the neurophysiological basis of intellectual growth as one theoretical cornerstone, Hunt builds his conception of learning and intelligence as a form of dynamic information processing dependent upon infantile experience.

In effect, Hebb (1949) concluded that experience is an essential mediator of neural connections and a requirement for the formation of so-called cell assemblies. These neural assemblies become relatively fixed functional units ("autonomous central processes") whose sequence and phasing in the associative cortex can only be formed by receptor inputs (i.e., sensory experience). Thus, it is the earliest experience or "primary" learning which forms much of the pattern for later information-processing capability in the system and serves as the "programmer of the human brain-computer" (Hunt, 1964, p. 242).

Evidence from animal studies of the effects of infantile experience on later learning lends substantial support to the above concepts and tends to negate consideration of a central nervous system that functions as a "passive switchboard" (Newell, Shaw, and Simon, 1958). Beach and Jaynes (1954) as well as Hunt (1961, chap. iv) review much of the work dealing with the enhancement of later learning by rich environmental stimulation in early life. Rats reared in darkness take longer to learn pattern discrimination than normals, and chimps reared in a darkened room for the first 16 months of life fail, initially, to show normal responses to moving objects in the visual field. Pets (cats and dogs) reared in the home perform better in learning situations than laboratory-reared animals. In addition, animals provided with the early experience of living with a variety of objects in their cages perform better in later learning situations and with less emotional interference than animals not exposed to such variations in the stimulus environment. The degree and permanence of this retardation depend largely upon the extent of deprivation. In the case of chimps reared in darkness, there is an eventual recovery of normal visual functioning if the deprivation does not go beyond an assumed critical point where physiological deterioration begins to occur (Riesen, 1958). Similarly, in human development, the ability to recover from the handicap of various forms of perceptual-motor deprivation (given sufficient time and opportunity to practice the requisite skills) indicates that, despite the importance of the early environment, maturational components cannot be ignored (Dennis and Najarian, 1957; Senden, 1932).

Although the behavioral evidence of the role of early learning has been impressive, the more recent works of Krech, Rosenzweig, and Bennett (1962) and Bennett, Diamond, Krech, and Rosenzweig (1964) have served to anchor this evidence in neural correlates. Behavioral measurement as well as chemical and neuroanatomical changes in the cortex of rats raised in enriched and impoverished environments (with and without designs and objects in the cage; variations in number of litter mates) have revealed significant differences in favor of the animals raised under conditions of greater environmental complexity. This improvement is evidenced by (*a*) superior learning ability on a variety of tasks, (*b*) neurochemical changes known to facilitate learning, and (*c*) increased quantity (weight) of cortical tissue in brain areas *specific* to those aspects of sensory stimulation provided by the environmental variables (e.g., greater development of the occipital cortex was related to greater environmental visual stimulation).

Evidence for early learning effects in children and "cumulative deficit" (decline in IQ scores) resulting from deprived environments have been reviewed extensively by Bloom (1964) and others (Anastasi, 1958; Bayley, 1955; Klineberg, 1963; Yarrow, 1964). Largely through studies of intellectual growth in twins reared apart, children separated from parents early in life by adoption, and effects of environmental deprivation in childhood, there has been mounting evidence for the potency of early environment in shaping later cognitive abilities. The extent to which such adverse environmental effects are reversible for retardation of higher-level cognitive skills in man remains poorly defined. But there appear to be extremes of social and cultural deprivation beyond which compensatory training provides only limited benefit (Zingg, 1940).

Bloom (1964) re-evaluates the data from longitudinal studies of the past four decades in an attempt to support a hypothesis of differential growth rate for human intellectual ability. He concludes that, in terms of intelligence measured at age 17, approximately 50 per cent of the variance can be accounted for by age 4 so that as much intellectual growth is achieved between birth and 4 years of age as is achieved for the remaining 13 years. (Assumptions of behavior overlap, absolute scaling, and a unidimensionality of measured intelligence, which are required for such a conclusion, remain open to contention.) Unfortunately, most of the evidence available has not dealt with specific mechanisms to explain conclusions regarding early environmental effects upon the child, and Bloom

(1964) feels that it is now necessary to bridge the inferential gap with more detailed and meaningful measures of the environment in order to relate these to cognitive performance.

This brief discussion of an extensive and complex topic is intended only to serve as background for the assumption upon which the balance of this review is predicated, that is, that the formation of cognitive and intellectual skills can reasonably be conceived of as developmental in nature and modifiable by variation in the environment. If this is granted, then how might changes be effected in early intellectual development through the use of appropriate child-rearing and educational practices? Hunt touches upon the need for such knowledge when he states: "Various bits of the evidence reviewed hint that if the manner in which encounters with the environment foster the development of intellectual interest and capacity were more fully understood, it might be possible to increase the average level of intelligence within the population substantially" (Hunt, 1961, p. 346). Similarly, Bloom feels that we are at a level where one can "specify some of the major characteristics of an environment which will positively or negatively affect the development of general intelligence or school achievement" (Bloom, 1964, p. 196). If cultural effects on intellectual functioning are, in some measure, "from the outside in" (Bruner, 1964), then the techniques by which this process can be influenced through parental practices are certainly an area of legitimate concern.

Three major aspects of the literature can be utilized to deal with the problem. The first is of primary concern for this review and deals with those studies that attempt to relate parental influences directly to some aspect of the child's cognitive performance. Second are the studies of child-rearing behavior in various social classes as linked with the evidence of intellectual achievements of children from these classes, and third is the experimental and descriptive literature dealing with educational techniques that have been used for developing cognitive skills in the very young child.

Direct Measures of Parental Influence

Research concerned with direct relations between parental practices and child development has tended to focus upon dependent variables concerned with physical development, personality formation, and behavior adjustment. Attempts to incorporate measures of cognitive skill and intelligence are relatively recent by comparison. Where such studies have been undertaken, they generally deal with children of elementary school levels, and they rely heavily upon retrospective reports by the mother regarding parental practices in early childhood. If there is a willingness to accept a relative continuity of home environment for the period of years from early childhood to the later grades and/or some measure of accuracy for mothers' retrospective reporting, then a number of pertinent studies to be considered in this review can provide insight into the nature of those family influences that might affect intellectual achievement.

One such study by Bing (1963) used sixty mothers of fifth-grade children. All of these children had similar total IQ scores and were divided by sex into "high" and "low" verbal groups. This grouping was based upon the contrast of verbal scores with spatial and numerical scores. For example, a "high verbal" subject was one whose verbal scores were high in relation to his numerical and spatial scores. Data were obtained from questionnaires and from interviews with the mother as well as from observation of an "interaction situation" during which the mother engaged in various problem-solving activities with the child. Responses on the retrospective questionnaire and interview indicated that mothers of "high verbal" children provided more verbal stimulation in early childhood (highly significant for boys but not for girls). These mothers also remembered more of the child's early accomplishments (significant for boys but not for girls), were more critical of poor academic achievement, provided the child with more storybooks, and let him take a greater part in mealtime conversations. Time spent reading to the child by the father was associated with high verbal scores for girls only, although no comparable association was found for reading time spent by the mothers with the child of either sex. The various sex differences that characterized these results were often difficult to reconcile on the basis of any previously stated hypotheses. In the observational situation, mothers of children with high verbal ability generally provided more assistance voluntarily, provided it sooner when requested by the child, and pressured the child more for improvement.

This influence of the mother's pattern of interaction and communication with the child appears to play a pivotal role in cognitive skill level, as is also evident in the work by Hess (1965). Utilizing the observational situation, Hess is presently conducting a series of studies with preschool children that require mother-child interaction in a problem-solving situation. His focus is on the way in which the mother assists the child in solving problems and the nature of the "cognitive environment" which she provides. Results indicate that, when mothers provide "restrictive language codes" (i.e., language that provides a smaller number of alternatives for action, fewer choices to be made, and fewer possibilities for thought), the child's problem-solving ability is diminished.

Maternal behavior toward the preschool child, which includes emphasis on verbal skill acquisition along with other phases of achievement, has also been shown to be related to measured IQ scores. Data obtained from parents of middle-class children from the Fels Longitudinal Study (Moss and Kagan, 1958) were used to develop a "maternal acceleration" score derived from ratings of "pressure" for the child's achievement, as evidenced by the mother in interviews. A significant relation between the child's IQ and maternal acceleration was found only for boys at the 3-year level but not for either sex in the 6-year age group. The study was essentially repeated in a second phase using another sample of children. The child's IQ scores at the 3- and 6-year levels were positively correlated with the mother's IQ and educational level, but the maternal acceleration score was, again, found to be related only to the boys' IQ at the 3-year level. The authors note that one possible explanation lies in the fact that four of six items on the 2½-year scale of the Stanford-Binet test are of the type that mothers who had high maternal acceleration scores emphasized (i.e., identifying objects by use, naming objects and body parts, and picture vocabulary).

There is evidence that early childhood achievement behaviors, as well as parental practices, are age- and sex-dependent in their predictive ability for later adult achievement behavior (Sontag and Kagan, 1963). Indications of sex differences were not only apparent in the Moss and Kagan study (1958), but Bing (1963) also reported that variables derived from the retrospective interview, which distinguished between high and low verbal groups, did so mainly for boys, while those from the contemporaneous observation situation indicated such differences primarily for girls. This finding of sex differences, based upon parental recall of earlier practices as contrasted with present behavior of the parent (observational data), represents a result that merits further verification. It is hardly surprising that mothers would respond differently to broad classes of behavior displayed by the male than they would for the female child (Sears, Maccoby, and Levin, 1957). Such differences for intellectual and achievement behaviors might also be culturally determined to some extent and could stem from differences in parental expectation for later intellectual and vocational achievement (Freeberg and Payne, 1965).

Age dependence has also become a variable of recent concern. Variations in the consequences of a parental practice, as a function of the child's age level at the time the practice is introduced, have been termed the "sleeper effect" by Kagan and Moss (1962). Evidence presented by these authors indicates that there may be critical periods in the child's development when a particular parental practice may be more effective in shaping later development than if it is introduced at other than the "optimum" age or developmental level. Obvious difficulties in evaluating research and defining suitable criteria of cognitive development are introduced by the need to identify such complex and incompletely understood effects of age and sex.

Another approach to uncovering pertinent aspects of parental influence is through the child's responses to questions about the home environment, an approach used by Milner (1951). First-grade children were classed as "high" and "low" scorers on the Haggerty Reading Examination and the Language Factors subtest of the California Test of Mental Maturity. The findings support the general pattern of subsequent studies, with the "high scorers" showing significantly more responses for such parental behavior-related items as: expressed appreciation for the time the mother spent taking them places and reading to them, possession of several or a great many storybooks, and the fact that the parents regularly read to them.

One of the most comprehensive, and apparently successful, attempts to relate parental influence to intelligence test performance of the child used data obtained from sixty fifth-grade students and from interviews with their mothers (Wolf, 1964). Those aspects of the home which were considered as most relevant to the development of general intelligence were incorporated as items in an interview schedule of 63 questions. The items were then used as a basis for ratings on 13 scales designated as "Environmental Process Characteristics." The correlation of the total score (which was a summation of the 13 scale scores) and the child's IQ score was a striking .69. Of particular interest for our purposes are the individual correlations of the 13 scales with the intelligence test score. The best relations were found for those scales dealing with the parents' intellectual expectations for the child, the amount of information that the mother had about the child's intellectual development, the opportunities provided for enlarging the child's vocabulary, the extent to which the parents created situations for learning in the home, and the extent of assistance given in learning situations related to school and nonschool activities. Dave (1963), using the same 63-item interview schedule as Wolf (1964) and apparently the same data, categorized the scales into five "Environmental Process Variables" that could be grouped to form an "Index of Educational Environment." The correlation of this overall "Index" with an "Educational Achievement Score" (composed of such areas as word knowledge, spelling, reading, and arithmetic computation) was found to be .80.

The findings from these two studies are indeed impressive as indications of parental influence on intellectual development. However, a number of the reported correlations between the intelligence measure and variables of social class are at odds with previous studies and require clarification. For example, the index of social class and parental education level were found to be unrelated to the child's intelligence test scores, whereas measures of this sort are customarily found to possess a moderate but significant degree of relation with intelligence. In any event, the general pattern of results from the several studies considered here is fairly consistent. Children of superior intellectual ability come from homes where parental interest in their intellectual development is evidenced by pressures to succeed and assistance in doing so, particularly in the development of the child's verbal skills.

Achievement

The concept of achievement has frequently been used as a criterion of performance for cognitive and intellectual development. As is the case for many of the criterion and predictor variables utilized in parent-child studies, the concept is not a unitary one. In this case it has been used to refer to "need," or motivation for achievement, measured proficiency, and opinions about achievement. Crandall lends some clarification to this widely used criterion variable. He distinguishes achievement variables from other behavior variables such as dependency, aggression, etc., on the basis of "positive reinforcement for demonstrated competence" and achievement situations from other social situations on the basis of the provision of "cues pertaining to some 'standard of excellence'" (Crandall, 1963, p. 418). Contrasted with these is the concept of achievement motivation or "need (n) achievement."

Several studies have attempted to relate specific parental child-rearing practices or attitudes to the development of either achievement behavior or achievement motives in the child. Ratings were obtained for: (*a*) achievement behavior in a nursery school free-play situation, (*b*) child-mother interaction in the home, and (*c*) mother reactions to child behavior (Crandall, Preston, and Rabson, 1960). The results depict a high-achieving child as one who is less dependent upon the mother for emotional support and whose mother frequently rewarded achievement efforts.

A series of studies conducted at the Fels Institute dealt with the relation of parents' attitudes concerning their own achievement to the achievement behaviors of their child (Crandall, Dewey, Katkovsky, and Preston, 1964; Katkovsky, Preston, and Crandall, 1964a; 1964b). The general findings of interest for this review include a similarity between intellectual achievement values that parents hold for themselves and those they expect for their child, as well as a relation between intellectual expectations and their participation with the child in intellectual activities. Academic achievement of children in the early grades and "general" parental behaviors (largely descriptive of "social climate") were found to be significantly related, but primarily with regard to mothers and daughters—such that mothers of academically competent girls were less affectionate and less nurturant toward their daughters than were mothers of less proficient girls. The essential distinction for fathers was a tendency for those who had academically proficient daughters to use praise more often and to criticize less. More "specific" variables, such as parents' expressed values for intellectual performance and satisfaction with the child's performance, were related to the child's achievement regardless of sex.

These findings of the Fels group are supported in general by the results of Callard's (1964) study with nursery school children and, in addition, by Rosen and D'Andrade (1959), who found that boys with high-need achievement scores had parents with higher aspirations for them and a higher regard for their competence and were fairly quick to disapprove if the child performed poorly. Biglin (1964), on the other hand, had little success in attempting to relate parents' attitudes (as measured by the Nebraska Parent Attitude Scale) to academic achievement when intellectual ability and socioeconomic status were controlled. The explanation for such differences would probably be found in the nature of the attitude scales utilized or in differences between interview results and those of attitude questionnaires. Moving from preschool and early elementary school to the high school level, some consistency of results can be demonstrated by reported relations of academic achievement with parental encouragement, approval, and sharing of activities (Mannino, 1962; Morrow and Wilson, 1961).

In the measurement of achievement, as for intellectual performance, the pattern of parental influence that emerges from these studies would appear to be sex-dependent as well as the result of overt parental pressures for achievement along with expressed attitudes indicating a high level of aspiration for the child.

Social Environment

One area of controversy that still requires clarification has centered about the social environment in the home and its effects upon the intellectual performance of the child. An early article by Baldwin, Kalhorn, and Breese (1945) reported that children reared in families characterized as Acceptant-Democratic-Indulgent showed higher IQ scores and more favorable changes in IQ, over several years, than children from authoritarian and rejecting homes. A controversy was sparked by Drews and Teahan (1957) who found that high achievers tend to have been reared in families where adult standards were not questioned and where mothers were more "authoritarian and restrictive." Hurley (1959) attempted to serve as mediator and re-evaluated the Drews and Teahan data (1957) to show that although mothers of high academic achievers tended to be more dominant and ignoring toward their children, mothers of "gifted" (high Binet IQ) children tended to be less so. Watson (1957) presented results that tend to favor the "permissive" home as one that stimulated intellectual activity of better quality. The controversy remains unresolved, and results have been difficult to reconcile simply on the basis of the techniques employed and the variables chosen.

To complicate the matter further, a similar and parallel controversy has arisen for what probably represents a related constellation of variables concerned with fostering dependence and independence in early childhood. It has been reported by Winterbottom (1958) that boys with high-need achievement had mothers who prompted earlier self-reliance and independence, while indulgent and overprotective mothers in Stewart's (1950) study had children who tended to be inferior in reading achievement. In support of this pattern, emotional dependence upon the mother by the preschool child was shown to be related to lower-need achievement and declining IQ scores, in a study by Sontag, Baker, and Nelson (1958). Shaw (1964) adds further positive evidence for early independence as a factor favoring academic achievement.

The trend toward agreement was upset, however, by Chance (1961) who found that first-grade children (particularly girls) whose mothers favored earlier demands for independence made less adequate school progress. Crandall et al. (1960) found that "neither maternal affection nor independence training was predictive of the children's achievement behavior." The results do indeed indicate, as Hurley (1959) has suggested, the "complex nature of relationships between maternal child rearing attitudes and children's behavior." Resolution of such a controversy can only be achieved by better understanding of the relations between those child-rearing variables that underlie the authoritarian-democratic, dependence-independence, and permissive-restrictive dimensions, along with greater precision of behavioral definitions for these concepts than has been shown in a number of the studies cited. Differences in criterion measures of achievement (i.e., academic performance, need achievement, measured intelligence) also require reconciliation in future attempts to deal with the controversy.

Cognitive Style

It has long been recognized that cognitive skill development and achievement are somehow related to personality characteristics. Linking of the causal sequence has been vague, however, until recent studies of cognitive style have attempted to deal with the relation of conceptual strategies in problem solving to personality correlates. Emotional dependence on parents, aggressiveness, self-initiation, and competitiveness in the preschool years were found to be predictive of intellectual growth, from an analysis of the Fels Longitudinal Study data (Sontag et al., 1958). The problem remains one of defining consistent, specific differences in the individual's approach to the environment. Kagan, Moss, and Sigel (1963) have established measures of distinctive cognitive (conceptual) styles in grade-school children that indicate "analytic" and "relational" (non-analytic) approaches which differentiate between males and females. These resemble the "field-dependent," "field-independent" dimension found by Witkin, Dyk, Faterson, Goodenough, and Karp (1962) who, in addition, attempted to relate the perceptual differences in cognitive styles to maternal influence in early childhood. "Field-independent" boys tended to be more resistant to social group pressure, showed greater consistency of behavior, used intellectualization as a defense mechanism rather than repression, and had mothers who encouraged greater autonomy and curiosity in early childhood. Hess and Shipman (1965) have argued that the child's style of response to problem-solving situations can be associated with the mother's ability to utilize verbal concepts in her interaction with him. Measures of cognitive style were obtained from a sorting task by Sigel (reported in Hess and Shipman, 1965) that defines the level and mode of abstraction displayed by the individual. One version of this instrument was used to obtain scores for the mothers' cognitive style and another was used for their children. Levels of conceptualization displayed by the mother were associated with the cognitive style and conceptual "maturity" of the child as well as with the child's performance on several problem-solving tasks. Cognitive style and levels of conceptual maturity were also found to be differentiated by the social status of the mothers and children.

Although the importance of maternal language style as a mediating factor may lead to stressing of environmental and situational variables in the shaping of cognitive patterns, the possibility of genetic influences has also been suggested, based upon two lines of evidence. First is the persistent finding of sex differences along the cognitive style dimensions reported by Kagan et al. (1963) and by Witkin et al. (1962). Second is a rather interesting discovery of unusual cognitive patterns among girls with Turner's syndrome, a genetic abnormality in the complement of x chromosomes (Witkin, Faterson, Goodenough, and Birnbaum, 1965). Intelligence test performance of twenty girls exhibiting Turner's syndrome was analyzed by these investigators using data from a study by Shafer (reported in Witkin et al., 1965). Significant discrepancies were found between verbal intelligence and ability on "analytical" tasks (i.e., perceptual organization skills characterized by such Wechsler Adult Intelligence Scale subtests as Block Design, Picture Completion, and Object Assembly). Having previously found strong relations between such discrepancies and scores on the perceptual field-dependence, field-independence dimension, Witkin et al. (1965) hypothesize strong field dependency for girls with the Turner syndrome.

Accuracy of Parental Evaluation and Report

A number of the studies that have been cited depend heavily upon the parents' (most frequently the mother's) evaluation of the child. It is, therefore, pertinent to consider this source of data in terms of its error contribution to any study.

Crandall and Preston (1955) compared mothers' self-ratings of their behavior with psychologists' ratings of this same behavior based upon observations, and found that the simpler maternal self-rating scales were not correlated highly enough with the more time-consuming observational ratings to be considered as a substitute. Significant agreement between scales, where it existed, depended upon the particular area of maternal behavior evaluated. Similar use of the observational situation by Zunich (1962) resulted in negligible agreement when questionnaire results were compared with observational ratings.

Other studies have demonstrated either a selective accuracy or general distortion of mothers' reports on developmental data and child-rearing practices (Mednick and Shaffer, 1963; Pyles, Stolz, and MacFarlane, 1935). This has been found even in situations where parents participated in a longitudinal study and were virtually "practiced" respondents (Robbins, 1963). Among such respondents, it was found that mothers displayed greater accuracy in recall of the child's early behavior than fathers when their responses were compared with prior reports obtained during the course of the longitudinal study. Hefner (1963) found overall agreement to be poor between mothers' reports 2½ years apart, with wide variation for different aspects of child development. Somewhat superior reliability was found for mothers' reports on first-born children and for those mothers whose husbands were of higher occupational level.

Sources of bias and questionable validity were also reported for selected areas of parent-child behavior with the interview technique (McCord and McCord, 1961). Attitude scale biases based on social desirability effects have been shown to influence responses on a number of widely used scales (Taylor, 1961). Yarrow (1963) discusses some of these problems in parent-child research and reviews a number of studies that indicate low agreement between parent-child data contemporaneously obtained and retrospective interview reports. Only Walters (1960) defends the questionnaire as preferable to the more time-consuming interview method for measurement of family behavior, but this is based exclusively upon criteria of economy and reliability.

Since the questionnaire or interview are often the only practical sources of information for studies of parent-child relationships, knowledge of the extent of the deficiencies of these instruments is critical. A review by Bell (1958) lends some perspective to the methodological considerations and to the means of improving the research design for the retrospective parent-child study. It seems evident that there is a need to combine parental reports with observational data or with other sources of verification where possible.

Social Class and Intellectual Growth

One major area of the research literature that bears a largely circumstantial relation to parental practices and intellectual characteristics of the child is concerned with performance of children from families of different social classes. Considerable detail exists regarding the behavior of parents of different social classes during various stages of child rearing, but rarely has there been any effort to relate specific practices to specific cognitive skills. For example, only brief mention of intellectual concomitants of achievement behavior is given in the Sears et al. (1957) widely quoted study of child-rearing practices. Others have been concerned largely with measures of personality and behavior adjustment that derive from practices which might logically be related to such measures (Havighurst and Davis, 1955; Kohn, 1959; Minturn and Lambert, 1964; White, 1957). The middle-class values that stress consideration, self-control, and higher educational expectation have been contrasted with lower- or working-class values of neatness, cleanliness, and obedience. These differences have tended to hold up from study to study, although Havighurst and Davis' (1955) evidence leads them to caution against generalizing too broadly from samples taken in geographically restricted areas to an entire social class.

Differences in intellectual achievement among children of different social classes have long been known to exist (Anastasi, 1958; Eells, Davis, Havighurst, Herrick, and Tyler, 1951), but any inference that these differences stem from particular parental behaviors has been tenuous at best. Attempts to explain variations in intellectual skill among social strata (Eells et al., 1951) have been based on the argument that intelligence tests, in general, favor children from middle and upper social classes. Efforts to devise "culture-free" tests have been made in order to overcome this supposed unfair advantage. However, even if adequate tests of this sort could be devised, they do not solve the problems resulting from poor early learning environments, since children of lower social class are, in fact, less likely to succeed in an academic setting. Questions remain regarding specific parental practices requiring revision if changes are to be effected. Jensen (1964) addresses himself to the evidence that supports the relation of the child's social class membership to verbal learning and reviews the literature in the areas of early experience, perceptual development, environmental deprivation, and laboratory studies of verbal learning in an attempt to show that it is the verbal deficit to which much of the lower-class cognitive disadvantage can be attributed.

Social Class and Deprivation

Declines in IQ during early childhood have been shown to occur repeatedly under environmental conditions of extreme cultural deprivation (Stoddard, 1943; Wheeler, 1932). Similar trends in measured intellectual ability have been used to support a "cumulative deficit" hypothesis for children of the lower socioeconomic classes (Deutsch, 1965; Deutsch and Brown, 1964; Wiener, Rider, and Oppel, 1963) and a conception of their retarded intellectual development as being the result of "cultural deprivation." Support for the deprivation pattern comes from work by Milner (1951), in which differences in reading ability could be attributed to differences in verbal interaction with the child by parents of high and low social class, and from similar findings by Deutsch (1965) that associate poorer language functioning with lower-class groups. Bernstein (1960) explains these differences on the basis of verbal styles in the use of language by different classes, along a "convergent" ("restrictive")- "divergent" ("elaborative") dimension. His concepts have served as a framework for examination of maternal verbal styles in relation to the child's cognitive behavior by Olim, Hess, and Shipman (1965). Language scales have been developed by these investigators which served to differentiate among mothers on the basis of social class—primarily middle- from lower-class mothers—with the middle-class mother exhibiting a more elaborate language style that includes a greater degree of complexity and a higher level of abstraction. Their evidence points to the mother's language usage as the mediating factor in the child's conceptual development, rather than to the child's IQ or the verbal IQ of the mothers. Class differences in maternal verbal style are credited with the superior problem-solving performance for middle-class mothers working with their children than is found for mothers and children of lower social status. In the view of Hess and Shipman (1965, p. 885), "the meaning of deprivation is a deprivation of meaning."

Lower levels of achievement motivation and expectation for lower-class children can also be assumed to occur from long-term social deprivation and to be passed along to the child by the parents (Rosen, 1956; 1959). Such differences are intimately linked to variations in the way the child learns to perceive the environment and its rewards for achievement. For example, lower-class children were found to perform more effectively for a material incentive, whereas a nonmaterial incentive is just as effective as a material one for middle-class children (Terrell, Durkin, and Wiesley, 1959). Battle and Rooter (1963) showed that lower-class Negro children perceived themselves as having far less control over reinforcement in the environment than did middle-class white children. Such differences in perception of incentives could be a major factor in the focus and orientation of achievement behaviors.

A note of caution is in order for continued use of variables of parent-child interaction dependent upon social class distinctions. Bronfenbrenner (1961) has concluded, from an analysis of changes in parent-child relations over the past 25 years, that there are decreasing differences among classes with regard to such practices. More recently, Caldwell (1965) analyzed items that were used to rate the home environment and family interactions in homes classified as low or middle class on the basis of the customary criteria. Only a few of a large number of items differentiated lower- from middle-class homes, and these were entirely on the basis of physical environment. Hopefully, more specific and direct evidence relating parental practices to the child's intellectual growth is becoming available which will lessen dependence upon the grossly differentiating characteristics subsumed under the rubric of "social class."

Techniques for Early Enhancement of Cognitive Skills

Systematically obtained evidence for parental use of specific instructional techniques to modify the young child's acquisition of cognitive skills is quite rare. A study by Irwin (reported in McCandless, 1961) indicated that working-class mothers who spent 10 minutes per day reading to the child, from 12 months to about 20 months of age, achieved improvement in "all phases of speech." Other available evidence of parental intervention is largely observational or anecdotal. Fowler (1962) summarizes a number of these "descriptive" surveys of gifted children who were early readers, including one with his own daughter. In such cases, children were generally exposed to instructional techniques developed by a parent, and the ability to read by age 3 was not uncommon. These same children often went on to outstanding intellectual achievement as adults.

One of the most extensive sources of potential didactic methods is the large number of studies by educators and psychologists who have evaluated techniques applied during the preschool years for modifying the child's intellectual development. The assumption is, essentially, that if such techniques have been effective they could constitute the framework for methods adaptable to parental use. The bulk of this evidence, to 1960, is covered in the comprehensive review by Fowler (1962) in which he summarizes the research which points to the possibility of modifying specific cognitive skills in children. His examination of the early studies, typified by those of Gesell (1954) and McGraw (1939), that attempted to support a maturational point of view, led him to conclude that the authors "often underplayed . . . the fact that specific training has invariably produced large gains regardless of whether training came early or late in development" (Fowler, 1962, p. 118). Studies cited on improvement of verbal memory and language, in that same review, point to the advantages of early verbal stimulation provided by oral, written, and pictorial material, as well as to the general experience gained in making observations and learning to discriminate between objects. Improvement in conceptual skills and increases in IQ scores were also shown to be amenable to early training attempts which teach higher-order verbal abstractions and provide broad verbal stimulation in play situations of the sort found in a nursery school setting.

Some of the more recent work, during the present decade, delves into the problem in broader scope, dealing largely with culturally deprived children of preschool age and the attempts to improve intellectual performance through specialized training methods (Deutsch, 1963; 1964). One such program by Gray and Klaus (1965) resulted in significant increases in IQ scores for deprived Negro children of preschool age following training programs over two summers and periodic visits to the home during the other months of the year. A control group showed the customary "cumulative deficit" in IQ scores over this same period of time. Further evidence from the Project Headstart Program of the U.S. Office of Economic Opportunity (Dobbin, 1965) has shown that preschool "enrichment" programs might reasonably improve intellectual and social skills. Evaluations of specific methods utilized in this program are now being undertaken and should constitute a rich source of instructional techniques.

Results in teaching young children from a variety of backgrounds to read at earlier ages than usual have been reported for a technique known as the Initial Teaching Alphabet (Downing, 1964) under large-scale evaluation in England. Attempts to apply programed instructional techniques as a means of hastening the acquisition of reading skills by the preschool child include those of Staats, Minke, Finley, Wolf, and Brooks (1964) and of Moore (reported in Hunt, 1964), who adapted the type-writer to a method of teaching letter recognition by having the child press the keys and observe the appropriate letter displayed. Unfortunately, this initial success has been dampened by Rosenhan's (1965) failure to duplicate Moore's results when the possible Hawthorne effect, resulting from the "publicity spotlight," is absent.

Although the programs that attempt to overcome environmental deficit seem certain to continue and expand, questions remain of just how extensively conceptual processes in the young child can be modified. Bruner's (1960) position is that almost any subject matter, if properly organized, can be taught at the grade-school or preschool level. At somewhat the other extreme is the essentially maturational position of Inhelder and Piaget (1958) who argue for specific levels of cognitive development that must be achieved before certain conceptual strategies can be learned (e.g., those basic to inductive reasoning). Ausubel (1965) would also doubt any likelihood of teaching certain concepts at the "pre-operational" stage in Piaget's system (i.e., to about age 7). However, he looks upon these conceptual stages as "nothing more than approximations" that are "susceptible to environmental influences" (Ausubel, 1965, pp. 11–12).

While it is not our intention to explore this controversy through all of the developmental stages, some noteworthy attempts have been made to deal with the teachability of "processes" or "central concepts" in Piaget's formulation at earlier age levels than Piaget (Inhelder and Piaget, 1958) had observed them to occur. With some reservations, trainability of young children on concepts of "conservation" and "transitivity" have been demonstrated by Smedslund (1961a; 1961b; 1963), but there is some question about the permanence of the results and whether the child is able to generalize the principles learned. Anderson (1964) achieved some degree of success with first-grade children in teaching problem solving that required a level of inductive reasoning usually reserved for much older children under the Inhelder and Piaget (1958) scheme. The learning was also shown to be relatively permanent and transferable. But the author believes that the children achieved this result using different strategies than those employed by adolescents or adults.

The major focus of research, stimulated by Piaget's work, seems to have shifted from attempts to support his postulated sequence of conceptual development, which appears to have been demonstrated reasonably well (Braine, 1959; Peel, 1959), to the more fruitful one of analysis of the strategies involved at such stages and appropriate programing of the material to be learned (Gibson, 1965).

Summary and Needed Research

The direction of recent research suggests that attempts to define parental influences on the child's acquisition of cognitive skills have begun to expand beyond the rather vague concepts of "enriched experience" and "widening of interests" that have served too often as explanations for poorly understood learning mechanisms. It is largely over the past decade that various aspects of parent-child interaction have been investigated in an attempt to define their influence upon specific modes of cognitive responses, with the most compelling lines of evidence pointing to a critical role for verbal patterns established by the parent. Included in these verbal patterns are the manner or "style" of communicating information to the child and the opportunities for verbal stimulation provided in the home (e.g., in the sheer amount of verbal activity and in the provision of books or other devices that supply a wide range of opportunity for language usage). Many of the social class distinctions in intellectual achievement, which consistently have been found, are likely to center around parental stimuli to the development of language skills as the mediating variable. But much more remains to be delineated regarding the dimensions of parental linguistic styles: the way in which these affect particular forms of verbal development and the patterns of parent-child communication which have an impact on specific verbal and problem-solving abilities.

Still other phases of parental practice that indicate some promise for differentiating levels, as well as areas, of cognitive skill development have been dealt with in the framework of permissive-restrictive environments in the home and parental pressures for achievement. If these variables were to be more clearly defined operationally—so that present inconsistencies in research findings can be reconciled—the next steps would require determining their likely interaction with one another and their relation to the important role that seems to mark communication and language.

Any description of the processes by which parental behavior influences the development of cognition would be augmented considerably by knowledge of the parents' perception of their role in rearing practices and its influence on cognitive growth. One of the major research gaps has been the scarcity of information regarding parents' attitudes toward their own potential influence upon intellectual development—particularly for parents of different social classes. In a laboratory setting it has been found that inconsistencies in experimental results can occur if there is a failure to deal with data regarding the mother's feelings about interacting with the child in a problem-solving situation (Beller and Nash, 1965). Perhaps some appreciation of the child's views of the learning situation and of his mother's responses would also be in order.

The most pertinent and systematically obtained results dealing with relations between parental practices and the child's level of cognitive skill development have been (and are likely to continue to be) achieved by observation in the laboratory setting as opposed to questionnaire methods. However, there remains the more ultimate validation that can only be derived from the broad range of daily rearing practices in a home or "home-like" setting. Data obtained from this source will be essential for defining the more complex aspects of parental influences in the modification of the child's cognitive performance.

References

Anastasi, Anne. 1958. Heredity, environment, and the question "how?" *Psychol. Rev.*, **65**, pp. 197–208.

Anderson, R. C. 1964. *Shaping logical behavior in six- and seven-year-olds.* Cooperative Research Project No. 1790A (Chicago, Ill.: University of Illinois).

Ausubel, D. P. 1965. Stages of intellectual development and their implications for early childhood education. In D. B. Neubauer (ed.), *Concepts of development in early childhood education* (Springfield, Ill.: Charles C Thomas), pp. 8–51.

Baldwin A. L., Joan Kalhorn, and Fay H. Breese. 1945. Patterns of parent behavior. *Psychol. Monogr.: gen. and appl.*, **58**, No. 3, Whole No. 268.

Battle, Esther S., and J. B. Rotter. 1963. Children's feelings of personal control as related to social class and ethnic group. *J. Pers.*, **31**, 4, pp. 482–490.

Bayley, Nancy. 1955. On the growth of intelligence. *Amer. Psychol.*, **10**, pp. 805–818.

Beach, F. A., and J. Jaynes. 1954. Effects of early experience upon the behavior of animals. *Psychol. Bull.*, **51**, pp. 239–263.

Bell, R. Q. 1958. Retrospective attitude studies of parent-child relations. *Child Develpm.*, **29**, pp. 323–338.

Beller, E. K., and A. Nash. February 1965. *Research with educationally disadvantaged preschool children.* A paper presented at the annual meetings of the American Educational Research Association, Chicago.

Bennett, E. L., Marian C. Diamond, D. Krech, and M. R. Rosenzweig. 1964. Chemical and anatomical plasticity of brain. *Science*, **146**, No. 3644, pp. 610–619.

Bernstein, B. 1960. Language and social class. *Brit. J. Sociol.*, **11**, pp. 271–276.

Biglin, J. E. 1964. *The relationship of parental attitudes to children's academic and social performance* (Lincoln, Nebr.: University of Nebraska). Unpublished doctoral dissertation.

Bing, Elizabeth. 1963. Effect of childrearing practices on development of differential cognitive abilities. *Child Develpm.*, **34**, 3, pp. 631–648.

Bloom, B. S. 1964. *Stability and change in human characteristics* (New York: John Wiley & Sons, Inc.).

Braine, M. D. S. 1959. The ontogeny of certain logical operations: Piaget's formulations examined by nonverbal methods. *Psychol. Monogr.: gen. and appl.*, **73**, No. 5, Whole No. 475.

Bronfenbrenner, U. 1961. The changing American child: a speculative analysis. *J. soc. Issues*, **17**, 1, pp. 6–17.

Bruner, J. S. 1964. The course of cognitive growth, *Amer. Psychol.*, **19**, pp. 1–15.

———. 1960. *The process of education* (Cambridge, Mass.: Harvard University Press).

Caldwell, Bettye. September 1965. *Infant and preschool socialization in different social classes.* A paper presented at the meetings of the American Psychological Association, Chicago.

Callard, Esther. D. 1964. *Achievement motive in the four-year-old child and its relationship to achievement expectancies of the mother* (Ann Arbor, Mich.: University of Michigan). Unpublished doctoral dissertation.

Chance, June E. 1961. Independence training and first graders' achievement. *J. consult. Psychol.*, **25**, pp. 149–154.

Crandall, V. J. 1963. Achievement. In H. W. Stevenson (ed.), *62nd Yrbk. Nat. Soc. Study Educ., Child psychology*, Part I (Chicago, Ill.: University of Chicago Press). pp. 416–459.

———, Rachel Dewey, W. Katkovsky, and Anne Preston. 1964. Parents' attitudes and behaviors and grade-school children's academic achievements. *J. genet. Psychol.*, **104**, pp. 53–66.

———, and Alice Rabson. 1960. Maternal reactions and the development of independence and achievement behavior in young children. *Child Develpm.*, **31**, pp. 243–251.

———, and Anne Preston. 1955. Patterns and levels of maternal behavior. *Child Develpm.*, **26**, pp. 267–277.

Dave, R. H. 1963. *The identification and measurement of educational process variables that are related to educational achievement* (Chicago, Ill.: University of Chicago). Unpublished doctoral dissertation.

Dennis, W., and Pergrouhi Najarian. 1957. Infant development under environmental handicap. *Psychol. Monogr.: gen. and appl.*, **71**, No. 7, Whole No. 436.

Deutsch, M. 1965. The role of social class in language development and cognition. *Amer. J. Orthopsychiat.*, **35**, 1, pp. 78–88.

———. 1964. Facilitating development in the preschool child: social and psychological perspectives. *Merrill-Palmer Quart. Behav. Develpm.*, **10**, 3, pp. 249–263.

———. 1963. The disadvantaged child and the learning process: some social, psychological and developmental considerations. In A. H. Passow (ed.), *Education in depressed areas*, Part II (New York: Bureau of Publications, Teachers College, Columbia University), pp. 163–179.

――――, and B. Brown. 1964. Social influences in Negro-white intelligence differences. *J. soc. Issues*, **20**, 2, pp. 24–35.

Dobbin, J. E. October 1965. *Observation of Project Head Start: a report on 335 Project Head Start centers* (Princeton, N.J.: Institute for Educational Development).

Downing, J. 1964. Teaching reading with i.t.a. in Britain. *Phi Delta Kappan*, **45**, pp. 322–329.

Drews, Elizabeth M., and J. E. Teahan. 1957. Parental attitudes and academic achievement. *J. clin. Psychol.*, **13**, pp. 328–332.

Eells, K., A. Davis, R. J. Havighurst, V. E. Herrick, and R. Tyler. 1951. *Intelligence and cultural differences* (Chicago, Ill.: University of Chicago Press).

Fowler, W. 1962. Cognitive learning in infancy and early childhood. *Psychol. Bull.*, **59**, 2, pp. 116–152.

Freeberg, N. E., and D. T. Payne. September 1965. *A survey of parental practices related to cognitive development in young children* (Princeton, N.J.: Institute for Educational Development).

Gesell, A. 1954. The ontogenesis of infant behavior. In L. Carmichael (ed.), *Manual of child psychology* (New York: John Wiley & Sons, Inc.).

Gibson, Eleanor J. 1965. Learning to read. *Science*, **148**, 1066.

Gray, Susan W., and R. A. Klaus. 1965. An experimental preschool program for culturally deprived children. *Child Develpm.*, **36**, 4, pp. 887–898.

Havighurst, R. J., and A. Davis. 1955. A comparison of the Chicago and Harvard studies of social class differences in child rearing. *Amer. sociol. Rev.*, **20**, pp. 438–442.

Hebb, D. O. 1949. *The organization of behavior: a neuropsychological theory* (New York: John Wiley & Sons, Inc.).

Hefner, Leslie T. 1963. *Reliability of mothers' reports on child development* (Ann Arbor, Mich.: University of Michigan). Unpublished doctoral dissertation.

Hess, R. D. September 1965. *Effects of maternal interaction on cognitions of preschool children in several social strata*. A paper presented at the meetings of the American Psychological Association, Chicago.

――――, and Virginia C. Shipman. 1965. Early experience and the socialization of cognitive modes in children. *Child Develpm.*, **36**, 4, pp. 869–886.

Hunt, J. McV. 1964. The psychological basis for using preschool enrichment as an antidote for cultural deprivation. *Merrill-Palmer Quart. Behav. Develpm.*, **10**, pp. 209–248.

———. 1961. *Intelligence and experience* (New York: The Ronald Press Company).

Hurley, J. R. 1959. Maternal attitudes and children's intelligence. *J. clin. Psychol.*, **15**, pp. 291–292.

Inhelder, Bärbel, and J. Piaget. 1958. *The growth of logical thinking* (New York: Basic Books, Inc.).

Jensen, A. R. 1964. *Social class and verbal learning* (Berkeley, Calif.: University of California). Unpublished manuscript on file at Library, Educational Testing Service, Princeton, N.J.

Kagan, J., and I. E. Sigel. 1963. Psychological significance of styles of conceptualization. *Monogr. Soc. Res. Child Develpm.*, **28**, No. 2, Serial No. 86, pp. 73–112.

———, and H. A. Moss. 1962. *Birth to maturity, a study in psychological development* (New York: John Wiley & Sons, Inc.).

Katkovsky, W., Anne Preston, and V. J. Crandall. 1964a. Parents' attitudes toward their personal achievements and toward the achievement behaviors of their children. *J. genet. Psychol.*, **104**, pp. 67–82.

———. 1964b. Parents' achievement attitudes and their behavior with their children in achievement situations. *J. genet. Psychol.*, **104**, pp. 105–121.

Klineberg, O. 1963. Negro-white differences in intelligence test performance: a new look at an old problem. *Amer. Psychol.*, **18**, 4, pp. 198–203.

Kohn, M. L. 1959. Social class and parental values. *Amer. J. Sociol.*, **64**, pp. 337–351.

Krech, D., M. R. Rosenzweig, and E. L. Bennett. 1962. Relations between brain chemistry and problem-solving among rats raised in enriched and impoverished environments. *J. comp. physiol. Psychol.*, **55**, 5, pp. 801–807.

McCandless, B. 1961. *Children and adolescents: behavior and development* (New York: Holt, Rinehart and Winston, Inc.).

McCord, Joan, and W. McCord. 1961. Cultural stereotypes and the validity of interviews for research in child development. *Child Develpm.*, **32**, pp. 171–185.

McGraw, Myrtle B. 1939. Later development of children specially trained during infancy; Johnny and Jimmy at school age. *Child Develpm.*, **10**, pp. 1–19.

Mannino, F. V. 1962. Family factors related to school persistence. *J. educ. Sociol.*, **35**, pp. 193–202.

Mednick, S. A., and J. B. P. Shaffer. 1963. Mothers' retrospective reports in child-rearing research. *Amer. J. Orthopsychiat.*, **33**, pp. 457–461.

Milner, E. A. 1951. A study of the relationships between reading readiness in grade one school children and patterns of parent-child interactions. *Child Develpm.*, **22**, pp. 95–112.

Minturn, L., and W. Lambert. 1964. *Mothers of six cultures: antecedents of child rearing* (New York: John Wiley & Sons, Inc.).

Morrow, W. R., and R. R. Wilson. 1961. Family relations of bright high-achieving and under-achieving high school boys. *Child Develpm.*, **32**, pp. 501–510.

Moss, H. A., and J. Kagan. 1958. Maternal influences on early IQ scores. *Psychol. Rep.*, **4**, pp. 655–661.

Newell, A., J. C. Shaw, and H. A. Simon. 1958. Elements of a theory of human problem solving. *Psychol. Rev.*, **65**, pp. 151–166.

Olim, E. G., R. D. Hess, and Virginia Shipman. September 1965. *Maternal language styles and their implications for children's cognitive development*. A paper presented at the meetings of the American Psychological Association, Chicago.

Peel, E. A. 1959. Experimental examination of some of Piaget's schemata concerning children's perception and thinking and a discussion of their educational significance. *Brit. J. educ. Psychol.*, **29**, pp. 89–103.

Pyles, M. K., H. R. Stolz, and J. W. MacFarlane. 1935. The accuracy of mothers' reports on birth and developmental data. *Child Develpm.*, **6**, pp. 165–176.

Riesen, A. H. 1958. Plasticity of behavior: psychological aspects. In H. F. Harlow and C. N. Woolsey (eds.), *Biological and biochemical bases of behavior* (Madison, Wisc.: University of Wisconsin Press), pp. 425–450.

Robbins, Lillian C. 1963. The accuracy of parental recall of aspects of child development and of child rearing practices. *J. abnorm. soc. Psychol.*, **66**, pp. 261–270.

Rosen, B. C. 1959. Race, ethnicity, and the achievement syndrome. *Amer. scciol. Rev.*, **24**, pp. 47–60.

———. 1956. The achievement syndrome: a psychocultural dimension of social stratification. *Amer. sociol. Rev.*, **21**, pp. 203–211.

———, and R. D'Andrade. 1959. The psychosocial origins of achievement motivation. *Sociometry*, **22**, pp. 185–218.

Rosenhan, D. L. February 1965. *Cultural deprivation and learning: an examination of method and theory*. A paper presented at the annual meetings of the American Educational Research Association.

Sears, R. R., Eleanor E. Maccoby, and H. Levin. 1957. *Patterns of child rearing* (Evanston, Ill.: Row, Peterson & Company).

Senden, M. von. 1932. *Raum- und Gestaltauffassung bein operierten Blindgeborenen vor und nach der operation* (Leipzig: Barth).

Shaw, M. C. 1964. Note on parent attitudes toward independence training and the academic achievement of their children. *J. educ. Psychol.*, **55**, 6, pp. 371–374.

Smedslund, J. 1963. Patterns of experience and the acquisition of concrete transitivity of weight in eight-year-old children. *Scand. J. Psychol.*, **4**, pp. 251–256.

———. 1961*a*. The acquisition of conservation of substance and weight in children, II: external reinforcement of conservation of weight and of the operations of addition and subtraction. *Scand. J. Psychol.*, **2**, pp. 71–84.

———. 1961*b*. The acquisition of conservation of substance and weight in children, III: extinction of conservation of weight acquired "normally" and by means of empirical controls on a balance. *Scand. J. Psychol.*, **2**, pp. 85–87.

Sontag, L. W., and J. Kagan. 1963. The emergence of intellectual achievement motives. *Amer. J. Orthopsychiat.*, **33**, 3, pp. 532–535.

———, C. T. Baker, and Virginia L. Nelson. 1958. Mental growth and personality development: a longitudinal study. *Monogr. Soc. Res. Child Develpm.*, **23**, No. 2, Serial No. 68.

Staats, A. W., K. A. Minke, J. R. Finley, M. Wolf, and L. O. Brooks. 1964. A reinforcer system and experimental procedure for the laboratory study of reading acquisition. *Child Develpm.*, **35**, pp. 209–231.

Stewart, R. S. 1950. Personality maladjustment and reading achievement. *Amer. J. Orthopsychiat.*, **20**, pp. 410–417.

Stoddard, G. D. 1943. *The meaning of intelligence* (New York: The Macmillan Company).

Taylor, J. B. 1961. What do attitude scales measure? the problem of social desirability. *J. abnorm. soc. Psychol.*, **62**, pp. 386–390.

Terrell, G., Jr., Kathryn Durkin, and M. Wiesley. 1959. Social class and the nature of the incentive in discrimination learning. *J. abnorm. soc. Psychol.*, **59**, pp. 270–272.

Walters, J. 1960. Relationship between reliability of responses in family life research and method of data collection. *Marriage Fam. Lvg.*, **22**, pp. 232–237.

Watson, G. 1957. Some personality differences in children related to strict or permissive parental discipline. *J. Psychol.*, **44**, pp. 227–249.

Wheeler, L. R. 1932. The intelligence of East Tennessee mountain children. *J. educ. Psychol.*, **23**, pp. 351–370.

White, Martha S. 1957. Social class, child rearing practices, and child behavior. *Amer. sociol. Rev.*, **22**, pp. 704–712.

Wiener, G. G., R. V. Rider, and W. Oppel. 1963. Some correlates of IQ changes in children. *Child Develpm.*, **34**, 1, pp. 61–67.

Winterbottom, Marian. 1958. The relation of need for achievement in learning experiences in independence and mastery. In J. Atkinson (ed.), *Motives in fantasy, action and society* (Princeton, N.J.: D. Van Nostrand Company, Inc.).

Witkin, H. A., Hanna Faterson, D. R. Goodenough, and Judith Birnbaum. 1965. *Cognitive patterning in high grade mentally retarded boys* (Brooklyn, N.Y.: Psychology Laboratory, Department of Psychiatry, State University of New York, Downstate Medical Center). Unpublished manuscript.

――――, Ruth B. Dyk, Hanna Faterson, D. R. Goodenough, and S. A. Karp. 1962. *Psychological differentiation: studies of development* (New York: John Wiley & Sons, Inc.).

Wolf, R. M. 1964. *The identification and measurement of environmental process variables related to intelligence* (Chicago, Ill.: University of Chicago). Unpublished doctoral dissertation.

Yarrow, L. J. 1964. Separation from parents during early childhood. In M. L. Hoffman and Lois W. Hoffman (eds.), *Review of child development research* (New York: Russell Sage Foundation), pp. 89–136.

Yarrow, Marian R. 1963. Problems of methods in parent-child research. *Child Develpm.*, **34**, pp. 215–226.

Zingg, R. M. 1940. Feral man and extreme cases of isolation. *Amer. J. Psychol.*, **53**, pp. 487–517.

Zunich, M. 1962. Relationship between maternal behavior and attitudes toward children. *J. genet. Psychol.*, **100**, pp. 155–165.

23   Cognitive Goals in the Nursery School*

ADA SCHERMANN, *University of Toronto*

This paper is an attempt at identifying the cognitive goals of nursery school education. Before attempting to describe such goals, it is necessary to know what it is that is to be considered. The term cognition or cognitive development is widely used at this time, and when studying the offerings of the various people working in the area of cognition the reader is often at a loss to find common elements between the studies, the term appearing to encompass almost every aspect of behaviour. English's (1934) *Dictionary of Psychological Terms* gives the following definition: "Cognition—a generic term for any process whereby an organism be-

* *Child Study*, Summer 1966, vol. 28, no. 2 (109). Reprinted by permission.

comes aware of or obtains knowledge of an object." Brunswick (1957) suggests, quite simply, that cognition is "the problem of the acquisition of knowledge." Bloom *et al.* (1956), in an attempt to classify educational goals, state that the "cognitive domain . . . includes those objectives which deal with the recall or recognition of knowledge and the development of intellectual abilities and skills." Cognitive development in the child may then be viewed in two ways; firstly, in terms of content or the precise knowledge a child possesses at any given moment, and secondly, in terms of the processes involved in development or the techniques which the child has at his disposal. Subsequent development may be seen as an increase in his amount of knowledge as well as in his use of additional techniques. For example, a fifteen-year-old not only knows more than a four-year-old, but the manner in which he deals with information is different. This imposes a dual function on the nursery school: the first is the provision of information, while the second involves the extension or advancement of the child's technical facility in both acquiring and processing information for himself. It is proposed here to explore the provisions that are needed to carry out this latter function.

Cognitive Skills: An Overview

Many writers (Fowler, 1962; Hunt, 1961) have pointed to the need for arranging the environment, in the first few years of life, in such a manner that a child's encounters with it will involve interactions that will stimulate his thinking. The need for activity (Anderson, 1957; Taylor, 1962) on the part of the child himself is stressed by writers on broad aspects of development as well as by those whose main concern is with intellectual development. Flavell (1963) notes "that there is no doubt that *l'homme piagetien* is assigned a very, very active role in the formation of his own cognitive world." The question may now be asked as to what types of verbal and manipulative activity are appropriate to the acquisition of knowledge and what techniques the child needs in order to achieve this goal. It will be suggested here that the activities involved in perceiving and conceptualizing are the most essential.

In his classification of children's thinking Russell (1956) points out that sensations are the raw material of thinking. While this is undoubtedly true, our actions are not based on pure sensations but rather on our perceptions in which we organize the information our senses convey to us. In order that we may carry out this organization with some measure of success, selection has to take place, not only in terms of the particular aspects of sensation that we choose to perceive, but also in terms of an adaptive overt response. Presenting children with stimuli is insufficient; we may have to ensure that the child is attending to and organizing these stimuli. The perception of young children is characterized by a lack of attention to detail, and so in many instances where attractive material does not ensure the selection of stimuli appropriate to the furthering of knowledge, a human agent using language as a guidepost may be necessary.

Cognitive development involves not only the development of suitable perceptual responses, but in addition a further organization at a conceptual level. Conceptualizing has its roots in perceiving but cannot be carried out adequately at a more complex level unless the child frees himself from the need for perceptual support and is able to cope with ideas or propositions (Inhelder and Piaget, 1958). The ability to cope with propositions need not concern those who deal with the typical three- or four-year-old for he is still in the stage of concrete operations. However, the nursery school child needs many experiences that will lay the foundation for the conservation that is essential to the intellectual growth that he will achieve during these early school years.

Discrimination is basic to conceptualizing, for if a child cannot discriminate he will be unable to classify material. He will also be unable to analyze and resynthesize elements or portions of a situation. In his attempts at classification he will need to abstract relevant elements, and in so doing he must learn to cope with conflicting cues and with non-essential cues. His generalizations will be on different levels, for different materials will need processing in a variety of ways. Attention may be focussed on the concrete or physical attributes of the stimuli, e.g. shape, colour or texture. Some stimulus attributes will lend themselves only to relational generalizing, e.g. large and small, heavy and light, or fat and thin. At an even more advanced level conceptualizing will not be on the basis of physical attributes but rather on the common meaning present in two situations, forcing the child to make a mediated type of generalization. To achieve this latter type of classification he will need to use class names, and here it is of some importance to see that a child is going beyond the label and not merely using it as an alternative name. It has been suggested by Brown (1965) that the naming practices of children probably depend largely on the naming practices of the adults in close association with them; hence class names should not be mistaken for class concepts.

It would be useless, or almost useless, to have developed a concept and be unable to communicate this knowledge to others. Language is therefore of prime importance in the cognitive domain. The capacity for naming or labelling, communicating, questioning and using language in an imaginative manner is all part of cognitive functioning. In addition the role of language in aiding perception and in remembering should not be overlooked. Opportunity for both delayed and immediate recall, as well as for recognition, provides a means of reviewing knowledge.

It will be clear from the foregoing that the nursery school environment should be so designed as to facilitate the progressive development of these various cognitive skills.

Sensory Stimulation

It has been stated that sensations are the raw materials of thinking; of immense importance, then, is the type of stimulation that is provided in the nursery school. A child should learn to use all his senses; visual, auditory, kinesthetic, tactile and olfactory stimuli should be present. In most well-run nursery schools there is a wealth of visual stimuli at all times. Auditory stimulation is usually attended to during specially arranged music sessions. However, the playroom, in which many different activities are occurring, presents interesting and changing auditory patterns, and children should be encouraged to be aware of the sounds accompanying each of these activities. Woodwork also provides an opportunity for practising auditory discrimination, and the outdoor playground with access to street noises gives another chance for the discussion of sounds. It is essential that names be attached to stimuli, whether they are auditory, visual, or of any other type. Materials such as the outdoor slide, climbing frame, and swing provide vivid kinesthetic stimulation. Indoor equipment should also offer opportunities for gross motor activity. To maximize tactile stimulation a variety of material is necessary. The doll corner enables the teacher to vary tactile stimulation; velvet, satin, fur, cotton, terry-cloth and silk all provide different experiences. Sand-paper, finger paints and the strings of an auto-harp will also help the child to gain a knowledge of his world through his sense of touch. In schools where lunch is served, olfactory stimulation presents no problems; in addition special efforts should be made to provide this type of stimulation, e.g. roses and newly mown grass. The fact that stimuli are the raw materials of thinking implies that successful stimulation will give rise to a train of ideas and consequently that language and manipulative activity will follow. It is insufficient to present stimuli without providing opportunity for response.

Research to date has shown that young infants prefer complex to simple stimuli (Fantz, 1965), and coloured to black and white ones (Staples, 1932). Not only do complexity and colour appear to play a part in orientation responses, but so does novelty (Berlyne, 1960). While complexity and colour are easy to provide, novelty is not an easy feature to introduce into a playroom for this implies change and young children seem to be more comfortable when things are kept in definite places and in some order. Predictability promotes security. The amount and kind of novelty and surprise that may be introduced into both the programme and the arrangement of material in the school need extensive research. It is the question of kind and degree that needs investigation rather than the presence or absence of novelty, for it is useless to present stimuli to which no orientation occurs and novelty is too important to neglect in this respect. Indicating stimuli on the part of the adult also determine orientation; comments such as "see," "listen," and "feel" are a part of stimulation.

If a child is to learn to process information he must use his senses to gain information. The teacher's task is to provide a variety of stimulation and to ensure that the child is aware of it.

Curiosity

Curiosity is another important element in early cognitive development. A distinction may be made between perceptual curiosity and epistemic curiosity. According to Berlyne (1960), "perceptual curiosity is reduced by exposure to appropriate stimuli," whereas epistemic curiosity is "that brand of arousal that motivates the quest for knowledge and is relieved when knowledge is procured." For satisfactory cognitive growth nursery school material should arouse both kinds of curiosity. Certain types of picture puzzles will give rise to perceptual curiosity, and when the puzzle has been put together the child's curiosity will be satisfied. Some puzzles, on completion, will initiate questioning indicating that epistemic curiosity has been aroused. For this to occur, the picture should be a colourful, complex one, depicting a novel situation involving some element of uncertainty or conflict. If the teacher's aim is to provide a stimulus to questioning, the manipulative aspect should involve little effort, with the picture being cut into a few simple shapes. If, however, emphasis is to be placed on the manipulative rather than the cognitive aspect, the puzzle could be divided into complicated shapes, with the picture being a relatively simple one. With some nursery school children it may be undesirable to combine the manipulative and informational aspects in one learning situation, as for these children the task would be too long. Children who show poor verbal development in that they are unable to phrase questions may need an alternative mode of response through which to display their curiosity. Stories told in serial form by means of puzzles would allow the child to ask his questions in a non-verbal manner.

Studies indicate that curiosity is "not at its maximum with complete ignorance but increases, up to a point, with increasing knowledge" (Berlyne, 1960). This finding suggests that the teacher should supply some information and then encourage both verbal and manipulative activity. It is noteworthy that when the information provided takes the form of a partially answered question and contains elements of conceptual conflict, curiosity is heightened. The availability of the teacher is vital to the development of curiosity as children address most of their questions to adults. In addition to supplying information to arouse curiosity, the teacher will also serve to reinforce the act of questioning by her approval of and readiness to answer each child's questions. Older and more experienced members of a group are also a source of information for younger and newer group members, and so it is likely that curiosity will increase in a situation where children are not confined with their age-mates. From the viewpoint of cognitive growth it may well be undesirable to separate the three-year-olds from the four-year-olds in the nursery school. The young child of today is the citizen of the future; perhaps the most important thing that we can do for him is to teach him to ask appropriate questions. Questioning is a skill that may be learned (Suchman, 1961). It is suggested here that learning begin in the nursery school for it is at this time that the child's natural curiosity is high. Teacher participation plus carefully selected material will nurture this natural curiosity, whereas an attitude of non-interference together with heavy reliance on the material will impede its growth.

Perceiving and Conceptualizing

These two aspects of cognition will be dealt with together for both are acts of classification and it is difficult to indicate precisely where perception ends and conceptualizing begins. Vernon (1952) describes four stages in the process of perceiving. The first stage involves a vague awareness of what is there. The second stage, that of the generic object, is one in which we become aware of the class of objects to which a stimulus belongs. At this stage in perception, naming and experience begin to play a large role. The stage of the specific object follows this, and it is at this point that the details of the particular object are noted. In the fourth and final stage the stimulus is identified, and the underlying meaning of the situation is apparent to the subject. He now knows how to deal with the situation as he understands the implications therein. A concept may be seen as a network of inferences available for use (Bruner, Goodnow and Austin, 1956). It is possible to identify an object as belonging to a particular category only when one has in fact had previous verbal or manipulative experience relating to the object. If names are known, classification is helped; if names are not known, classification may be impeded. Probably the greatest difference between a child's perception and that of an adult occurs at this stage as the child has a limited number of inferences available for use.

Observation is important at the third stage in perception where details need to be noted. Despite the fact that children tend to have global perception (Werner, 1948), material should provide opportunity for the consideration of detail, the analysis of which is dependent on discrimination. Nursery schools abound with tasks in which material requires sorting on the basis of physical characteristics. While there is therefore no lack of opportunity for this type of concrete generalization and similar generalizations involving relational aspects, one sees fewer opportunities for classification on the basis of meaning. Administrative convenience often determines the lay-out and housing of material in the nursery school, and this tendency to keep materials separate is of little help to the child. The child's play world is arranged in too orderly a manner; on many occasions he should be given the opportunity to order things in his own way. When a child wants to play with blocks, he finds them in a neat pile or in a box and he does not have to select them from a box containing other materials. Neat separation of materials will not enhance discrimination or creativity, for creative thinking involves using familiar things in new combinations. The young child who is allowed only one set of material at a time will have little opportunity for practising creative thought. Torrance (1965) has stressed the fact that creative thinking needs to be reinforced. Too many young children are negatively reinforced if they dare to use a book as the roof for a house.

This does not mean that the nursery school playroom should present a continuously chaotic appearance, but some mixing of materials followed by reclassification would provide opportunities for discrimination. This exercise should not be limited, for example, to putting the blue blocks in the blue box, nor should it be solely on the concrete basis, but it should also allow for relational generalizations such as putting together small objects, objects that will roll (e.g. chalk, a jar, a ball), or things that may be pasted on to paper (e.g. beads, corrugated paper, bits of material). New classifications should be encouraged as new activities and games are introduced. This would be the beginning of practice in abstraction, for in arriving at new ways of classifying material children would have to neglect many aspects of each object and concentrate only on the elements essential to the new grouping. In addition, conflicting cues would have to be considered; for example, if a piece of chalk is stood on end it will not roll, and a half-inch cube, although small, will be large compared to a bead. These conflicts would have to be resolved through manipulative exploration and discussion. What a young child sees depends largely on the arrangement of the stimuli. He needs experiences such at matching, counting, and serial ordering, in which material can be rearranged; at the same time he will learn that the rearranged material remains invariant in quantity. Here again, language plays an important part.

Without language the nursery school experience is incomplete. Language is one mode of sensory stimulation, is vital to curiosity, and helps in perception. Much perceptual learning has already taken place by the time a child enters nursery school. He has achieved a constancy in many areas and is accomplished in figure-ground perception. Where there has been failure to learn in these areas, re-education should include language and not be confined to manipulative activity. The child moves from perception of real three-dimensional objects to flat pictorial representations and in developing programmes to promote perceptual growth this should be taken into account. The nursery school child should be talked to about his world and should be encouraged to talk about it and to recall experiences just after they have occurred. After lunch, the food should be discussed; after outdoor play the weather and the games played are topics for practising recall. Routines afford unique opportunities for teaching concepts. In the cloakroom the child can gain new insights in terms of the special activities that occur only in this situation. For example, he stands *up* and slips *into* his coat, and sits *down* to take *off* his shoes. His body image becomes more clearly differentiated as he puts a shoe on one foot and then on the other. Terms such as left and right come to have meaning, for the left shoe will not fit the right foot. The toilet routine offers opportunity for hearing different sounds, but all these will be missed if the child has no words to attach to these sensations. The language of taking off your coat is as important as the act itself. The three-year-old does not learn language from his peers, but from adults, and the nursery school adult with whom he spends, in some instances, the larger portion of his day has a great responsibility in the language area. Language is a means of self-expression and the young child needs help in the development of this skill, for its development cannot occur unaided.

The Teacher's Role

The role that the nursery school should play in fostering intellectual skills has been the subject of discussion on many occasions. Most people agree that a materially enriched environment is desirable; it is the part played by the adult that arouses the emotions of the debaters, with views ranging all the way from complete non-interference to direct, active teacher participation. It is proposed here that the teacher of today needs to play an active role in both talking with the child and sharing in his activity. This will require highly trained and skilled teachers whose participation will constitute enrichment of, but not rude intrusion into, the child's life. The teacher's aims are:

1. to provide a variety of stimulation;
2. to ensure suitable orientation responses to stimuli;
3. to arrange for practice in perceptual and conceptual activities;
4. to supply the reinforcement necessary for learning in this area;
5. to motivate the child to carry out knowledge-seeking responses and especially to help him to develop achievement motivation and competence motivation;
6. to encourage and provide a model for language growth;
7. to promote exploratory motor and verbal activity.

To carry out these functions the teacher will need to be an astute observer and a skilful conversationalist, for the activities involved in cognitive growth should occur easily and naturally in the programme without special practice sessions having to be arranged. The teacher needs to keep these aims in mind during her casual conversations with the children. She needs to know why she has made a comment and what purpose it has served. Has her comment sparked curiosity, has it had a motivating or reinforcing function or has it increased the child's knowledge or set him on his way to acquire information for himself? Analysis of teachers' conversations with children could play an important part in teacher training. Verbalization should aim at shaping cognitive skills. The teacher will require a detailed knowledge of the processes of learning and thinking to perform this function successfully. To help the teacher, new ways of testing cognitive skills will be required, for each child will have to be catered for in terms of his uniqueness. The individuality of each child's level and style of cognitive functioning is her intimate concern. Cognitive development is a long, slow process which will be slowed down even more if the teaching staff is moved around too often; teacher continuity is an important factor if the teacher is to be thoroughly familiar with her children.

Activity depends on social, emotional and motor growth as well as on cognitive growth, which cannot therefore be understood in isolation. Cognitive functioning must be seen as one aspect of a child's total behaviour pattern. The nursery school teacher will have to have specialized knowledge in all these areas of development in order to deal intelligently with any one aspect of development. Knowledge of the social setting in which the children live may significantly influence the type of programme the school should offer, as studies (Deutsch, 1964) are demonstrating the adverse effects on development of certain types of environment. The nursery school would do well to aim at counteracting these poor conditions.

Much basic research is needed in the cognitive area. The manner in which early functioning is related to subsequent growth needs to be explored. Longitudinal studies, despite their time-consuming disadvantage, are likely to provide us with the most valuable data. Individual case studies in which a detailed clinical approach is adopted would also be worthwhile. An approach in which cognitive development is related only to chronological age is insufficient; individual differences and patterns of growth are far more important to the nursery school teacher than are age norms. A study in progress by Millichamp and Langstaff* is one in which the relationship between patterns of cognitive functioning and mental health status is being investigated. Interpersonal affiliation will also be viewed in relation to cognitive development. The longitudinal nature of this research in which the outcome of early patterns will be seen in terms of later functioning should provide the type of data that will assist in designing programmes for individual children. A study by Schermann (1965) is suggestive of the type of easily administered test needed to give the teacher information about a child's level of thinking Results show that some four-year-olds are unable to carry out simple matching tasks, whereas others are capable of making far transpositional judgements; these latter have this technique well established, and they are easily identified. In addition the test distinguishes between those children who are able to give elaborate verbal explanations and those who are able to discriminate correctly between shapes, sizes and colours but are unable to explain why they have made a particular choice. Children falling into each of these categories need very different experiences. That these early experiences may be important to the child's future development is highlighted by the fact that success on this test at four years is significantly related to high reading achievement at the end of grade one. Many aspects of perception probably have critical periods during the nursery years, and await exploration.

There has been a great deal of talk in the past about leaving the child to realize his own potential in his own time. At the present time psychologists are questioning how this potential comes about. Evidence is accumulating to the effect that reaction potential is itself determined to a larger extent by the early environment than was previously thought to be the case (Hunt, 1961). The importance of the early years is to be seen in Bloom's (1964) comment that "in terms of intelligence measured at age 17, about 50% of the development takes place between conception and age 4, about 30% between ages 4 and 8, and about 20% between ages 8 and 17." Today society is looking to the educational system to attempt to raise the level of each child's cognitive ability, not merely to

* This investigation is supported by Mental Health Grant No. 32, and is being carried out at the Institute of Child Study, University of Toronto.

educate each according to his ability. Individual needs must be taken into account; it is not sufficient to provide children with equal opportunities. The educator of today must challenge each child in realistic terms, that is, in terms of his uniqueness. It is time to forget about norms and averages and to allow children the luxury of being individuals. Routines are important, but so is departure from routine, for these moments of divergence are when we exercise cognitive skills. The role of the nursery school is to provide the opportunity for the child to exercise the skills he brings with him to school, and to foster those which he lacks.

References

Anderson, J. E. 1957. Dynamics of development: system in process. In D. B. Harris (ed.), *The concept of development* (Minneapolis, Minn.: The University of Minnesota Press).

Berlyne, D. E. 1965. *Structure and direction in thinking* (New York: John Wiley & Sons, Inc.).

———. 1960. *Conflict, arousal, and curiosity* (New York: McGraw-Hill, Inc.).

Bloom, B. S. 1964. *Stability and change in human characteristics* (New York: John Wiley & Sons, Inc.).

———. 1956. Taxonomy of educational objectives. *The classification of educational goals, handbook I: cognitive domain* (New York: David McKay Company, Inc.).

Brown, R. 1965. How shall a thing be called? In P. H. Mussen, J. J. Conger and J. Kagan (eds.), *Readings in child development and personality* (New York: Harper & Row).

Bruner, J. S., J. S. Goodnow, and G. A. Austin. 1956. *A study of thinking* (New York: John Wiley & Sons, Inc.).

Brunswick, E. 1957. Scope and aspects of the cognitive problem. In J. S. Bruner *et al.*, *Contemporary approaches to cognition* (Cambridge, Mass: Harvard University Press).

Deutsch, C. P. October 1964. Auditory discrimination and learning: social factors. *Merrill-Palmer Quart.*, **10**, pp. 277–296.

English, H. B. 1934. *A student's dictionary of psychological terms.* Fourth ed. (New York: Harper & Row).

Fantz, R. L. 1965. The origin of form perception. In P. H. Mussen, J. J. Conger, and J. Kagan (eds.), *Readings in child development and personality* (New York: Harper & Row).

Flavell, J. H. 1963. *The developmental psychology of Jean Piaget* (Princeton, N.J.: D. Van Nostrand Company, Inc.).

Fowler, W. March 1962. Cognitive learning in infancy and childhood. *Psychol. Rev.*, **59**, pp. 116–152.

Hunt, J. McV. 1961. *Intelligence and experience* (New York: The Ronald Press Company).

Inhelder, B., and J. Piaget. 1958. *The growth of logical thinking: from childhood to adolescence* (New York: Basic Books, Inc.).

Russell, D. H. 1956. *Children's thinking* (Boston: Ginn & Company).

Schermann, A. 1965. A paper read to the Conference on Nursery Education, Toronto, Canada.

Staples, R. April 1932. The response of infants to colors. *J. exp. Psychol.*, **15**, pp. 119–141.

Suchman, J. R. June 1961. Inquiry training: building skills for autonomous discovery. *Merrill-Palmer Quart.*, **7**, pp. 147–169.

Taylor, J. G. 1962. *The behavioral basis of perception* (New Haven, Conn.: Yale University Press).

Torrance, E. P. 1965. *Rewarding creative behavior* (Englewood Cliffs, N.J.: Prentice-Hall, Inc.).

Vernon, M. D. 1952. *A further study of visual perception* (Cambridge, Mass.: Cambridge University Press).

Werner, H. 1948. *Comparative psychology of mental development*. Revised ed. (Chicago, Ill.: Follett Publishing Co.).

PART **5** *The Promise of Head Start*

Among the many programs arising from the "war on poverty," Project Head Start currently stands in an enviable position. Reports from every geographical area of the nation, with few exceptions, point to this innovation as having great potential for altering the cycle of educational retardation of children from low income homes. Additionally, the success of Head Start is producing great interest in the widespread establishment of programs in early childhood education.

Operation Head Start was designed to assist communities in financing Child Development Centers for children of limited opportunity at the pre-kindergarten or pre-first-grade level. Created by the Economic Opportunity Act of 1964, Head Start programs are financed up to ninety percent of cost by the Office of Economic Opportunity. Community Action Agencies organize the programs on a community-wide enrollment basis. Sponsoring agencies provide health, social services, and educational activities.

Head Start programs are tailored to local needs. Teachers are given intensive training prior to working directly with the children. And very importantly, for the first time on a large-scale basis, teachers, social workers, members of the medical profession, neighborhood volunteers, parents, and others have been pooling their resources to accomplish the goals of the program. It appears relevant to assert that neither these goals nor most of the programs emphasized academic content or the common "school readiness" approaches. Rather, they focused upon providing those social experiences commonly experienced by most children but unavailable to those from impoverished homes. The Office of Economic Opportunity* suggested several broad goals, including improving health, confidence, self-respect, dignity, and

* **Office of Economic Opportunity,** *Project Head Start* **(booklet), Washington, D.C., 1965.**

277

peer relations, strengthening family ties, providing opportunities for meeting various community helpers, broadening horizons, and increasing language competencies through varied social experiences. The imaginative experimentation reported throughout this volume will undoubtedly lead to a heavier cognitive focus in future programs.

During the summer of 1965 over 550,000 children in approximately 2500 Child Development Centers participated in Head Start programs. After participating in the planning of Head Start, Keith Osborn visited centers around the country during their initial summer operation. His report, though not statistical, leaves little doubt of the concern of many different groups in making Head Start a success. Osborn believes that low pupil-teacher ratio was instrumental; that the benefits are multiple; that the impact will influence the entire educational field toward downward extension of schooling.

Some of the early research findings on experimental preschool programs are reported by Clay V. Brittain. The results are predominantly positive. However, over extended periods, gains in certain programs were no longer evident. This, however should not necessarily reflect upon Head Start but on the programs that follow: Brittain suggests that findings be analyzed according to the types of programs, initial entrance age, length of program, and the training of participating teachers. A crucial issue may well be regimentation, characteristic of public school programs, versus the child development centers' permissiveness concept.

The "Six Months Later" study, reported by Max Wolff and Annie Stein, was designed to evaluate the effects of Head Start on first-grade readiness. The initial results generally favored Head Start children over non-Head Start children on school readiness measures, and teachers indicated an initial adjustment advantage for Head Start children. But after six to eight months had elapsed there was no significant difference between the scores of Head Start children and their peers on the pre-school inventory. None of the teachers replying felt that Head Start helped the child relate to a teacher. Such studies tend to elaborate the limitations of short-term research on the effects of Head Start. Consequently, we look to the future for clearer direction.

Following the second year of year-round Head Start classes, William Brazziel analyzed the effects of Head Start on the lives of children and adults involved. Although numerous research organizations are conducting studies, at this time certain aspects defy measurement and others require subjective description. Yet some answers are readily available. A minimal gain from Head Start is now regarded as "from five to ten points in I.Q. and from twenty to twenty-five points on school readiness tests." There is a major problem of maintenance of such gains in the elementary grades. In essence, it appears that public schools have a long way to go in catching up to the spirit of Head Start. Some radical departures from the ordinary are in order.

A program to evaluate Head Start-produced changes through focusing upon the mutually interactive effects of the child and the teacher is being carried on by the staff of the Child Development Evaluation and Research Center at the University of Texas. This has resulted in the development of several new evaluative instruments for assessing teachers' classroom behavior relative to children. Edward Earl Gotts and John Pierce-Jones report that Head Start children entered first grade with greater readiness to learn; teacher "authoritarianism" increased with years of experience; teachers from minority groups had more authoritarian attitudes; Head Start teachers approached children with greater confidence and optimism and viewed those children with Head Start experience more favorably than did other teachers. These writers recognize the need to direct attention toward the parental-environmental setting and to continue imaginative investigations along longitudinal lines.

As preschool programs become firmly established in public schools, Head Start programs are coming increasingly under public school control. Erwin Knoll points out that Title 1 funds are being used to supplement O.E.O. funds for the establishment of preschools. Many educators believe that such programs will become permanent fixtures of the public school system. The failure of many primary grade programs to sustain Head Start gains leads the editor of this volume to suggest that Head Start has more to offer public schools than vice versa in the education of disadvantaged children. Indoctrination of Head Start with the rigidity of typical public schoolism could well prove fatal for Head Start *and* for the disadvantaged.

24   Project Head Start—An Assessment*

KEITH OSBORN, *Merrill-Palmer Institute, Detroit, Michigan*

During the past summer over 550,000 children in approximately 2,500 Child Development Centers throughout the country participated in a preschool program formally known as Project Head Start. Project Head Start is one of several Community Action Programs operated under the Office of Economic Opportunity. This project represented the largest program for young children ever sponsored by our government.

Geographically speaking, there were programs as far north as the Arctic Circle; as far south as American Samoa; as far east as the Virgin Islands; as far west as Guam. Children came from rural and urban areas, from Indian reservations and Eskimo villages, from migrant groups and "the Hollows" of West Virginia. In some counties one out of three children who entered kindergarten or first grade this fall were in Head Start programs during the summer.

The project also involved over 100,000 adults—parents, teachers, physicians, psychologists and other professional and volunteer workers. It is noteworthy that while the actual operation of the program could be administered by any local nonprofit organization, over 80 percent of the centers were sponsored by local school systems.

These general facts can give the reader some idea of the scope of the project.

The growth and time element of Head Start are rather remarkable. Implemented in June of 1965, the program was not conceived until November 1964. A Planning Committee was formed during that month composed of outstanding professional leaders, including George Brain, James L. Hymes, Jr. and Jack Neimeyer. A Project Director, Julius B. Richmond, M.D., was named in February.

During the early planning stages the project was referred to as the Kiddie Corps and it was felt that perhaps fifty to one hundred thousand children would be involved in an eight week summer program. By late February the response of local communities was so great (approximately 65 percent of all counties in the U.S. wanted programs) that the projected enrollment was estimated between five and six hundred thousand. While the basic outlines of the program were formulated between November-

* *Educational Leadership*, November 1965, vol. 23, no. 2. Reprinted with permission of the Association for Supervision and Curriculum Development and Keith Osborn. Copyright © 1965 by the Association for Supervision and Curriculum Development.

January, for all practical purposes the actual work of the project (community planning, funding, orientation of teachers) took place over a period of four months. At this writing plans are being considered to: (a) initiate programs to "follow-up" on Head Start children, (b) to begin year-around programs wherever possible, and (c) plan for the second Head Start program for the summer of 1966.

Observations

Since research data on the project are not available at this early date, the following statements are based on my observations of the program.

1. THE CONCEPT OF THE CHILD DEVELOPMENT CENTER. One of the most significant aspects of the project is the general idea of a Child Development Center, since Head Start encompasses more than an educational program *per se*.

The Child Development Center is both a concept and a community facility. In concept it represents drawing together all the resources—family, community and professional—which can contribute to the child's total development. It draws heavily on the professional skills of persons in education, health, nutrition, and social services. It recognizes that professional and nonprofessional can make a meaningful contribution. It emphasizes the family as fundamental to the child's total development and the role of the parents in developing policies and participating in the program of the center.

As a community facility the Child Development Center is organized around the classroom and the play area. It provides a program for health services, parent interviews, feeding of children, and meetings of parents and other residents in the community. This concept recognizes that some children have been deprived in many areas—and that the lack of intellectual stimulation is only one of several gaps for the children of the poor. While the concept of nursery school is sound, the concept of a Child Development Center seems more appropriate for the children served by Head Start.

My observations of programs throughout the country reinforce this belief. Many children received early diagnosis of medical problems which were unknown to the parents. In some instances dental diagnosis showed that a "slow learning" problem was in reality a dental problem. In other cases a "discipline problem" turned out to be a medical one.

Most of the children in Head Start were provided with at least one hot meal each day. One teacher told me, "Head Start is providing several of the children in my group with the only substantial meal they receive."

2. TEACHERS AND PROGRAM. Approximately 40,000 teachers served in

Head Start Centers during the summer. Many of these teachers had not had previous experience with children of this age and cultural milieu. As a result there were instances in which third and fourth grade teachers taught miniature versions of these grades and treated the children more like preadolescents than like preschoolers.

Some of the centers were more concerned with seating arrangements and school readiness *per se*. A number of centers concentrated on teaching of reading and numbers and failed to provide a program which would make up for earlier cultural losses in these children.

In some instances the children were highly regimented and programs were lacking in flexibility, thus many golden opportunities were missed for individualized instruction of children. It is unfortunate that more centers did not provide programs which could meet both individual and group needs. I would quickly add that this shortcoming was not due to lack of staff—the teacher to pupil ratio in Head Start was 1 to 13 and the adult to child ratio about 1 to 5. Rather it was usually a lack of imagination on the part of the teacher.

Fortunately, the majority of teachers did capitalize on the small group and did make the transition to preschool types of curriculum. Activities included art, stories, science activities, creative play and visits to various community facilities. These programs were designed to stimulate children's thinking—but, in contrast to situations mentioned earlier, the curriculum was geared to the interests and abilities appropriate to children of this age.

I feel much of the success of the program was due to the factor of class size. For years educators have asked for small groups and Head Start has demonstrated the value of such class size. The most consistent comment from teachers was in terms of class size and their feeling that substantial gains were possible since they could provide each child with maximum individualized instruction. Whether or not communities will ultimately bear the high cost of small group instruction is another matter. However, this may be the price we must pay for earlier deprivation.

I also believe that the program will ultimately affect the entire educational field in another way. Everywhere I went, school administrators were discussing ways to extend school downward. I feel the most immediate change will be a rise in kindergarten programs in school districts where no program exists; in other districts, there will be a move to extend schooling to three and four year olds.

Perhaps Head Start's biggest contribution has been its effect on the teacher himself. This could be seen in three ways: (a) alerting the teacher to the needs of the poor, (b) seeing the progress which could be made in eight weeks in a small group setting, and (c) a commitment on the part of the teacher to follow through with these children in the fall.

3. PARENTS AND COMMUNITY.   Just as the quality of teaching varied, so did the quality of work with parents and with the commitment of the community. In some centers parents participated fully in all aspects of the program. Parents served as committee members and, in several instances, as committee chairmen of the center. Parents also served as teacher aides, story tellers, cooks, carpenters and secretaries.

This type of participation is a basic part of the philosophy of the Community Action Program. I am convinced that this philosophy is sound and is justified. By and large parents of culturally deprived children are as concerned with the welfare of their young as any other parents. Perhaps even more so—since these parents know the long term effects of an inadequate education. At one center a Head Start father told me that his teenage son had more respect for him since he had assumed a role of importance in his community. A number of parents talked of returning to school. Many parents went to the Public Library for the first time to obtain books for themselves and their children.

In some centers, however, there was little or no parent participation. Part of the lack of parent participation was doubtless due to the "crash" aspect of the program, since some communities were unable to mobilize their parents as quickly as others. However, we encountered many instances—often in programs run by the local school system—where no real effort was made to include parents in any way. If this program is to be more than first aid, we must bring parents into the center and include them in all aspects of the program.

4. THE CHILD.   Research data and success in school this fall will ultimately provide the information as to how successful the Child Development Center was in providing children with a head start into life.

But for me—as well as many teachers, physicians, social workers and others who worked actively in the program—the day to day, here and now experience which the children received made the program a success.

There were some dramatic instances of children who had never seen themselves in a mirror or children who used a telephone for the first time.

But for nearly all of the children there was a "first" at painting, crayons, child-oriented facilities, or visits to the zoo, supermarket and the fire station. Many situations which middle-class children take for granted, the Head Start child experienced for the first time. Many of these youngsters had never had a book read to them.

Certainly the Child Development Center cannot in eight weeks make up for four years of deprivation. It did not attempt to do so. Rather the program attempted to provide some of the medical, nutritional and educational advantages the children of more affluent parents enjoy. It attempted to give these children a better beginning—or as we at the Office of Economic Opportunity called it—a Head Start.

EDITOR'S NOTE: Ordinarily a letter of transmittal is just that—it transmits. However, the letter that accompanied Keith Osborn's article did more than transmit. It gave a sense of the excitement and almost of exaltation felt by many of the persons responsible for initiating and carrying out the pioneering venture for young children that was called Project Head Start. The letter follows:

Saturday
Sept. 11, 1965

Dear Robert:

During Head Start, I was brought to Washington by the Office of Education as Educational Consultant (three days a week) and placed on temporary assignment to the Office for Economic Opportunity with Project Head Start. I went in February so I had the opportunity to see the project grow from infancy.

I must admit the past few months have been the most exciting in my life. As one who taught as a nursery school and kindergarten teacher, it was gratifying to see others become equally interested in the education and welfare of young children.

There were some problems (at times we referred to the project jokingly as "Head Ache" and "Head Shrink") but many more satisfactions —I hope I have presented both fairly. However, I am really prejudiced and perhaps much too close to the Project. It was a huge success. In spite of some poor teaching—there were many more examples of great teaching—and of teachers and administrators who worked long hours on short notice to insure success of the program.

I wish I knew how to tell this part of the story—the many nonprofessionals (the secretaries at OEO and other personnel who worked 12-15 hours every day between February and June—because they wanted these children to have a Head Start in school—the bus driver in West Virginia who took time off from his regular job and went to the Center to have juice and crackers with "his" children because they asked him to. The Head Start Center in Mississippi that met in a church which was burned to the ground by some whites—and they opened the next day in a tent. The farmer who lived near an Indian Reservation and who each morning saddled his horse, forded a river and picked up an Indian child—who would not have attended a Center otherwise. An ADC (Aid-to-Dependent-Children) mother who worked four hours daily in one center—without pay—she paid a baby-sitter to care for her other children—why? Because she wanted these children to get the schooling she never had. The Kentucky principal who worked at two jobs for four months so his county could have Head Start. The Negro principal in Georgia who will probably lose his position in the school system because of his stand in following the "spirit" that Head Start is for *all* children regardless of color. Numerous consultants who, on an hour's notice, dropped everything and flew all over the country to help communities plan for Head Start. I visited one cook (a volunteer) working in a "tenant farm" center—there were no fans and only one small window in the kitchen—the temperature was 97° outside—she was cooking fried chicken and baking rolls for the children. Or even the school superintendent who received funds for 30 migrant children and then returned the funds because the families moved before the Center opened.

I don't know how you tell these stories in an article—it is really unfortunate—since they represent the true flavor of Head Start.

Sincerely,

Keith (Osborn)

25   Some Early Findings of Research on Preschool Programs for Culturally Deprived Children*

CLAY V. BRITTAIN, *Children's Bureau, U.S. Department of Health, Education, and Welfare*

One of the most salient recent educational movements in this country is the widespread development of compensatory programs for culturally deprived children, especially at the preschool level. Project Head Start, sponsored by the Office of Economic Opportunity, alone reached well over half a million children in its first year of operation, and thousands of preschool children are enrolled in other programs for the disadvantaged. Although designed primarily to serve educational ends, the value of these programs goes beyond education in any narrow sense. Based on premises about the potential effectiveness of early compensatory intervention as a means of breaking intergenerational cycles of economic and cultural deprivation, the effects of preschool enrichment programs promise to have important meaning for child-care programs generally. Given their recency and their proliferation, exhaustive treatment of the subject now would be premature; but a preliminary examination of some of the preschool programs and early findings of research concerning their effects is not untimely.

A basic consideration in the development of compensatory educational programs is the observation, by no means recent, that children from poverty-ridden homes tend to do poorly in school. They come to school less well prepared than middle-class children and fall further behind each year. The main effect most often expected from preschool enrichment programs is a change in this tendency, that is, the child's involvement in

* Reprinted from *Children*, July–August 1966, vol. 13, no. 4, published by the Children's Bureau, Welfare Administration, U.S. Department of Health, Education, and Welfare.

such a program becomes a means of improving his readiness for school and, in turn, his academic achievement.

The focus on this end does not preclude concern about and provision for other types of outcome; however, the early findings pertain almost exclusively to educational effects. Before examining these findings, let me mention the rationale underlying the programs and the followup studies which evaluate them.

These programs are shaped largely by assumptions about the characteristics of "culturally deprived" children which underlie their inferior academic performance. These characteristics, which follow patterns of both cognitive and affective deficit—at least from the middle-class point of view—include poor language facility, constriction in dealing with symbolic and abstract ideas, narrowness of outlook because of the narrowness of the familiar environment, passivity and lack of curiosity, low self-esteem, and lack of motivation for achievement.

In developing enrichment programs, the longer range goal of improving academic achievement becomes the proximal goal of modifying these features in the psychological makeup of the "culturally deprived" child; thus, plans for systematic evaluation include both the long-range assessment of school achievement and the assessment of more immediate psychological changes, typically as they are reflected in test scores. Early findings are mainly of the latter type, though this is not exclusively the case.

Early Results

Although the preliminary findings concerning the effects of preschool enrichment programs are predominantly positive, this is not universally so. Gains in IQ scores and augmented language-cognitive ability have been found in several followup studies, along with indirect evidence of greater interest in school and motivation for doing schoolwork. But this is not evenly true; some followup studies have not found such effects. I will here examine both types of findings.

Two of the earliest programs are the Peabody Early Training Project (Gray and Klaus, 1965) near Nashville and the program of the Institute for Developmental Studies (Goldstein, 1965) directed by Martin Deutsch in New York City. Although the directors of both projects emphasize the importance of long-range followup studies to determine program effectiveness, preliminary results have been reported. From the Peabody project, Gray and Klaus (1965) report substantial increase in IQ scores, as measured by either the Stanford-Binet or the Wechsler Intelligence Scale for Children (WISC), among children in the program as compared with those of

children in control groups. There were gains of 5 and 6 points in two treatment groups and losses of 4 and 6 points in two control groups. Children
in treatment groups also had higher scores on the Peabody Picture Vocabulary Test and the Illinois Test of Psycholinguistic Ability, and when
they entered the first grade they performed better on reading readiness
tests. From the Institute for Development Studies, Goldstein (1965)
reports comparable differences in Stanford-Binet IQ scores between children attending the experimental preschool program and controls. As in
the Peabody project, there were apparently control group losses as well
as experimental group gains. Also, as before, the experimental group performed better on the Peabody Picture Vocabulary Test. In both programs, gains in the early experimental groups had been maintained for
about 2 years.

From an experimental nursery school program in Philadelphia, Beller
(1965) reports similar findings. The children gained about 6 points in
Stanford-Binet IQ scores from mid-year in the nursery school to mid-year
in kindergarten. Also, at the time of testing in kindergarten, the nursery
groups were on the average about 8 points higher in IQ scores than control
children with no nursery school experience. The nursery groups performed better than the control groups on the Peabody Picture Vocabulary
Test. A group verbal intelligence test (Philadelphia Verbal Abilities) also
reflected the effects of nursery school, but results of an individual non-
verbal test (Goodenough Draw-a-Man) showed no consistent difference
between the nursery and control groups.

In addition to test scores such as these, there are other indications of
the effectiveness of preschool enrichment programs. Weikart, Kamii, and
Radin (1964) report from a study in Ypsilanti, Mich., that children who
had been in the preschool program had better kindergarten attendance
records than the control group children. They were also rated higher by
their kindergarten teachers on interest in subject matter, initiative, verbal
communication, imagination, and possessiveness toward the teacher.

In the Philadelphia study (Beller, 1965), the nursery school children
were rated as more casual, expressive, and flexible than the control group
children in reaction to test and learning situations in kindergarten.

Less systematic but interesting impressions were reported in the other
preliminary studies I have mentioned. Goldstein (1965) cites statements
from parents concerning the positive effects on other children in the
family of the child's involvement in the enrichment program of the
Institute for Developmental Studies. And Gray and Klaus (1965) report
indications of effects of their early training project on culturally deprived
children not enrolled in it.

There are, in addition, many instances of impressionistic judgment
of the good effects of small enrichment programs for which systematic

followup is not feasible. Such impressions seem to be universally favorable, in most instances highly so.

But there is another and more cautionary side to the picture. Although there are few studies with negative findings, the results of these studies are too important to be ignored. The most unequivocally negative findings to date, it seems to me, are reported by Alpern (1966) from a program in Indianapolis, Ind. He reports that 5-year-old children who attended a preschool program for 7 months made substantial gains on the Metropolitan Readiness Test, but so did children in the control group. In both groups, gains were statistically significant, but group differences were not. Both made slight and nonsignificant gains in Stanford-Binet IQ scores. On the bases of these findings, he is strongly skeptical about the value of short-range preschool programs. A followup study 17 months later showed no difference between experimental and control subjects in first grade scores on the Metropolitan Readiness Test or in ratings by teachers of academic motivation and progress.

Maintenance of Gains

But even when good effects of preschool programs are evident in gains in test scores and observable behavioral changes, are they maintained over extended periods of time? This is a crucial question which can be answered only by long-range followup studies. However, the findings reported by Weikart and others (1964) from the Ypsilanti study are especially significant. At the time of the followup study, three small groups of children had been admitted to the prekindergarten program. These groups, together with control groups, were called "waves." Children in wave 0 entered in the fall of 1962 as 4-year-olds and had, at the time of reporting, spent 1 year in the experimental nursery and 1 year in kindergarten. Wave 1 entered in 1962 as 3-year-olds and had spent 2 years in the nursery. Wave 2 children entered in 1963 as 3-year-olds and had spent 1 year in the nursery.

Scores on the Peabody Picture Vocabulary Test, the Illinois Test of Psycholinguistic Ability, the Gates Reading Readiness Test, and the Stanford-Binet Intelligence Scale all provided indications of the effects of attending nursery school, but the findings of interest pertain to Stanford-Binet IQ score changes. In all three waves, the experimental and control groups diverged during their first year in the program and at the end of the year group differences were impressive. But for waves 0 and 1, this trend was reversed during the second year. At the end of the second year, the group differences were no longer statistically significant.

Similar findings have been reported by Larson and Olson (1965) from a program in Racine, Wis. At the end of a year in a well-designed kindergarten program, the experimental group performed substantially better than a comparison group in scores on the Illinois Test of Psycholinguistic Ability. But by the end of the first grade this and other signs of superiority in the children in the experimental group over the children in the control group were no longer evident.

Preliminary findings, however, are not consistent on the extent to which gains from these preschool programs are maintained. As noted above, gains in IQ scores that had already persisted for 2 years were reported from the Peabody project and the Institute for Developmental Studies.

Precisely how we should interpret these initial results is not clear. The extent to which they are regarded optimistically probably would vary from one reader to another. But it seems neither rash nor unduly pessimistic to suppose that the variability they reflect will continue to be evident, even in less preliminary findings. Imperfections in assessment methods would of course be enough to assure variability. But programs of early enrichment differ from one another so extensively they almost assure different results.

Program Differences

Getzels (1965) has described these program differences in terms of the different underlying assumptions which the programs reflect about the deficiencies of the culturally deprived child. Present preschool programs for culturally deprived children, he suggests, may fall into these three broad categories:

1. Programs based on the assumption that differences between the culturally deprived child and the middle-class child are matters of degree rather than of kind. Hence, if a given type of nursery program is good for the middle-class child, it is also good for the culturally deprived child. The aim in these programs is to provide supplementary experience.

2. Programs based on the assumption that what culturally deprived children mainly lack is familiarity with school-related objects and activities. The aim here is to provide academic-preparatory preschool experience.

3. Programs based on the assumption that the culturally deprived child differs fundamentally from the middle-class child in self-concept, language, values, and perceptual processes. The aim here is to provide compensatory experience sufficient to modify these environmental effects.

As results accumulate, findings should be analyzed in relation to some such typology of programs as Getzels describes. But there are also more simple program differences on which results should probably be examined. They include ages of children at entrance, program duration and amount of time children spend in it, staff characteristics, and the nature and amount of parental involvement in the program.

The interprogram variation in initial ages of the children spans a difference of about 2 years, and the entrance age varies from 3 years in some programs to 5 years in others, but modally the entrance age seems to be 4. In view of what is almost the *raison d'etre* of the preschool programs—that is, early intervention is crucial—an examination of results in relation to age differences should be significant.

The programs vary in length from a few weeks or months to several years. They also vary in the amount of time the child spends in the program: from sessions of 2½ or 3 hours a week to sessions of 5 hours for 4 or 5 days a week. Economics indicate the desirability of examining possible relationships between time dimensions and program results.

Two types of program variations in terms of staff characteristics have a bearing: differences in professional training and experience and differences in personal characteristics. With respect to the first, there are several staffing patterns. For example, some programs use both professional and nonprofessional teachers; others use only experienced and certified teachers. Comparative data reported by Beller are significant here. In one program, all teachers had at least 1 year of experience in teaching culturally deprived children; in two others the staff included inexperienced teachers. Differences favoring the experimental group were more clearly evident in the first program.

The second type of variation in staffing is represented by the Peabody Early Training Project (Gray and Klaus, 1965). All of the children in this program are Negro. In the assignment of staff members, attention was given to balanced representation in sex and color to provide the children with appropriate role models. The consequences for achievement motivation should be particularly significant.

Minimal level of parental involvement is no doubt essential for the success of any program, but there are at least three types of interprogram variation in parental role. Programs differ in (1) the degree of parental commitment prerequisite to the child's enrollment in the program, (2) the level of parental involvement in the educational processes of the program, and (3) the means of enlisting and encouraging parental involvement. It might be valuable to look at these in terms of different effects on the parents as well as on the children. But more than this, such program differences probably make a difference in the types of children served and in attrition rates, both of which are highly important in interpreting different results.

Focus and Goals

Careful analyses of programs would undoubtedly reveal other, and perhaps more significant, differences. But whatever the program differences in terms of which results are analyzed, it seems highly important that the ends desired not be narrowly conceived. In this connection, the focus on school readiness and the improvement of academic achievement is not necessarily at the expense of concern about and provision for other types of outcome. In several instances, followup plans call for the assessment of the effect of the program on the child's development in its multiple dimensions. In the Baltimore Early School Admissions Project (1964), for example, research studies will assess such health and physiological effects as changes in height, weight, and dental and bone development. It will also assess the effect of the program on the child's emotional development and interpersonal behavior. This broad assessment will increase the relevance of the findings for child-care programs generally.

But even in terms of educational effects per se, it is important that criteria of desirability not be narrowly construed. Findings reported by Kitano (1964) may illustrate a crucial issue here. In his study, he found that children who had been enrolled in a child-care center housed in a public school were rated by their teachers in the early elementary grades as less well adjusted to school than control children not enrolled in such a program. He suggests that this difference may have been due to the assertiveness and spontaneity nurtured in the permissive atmosphere of the child-care center but not regarded as appropriate in the more highly regimented elementary school classrooms.

This possibility points up the importance of the questions raised in Getzels' paper (1965): "*Can the standards of today's school be taken safely as the model for the transformation of the culturally deprived child? Is this what we want for our children, or should some thought be given as well . . . to the transformation of the school itself?*"

References

Alpern, G. D. 1966. *The failure of a nursery school enrichment program for culturally deprived children.* A paper presented at the 1966 meeting of the American Orthopsychiatric Association, San Francisco, California.

Baltimore Public Schools. 1964. *An early school admissions project progress report* (Baltimore, Md.: Baltimore Public Schools).

Beller, E. K. 1965. *Annual report of research in the Philadelphia experimental nursery school project.* Philadelphia Council for Community Advancement. Mimeographed.

Getzels, J. W. July 1965. Preschool education. In *Contemporary issues in American education.* Papers prepared for the White House Conference on Education, Washington, D.C.

Goldstein, L. S. June 1965. *Evaluation of an enrichment program for socially disadvantaged children* (New York: Institute for Developmental Studies, New York Medical College).

Gray, Susan W., and R. A. Klaus. December 1965. An experimental preschool program for culturally deprived children. *Child Develpm.*

Kitano, H. H. 1964. *The child-care center: a study of the interaction among one-parent children, parents, and schools* (Berkeley, Calif.: University of California Press).

Larson, R. G., and J. L. Olson. July 1965. *A pilot project for culturally deprived kindergarten children: final report* (Racine, Wisc.: Unified School District No. 1). Mimeographed.

Weikart, D. P., C. K. Kamii, and N. L. Radin. June 1964. *Perry preschool project.* Progress report (Ypsilanti, Mich.: Ypsilanti Public Schools). Mimeographed.

26   Head Start Six Months Later*

MAX WOLFF, *Center of Urban Research*
ANNIE STEIN

The "Six Months Later" study, made in the fall of 1965, compared kindergarten children who had participated in the Head Start program with their classmates who had not. We hoped to learn whether there were any differences in readiness to enter regular first-grade classes; to ascertain in what areas of "readiness," if any, the Head Start children were advantaged and to measure such differences; to gain insights into the influence of the kindergarten experience itself and its effect on the social and educational initial head start of the children who had had preschooling.

The children studied attend the kindergartens of four public elementary schools in New York City. The Head Start children in these schools attended three Head Start centers that were chosen for this case study with the help of the Early Childhood Division of New York City's Board of Education. The criteria for choice were 1) that the centers were con-

* *Phi Delta Kappan*, March 1967. Reprinted by permission.

sidered to be "very good to excellent" by the supervisory staff of the summer Head Start program and 2) that one was all-Negro, another predominantly Puerto Rican, and the third mixed in racial and ethnic composition.

Four measures of social and educational "readiness" for first-grade work were selected for comparisons: the child's initial adjustment to classroom routines and the length of time it took him to become fully adjusted to school routines; his behavior towards his peers and towards the teacher; his speech, work habits, and listening habits; and his educational attainments.

The parents' interviews, conducted by trained interviewers who visited the parents in the home, enriched the study by bringing to it the immense enthusiasms of the parents for the Head Start program.

An equal number of parents of children who had not had Head Start, matched by school, child's teacher, and the ethnic background, age, and sex of the child, were interviewed as well.

The Caldwell Pre-school Inventory was administered to all the Head Start children in the 30 classes and to a control group of all their classmates in 15 of the 30 classes. Needed information on the evaluation of the test itself was gathered in addition to the data on the achievement of the children. Comparisons were made between Head Start and non-Head Start children and between Negro and Puerto Rican children in different class settings. These test results were used to check the independent teacher rankings of the children's readiness for first-grade work.

1. Head Start children tended to be ranked high in their kindergarten classes (first to third deciles) in greater proportions than children who had not had Head Start, after six months of kindergarten. They appeared with less frequency in the bottom three deciles of the class than non-Head Start children.

In the all-Negro school, the top 30 percent of the ranks held 33 percent of the Head Start children and only 26 percent of the non-Head Start children. Only 18 percent of the Head Start children were found in the bottom 30 percent of the class, contrasted with 42 percent of the non-Head Start children. In the Puerto Rican schools, Head Start children predominated in the upper three deciles, 37 percent Head Start to 26 percent non-Head Start for one school and 50 percent Head Start to 28 percent non-Head Start for the other. There was less difference in the bottom three deciles of the class for these schools.

In the mixed school, exactly the opposite result was obtained. Head Start children appeared with less frequency than non-Head Start children in the upper ranks and with greater frequency than non-Head Start children in the lower ranks. Non-Puerto Rican white children who attended this mixed school (coming from a middle-income housing project in the neighborhood) were ranked higher by the teachers than the Negro and Puerto Rican children.

The enthusiasm of the parents for the Head Start program was unanimous. Parents reported in detail the specific gains they felt their children had made. The majority of the parents sought "better preparation for kindergarten," including primarily the social gains of becoming accustomed to the routine of going to school, of playing with other children, and of getting used to the teacher-child relationship. Twenty-three percent sought specific educational gains for their children.

The youngsters who had the Head Start experience seemed to remember it well and pleasurably.

2. When interviewed, the teachers differed in their evaluation of the influence of Head Start of the child's initial difficulties in coming new into the class. Dated analysis showed that those teachers who had fewer than 25 percent Head Start children in their classes thought that Head Start had made no difference. Where Head Start children made up 50 or more percent of the class, the teachers all thought Head Start had helped the individual child's initial adjustment.

Of the 14 teachers interviewed, nine felt that any initial advantage in social adjustment to school evidenced by Head Start children had disappeared after the first few months of kindergarten. Of the four teachers who thought the advantage had persisted, three had been closely associated with the Head Start program, two as directors, and one as a teacher in the program. One teacher attributed any later advantage or disadvantage solely to the individual Head Start teacher the child had had.

For all four schools combined, Head Start children had a very substantial advantage over non-Head Start children in initial adjustment.

The ratings present a much more consistent picture of the Head Start children's initial advantage over non-Head Start children than that given by the same teachers when directly asked the question. Sixty-four percent of the Head Start children as against 40 percent of the non-Head Start children were rated *1* in initial adjustment. Combining ratings *1* and *2*, we found that 91 percent of the Head Start children adjusted in a short time as against 69 percent of the non-Head Start children. By the end of September, Head Start children still maintained a lead in later, full adjustment, although the lead was lessening. By the end of October, 88 percent of the Head Start children were fully adjusted and 81 percent of the non-Head Start. By the end of November, most of the children were fully adjusted to the school routines and any advantage held by Head Start children had vanished. This finding does conform to the majority of the teachers' reports to the interviews in answer to the direct question.

Of the 14 teachers interviewed, only seven thought that Head Start children were better adjusted to their classmates than non-Head Start children.

None of the 12 teachers who answered the question felt that Head Start had helped the child relate to a teacher. One other teacher, the one rated best by the observation team, felt that if the child had a poor Head Start teacher he would have a harder time relating to the kindergarten teacher than a non-Head Start child who had not had previous experience.

The parents' descriptions of the nature of changed behavior were informative. Negro parents tended to report that the children seemed more "organized" in their behavior; that they were able to play by themselves for longer periods of time constructively. The Puerto Rican parents found that the children played better with their sisters and brothers and were more relaxed at home.

The contrast between the learning standards set by teachers in the three minority-group schools and in the ethnically mixed school was striking. The actual learning of concepts was listed as being of first importance by two out of the three teachers in the mixed school, with the third teacher listing it third out of six important preparations for first-grade work. In the Negro school, only one of the three teachers even mentioned the learning of concepts, and she listed it second in importance to a social attribute. In one Puerto Rican school two out of four teachers mentioned it, but listed it last. In the other, "learning concepts" was mentioned by three of the four teachers, but given last place in importance by two of them and fourth in importance by the third.

3. There was no significant difference between the scores of Head Start children and their classmates in kindergarten who did not have Head Start, as measured by the Pre-school Inventory six to eight months after the summer Head Start experience.

Head Start children's mean ratings in the minority-group schools were slightly better than those of non-Head Start children, with the reverse true in the mixed school.

Head Start parents, however, generally thought their children had learned a great deal; only 12 percent thought their children had learned "none or very little" in Head Start.

Pre-school Inventory mean scores were only slightly higher for the children who had had six to eight months of "good teaching" over mean scores for those who had "poor teaching." We can conclude that whether the teacher is good or poor, none of the children learn very much, although there is a great readiness for learning in the good teacher's class. These facts probably reflect a paucity of direct learning in the kindergarten curriculum.

In the good teachers' classes, however, Head Start children scored consistently higher than non-Head Start children. In poor teachers' classes, Head Start children scored consistently lower than non-Head Start children.

There was almost unanimous agreement by the teachers that Head Start children helped the whole class adjust to the regular school routine. Only two teachers felt they had made no difference in the speed of class adjustment to routines.

27   Two Years of Head Start*

WILLIAM F. BRAZZIEL, *Virginia State College, Norfolk Division*

Project Head Start, the antipoverty preschool program, is completing its second year of year-round classes at this writing and planners are preparing for a third summer of Head Start classes and activities. Approximately 1.3 million children have been enrolled in the program in 2,400 communities. This includes 561,000 children in the 1965 summer program, 575,000 children in the 1966 summer program, and 171,000 in full year programs.

Head Start has been referred to as the country's biggest peace-time mobilization of human resources and effort.

Administrators and faculty of the program, together with interested persons from various areas of endeavor, are now beginning to analyze its effects on the lives of the children and adults involved. What has been the impact on cognitive and affective behaviors of the children? The parents of these children? The general community? The teachers of schools which received Head Start "graduates"? Some answers are readily available. Some aspects defy measurement, others require subjective descriptions of changes in intangible factors such as changes in community attitudes toward education. A broad program is under way to evaluate and assess the impact of the program. The Division of Research and Evaluation of Project Head Start is directing most of the study. It has contracted with colleges and universities, the Educational Testing Service, and with independent research organizations for studies. Independent research and evaluation is also proceeding at a few colleges and universities and in some school systems.

---

* *Phi Delta Kappan*, March 1967. Reprinted by permission.

What Head Start Provides

Assessments of Head Start involve the analysis of impact of a program of child development with six major aspects. These are: the educational program, health services, social services, psychological services, nutrition, and the parent-participation program.

The educational program is designed to help the children develop vocabulary and verbal fluency, spontaneity in expression, familiarity with school routines, trust in and rapport with teachers, interest in books, a motivation to want to learn to read, and a broadened concept of the world around them. Cultural enrichment is stressed in the educational program and teachers are encouraged to utilize community resources for exposure to enrichment experiences. The 2,000 children in a summer program in Norfolk, Virginia, for example, used the entire Hampton Roads metropolitan complex as a "classroom." Walking tours of the immediate community and visits to the downtown area, to Norfolk's Azalea Gardens, to the airport and zoo, to Colonial Williamsburg, to Jamestown and Yorktown and other places of interest were part of the enrichment efforts.

Classroom experiences in the educational program are similar to nursery and kindergarten routines, with a much heavier emphasis on labeling, describing objects, work in tactile activities such as modeling dough and tempera, soap and finger painting, and provision of opportunities for children to talk about themselves and their projects and experiences.

The following is an outline of a full day program (8:45 to 3:30 P.M.) of activities:

8:45– 9:15	Arrival and Independent Activity
9:15– 9:30	Morning Assembly
9:30– 9:50	Nourishment, Story
9:50–11:00	First Work Period
11:00–11:45	Outdoor Activities
11:45–12:30	Lunch
12:30–12:45	Clean-Up
12:45– 1:40	Rest
1:40– 2:05	Refreshments, Story
2:05– 3:10	Second Work Period
3:20– 3:30	Afternoon Assembly
3:30	Dismissal

Classes in Head Start are limited to 20 children, with 15 recognized as ideal. Each class has a teacher and an aide. Both have received special training in a Head Start teacher training institute. The importance of this small teacher-pupil ratio cannot be overemphasized. The high priority activities listed above require much individual attention by the teaching staff. A typical work session might have two children talking on the toy telephones, four talking to the hand puppets, three telling the teacher a story (sometimes simultaneously), two caring for the pets, and so on. This requires an exceptional amount of manpower.

The program of nutrition attempts to establish good nutritional practices by providing food for the children and working with parents to foster insights and appreciations regarding proper nutritional practices. Good nutrition, of course, influences physical and mental functioning in school activities.

Most programs include a mid-morning snack and lunches. In a 100-child center in a summer program in Norfolk where breakfasts and snacks were served, every child but one gained weight. The one exception was a child who was intermittently ill during the program. Serving free and low-cost breakfasts and lunches is now a valuable aspect of compensatory programs of many schools using Elementary and Secondary Education Act funds.

The health services are designed to provide more adequate and more accessible medical resources to the children. An ideal program provides a complete medical evaluation of each child and remedial care to correct conditions that would impede the academic and social development of the child. Children are given a complete examination and are screened for vision, hearing, speech, anemia, tuberculosis, diabetes, and dental defects. Immunizations are checked and completed if necessary, a psychological examination is completed, and the results of all tests and examinations are discussed with parents. Most important, social workers at the Head Start centers explore every possible community resource for referral of children needing attention. Also, the complete medical records are forwarded to the schools for further attention of staff of the school health programs.

Social service staffs in Head Start try to identify special and immediate needs for clothing, food, books, and toys which arise as a result of the child's participation in Head Start. Clothing banks are among the most prevalent needs. Families are often appraised of social services and helped to avail themselves of them. In many cases, parent-child counseling is also given. The intent here is to bring the parent gently to realize impediments to learning that a given child-rearing practice might engender and to have this practice altered.

School psychologists are utilized in pre- and post-testing in the programs and in diagnosis of special problems of children. Referrals to community child guidance clinics are also made, and some child play therapy for mildly disturbed children is carried on in the more advanced centers.

The parent-participation program has been called the most important auxiliary activity. The emphasis here is on parent involvement. The reasoning follows the axiom that parents who can help plan and execute an activity which affects their family so much will be more willing to support this activity and, most important, be willing to strengthen home life in any way possible to help their children develop.

Hence parents are encouraged to help select the sites for projects, plan the program, prepare the center for the children, carry out field trips, play games, tell stories, and, in short, become a valuable part of the resources of the center. By attending the training meetings, reading the literature, and talking to professionals and to each other, many of the finer points of child development become a part of a parent's understandings and appreciations. Folklore is easily replaced in home practices. Also, these parents tell others in the churches, lodges, and other social units. The word spreads.

A fine example of parent participation is the Whites Chapel Summer program in Shelby County, Tennessee. This program is directed by Mary Terrell who has had wide experience in developing readiness programs for deprived children (Brazziel and Terrell, 1962). The staff at Whites Chapel promotes adult involvement with the slogan: "Let's get every parent and every resident involved. Other people are willing to help us; let's help ourselves." Parent involvement at Whites Chapel is almost always 100 percent. Parent conferences are well attended and the center overflows with materials and equipment contributed by the parents—low-income parents. Volunteer workers are plentiful and a continuous child development seminar is in progress. Whites Chapel parents are learning a lot about how to develop their children, most of it will be assimilated and passed on to succeeding generations.

Assessment of Academic Gains

As noted, both tangible and intangible gains are hoped for by Head Start planners. Readiness for formal schools is the prime wish; gains in achievement and achievement motivation are important corollaries. It is also hoped that parents and other adults will know more and do more about preparing underprivileged children for school by providing the psychological, social, and physical support necessary for achievement motivation and success. Put differently, it is hoped that a change in community ethos will result. This spirit will be apparent in the efforts of parents of younger children to apply the new techniques they have learned in the development of the children's intellect. Just as important, it will be apparent in increased efforts on the part of the greater community to help these parents succeed. Greater concentrations of health services in low-income communities is only one example of such effort.

A minimum academic gain from Head Start experiences is coming to be regarded as an increase of from five to 10 points in I.Q. and 20-25 points on school readiness tests. Evaluators of the Lawrence Township, N.J., project reported a 20-point I.Q. gain (Hyman and Sill, 1965). The readiness test gains are perhaps more important, as readiness tests have a very high correlation with children's success in learning to read and write. They stress word meaning, matching, numbers, copying, and sentence structure. Children scoring in the "poor risk" range usually fail to learn to read successfully in the first grade. Children scoring in the average range usually do well.

Extensive analyses of test data were carried out for a 10 percent sample of 1965 summer program children. In addition, Leon Eisenberg of Johns Hopkins University made an intensive study of children in the Baltimore program. Both efforts documented the I.Q. reading readiness gains. Analyses of pre- and post-testing in Chesapeake, Virginia, provide an example of gains in a standard, well-run program. The median readiness gain of the 700 children enrolled there rose from the 10th to the 28th percentile. The Metropolitan Readiness Test was used. The program was operated for eight weeks. The number of poor risks (38 percent) was cut in half and the number of children with scores of average or above was more than doubled (from 14 to 32 percent). Twenty-seven of the children scored in the superior range on the post-test compared to six on the pre-test (Chesapeake Public Schools, 1965).

Some follow-up testing has been done to ascertain the degree of persistence of I.Q. gains as the children move through the grades in the schools. The results have varied. Ivor Kraft has questioned the validity of the gains because of this variance. Generally speaking, the I.Q. gains persist where school systems have strong Title I ESEA programs in the lower grades and tail off where this is not the case.

It must be pointed out here that I.Q. gains and persistence of I.Q. gains might very well be a faulty premise from which to judge. I.Q. gains are eye-catching and emotion-generating but the true test of preschool experiences is the performance of the children in learning to read, write, and do numbers in school; their understanding and appreciation of school routines; and their achievement motivations for school work. This performance is measured by *achievement* tests, analyses of age-grade records, school persistence and attrition, and teacher opinion. I.Q. tests are not the correct instruments here.

Further, the white-blue collar differences in I.Q. scores are now familiar to all and the inherent weaknesses of these tests in this respect are also widely recognized. The large majority of underprivileged children are from blue-collar families. The styles of life upon which a good I.Q. test is based are different. But many schools have an entire school population of these children and their *achievement* scores are in the normal range. Grade-level texts and curriculum guides can be used. The children persist in school and some go on to further study. These must be the broad goals not only of Head Start but of Title I and other compensatory programs in this country. I.Q. gains as a major criterion seem narrow and restrictive in this respect and quite irrational when weaknesses in the instrument are considered. Questions of I.Q. aside, there is still a major problem of maintenance of basic academic gains of Head Start in the elementary grades. This problem seems especially acute in schools where little has been done to develop instructional programs to build on Head Start experiences. A full, 1966, report to the Office of Equal Opportunity on some of the New York City experiences, made by Max Wolff of Yeshiva University, documented this situation to some extent.

Edmund Gordon, director of research and evaluation for Head Start, noted that while the Wolff report involved neither rigorous matching of experimental and control groups nor rigorous control of post-Head Start experiences, it did reemphasize significant concerns regarding both the quality of Head Start and post-Head Start experiences. These concerns, Gordon noted, were stated in clear terms at the initiation of the project and have since been given high priority in the planning and policy evaluations of the Head Start staff (Gordon, 1966).

Developing kindergarten and lower elementary school programs which continue Head Start experiences is a serious and critical challenge. After studying additional evaluation reports of this situation, Sargent Shriver and the Head Start staff developed a six-point proposal for such a program. Termed Project Keep Moving, the program was outlined by Shriver at the annual meeting of the Great Cities Research Council in November, 1966. The program calls for:

1. An across-the-board reduction in pupil-teacher ratio in depressed areas to correspond with that of Head Start, namely one teacher to every 15 children.

2. Use of teacher aides and volunteers in every classroom.

3. Establishment of programs of tutorial assistance.

4. Greater involvement of parents through neighborhood school councils and community associations.

5. Provision of an adequate supply of equipment and supplies and a broader use of electronic teaching aids.

6. Assignment of child development specialists to the primary grades for diagnosis of obstacles to the individual child's progress.

Shriver termed Project Head Start "a short-term experience—a shot of educational adrenalin whose effects can wear off in the grinding boredom and frustration of the slum classroom." He urged school people to pick up the challenge of Project Keep Moving (Shriver, 1966).

None of Shriver's proposals is new, but few school systems have felt the need or had the money to put them into effect in the past. We now seem to have a fine opportunity to do this by utilizing ESEA funds and the widespread community support for early education.

Assessment of Impact

Assessments of impact of Head Start in communities is more difficult than measuring behavioral changes in children. Undoubtedly, a fine potential exists for promoting desirable concepts and attitudes regarding child development. The three major newspapers in Hampton Roads, for example, carried an average of four news accounts each over a twelve-week period at the inception of the program. The three television and eight radio outlets gave comparable coverage. Officials and teachers of the program were interviewed and quoted and the mayor of one of the cities in the area posed for newspaper pictures with one of the children on his knee. In all, it was the most intensive media exposure ever given a program of education in the area. Media coverage has diminished considerably, of course, but the neighborhood discussions continue as parents plan, discuss, and work in the program. Much is no doubt being learned by the parents.

The Research and Evaluation Division of Head Start has contracted for several studies to analyze this impact. One immediate and important finding of program planners and evaluators is that a high degree of sensitivity surrounds the use of the labels "culturally deprived" and "culturally disadvantaged." There is resentment of the descriptive litany which has grown to describe the deficiencies of the children, their parents, and their homes and communities. This is a healthy resentment and indicates that these parents actually *share* the educational values of school people more than was previously realized. Robert Havighurst (1966) has noted similar sensitivity in compensatory education programs. A use of softer terminology is surely indicated. A Harlem housewife spelled out this need explicitly in explaining the reasons for picketing a new intermediate school in the fall of 1966. She said the pickets were demanding quality education and that they did not want to be told that the children weren't learning because mothers were often heads of the households or because they had cornflakes instead of poached eggs for breakfast.

A potentially valuable program of parent education has been initiated by the Woodward, Iowa, public schools. It is called "Project Home Start." It consists of adult group meetings, home visits, and prekindergarten (or Head Start) evaluations. The project operates a loan program for books and toys and promotes the purchase of others. A comprehensive child development discussion program is offered. ESEA

Title I funds are used for the program. A good example of Head Start parent involvement was outlined earlier in the description of the Whites Chapel Tennessee program.

The importance of gains in knowledge in this area should not be underestimated. Many investigators have come to the conclusion that although parents of underprivileged children revere education and want the best for their children, there is a debilitating lack of know-how regarding the development of verbal, curious, trusting children with high achievement motivation. This development of parental know-how should also become a prime goal in compensatory education in America. To do less is to opt for compensatory programs well into the future of this country, it would seem.

The Future

In the months and years ahead, energy and effort will be directed toward improving and expanding Head Start programs. Expansion is especially needed in the year-round programs. An ideal program would involve nearly two million children and some 70,000 teachers. Quality control will be a great challenge in this expansion. There is a need, too, for the development of publicly supported kindergartens in some states. At least one state (Virginia) has passed legislation authorizing state support for kindergartens, probably as a result of the great public interest in early education engendered in part, at least, by Head Start. Public kindergartens would enable Head Start programs to concentrate more on the younger children (ages 3–4) instead of serving as de facto kindergartens, as is presently the case in many places.

There has been much discussion and more than a little speculation regarding the transfer of Head Start to the Office of Education. Many debate the wisdom of such a move, pointing out the necessity for freedom to innovate and negotiate with local communities which might not be possible within a larger agency. On the other side are those who urge a "permanent institutionalization" of the program and the advantages of the haven of such an agency as a protection from the vicissitudes and turmoil of political life. It is probably unwise to try to predict what will happen in this respect.

It seems safe to predict more changes in the approaches to early education in this country, however, and this includes the primary years of the elementary schools in depressed areas. Even such conservative (but public-spirited) men as John McCone are urging federal outlays of $4–5 billion per year to build the classrooms, hire the teachers, lower the class size, and provide the technology necessary to provide underprivileged children with a good education (Alsop, 1966). History books of the future will record the Sixties as the era when Americans tried very hard to reshape their schools to make educational opportunity more nearly equal. Head Start will probably be recorded as one of several programs which were at the cutting edge and which helped point the way in this mammoth, heart-warming effort.

References

Alsop, Joseph. December 19, 1966. Report of John McCone's address to the Advertising Council of America. *Washington Post.*

Brazziel, William, and Mary Terrell. April 1962. For first graders: a good start in school. *Elem. Sch. J.*, pp. 352–355.

Chesapeake Public Schools. 1965. *Growth of pupils in Head Start* (Chesapeake, Va.: Department of Research, Guidance and Testing, Chesapeake Public Schools). Monograph.

Gordon, Edmund. November 1966. *Evaluation of the Wolff report* (Washington, D.C.: Office of Economic Opportunity). Mimeographed.

Havighurst, Robert. 1966. *Education in metropolitan areas* (Boston: Allyn and Bacon, Inc.).

Hyman, Irwin, and Deborah Sill. 1965. *A research report on the 1965 summer Head Start program in Lawerence township public schools* (Lawerence Township, N.J.: Public Schools). Monograph.

Kraft, Ivor. September 1966. Head Start to what? *The Nation*, pp. 179–182.

Shriver, Sargent. November 1966. An address to the Annual Conference of the Great Cities Research Council, Milwaukee, Wisconsin.

28   Evaluating Head Start Inputs and Outcomes*

EDWARD EARL GOTTS, *Indiana University*
JOHN PIERCE-JONES, *The University of Texas at Austin*

When Project Head Start (PHS) was launched in the summer of 1965, one of the problems immediately confronting its supporters was the

* A paper prepared especially for this book of readings.

gathering of information about the effectiveness of the program in accomplishing its stated aim, i.e., to make children identified as "disadvantaged" more ready for entry into the public schools. The problem was one of basic interest to those persons who were already engaged in psychoeducational research, so it was natural that some of them should have become involved in the evaluation task. While educational researchers were perhaps more ready than others to take up the challenge of the assignment, they were not in a uniquely favorable position tactically, because they were dependent upon the same evaluation tools that had been developed for use with the general school population. Thus, as will become evident from this report of evaluation research "in progress," much of the initial work has been directed toward developing new and more appropriate evaluation tools for use with disadvantaged children.

Conceptual Model

In addition to the tools of evaluation research, e.g., tests, rating scales, and others appropriately obtained behavior samples, one has need of a viable framework or conception to guide his efforts. The work of the Child Development Evaluation and Research Center at the University of Texas has been cast into a social-environmental model of the school's operation—a model outlined by Pierce-Jones (1966) which specifies that such changes as occur in PHS children are themselves functions of "input" variations which depend interactively upon (a) characteristics of teachers and (b) initial status of children on such factors as might undergo change. That is to say, changes in children cannot be specified either in terms of the child alone or of the teacher alone, but only in terms of their mutually interactive effect. One might also direct attention to the home and physical environment, although the focus of the evaluation reported here has been the teacher and child interaction. The relation of this conceptual framework to the evaluation process is shown schematically in Figure 1.

The input of the child was defined in terms of his initial status on the *Peabody Picture Vocabulary Test* (PPVT), the *Sequin Form Board* (Arthur Revision), the *Bender Visual-Motor Gestalt Test* (Hubbard Adaptation), and Caldwell's *Project Head Start Preschool Inventory* (PSI). These instruments relate to each of the characteristics on which

FIGURE 1   Schematic Representation of Multiple Interacting Factors Operating Through Head Start Center Programs to Produce and Predict Changes in Educational Development and in the Extra-School Environment.

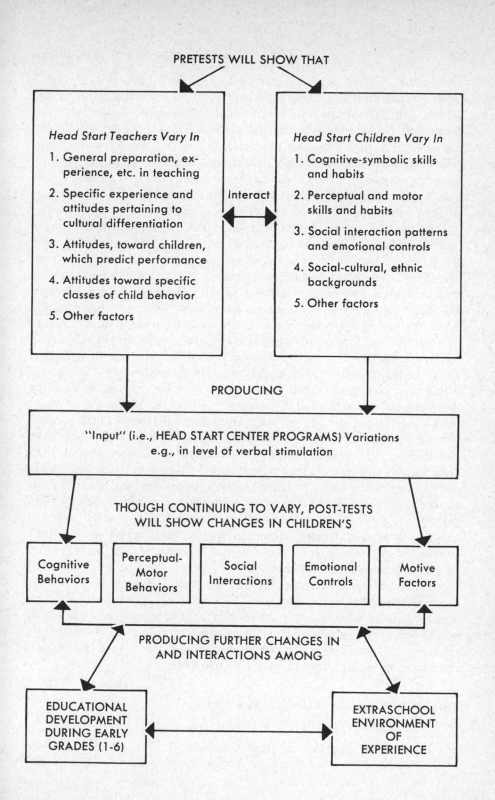

Head Start children are hypothesized to vary in Figure 1. The teacher input contribution was assessed by use of the *Observer's Rating Form* (Pierce-Jones, Caldwell, and Linn, 1966), *Minnesota Teacher Attitude Inventory*, *Dimensions of Teachers' Opinions* (Pierce-Jones, 1965), *Behavior Classification Checklist* (Pierce-Jones, 1965), *Need for Assistance* (Pierce-Jones, 1965), and *Child Attitudes Survey* (Pierce-Jones, 1965). Since the characteristics of these various instruments have been discussed elsewhere extensively, attention here will be directed only to the major results of their use in the present evaluation task.

As the reader is no doubt aware at this point, the conceptual model describing Project Head Start change in children, when coupled with the above measures, leads to a vast array of predicted outcomes. Without exercising considerable editorial restraint, the present writers would find themselves expounding at book length regarding the actual results and their implications for current educational practice and research. Thus, for expository convenience, the reader's attention will be directed to results of a number of studies arising from the above model and measurements. In this way it will be possible to traverse in a limited space the major results of an entire program of studies.

Before commencing this, however, it will be relevant to describe the personnel and setting of these studies. From the beginning of Head Start classes in the summer of 1965, this Center performed basic evaluation of program centers throughout Texas. In the process, data were gathered on 1256 PHS teachers and on several smaller samples of PHS children, on through the time that these children entered first grade and became well known to their teachers, i.e., about mid-winter, 1966. As the need for more systematized evaluation procedures became evident, this Center became a regional evaluation facility for six states in the Southwest and Rocky Mountain region. Since these more recent studies are still in progress, discussion will be restricted to the follow-up into first grade of an initial group of Texas children who attended Head Start classes during the summer of 1965. Whereas these teachers and children may be presumed to be similar in many ways to their counterparts in other parts of the country, differences may exist which would affect the generalizability of results reported here. Nonetheless, these results should prove suggestive of outcomes that would be obtained elsewhere, if similar procedures were followed.

Predicting Cognitive Changes in Children from Teacher Behavior Styles

Linn (1966) hypothesized that a knowledge of teachers' behavioral styles, measured by the *Observer's Rating Form* (ORF), would be significantly predictive of cognitive changes in children on the PPVT and on scales of the *Preschool Inventory*. Use of the ORF conceptualizes "input" and makes it measurable, not in curricular terms, but in terms of the teacher's classroom behavior relative to children, i.e., in terms of her "style" of working with her pupils. Linn found that changes in children's PPVT scores occurring between their entry into Project Head Start and the middle of their first grade training could be predicted from a knowledge of ORF-measured teacher style. Likewise, difference scores on scale II of the Preschool Inventory, representing "Personal-Social Responsiveness," were predictable from the same. When other teacher-related information was added to the ORF, e.g., MTAI, Behavior Classification Checklist, and Child Attitudes Survey, the capacity to predict changes in children's cognitive functions increased. At least 40 percent of the variability in children's changes on the PPVT, *Sequin Form Board*, and scales of the *Preschool Inventory* representing "Personal Control," "Verbal-Social Skills," and "Developmental Standing" could be accounted for from a knowledge of the foregoing teacher characteristics.

Finally, predictive success increased even more when the interactive model was implemented by combining the above teacher variables with children's scores obtained during initial testing. Under these conditions, the predictable variance in change scores rose from 40 percent to over 60 percent for all of the above-mentioned child variables except "Developmental Standing." Clearly the teacher's behavior and personal characteristics *do* matter in the Head Start classroom when the question at issue is the child's intellectual growth. Nor should it be surprising that the child's initial level of functioning also influences the outcomes.

Teacher Behavior as a Function of Teacher Characteristics and Child Attributes

Our general conceptual model suggested that teacher behavior in the classroom should be a joint function of the teacher's prior experience, i.e., "what she is like," and of the children with whom she interacts. In terms of the measurements used, therefore, ORF ratings for teachers should have proved to be predictable from the measures of child functioning and from a knowledge of teachers' attitudinal characteristics, e.g., as measured by the MTAI and *Behavior Classification Checklist*. From 37 to 51 percent of the variability of teacher rating scores on the eight scales of the ORF could, in fact, be accounted for by a best-weighted set of teacher and pupil attributes as predictors.

The foregoing means that ratings by trained observers of teachers along such dimensions as "Stimulation of Cognitive Development," "Providing Warmth," "Showing Child Respect," "Encouragement of Motor Skills," "Teachers' Dependency," "Providing Reinforcement," "Perceptual-Emotional Control," and "Middle-Class Orientation" could be substantially anticipated from self-report information supplied by the teacher and from test results obtained on children. That the information about child attributes is important to understanding the teachers' classroom behavior is evident from the fact that from 10 to 17 percent less of the teachers' behavior variability on the above listed eight ORF scales could be accounted for by the teacher self-report measures taken by themselves.

Comparisons of Head Start
and Non-Head Start Children

No control sample (at least in the conventional sense) was included in the initial Texas Head Start evaluation. It was possible later, nevertheless, to designate a group of non-Head Start children who would have been eligible for Head Start, and thus to compare them with the Head Start sample to determine whether Head Start children functioned more effectively in first-grade classrooms. All of the instruments administered to Head Start children, except the PPVT, showed them to be functioning at a higher level *in the first grade* than did the comparison sample of non-Head Start children. Taken together, these results strongly suggest that Head Start children did enter first grade with greater readiness to learn than did other disadvantaged children who had not been in Head Start. Still, it is not possible to rule out initial differences in the degree of disadvantagement of the Head Start and non-Head Start groups that were compared, since the latter were not seen until after their entry into first grade. This weakness of the research design should be remedied in future studies where the question at issue is the comparison of Head Start effects with the null condition.

Predicting Teacher Attitudes
toward Project Head Start
and Project Head Start Children

In an effort to relate teacher attitudes to various background or demographic characteristics, Boger (1966) tested two major hypotheses: 1) Teachers who are members of minority groups that have experienced social disadvantagement are more accepting of and optimistic toward Project Head Start than are teachers whose origins are in the majority group, i.e., the English-speaking and fair-skinned. 2) Teachers of minority group membership have more authoritarian attitudes regarding the management of child behavior than their majority group counterparts. Boger thus viewed attitudes as "residues" of the teacher's prior experience, which act to influence her approach to new situations. Using a variety of criterion statements, Boger obtained general support for both hypotheses. He found, further, that, with increasing years of teaching experience, there was a *decrease* in the variability of teachers' attitudes of optimism and acceptance. It is not known whether this is due to changes which occur in individual teachers with increasing years of experience or because the more variable teachers disappear from the total pool of active teachers at an earlier time. The degree to which a teacher appeared to be "authoritarian" or "democratic" in orientation was likewise found to be related to years of teaching experience.

One problem inherent in comparing minority group teachers with those of the majority group is that there are initial differences of social class which may, in part, have been responsible for the more authoritarian attitudes of the minority teachers. That is, because the lower-class culture tends to be more adult- than child-oriented, as compared with the middle-class culture, the differences in teacher authoritarianism may be as much related to social class membership as to minority status. In any event, Boger's findings point to the need for further investigation of the relationship of teaching experience to ethnic background, as they operate interactively to influence teachers' attitudes toward disadvantaged children and toward programs of compensatory education.

Concomitant studies of teacher characteristics further suggested that the teacher task force which helped to launch Head Start was marked by strong feelings of enthusiasm and by confidence in the program and in the ability of teachers to work effectively in it. As in the Boger study, teachers from minority groups and teachers who had worked with children similar to those in Head Start showed even greater confidence in themselves and the program. The general conclusion from these lines of evidence would be that teachers who are able to empathize with the disadvantaged child, either by virtue of prior participation in the environment of disadvantagement or by having had competence-producing experiences with disadvantaged children, approach the job of teaching such children with greater confidence and optimism.

Teacher Comparisons of Head Start and Non-Head Start Children

In addition to the differences observed in children's test scores, as reported above, it has been possible to determine whether Head Start and non-Head Start associated first-grade teachers had differing reactions to Head Start and non-Head Start children. As in the preceding studies, because there were no existing instruments suitable for this purpose, one was developed to permit this comparison of outcomes, the *Teachers' Survey Form* (TSF). Data were collected in January, 1966, from 473 Texas first-grade teachers who had taught both Head Start and non-Head Start children in their classes. Slightly over half of these teachers had taken part in Project Head Start during the summer of 1965.

The Teachers' Survey Form asked teachers to mention children in their classroom who stood out 1) in learning proficiency, 2) in likelihood of becoming a school dropout, and 3) in intellectual curiosity. Only subsequently were the named children identified as either having or not having taken part in Project Head Start for Summer, 1965, thus controlling for the possible direct knowledge of the teacher regarding the child's participation. By fairly clear margins, Head Start children were more often named for (1) and (3) and less often for (2) than were non-Head Start children, by first-grade teachers who had taught pupils from both groups.

Then, on a series of other items, direct comparisons were invited from teachers regarding Head Start versus non-Head Start children. These were analyzed to determine whether teachers who had participated in Project Head Start saw children differently. For a great number of the possible comparisons, Head Start trained children were perceived more favorably by both groups of teachers, although the Head Start-participating teachers tended to view them more favorably than did the other teachers. This almost overwhelming edge for the Head Start children was found for almost all of the attributes that Project Head Start was designed to improve.

Summary and Conclusions

Five separate lines of investigation of Head Start outcomes have been conducted within the framework of a more encompassing program of evaluation research. Various teacher and child inputs have been shown to be mutually interactive in a predictive sense. When these studies began, instruments for measuring the culturally different were almost nonexistent. During the initial round of studies, the Child Development Evaluation and Research Center developed a number of new instruments, particularly for the assessment of teacher characteristics and behaviors. The *Preschool Inventory* was likewise prepared by other Head Start-involved research persons to measure child characteristics. As work has progressed up to the present, the basic weaknesses of the available measures of child functioning have become painfully apparent. Thus, we find ourselves currently attempting to remedy this deficiency by devising a series of instruments better suited to determining the cognitive, emotional, motivational, and behavioral readiness of the disadvantaged child. As more appropriate instruments emerge, it is to be expected that some of the previously inconclusive findings will yield more definitive results.

While some satisfaction is to be derived from the substantial increases in school readiness observed in Head Start-prepared children, and while some confidence can be placed in the predictability of these results, other basic questions remain at issue. No attention has been given to the parental-environmental setting and its predictive relation to the disadvantaged child's functioning. In addition, little is known of the persistence of changes observed in Head Start-trained youngsters. We are currently analyzing late second-grade data in an effort to answer this last question, but it will be some months before final results are available. There is, then, much promise suggested by available evaluation results, but the need for continued imaginative research along longitudinal lines is the real challenge to be faced.

References

Boger, R. P. 1966. *Sub-cultural group membership and attitudes of Head Start teachers* (Austin, Tex.: The University of Texas). Unpublished doctoral dissertation.

Linn, Emma L. 1966. *The socially disadvantaged child: teacher correlates* (Austin, Tex.: The University of Texas). Unpublished doctoral dissertation.

Pierce-Jones, J. September 1966. *Outcomes of individual and programmatic variations among Project Head Start centers, summer, 1965.* Final report to the Office of Economic Opportunity (Austin, Tex.: The University of Texas).

———. March 1965. *Orientation to school mental health consultation* research at the University of Texas. Progress report to the Inter-professional Research Commission on Pupil Personnel Services (Austin, Tex.: The University of Texas).

———, B. Caldwell, and Emma L. Linn. 1966. *The observer's rating form* (Austin, Tex.: Child Development Evaluation and Research Center, The University of Texas).

29   Will Public Schools Control Head Start?*

ERWIN KNOLL, *Newhouse National News Service, Washington, D.C.*

Washington, D.C.—To Sargent Shriver, director of the U.S. Office of Economic Opportunity, Project Head Start is "the greatest success" of the Administration's war on poverty. To President Johnson, the year-old preschool program is "a landmark, not just in education but in the maturity of our own democracy." To congressional critics of federal antipoverty programs Head Start is the one achievement that deserves full financial support. And to a growing number of educators it is all these things plus—plus a king-sized administrative headache that threatens, in some cases, to undermine the effectiveness of this promising advance in U.S. education.

When the first plans for Head Start were announced in February 1965, some farsighted observers recognized it at once as the beginning of an educational revolution. The infusion of federal funds, the national impetus of the war on poverty they predicted, would create a strong and permanent position for preschool education as a public responsibility. Other experts were more pessimistic. The effort was too hasty, they said, and the plans for follow-through were virtually nonexistent. "The best preschool program," Martin Deutsch warned, "can do more harm than good if the children don't have an appropriate kindergarten program into which they can step—and if the early grade years are not designed to carry through what was begun in the preschool program."

Since last summer, both optimists and pessimists have had ample occasions to congratulate themselves on their prescience. In fact, accomplishments as well as problems under Head Start have surpassed all expectations.

Last summer's eight-week Head Start program, financed at a total cost of $95 million (including $83 million in federal antipoverty funds), enrolled more than 560,000 children in 13,344 child development centers located in 2,398 communities. More than 40,000 professionals—teachers, social workers, physicians, nurses, psychologists—were employed, and they had the assistance of 45,000 nonprofessional neighborhood residents. Shriver estimated that 250,000 unpaid volunteers aided the program—"the greatest voluntary effort in peacetime this country has ever known."

There were problems, to be sure. Last-minute grants left little time for planning or teacher preparation. Enrollment standards were confused, and some congressional critics complained that their children had been recruited for the antipoverty effort. Issues of church-state conflict arose where Head Start programs were placed in religious institutions. In the South, the inevitable disputes arose over segregation. Some projects were dropped when local officials proved unwilling to operate centers on a biracial basis. Others were funded, and O.E.O. later conceded that Head Start projects had, in some instances, violated federal desegregation policies. Where Head Start was associated with civil rights efforts—notably in the case of the Child Development Group of Mississippi—the program came under heavy fire from segregationists.

But by and large the summer effort was a notable success. Julius B. Richmond, the director of Head Start, was able to report that pupils showed "significant gains in educational achievement and mental ability." He cited these results of standardized testing:

Members of the Johns Hopkins University department of child psychiatry found that Head Start pupils gained 30 to 40 points on the Peabody Picture Vocabulary Test, as compared with children not enrolled in the preschool program. Head Start pupils also gained about 10 points in a standard I.Q. test.

Investigators of the Staten Island Mental Health Society measured a gain of 14 months in performance on a test designed to measure intellectual ability.

Observers at the University of Texas found that first grade teachers reported Head Start children to be more proficient in learning, more intellectually curious, and better adjusted to the classroom than other children.

In Clovis, Calif., children in Project Head Start showed a gain of 4 to 12 months on intelligence test performance during a six-week preschool program.

Richmond also said the health screening program instituted as part of Head Start found "significant health defects" among one-third of the participating pupils. Defects ranged from active tuberculosis and conditions requiring open heart surgery to dental caries.

As was predicted, follow-through on the summer program's achievements posed difficulties. Some of the health defects uncovered remain uncorrected, and some of the educational gains, observers believe, have been dissipated where children entered regular classrooms that were unprepared to capitalize on the "head start" of the summer session.

But the major problems of Head Start have been associated with the effort to establish the program on a year-round basis. Last month, however, President Johnson announced that Head Start definitely would operate on a year-round basis with a follow-through program for those enrolled in last summer's programs that would include home visits, special tutoring, field trips, and medical and social care.

Financial problems of the preschool program are associated with the across-the-board tightening of spending on domestic programs owing to the rising cost of the war in Viet Nam. No official figures are available on the amount that might have been budgeted for Head Start if military spending had been continued at last year's level, but it is certain that the program would have been expanded at a considerably greater rate. In testimony before the House education and labor committee this spring, Shriver said a Head Start appropriation of $450 million could be used "effectively" in fiscal 1967. The Administration has asked for $300 million—enough to support a summer program at approximately last year's level and provide year-round classes for about 210,000 children. Officials estimate that about four million children who meet O.E.O.'s definition of poverty are in the 3 to 6 Head Start age bracket. Less than a sixth is therefore being served by the current scope of the Head Start operation.

Juggling of Head Start applications in an effort to stretch out the available funds has strained administrative procedures which were, to begin with, not noted for their efficiency. To the frustration of applicants, regulations have been devised, revised and improvised while school systems and community antipoverty agencies waited for grant approvals. And problems at the federal level have been matched by local difficulties. Neither space nor staff are available on a year-round basis as they are during the summer months.

Complicating the situation still further is the fact that federal funds under Title I of the Elementary and Secondary Education Act of 1965 are also available for preschool programs serving disadvantaged pupils. In fact, early applications for Title I grants indicated that about one-third would be directed at preschool efforts.

Unlike O.E.O.-sponsored programs, Title I funds require no local 10 per cent matching of federal funds, nor do they impose the rigid standards of enrollment and staffing demanded by the antipoverty agency. In some instances, local school systems are taking maximum advantage of both E.S.E.A. and O.E.O. funds to mount broad-gauged preschool programs. Elsewhere, however, proposed projects have bogged down in confusion—and even competition—between the two federal programs. Jurisdictional squabbles have developed between school authorities and antipoverty boards, with resulting delays and disappointments. At the federal level, coordination between O.E.O. and the U.S. Office of Education has only recently been established and is not yet fully satisfactory.

Federal officials tend to dimiss these problems as the inevitable "growing pains" of a new and revolutionary program. Looking ahead, some predict that preschool programs will eventually come under the full jurisdiction of the Office of Education, while localities establish them as permanent features of their school systems. This, it appears, was the desire of delegates to last summer's White House conference on education. Summarizing their discussion of preschool education, New York State Commissioner of Education James E. Allen, Jr., said:

"The continuation of Head Start and other such preschool programs was deemed essential. The incorporation of such programs into regular school programs was considered to be highly desirable, with the provision that the cooperation and involvement of the whole community and its whole resources be continued. And paramount in the deliberations on the subject of preschool education was an all-pervading feeling that the momentum of Head Start should not be lost."

PART **6** *Cognitive and Affective Bases for Learning to Learn*

The existence of a learning set wherein the learner develops a particular approach to solving a problem that he can use effectively in attacking other problems is conceptualized as "learning how to learn." Susan Harter believes that learning how to learn should be distinguished from the more simple fact or response learning. Both are important for the purposes of school learning. The learning set model would apply to the learning of certain concepts that could be generalized to learning in related tasks. At the same time the youngster would be learning specific facts. A careful analysis of the types of learning which characterize the school behavior or subject to be learned would be an essential initial step.

Learning set learning, as described by Harter, is more complex than the learning of facts, requiring more extensive and complex planning by the teacher. To achieve such learning it would seem that the child is required to grasp the underlying principle, to "catch on" to principles common to solving a task when the elements of the problems being attacked are different. This view is not in character with "insight" learning whereby a solution is grasped immediately, for even such learning as this is dependent upon previous learning. Harter warns that the search for a *single best example* for learning set learning may be inappropriate; that diversity of attack is to be expected.

Ivor Kraft assumes a dim view of "learning how to learn." The reader should recognize at this point that the phrase receives different meanings from different people. Kraft explores several meanings—problem solving, sequential stage achievement, and acquiring "study habits." There is no need, he says, for humans to learn learning for we are born with enormous learning capacities. Most learning failure is because of disinterest or lack of motivation. Children are quite proficient in

319

learning the new mathematics but practically none are learning the *new race relations*. The basic skills of learning information are not nearly as difficult to instill as learning *what* to learn, how deeply to learn, and learning what not to learn. We have been far from successful in promoting the learning of wisdom and compassion.

It would appear that "learning how to learn" is essentially a way of describing readiness for learning. Such a phrase, implying movement and sequence, would indeed appear to represent a more dynamic view of children's preparation for learning tasks than the commonly abused readiness concept. The practices of many teachers and the content of many readiness materials reflect an extremely narrow view of preparation for achievement of particular tasks.

Regardless of the terminology used, learning is subject to both cognitive *and* affective considerations. Glenn R. Hawkes believes that the bases for early educational experiences must be regarded in the broadest sense. A facilitating emotional climate is essential to the development of a positive self-image. And one's feelings about self will play an important role in learning. Helping children to understand themselves involves communication in many forms. A climate for unbridled expression —speaking, playing, gesturing—is necessarily a climate for exploring, thinking, creative inquiry, sharpening and broadening concepts. Whether this is labeled "learning" or "learning how to learn" is less important than the fact that it is taking place. In either event, basic attitudes about one's self are fundamental in establishing a scheme of learning patterns that are prerequisite to the development of more complex patterns.

Daniel A. Prescott cites research to show that young children deprived of the nurturance of love fail to achieve their best growth physically, intellectually, and emotionally. This is supported by studies of notable psychologists and anthropologists. Yet, the word "love" fails to appear in the majority of books on human development and educational psychology. Serious and scientific study of the effect of love on humans is almost nonexistent. Examination of the biographies of three great men—Kagawa, Gandhi, and Schweitzer—revealed that each affirmed that love was a central dynamic in his accomplishments. Prescott develops a number of theses about love. He then proceeds to explain these and moves to a pertinent question: What roles can love play in human development? Believing that the question will be answered by researchers in the near future, a series of hypotheses as to probable findings are presented. Implications for the education of preschool children place heavy emphases on the establishment of warm relationships between the *adults*—parents, teachers, administrators—who live with children. If one is to transmit love and respect to children he must reciprocate love and respect with his peers.

Another important variable in the establishment of bases for learning is that of play. Play is an inherent right of every child and, contrary to popular notion, offers unlimited opportunities for learning. Two forms of play, according to Millie Almy, hold legitimate places in the nursery school curriculum. One is self-initiated activity, the other is adult-prescribed activity. Presently, adults are prescribing more of the child's play activity toward the development of specific and basic concepts. Almy reviews some of the tenets of psychoanalytic theory, theories of Piaget, and selected research in cognitive development regarding what constitutes a proper balance between structured and spontaneous play. Definitive answers, as one would expect, are not forthcoming. Uniquely personal dimensions leave much to the teacher's artistry and sensitivity. Such behavior should open new cognitive possibilities for the child in directed play activities. But to limit the child solely to structured play would be to deny him the opportunity to initiate and test his own ideas in spontaneous play, or in Piaget's words, "the opportunity to invent and reinvent for himself."

30   Learning How to Learn*

SUSAN HARTER, *Yale University*

If teachers were asked to imagine a utopian classroom situation, their descriptions would probably include children who are eager, attentive, and curious—in short, good learners. Unlike the educator, the researcher does not deal so much with reactions as he does with what lies behind them. He necessarily focuses on selected aspects of the learning process.

There has been an increasing amount of research directed toward examination of complex learning processes and problem-solving behaviors, and it promises to enrich considerably our understanding of how children learn. One recent and exciting chapter in the history of the study of learning and cognitive processes will be the focus of this article— namely, a kind of learning that we call "learning set learning."

The process was first formally demonstrated by Dr. Harry Harlow in his primate laboratories at the University of Wisconsin. Previous to this, it had consistently been observed that when monkeys were given a simple discrimination task in which they were repeatedly presented with two objects, one of which concealed a food reward, they gradually came to learn which object was the correct one. This learning resulted after a relatively long process of trial and error behavior in which errors were gradually eliminated until eventually the monkeys chose the correct object every time.

The significant discovery revealed in subsequent research came when these same animals were given further training on a series of similar problems in which the objects *differed* from problem to problem. It was found that, with each successive problem, the monkeys learned with greater efficiency until eventually they might solve such problems in a single trial.

The critical distinguishing feature of this type of learning is that, since the objects change from problem to problem, the improvement in learning ability over the series of problems demands that the learner discover a general solution applicable to problems of a similar nature. For this type of discrimination learning task, in particular, the concept underlying the solution may be most directly stated as: "If the reward is not under one object of any pair, it will always be under the other." It is only when this concept is mastered that the learner can rapidly solve problems later in the series, without lengthy trial and error.

More generally, this type of inter-problem learning has been viewed as representing the formation of a learning set in which the learner develops a particular method of approach whereby he can rapidly learn or solve problems of a similar nature. Doctor Harlow has also suggested that this type of process be conceptualized as "learning how to learn." Thus, with experience on a variety of different problems that have a common basis for solution, the individual learns how to learn solutions to such problems with maximal speed and efficiency.

Classroom Application

These initial research efforts have sparked considerable interest in the applicability of such principles to the learning of children, since our general observations indicate that a significant amount of the learning that occurs in the developing child involves "learning how to learn" various skills and methods of approaching subject material. In the school situation, for example, a child learns how to read, in addition to learning the precise meaning of specific words. In learning how to read, he must master a method involving a set of principles and grammatical rules that he can apply to new verbal material.

Our research with children suggests that, in certain important respects, learning how to learn represents a different and more complex type of process than that observed in more simple learning, as, for example, in the learning of a specific response or fact. In terms of the formal characteristics and their implications for educational practice, such findings suggest that it may be fruitful to maintain a distinction between these two types of learning.

On the one hand, a significant amount of school learning would seem to fit the learning set model in which the child learns certain concepts or rules that he can subsequently apply to tasks or problems that are similar in nature, although they may vary in content. On the other hand, the child must also master a considerable amount of factual material, where the learning task requires the acquisition of a large number of specific facts that define particular areas of knowledge.

Help for the Teacher

An appreciation of this distinction may aid the teacher in promoting more effective learning of both types. A first step in applying this approach would seem to demand a careful analysis of the type of learning that best characterizes each school subject. Often *both* types of learning are represented, although the balance may differ from subject to subject.

In science courses, for example, a child is expected to learn *how* to use our system of weights and measurements and *how* to read various temperature gauges. But he also is expected to learn *that* there are 36 inches in a yard and *that* water boils at 212 degrees. In arithmetic, a child must learn how to add, subtract, multiply, and divide, but he must also learn certain specific answers, as, for example, the multiplication tables.

These examples suggest the validity of an approach to education that distinguishes between those situations that require learning how to learn or how to perform certain mental skills and those that demand memorizing specific facts. Thus the *product* of learning is different for each type.

Never-ending polemics revolve around the issue of whether the teacher should resort to rote learning and memorization or should appeal to some other method, under the assumption that mere drill gives a child little or no insight into what he has learned. Compromising resolutions implying that the answer lies somewhere in between may provide a superficial sense of satisfaction; however, their very vagueness makes them of little practical value. A more promising hypothesis may be derived from our understanding of the two types of learning I have mentioned. The task of the teacher as well as the learner will be different for each.

Where factual knowledge represents the desired end product of learning, the necessary and appropriate methods involve drill and repetition. The teaching and learning task in such cases may be simultaneously less difficult and less interesting. Although the imaginative teacher may devise game-like approaches to facilitate this type of learning, the basic process involves the repeated practice and memorization of specific items or facts.

Bigger Challenge

In contrast, the very nature of "learning set learning" requires different and more complex methods and, therefore, the challenge—and perhaps the difficulty—of teaching is significantly enhanced. The process by which a learning set—for example, learning how to multiply—is acquired depends on practice, but practice quite different from the rote drill necessary for the learning of factual material. Learning set formation or the development of the ability to comprehend and apply a particular method, concept, or solution requires repeated exposure to a variety of situations or problems that are similar, in that each embodies a common solution, but which differ in their content or their specific elements.

The lesson planning appropriate for this type of learning is necessarily more extensive and elaborate. It requires the construction of a series of examples analogous to the series of problems presented to Harlow's monkeys, where the same basic process, principle, or solution is appropriate and where the specific content varies from example to example. The clearest illustration of this method is evident in mathematics where the child is asked to solve a series of arithmetic problems, each of which has different numbers but requires the application of the same mathematical principle.

The Need to "Catch On"

Because this type of learning is more indirect, it represents a more challenging teaching task. In the final analysis, it requires the child's ability to recognize the underlying principle, to "catch on," to "get the idea," to grasp the common nature of the solution in the presence of differences between the elements of particular problems or examples. Thus, wherever "learning set learning" is involved, the teacher must keep in mind that the key to the child's understanding lies in his appreciating conceptual similarity in the face of contextual difference. This realization will guide the choice of material, since it demands the selection and presentation of examples that have sufficient diversity in terms of content, but sufficient similarity in terms of the principles that the child is expected to learn.

One final discovery from our study of "learning set learning" has important implications for education. Formerly, the view was held that certain learning is best characterized as a process of "insight," whereby a solution is grasped or learned immediately. Descriptively, the experience is best communicated by phrases such as "That's it!" "I get it!" "Eureka!"

What our recent research has indicated is that the apparent abruptness of such "insightful" learning is dependent largely upon previous learning and practice with similar, though not identical components. Frequently it is difficult to appreciate the nature of this process. The precursors of this ability to demonstrate "insightful" learning are common experiences that we often overlook in our analysis of the learning history of the child or adult. In part, this results from the fact that these experiences are so ubiquitous and inevitable. However, this early general learning involving exposure to a variety of situations is essential in order for more efficient learning to take place at some subsequent point in development.

Room for Searching

In terms of educational practice, this suggests that the search for some *single best example* or exercise by which the child may grasp the principle may be an inappropriate and fruitless one for certain kinds of learning. The more laborious procedure, involving practice with a variety of problems in which there is a common solution, cannot be short-circuited.

There still is considerable room for searching in our attempts to sensitively program the appropriate series of learning experiences whereby we may assist the child in learning how to learn. In the classroom, it is the teacher who dons the mantle of researcher to the extent that he must experiment with a variety of possible approaches. It is only through these efforts that the practical value of the distinction between the two methods of learning can be assessed. Back in our laboratories, we researchers eagerly await the results.

31   "Learning How to Learn": Myth or Reality?*

IVOR KRAFT, *Division of Research, Children's Bureau, Department of Health, Education, and Welfare*

Definitions of education are bountiful and boundless. They begin nowhere and end everywhere. Almost anything will do: education is life, education is schooling, education is the three R's, education is growing. A very popular one these days has it that education is "learning how to learn."

It is becoming very fashionable among some educators and psychologists to warn parents that early learning is intricate and crucial, not for the exceptional child, but for all children. One writer solemnly tells us that "by the time an American child is six and in the first grade, time is already running out for him" (Rambusch, 1962). What a pity that a human being with a life expectancy of 70 or more years has to feel that at the age of 6, time is already running out. Whatever would have become of Andrew Jackson, the 7th President of the United States and

* *The Journal of Negro Education*, Fall 1964. Reprinted by permission.

a man who did not properly learn to read and write until he was in his third decade (and he never did learn correct English) if he and those who had faith in him simply concluded that for a post-adolescent functional illiterate time had already run out?

Other writers are warning us that whether children will be blessed or blasted for life might well depend on their exposure, prior to age 5 or 6, to structured learning methods and materials, reading readiness exercises (or reading skill itself), teaching machines, and systematic training in problem solving. The implication is that if they do not learn by the time they reach the first grade, perhaps they never will.

The learning how to learn slogan is a very attractive one; we are positively eager to believe in it. Just imagine: if instead of providing the student with miscellaneous facts, skills, and attitudes we can give him the basic formulas for learning how to learn, then we have set him up once and for all. He is close to being intellectually invulnerable, since despite gaps and lapses in his knowledge he can always trot out an appropriate formula (especially "scientific method") and proceed to learn.

Also, if we accept this formula we are armed with a decisive and useful explanation for all those cases in which children and adults fail to learn. We can say, quite simply, that the individual failed to pass successfully through the crucial stage (or perhaps stages) of the learning how to learn process. We then possess a portmanteau explanation for at least half the ills of modern society.[1]

Alas, the theory is completely without supporting empirical or experimental evidence. So far we have not been able to identify any process of learning how to learn.[2] If there were such a process, then presumably there would be something like "learning how to learn how to learn" and so on in an infinite series of regressions. In actuality there is only learning, but it happens to exist in many guises.

If by learning how to learn, however, we mean nothing more

[1] Perhaps the foremost representative of this viewpoint in our day is H. G. Rickover. See his *Education and Freedom.* New York: E. P. Dutton, 1959.

[2] Since the epoch-making researches of Pavlov, we have seen the enormous growth of a literature on the physiological, psychological, and mathematical aspects of learning in animals and human beings. None of this can be said to have uncovered a clear-cut "learning how to learn" mechanism or set of mechanisms. Among many other treatments, see for example the following: Ernest R. Hilgard, *Theories of Learning.* New York: Appleton-Century-Crofts, 1956; O. Hobart Mowrer, *Learning Theory and Behavior.* New York: John Wiley & Sons, 1960; O. Hobart Mowrer, *Learning Theory and the Symbolic Processes.* New York: John Wiley & Sons, 1960; Lester D. and Alice Crow (eds.), *Readings in Human Learning.* New York: David McKay, 1963; and N. L. Gage, "Toward a Cognitive Theory of Teaching," *Teachers College Record,* 65:408–412, February, 1964.

than the rather common process of acquiring a cluster of "study habits" (time budgeting, neatness, checking your work, beginning and ending on time, regular review, and so forth) then this is probably a useful phrase, because such habits of study do indeed help to make the learning processes more effective. They are far from being essential or sufficient to the learning process, however, because it is well known that many highly creative and intellectually powerful individuals study, learn, and work in very unconventional and even disorganized ways which do not entail neatness, careful scheduling, systematic checking, and all the rest.

But if by learning how to learn we mean that people actually do undergo a defined sequence of training, so that by experiencing a stipulated series of exercises or intellectual revelations they move from one point in their lives where they did not know how to learn over to another point where it can be said of them that they have "learned learning," then this is a very misleading way to regard human life and human learning. As a way of regarding the goals or substance of education, it may lead us into dark and ominous corridors.

In any deeper or serious sense there is no need for a human being to "learn learning." With the exception of a tiny per cent of defective human beings, all of us are born with enormous built-in capacities to learn. On the primitive biological level, crucial "learning" has occurred before birth. On the sensory-motor and psychological levels, extraordinary mechanisms of learning are activated immediately following birth. The school is as often a device for capturing and confining learning as it is a means of promoting or generating it. So powerful are the innate drives and mechanisms of learning that we do not easily succeed in unlearning how to learn. Indeed, in many respects what we call psychosis or mental illness is a kind of violence of unlearning or anti-learning.

Why then do so many people fail to learn? Is it because they are incapable of mastering the basic skills of learning? There are two good answers to this question. The first is that the question itself is a mistake, that people have indeed learned and over-learned many things, although we may not agree that they are the important or proper things. The second answer is that people do not learn because most of them are basically disinterested or unmotivated when it comes to facing directly the vast domains of knowledge that lie beyond their most immediate concerns. In other words, most human beings are spiritually-intellectually very lazy.

When it comes to proving the validity of both these answers, Nazi Germany is still our best case study.[3] Strangely enough, Nazi Germany had a system of schooling which ranked very high on all dimensions of a so-called "learning how to learn" scale of excellence as applied to classroom practice. The teachers were well-trained and energetic, the curricula were systematic and orderly, teaching was methodical and precise, and discipline was exemplary. Logic prevailed, the rules worked, and there were very few functional illiterates (in America we have always had millions). It can be said that there was a lot of learning going on in Germany, and what the Germans did learn they learned very well and put into solid practice. In his writings, Robert M. Hutchins often points out that 25 per cent of Hitler's SS troops held the doctor's degree (Hutchins, 1963). (I cannot vouch for Hutchins' statistics, but the point is well taken.) The trouble with this superficially top-notch system of education was simply this: what the German people actually learned—and failed to learn—turned out to be appalling in the extreme.

It is very incorrect to retort that all of Nazi-promoted learning was pseudo-learning. Despite certain peculiarities Nazi science was competent and capable of making important discoveries. It was only when it came to confronting certain vast domains of knowledge concerning ethics, history, philosophy, and human relations that the entire German nation was rendered apathetic, disinterested, and unmotivated. Some things they had learned very well, including when to be apathetic, but into those vast and crucial domains of true knowledge and learning, beyond the crudest facts and the emotional bias, they were somehow not ready or able to venture.

There is a very important lesson here which the ardent preachers of learning how to learn have not yet assimilated. To put it bluntly, that lesson has to do with confronting those elements in our systems of schooling which resemble Nazi-promoted learning. Of course, they are not anywhere as blatant as those in Hitler's Germany, but they are there nonetheless.[4] There are some very bright adolescents in the South and

[3] For useful accounts of Nazi education, see the following: Erika Mann, *School for Barbarians*, New York: Modern Age Books, 1939; Robert Ulich, "Education in the Nazi Reich," *The Harvard Educational Review*, 13:101–118, March 1943; Hans Liebeschuetz, "The Social and Educational Background of the Nazi School System," *The British Journal of Educational Psychology*, 11:197–204, November 1941; Edward J. Kunzer, " 'Education' Under Hitler," *Journal of Educational Sociology*, 13:140–147, November 1939; and the ordinance of the Reich Minister for Science, Education, and Popular Development, of January 29, 1938, on the reorganization of secondary education in Germany, which appears in translation in *The Educational Forum*, 3:81–95, November 1938.

[4] For an interesting comparison of common kinds of historical distortions in the texts of pre-war Germany and our own texts dealing with Negroes in American History, see in particular R. John Rath, "History and Citizenship Training in National Socialist Germany," *Social Education*, 13:309–314, November 1949, and then Patrick J. Groff, "The Abolitionist Movement in High School Texts," *The Journal of Negro Education*, 32:43–51, Winter 1963.

even a few very good high schools. Do the students learn how to learn? Some of them are learning effectively indeed the new physics and the new mathematics and the new grammar. But practically none of them are learning the *new race relations*. You cannot learn how to learn that. Either you learn it or you do not, and it is not taught in the secondary schools of the South (nor in many Northern ones for that matter), where even the brightest adolescents have shown themselves to be capable of extremely bigoted and spiteful behavior towards the token handfuls of Negro youth who are admitted to the classrooms. But what is ultimately of importance to the South, the new mathematics or the new race relations? Can we afford to set up our curricula and organize our high schools in such a way as to give youth the impression that good mathematics is more important than good human relationships? All of history, not only the last 30 years, proves otherwise.

If we take a close look at the history of education this becomes readily apparent. We have a rich and fact-crammed history of schools and schooling that goes back at least 3,000 years. In this history are many tales and documents which show us how political parties, emperors, religious leaders, and governments were able to establish and dissolve systems of schooling. But we do not have a single, authenticated case of how a school or a body of schools managed to topple or even seriously shake a government. As compared with the influence of society on the schools, the influence of schools on society has been negligible.[5]

In other words, we learn from history that heretofore it has not been the formal rules and skills of learning, the logic of mathematics and science, which ultimately determined what relationships and systems of society would prevail among men. This does not mean that it is the other way around, that social systems can actually alter or demolish the laws of science. This is certainly not the case. But it does very much mean that human societies can ignore, suppress, and even violate those laws and the ethical implications that flow from them. Inhumanity and injustice are the result.

We must reject the false notion that good laboratories and curriculum reform will automatically make for improved education, that to make education better we merely need to make it more efficient, more logical, and more elegant. Just because a school has a high reading level and lavish reading clinics does not in itself mean that better human beings are developed in that school. The child may be a voracious speed-demon of

[5] One of the best and most enlightened histories of education, and one that does not obscure this important point, is still that of William Boyd, *The History of Western Education* (5th ed. enlarged). London: Adam & Charles Black, 1950. Consult in particular his treatment of 20th century education, pp. 404–457.

a reader performing at the "umpteenth" reading level. This does not mean that he reads intelligently or selectively or knows how to apply what he reads. There are tests for reading comprehension, but there are no tests for "wise and compassionate reading," which is the supreme skill that teachers ought to be aiming at.

Wisdom and compassion are not easily taught or easily grasped. The basic skills of learning, on the other hand, are not nearly as difficult to instill in a youngster as is commonly supposed. True enough, some retarded and emotionally disturbed children may need painstakingly to be taught learning skills. Most children need to be *taught*. When they are very young they need to be taught how to begin and end tasks, how to pay attention, how to sit in a circle without raising a rumpus, how to enjoy intellectual effort, how to share gracefully, and many other things which become the curriculum of nursery and kindergarten schools but which also can be learned from a competent mother or well brought up older brother or sister. (Incidentally this is one reason why intensive pre-school education is not very important for most children from good middle-class homes, whereas it can be very significant for slum children from poor, messy homes (Passow, 1963).)

Later, when the child is in primary or grammar school, he needs to be taught the 3 R's, something about science and the planet and how his body works, and also a rudimentary appreciation for the creative and esthetic side of life. Still later, in secondary school, the youth must be given a chance to test out where his own strengths lie, to advance and synthesize in a human framework some of his prior learning, and to become familiar with some of the great unsolved problems and controversial issues of our age. This is where our high school education breaks down: we are afraid to trust youth with the kind of knowledge and commitment that might cause them to challenge the faith of their fathers. But what is the purpose of learning and education if not to give the youth the wherewithal to abandon or reaffirm the faith of their fathers? Giving the younger generation a liberal and liberating education, and not merely "schooling," is the riskiest business the older generation can undertake.

Some educators claim that the art of learning is equivalent to the art of posing proper and relevant questions in a proper form. We have learned how to learn when we have become skilled in the formulation of "researchable queries."

There is some truth in the belief that a well-educated person must know how to confront his environment with incisive and logical questions that will evoke useful responses. But this, too, is for the most part a built-in tendency of the human being. After all, even a bright four year old is capable of asking one of the supreme questions: who made God? And of rejecting or ignoring the pat or bumbling answers. And so the bright four year old comes to understand *not knowing, not learning*, the fact that there is something fishy going on around here. This is all to the good, for if he does not let go of the sense of the fishy, of the sense of *not knowing and yet needing to find out*, he is on his way to being an intellectually emancipated human being for whom the learning process never ends. This is equivalent to saying that no human being ever ultimately and totally learns. Being man, it is our lot to learn only a little and a little at a time, although it may seem like much.

Other educators claim that the best synonym for learning how to learn is problem solving. They believe that the chief aim of the school is to promote proficiency in solving problems.

Some people are better than others at solving problems. This is undeniable. The child psychologist is an expert in advising parents on problem children, but he may be hopeless before the problem of repairing his broken-down car. The automobile mechanic can solve problems presented by faulty carburetors and tired motors, but he is often not much good at answering questions having to do with higher mathematics. The mathematician is proficient in finding solutions by manipulating abstract rules, but he may be a failure when it comes to rearing his children. And so it goes.

It cannot be doubted that human beings are born and develop with varying capacities for different kinds of learning—we lump it together and call it "intelligence"—but there is no such thing as a general problem-solving capacity. It is true that some people put themselves out more, are more energetic, and thus learn more ways to solve more kinds of problems. It is also true that in some people the innate intellectual capacities are masked or smothered by bad events, and these people go through life solving fewer problems in fewer ways.[6] But now we are talking about motivation and chance and the fact that in many respects the world is a treacherous and unfair place—we are not talking about pure problem-solving.

Does this mean that children cannot be taught to learn more effectively, to solve problems more efficiently? Beyond any doubt they can be so taught. In addition to good study habits mentioned above, they can also be brought to see the importance of drill, the need to memorize basic facts, the use of reference books, the difference between fact and opinion, and many other things too numerous to mention. All this will be of some help in solving problems. Above all, they can be brought to control their interest or dedication to certain learning tasks by diminished or heightened levels of motivation, and controlling these motivational

[6] It is now fashionable to call such individuals "culturally deprived," although it is usually more accurate merely to identify them as being poor.

levels becomes a powerful tool in the hands of the gifted teacher. But none of this amounts to learning how to learn, nor does it make for a genuinely learned human being.

Conclusion

Learning how to learn is a small problem (but perhaps a big task) which millions of ordinary human beings master every day without the help of the schools or teachers. Knowing *what* to learn, how much to learn, how deeply to learn, how to use what is learned, and what not to learn—these are the enduring and never-ending challenges to the human race. It has never been a chief mission of the schools to teach us how to learn. Man possesses the power to learn and knows that he possesses that power. He stands in need of profound help, as always, in deciding how to apply that power. To assist in providing that help is the ever-new and now much more challenging mission of the schools.

References

Hutchins, Robert M. 1963. *Science, scientists, and politics.* An occasional paper on the role of science and technology in the free society (Santa Barbara, Calif.: Center for the Study of Democratic Institutions).

Passow, A. Harry (ed.). 1963. *Education in depressed areas* (New York: Teachers College, Columbia University Press).

Rambusch, Nancy McCormick. 1962. *Learning how to learn, an American approach to Montessori* (Baltimore, Md.: Helicon Press, Inc.), p. 7.

32   Building Self-Image in Preschoolers*

GLENN R. HAWKES, *University of California, Davis*

Social living forms the base for preschool educational experiences. Both social living and educational experiences need to be regarded in the broadest sense if we are to understand the total impact of early school

* *The Instructor*, January 1966. Reprinted by permission.

experiences on the young child. All of a child's experiences are educational, and social living involves the child's growing concept of himself and his concepts of others. This makes the early primary curriculum harder to understand, and, for that matter, harder to explain.

As children grow and develop, they learn from their associates who they are—their language, values, preferences, attitudes, and their own worth. This learning is largely a process of socialization and personality development, not instruction per se or assigned lessons. This process involves adult-child interaction.

The initiative for effective interaction falls upon the teacher. It is her job to create a climate which fosters development in a positive manner. To do this she must understand the importance of his interaction, and a great deal about the psychological and physiological development of children. The teacher must be constantly cognizant of the child's need to know who he is, that he is valued, and that he has the freedom to explore the fulfillment of his needs.

The ability to interact effectively in social situations depends on many factors. The child's self-image is a very important factor, but probably the least understood. The preschool teacher must do everything in her power to help build an adequate and developing self-image for the child. This self-image comes from many kinds of interactions. However, the child mainly gains this image from the telling reflections of adults around him. A look, a touch, or a word can convey a definition of himself that becomes a part of his growing concept of himself as a person.

> Mark's preschool teacher, aware of his lack of muscle coordination in climbing on the jungle gym, used encouragement and verbal approval to help him see what he could do, rather than what he could *not* do. She noticed real progress because of positive reflection. He became more confident and ventured further, gradually building his skill.

The child's growing concept of himself takes constant defining and redefining. It is not full-blown with one interaction, nor is it ever complete. (Even we adults seek new definitions and reassurances that we are who we think we are. If those with whom we interact see us in a more—or less—positive way, we are prone to change our self-image.) Consider the child's greater plasticity and the smaller reservoir of reassurances he has been able to establish. One can easily understand the critical need for image-building in the young child as he struggles toward adulthood.

Image-building is also a function of the people with whom the child interacts. Parents and family are usually very important people in this respect. So is the teacher, because of the rise in early childhood education opportunities and because our way of life is changing. The impact of urban and suburban living on the young child has denied him the rich interaction potential of the extended family. We are prone to live in small family units, isolated, yet living in ever closer proximity to our neighbors. This living arrangement offers a limited, usually biased sampling of reality in relationship to people. Interaction potential is reduced because families seek similar families with which to interact, in spite of the fact that parents have ever rising aspirations for rich growth opportunities for their children.

With the growing absenteeism of father and mother, more and more image-building falls upon the nonparents with whom the child associates. If the goals of the nonparents are incompatible and inconsistent with those of the parents, the child is faced with a blurry, confused image of what he is and ought to be.

A preschooler needs a variety of images fed to him. But these images must have common elements or he will be confused and dismayed, with little conception of where he is and where he ought to be going.

Young children desire the correction of their liabilities. Their feeling of worth is enhanced when an adult shows concern for them and gives them moments of undivided attention. Even if nothing more than a bond of communication is accomplished in this process, the effort has been worthwhile and the avenues are open for the next interaction in image-building.

An effective preschool teacher knows the value of the peer group in image-building. Preschoolers particularly need help in clarifying who they are in relation to children of the same size with the same sort of needs. An effective teacher lubricates the wheels of this type of inter-action.

"Your finger painting is all yellow and blue, Ned. We'll put your name on it and hang it up where everyone can see it."

"Sally has found a worm. Everyone can come and Sally will tell us how she found it."

"You did a nice job of waiting for your turn, Ralph. Now you may have your turn with the swing."

Such statements as these from teachers may help a child see himself more clearly. It may help him clarify his place in the group—his worth to peers. Letting a child experience success helps him learn he can be successful, not only as an individual but also in social living.

The resultant behavior of successful image-building shows up in the child's ever increasing awareness of his own autonomy. He shows more self-direction in his behavior. He has a clearer notion of his goals and how to achieve them. If he does not succeed in reaching his goals, he more easily modifies them or the method by which he intended to reach them. Consider this incident:

Early in the spring Mary asked her nursery-school teacher for a small plot of ground on the play yard so she could plant some seeds.

The teacher marked out a small square which was to be for Mary to build her garden. She cultivated the area and then planted some radish and carrot seeds. Shortly after the plants began to emerge from the ground some of the children in the group played too rough nearby and the seedlings were destroyed. The teacher was disturbed because the project was one of Mary's first. She talked to Mary about the "accident" —hoping to help her accept what had happened.

Mary's response was somewhat philosophical in nature, "Oh, well, they didn't mean to do it. I can plant my garden all over again and this time I'll put up a fence to keep people out. Or maybe I should put it back in the corner where it is out of everyone's way."

Mary was able to keep her goal in mind while modifying her means so she could achieve success and retain her view of her rights and the rights of others in the group. Such social perceptiveness lays the groundwork for complicated social interaction and concern on a much more complicated level.

Social living requires that a person learn to be a partner if he is to get along in the world. It is possible to achieve some goals on "one's own." However, in this modern world, it is not possible to be an isolate. The basics of social living require that a person have a self-image of worth and worthwhileness. The preschool program provides "helping people" who lay the groundwork for later learnings . . . interesting people— children and adults—with interesting tasks build the self-image. This is where social living begins.

A successful preschool program teaches "I like me because I am worthy of being liked and I can do things. I like teachers because they like me and they help me. I find pleasure in relationships with other children because I can trust them and I am safe with them." Every child who develops a positive self-image of himself and who learns to function in social situations represents a valuable addition to the total educational scheme. This is one very important contribution of preschool education.

33   Helping Children Understand Themselves*

GLENN R. HAWKES, *University of California, Davis*

Understanding himself is one of the most important achievements any human being can strive for—understanding, insofar as possible, his own

* N.E.A. Department of Elementary, Kindergarten, Nursery Education. Reprinted by permission.

needs and wants, his own emotions, his own aspirations, his own strengths and liabilities, and his own behavior. With understanding may come an appreciation of himself as an individual, a unique person of much importance. The achievement of such understanding can begin early in a child's life, and should if it is to keep pace with his physical and emotional growth as he moves from one stage of development to another.

Helping children understand themselves means helping them to understand personal emotional disturbances and to find suitable fulfillment of their own unique needs. Providing such help is a big order for teachers and for parents. When adults understand themselves, they find it easier to understand children, but understanding oneself is one thing and making the most of that knowledge is another, at any age. Learning to understand oneself is a project with a definite goal—being able to live and deal with the complicated world of today with satisfaction and joy along the way, and becoming a loving and lovable person.

Child Behavior

Children's misbehavior is not motivated by a desire to be disagreeable. It results from an overriding need to achieve a goal when the child cannot perceive a better way at the moment, or when he has forgotten the more socially acceptable patterns of behavior which have not as yet become established as habit. At other times more immediate needs may overpower self-control. When this happens, if an adult in a nonpunitive way either calls the child's attention to the lapse or suggests a more acceptable practice, the child may be able to recover his self-control and work out his own solutions. Sometimes misbehavior is caused by a child's need to get back at what he sees as unreasonable and/or punitive behavior by the adult. The mature adult, aware of this possibility, should analyze the situation and change either his own behavior or the child's perception.

The important point in handling misbehavior is for the adult to support and strengthen the child's ability to meet threatening situations and resolve inconsistencies in ways acceptable to himself and others. Timing is important in helping children understand themselves and their problems, and the time is *now*. Treatment is more effective if it is contiguous with the problem but should never be initiated in the heat of disturbance.

Communication between children and adults is a critical phase of any effort to help children learn to understand their behavior. Speech is only a part of the communication process however. Either the child or the adult may convey his thoughts and their meanings through posture, tone of voice, stance, gestures, facial expressions, or the way he keeps his distance. Nonverbal behavior can be even more forceful than words, and more helpful. The need for understanding the effect of nonverbal communication—an unending one—is especially important in working with young children, since they have not yet mastered the complexities of verbal communication.

Most children need to be able to talk freely at times with an adult, often someone outside the home. They need an opportunity to put thinking into words, try out ideas, refine or clarify concepts, release feelings, or even to look at themselves. The adult must be a good listener who does not preach or express horror or exasperation at what he hears. For a child's openness to adult help can be and often is smothered by censorious listening. This is the time to learn more about the child, gather data from which an interpretation can be made, and discern directions for help. A child needs assurance and seeks the guidance of an adult if he is secure in the knowledge that confidence will be respected. A child needs to feel that *he* is loved even when his actions are not accepted—"She likes *me* but she doesn't like what I'm doing."

Deep inside, children are favorably impressed and their self-concept is enhanced when an adult shows concern for them and gives them even a pittance of undivided attention. Even if nothing more than a bond of mutual confidence is accomplished in trying to help children understand themselves, the effort has been worthwhile.

If tact and patience are exercised, guidance of children in the correction of their liabilities can contribute to their self-understanding and help them capitalize on their unique abilities. Seeing the situation from a child's viewpoint, accepting the child's feelings at the moment, and looking for what the child is trying to accomplish are all important if he is to be helped in self-understanding.

Social Encounters

Children need to feel socially secure, to feel valued by their peers. Discovering how a child feels about his place in his circle of friends or playmates may be the key to understanding him and the key for finding ways to help him help himself.

A conversation between an unhappy child and his teacher may help him see his problem more clearly. Often the child needs a "map of reality" to help him view the problem as it really is. The adult's carefully chosen questions may help him find the answer to his questions within himself. For instance . . .

> Cynthia and Mark had been busy in the "housekeeping corner" for well over an hour when Mark suddenly announced his intention to quit playing with girls and to begin real boy play. Cynthia resorted to tears

to keep Mark, and he responded by calling her "cry-baby" and moving away. The teacher quietly took in the situation and by careful and skillful responses to Cynthia's tear-filled sentences helped Cynthia understand the situation. Mark had really played a long time; he was still her friend; there were other children who would like to play with her; and there were many other available activities.

A youngster may have doubts and misunderstandings that need to be clarified and settled.

Gary, an eager, enthusiastic nine-year-old, seemed suddenly to have developed an inordinate fear of animals, especially dogs. His fear was so out of character for him that it caused difficulty with his fellow students. One day after a particularly trying session when a stray dog got on the playground, the teacher talked over the problem with Gary. Careful and skillful discussion led to the discovery that, after being warned about the dangers and horrors of rabies, Gary had developed an irrational fear of dogs that was too strong to cope with. His vocabulary and concepts were too limited for intelligent seeking of information.

Sometimes a child may have strong feelings that can be a problem if nothing is done about them. Rage and foul language may be the outlet he has discovered to clear the air for him. If secure in the teacher's acceptance of him, he can be helped to understand his feelings and find less destructive ways of getting release.

Harry, an athletically able fellow who played to win, let out a stream of oaths when he was called out on a close play at third base. The student teacher recognized that this was common language in Harry's home and shortly afterwards made an opportunity to talk with the boy about different patterns of speech. In a man-to-man fashion the student teacher tried to help Harry see that his choice of words needed to be in keeping with his audience, that English has indeed many colorful words, and that in the big leagues foul language sometimes results in a fine. Thus the need to increase his vocabulary and to have drill and practice in language usage was presented and the boy was helped to find other emotional outlets when words were inadequate.

Feelings of anxiety or guilt may bother a child, but if he can talk to someone he trusts his feelings will be soothed and the cause of his unhappiness will fall into proper perspective.

Joe, a popular sixth-grader, developed a sudden dislike for outdoor play periods. When the other children in his class flocked to the play yard he would find some excuse to tarry and became belligerent for no apparent reason. Each day the situation seemed to be worse until Joe's teacher felt action had to be taken. A quiet talk in the classroom after the other children had gone outside revealed that Joe had broken his glasses twice while playing ball. His parents had warned him the first time to be more careful, and on the second occasion had forbidden him to wear his glasses during recess period. But to keep his status as the best man at bat he had to wear his glasses to see the ball. Helping Joe spill his feelings and thus reveal the cause of anxiety led to a program of positive action. His parents were consulted and arrangements were made to protect his glasses while Joe was at bat.

Personal Limitations

Circumstances that a child feels neither he nor anyone else can change may worry him, but talking about the problem and his feelings about it may help him acquire a comfortable sense of acceptance.

> No matter how much Timmy stretched he could not slip the strap of the tumbling pad over the high hooks on the gym wall in order to get the mat down. After repeated attempts he would become annoyed and hostile toward the hooks and the activity and show frustration about his size. A skillful teacher talked to him about how we are all different and all have inadequacies. This was a new concept to Timmy. After he was helped to think through ways of solving his problem and to admire persons like Franklin D. Roosevelt who have overcome physical incapacities, he began to volunteer and to play a leadership role for tasks not requiring size.

In groups, difficulties sometimes can be overcome if the members have a keen appreciation of each other or if they can understand why certain conditions have arisen as a result of their own behavior.

Feelings of hostility and aggression are common among children, partly because such feelings are tied up with normal development. The child may overreach his physical capacity and resort in frustration to hostile and aggressive behavior. Other instances of hostile behavior may be generated by nudging of ambitious parents, academic standards which cannot be met, unfair competition, failure to get attention, or unfulfilled ambitions.

When a child's hostility turns into aggression toward another child or himself, the teacher can suggest that he let off steam by turning to the work bench, modeling clay, punching a pillow or punching bag, running, or digging. All of these are harmless outlets for feeling. By accepting and interpreting the child's behavior with the child, the teacher shows the child that he understands and thus helps the child understand and cope in turn with his own hostility.

Environmental Factors

Situations which the child cannot understand because of limited experience may arouse undesirable traits which can become routine behavior. For instance, repeated incidences of unfriendliness may cause a child to become habitually easily offended. An adult can seek to avoid such situations and at the same time help the child develop self-confidence and social maturity. Time, experience, and success in meeting problems will help the child grow in understanding and relate positively to new events.

Learning to accept limitations gracefully, if not cheerfully, is a useful lesson for a lifetime. There are the practical limits of time, space, and money; the regulations of government, school, and home; the rules of the game; and the requirements of work. When a child understands that all people, whatever their ages, must live and work within limits of one kind or another, he begins to appreciate the routines and structure of life that cramp his desires.

> Bill's discovery that his father could not leave work at his whim or without cause seemed to change Bill's viewpoint. Heretofore he had been rebellious at attending school on Opening Day of the baseball season or going to a special scout meeting on the night of his favorite television program. But when he found fathers also have restrictions, the explanation that "we all have limits" seemed to make sense.

Helping children understand the need for cooperation in group living at school and in the home calls for diplomacy of the highest order. All too often adult values and demands are imposed on a child with little consideration of his rights as a human being with desires and goals of his own, just learning to understand himself.

Children sometimes see themselves as bad, unworthy, or inadequate. Many times a child's naiveté and inexperience produce unacceptable behavior in a social situation for which he is punished without explanation. The resulting feeling is shame. Sometimes a child is compared with a sibling or another student, is found wanting, and is left feeling inadequate. Or he may be placed in a competitive situation where success is impossible. Because children have not reached adults' expectations or have not been able to please, they become hostile toward the world and experience failure. Such feelings of shame, inadequacy, failure, and the like all can have only one effect on a child: he feels defeated—no good, unwanted, incapable of "becoming."

Contrast this self-concept with that of a child who is encouraged to reach higher, supported when he does not quite succeed, praised for every bit of progress. Talking over failures with someone who cares and understands helps the child to develop a more positive self-image or self-concept. Understanding that others experience difficulties in the school, the home, and the neighborhood may be a comfort to some children. The reflection a child sees of himself is the one painted for him by the adults in his life, for even his peers accept the label assigned him by his teacher and parents.

Helping a child understand how his actions are linked to his feelings and the feelings of other people for him may help a child accept himself as a succeeding-failing, adequate-inadequate, good-bad person, but always a person who is worthy, striving, and growing.

> Each day when Darren arrived at nursery school he would seek Linda out and tell her he was going to eat her up, at which Linda would run and hide. The teacher finally concluded that possibly Darren wanted to play with Linda but was uncertain how to make an approach. When she asked if Darren wanted this, he said "yes," so she helped the two children get together for play. Darren no longer needed to "eat up" Linda and they found a mutual interest in horses which became a bond between them.

Sooner or later, a child must learn to be a partner if he is to get along well in the world. Some goals may be attained by an individual, but others require the cooperation and contributions of others. By setting up tasks that require two or more children to work together, the teacher helps each child to experience the thrill of cooperative achievement and learn that a personal goal can be reached through the group's joint effort.

> A classroom group was challenged to devise some novel way of sharing their creative work with other children. The teacher suggested that they might want to combine efforts and talents, knowing that one sensitive, highly creative, shy girl needed to be appreciated by her classmates. The next step, getting Linda and three others into a committee, was easily managed. In this small group Linda blossomed. Her ideas were picked up and embellished. While she sketched the illustrations for a story whose plot had been cooperatively worked out, another girl wrote the single line captions, and the third constructed a strong book covering. And Linda's brother's kindergarten class was the richer by one picture book.

Learning

Learning how to learn and how to find joy in learning might be called "creative inquiry." No one can learn all he needs to know; he can only discover his own assets and limitations, and learn how to learn and how to acquire and use new ideas, knowledge, and ways of doing things. A child's questions indicate his need to learn. As a teacher builds experiences to supply the information desired, the child gains insight into the process of learning and sees himself as the dynamic force.

This support of the child's quest and a teacher's enthusiasm for new learning, new ideas, and new developments in old ideas foster a child's curiosity about the world around him—what he sees, what he hears, what he feels. Such encouragement, his involvement, and his recognition that the teacher values his contributions to the learning situation and shares in his discoveries and enthusiasm help a child find satisfaction in learning.

He learns how to direct and satisfy his curiosity. He gains both increased insight into the effect of his personal behavior and the cause of his failures, and the ability to manipulate circumstances. The teacher's skillful use of a wide variety of learning materials and opportunities—games, records, tapes, films and filmstrips, pictures, manipulative and technological materials and equipment, books, and magazines—fosters the development of a child's understanding of his intellectual potential and how to fulfill it.

The exchange of ideas among children encourages them to seek further information, to think about what they know and what they have learned from others, and to put it all together to become a part of their own reservoir of information and opinion. Successful communication of ideas among children usually is spontaneous. The teacher listens and enters the discussion only if his information or opinion is needed.

These basic attitudes about learning are increasingly important in setting up the total scheme of learning patterns that will be a part of a child's life always.

Conclusion

The value of any understanding must be judged in terms of its effects, both immediate and indirect. Children's understanding of themselves must be appropriate to their ages.

How does one know when a child is making progress in understanding himself? Observation of his general behavior indicates—

- A feeling of safety and security.
- A sense of belonging.
- An impression of adequacy—self-reliance, independence.
- A realization of himself as a person.
- A spirit of happiness—contentment in small pleasures, delight in humor.
- Assurance in meeting his own needs.
- Flexibility and buoyancy—the ability to find pleasure in an alternative when he cannot do what he first chooses.
- An aptitude for dealing with realities—mistakes, circumstances beyond his control, conflicts within himself and with others.
- A sensitivity to other people and how they feel.
- A recognition of the normal range of emotions and reasonable control over behavior.
- An ability to work—to plan and carry out a project.
- Ease and poise in meeting and communicating with his peers and with adults.

Every child who learns to understand people in general and himself in particular represents a contribution made by the people who have helped him to learn.

References

Association for Supervision and Curriculum Development. 1962. *Perceiving, behaving, becoming* (Washington, D.C.: The Association, a department of the National Education Association).

Hawkes, G. R., and D. Pease. 1962. *Behavior and development from 5 to 12* (New York: Harper & Row).

Jenkins, G. G. 1961. *Helping children reach their potential* (Glenview, Ill.: Scott, Foresman and Company).

Osborn, D. K. 1957. Open and closed avenues. *Discipline*. M. Rasmussen (ed.), Bulletin No. 99 (Washington, D.C.: Association for Childhood Education International), pp. 13–17.

Peters, H. J., A. C. Riccio, and J. J. Quaranta. 1963. *Guidance in the elementary school—a book of readings* (New York: The Macmillan Company).

Rasey, M. I. 1957. Interpreting discipline. *Discipline*. M. Rasmussen (ed.), Bulletin No. 99 (Washington, D.C.: Association for Childhood Education International), pp. 4–9.

Waring, E. B. 1952. *Principles for child guidance*. Extension Bulletin No. 420 (Ithaca, N.Y.: Cornell University).

34   The Role of Love in the Education of Pre-school Children*

DANIEL A. PRESCOTT, *Institute for Child Study, University of Maryland*

It often happens in human affairs that scientists gain their first insights by studying illnesses and mishaps. When things go wrong, the causes which produce the undesirable happenings are sought, and, as these negative factors are understood, an initial and partial vision is gained into the more important positive forces that govern phenomenon being investigated. It was so with love.

During the past three decades students of the health and growth of young children arduously have been tracing the physical, social, economic,

* *The Journal of Education*, January 1966. Reprinted by permission. The World Council of OMEP (Organisation Mondiale pour l'Education Préscolaire) has also kindly given permission to print this address by Dr. Prescott to the World Congress of OMEP held in Athens.

and psychological factors which underlie disturbances in physical growth, which are responsible for emotional maladjustment, or for the malformation of character in the early years of life. Over and over again they have discovered a deficiency factor, the absence of something needed, to be primary in the causation of these undesirable happenings. Expressed most simply, the absence of love, or the inadequate expression of love, seems to have been indicated repeatedly as one of the major causations of these distortions of development.

Only a few of these revelatory studies will be mentioned here, because I wish to go on rapidly to consider in more detail what love really is, and what its positive role in human development may be. For it is small use to say that maladjustments and limitations of development ensue from the absence of love unless one is able to describe positively the nature of the force which must be created to alleviate the maladjustment and to bring about the conditions necessary to the full realization of human potentialities.

In the United States during the past thirty years the custom has developed of having babies born in hospitals rather than in the home. This has come about in order that both the mother and the child could receive better medical attention and more hygienic care. And, in fact, both maternal and infant mortality rates have been reduced greatly by this practice. However, the procedure developed of taking the child from the mother in the delivery room and of keeping him most of the time for some days in a special nursery with other infants, rather than of placing him in the bed or even in the room with his mother. His needs were cared for by specially trained nurses, except that at certain intervals he was taken to his mother for feeding and then returned to his bassinette in the nursery.

Under these conditions many children developed nutritional difficulties and, in some, a special illness, called marasmus, which means wasting away, was identified. This was described by Bakwin in 1942. Subsequently, Dr. Margaret Ribble of New York published several books and articles about this phenomenon. Indeed, as early as 1937, Dr. David Levy, a psychiatrist, published an article in the *American Journal of Psychiatry*, called "Primary Affect Hunger." In this he made it clear that infants and young children cannot thrive on food and physical hygiene alone but must have the added nurturance of love, fondling and contact with their mother's bodies if they are to grow physically healthy and emotionally adjusted. In this connection, also, Bevan Brown has written extensively on the importance of breast feeding for later physical and mental health. The absence of love and of the nurturance patterns which are the natural expressions of love seems to be an important factor in the causation of nutritional illnesses in infants.

There is a second line of evidence pointing to the important role of love in the development of children. War and its aftermath disturbed the home life of millions of children and orphaned countless thousands. Institutions have had to be developed in many countries to care for these children separated from their parents. The physical, mental and emotional development of these institutionalized children has been the object of much study by scientists because, under institutional conditions, they did not flourish as well as children at home.

Dorothy Burlingham and Anna Freud in their book, "Infants Without Families," William Goldfarb in a series of articles in the *American Journal of Orthopsychiatry*, John Bowlby in a *World Health Organization Monograph* in 1951 and in an article in the *Journal of Mental Science* in 1953, Rene Spitz in a very telling series of research studies as well as Beres and Obers—all have shown that young children separated from the love of their parents languish and fail to achieve their best growth both physically and intellectually. They also develop unwholesome emotional reactions under usual institutional conditions. But happily, this has not been true in those institutions where they have had regular, extensive, intimate and continuing person-to-person contacts through time with one particular adult who valued them highly. Again the accumulated evidence is very powerful that a child must have more than adequate nourishment, good physical care and systematic instruction if he is to achieve the full development of his potentials. A person-to-person relationship which can only be called love, together with the day-to-day interactions implied by this love relationship, is necessary to provide the emotional climate essential to wholesome development.

Anthropologists who have studied the family and child-rearing customs of many cultures supply a third line of evidence of the vital role of love in the development of the pre-school child. Wayne Dennis in "The Hopi Child," Margaret Mead in "From the South Seas" and Ashley Montagu in "The Direction of Human Development," to mention only three among many, have supplied detailed descriptions of child-rearing practices in different cultures and of the psychological aftermaths of these customs in the human personalities produced by them. Ashley Montagu (op. cit., p. 245) has generalized on these findings of cultural anthropologists as follows:

> We know from the observation and study of many peoples that the well-integrated, cooperative, adult personality is largely the product of a childhood which has enjoyed a maximum of satisfaction and a minimum of frustration. We also know the obverse to be true, that the disintegrated, non-cooperative adult personality is largely a product of a childhood which has suffered a maximum of frustration and a minimum of satisfactions to young children and that the absence of love nearly always builds up a disturbing number of frustrations.

Thus, we have three lines of evidence from scientific research, all of which show that love is vital to optimum growth and to wholesome personality development in infants and young children.

But what is the nature of this person-to-person relationship which infants and young children must experience to achieve a healthy becoming and which I have chosen to call love? The validity of the term "love" also must be tested against available scientific evidence and its essential qualities must be defined most carefully. Accordingly the remainder of this paper will address itself to three questions:

1. Is love a reality or only a delusive romantic construct of our culture?
2. If love is a reality, what are its essential qualities?
3. If love is a reality, what is its role in human development?

In preparing this paper I examined dozens of books on human development, educational psychology, cultural anthropology, sociology, psychiatry, and biography. In the majority of the books on human development and educational psychology the word "love" did not occur. When it did occur it was used without definition for the most part. I feel that if love is a reality, we need seriously and scientifically to study its influence on human lives and to learn what conditions are favorable to its enhancement and fulfillment. If it is not a reality, we shall need to study the reasons for the emergence of so strong a myth, so frustrating an aspiration, so delusive a pretension. There is a remarkably small amount of scientific material now available about the nature of love.

A very brief review of the ideas found in some of the books examined comes first. Breckenridge and Vincent, Strang, and Barker, Kounin, and Wright, all mention love as a reality. The general idea expressed is that love markedly influences behavior, development, and adjustment. One notes a vagueness about the nature of love as a positive force and finds much more specificity about the negative effects of lack of love and of inappropriate use of love relationships. Kluckhohn and Murray give a great amount of material about sexual behavior and about family processes but no discussion of love as such.

James Plant clearly regards love as a reality but does not define it. In his view, love affords children a basic security, a sure feeling of belonging. Insecure, unloved children show anxious, panicky symptoms that contrast with the aggressive over-compensation of inadequate children. Confusion about their security often arises in children as they try to meet the learning and behavioral demands set for them by the authority of their parents and of society, and, again, as they struggle for independence.

Harry Stack Sullivan defines love in these terms:

> When the satisfaction or the security of another person becomes as significant to one as one's own security, then the state of love exists. He

goes on to say that when one loves one begins to feel human in a sense in which one has not previously felt human . . . one begins to appreciate the common humanity of people.

Overstreet says:

> The love of a person implies not the possession of that person but the affirmation of that person. It means granting him gladly the full right to his unique humanhood. One does not truly love a person and yet seek to enslave him—by law, or by bonds of dependence and possessiveness. Whenever we experience a genuine love we are moved by the transforming experience toward a capacity for good will.

Fromm coins the term "productive love" because the word love as popularly used is so ambiguous. The essence of love, he contends, is the same whether it is the mother's love for a child, our love for man, or the erotic love between two individuals. Certain basic elements are characteristic of all forms of productive love. They are *Care, Responsibility, Respect*, and *Knowledge*. He says:

> Care and responsibility denote that love is an activity, not a passion . . . the essence of love is to labor for something, to make something grow . . . Without respect for and knowledge of the beloved person love deteriorates into domination and possessiveness. Respect . . . denotes the ability to see a person as he is, to be aware of his individuality and uniqueness . . . Love is the expression of intimacy between two human beings under the condition of the preservation of each other's integrity . . . To love one person productively means to be related to his human core, to him as representing mankind.

Fromm also contends that love of others and of ourselves are not alternatives:

> The affirmation of one's own life, happiness, growth and freedom is rooted in one's capacity to love . . . If an individual is able to love productively he loves himself too . . . Selfishness and self-love, far from being identical are actually opposites . . . The selfish person does not love himself too much but too little, in fact he hates himself . . . He is necessarily unhappy and anxiously concerned to snatch from life the satisfactions which block himself from attaining . . .

The recurring mention in the literature of the relatedness of love for self (self-respect), love for other individuals, and love for mankind led me to examine biographies and writings of three men who have lived lives of great devotion to mankind: Kagawa, Gandhi and Albert Schweitzer.

Kagawa says:

> Love awakens all that it touches . . . creation is the art of life pursued for love . . . Love is the true nature of God . . . In social life human beings meet and love one another through a material medium . . . Love spins garments for itself out of matter . . . through love eco-

nomic life appears as the content of the spiritual . . . Real construction of society can be accomplished only through the operation of education through love . . . Love is identical with activity . . . It means creating existence where there has been none . . . If we view economics so, the study of it changes into a science of love . . . Art must create externally beautiful objects and internally it is itself love.

The practical social and political application of love has worked several miracles in India during our times. Gandhi said:

To be truly non-violent I must love my adversary and pray for him even when he hits me . . . We may attack measures and systems. We may not, we must not attack men. Imperfect ourselves, we must be tender toward others . . . forgiveness is more manly than punishment. *Gandhi told landowners*, Landlords should cease to be mere rent collectors. They should become trustees and trusted friends of their tenants. They should give peasants finity of tenure, take a lively interest in their welfare, provide well-managed schools for their children, night school for adults, hospitals and dispensaries for the sick, look after the sanitation and in a variety of ways make them feel that they, the landlords, are their friends.

Gandhi contended that God is love and can be known only through action. Faith does not permit of telling. It has to be lived and then it is self-propagating.

Albert Schweitzer is another extraordinary international figure who has accomplished the apparently impossible during the past fifty years. He has tremendous reverence for life and respect for the dignity of all human beings, and he believes that love is the great force of the universe. He says:

By the spirit of the age the man of today is forced into skepticism about his own thinking in order to make him receptive to truth which comes to him from authority . . . (but) it is only by confidence in our ability to reach truth by our own individual thinking that we are capable of accepting truth from outside . . . Man must bring himself into a spiritual relation to the world and become one with it . . . Beginning to think about life and the world leads a man directly and almost irresistibly to reverence for life . . . the idea of love is the spiritual beam of light which reaches us from the Infinite . . . in God, the great first cause, the will-to-create and the will-to-love are one . . . In knowledge of spiritual existence in God through Love he (man) possesses the one thing needful.

Each of the three men whose biographies were studied was a man of action who accomplished the seemingly impossible during his lifetime in the first half of this, our twentieth century. Each affirmed that love was a central dynamic in his accomplishment—love of mankind, and love of God. Theirs certainly was "productive love." We may therefore regard our first question as answered in the affirmative. Love does exist. It is a potent reality. It has been validated by men of science as well as by those three extraordinary men of action.

Now what about the nature of love? On the basis of my research I have developed a number of theses about love. They will be presented with brief mention of the degree to which they seem to be supported by the ideas found in the material already cited.

1. Love involves more or less empathy with the loved one. A person who loves actually feels with and so shares intimately the experiences of the loved one and the effects of experiences upon the loved one. Sullivan indicates something of how this comes about: "If another person matters as much to you as you do yourself, it is quite possible to talk to this person as you have never talked to anyone before. The freedom which comes . . . permits nuances of meaning, permits investigation without fear of rebuff which greatly augments the consensual validation of all sorts of things."

2. One who loves is deeply concerned for the welfare, happiness, and development of the loved one. This concern is so deep as to become one of the major values in the organized personality or "self-structure" of the loving person. All sources studied seem to agree on this proposition. It is especially validated by the lives of Kagawa, Gandhi and Schweitzer. Each of them has shown by his actions through the years that he values the human beings whom he serves not only as much as he values himself, but even more.

3. One who loves finds pleasure in making his resources available to the loved one, to be used by the latter to enhance his welfare, happiness, and development. Strength, time, money, mind—indeed all resources—are happily proffered for the use of the loved one. This implies that a loving person acts with and on behalf of the loved one whenever his resources permit and the action is desired by the loved one. The loving person is not merely deeply concerned about the welfare, happiness, and development of the beloved; he does something to enhance them whenever possible. All sources seem to agree on this proposition, too.

4. On the one hand the loving person seeks a maximum of participation in the activities that contribute to the welfare, happiness, and development of the loved one; on the other hand the loving one accepts fully the uniqueness and individuality of the loved one and accords him freedom to experience, to act, and to become what he desires. This thesis is agreed to by nearly all of the sources consulted.

5. Love is most readily and usually achieved within the family circle, but can be extended to include many other individuals, or categories of people, or all of humanity. In the case of Schweitzer it also includes all living things and the Creative Force of the universe—God. In the same

way a person can advantageously experience love from a limitless number of other human beings and living things. Of course, genuine full love is hard to achieve even with a few persons, as several of our sources pointed out. But this is not proof that with greater scientific understanding of its processes we cannot create conditions that will favor its broadening.

6. The good effects of love are not limited to the loved one but promote the happiness and further development of the loving one as well. Love is not altruistic, self-sacrificing, and limiting for the one who loves. On the contrary, it is a reciprocal dynamic which greatly enriches the lives of both. This idea is not too clearly stated in a number of our sources but seems implied where not stated, in nearly all.

7. Love is not rooted primarily in sexual dynamics or hormonal drives, although it may well have large erotic components whether between parents and children, between children, or between adults. Fromm seems to support this position when he says that the essence of productive love is the same no matter who is concerned.

8. Love affords many individuals fundamental insights into and basic relationships to humanity and to the forces that organize and guide the universe. It gives many persons a basic orientation in the universe and among mankind. It can become the basis for faith in God. I was surprised to find support for this thesis from all sources. For example, Plant affirms that:

> From early adolescence on, the Church gives a great many children a sense of belongingness which has greater continuity and certainty for the individual than anything provided by his parents.

Each of the other sources also intimated that love is a great aid in the developmental tasks of orienting the self toward the rest of mankind and within the universe toward God.

These eight theses, I hope, may be of some aid in analysing the nature of love and the processes by which it develops. Admittedly they represent only a first and faltering attempt. But if they are sufficient to focus more scientific attention and research on love, the purpose of this paper will have been accomplished.

Now we address ourselves to the third question. Since love does exist, it potentially can become a reality in the life of every human being. Then, if our theses regarding the nature of love are true, what roles can love play in human development? This question will be answered during the next decade, I hope, by a whole series of researches. The findings should fill many monographs and some books. In the meantime I should like to propose a series of hypotheses as to the probable findings of these researches, in the hope of suggesting profitable research leads.

The first hypothesis is that being loved can afford any human being a much needed basic security. To feel that one is deeply valued because one *is*, rather than because of the way one behaves or looks, is to feel fundamentally at home whenever one can be with the person who loves one so. From earliest infancy to most advanced age this feeling of being deeply valued is an important precondition to meeting life's challenges and expectations, to doing one's best without unhealthy stress.

The second hypothesis is that being loved makes it possible to learn to love oneself and others. The capacity of infants for empathy, before language development makes more explicit communication possible, permits the feeling of the nature of love very early in life. The closeness of mutual understanding among pre-adolescent peers makes its joyous expansion natural. The hormonal creation of unrest in the presence of peers of the opposite sex pushes its further development until it is stilled by intimate sexual sharing of vivid life in marriage. The mystery and the creative fulfillment that comes with the first baby begins a cycle of nurturance and guidance of a rapidly developing new personality that brings tremendous fulfillment through the years. But this wonderful growth and enrichment of life by love seems possible only to those who first were loved by others. Indeed we suspect that a person who has never been loved cannot fully respect and love himself but must always restlessly be reassuring himself as to his fundamental worth.

Our third hypothesis is that being loved and loving others facilitates the winning of belonging in groups. Of course, winning roles in group activities requires that the individual have knowledge and skills that are valuable in carrying on the activities of the group, for example, being able to act in conformity to group customs and codes. Being loved contributes to none of these skills, but being secure through love and being able to give love favors personality characteristics that are easy and attractive in group situations. Such a child or youth has no reason to lord it over others, to be aggressive and hostile, or to be shy and withdrawing. Such children do not need constantly to climb in status by calling attention to the failures and inadequacies of others.

A fourth hypothesis is that being loved and loving in return facilitates identifications with parents, relatives, teachers, and peers by which the culture is internalized more readily and organizing attitudes and values are established easily. When one feels loved and loves in return it is easy to learn that which is expected, it is easy to believe that which one's objects of love believe, and it is easy to aspire in the directions encouraged by one's objects of identification. The unloved child feels so much insecurity that he scarcely dares to try his wings in learning. Or he is so full of hostility that he tends to reject what he is told and to refuse to meet the expectancies that face him as a way of demonstrating his power to himself. Obviously the readiness of loving persons to provide meaningful experiences and to aid him in the learning process are further facilitations that give great advantages to loved children.

Our fifth hypothesis is that being loved and loving facilitates adjustment to situations that involve strong unpleasant emotions. When a loved child fails at something, the failure does not cut so deep as to make him doubt his basic worth, because he is still secure in that love relationship. Consequently he is more easily reassured and encouraged to try again and again. In contrast the unloved child who fails is in double jeopardy. To his insecurity is added the feeling of inadequacy and the world looks blacker and blacker. When a loved child is frightened, he can literally or figuratively take the hand of the person who loves him, approach and examine the terrifying situation, learn its true dimensions, and more readily find the courage to face it. But terror to the unloved child is unfaceable and overwhelming. Fearful things must be avoided at all costs, and if they enter and remain in the child's field they may result in physical illness or emotional breakdown. Punishments, penalties, and the demands of authority are bearable for loved children because they do not imply rejection or fundamental lack of worth. Consequently they are analyzable by the loved child, who more easily can perceive their meaning and take them in stride. But to the unloved child these things may be taken as indicators of personal rejection or of unfavorable status. Resentment, rebellion against authority, hostility against peers who seem more favored, or fundamental doubts of one's own worth ensue.

The implications of this paper for the education of pre-school children I think must be quite clear. But it may not be out of place to state a few of them briefly.

1. Children from homes where they are surrounded by a climate that is rich in love—between their parents, between their parents and themselves, and between siblings, do not need to find love awaiting them at the nursery school or kindergarten, though it will do them no harm if found there, too.

2. Children from homes where love is absent or ill-expressed need to find a personal relationship based on love in the nursery school and in the kindergarten. In fact the finding of such a relationship is their main hope of avoiding later maladjustment and failure to achieve satisfactory love relationships as adults.

3. It is necessary that teachers in the nursery school and kindergarten have a full knowledge of the quality of the interpersonal relationships which exist in the homes of each of their pupils because this information

is necessary to a real understanding of the behavior of each child and of his needs. In turn, this understanding is prerequisite to the making of wise decisions when interacting with the child and guiding his actions.

4. The gathering of this information about the emotional climate in which each child lives must be done very carefully, and requires considerable training. It must be recorded objectively and the records must be safeguarded with the greatest care. This implies that a strong code of professional ethics must govern all who have access to this information.

5. Only persons who have achieved the security of knowing that they are loved should be employed as nursery school teachers because persons who lack this security will be unable to build the kinds of relationships needed by certain children.

6. The nursery school and kindergarten must be administered in such a way that relationships between the director and the teachers, between supervisors and the teachers and among the teachers themselves will be warm, mutually-valuing and mutually assisting each other in all daily matters. The spirit in which the school is administered does much to create the climate in which the pupils live.

It is my firm hope that more and more children will be nurtured in a climate of warm love and deep respect for them as human beings. For I am sure that love gives the feeling of security to the human individual, that security gives rise to respect and acceptance of other people, and that this permits action in cooperative endeavors for the common good. And as we learn to work together for the common good, peace will be established among nations as the only sound and reasonable basis of human relationship because we mutually love and value each other's self-realization as much as our own.

35   Spontaneous Play: An Avenue for Intellectual Development*

MILLIE ALMY, *Teachers College, Columbia University*

Early child education has just been rediscovered. Psychologists interested in learning and cognition, linguists, mathematicians, physicists, economists, anthropologists and representatives of other scholarly disciplines are beginning to recognize that a child's experience in the years before he is six

* *The Bulletin of the Institute of Child Study*, November 1966, vol. 28, no. 2. Reprinted by permission of the author.

may influence not only his attitudes toward intellectual ideas, but his actual abilities for grasping them.

This is no new idea to the nursery educator and one might anticipate that she would welcome new support for it. On the whole she has, but too often attempts at cooperative exploration of the implications of the idea that children really learn in nursery school have come to nothing or have ended in mutual distrust. Many different factors contribute to this state of affairs, but perhaps most crucial has been a lack of mutual understanding of the nature and function of play in the cognitive life of the young child.

Nursery educators, since the very beginning of the nursery school movement, have regarded play as an inherent right of the child (Omwake, 1963). Moreover they have long identified the child's play with experimentation that offers unlimited opportunities for learning (Johnson, 1928; Goldsmith, 1946). In this regard, they are in complete accord with their colleagues in other professions, though the latter may more recently have given up the layman's notion that play is merely "nonconstructive and unrealistic behaviour" (Mussen, Conger and Kagan, 1963, p. 269).

Suppose, however, that the nursery educator and her colleague visit a typical nursery school classroom together. The activity is kaleidoscopic, as children flow out of one small group and into another. Domestic themes merge with transportation themes as the husbands from the housekeeping corner become the truck drivers delivering cement to the construction workers in the block corner. This is play. It represents "important learning" for the nursery educator. Her colleague is baffled. He sees no apparent beginning, no apparent end, little "structure," and surprisingly little teacher participation. What he had in mind is quite different: equipment more obviously designed to teach specific concepts, teacher-directed games to stimulate language and thought, and less or none of the same kind of activity he observes in his own children's play at home. At this point collaboration often ceases. The nursery educator is horrified at her colleague's notion of "play." He is unconvinced of the validity of her notion of "learning."

Progress can only be made when a clearer differentiation is made between two forms of play, both important to intellectual development, both holding legitimate places in the nursery school curriculum, but each having certain specific characteristics. The first form of play, the one so highly valued by the nursery educator, is activity that is self-initiated by the child. It is lacking in structure, other than that given it by his interests and his imagination. The second form is adult-prescribed activity, initiated and directed by the nature of the equipment (Omwake, 1963).

Traditionally (if an institution with something less than fifty years of existence can properly be said to have a tradition), the greater portion of the nursery school day has been allotted to play of the first kind. Even during so-called "work" periods, when many children painted or made things at the carpentry bench or built with blocks, strong elements of spontaneous play were usually present. During the years when emotional and social development received primary emphasis in most nursery schools, this type of play predominated. But a combination of circumstances has recently begun to call into question the proper balance between the two forms of play.

The new proponents of the importance of early learning do not discount the importance of the child's spontaneous inclination toward play. They would indeed capitalize on it. O. K. Moore, for example, avers that his "prepared learning environment" simply shapes the investigative, manipulative, repetitive behaviour characteristic of the normal child's play into the responses involved in learning to read. J. McV. Hunt (1961), in *Intelligence and Experience*, a volume that devotes many pages to Piaget's views on the function of play in intellectual development, makes a general proposal for "governing the encounters" young children have with their environments. He specifies that these encounters should be enthusiastically relished by the child since they are to be "matched" to his developing abilities, providing enough challenge to be interesting but not so much as to be frustrating. Not surprisingly, Hunt and others with similar concerns for the early intellectual experience of young children have been much attracted to the Montessori method since its apparatus is designed to pattern the child's play toward the eventual development of specific and basic concepts. The possibilities for intervention in the child's play in order to give it particular meaning have also been given impetus in revised curricula for elementary schools. J. S. Bruner's (1961) much quoted hypothesis that "any subject can be taught effectively in some intellectually honest form to any child at any stage of development" has added weight to the notion that at least some elements of the fundamental ideas of the disciplines should be taught in the kindergarten, and perhaps also in nursery school.

What does this mean for the nursery school curriculum? Is spontaneous, free-flowing, self-initiated play to be replaced by structured play where the cognitive culmination can be clearly foreseen (by the adult at least) from the outset? Perhaps—if nursery educators and their colleagues fail to appraise adequately the cognitive elements in spontaneous play, and if nursery teachers continue, as some have in recent years, to abdicate their responsibility for nurturing these elements.

Those who must make decisions as to what constitutes a proper balance between structured and spontaneous play can find little to guide them in either psychological or educational research. There is substantial evidence that both children and animals, deprived of opportunities for play, fail to learn as effectively as those who have freedom to manipulate and explore. But the issue here is a different one. Should the nursery school, an educational institution, assume responsibility for an activity that healthy children are going to initiate and carry on regardless of whether they happen to be enrolled in a nursery school? What justification, if any, can be found for the deliberate inclusion of such activity?

For possible answers to these questions we turn, initially, to a re-examination of some of the tenets of psychoanalytic theory that have in one way or another profoundly influenced the thinking of nursery school educators at least since the early 1940's. Next we look to the theory and experiments of Piaget, whose ideas about the nature of intellectual development are only now beginning to permeate American psychology and education. Finally, we also give brief consideration to some current research in cognitive development.

Psychoanalytic Views of Play

One has only to put on the spectacles provided by psychoanalytic theory to see in the spontaneous play of young children some of the most elementary human emotions laid bare. Love and hostility, anxiety and aggression, sympathy and jealousy are all there together with a great variety of fantasies and defensive manoeuvres. But play, as some of the earliest psychoanalytic studies of children clearly indicated, reflects much more than emotion alone. Its emotional, physiological and intellectual aspects are interwoven and only logically separable. "In actual experience they are closely associated, developing together . . . almost from the beginning and growing the one out of the other as well as reacting the one upon the other" (Griffiths, 1935, p. 269).

This cohesiveness is perhaps nowhere better illustrated than in the work of Susan Isaacs (1930, 1933) who, as one of the first to conduct a nursery school based on a psychoanalytic theory of development, entitled the first volume of her observations, *Intellectual Growth in Young Children* and the second, *Social Development in Young Children*. Anna Freud, long concerned with the ramification of psychoanalytic theory for education, observes that the thinking of the young child is often brilliant (she arrives at solutions to problems that may amaze the adult), but it is not solidly based (A. Freud, 1963, pp. 179–180). It is bound neither to logic nor to reality. This is nowhere more apparent than in spontaneous play. In a somewhat similar vein, Lili Peller (1952) notes that play is largely wishful thinking. Accordingly, solving a problem through play appears the opposite of intellectual problem solving. Nevertheless, play and reasoning have several common elements. Neither has direct and immediate consequences in the outer world. In both, certain elements of reality are selected and varied. Both are far quicker than is direct action in reality. Isaacs (1950, p. 104) identifies an "as if" orientation in both play and reasoning. One plays or thinks *as if* the world were ordered in a certain way. Such an orientation serves to overcome the obstacles of space and time. Peller (1954) also comments that play like reasoning is precipitated by an experience that is not satisfactorily completed. Play provides the opportunity not only to savour whatever pleasurable aspects the experience had, and in various ways to work out compensations for its hurts, but also to understand it.

For such a view of spontaneous play, one might well conclude that it provides a setting for the exercise of certain of the abilities involved in thinking and reasoning. It is as though at this period the child, freed from the handicaps eventually to be imposed by logic and some of the realities of space and time, could try out incipient intellectual powers.

Clearly, however, play in the usual nursery school setting does place any number of reality-based limitations on the child. A doll-carriage may serve equally as cradle, shopping cart or delivery van, but it will not go through an opening that is too narrow for it. A block construction can be the Empire State Building, or a satellite on its launching pad, but it will not stand unless it is properly balanced. Each such instance constitutes a challenge, to which the child can respond in various ways. With emotion clearly in the foreground, he may cry, or kick, or leave the scene. More playfully, he will incorporate the physical realities into his fantasy. The carriage changes its destination, the Empire State blows down, the satellite blasts off prematurely, or play retreats while reasoning comes to the foreground and a problem is solved. A new gate is constructed. The blocks are rearranged.

Anna Freud (1963) underlines the importance of achievement of these sorts where the child solves a problem independently of adult praise and approval. It represents the capacity the child has for deriving pleasure from task completion and problem solution. This aspect of the child's development, although for a time rather neglected in psychoanalytic theory, has long been recognized by Anna Freud and has figured prominently in the formulations of psychoanalytical ego psychology. In a recent monograph, R. W. White (1963), reviewing the history of psychoanalytic and specifically its ego psychology, also cites more academically oriented research in child and animal psychology dealing with manipulative behaviour, curiosity, and explorative play. He proposes the incorporation into the psychoanalytic theory of development of a new motive, *effectance* or the active tendency to influence the environment.

The theoretical issues involved are of little interest here. What is relevant is the fact that psychoanalytic theory has for so long regarded the young child's spontaneous play as a reflection not only of his emotional conflicts, but also of his developing intellectual competence. Despite this, it appears that many nursery schools (there are notable exceptions), including both those acknowledging a psychoanalytic orientation and those influenced less directly by the general infiltration of psychoanalytic thought into child psychology, have been so pervasively and persistently preoccupied with the emotional aspects of play as to neglect its intellectual connotations.

The symptoms of such preoccupation are varied. One is the teacher's assertion that the children "learn through their play," an assertion accompanied by an inability to describe that learning in any terms other than those having to do with emotional or social adjustment. To say that the children are "forming concepts" in their play is not enough. One needs to know what concepts are revealed and at what level of adequacy.

A second symptom of preoccupation with the emotional is apparent lack of involvement of the teacher in the intellectual life of the child. She is an observer who intervenes to arbitrate disputes and to comfort the frustrated. But she seldom rearranges the environment to confront the child with a possibility for reducing his frustration by solving a problem. She sometimes notes the intellectual confusions his play reveals (they become part of her repertoire of amusing incidents) but she feels no particular responsibility for providing experience in play or elsewhere to correct misconceptions.

A third indication of disregard of the intellectual is the striking similarity (in some instances one could say identity) of materials and equipment, and indeed of much of the play itself, from one classroom to another, whether the children are three-year-olds, four-year-olds, or five-year-olds.

Perhaps what is lacking here is a clear sense of developmental direction. "The playing child," says Erikson (1959, p. 85), "advances forward to new stages of real mastery." The advance proceeds along two fronts, one related to association with peers, the other to the use of toys and equipment. Along both, the child, in a sense, moves out of himself to confront reality more effectively.

At first, the nursery school child treats other children as things. Gradually he learns "what potential play content can be admitted only to fantasy, and only to play by and with oneself, and what content can be shared with others" (Erikson, 1959, p. 85). This is an essential step toward the intelligent grasp of ideas other than one's own. The child also makes intellectual progress as he uses toys and equipment. "If the first use of the thing world is successful and guided properly, the pleasure of mastering toy things becomes associated with the mastery of conflicts which were projected on them and with the prestige gained through such mastery" (Erikson, 1959, p. 85).

The goal, of course, is not the mere mastery of toys but the understanding of the larger physical and social environment, and one's place in it. For the three- or four-year-old child's nursery school teacher to see his becoming a five- or six year-old through his play, and to help him to become so, need not be to push or pressure him, but rather to nurture basic abilities as they are developing. That this is no easy task is readily granted. Children do not all progress in the same fashion nor at the same rate. What may be an intriguing challenge to one child, offers real threat to another. Furthermore, most nursery school teachers, with the possible exception of those whose professional education is very recent, have very hazy notions about cognitive advances they might reasonably expect to observe and to promote during the nursery school years. Their uncertainty reflects, in part, the research available to teachers. This literature is considerably better at describing the nature of the concepts children of these ages are likely to have than it is at delineating the processes involved in their formation. Despite its inadequacies, however, a considerable body of research literature dealing with cognitive processes in young children is now accumulating. Some of it has direct relevance to the place of play in the child's intellectual development. Much has been stimulated by the theories and investigations of Jean Piaget.

Piaget's Views

Perhaps no single investigator in the world has given more attention to cognition in children than has Piaget. His volume, *Play, Dreams and Imitation in Childhood* (1962), describes the evolution of the child's thought as revealed in his play from infancy through the period of early childhood. Its illustrations are drawn from his observations of his own three children. Another volume, *The Early Growth of Logic in the Child* (Inhelder and Piaget, 1964), includes "experiments with children as young as two years, and deals with the development of the ability to classify objects on the basis of their similarities, and to arrange them in order on the basis of some attribute on which they differ." Piaget has also investigated children's concepts of space, geometry, number, quantity, time, and velocity, but in these areas he has included relatively few subjects younger than five.

Piaget's theory of the development of intelligence encompasses the infant's sucking, looking, and grasping and the adolescent's ability to deal with abstract logical propositions, and attempts to describe the evolution of the latter from the former.

As the child grows and his experience increases, one might say that he mentally stores more and more information, and constructs new and more effective ways of retrieving and applying it. In infancy, information is stored in patterns-of-action (schemas). The baby "knows" his environment through what he can do with it. By the time he is established in elementary school he has an array of relatively stable concepts with which to apprehend his world. Such stability comes only as the child's perceptions and actions and the information he derives therefrom are adapted to the ways others perceive and act. Thinking becomes less egocentric and more socialized.

Piaget describes the adaptive processes involved as consisting on the one hand of *accommodation*, in which the child's behaviour, or more specifically his thinking, conforms to fit the outer reality, and on the other hand of *assimilation*, in which the child integrates the information thus gained into his already existing systems of meaning. The two processes are reciprocal though at any given point in development they may or may not be in equilibrium. For example, most children make a kind of verbal accommodation in learning to count to five considerably before the counting experience becomes sufficiently well assimilated for them to have a stable concept of fiveness. Piaget identifies instances in which accommodation is ascendant over assimilation as instances of imitation. Conversely when assimilation takes priority the child is seen as playing. Obviously in spontaneous play as here defined, imitation is not ruled out. Children imitate adults, other children, animals, even machines. But the predominant process in most of spontaneous play seems to be assimilation. "Play constitutes the extreme pole of assimilation of reality to the ego while at the same time it has something of the creative imagination which will be the motor of all future thought and even of reason" (Piaget, 1962, p. 162).

Although, as Piaget indicates, there is no reason to think that the child believes in everything he plays (we are reminded of the child who proposed that he and his playmate "pretend we are not playing pretend"), the content of the play and extent of its egocentricity reveals something of the child's progress toward more socialized thought. To view that progress as Piaget does, one needs to contrast the thinking of an average four-year-old with his brother or sister who has reached the age of seven.* Typically, the latter is not only more objective, that is, less inclined to be able to view the world only from the limits of his own perspective, but is also more conceptual in his thinking. Where the younger child tends to be taken in by the appearance of things—he will think, for example, that there is more to drink when the water from one vessel is poured into two or more smaller ones—the older one is not deceived by such transformations. Where the older child can mentally manipulate the relationships between two or more variables (think "operationally" in Piaget's terms), the younger child tends to focus on first one, and then another.

The growing awareness that objects have many properties, that they can be viewed along different dimensions, and that they can be classified in a variety of ways is, Piaget believes, a product of the child's activity with them. Through manipulation—touching, lifting, holding, arranging, sorting and so on—the child begins to take note of similarities among the objects he encounters. In like fashion he comes to pay attention to differences in objects that are alike in some respects and differ in others. Eventually, just as he can sort an array of objects into collections that have one or more similar attributes, such as form, colour, and weight, he can order them on the basis of their differences, arranging them from smallest to largest, darkest to lightest, softest to hardest, and so on. In these activities, Piaget sees the origins of truly conceptual thinking. Such thought implies the existence of a system whereby the individual can identify the defining attributes of a concept and the extent to which a particular instance of the concept may vary and still be included in the class, and at the same time deal with the intricacies of inclusion in more than one class.

At first glance, the ability to arrange experience in logical categories seems far removed from spontaneous self-initiated play as here described. Would it not more likely be a product of structured, teacher-arranged play? Clearly, the latter kind of play contributes. But Piaget seems to suggest that structured play may not be sufficient, particularly for the younger children. The reason lies in the necessity for the child to take in reality in his own egocentric and affect-laden way before he can adapt to the system of logical thought that characterizes adult thinking. Piaget (1962, p. 166) states his conviction thus:

* When Piaget attributes a particular way of thinking to a specific age level, he refers to the age at which three-quarters of the children in his studies thought in this fashion. Some of them would have reached that mode of thinking by six, some as early as five. The ages he reports are also specific to Geneva, Switzerland. (Piaget, 1964.)

Why is there assimilation of reality to the ego instead of immediate assimilation of the universe to experimental and logical thought? It is simply because in early childhood this thought has not yet been constructed, and during development it is inadequate to supply the needs of daily life.

According to Piaget, the construction of logical thought depends not only on the child's activity with material things, but also on his social collaboration with other children. Characteristically, the preschool child has difficulty in conceiving a point of view different from his own. But interaction with his peers in the social give-and-take of spontaneous play confronts him with the necessity of accommodating himself to their ideas. Presumably, since these ideas are not so strikingly different from his own as may be those of the adults, adaptation is more readily made to their thought than to the thought of the older person. ". . . doing things in social collaboration, in a group effort . . . leads to a critical frame of mind, where children must communicate with each other. This is an essential factor in intellectual development" (Piaget, 1964, p. 4).

Clearly, Piaget's theoretical formulations regarding the function of play in the intellectual life of the child can be used to support the contention that spontaneous play has a legitimate place in the nursery school and kindergarten curriculum. Unfortunately, neither Piaget nor others who are espousing or testing his theories have carried on the experimental work necessary to reveal the intricate relationships between the intellectual experience the child has during this period and his later conceptual development. Most of the experimentation that has been done so far deals with various possibilities for facilitating the transition from the intuitive, perceptually dominated thought of the preschool period, to the logical, "operational" thinking of the older child. Such a transition is manifested in the ability to "conserve." The child who has made such a transition no longer insists that the quantity of a ball of clay changes as it is elongated, or that there are "more" blocks when they are spread over a large area than when they are bunched together. Several studies (Almy, 1966, pp 40–48) have revealed the difficulties involved when short-term training procedures are used in an attempt to accelerate the child's progress toward his transition. On the other hand, some of the work, notably that of Smedslund, suggests that procedures that lead a child to question the adequacy of his own responses and consequently re-think them may be more effective. Progress, accordingly, comes only as the child experiences some dissatisfaction with what he already knows. From this one might argue that spontaneous play provides not only a good means for practising and thus consolidating or assimilating what one knows, but also for confronting or accommodating to situations that may challenge and potentially revise that knowledge.

It is Piaget's view that the child's response to instruction from without is always relative to whatever internal construction he has already developed (Flavell, 1963, p. 406). Such a view supports the idea that the curriculum should provide some balance between adult prescribed experiences that are intended for all the children, and those that are oriented to the individual child.

Individuality in Cognition

While some investigators are concerned with tracing the steps in intellectual development that seem to be common to the majority of children, others attempt to isolate the factors that make for individual differences in cognitive activity. For example, one group (Kagan, Moss and Sigel, 1963) has identified certain stable cognitive preferences or "styles" among individuals of adequate intelligence that can be traced back to the nursery school years. Some children tend to analyze and seek out details in scanning their environment. Others tend to respond to the field as a whole. Grossly, the analytic children appear to be less impulsive, less hyperkinetic, more apt to become absorbed in tasks and to be oblivious to distraction than their equally intelligent but non-analytic peers. In a group of adults studied from infancy these differences seemed to be as apparent in spontaneous play in the nursery school as they were in their responses to assigned cognitive tasks in later years. Interestingly, the differences are much greater for boys than for girls.

Cognitive "style" represents a dimension of child behaviour of which nursery educators have likely long had an intuitive but vague awareness. Many view it as a personality variable or emotional response, not necessarily identified with the way the child copes intellectually.

Further information on individuality in cognitive development can also be anticipated as more reports come in from work currently in progress with children from disadvantaged homes. Most of the investigations so far have pointed up their deficits in perceptual learning and in the acquisition of concepts.

Hunt (1961), drawing in part on Piaget, has proposed that a better match between children's cognitive organization and the educational experiences provided might serve to improve their cognitive functioning. Factors similar to those subsumed under "cognitive style" may need to be taken into account in the matching process.

Another manifestation of individuality in cognition receiving considerable attention of late is often labelled "creativity." The term means different things to different investigators. Nor is it certain how many of these meanings are shared by the nursery educator, who has long been ostensibly concerned with its nurture. Nonetheless it seems clear that connections may be found between certain aspects of spontaneous play, and performance on some of the cognitive tasks that are currently being used to appraise creative thinking (or potential for it). Nina Lieberman (1964) for example, found some association between teachers' ratings of the "playfulness" of kindergarten children, and the "divergent thinking" factors of "ideational fluency," "spontaneous flexibility" and "originality" as measured on cognitive tasks derived from work by Guilford and Torrance.

A great number of other studies dealing with various aspects of cognition in children of nursery school and kindergarten age might be included here. Some provide information directly relevant to early childhood, and implicitly to children's play. Other studies are so specific to a given theoretical issue and a given experimental condition that any generalizations must await further experimentation in more naturalistic settings. Obviously there is also great need for further investigation of children's cognitive activity during spontaneous play. To what extent does it reflect fantasy, and to what extent is there evidence of learning through encounters with the physical environment and with one's peers? Despite the lack of completely definitive answers to these and related questions, the available theory and research clearly support the idea that spontaneous play can contribute importantly to the young child's developing intelligence. What then are the implications for the curriculum?

Understanding and Supporting Spontaneous Play in the Nursery School

We start with the assumption that the nursery school, serving as a specially prepared educational environment, and under the direction of teachers who have had special professional training, should provide something more as a setting for spontaneous play than does a typical home setting. This "something more" is a function of the teacher's ability to analyze or diagnose cognitive functioning as it is revealed in play, and in the light of that analysis, to make further provisions for the children's development both in their play and in other aspects of the curriculum.

The analysis here proposed is not intended to supersede the appraisal of emotional, personality, or adjustment factors that skilled nursery school teachers have always made, but rather to underline the importance of another dimension of that appraisal.

Teachers have long studied children's spontaneous play for evidence of their motivation, their ways of coping with anxiety, their developing concepts of themselves. No less important, to some extent interwoven, and yet to some extent separable is evidence regarding the children's curiosity, their interest in investigation, in problem solving, and in mastery. The extent to which children manifest such motivation reflects in part the history of their experiences in their family, and the kinds of pressure, encouragement, and defeat they have known there. But it is also a product of the expectations for and support of the learning they encounter in the nursery school.

Similarly, the concepts the child reveals in his play reflect not merely the information he has gained outside school, but also in school. Teachers might well watch and listen to spontaneous play not only for evidence as to what information the children have, but also how it is organized and categorized. What attributes or properties do the children notice as they encounter objects and materials? How effectively do they label these and other experiences? What kinds of relationships enter into their awareness? What kinds of reasoning are revealed in their play? Do they proceed from one particular instance to another particular instance, picking up some similar elements, or are they beginning to weigh situations more deductively? What kinds of inferences and generalizations can they make? What sorts of contradictions do they notice? To what extent do they see situations only from their own point of view, and to what extent can they stand, as it were, in another's place?

These are the kinds of questions that teachers need to consider if they are to appraise the cognitive levels at which each of the children is functioning, and if they are to provide experience to further cognitive development. Obviously whatever information can be gleaned from spontaneous play will serve to supplement what is known from the child's functioning in other parts of the curriculum.

Such dimensions in intellectual behaviour as cognitive style and playfulness can also be appraised in the child's spontaneous play. What implications these may have for the child's further instruction, either in the nursery school or later, are by no means clear. Perhaps they represent orientations toward learning that had best be respected throughout schooling. Or perhaps it is possible to encourage children to shift orientations according to the tasks at hand.

In general, such analysis or diagnosis as has been proposed here is for the teacher's own and rather immediate use in planning for individual children and for the group as a whole. Closer attention to both the level of the child's cognitive functioning and the apparent content of this thought should provide the teacher with many possibilities for stimulating further thought and providing him with further information.

The content of many of the activities typically provided in the nursery school curriculum might well reflect this analysis. The trips that are arranged for all or for part of the group, the visitors that are invited to share experiences with the children, the books and pictures, the natural science observations and experiments that are introduced can all be chosen not simply because children of these ages have tended to enjoy them, but because they offer appropriate possibilities for extending or strengthening the knowledge of these particular children. In like fashion some of the teacher's cues as to the kinds of structured games, puzzles, and so on to be provided can come from her expanded knowledge of the children's cognitive abilities as revealed in their spontaneous play.

So far as the balance between spontaneous and more structured play is concerned, it seems likely that the more the teacher knows about the ways in which each child functions, the more apt she will become in maintaining an appropriate balance. Erikson's (1959, p. 83) observation that some elementary school children learn more readily from directed instruction, others from guided play, is somewhat supported by the investigations of cognitive style, and may have relevance for nursery school children as well. But to limit the play of the younger child solely to that structured by the adult would not only run counter to the child's typical way of life, but would be to deny him the important opportunities to initiate and test his own ideas and schemes in spontaneous play. Further, play at this stage of development is not simply an avenue for moving ahead in the acquisition of knowledge and skills. It serves equally as a place where past experience is confronted (sometimes over and over) and eventually consolidated.

Because there are these uniquely personal dimensions to the child's spontaneous play, one might question whether it is appropriate for the teacher to intervene in it at all. But children normally do look to the teacher for some help, particularly in keeping their behaviour within acceptable bounds. She must at least step in when the play seems to be leading toward physical harm or the destruction of valued property. Beyond this, the amount and kind of direct intervention seems to be largely a matter of the teacher's artistry and sensitivity. Less directly, the teacher can set the stage for the child's play, and accordingly open new cognitive possibilities for it. Rearranging materials and equipment and introducing those with which the children are not familiar are obvious means to this end. Creating opportunities for children to associate with different playmates may also be appropriate.

If there is to be a continuous appraisal of play and the way it serves the development of each child's powers, teachers cannot be responsible for many children. The task demands keen awareness of each child, what he does and how he thinks today, where he was yesterday and where

he may go tomorrow. In a sense nothing that has been suggested here
goes beyond what some nursery school teachers have done intuitively, if
not always with explicit consciousness, for years. Today there is available
enough information about cognition in play that one can hope that
nursery teachers will become truly articulate about what they do and
how the children respond. There is also need for much more study and
research into the nature of play, and what it means in the life of the
young child.

References

Almy, Millie, 1966. *Young children's thinking* (New York: Teachers
     College, Columbia University Press).
Bruner, Jerome S. 1964. The course of cognitive growth. *Amer. Psychol.*,
     19, pp. 1–15.
————. 1961. *The process of education* (New York: Random House,
     Inc.).
Erikson, Erik H. 1959. *Identity and the life cycle* (New York: Interna-
     tional Universities Press, Inc.).
Freud, Anna. 1963. The concept of developmental lines. In Eissler, Freud,
     Hartmann and Kris (eds.), *Psychoanalytic study of the child*, vol.
     18 (New York: International Universities Press, Inc.), pp. 245–265.
————. 1952. *The ego and the mechanism of defense* (New York: Inter-
     national Universities Press, Inc.).
Goldsmith, Cornelia. (n.d.) Good education for our young children—
     what is it? *Good Education for Young Children* (New York: Na-
     tional Association for Nursery Education), pp. 5–12.
Griffiths, Ruth. 1935. *A study of imagination in early childhood and
     its function in mental development* (London: Trench, Trucker &
     Co., Ltd.).
Hunt, J. McV. 1961. *Intelligence and experience* (New York: The Ron-
     ald Press Company).
Inhelder, Bärbel, and Jean Piaget. 1964. *The early growth of logic in
     the child* (New York: Harper & Row).
Isaacs, Susan. 1933. *Social development in young children* (London:
     Routledge & Kegan Paul Ltd.).
————. 1930. *Intellectual growth in children*. Sixth ed. (London: Rout-
     ledge & Kegan Paul Ltd.).
Johnson, Harriet. 1928. *Children in the nursery school* (New York: The
     John Day Company, Inc.).
Kagan, J., H. A. Moss, and I. E. Sigel. 1963. Psychological significance

of styles of conceptualization in basic cognitive processes in children. J. C. Wright and J. Kagan (eds.), *Monogr. Soc. Res. Child Develpm.*, **28**, 2.

Lieberman, Josefa N. 1964. *Playfulness and divergent thinking: an investigation of their relationship at the kindergarten level* (New York: Columbia University). Unpublished doctoral thesis.

Moore, Omar K. *Early reading and writing* (film).

Mussen, Paul H., John J. Conger, and Jerome Kagan. 1963. *Child development and personality*. Second ed. (New York: Harper & Row).

Omwake, Evelyn. 1963. The child's estate. In A. M. Solnit and S. A. Provence (eds.), *Modern perspectives in child development* (New York: International Universities Press, Inc.), pp. 277–594.

Peller, Lili E. 1954. Libidinal phases, ego development and play. In Eissler, Freud, Hartmann and Kris (eds.), *Psychoanalytic study of the child*, vol. 9 (New York: International Universities Press, Inc.), pp. 178–198.

———. 1952. Models of children's play. *Ment. Hyg.*, **36**, pp. 66–83.

Piaget, Jean. March 1964. Cognitive development in children. The Piaget papers in R. E. Ripple and V. N. Rockcastle (eds.), *Piaget rediscovered: a report of the conference on cognitive studies and curriculum development* (Ithaca, N.Y.: School of Education, Cornell University), pp. 6–48.

———. 1962. *Play, dreams and imitation in childhood* (New York: W. W. Norton & Company, Inc.).

White, Robert W. 1963. Ego and reality in psychoanalytic theory. *Psychol. Issues*, **3**, 3.

The development of literate behavior in children takes
on new urgency when we realize the close association
between linguistic skill and school success. Linguistic
deficiency, characteristic of disadvantaged children, is
also indicative of conceptual deficiency. Collectively,
these deficiencies set boundaries for school progress and
result in a cumulatively negative self-concept for the
young child.

The failure of compensatory programs to erase the
effects of early linguistic restriction is presently encouraging a great deal of linguistic experimentation. Such
experimentation appears to represent one of three possible alternatives in the education of the disadvantaged,
assuming the goal of academic equality. The first is to
start earlier; the second, to operate on a different set of
assumptions than those that have produced large measures of past failure; the third is to give up the goal
of academic equality across cultural group lines—obviously no one is willing to make this concession. Therefore, starting earlier and developing imaginative programs will continue to occupy our attention.

A structure-process approach to cognitive development and literacy in disadvantaged children is proposed
by Joe L. Frost and Thomas Rowland. Assuming an
inextricable relation between literacy and cognition and
an invariant sequence of development (with the possible exception of mutation of sequence due to severe
deprivation such as is found in some orphanages), the
authors proceed to trace the developmental process of
literacy. The cultural variable, extremely influential in
linguistic development, is recognized to produce marked
variations in oral language behavior between middle-class
and lower-class groups. Bernstein calls these patterns
elaborated and restricted codes. The theoretical position
of Frost and Rowland accepts a cognitive and linguistic

371

hierarchy; certain prerequisite abilities essential for concept attainment are dependent upon subordinate concepts. One terminal concept, oral language proficiency, operationally described as elaborative language (essential to the production of literacy), is described graphically. The authors contend that *time* per se is an irrelevant variable in the cognitive hierarchy but that the *timing* of educational encounters is critical. That is, learning does *not* depend upon chronological age, neither *should* teaching; learning *does* depend upon accumulated conceptual structure, so *should* teaching. The challenge to educators is to devise imaginative tools for assessing developmental levels and to develop appropriate teaching encounters.

The struggle between the "correctionists" regarding *how, when*, and *where* language intervention should occur is appropriately moderated by Beryl L. Bailey. One thing is clear: we cannot depend upon chance and piecemeal correction of dialect forms. This does not imply an either-or approach. Both goals—personality adjustment and language development—can be parts of the school curriculum. The teacher may structure short periods for the learning of language forms in *rote fashion*. There is ample time in the course of the total day for informal verbal interaction with peers and adults. Reliance on environmental enrichment alone to overcome deficiencies reinforced since birth *is optimism indeed*.

Several widely held misconceptions about linguistic phenomena are examined by Vivian Horner: (1) verbal deficiency may imply some sort of abnormality; (2) teachers fail to distinguish between *speech defect* and *language deficit*; (3) teachers may engage in *linguistic chauvinism*, believing that dialect must be eliminated and replaced by "pure, intrinsically superior standard language"; (4) continuous "correction" of speech subordinates the *use* of language to the *form* of language. Horner emphasizes the need for greater flexibility and sophistication in remediation efforts, specified by examination of the individual child's entering repertoires.

Courtney B. Cazden reviews four strands of research in child language: (1) nonstandard versus standard English; (2) the mediators by which environmental variables (for example, social class) affect language development; (3) problems which dialectical differences pose for the establishment of developmental scales; (4) individual and group differences in communication.

Although much is known about language development, the factors that mediate language retardation among lower-class children are largely unexplored. The theoretical position of Basil Bernstein concerning elaborated and restricted verbal codes, though categorically positioned by Cazden for purposes of clarity, suggests implications for a number of linguistic problems. Bernstein's theory reaches beyond verbal behavior to cognitive functioning. Modes of speech have great influence on the behavior of the individual. They are seen as bearers of "social genes." Although it is clear that there is more to cognition, culture, and communication than what is revealed by speech, all are intimately interrelated.

For the child who is familiar with the elaborated code of the middle class, school presents experiences for symbolic and social development or, if you will, continuity. For the child sensitive to the restricted code of the lower class, school typically represents symbolic and social change, or discontinuity. The educational institution, then, may carry certain alienating features to be altered.

While Bernstein concentrates upon the interlaced nature of social interaction and language, Robert D. Hess and Virginia C. Shipman draw upon his work to explore modes of translating cultural experience into cognitive behavior and academic achievement. Specifically, they proceed from three hypotheses: (1) the behavior that leads to social, educational, and economic poverty is learned in early childhood; (2) the central quality involved is a lack of cognitive meaning in the mother-child communication system; (3) the growth of cognitive processes is mediated by the range of action and thought alternatives. Their research group of 160 Negro mothers and their four-year-old children was selected from four different social status levels. Social class differences were found on verbal and cognitive variables. The emerging picture is that "the meaning of deprivation is a deprivation of meaning."

36   Cognitive Development and Literacy in Disadvantaged Children: A Structure-Process Approach*

JOE L. FROST, *The University of Texas at Austin*
THOMAS ROWLAND, *New York University*

A literate control of language is primary evidence of the development of adequate cognitive structures in the educational encounters of children. Without such evidence, education cannot be presumed to have occurred, and to the degree that such evidence is forthcoming, the teacher may assess the level of success which she and the child have achieved. When literacy and cognition are so intimately conjunctive, one being the essential evidence of the other, it is necessary that educators of children give careful examination and consideration to this concept. This is even more critical when there is planned intervention, as in the re-education of the disadvantaged child.

The critical nature of the cognition-literacy concept defines the purposes of this section; namely: (1) to trace some socio-environmental factors affecting the development of cognition; (2) to examine a sampling of prior cognition theories; and (3) ultimately, to propose and demonstrate a model for the instruction of children, particularly disadvantaged children.

The authors believe that the development of intelligent behavior and the exercise of literacy are one and the same function, and any contrived separation of the two is artificial under ordinary circumstances. This means that without physiological impairment such as brain damage or sensory deprivation, the human being manifests developed intelligence by his control of language, though not usually limited specifically to an oral manifestation of literacy.

Accepting as the ultimate goal of education the development of intelligent behavior appropriate to the student at a particular time and stage of development, the educator is compelled to define specifically his measures of progress toward his objective. We have identified as the critical measure of intelligence mastery of the *primary linguistic skills*. The most basic linguistic skill appears, at this stage of our conceptualizations, to be the development of verbal behavior, including both *speaking and listening*.

---

* A paper prepared especially for this book of readings. The theme is developed in greater detail in Joe L. Frost and Thomas Rowland *Curricula for the Seventies* (Boston: Houghton Mifflin Company, in press).

Verbal behavior is defined, therefore, as *the* primary linguistic skill and is held to be essential for additional achievement of the developmental sequence. The *secondary linguistic skills*, such as reading and writing, are dependent upon mastery of the primary skill, but after intensive planned educational intervention appear to develop a high degree of autonomy from the primary skill. Such autonomy is necessarily dependent on the cognitive capabilities of the learner and the abilities of the educator.

The critical role of verbal behavior in the development of intelligent behavior is most cogently discussed in the work of the Soviet psychologist, A. R. Luria (1959), who holds that speech not only has semantic and syntactic functions, but also has a pragmatic or directive function. This final function is seen to be demonstrated by the control words have over the activity of children and in the way children use words to control the behavior of significant other people. He states that the semantic functions of speech eventually become dominant as the human begins to internalize control of his own behavior.

Luria indicates a sequence of stages in the child's development of verbal control of behavior; namely impellant (Go!), inhibitory (Stop!), regulatory (Come here!), and self-regulatory (I will go there). These stages of the verbal control of behavior are seen to develop during the period which Piaget (1947) has identified as the stage of sensory-motor intelligence. It should be noted that Piaget does not specify this as *a stage* in intellectual development, but *identifies it as a particular and unique type of intelligence*. Brunerians would see this as occurring during the enactive (1964) stage. In all instances, the sequential developments are seen to be supportive of a hierarchical system of cognition, and the development of the critical hierarchies cannot be linked to time. In human development time is a backdrop against which sequences transpire, but time itself is in no way legitimately a factor of significant importance. It is the *necessary and invariant* sequence which is important in the development of intelligence.

Bearing in mind the essential invariancy of sequential development, insight is gained into some of the most pressing linguistic problems of the disadvantaged child. The environment from which he comes has not adequately prepared him in most instances for the verbal experiences he will encounter in the classroom.

Any depth understanding of the disadvantaged child necessarily begins with a realistic recognition of the prevalent ignorance of level of concept development in the pre-school child. Stott and Ball (1965) state that the assessment of the intellectual development of first-graders is currently *unreliable and inconsistent*. This lack of understanding marks the educational novice as the great "unknown factor" in education, especially should he arrive at school from a disadvantaged background, the implications of which we are only beginning to understand. This child's prior learning has been in an environment which is often only tangentially related to the school and often may be conceived of as hostile to the school, which is viewed as the institution of an unfriendly but dominant society. At best, the model for his social learning and personality development (Bandura and Walters, 1963) is not in the classroom with him. The school is in a state of naive ignorance with no records of what the incoming child knows; what concepts he has developed; no understanding of how this child may perceive the world; and to date no accurate way of overcoming this institutional stupidity.

On these grounds, teaching begins.

In order to make some realistic appraisal of the child's linguistic needs to begin his educational experience, the educator is obliged to delve below the superficial characteristics of the youngster entering school for the first time. *Literacy begins to develop from birth*, and for most children follows a general *continuous* pattern which eventually facilitates his mastery of the literacy requirements of schools. For the disadvantaged child the pattern is frequently one of *discontinuity and resultant failure*. To understand the impact of this discontinuity in the child, it is necessary to turn to some considerations of linguistic development during infancy and early childhood and to consider the importance of continuity in the development of literacy.

Continuities exist when a child's development has progressed in an appropriate manner. Such continuities imply that the expectations and environmental conditions of the classroom will be *harmonious* and consistent with the child's linguistic repertory or level of cognitive development. In other words, the school will not represent a development break or radical change, but there will be continuous interaction between the home and school environments. Conceptual retardation in any form represents *discontinuity* or radical departure from the appropriate developmental sequence. For this child the school may be a frightening place, populated with demanding and unintelligible beings who have no relevance to his conceptual framework. By analogy, for this child home and school are like water and oil—they do not mix. It is not unusual that should such a child adopt the expectations and values of the school, he will become a social outcast in his home environment (Rowland and McGuire, 1967).

Literacy During the Pre-School Years

Learning begins with birth. It is an inevitable human encounter between the organism and the environment. There is substantial evidence that learning may begin prenatally (Grier, Counter, and Shearer, 1967). Learning in the postnatal environment may initially be passive, where the child receives stimulation from the environment, particularly from other human beings as he begins to interact with the significant adult figures in his world. Quickly he learns to manipulate and modify his world and to adapt his behavior to gain satisfaction of his needs, marking the first efforts at expressive behavior and communication. At this point in development, his literacy is crude and primitive, involving primarily oral noises and physical movement. It entails a great deal of practice for the infant, but it is practice with a purpose. Adults reinforce the early communication patterns by responding in a positive way or they may be extinguishing the behavior by aversive and negative responses.

A differentiated and flexible language system ordinarily develops in a sequential manner. Opportunity to actively exercise this developing language facility is indispensable to later more articulate use of language. Unfortunately, not all children are exposed to sufficient communicative interaction during the critical pre-school years for adequate linguistic skill to develop. The child of large families may find himself "left out" before age two for the mother has a new baby, he may learn that adults do not welcome "interference" of children in adult conversations, or communication with adults may result exclusively in the child reacting to harsh demands.

Linguistic development during the early stages will tend to depend upon imitation. The normal child learns the language of his home but the congenitally deaf child does not learn to speak at all because he is deprived of opportunity for imitation. It is also evident that the child of English-speaking parents learns English to the exclusion of all other languages, the Spanish child learns only Spanish, if the parents speak only one language. The disadvantaged child may be deprived of close interaction with the all-important mother figure who may lend linguistic and emotional support. Ordinarily he is not deprived of opportunity to imitate sounds and behavior patterns but he is deprived of opportunity to imitate language and behavior patterns that will serve him well in school.

The Culture of Poverty

Since the child we are principally concerned with here is the current generation of the culture of poverty, the authors believe digression to gain further understanding of this phenomena is justified. In view of the current concern with poverty, we are correct in assuming that this state of impoverishment is an enemy of education and society. War demands a victor and a victim, and obviously poverty is to be the victim.

Yet it is difficult for most Americans to identify poverty specifically. This confusion exists beyond the usual common sense definitions of most people, and is evidenced in much current writing about the subject, even in the writings of educators. There tend to be two evaluations of poverty. One evaluation stresses the neglected capacities of the poor for self-help, leadership, and community organization. The opposing view, which is also frequently found in current literature, is that the poor are shiftless, mean, violent, evil, criminal, sordid, and immoral. Writers holding this second viewpoint tend to call the effects of poverty irreversible and destructive on the characteristics of the individuals. Fortunately for the disadvantaged child and his teacher, neither view is completely correct.

Oscar Lewis (1966) summated much research among the poor of many nations. The culture of poverty, his term, is identified as a valid subculture with its own structure and rationale, a way of life handed on from generation to generation along family ties. It is not a matter of deprivation or disorganization but is a culture in living and a set of solutions for problems. Poverty has no respect for national boundaries nor ethnic groupings, and its practitioners are similar in the structure of their families, interpersonal relations, spending habits, value systems, and orientation in time.

Poverty is a cash economy with a persistently high rate of unemployment and underemployment at low wages. It ordinarily provides no social, political, or economic organizations, and once the culture of poverty has come into existence it tends to perpetuate itself. Lewis says (1966, p. 21):

> By the time slum children are six or seven, they have usually absorbed the basic attitudes and values of their subculture. Thereafter they are psychologically unready to take full advantage of changing conditions or improving opportunities that may develop in their lifetime.

A trait of the culture of poverty is its *nonintegration with the major institutions of society such as schools.* This is a reflection of segregation and discrimination, fear, suspicion, and apathy as well as the development of alternative institutions and procedures within the subculture. It is not unusual to discover that females within a subculture family are not expected to seek education. That is not their purpose in life, but rather they are to be mothers and wives, vocations which do not call for education within the context of the subculture. Yet families in the culture of poverty do not tend to cherish childhood as a specially prolonged and protected stage in the life cycle. Sex initiation comes early in life and sex role identification usually poses little difficulty for the lower class child. Families tend to be mother-centered, and sibling rivalry for the limited goods and maternal affection is often intense. There is little or no privacy in the culture of poverty and often practitioners within the subculture have strong feelings of fatalism, helplessness, dependence, and inferiority.

Children from the culture of poverty tend to have weak self-concepts, a strong present-time orientation with little ability or disposition to defer gratifications and plan for the future. There tends to be a high tolerance for psychopathology of all kinds.

Language and the Disadvantaged

The language of the culturally disadvantaged is usually *informal or restricted*. Simple in nature, it lacks the breadth and depth necessary for precision about ideas or emotions. It tends to be severely inhibited because of a deficiency in concept development. The language of these children tends to be repetitious and dull, colorless and unimaginative—reflecting the environment within which they exist.

On the other hand, middle-class children tend to use formal, elaborate, and imaginative language patterns, learned from their parents and peers. Their language is grammatically more precise, more complex, and allows for elaborations of meaning and subjective feelings. Therefore, the disadvantaged child's language development is delayed during infancy and early childhood because of the absence of formal language interaction. Their world is a noisy world *but* a relatively fixed verbal world.

Language among the culturally disadvantaged may often bear a systematic relationship to the physical movements which stimulate the original concept of the word. Often the disadvantaged are unable or unwilling to make the transformation of verbal patterns to bring about a higher level of symbolism. These people may never reach a stage of formal symbolism. Jean Piaget (1936) and Roger Brown (1965) have concluded that there are cultures where no one reaches this level of intellectual development.

Simpler forms of non-verbal symbolism are prevalent in the culture of poverty and may involve movement representing direct transformation of physical movements, *i.e.*, the symbol possesses a remarkable relationship to the direct action. Many such symbols are not only inappropriate for the educational encounter but are socially repugnant to the middle-class teacher.

Readiness for the Educational Encounter

The culture of poverty, the development of cognitive structures and the concurrent literacy skills, and each interaction with the environment summate to produce what is commonly known as readiness. The child eventually arrives at the school and if his background has done an appropriate job, the task of the teacher and school is usually uncomplicated. On the other hand, the disadvantaged child most often arrives with serious academic impediments.

Piaget (1966) offers important insight into the nature of child development, emphasizing four deductions important for education; namely:

1. The stages of intellectual development are *sequential*, each being necessary for the stage that follows though the rate of development is highly variable. Each stage is characterized by the development of concepts, sequentially organized from simple to complex, development to a more complex stage being dependent upon successful attainment of a conceptual structure characteristic of the early stage. This supports the view that readiness activities should be individualized.

2. The manifestation of the development of intelligent behavior is dependent upon cognitive development and attempts to move a child from one stage of intellectual development to another are seen as futile. Support for this was demonstrated by Wallach (1963) and Smedslund (1961), both of whom made attempts by tutorial enrichment to bring about a development increment, and both attempts were unsuccessful unless the child was near the point of readiness for the next stage at the time of enrichment. This does not contradict the contention that children can be taught any subject in some academically honest way at any point on the developmental continuum (Bruner, 1960), for Piaget himself (1948) ridiculed educators who contended that young children could not handle abstract concepts. The point is that time is of no concern, for we have substantial evidence from the research of Rosenzweig (1966) that the cerebral cortex can be enlarged by placement in an enriched environment, both when the enrichment occurs from birth and when enrichment is intervened at adolescence.

3. The child's motivational factors are important to success in the educational encounter. Piaget (1947) identifies a homeostatic (balanced state) motivational model which he calls *equilibration*. Equilibration involves *adaptive behavior* with two invariant functions; namely, *accommodation*, which is the adaptive change of the organism to external circumstances, and *assimilation*, which is the incorporatin of the external into the internal organization with transfer, *i.e.*, generalization to new circumstances and situations.

4. Intelligence functioning leading to comprehension is facilitated by opportunity to invent and reinvent and to teach too quickly a concept that would result from thought and reflection may hinder the child from discovery for himself.

All of this implies that efforts to develop literacy in school-age children will fail if existing conceptual structure is disregarded, and as demonstrated conceptual (cognitive) structures are hypothesized to exist in hierarchical form, so that deficiencies or inadequacies in early learning weaken the entire structure of intelligent behavior, as does inappropriate (for the expectations of the school) learning among the disadvantaged. From this viewpoint much of education, especially with the disadvantaged, may rightly be considered as intervention for remedial purposes. It also implies that the indiscriminate use of standardized materials such as enforced use of a basal reading text for all students in all schools represents *educational miscarriage and injustice*.

Readiness and Early Reading

Educational research, including the USOE first-grade reading studies, continues to provide evidence that there is no *best* method of teaching reading. The first-grade reading teacher who is able to provide additional stimulation for more of her children consistent with developmental levels appears to be most effective regardless of method. Yet we should consider the types of learning that are not measured by common data-gathering instruments. Among these are the most desirable outcomes of teaching—attitudes, appreciations, insights, habits, etc. Should these learnings be carefully measured we may learn that certain approaches are more effective than others under particular circumstances.

In the absence of clear direction regarding the most effective method, we must rely heavily upon what is known about the developmental character of children in striving for language continuity.

The disadvantaged child may have serious language difficulties. His vocabulary may be limited to such words as "nope," "naw," "un huh," "uhuh," "cuz," or certain profanities that shock the middle-class teacher. It is quite logical to expect that the child has learned such language because he has heard this language from the people around him. This has been the sole medium available to him. Or the child may not speak at all, because the powerful factors of fear and anxiety have had their effects on his developing personality.

Studies by Frost (1967) concluded that the vocabulary growth of children in an Arkansas migrant school was insignificant beyond the ages of five or six. That is, the child of five or six demonstrated essentially the same vocabulary level as the youngster of 15 or 16. This suggests, among other things, that the schools have been remarkably ineffective in promoting literacy. It follows that the child with a restricted vocabulary is also a restricted reader, for reading has its roots

in oral language and related meanings which accompany language proficiency.

These related concepts that the child has programmed in his cognitive structure are the basis for all intelligent functions and impose
boundaries for the child's progress in school. These meanings, brought
to school by the child, have been shaped by the nature and quality
of living with others, and they may be intensified and broadened
through environmental enrichment or they may be restricted by depriving the child of multiple opportunities to use his avenues of learning
—the senses—in rich, meaningful ways.

This means that *readiness training should be continued* for the disadvantaged well into the elementary school years. It does not follow that
all attempts to teach the child to read will fail for reading may well begin,
using the basic vocabulary of the child. The basic vocabulary is that which
the child has, understands, and uses. It can be built upon—slowly. The
child can be taught to read as readiness training continues, for reading
readiness involves much more than vocabulary—the disadvantaged child
may be quite mature physically, though the chances are good that he
suffers some deficiencies. And he may be quite mature emotionally, but
the teacher will have to work hard to keep him that way in the new,
strange world of the classroom. Reading instruction *can* proceed, but
we must be quite careful to create appropriate situations for it to proceed
in a natural fashion. The social and emotional effects of inability to read
for the eight-, nine-, or ten-year-old are infinitely greater than the possible
ill effects of *teaching with care*. Even limited success in reading at age
six or seven can open the doors to a lifetime of continued linguistic
development. Reading is too important and society too unaccepting to
delay for reasons other than illness or injury.

Teaching the Disadvantaged

Delay of language development during the early years results in
almost irreparable damage in academic relations. The child arriving at
school with inappropriate language will be hard put to communicate
with many of his peers and particularly with his teacher. Since the school
typically offers few problem-solving situations that would reinforce the
strengths of the disadvantaged child's culture, and opportunities for
development are effectively foreclosed. Loretan and Umans (1966) say:

> Many situations arise where the teacher and the student *never* make
> contact. The situation is similar to that of a Spaniard and a Portuguese

talking to each other with neither one quite knowing the other's language.

A common technique in language study is to teach the child to imitate the teacher's speech. This is often done through negative ways which do not take into account the child's prevailing conceptual structure nor the need for developing self-concept. In the presence of an incorrect response by the child, Spicker (1966) suggests a "corrective feedback" approach: "If a child labeled a cow as a *moo-moo*, the teacher would state, 'Yes, this is a cow, and cows say *moo-moo*,' rather than 'No, this is a cow.'"

The teacher may *guide* the child toward more acceptable language use and ultimately toward the achievement of literacy. Such guidance should be on the child's terms. Piaget in his *Judgment and Reasoning in the Child* (1924) and in his other works, provides a model for the teacher attempting to make such an approach to the child. In his work the child answers questions, and his answers are the data for the Geneva research. Answers are *not* considered correct or incorrect, but rather evidence of the level of the development of intelligent behavior. For the teacher, the verbal behavior or level of literacy is concrete evidence of the starting point for the child's education. From that point education is a matter of change, often *radical change*, but the beginning of the educational encounter is brought *to the school* by the child, *from* the environment which has shaped and educated him until the moment of formal education begins.

If the point of beginning is incongruous with the expectations of the school, the teacher should recall that the burden of communication, without which there will be no guidance or education, rests with the more completely educated—*her*, as the representative of the educational institution with a direct social charge to control and guide change in the child.

The reconciliation of the home and the school is the task of the teacher, for the child cannot effectively reconcile environmental differences if the divergence is too great (Frost and Hawkes, 1966). Such reconciliation will need constant referral from the unfamiliar school environment to the home environment familiar to the child. This of course presumes the teacher *understands* and is *intimately* familiar with the environment from which the disadvantaged child comes to the school.

A number of promising programs for developing literacy are currently in the experimental stage. One program for five-year-olds (Sterns, Hodges, and Spicker, 1966) is designed on the assumption that "elaborative representational language is necessary to the development of symbolic thought, to verbal mediation skills, and to school success, every activity taking place in the classroom is seen as an opportunity to elicit elaborate language and to reinforce its use." Although the principal theme of the program is language development, techniques and materials for improvement in socialization, self-concept, fine-motor skills, time perspective, and achievement need are also stressed.

A similar language remediation program was conducted by Spicker (1966) with educable mentally retarded children. He concluded that language *intervention* programs should: (1) be used in conjunction with a total curriculum emphasizing language development throughout the day; (2) stress elaborative language rather than labeling language; and (3) be continued as a part of the on-going program. Spicker placed special emphasis on teaching a wide variety of words needed to describe the environment, discrimination of objects in terms of size, shape, color, texture and function, building accurate grammatical order and syntax, increasing sentence complexity, and using a wide range of conjunctions and subordinate clauses.

An experimental language project at The University of Texas (Horn, 1966) consists of an instructional program in oral language and is designed to phase into beginning reading. The program is being conducted in the San Antonio Public Schools, San Antonio, Texas, and focuses around five organizing elements: intervention into the conceptual; linguistic and experiential structures of the children with the purpose of dimensional increase through the coordination of learning principles; and a discovery-oriented science program.

Three common techniques for language development—imitating the teacher's speech, building on the child's present language, and teaching standard English as a second language—are indicative of limited aspects of a total program. Obviously a child needs to *speak* a language well enough to manifest appropriate conceptual development for approaching reading and other secondary literacy tasks successfully. He may, however, retain a pronounced regional dialect throughout life with no apparent effect upon reading standard printed English. Loretan and Umans (1966, p. 41) say:

> A child does not *need* to change his speech pattern in order to learn how to read. Standard, printed English is the same, whether one speaks the dialect of the North, of the South, of New England, or of the West. People speaking all the dialects of immigrants to the cities learn to read the same printed words. Therefore, the argument that retraining of speech patterns is needed in order to teach reading is not based upon fact.

There is little prospect for the severely word-restricted child to read before a degree of verbal sentence fluency is achieved. But if the child is verbally promiscuous, he may successfully engage in reading as standard speech patterns are being established.

Literacy and the Structure-Process Approach
to Cognitive Development

Specific techniques similar to those discussed above may serve as cues for the educator in determining their own classroom behavior, and this often is the greatest value of much research. However, specific instances are severely limited and the greater need is for a general approach which is applicable in many different situations with divergent groups of learners. The *structure-process* approach to cognition (Rowland, 1967) is just such an approach and has been formulated in an attempt to bridge the gap between the psychological laboratory and the classroom.

Any theory which attempts to go from the principles which have been tested in basic research, *i.e.*, research on learning with no regard for its educational relevance, to an application in the classroom is necessarily making a "leap of faith" which leaves many gaps. This is typical of theory building, where the initial system is laid out, experiments are designed, and the concepts of the theory are tested. Eventually the theory is evaluated and reformed until it becomes strong enough and its application is broad enough to merit general acceptance or recognition. The *structure-process* approach is a calculated move toward the classroom.

In the structure-process approach, cognition is defined as the *exercise* of the higher mental processes, totally dependent upon but *essentially different* from the organism's learning processes. Intelligence, which embraces both learning and cognition, is defined as the organism's ability to adapt to increasing complex and sophisticated internal and external environmental situations and stimuli. In this conceptualization, learning and cognition are seen as separate but correlated and interdependent factors of intelligence, with integral relationships to the neurophysiology of the brain.

A review and synthesis of some related research reports in the area of cognition is necessary in order to propose a model for intervention, which will incorporate some of the most common elements of the psychology of cognition into the educational encounters of public school children. A concept which appears to have *communality* among the theories of many psychologists, though differently labeled, will be accepted as valid. A common concept will be examined as a possibility in the instruction of children. Following the presentation of the theory, its application to the classroom will be discussed as it relates to the development of literacy. No one content area is seen by the authors as a limitation to the theory's applicability. It is felt that any content field can be adequately handled within the framework of the structure-process model for literacy.

We recognize that this is only a limited approach to Bruner's sweeping manifesto for the evolution of a "prescriptive theory of instruction" (1966, p. 40). We are also aware of the criticism of educational psychologists for their "molecular" approach to an entire classroom. These critics accuse educators and educational psychologists of never seeing a whole child because they are so busy examining one little "need." Perhaps there is justice in the accusation of never seeing the forest for looking only at the trees—yet there seems to be great wisdom in this approach. For example, if we attempt to attack the massive problem of poverty and deprivation *in toto*, we are almost predestined to failure, the problem is so monumentally unmanageable. If, however, we adopt a "molecular" approach and attempt to begin a remedy by intervening in the educational experiences of the children from the culture of poverty, perhaps there is a chance for some degree of success. It would seem the odds are on the side of a molecular approach instead of a massive confrontation with the "whole."

It should be recognized also that the *principles* evolved from the consideration of only one facet of an admittedly much larger problem, hold possibilities for application in the larger area. With this in mind, our point of view is felt to be justified.

Cognition: Review of Some Positions

Cognition as a distinct field for study in psychology is somewhat "new." Van de Geer and Jaspars in 1966 contributed the first chapter on "Cognitive Functions" to appear in the *Annual Review* in which they defined cognition as "the field of thought processes" (p. 146). Harlow in 1949 proposed "learning set" and implied that intelligence is learned and could be cultivated by teachers, and such "set" supplies the basis for insightful problem-solving.

Gagne (1962) approached cognition in terms of "abilities," and produced an ordered hierarchy of types of learning. In another approach, Gagne discusses "productive learning" which he defines as a change in human behavior which permits the individual to perform successfully on an entire class of specific tasks, and when performance is changed, the acquisition of a *capability* is assumed. In productive learning there are two major variables: knowledge (that which the learner brings to the task) and instructions. In defining knowledge Gagne constructs a hierarchy of subordinate knowledges or capabilities, called learning sets. Gagne concludes that productive learning is a matter of transfer of training from component learning sets to a new activity which incorporates these previously acquired capabilities. Gagne identifies the major methodological implication of his study as the need for investigations for productive learning to deal intensively with the kinds of variables usually classified as "individual differences," and states that the measurement of general proficiency is undependable in revealing much of the important variability in the capabilities brought to learning tasks. This seems to lend support to a major assertion of this paper: *current attempts to measure a child's learning in traditional education are generally failures, and tend to ignore the child's educable potential.* For example, no formal attempt is made to determine the capabilities already established in the child's cognitive structure, and should his current level of cognitive development not fit the defined curriculum, his knowledge is ignored or intense attempts at extinction are carried out. This is especially true in the culturally different child such as the Negro or the Latin American.

G. A. Ferguson (1954, 1956) outlined his approach to cognition, the salient features of which are: (1) the abilities of man are attributes of behavior; (2) biological features of man fix limiting conditions; (3) cultural factors are prescriptive; (4) abilities emerge through a process of differential transfer; and (5) positive transfer explains the concept of a general intellective factor. Ferguson views learning as a process whereby the abilities of man become differentiated, and defines ability as: (1) performance in any situation; (2) a factor in the methodology of factor analysis; or (3) some attribute of the state of the organism. Ferguson explicates transfer as a mathematical function, when two variables are so related that the values of one are dependent on the values of the other, implying concomitant change, *i.e.*, change in performance on one task will result from practice on another. He implies that his approach will consider: intraindividual variability in ability patterns; and the emphasis on environmental factors in the formation of abilities. If such is the case, and it is here assumed to be so, this theory has remarkable significance for education, particularly in conjunction with the work of Gagne and the more recent work of Olson (1966) as an associate of Jerome S. Bruner.

Olson accepts Bruner's (1964) three processes by which people know things: (1) enactive—by doing it; (2) iconic—through a picture or image of it; and (3) symbolic—through some symbolic means such as language; as well as Bruner's (1956) ideal strategies. Olson's work revealed three strategies in children which he calls: (1) searching (approximately three years), a quasi-systematic search of the stimulus situation; (2) successive pattern matching (five years), a concentration on the pattern and model; and (3) information-selection (seven years) where the child tends to eliminate redundancy and is more likely to achieve the solution to a problem with a minimum of information. To move to information selection tends to require that the child be able to deal with not one image at a time, but rather with the properties or features of several images simultaneously, as well as the ability to construct a hierarchy of distinctive features.

Any consideration of current studies of possible classroom adaptation would be greatly devaluated without consideration of Piaget. His profound and elegant work, *Psychology of Intelligence* (1947), translated in 1950 by D. E. Berlyne, contains the substance of a series of wartime lectures in which Piaget defined intelligence in relation to adaptive processes in general. Piaget postulated that the act of intelligence consists essentially in "grouping" operations according to certain definite structures. Piaget conceives of intelligence as the form of equilibrium towards which all cognitive processes tend. In another work he discusses how a child comes to understand numbers (1953). He distinguishes between a child's ability to rotely name numbers and actual concept attainment. Piaget states that children must grasp the principles of *conservation of quantity* before they can develop the *concept of number*. The ability to coordinate different perspectives does not come until the age of nine or ten, about the same time the child can distinguish between and coordinate the different possible perspectives demonstrating a grasp of projective space in a concrete or practical form. Piaget's conservation principles arise in various forms: conservation of length, and conservation of distance and a prerequisite to the construction of geometrical concepts as well as the formation of the concept of number. Measurement (a derived concept) involves the additional logical operations of the process of division and displacement or substitution, allowing the child to apply one part upon others and build a system of units.

Evaluation

Throughout the distinguished studies which have been considered as fundamental to this paper, there appears a common element or factor in cognitive development which may be conceived of as a set of equivalences:

Psychologist	Common Elements
Gagne	capabilities
Ferguson	abilities
Olson (Bruner)	strategies
Piaget	principles
Harlow	learning sets

It should be kept in mind that this set of equivalences is only a partial listing. Other equally prominent psychologists could be added, *e.g.*, Miller, Galanter, and Pribram's (1960) T-O-T-E variables, "plans, strategies, and tactics."

Assuming certain prerequisite abilities necessary for concept attainment, which function in a cumulative manner, the educator should be able to subdivide a specific intellectual task into its subordinate or fractional concepts or units necessary for mastery. We further assume the cognitive structure desired for mastery may be identified as terminal behavior and that all ultimate conceptual goal behaviors are supported by subordinate concepts. Based on these assumptions, education may proceed in a controlled and planned manner of successive, cumulative mastery of the subordinate concepts as illustrated in Figure 1. For hypothetical pur-

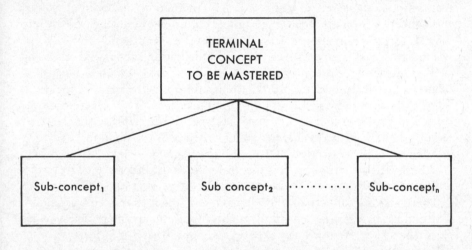

FIGURE 1

poses we may identify the "Terminal concept" as the behavioral change we seek to effect, in this instance, it would be *the development of verbal literacy*. The subordination concepts on which literacy would depend might be: pronunciation, enunciation, ability to express clearly and logically a train of thought, the ability to retrieve words and their appropriate meanings from the cognitive memory structure, and any other of an almost unlimited number of concepts on which the exercise of literacy essentially depends.

Accepting the probability of some common element, we have made the assumption that determination of the level of cognitive development is made more accurate by bypassing the motor skills necessary for writing. We accept the theoretical construct of a *cognitive hierarchy*, defined in this section in a very limited, two-dimensional manner.

In order to achieve this conceptual breakdown, the concept needs first to be carefully defined, and the subordinate abilities to be mastered should command individual specification. Also, it should be remembered that each subordinate concept *may in turn be a terminal concept*, and would then rest upon lower order concepts before contributing to the ultimate concept achievement, as shown in Figure 2.

For example, having specified our terminal concept, the next task at this point is to *identify and define* some relevant subordinate concepts (Subordinate Concept$_x$ in Figure 2) on which literacy depends. Earlier several were named and the educator planning the experience would be free to choose one at random; for example, the ability to express clearly and logically a train of thought. This will involve choosing the right word, using it correctly and appropriately, so that the desired meaning may be communicated to a listener. This definition makes it clear that this concept is in itself somewhat complex and may be broken down into what is identified in Figure 2 as "lower level concepts."

Lower level concepts demand equal definition, and again choosing at random the educator may select one from many available dimensions of the subordinate concept, for example, the task of selecting the right word so as to communicate meaning to the listener. This selection of the right word for communication purposes will, in turn, rest on many other factors, including the developmental experiences of the child in associating words with objects or ideas and implying meaning.

Thus, the structure-process hierarchy leads us directly into the *home and school environment*. A recent study by Agranoff (1967) dramatically demonstrates the effects of the environment on learning and retention. The child's success will depend inevitably upon the appropriateness of his experience background. Each experience, appropriate or otherwise, contributes substantially to the development of cognitive hierarchies upon which the child necessarily depends as he attempts to demonstrate literacy. A void or deficit in a lower level concept would be seen to create serious deficiencies in the child's adaptive abilities and, therefore, would handicap him in the ongoing educational encounter. Failure would lead to failure and eventually to frustration, and the culture of poverty would perpetuate itself again and again.

Application of the Model to a Primary Linguistic Skill: Oral Language

THE ELABORATE LANGUAGE SERIES. An approach to the developing mastery of oral language is the Elaborative Language Series published by Educational Media Laboratories (Frost, 1967). The theoretical foundations of the series are the same as discussed herein. The series is a *practical application* of the theory, which structures oral language lessons around

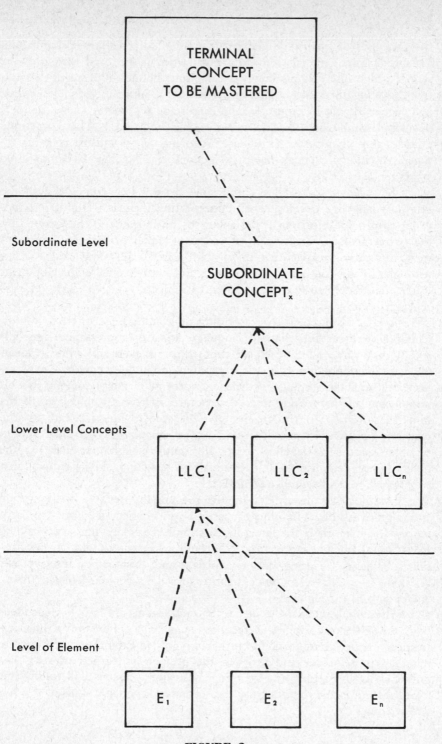

FIGURE 2

the processes of observation, experimentation, description, classification, and prediction. Language development is held to proceed through four stages, which like Piaget's stages are not time-bound. The stages proceed from *labeling* to *comparative*, to *creative* and ultimately to *elaborative* language as shown in Figure 3. The final stage represents a level of ideal development, but not all learners will achieve the ideal. There are some cultures and subcultures, particularly segments of the culture of poverty, where the individual may never go beyond the labeling or comparative stages.

The series proposes a set of lessons, designed to coincide with the stages of language development, incorporating materials (filmstrips, records) to provide vicarious experiences to the learner, on the assumption that when actual interaction in the form of direct experience is impractical, a vicarious experience may, with careful planning and follow-through, be the initiation of concept and oral language development, leading ultimately to literacy. The actual objects, when present, are systematically utilized.

No effort is directed to prescribing time limitations for these lessons. Children with severely limited language skills, *e.g.*, pre-school-age culturally disadvantaged children are exposed to visual stimuli (filmstrips) of objects commonly found in the classroom (following concrete exploration) and to audio stimuli (recorded narrator or teacher) for oral modeling of language form and sentence structure. Behavioral objectives of the initial lesson are: (1) the child should be able to identify and say the names for objects commonly found in the school; (2) the child should be able to use these labeling words in complete sentences; and (3) the child should demonstrate improvement in speaking skills—enunciation, pronunciation, and sentence structure.

Subsequent lessons are designed to sequentially develop oral language and cognitive skills. The objects, patterns, and concepts learned in early lessons form the basis for later, more complex lessons. The series moves from "using labeling words" to "color and geometric shapes," "classification," "polarity," "using action words," and "using position words." Speaking in complete sentences, approximating a standard dialect form, is emphasized throughout.

Fully cognizant that the success of such lessons are largely dependent upon the skill and flexibility of teachers, suggestive follow-through activities are intended to move children through guided exploration of concrete materials to reinforce and broaden the previously learned primary linguistic skills of listening and speaking. Subsequent lessons will follow this established rationale to phase into the secondary linguistic skills of reading and writing.

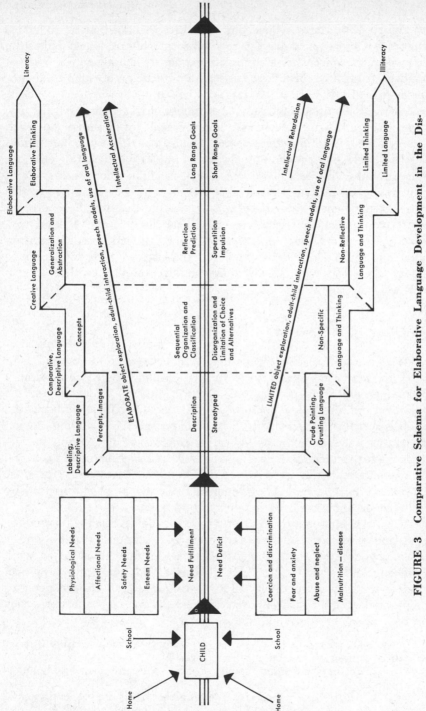

FIGURE 3 Comparative Schema for Elaborative Language Development in the Disadvantaged Child. (Reprinted from Joe L. Frost, *Teacher Orientation Handbook*, The Elaborative Language Series. Educational Media Laboratories, Austin, Texas. 1967. By permission.)

Figure 4 illustrates a hierarchy of concepts contributing to verbal literacy. It is not assumed that this represents the only possible combination or sequence of concepts. Yet such defining and redefining to the point of specificity is essential for precise evaluation of teaching-learning behaviors. The degree of relevance to be assigned the various lower level concepts underlying elaborative oral language functioning remains speculatory.

In regard to the secondary literacy skill of reading, however, Holmes' (1960, 1965) Substrata Factor Theory has resulted in illustrations of relative complexity and dimensions. Holmes (1960), for example, demonstrated (with college students) that the first order factors underlying power of reading (terminal concept) were perception of verbal relations, intelligence, vocabulary in isolation, and fixations. Second order factors were general information, vocabulary in isolation, and prefixes. Third order factors were general information, phonetics, word discrimination, and suffixes. Additional studies of this nature are sorely needed to synthesize the learning tasks of young children and make them educationally manageable.

Continuity in the School

We have seen the wide gaps that exist between readiness and associated developmental factors for different cultural groups. Discontinuity becomes progressively pronounced as the child lives in school, for the typical pattern is to follow one of two courses: (1) artificial (guesswork) readiness activities are pursued for indefinite periods while reading instruction *per se* is delayed; the child suffers progressive retardation in prerequisite (for reading) skill development; (2) reading instruction is begun and readiness activities are terminated. The child may never experience real success, for conceptual development from this point is restricted by over-reliance upon symbolic activities.

Language continuity can exist for the child as reading instruction begins and as readiness activities (concrete and vicarious) proceed on the basis of diagnosis of pertinent needs. The reader may refer to the work of Gordon (1966) and Otto and McMenemy (1966) for diagnostic procedures. A program of continuity uses the language (reflecting conceptual complexity) of individual children as the basis for language instruction and rests upon these assumptions:

1. Oral language is the basis for reading instruction. Emphatically there is no other base upon which to build.
2. Reading and other communicative skills are inextricably interrelated.
3. The basic vocabulary of a child is that which he has, understands, and uses. There is no other "basic" (to the child) vocabulary.

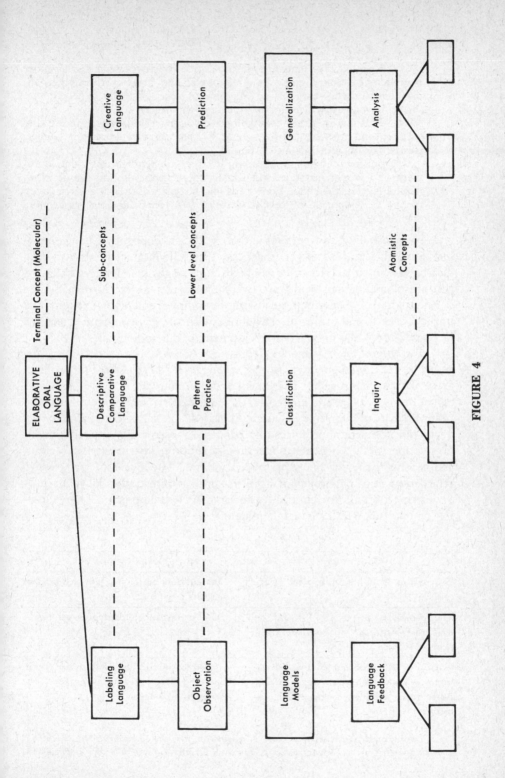

FIGURE 4

4. Reading, like language in general, is presently regarded as more psychological than logical, attaining power and function through meaningful interaction with people and objects. Yet it is fully expected that scientific inquiry will ultimately reverse this state.

5. Fluency in reading is gained through reading easy, interesting material and through reinforcement by success. Code breaking ability, formal and informal, is also essential.

6. Successful beginning reading is largely dependent upon the attainment of a proper match between instruction, materials, and the developmental level of the child. This prevailing but critical theme lends urgency to the development of teacher repertoires for diagnostic-prescriptive teaching.

The prevailing and perhaps most significant concept in education—individual differences—is yet unaccepted in school practice. It has been clearly shown that children develop through stages of cognitive behavior that are characterized by certain predictable tasks to be learned. Simple conceptualization is prerequisite for more complex conceptualization. The quality, nature, and extent of encounters with the environment determine in large degree the cognitive development of an individual.

A common error made by schools is the misunderstanding and disregard of the conceptual structure of disadvantaged children. The problem exists for all children, but it is more acute among the socially disadvantaged because of extreme deprivation of experiences which normally result in mature cognitive behavior. This, of course, directly affects language development and the reading process. Consequently, the attainment of a proper match between conceptual structure, instructional materials, and teacher behavior takes on new urgency. The cycle of progressive retardation may be broken if teachers and administrators develop programs that provide for continuity in language development. The following comparisons* offer general guidelines.

Continuity	Discontinuity
Instruction follows individual diagnosis.	Instruction is based on group test results.
The program moves from aural to oral to print. A multi-sensory approach is used.	The program concentrates on print.
Creation of problem-solving situations for development of thinking processes. Children begin with familiar problems.	Problem-solving largely limited to answering direct questions or reactions to printed exercises.

* Reprinted from *Issues and Innovations in the Teaching of Reading.* Joe L. Frost (ed.). Chicago: Scott Foresman and Co., 1967. By permission.

Continuity	Discontinuity
Readiness training (concrete and vicarious) continues as the child learns to read.	Reading delayed as readiness activities (vicarious) proceed or readiness training concluded as reading instruction begins.
The basic vocabulary for beginning reading is unique to each child.	A "basic" vocabulary is prescribed by books used for beginning reading.
No attempt is made to separate reading and other language arts.	Language arts are taught separately.
Skills are learned through reading and/or taught according to need.	Skills are taught to all children according to a predetermined schedule.
Skill in reading is developed through reading widely from various types of material.	A large proportion of the time allowed for reading is spent in assigned reading or "skills" work.
Individual one-to-one contact helps to promote fulfillment of affectional needs of the disadvantaged, promotes oral expression for backward children leading to facility in group expression. One-to-one contact can ensure regular successes for each child. The study of children's unique needs is facilitated.	Rigid group teaching fails to provide for close personal interaction essential for the disadvantaged. Oral expression may be repressed by anxiety in a group situation, particularly in group with higher-status individuals. Regular success is difficult to attain.
The use of familiar speech, objects, pictures, and books, allow the disadvantaged to feel comfortable in the classroom. Motivation is easier to achieve.	A totally unfamiliar classroom scene is too threatening for motivational purposes.
Conceptual development is enhanced through systematic, guided object exploration and manipulation. The teacher utilizes the natural exploratory tendencies of children. Frequent trips with opportunities to engage in conversation with other children and adults are provided.	Conceptual development is progressively retarded by provision of inappropriate materials — workbooks, worksheets—that are often unrelated to the needs of the disadvantaged. Exploration is inhibited by the absence of manipulatory materials and freedom to move about the classroom. Unrealistic field trip policies restrict linguistic and conceptual development.

From the beginning of school the child is encouraged to share his ideas with others through the use of words, pictures, and objects. The teacher records the child's stories in his own language. The child reads the stories to his classmates. Many reading materials are developed by the children themselves, no artificiality, no watered-down vocabulary. Through hearing the child's stories, the teacher becomes more aware of his conceptual level and uses this as a basis for continuing readiness activities and for developing further reading skills.

As the child progresses, he begins to see the similarity of his writing to that of others. He recognizes words that are used repeatedly in his language and in the language of his peers. Eventually he learns that books contain the same words that he uses and that they can be fun to read.

Concurrent with the utilization of the child's present language in beginning reading, activities are designed to foster more elaborative language. These activities may be integrated with science, social studies, and mathematics programs. Concept development is enhanced through active, guided, exploration, categorization, classification, and manipulation of concrete materials, leading to increasing abstraction. Art, music, and physical education activities are adapted to develop concepts of color, form, space, time, etc. In other words *structured language lessons* are best used in a total curriculum context. All this requires the participation of a highly perceptive teacher. For it is clear that only those teachers possessing a greater than average degree of empathy, sensitivity, and perceptiveness will make any positive difference with culturally disadvantaged children.

We can ensure the attainment of literacy for most disadvantaged children through a program of continuity built upon the oral language of the child, based on a *structure-process* approach incorporating the concepts implied by a hierarchical structure. Since it is clear that language—reading, writing, speaking—is functionally dependent upon cognitive development, the challenge to teachers is to construct a program that builds upon existing structures, and systematically utilizes the inherent cognitive processes of the human organism.

Importance to Education

The structure-process theory of literacy and cognition is brought into meaningful focus when it is realized that literacy and cognition are *essential to any subject matter area.* The learner is expected to be literate in science, mathematics, social studies, physical education, or any other content which he is required to or chooses to master. From this viewpoint the structure-process approach is applicable to all classrooms and all content material and is therefore a valid theoretical approach to the *development of intelligent behavior* and *curriculum design and construction.* Promising implications for teacher training (in-service and pre-service) are now being explored.

This approach forces the educator to *define specifically* the concepts needed for literacy in the chosen area. *In order to make such a definition, the area will necessarily be understood in depth, for it is impossible to analyze a concept into its contributing components without a thorough knowledge of the concept in the first place.* The approach also forces educators to be constantly aware of the multi-dimensionality of cognition, and the critical cognitive processes.

A second major contribution is that, assuming concept mastery on the part of the teacher, the approach *facilitates the essential analysis* into components for instruction. No concept is considered to be a complete entity, but rather to be directly related to the interacting experiences of the learner. In some form, at some time, the learner will need to manipulate the environment directly or vicariously. Perhaps this is a realistic starting point for much of education.

The structure-process approach supplies education with a logical thought pattern which could easily serve as the "map" for curriculum design. Literacy is evidence of mastery, and if literacy is not demonstrated then no conceptual development may be assumed. All concepts are learned and the teacher is the stimulus or stimulator of most organized learning within the standard framework of education.

Thus, the role of the teacher is somewhat clarified when she is conceived as the stimulus or stimulator of learning. Her guidance function is but another dimension of this stimulus role. Through this concept, a bridge between education and research in the traditional and basic learning theory of psychology is established, hopefully bringing many of the theoretical laws previously confined to psychological laboratories to bear upon an urgent empirical and practice need in the classroom.

In summary, this entire approach has been formulated with the view of establishing a working relationship between two closely allied but often dissimilar sciences concerned with human behavior: psychology and education. The role of the first is to understand behavior, while the role of the second is to change behavior. Like literacy and cognition, one is considered the essential and dependent function of the other, for the foundation of change is understanding.

References

Agranoff, Bernard W. June 1967. Memory and protein synthesis. *Sci. Amer.*, **216**, 6, pp. 115–122.

Bandura, Albert, and Richard Walters. 1963. *Social learning and personality development* (New York: Holt, Rinehart and Winston, Inc.).

Brown, Roger. 1965. *Social psychology* (New York: The Free Press).

Bruner, Jerome S. 1966. *Toward a theory of instruction* (Cambridge, Mass.: Belknap Press).

———. 1964. The course of cognitive growth. *Amer. Psychol.*, **1**, 19, pp. 1–15.

———. 1960. *The process of education* (New York: Vintage).

———, et al. 1956. *A study of thinking* (New York: John Wiley & Sons, Inc.).

Ferguson, G. A. 1956. On transfer and the abilities of man. *Canad. J. Psychol.*, **10**, 3, pp. 121–132.

———. 1954. On learning and human ability. *Canad. J. Psychol.*, **8**, 2.

Frost, Joe (ed.). 1967. *Issues and innovations in the teaching of reading* (Glenview, Ill.: Scott, Foresman and Company).

———. 1967. *Orientation handbook*. The elaborative language series (Austin, Tex.: Educational Media Laboratories).

———, and Glenn R. Hawkes (eds.). 1966. *The disadvantaged child* (Boston: Houghton Mifflin Company).

Gagne, Robert M. 1962. The acquisition of knowledge. *Psychol. Rev.*, **69**, pp. 355–356.

Gordon, Ira. 1966. *Studying the child in school* (New York: John Wiley & Sons, Inc.).

Grier, J. B., *et al.* 1967. Prenatal auditory imprinting in chickens. *Science*, **155**, pp. 1692–1693.

Holmes, Jack A. 1965. Basic assumptions underlying the substrata-factor theory. *Reading Res. Quart.* (Newark, N.J.: IRA).

———. 1960. The substrata-factor theory of readings: some experimental evidence. *New frontier in reading* (Newark, N.J.: IRA).

Horn, Thomas D. 1966. Three methods of developing reading readiness in Spanish-speaking children in first grade. *Read. Teach.*, **20**, pp. 38–42.

Lewis, Oscar. October 1966. The culture of poverty. *Sci. Amer.*, **215**, 4, pp. 19–25.

Loretan, Joseph O., and Shelley Umans. 1966. *Teaching the disadvantaged* (New York: Teachers College, Columbia University Press).

Luria, A. R. 1966. The directive function of speech in development and dissolution. In R. C. Anderson and D. P. Ausubel, *Readings in the psychology of cognition* (New York: Holt, Rinehart and Winston, Inc.). Also in *Word*, 1959, **15**, pp. 341–352.

Miller, G. A., *et al.* 1960. *Plans and the structure of behavior* (New York: Holt, Rinehart and Winston, Inc.).

Olson, D. R. 1966. On conceptual strategies. In J. S. Bruner, *et al.*, *Studies in cognitive growth* (New York: John Wiley & Sons, Inc.).

Otto, Wayne, and Richard A. McMenemy. 1966. *Corrective and remedial teaching* (Boston: Houghton Mifflin Company).

Piaget, J. 1966. *Psychology of intelligence*. First ed., 1947 (Totowa, N.J.: Littlefield, Adams).

———. 1965. How children form mathematical concepts. In P. H. Mussen *et al.*, *Readings in child development and personality* (New York: Harper & Row). Also in *Sci. Amer.*, November 1953.

———. 1952a. *Judgment and reasoning in the child* (New York: Humanities Press, Inc.).

———. 1952b. *The origins of intelligence in children*. First ed., 1936 (New York: International Universities Press, Inc.).

———. 1948. *The moral judgment of the child* (New York: The Free Press).

Rosenzweig, M. R. 1966. Environmental complexity, cerebral change, and behavior. *Amer. Psychol.*, **4**, 21, pp. 321–332.

Rowland, Thomas. April 1967. *Cognitive development in children: a model for intervention*. A paper read at the 14th Annual Convention, Southwestern Psychological Association, Houston, Texas.

———, and Carson McGuire. July 1967. The development of intelligent behavior III: Robert W. White. *Psychology in the Schools*, **5**, 3.

Smedslund, J. 1961. The acquisition of conservation of substance and weight in children, III: extinction of conservation of weight "normally" and by means of empirical controls on a balance scale. *Scand. J. Psychol.*, pp. 85–87. Also in R. C. Anderson and D. P. Ausubel, *Readings in the psychology of cognition* (New York: Holt, Rinehart and Winston, Inc.), 1966, pp. 602–605.

Spicker, Howard H. October 1966. The remediation of language deficiencies of educable mentally retarded children. *Ed and the Training of the Mentally Retarded*.

Sterns, Keith, *et al.* 1966. *A diagnostically based language curriculum for psycho-socially deprived preschool children*. Interim report (Washington, D.C.: Office of Education, Department of Health, Education, and Welfare).

Stott, L. H., and R. S. Ball. 1965. Infant and preschool mental tests: review and evaluation. *Monogr. Soc. Res. Child Develpm.*, **30**, No. 3, Serial No. 101.

Van de Geer, J. P., and J. M. F. Jaspars. 1966. Cognitive functions. *Annual Rev.*, **17**, pp. 145–176.

Wallach, M. A. 1963. Research on children's thinking. In the 62nd Ybk. Nat. Soc. Study Educ., *Child psychology* (Chicago, Ill.: University of Chicago Press).

37   A Crucial Problem in Language
Intervention as It Relates
to the Disadvantaged*

BERYL LOSTMAN BAILEY, *Yeshiva University*

Within the ranks of the language teachers, the struggle, long joined, continues unabated between the forces of the "creativists" on the one hand, and those of the "correctionists" on the other. The recent interest in the language development of the disadvantaged has given new impetus to the struggle, which has now broadened to include not only the *how* implied above, but also *when* and *where* intervention should take place.

Those who argue for creativity and for freedom of expression are deeply concerned lest children whom they find largely non-verbal should be suppressed in their efforts to communicate with adults, and as a result wind up having no language at all. Language, they argue, is a tool which is sharpened by constant use, and unless the child is encouraged to use his language freely, he will never become truly verbal.

The purists, on the other hand, are committed to the doctrine of correctness in speech, and argue for early training in proper usage, with its emphasis on *correct* grammar, *correct* pronunciation, and the *right accent*. This group contends that appropriate language, like other appropriate social behavior, is the key which will open doors to upward social mobility. Therefore, the sensible thing to do is to drill the child in the use of the correct forms. Some go so far as to contend that every class should be an English class, and that all teachers should stand constant guard over the language of the children. The evidence, however, points to the fact that this approach is rarely as successful as its protagonists think it should be.

One thing seems clear. As we examine the language of the disadvantaged, we find more and more that it deviates structurally and formally from that of the larger culture, and that we cannot depend on chance or piecemeal correction of the dialect forms to achieve our goal. New patterns have to be taught—the copula with its diverse present tense forms (*am, is, are*), the sibilant ending on possessive nouns, the singular-plural distinction in the present forms of verbs, to name a few of the features of the standard which do not occur in the child's dialect.

Although this article is restricted to the classroom situation, it must

* *IRCD Bulletin Supplement*, Summer 1966, vol. 11, no. 3A. Reprinted by permission.

be remembered that a good deal more language learning takes place outside the classroom than within it, and this may in large measure be responsible for the traditional emphasis in schools on correctness, which was not likely to be taught anywhere else.

It is equally obvious, however, that unbridled freedom of expression may leave the child insensitive to the very features of the language which may militate against his social and economic progress. The understanding middle-class mother does not let her child prattle wildly on, but intervenes at appropriate moments, providing the vocabulary item which the child doesn't know, articulating more clearly an ill-perceived phrase, or correcting a grammatical pattern. The disadvantaged child, with far less opportunity for interaction with adults, is less likely to receive the benefits of such correction in these formative years, and even if he does, the forms he learns will surely be those of the language of the sub-culture, rather than those of the school.

The classroom teacher is therefore faced with a dilemma which must be resolved to the satisfaction of all concerned. More likely than not, she will have been brought up in one or the other school of thought, and will see her role either as that of nurturing uninhibited, well-adjusted personalities, capable of conceptualizing their universe and of utilizing language to adequately communicate such conceptualizations, *or* as that of shaping the child's linguistic performance so that the *rules* of the standard language are always observed.

This is, however, not an "either-or" situation. Both goals must be achieved within the framework of our school structure and, since it would appear that the approaches are mutually exclusive, then *some* provision must be made in the curriculum for both types of activity. While there is a consensus that the opportunities for language development must be provided throughout the school life (beginning with the pre-school years), that the environment must be enriched to provide exposure to good literature and good language models, and that the children must be stimulated and encouraged to imitate the models and to use the new vocabulary items provided by their new experiences, not nearly so much agreement attaches to the amount of attention to be given to the so-called incorrect usage.

I would like to suggest here that there is room for both approaches throughout the curriculum, and, what is more, that the sooner the intervention takes place, the better. I would suggest, too, that the two be kept separate, that is, that a short period of the school day be reserved for drills in correct usage, in which utterances are initiated not by the children, but by the teacher, who will have chosen the patterns to be drilled from the children's experience. This means that the teacher must be equipped with the linguistic tools necessary to diagnose the areas of greatest deviation in the children's language, and she must be prepared, with the use of appropriate props and reinforcement, to structure situations in which the forms to be learned will be drilled in rote fashion. For the pre-school child the drills can be built into a play situation; as they grow older, the props will be gradually removed, and the drills as well as the rules underlying them will become the sole content of the language lesson period.

The argument for the separation of these types of activity is based on the fact that there is no necessary link between verbalness or the ability to communicate one's conceptualizations and proficiency in the use of the forms or structures of a given language. We have yet to prove that, if the language of the school were that of the sub-culture, there would be any great difficulty in getting children to express their concepts succinctly and appropriately. But given, as we have been in our disadvantaged populations, 1) a language which has not been developed or expanded to articulate high-level intellectual concepts, and 2) a society in which all such tasks are performed within the framework of the standard language only, then there seems to be no alternative but to equip the disadvantaged child with 1) the forms and structures of the standard and 2) the opportunities for developing the ability to use these forms and structures for higher intellectual tasks.

The time has come for us to renounce the useless polemics as to which course should be followed. We simply cannot leave the dialect of the disadvantaged alone. To rely solely on environmental enrichment to supply their linguistic deficiencies is being unduly optimistic. Until schools are so structured that the disadvantaged child can have one-to-one interaction with a suitable adult model, or until the disadvantaged child can be placed in integrated situations in which peer-group pressure will serve to modify his language, we must provide, *throughout the curriculum*, (and here even the Head Start programs are included) some opportunity for drills in those forms or patterns of the standard which are foreign to the child's dialect, to supplement the enrichment phase of his training. The question, then, is not one of which approach, but one of degree— how much of each ingredient is optimally beneficial at each stage—and it is to this task that our research must now be directed.

38 Misconceptions Concerning Language in the Disadvantaged*

VIVIAN M. HORNER, *Yeshiva University*

In a recent survey of the language situation in Head Start programs, linguist Donald G. Reiff (Reiff and Pere, 1966) brings under close scrutiny several widely held misconceptions about linguistic phenomena. In an attempt to clarify persistent confusion about language demonstrated in both teaching and research, he discusses a number of attitudes and practices which have been rather unproductive in determining the nature and extent of language problems in disadvantaged children and in suggesting feasible solutions.

Most sweeping in its effects, perhaps, is the almost universal assumption that a *verbal deficiency* implies some sort of *abnormality*. What is accepted as the "norm" is the language patterns of the white, middle-class child of educated parents, though such a child may well be in the minority. This view is reified by research, which must rely upon measuring instruments and analytic techniques designed for and standardized on middle-class populations. Reiff indicates one of the dangers:

> The fact that intelligence quotients and measures of mental age depend highly upon verbal information . . . does not deter those who attribute poor verbal performance to low intelligence, less than appropriate mental age figures, or deficient cognitive development.

The simple fact is that the kinds of "defects" identified reflect little more than the structure of the instruments used to identify them. Reiff urges that caution be exercised in assessment:

> [Our first need is for] honesty in the recognition of assumptions which lead to the construction of hypothetical notions of 'normalcy' and 'deficit.' *Difference* is the term we need; the negative aspects of difference become apparent only on examination of the *implications* of difference.

A similar point is made with regard to a widespread failure to distinguish between a *speech defect* (an organically determined, pathological problem requiring therapy) and a *language deficit* (a behaviorally determined problem, remediable by teaching). This confusion frequently leads to a referral of all "language problems" for speech therapy. Thus overloaded speech therapists find themselves with clientele ranging from the

* *IRCD Bulletin Supplement*, Summer 1966, vol. 11, no. 3A. **Reprinted by permission.**

child whose cleft palate interferes with the acquisition of intelligible speech to the child who does not talk at all to the child whose "problem" is that he did not score well on the PPVT. Clearly it is a responsibility in which the teacher should share, but this is evident only if a basic distinction is made.

Similarly, there seems to be a general confusion between dialect-determined pronunciation patterns and articulatory defects:

> Slowness in acquiring 'the sounds of the language' appears to be a commonly observed phenomenon in the culturally deprived, though one searches in vain for a description of what speech sounds these children are expected to acquire, and whether or not the sounds they do not acquire are part of the dialect they are acquiring.

The Negro child's "Come wif' me" is labelled "substitution" or "distortion" despite the fact that the child demonstrates a phonological pattern consistent with that of his own speech community. This labelling probably derives from the use of articulatory tests, which are constructed on the basis of a hypothetical norm, never described, and which are standardized on a different population. Yet scores are readily translated into descriptions of "articulatory immaturity" and "developmental lag." Such terms are meaningless in the absence of an existent and carefully specified *norm for these children*.

Another set of misconceptions stems from a kind of naïveté which is best described as *linguistic chauvinism*. Perhaps the best known example of this is the linguists' Miss Fidditch, a fictional English teacher, who spends all her class time issuing edicts against the use of *ain't* and double negatives. Her archaic conception of grammar as "correctness" rather than as a description of the way people use language has set for her the primary teaching goal of eliminating "dialect"; nothing must remain but the "pure, intrinsically superior standard language." For the sophisticated student of language, "dialect" is recognized as the way of referring to the collective speech patterns of one subcommunity as opposed to those of any other subcommunity. Everyone speaks a dialect (or several) and it is only an accident of history that one ("standard") currently occupies a position of prestige with respect to the others. Thus, to the linguist, Miss Fidditch is an amusing figure. The humor is lost, however, in observing that her attitudes are still very much with us. So much so, in fact, that the National Council of Teachers of English (1965) task force on language programs for the disadvantaged found it necessary to caution against concern with nonstandard English dialect at the preschool level *except to the extent that it interferes with learning*.

A danger inherent in continuous "correction" of speech is that effort is wasted on *form* at a time when it is far more important to help the child become proficient in the *use* of language. Furthermore, "correction" constitutes punishment for the child's attempt to communicate verbally, and may serve to inhibit further attempts to speak in the classroom.

Reiff points up another manifestation of this linguistic chauvinism in attitudes toward children who are native speakers of foreign languages, and whose English is either nonexistent, not fully developed, or "accented." The middle-class community strongly supports the notion of English as "superior," and any one who does not speak it, or who speaks it with a foreign accent, is considered by definition to be part of the "disadvantaged" population. Arthur Rubel (1966) discusses some of the effects of such attitudes in the Southwest:

> The importance imputed to the control of English language skills may be inferred from a wide-spread pattern in which school administrations prohibit young scholastics from speaking Spanish on or near the school grounds . . . it is difficult indeed to overemphasize the practical *and* symbolic importance which administrators and teachers attach to the acquiring of English and the loss of Spanish by young school children . . . I can think of no other punitive program which has had so contrary an outcome as the one just described . . . not only is Spanish heard whenever a supervisory teacher is not in the immediate vicinity, but the very prohibition itself has increased the importance which spoken Spanish has for the Mexican-American and the Southwest. The ban is considered one more instance of the denigration of the entire traditional way of life of Spanish-speaking Americans by the dominant Anglo-American group.

Such inflexible policies, dictated by the dominant social ideology, are translated into practices which fail entirely to consider level of performance in the native language, and lead to a generalization of "verbal inadequacy." The verbal demands on the non-English-speaking child are enormous in this light; no less enormous is the teaching task. This hard-headed position forces once more a concern with *form* at a time when *function* is the critical issue. Reiff concludes:

> The 'absolute' verbal skills of the individual, in his native language first (or his native dialect) and in English second, is necessary to gain a full picture . . . it may well be that before a child can become verbal in English to a sufficient degree to ensure his success or at least remove any limiting factors for his future education, he must become verbal in his native language or dialect.

What seems clearly indicated by Reiff's discussion is a need for greater sophistication and flexibility in the conception and identification of verbal deficiencies, if we hope to design effective techniques for their remediation. We need to shift from our present global attack on "the language problem" to a sharply focused attack on "language problems" specified by examining the individual child's entering repertoires in the light of all the linguistic and behavioral information currently available.

Such a change in orientation should lead to more meaningful research and to instructional programs which will establish the kinds of verbal repertoires which enable the child to control his environment more effectively.

References

National Council of Teachers of English. 1965. *Language programs for the disadvantaged.* NCTE task force report on teaching English to the disadvantaged (Champaign, Ill.: National Council of Teachers of English).

Reiff, Donald G., and Pere Julià. 1966. *The language situation in Project Head Start centers,* 1965. Final report (Washington, D.C.: Office of Economic Opportunity, Office of Research and Evaluation, Project Head Start, Contract OEO-932).

Rubel, Arthur J. February 1966. *Some cultural anthropological aspects of English as a second language.* A paper presented at the American Educational Research Association Symposium.

39   Subcultural Differences in Child Language: An Inter-Disciplinary Review*

COURTNEY B. CAZDEN, *Harvard University*

The argument over whether children from Harlem or Appalachia should be called "culturally different" or "culturally deprived" is more than an empty terminological dispute. It reflects a basic and important question: Is the concept of cultural relativity valid in this subcultural context or not? More specifically, in what ways is the language used by children in various subcultural groups simply different, and to what extent can the language of any group be considered deficient by some criteria? It is the purpose

* *Merrill-Palmer Quarterly*, July 1966, vol. 12, no. 3. Copyright 1966 by The Merrill-Palmer Institute. Reprinted by permission. An earlier version of this review was submitted as a special qualifying paper to the Harvard Graduate School of Education. The author is grateful to Professors Robert Anderson, Roger Brown, and Robert Dreeben for helpful comments and criticism. This revision was supported by Contract OE5-10-239 of the U.S. Office of Education with the Center for Research and Development on Educational Differences, Harvard University.

of this paper to explore a large body of literature bearing on the basic question.

Necessarily, this review of the literature will be an inter-disciplinary one. Linguists describe the nonstandard dialects of English in formal ways. Developmental psychologists find variations in the rate of language acquisition by children that correlate with variations in status characteristics, e.g., of social class or ethnic background. Anthropologists and sociologists suggest that not only language, but speech, is structured. Under the heading of ethnography of communication or socio-linguistics, they examine the inter-individual functions that language serves in subcultural settings. Lastly, experimental psychologists studying the intra-individual, or mediational, role of verbal behavior are becoming interested in the individual and group difference among their subjects.

I will discuss these four strands of research in turn, not trying to list all the studies and their findings but concentrating instead on an analysis of significant issues. However, even though some of this work has been stimulated by pressing educational problems, the educational issues would require such a lengthy discussion in themselves that they must be considered as falling outside of the scope of the present paper.

Nonstandard versus Standard English

Dr. Martin Luther King, speaking in Selma, Alabama, just before the civil-rights march to the state capital, said:

> Those of us who are Negroes don't have much. We have known the long night of poverty. Because of the system, we don't have much education and many of us don't know how to make our nouns and our verbs agree. But thank God we have our bodies, our feet and our souls (*New York Times*, March 22, 1965, p. 1).

As will be seen, Dr. King's example is pertinent in a discussion of standard and nonstandard English.

Standard English has been defined as "the particular type of English which is used in the conduct of the important affairs of our people. It is also the type of English used by the socially acceptable of most of our communities and, insofar as that is true, it has become a social or class dialect in the United States" (Fries, 1940, p. 13). Nonstandard English, by contrast, refers to dialects which deviate from the standard in pronunciation, vocabulary, or grammar. Social or class dialects are thus usually grouped into three main types: Standard English, common or popular English, and vulgar or illiterate English. However, the methods of distinguishing or describing the latter two types also vary in themselves.

Methods of Describing Nonstandard English

The differences between nonstandard dialects and Standard English have been described in three principal ways: in terms of frequency of errors, of contrastive analysis, or of transformational grammar. The oldest method, now discarded, is simply to count "errors" or deviations from Standard English and express the sum as a percentage of total use of a particular part of speech (e.g., pronouns), or as a percentage of total words used. Three studies of child language (Templin, 1957; D. R. Thomas, 1962; Loban, 1963) provide information on such deviations. All three find that verb usage is the most frequent source of errors: specifically, violation of subject-verb agreement; deviant use of the verb *to be*, "especially for Negro subjects whose parents have migrated from the rural South" (Loban, 1963, p. 52); use of present for past tense; and use of *got* for *have*.[1] Other frequent errors are wrong forms of the pronoun, double negatives, and the use of *ain't*.

A second method is to describe nonstandard forms of English in terms of a contrastive analysis, a technique adapted from research on foreign language teaching. This defines the points of maximum interference between the phonology, morphology or syntax of the speaker's native language and the "target language" which he is trying to learn. Thus a contrastive analysis would pinpoint, for example, the problems of learning English for a native speaker of Hindi. The same technique could be applied to the teaching of Standard English to speakers of nonstandard dialects.

However, this method entails making a separate analysis for each nonstandard dialect—regional, foreign-language background, or social class. Work is now in progress for Negro and Puerto Rican speech in New York City (Labov, 1965); for Negro and white middle- and lower-class speech in Chicago (Davis and McDavid, 1964; Pederson, 1964); for the speech of Negro students at Tougaloo College, in Mississippi (Beryl Bailey)[2]; and for the speech of school children in Washington, D.C. (Center for

[1] This last instance deals primarily, of course, with *got* used as a transitive verb in a present-tense construction for *have* in the sense of "to possess, own, hold," etc., not with *got* as a past participle used with some form of *have* as an auxiliary verb. The writer recognizes that any discussion of *got*-versus-*have* is soon diverted into historic arguments on English usage, divergent British- and American-English practices, literary precedents running from Shakespeare to Shaw, and so on and so on—all of which are beyond the scope of this review. Moreover, it is my impression that the use of *got* is increasing among speakers of Standard English; built into the definition of Standard English is the concept of the changing norm.

[2] Personal communication from Beryl Bailey, 1964.

Applied Linguistics, 1965). These are particularly promising studies of language behavior and the psychological and sociological factors related to it. The Center for Applied Linguistics is also stimulating as well as coordinating activities in this field.

The third method uses the approach of "transformational grammar." Very briefly, each dialect is described in terms of the rules underlying it (descriptive, not prescriptive rules), and the rules for different dialects are then compared. A readable exposition of the basic theory is set forth by O. C. Thomas (1965). Rosenbaum (1964, p. 30) comments that the transformational approach "permits a precise and insightful characterization of the relatedness between grammatical systems" and notes some of the ways in which it seems to hold promise for dialect study. To date, the only example of this approach is Klima's (1964) analysis of the use of interrogative and personal pronouns in four "styles"—elegant or literary English, two intermediate styles, and vulgar English as found in the novels of Nelson Algren.

Nonstandard English as Deficient

There are both social and psychological criteria by which nonstandard speech might be considered deficient. The evidence on social grounds is the more conclusive. There is little question that speaking a nonstandard dialect is a social liability, creating a barrier to the speaker's acceptance in the dominant culture. As Jespersen ([1946], 1964, pp. 70–71) has observed:

> [It is to the advantage of the children to speak Standard English] not only materially, because they can more easily obtain positions in society which now—whether one approves it or not in the abstract— are given by preference to people whose speech is free of dialect, but also because they thus escape being looked down on on account of their speech, and are therefore saved from many unpleasant humiliations. Apart from all this, merely by reason of their speaking they have a better chance of coming in contact with others and getting a fuller exchange of ideas.

Putnam and O'Hern (1955) provide recent evidence that features of nonstandard speech are indeed perceived and negatively evaluated by Standard speakers. Just which features elicit the most unfavorable reactions from teachers, employers, etc., is one of the points under study in several of the contrastive analyses referred to earlier.

Whether nonstandard English is, in addition, a cognitive liability to the speaker is much harder to determine. First, Standard English might be a more powerful means of communication. But all other things, such as vocabulary, being equal there is no evidence that this is so. "It is generally the very small points that are fixed upon as objectionable, often insignificant things that hardly affect the value of the language as a means of communication" (Jespersen [1946], 1964, p. 56n.).

Second, the child who speaks a nonstandard dialect may have difficulty understanding his teacher and his schoolbooks. The evidence on this point is unclear. Cherry (1964) reports a pioneer attempt to use the Cloze technique "to evaluate the extent to which information is successfully communicated from teachers to pupils of various social backgrounds and the degree of effective communication among children from different social backgrounds" (p. 23). Words were deleted according to a predetermined sequence from samples of teacher and peer-group speech, and the child's comprehension was measured by his ability to replace the exact word or suggest a substitute that made semantic or grammatical sense. Despite methodological problems in oral presentation of the speech samples and in the reliability of the scores, there were three major results: (1) social-class differences in understanding teacher speech were more apparent among fifth-graders than first-graders, but this effect was not maintained when intelligence was controlled statistically; (2) there were no social-class differences among fifth-graders in comprehending lower-class peer speech, but middle-class children were significantly superior to lower-class children in comprehending middle-class peer speech, and this effect was maintained even when intelligence was controlled; (3) Negro-white differences in these receptive language skills were virtually absent. In interpreting these results, we should note that while lower-class fifth-graders had more trouble understanding middle-class peer speech, the decreased comprehension across social-class lines was not reciprocal. The middle-class children understood lower-class peer speech as well as did the lower-class children. This finding suggests that dialect differences are confounded with other linguistic variables, such as vocabulary load and utterance complexity.

Here is a key problem. It is hard to determine whether nonstandard dialects are, "other things being equal," just as good a means of communication as Standard English. For such "other things" as the total repertoire of words and grammatical patterns are, in fact, rarely equal. Fries (1940, p. 287f.) reached the following conclusion:

> Over and over again . . . it appeared that the differences between the language of the educated and that of those with little education did not lie primarily in the fact that the former used one set of forms and the latter an entirely different set. In fact, in most cases, the actual deviation of the language of the uneducated from Standard English grammar seemed much less than is usually assumed. . . . The most striking difference between the language of the two groups lay in the fact that Vulgar English seems essentially poverty stricken. It uses less of the resources of the language, and a few forms are used very frequently.

Fries's language samples were taken from the correspondence of American citizens with agencies of the federal government, and it could be argued that the writers of Vulgar English were particularly impoverished in meeting the demands of that task. However, Loban obtained comparable results from an analysis of oral language of children in an informal interview. Thus it seems unlikely that the relative position of high and low social-class groups on a richness-impoverishment dimension can be explained wholly in terms of each given situation.

Loban (1963) used a two-level analytical scheme developed for his research. In the first level, utterances were classified into one of nine structural patterns—e.g., subject-verb-object (*George eats onions*), or subject-linking verb-predicate nominative (*Onions are roots*). In the second level, the component parts of these nine patterns were examined. From a comparison of the speech of a high group and a low group, selected on the basis of language ability but contrasting on socio-economic status as well, Loban (1963, p. 46) concludes:

> All these subjects . . . use the relatively few structural patterns of the English language. Thus structural pattern reveals less remarkable differences than does dexterity of substitution *within* the patterns. The important differences show up in the substitution of word groups for single words, in the choice and arrangement of movable syntactic elements, in the variety of nominals, and in strategies with prediction.

In other words, there is evidence that not only do nonstandard dialects use different rules once a particular construction has been selected (the so-called "errors") but, more importantly, people speaking these dialects tend to use fewer of the optional constructions in their native language and to fill all the slots in their constructions from a smaller set of words.

Sometimes a single utterance can be categorized in several ways. Take the case of verb usage and, specifically, this example heard from a five-year-old in a day-care center: *My Mommy help me*. It can be considered as containing an error at the morphological level of linguistic structure in the failure to observe subject-verb agreement in the third person singular. Such errors are common in nonstandard dialects, as has been seen above. But the same utterance can be considered evidence of impoverishment, in failing to encode a particular meaning in a unique way by taking advantage of the rich possibilities afforded by English verb auxiliaries. The weakness of *My Mommy help me* as a communication lies in the use of an unmodified lexical verb instead of one of many alternatives, such as *My Mommy did help me* or *My Mommy would have helped me*. (However, see Stewart, 1965 for evidence that nonstandard dialects make different, not simply fewer distinctions.) Further, since the use of unmodified lexical verbs like *help* precedes developmentally the emergence of more complex constructions, the same utterance can be considered an example of retardation. I will suggest later that such ambiguity in interpretation poses a serious problem in the attempts to establish dialect-free scales of language development.

The question of whether nonstandard dialects are deficient or just different is sometimes glossed over by the statement "you can say anything in any language." It may be true that any language has the resources available, in words and grammatical constructions, to encode any meaning in some way (although Hymes, 1961, offers an opposing view). What is meant by such "resources" is the contents of a complete dictionary. In this sense English is as good as, but not better than, French or Russian. However, when we shift from the difference between English and French to that between the speech of a middle-class child and a lower-class child, we aren't looking at the total of what is available in language as a set of symbols but only at what is actually used by certain individuals at the moment of framing an utterance. This is one distinction between language and speech, and it's a sign of confusion between the two to inject the idea that "one language is as good as another" into the controversy over the verbal inadequacies of children in some subcultural groups.

In general, then, it is probably true, to quote Loban (1963, p. 85), "Subjects who are rated as most proficient in language are also those who manifest the most sensitivity to the conventions of language. The subject who, despite unconventional usage, exhibits verbal linguistic skill is the exception." But while a correlation between deviation from Standard English and impoverishment exists, it can't be explained on any intrinsic grounds. The causes must therefore lie in historical and sociological factors—such as isolation, discrimination, or distance from foreign-language background—and the degree of correlation will therefore vary from one subcultural group to another.

Stages on a Developmental Continuum

The findings of those studies of language development that make subcultural comparisons have become rather widely known. Therefore I will devote less space here to a summary of that work than to two related topics: an outline of the mediators by which such gross environmental variables as social class may affect language development, and an exploration of the problems which dialectal differences pose for the establishment of developmental scales.

Studies of Language Development

In addition to the work of Templin (1957), D. R. Thomas (1962), and Loban (1963) already touched on, the studies by Irwin (1948*a*,

1948*b*) and Lesser, Fifer, and Clark (1965) should be mentioned. Research by various members of the Institute for Developmental Studies (e.g., Deutsch, 1963; John, 1963; Keller, 1963; Cherry, 1965; Deutsch and B. Brown, 1964; John and Goldstein, 1964) is cited elsewhere in this review. Except for the work by Lesser, et al., these studies divide their subjects by social class only. They deal with three aspects of language development: phonology, vocabulary, and sentence structure (today more often termed grammar). The findings can be quickly summarized. On all measures, in all the studies, children of upper socio-economic status, however defined, are more advanced than those of lower socio-economic status. Nevertheless, some points merit additional comment.

PHONOLOGY. Irwin's (1948*a*, 1948*b*) work is striking in that it pinpoints the early age at which environmental differences impinge on phonological development. Comparing the number of sound types and tokens produced by infants from birth to 30 months, he found that the infants from higher-status families had significantly higher scores for the last year of the period than did those from lower-status families. In other words, the developmental curves separated at 18 months of age.

VOCABULARY. The study by Lesser, et al. (1965) is included here because language development was measured with a vocabulary test, but the import of this research extends beyond that to intellectual development as a whole. The purpose was to examine the pattern of four mental abilities (verbal, reasoning, numerical, and space) among first-grade children in New York City from middle and lower social-class groups and four ethnic backgrounds—Chinese, Jewish, Negro, and Puerto Rican. Care was taken in preparing the test materials and in obtaining examiners from the child's own subcultural group to insure that "observed differences . . . reside in the respondents and not in the test materials themselves" (p. 13). Verbal ability was measured by a 60-item vocabulary test, one-half pictures and one-half words, administered in the child's native language, or English, or a combination of both.

Probably the most important finding is that ethnic background and social class have different effects. Ethnic background affects the pattern of mental abilities, while social-class status affects the level of scores across the mental-ability scales. Specifically, on *verbal ability* Jewish children ranked first (being significantly better than all other ethnic groups), Negroes second and Chinese third (both being significantly better than the Puerto Ricans), and Puerto Ricans fourth. On *space*, by contrast, the rank order was Chinese, Jewish, Puerto Rican, and Negro children. But in all four ethnic groups, on all scales and subtests, the middle-class children were significantly superior to the lower-class children. As Lesser and his co-workers (1965, p. 83) observe:

Apparently, different mediators are associated with social-class and ethnic-group conditions. . . . The importance of the mediators associated with ethnicity is to provide differential impacts upon the development of mental abilities, while the importance of mediators associated with social class is to provide pervasive (and not differential) effects upon the various mental abilities. This conclusion allows selection among several explanations offered to interpret cultural influences upon intellectual activity.

The same investigators also found that social-class position has more effect on mental abilities for the Negro children than for other groups, and that on each mental-ability test the scores of the middle-class children from the four ethnic groups resemble each other more than do the scores of the lower-class children. All the findings are discussed in the light of previous studies. For instance, the superior verbal ability of the Jewish children appears in many other studies. On the other hand, the verbal inferiority of the Puerto Rican children has been contradicted by other evidence (e.g., see Anastasi and De Jesús, 1953). Lesser, et al. discount the possible effects of bilingualism.

Although measures of vocabulary consistently yield social-class differences in the scores, significant questions relevant to the difference-deficiency issue remain unanswered. Tyler says that "lower-class children use a great many words, and a number of them use these words with a high degree of precision; but facility with words commonly used by the lower classes is not correlated with success in school" (Eells, Davis, Havighurst, Herrick, and Tyler, 1951, p. 40). Does Tyler mean that children from different status groups know and use different words? If so, how can this be reconciled with Templin's (1957) results on the Seashore-Eckerson Test in which the sampling of words from an unabridged dictionary results in a bias in the direction of common, easier words (Lorge and Chall, 1963)? Or how can it be reconciled with the results obtained by Lesser, et al. on the tests described above? Or does Tyler mean that lower-class children use "slang" from a different "dictionary"? How does this relate to Nida's (1958, p. 283) suggestion that "subcultures have proportionately more extensive vocabularies in the area of their distinctiveness"? Can one speak of the vocabulary of an idiolect or a dialect as structured? Is Tyler implying that, even for vocabularies similar in size, children from different groups may know fewer words in common than children from the same group? Conceivably, quantitative measures may conceal wide variation in overlap.

It has also been remarked that the language of the lower-class child is rich in something called "expressiveness." Cohn (1959, p. 439) speaks of "the great power of lower-class language to express emotions, a power ordinarily exploited with a clear conscience only by novelists." Is this just a romantic view in which the clichés of one subculture are perceived as creative expression by the listener from a different culture? Or does it mean that lower-class children use a small vocabulary in varied and novel ways, compensating by inventive encoding for what they lack in availability of single words? Or does it refer not to language as a code but to what it is used to say?

SENTENCE STRUCTURE. The most common measure of development in sentence structure, or grammar, is mean length of response (MLR), usually in words although it should be in morphemes. The validity of such a global and summary kind of measure rests on the widespread finding that it increases with age, and on more recent discoveries by Brown and Fraser (1964) and Bellugi (1966) of a close correspondence between mean length and the emergence of specific grammatical features in the speech of children under 4 years of age. We should not assume, however, that the correlation between length and complexity remains high at older ages. An average can include very short and very long. Thus, even if the MLR for two status groups were similar, the lower-status children might be speaking either in short sentences or connecting simple strings of words with "and" while the upper-status children utilize more complex syntactical patterns.

In a frequency distribution of the written sentences from Standard English and Vulgar English samples, Fries (1952, pp. 291–292) found that even though average lengths were similar, 23.46 and 23.16 respectively, the mode (most frequent length) in Standard English was 21 words, while Vulgar English had a mode of only 11 words but included more very long sentences. The same phenomenon can explain Templin's (1957, p. 79) finding in her study of children 3–8 years old, that while the MLR is the same or higher for upper-status children at all ages, the standard deviation of length-of-response scores is the same or higher for lower-status children above the age of 4 years.

Mediating Variables

In measuring aspects of the environment which correlate with the growth of intelligence and academic achievement, Wolf (1964) and Davé (1963) distinguish between *status* and *process* variables. Examples of status variables are the income of the family and educational level of the parents; examples of process variables are the nature of intellectual aspirations for the child and the academic guidance provided in the home. In short, the contrast is between what parents are and what they do. In a sample of all the fifth-grade children in a Midwestern community, Wolf obtained a multiple correlation of +.76 between the process variables and intelligence; Davé obtained a multiple correlation of +.80 between the process variables and achievement. These contrast with usual correlations of +.40 to +.50 between intelligence or achievement and usual measures of socio-economic status. (See Bloom, 1964, pp. 24 and 79, for summaries of these two studies.)

In this sense, the widespread finding of a significant positive correlation between social class (a cluster of status characteristics) and the rate of language development begs the important question of what mediating process variables may be operating. I have therefore adapted the categories used by Gray and Klaus (1964) and will outline the features of the environment that may be critical under three headings: context, or the non-verbal setting in which the language occurs; stimulation; and responses to the child's speech. Some of these may have a "differential" impact on language development, while others may have a more "pervasive" impact on cognitive development in general (Lesser, et al., 1965). Unfortunately, we are not yet able to separate these two sets of variables.

CONTEXT. Five features of the non-verbal context may be important: the affective quality, whether the child talks to adults or other children, how varied the contexts are, the prevailing signal-to-noise ratio, and conversation versus television. These will be discussed in order.

1. Affective Quality—There is widespread emphasis on the key role in language development of the mother-child relationship. It is difficult to test the specific influence of that relationship, however, because warm feeling and lots of talk tend to occur together. This confounding is present when home care is contrasted with institutional care (e.g., Provence and Lipton, 1962). It is also present when the home environments of high and low scorers on reading readiness tests are compared (Milner, 1951).

2. Adults versus Children—Children talk with adults and other children, and the relative amounts of such talk vary greatly among subcultural groups. Which has the greater influence on language development is still an unresolved question. On one side of the issue are those linguists who argue that children speak more like their peers than like their parents. This is the view of Jespersen (1922) and Hockett (1950). And more recently, Stewart (1964, p. 14n.) has observed:

> It is easy to find cases involving second- or third-generation Washington [D.C.] Negro families in which the parents are speakers of a quite standard variety of English, but where the children's speech is much closer to that of the newer immigrants [from the South]. . . . This phenomenon, incidentally, seems to support the theory that children learn more language behavior from members of their own peer group than from their parents, and suggests that educator concern over the quality of "language in the home" may be misplaced.

On the other side are those psychologists who offer convincing evidence that the speech of children without siblings, who presumably have more opportunity for conversation with parents, is generally superior. Examples can be found in the studies of Koch (1954), Nisbet (1961), and most recently in Vera John's finding[3] of a birth-order effect on language development within a sample of lower-class Negro children.

No doubt, studies of conversation among children could help resolve this issue, but such studies are rare. One example is Smith's (1935) analysis of the mean length of utterance of 220 children, from 18 to 70 months in age, in two situations—at play with other children and at home with adults. The children used longer sentences in conversation with adults, probably because they answered fewer questions, gave fewer imperatives, and generally engaged in more connected discourse with less active play and fewer interruptions.

Only a possible direction for resolution of these seemingly conflicting claims can be suggested. Extrapolating far beyond the present evidence, and using a computer analogy, I wonder if the opportunity to talk with adults may largely determine the complexity of the "programs" for constructing and understanding utterances which a child can handle, while conversation with peers has more effect on specific details of those "programs" such as features of phonology and morphology.

3. Contextual Variety—A child's language develops within contexts of greater or less variety. Deutsch and Brown (1964) suggest that variety in family activities increases verbal interaction. Ausubel (1964) writes of the desirability of a wide range of objects which can serve as referents for speech. John and Goldstein (1964) report that a group of lower-class Negro four-year-olds had trouble on the Peabody Picture Vocabulary Test with such action words as *digging* and *tying*. They suggest that a word like *digging* differs from one like *Coca Cola* in the stability of the word-referent relationship: "Gerunds such as *tying* were failed, not because the children were deficient in experience with the referent, but rather because they had difficulty in fitting the label to the varying forms of action observed and experienced" (p. 269). They argue that the process of generalization and discrimination involved in learning the meanings of more abstract words does not come about simply through "receptive exposure" to many examples but through "active participation" with a more verbally mature individual (p. 273). The benefits of variety in non-verbal experience may depend on the availability of help in encoding that experience in words.

Varied surroundings can stimulate and reinforce different functions of language. Bernstein (1962a, p. 32) contrasts "restricted" and "elaborated" codes, and asserts that working-class speech is characterized by a

[3] **Personal communication from Vera P. John, 1965.**

restricted code which "is played out against a background of communal, self-consciously held interests which remove the need to verbalize subjective intent and make it explicit." It may be that during the period of language learning those children who are confronted with a narrow range of close personal contacts learn only the economical mode of communication that suffices within that small circle. A related hypothesis is suggested in Frake's (1961) study of folk taxonomies: ". . . the greater the number of distinct social contexts in which information about a particular phenomenon [e.g., skin disease] must be communicated, the greater the number of different levels of contrast into which that phenomenon is categorized" (p. 121).

4. Signal-to-Noise Ratio—Deutsch (1963) discusses the relevance to language learning of the overall signal-to-noise ratio prevailing in the daily environment. One characteristic of slum living which may contribute to language retardation is the high noise level, not only in the literal sense of noise but in the minimum of non-instructional conversation directed toward the child. This situation is ideal for inducing habitual inattention. The child may learn to "tune out" both meaningless noise and the occasional meaningful stimuli, with the result of an absolute decrease in effective stimulation.

5. Conversation versus Television—Lastly, what about television? Children from lower-status groups watch as much TV as high-status groups, if not more (Keller, 1963; Wortis, et al., 1963). Why isn't this extra language stimulation more beneficial? Is the critical difference passive listening to a monologue versus active participation in a dialogue? If so, then what of the supposed benefit of listening to stories? Is attention to language reduced when it is embedded in the context of constantly changing visual stimuli. There is evidence that TV has some positive effect on vocabulary (Schramm, Lyle, and Parker, 1961), but research is needed on what children attend to while watching TV and how they process the language heard in this context.

STIMULATION. Language stimulation can vary both in quality and in quantity. The quality of the stimulus in turn can vary along lines of conformity to Standard English, variety, and sequence.

1. Conformity to Standard English—Ervin-Tripp (1964, p. 163) states "Children's grammar converges on the norm for the community in which they live." If that norm is not Standard English some of the effects may resemble retarded speech, as we have seen, and may be unfortunate from other standpoints. But when we study the rate of language development as such, a child's progress should be judged in terms of his approach toward the norm for his particular language community. Whether the nature of that norm can itself affect development is an open empirical question.

In the studies cited earlier, Wolf (1964) and Davé (1963) found that a rating of opportunities provided in the home for enlarging vocabulary and using a variety of sentence patterns correlated highly with both intelligence and achievement, while a judgment by the interviewer of the quality of language usage of the mother did not. Davé (1963, p. 114) was thus led to observe, "This may imply that the quality of language usage of the parents, and the extent of verbal interaction among family members, are quite independent characteristics."

2. Linguistic Variety—Variety in the non-verbal setting in which language occurs has already been discussed; here we are dealing with the variety in the words and grammatical patterns which the child hears. Razran (1961, p. 126) reports a Soviet experiment on the role of both kinds of variety in the development of lexical meanings. A group of nine children, 19 months old, were given 20 simultaneous exposures to a book and a sentence about a book. Three children received a single book and a single sentence; three received a single book and 20 different sentences; and three received 20 different books and a single sentence. Learning, as measured by the child's ability to select a book from a group of objects, was greatest for the varied language group, next best for the varied referent group, and practically nonexistent for the first group.

Another approach uses the "type-token" ratio. Briefly, the number of tokens—e.g., the total number of instances of plural nouns that a child hears—is an indication of the sheer quantity of language stimulation. The number of types—e.g., the number of different nouns which the child hears pluralized—is a measure of variety. Miller and Ervin-Tripp (1964) have asked whether greater variety, as measured by the type-token ratio, plays a role in the development of grammatical meanings, specifically in the child's developing use of the plural inflection. Starting from non-contrast (e.g., using *boy* for both singular and plural), the child occasionally uses contrasted forms, then correctly contrasts all familiar words, and finally generalizes to irregular nouns (*foots*) and, in an experimental situation, to nonsense words (*biks*). Contrast with familiar forms always precedes generalization to nonsense forms, but the time lapse between the two stages varies. Miller and Ervin-Tripp (1964, p. 33) therefore point out, "We do not know whether it is the variety of types or the frequency of tokens showing contrast which is crucial in determining the length of time before generalization occurs." The question at issue is whether increased variety, often termed "richness," adds anything to increased quantity alone. It is at least a hypothesis to be explored that variety does aid the child, in and of itself; and, conversely, that language that is impoverished is harder to learn, not easier.

Three arguments can be suggested for this hypothesis. First, if as

Cofer has commented, "learning of inflectional and syntactical skills is akin to concept formation" (Cofer and Musgrave, 1963, p. 198), then variation in irrelevant features (e.g., particular count nouns) may aid learning of the concept of inflectional marking of plurality. Second, increased variety of language stimulation may enhance attentional processes in the child (Fiske and Maddi, 1961). Third and purely theoretical, if the process of first language acquisition is akin to scientific theory construction in which hypotheses are tested against available data, as the transformational grammarians argue, then a meagre set of data could be a hindrance. Fodor (n.d.) makes this argument explicit:

> If parents do simplify the syntax of their speech when they address children they may make it *harder* for the child to learn the correct syntactic analysis of his language. Rules that hold for selected sets of simple sentences may have to be abandoned in the light of examples of sentences of more complicated types.

In contrast to variety are well-learned routines. These may include sentences such as *I don't know*; they may also include bits of nursery rhymes and songs and, perhaps most important of all, phrases from books read to the child many times. It has been a long time since Carroll (1939, p. 222) suggested, "An interesting investigation could be set upon the hypothesis that learning of rote material is an important factor in speech development." That investigation still remains to be done.

3. Sequence—In analyzing the detrimental effects of the slum environment, Deutsch (1963, p. 168) suggests that "in addition to the restriction in variety . . . it might be postulated that the segments made available to these children tend to have poorer and less systematic ordering of stimulation sequences, and would thereby be less useful to the growth and motivation of cognitive potential." Variety can be described in absolute terms, e.g., by the type-token ratio, but sequence cannot. For while an optimal sequence may incorporate some absolute dimension of complexity, there remains as a relative component the "match" between the stimuli the child encounters in his environment and the cognitive structures which determine his readiness to respond to them (Hunt, 1961).

This match can be improved in two ways. The adult might provide a rich and varied supply of stimuli and let the child find what he needs. This was the principle involved in the self-selection feeding practices of some years ago; it is also the principle recommended by the Montessori method (Hunt, 1964). Applied to language development, this principle would predict that if a child has the chance to hear a sufficiently varied and large sample of well-formed sentences, he will take from it what he needs for the acquisition of his own language system. Alternatively, the adult might preselect certain stimuli for the child. Such preselection could be either purposeful or fortuitous. For first language learning it would have to be fortuitous, since no one knows enough about what the child is doing to plan his curriculum.

4. Quantity—Finally, the language stimulation available to a child can and does vary in quantity. It seems intuitively obvious that differences in quantity should affect language development, although frequency of exposure may matter only up to some threshold, beyond which no additional benefits may accrue. But severe problems face any attempt to separate the effects of frequency of stimulation from the effects of responses to the child's speech.

RESPONSE TO THE CHILD'S SPEECH.   It is still an open question whether some category of response, such as reinforcement or feedback, is necessary or at least very helpful to language development, or whether rich stimulation or exposure is sufficient. For the most part, the theoretical controversy is carried on between experimental psychologists who attempt to substantiate their theories of human learning by fitting them to the child's strikingly successful acquisition of language (e.g., Staats and Staats, 1963), and linguists and their cognitive psychology associates who derive implications for the process of acquisition from the transformational model of language structure (e.g., Fodor, n.d.; Lenneberg, 1964; Katz, 1966; McNeill, 1954). A review of the arguments is outside the scope of this paper. I will only suggest one way in which reinforcement may apply, then review several empirical studies.

Whether reinforcement applies to any of the actual content of the language learning process—to any aspect of phonology, vocabulary, or grammar—it may apply to the child's interest in, valuing of, and motivation toward language. It may affect his attentiveness, regardless of what is happening while he is attending. It seems to me that some global effect such as this, ill-defined as it is, is necessary to explain the role of the Jewish tradition in consistently producing an impact in the direction of superiority in verbal development. (See Lee, 1960, for a description of this subculture.) At the opposite extreme is the isolated and hopeless situation of many mothers on Aid to Dependent Children, where "the reduction of absolute power undercuts the motivation for protracted verbal exploration of action possibilities" (Strodtbeck, 1965, p. 108).

Studies of infant vocal behavior have been widely cited in support of reinforcement theories of language learning. Detailed comparisons have been made of caretaking activities of parents in homes and of adults in institutions (Rheingold, 1960, 1961; Provence and Lipton, 1962). There is notably more talking to the infants at home—five to nine times as much, according to Rheingold's time-sampling data. There is likewise more vocalizing by the infants themselves. Experimental studies with infants—such as those of Rheingold, Gewirtz, and Ross (1959) and Weissberg's (1963) carefully controlled follow-up study—offer convincing evidence that reinforcement rather than stimulation is operating. But it is questionable whether any results should be generalized across the discontinuity which separates pre-linguistic babbling from true verbal behavior.

Irwin's (1960) experimental study with slightly older children has been widely cited in support of the value of added stimulation. He induced working-class mothers to read to their children for 20 minutes a day from the time the children were 13 months until they were 30 months old. The result was a significant increase in production of speech sounds, both in tokens and in types. Irwin interpreted this result as a response to the systematic increase in the "speech sound stimulation" (1960, p. 189). While reading could indeed have provided an increased quantity of stimulation alone, it is possible and even likely that in the course of reading the mothers also responded to the vocalizations of the child which the reading may have prompted. Moreover, we do not know how this induced attention to the behavior of her child may have affected the mother's response to him during all the non-reading parts of the day. Once a child has started to speak, it is not feasible to withhold response even for experimental purposes. Consequently, the effects of exposing a child to language and of responding to his language become confounded.

It is commonly assumed (e.g., Ausubel, 1964; Bloom, Davis, and Hess, 1965) that where language has developed well something termed "corrective feedback" has been in ample supply. For this to exist, the child must make errors and the adults must recognize those errors. Parents do seem to correct errors in naming, e.g., of *cat* for *dog*, and feedback may be very important for the learning of vocabulary. But errors of a non-referential nature seem to be largely ignored.

Miller and Ervin-Tripp (1964, p. 26) give this summary of errors in the speech of two-year-old and three-year-old children:

> Most of the mistakes or deviations from the model can be classified as omissions (*I'll turn water off* for *I'll turn the water off*), overgeneralization of morphophonemic combinations (*foots* for *feet, a owl* for *an owl, breaked* for *broke*), the incorrect use of a function word with a subclass of a lexical class (using *a* with mass nouns and proper nouns), or doubly marked forms (adding the possessive suffix to a possessive pronoun, *mine's*).

While no frequency counts are yet available, it is safe to say that except for the category of omissions the proportion of errors in the young child's speech is remarkably small. Furthermore, it is my impression that adults without special training do not "hear" such errors even when they are made. Persons trained to be attentive often cannot catch them except under special conditions, such as repeating tape recordings at half-speed. Ordinarily, we hear what we expect to hear— normal English speech. Not surprisingly, R. Brown and his colleagues (conference discussion in Cofer and Musgrave, 1963, p. 203) found "little correction of children's speech by their parents." Furthermore, there is no evidence that the non-verbal responses of adults match in any way the degree of the child's approximation to the adult model.

Sentences containing errors of omission are one exception to the generalization that errors of a non-referential nature are largely ignored. Such sentences constitute the typical "telegraphic speech" of the young child (Brown and Bellugi, 1964; Brown and Fraser, 1964), and a gradual filling in of the omitted morphemes is the most prominent change characterizing the child's acquisition of grammar. From transcriptions of the speech of two children with their respective graduate student parents, Brown and his colleagues discovered that to the child's telegraphic utterance, e.g., *Mommy lunch*, the parent often responds with the nearest complete sentence appropriate to the particular situation, e.g., *Mommy is having her lunch*. To the content words of nouns, verbs or adjectives in the child's speech, the parent adds mainly the functors: auxiliaries, prepositions, articles, pronouns, and inflections.

Expansions seem to constitute perfect examples of feedback. In fact, they constitute the one category of adult responses where the nature of the assistance to the child can be specified. Again, to quote Brown and Bellugi (1964, p. 143):

> By adding something to the words the child has just produced one confirms his response insofar as it is appropriate. In addition, one takes him somewhat beyond that response but not greatly beyond it. One encodes additional meanings at a moment when he is most likely to be attending to the cues that can teach that meaning.

In discussing the optimal sequencing of stimuli, I suggested that if it does occur in the language learning process it must occur fortuitously. Expansions, by their very nature, provide such sequencing. No one has suggested that parents expand with any conscious tutorial intention. It seems simply to be one spontaneous way of keeping the conversation with a young child going.

Discovery of the category of expansions make possible a new attempt to separate the effects of exposure and contingent response. At first it seemed this might be possible even in natural observations, and that it would therefore be informative to compare the emergence in the child of grammatical constructions heard in the adult's non-expanding speech with those appearing in the adult's expansion of the child's telegraphic utterances. Brown[4] found that for his two subjects the order of emergence of some 40 different grammatical constructions can be well predicted (rank order correlation near .80) by the frequency with which the same constructions are used by the mothers. But the constructions more often used in the parents' non-expanding speech were also the ones more often expanded. The confounding of the two variables was still present.

Part of the present writer's own research (Cazden, 1965) was an experiment designed to separate adult expansions from adult modeling of well-formed sentences. The subjects were 12 Negro children, 28–38 months old, attending an urban day-care center. One group (expansion) received 40 minutes a day of intensive and deliberate expansions; another group (modeling) received 30 minutes a day of exposure to an equal number of well-formed sentences which deliberately were not expansions. One of two tutors, trained for the research, talked with each child in these two groups in an individual play session every school day for three months. A third group (control) received no special treatment. Six measures of language development were used, one being a structured sentence imitation test. The other five were measures of spontaneous speech—mean length of utterance, complexity measures of noun and verb phrases, percentage of copulas supplied, and percentage of sentences which included both subject and predicate.

Contrary to predictions, the children who received the non-expanding language stimulation gained the most. One possible explanation is that as the concentration of expansions goes up, in this case far above that occurring in natural conversation, the richness of the verbal stimulation goes down. By definition, expansions are contingent on the child's speech, in content as well as in timing. To the extent that they are pure expansions, just filling in the child's telegraphic utterance to make it a complete one, they will have less variety of vocabulary and grammatical patterns than the adult's non-expanding speech normally contains.

In summary, a tentative resolution of the stimulation-reinforcement controversy can be suggested. Reinforcement, in the classical sense, probably operates to increase vocalizations at the babbling stage of infancy. But once true language begins to develop there is no clear evidence that any specific kind of adult response, verbal or non-verbal, aids the child's progress. Natural observations and the few existing manipulative studies are consistent with the hypothesis that it is the amount and richness of language stimulation available in the context of face-to-face interaction which is most important. Differential access to such stimulation by children from different subcultural groups can be explained by differences in the conditions of their lives, as outlined above under "Context."

[4] R. Brown. Unpublished memorandum, 1964.

Developmental Scales

There is general hope that current research on the acquisition of language[5] will eventually make possible developmental scales which will be more valid measures than mean sentence length (Carroll, 1961). Little consideration has thus far been given to problems which dialect differences pose in establishing such scales. Ervin-Tripp and Miller (1963, p. 126) recognize the problem: "Adult usage differs in the various subcultures of any community. A good developmental measure for general use should include only those features common to all adult speech in the presence of children." The author faced this problem in the research reported above (Cazden, 1965). I needed to measure the grammatical development of working-class Negro children, but had to devise scales from data on the language of two children from graduate-student families. Because that experience suggests that the problems posed by dialect differences will not be easily solved, it will be recounted in some detail.

The grammatical structure of child speech can be scaled along at least three dimensions—developmental sequence, structural complexity, and conformity to Standard English. Complexity undoubtedly influences the sequence of emergence but is not in any one-to-one correspondence with it.

Two examples may clarify this point. Brown and Bellugi (1964) have studied the development of the noun phrase. They found that in the first stage any modifier was used with any noun. When the differentiation process began, articles were separated out of the class of modifiers. The children said *A blue flower* but not *Blue a flower*. Only later did they use two modifiers other than articles before a noun (*My blue flower*). Therefore, on a weighted index, *Flower, Nice flower, A blue flower*, and *My blue flower* may be scored from 1 to 4, respectively. There is no objective difference in complexity which dictates this separation of articles from other modifiers. *A blue flower* and *My blue flower* each contain three units in a common pattern. Yet the developmental sequence is clear.

Verb forms present a contrasting case. The sequence of *I drop, I dropping*, and *I'm dropping* represents both increasing complexity and sequence of emergence, and the forms may be accordingly scored 1, 2 and 3, respectively. But what of the past tense *dropped*? On the basis of complexity it should be grouped with *dropping*, as a verb plus one additional element, but its period of emergence is definitely later. If we knew exactly when it appeared in relation to other forms, it could be

[5] See Bellugi and Brown (1964) for a report on current research in this area.

scored accordingly. Since we don't know, the decision has to be made on grounds of complexity: *dropped* thus receives 2 points.

Conformity to Standard English is another possible criterion—one I deliberately did not apply. Thus *a trees* and *a coffee* were each given full credit on the noun-phrase index. But conformity did intrude. Sometimes deviations from Standard English left the meaning ambiguous. If the child said *Her go upstairs*, clearly *her* was being used in the subject position. But if the child said *He wet him bed*, it was not equally clear whether *him* was being used as a possessive pronoun. Sometimes nonstandard forms raised problems in scoring even when the meaning was clear. The children in my sample often used an auxiliary with an unmodified verb, such as *He's go* or *I'm put*. These patterns hadn't been anticipated, since they had not appeared in Brown and Bellugi's data. Strictly on a criterion of complexity, *I'm put* would be counted as two verb elements, along with the more familiar *He going* or *I putting*. Dialect differences also made it impossible to measure the use of negation. Basis for such an analysis had been provided by Bellugi's (1966) study of the sequence of emergence of particular negative forms, but many of the utterances of the subjects in my study could not be placed on Bellugi's scale. First, the frequent use of *got* and *ain't got* produced a construction where the negation appeared after the verb, as in *I got no crayons*. Second, multiple negatives (*I not kiss no people*) were more frequent and seemed to appear at earlier stages than in Bellugi's data. In the end, I gave up the attempt to do this analysis.

I have already suggested that, ideally, a child's language development should be evaluated in terms of his progress toward the norms for his particular speech community. My reliance on complexity more than on developmental sequence as a criterion for evaluation helped make possible the transfer from one dialect to another. A scale which accepts alternate forms of the complexity on which it is based can be applied cross-culturally more appropriately than one based on sequence of emergence. Though the latter is otherwise the superior criterion, it is more likely to penalize departures from a preconceived norm. This issue of "dialect-fair" scales of language development may become as significant in the future as that of "culture-fair" tests of intelligence has been in the past.

Different Modes of Communication

To view the language of subcultural groups as different modes of communication, it is necessary to go beyond the structured system of symbols and the rate at which parts of that system are learned to the

functions the language serves in actual verbal behavior. This requirement is one version of the contrast between language and speech, which
is at once so important and subject to many interpretations.

The two main categories of language functions are, as Carroll (1964,
p. 4) has stated them, "(1) as a system of responses by which individuals
communicate with each other (inter-individual communication); and
(2) as a system of responses that facilitates thinking and action for the
individual (intra-individual communication)." In this paper I use the term
"mode of communication" to refer to both subsystems of language functioning, which are somehow intimately related. I say "somehow related"
because we do not know how overt speech becomes internalized into
covert thought, particularly in the case of the growing child (John,
1964). Of great importance for the study of subcultural differences in
child language, we don't know how variation in the use of language for
inter-individual communication affects its use as an intra-individual cognitive tool. For reasons that have to do with the intellectual history of the
behavioral sciences,[6] the two functions of language have been studied in
separation. One reason for subsuming my discussion under one term,
"different modes of communication," is to emphasize the importance
of their relationship.

Inter-individual Communication

A statement by Hymes (1961, p. 57) is immediately pertinent here:

> In a society, speech as an activity is not a simple function of the
> structure and meanings of the language or languages involved. Nor is
> speech activity random. Like the languages, it is patterned, governed by
> rules; and this patterning also must be learned by linguistically normal
> participants in the society. Moreover, the patterning of speech activity
> is not the same from society to society, or from group to group within
> societies such as our own.

How speech activity is patterned is the focus of a new inter-disciplinary
study, the ethnography of communication. More recent publications by
Hymes offer both an overview of the field (Hymes, 1964b) and a
provocative discussion of the inadequacies of the description given by
the transformational linguists of the capabilities of language users (Hymes,
1964a). Overlapping with an ethnography of communication, but not
confined to naturalistic observations, is another inter-disciplinary field,
socio-linguistics (see Ervin-Tripp, 1964). Both deal with the questions of
who says what to whom, how, and in what situations.

Studies of subcultural differences in inter-individual communication have been carried out by Bossard (1954), Schatzman and Strauss

---

[6] In this regard, see Hymes (1963) for the viewpoint of those in the field
of linguistics, and Cronbach (1957) for those in psychology.

(1955), Bernstein (1959, 1960, 1961, 1962*a*, 1962*b*), Loban (1963), and Lawton (1964). (The work of Hess and his colleagues will be considered in the next section.) These studies are quite different, and the story of their work will not be a connected one. But each raises interesting issues for further exploration.

Bossard (1954) was a pioneer in what used to be called "the sociology of language." He analyzed the mealtime conversations of 35 families and found differences in amount of talk per unit of time, in range of vocabulary, in the use of imagery, in the extent to which children were interrupted, and in whether the talk was child- or adult-centered—with social class "the most important line of cleavage in our language records" (pp. 190–191). Studies by Milner (1951) and Keller (1963), previously cited, found that lower-class children are more apt to eat alone or with siblings, and less apt to eat with adults, than middle-class children. What Bossard's work indicates is that children not only participate in different speech situations, but that even where the situation is a common one, family mealtime conversations, the patterns of speech activity vary along social-class lines.

The study by Schatzman and Strauss (1955) is included here even though the subjects were adults, because it raised important questions about inter-group versus intra-group communication. Twenty subjects, 10 upper-status and 10 lower-status individuals selected from the extremes of income and education, were interviewed in a small Arkansas town after a tornado. The authors summarize the difference in the resulting narratives of members of the two groups:

> The difference is a considerable disparity in (a) the number and kinds of perspectives utilized in communication; (b) the abilty to take the listener's role; (c) the handling of classification; and (d) the framework and stylistic devices which order and implement the communication (p. 329).

In analyzing these differences, Schatzman and Strauss express two different ideas. On the one hand, they say that the upper-status subject is better able to make his meaning explicit because he has been more often in situations where this is necessary, whereas the lower-status subject is accustomed to talking about his experiences only with people with whom he shares a great deal of previous experience and symbolism. By this view, the experience of the upper-status speaker has taught him how to encode more information. Yet, on the other hand, the authors also seem to assert that the important variable is not how much information the speaker has encoded, but the extent to which communication of it from speaker to listener may be impeded by "differential rules for the ordering of speech and thought" (p. 329). These rules, describing the structure of speech, are independent of those describing the structure of language, referred to earlier in the discussion of dialects. Subcultural differences in both kinds of rules may have been tapped in Cherry's (1965) study of communication in the classroom.

Bernstein's work in Great Britain is cited in virtually every discussion of the influence of subcultural differences—in this case, social class— on language and cognition. It is cited, but rarely is it subjected to the analysis it deserves. He set out "to find a way of analyzing some of the interrelationships between social structure, language use, and subsequent behavior" (Bernstein, 1962a, p. 31). He postulated the existence of two codes, restricted and elaborated. These are defined in terms "of the probability of predicting which structural elements will be selected for the organization of meaning"—highly predictable in the first case, much less so in the second. Further, the first is considered to facilitate "verbal elaboration of intent," the second to limit "verbal explication of intent" (Bernstein, 1962b, p. 233).

So far, he has reported one experiment testing three hypotheses related to these codes: that they can be distinguished, that their use is associated with social class, and that their use is independent of measured intelligence. For a non-linguistic measure of the verbal planning functions associated with speech, he drew on Goldman-Eisler's (1958) research on the nature of hesitation phenomena. Goldman-Eisler differentiates between two kinds of gaps in the continuity of speech-production: breathing, related to the motor dimension; and hesitations or pauses, related to the symbolic dimension. Measuring the frequency and duration of pauses, she found that they anticipated a sudden increase in information as measured by transitional probabilities:

> Fluent speech was shown to consist of habitual combinations of words such as were shared by the language community and such as had become more or less automatic. Where a sequence ceased to be a matter of common conditioning or learning, where a speaker's choice was highly individual and unexpected, on the other hand, speech was hesitant (1958, p. 67).

Using Goldman-Eisler's procedures, Bernstein analyzed the verbal behavior of a group of 16-year-old boys. From 61 lower-status messenger boys and 45 (British) "public school" boys he selected five subgroups of 4 or 5 boys each, arranged so that their speech patterns could be compared while holding social class or verbal and non-verbal intelligence constant. An unstructured discussion of capital punishment was held with each subgroup, with only one special provision: "It was thought the working-class group would find the test situation threatening and that this would interfere with the speech and consequently all working-class groups had two practice sessions (one a week) before the test discussion" (1962*a*, p. 37). Analysis of the recorded group discussions confirmed all three of his hypotheses in regard to the "codes."

Bernstein (1962*b*) acknowledges the limitations of a small sample and a discussion topic which may not have had the same significance for the two social-class groups. But he has not raised the question of the possible effect of the two practice sessions on the fluency of the working-class speech. Fluency, as measured by the hesitation phenomena, was taken as the operational definition of predictability, and that in turn was the defining attribute of the restricted code. Any influence of the practice sessions would have been in the direction of greater fluency. But sound research procedures requires that bias, if unavoidable, should work against one's hypothesis, not for it. The experiment has since been replicated by Lawton (1964)—but the analysis of the hesitation phenomena is not yet available and he does not indicate whether he repeated the practice sessions for the working-class group.

Of greater importance is that Bernstein's theory reaches beyond verbal behavior to cognitive functioning in general. He believes that differences in the habitual modes of speech arise out of "a different way of organizing and responding to experience" (1959, p. 312), and that they accordingly "create and reinforce in the user different dimensions of significance" (1960, p. 276). In other words, speech is seen as both effect and cause: "In some way the form of the social relationship acts selectively on the speech possibilities of the individual, and again in some way these possibilities constrain behavior" (1962*a*, p. 31). Further, he believes that the nature of the restricted code has far-reaching implications for the behavior of its speakers: a low level of conceptualization, a disinterest in process, a preference for inclusive social relationships and group solidarity, and socially induced conservatism and acceptance of authority (1961, pp. 300–303).

With these last assertions we are right in the middle of the well-argued controversy over the Whorf hypothesis that language conditions our perceptions of and responses to the environment. Bernstein's version of that hypothesis may be a particularly interesting one. Whorf was interested in the influence of the structure of language, whereas Bernstein is interested in the influence of the structure of speech activity Hymes (1964*b*, p. 20) suggests that the latter is the more fundamental question: "What chance the language has to make an impress upon individuals and behavior will depend upon the degree and pattern of its admission into communicative events." But Bernstein's formulation is a hypothesis, nonetheless.

It is not possible to review here the arguments for and against the strong ("language determines") and the weak ("language predisposes") versions of the Whorf hypothesis. It is sufficient to report the wide-spread agreement that evidence of differences in language, no matter how extreme, cannot be used both to suggest and to prove differences in feeling, thought, or other non-verbal behavior. The claimed effects of language or speech differences on ways of perceiving or responding must be demonstrated and not merely assumed, and their proof must involve independent measures of linguistic and non-linguistic behavior (Carroll, 1958). Since all of Bernstein's data deal with speech, there is so far no supporting evidence for the broader implications of the differences he reports.

Bernstein is dealing with a topic of great interest today, and he has engaged in theory construction in a field where theory is sorely needed. The danger is that those reading the widespread references to his work may take his assertions as proven fact, rather than as hypotheses to be tested. The result could be a stereotype of working-class children and adults as unfortunate as the now-discredited stereotype of limited genetic potential. Schorr (1964, p. 911) retells a poignant admission by sociologists that, "according to all that they knew of it, the [civil rights] sit-in movement should never have happened." At least sociologists were in no position to make their erroneous prediction come true. But educators are among the readers of the frequent references to Bernstein's work, and through them the danger of a self-fulfilling prophecy is a real one.

One other point merits examination before leaving Bernstein's work. Earlier, I mentioned that he found a social-class difference in the use of what he calls "egocentric" and "sociocentric" sequences. The former refers to the sequence *I think*, which is more used by middle-class speakers. The latter refers to terminal sequences such as *isn't it, you know, ain't it, wouldn't he*—"sympathy circularity sequences" (1962*b*, p. 223)—used more by lower-class speakers. Bernstein considers both egocentric and sociocentric sequences to be ways of dealing with uncertainty, with quite different results. For example, he has stated (1962*b*, p. 237):

> Inasmuch as the S.C. [sociocentric] sequences . . . invite implicit affirmation of the previous sequence, then they tend to close communication in a particular area rather than to facilitate its development and elaboration. . . . The "I think" sequence, on the other hand, allows the listener far more degrees of freedom and may be regarded as an invitation . . . to develop the communication on his own terms.

His interpretation of the function of these two modes of communication contrasts with one of Loban's findings. Loban (1963, pp. 53–54) has reported:

> Those subjects who proved to have the greatest power over language by every measure that could be applied . . . were *the subjects*

who most frequently used language to express tentativeness. . . . These
most capable speakers often use such expressions as the following:

> It might be a gopher, but I'm not sure.
> That, I think, is in Africa.
> I'm not exactly sure where that is.

The child with less power over language appears to be less flexible
in his thinking, is not often capable of seeing more than one alternative,
and apparently summons up all his linguistic resources merely to make
a flat dogmatic statement.

Remembering that his high language group was also higher in socio-
economic status, we see that Loban, in a study of elementary school
children in California, and Bernstein, in a study of adolescents in
England, both found that higher-status subjects say *I think* more than
lower-status subjects do. What is striking is the ease with which two
interpretations are placed on the common finding. Bernstein contrasts
I think with *ain't it*, and finds an egocentric-sociocentric contrast. Loban
groups *I think* with *I'm not exactly sure* as examples of cognitive
flexibility.

Intra-individual Communication

The use of language as a cognitive tool for intra-individual communication places its own demands on some special set of inner resources.
Jensen (1966) sees it as depending on the existence within the individual of a hierarchical verbal network "which environmental stimuli,
both verbal and non-verbal, enter [into] and ramify. . . . A great deal
of what we think of as intelligence, or as verbal ability, or learning
ability, can be thought of in terms of the extensiveness and complexity
of this verbal network and of the strength of the interconnections between its elements." There are at least two variables here: the number of
elements and the quality (which could be further subdivided at least
into complexity and strength) of their connections. In discussing measures of vocabulary, I reported studies which found subcultural differences
in the repertoire of words or grammatical patterns available or used. A
repertoire can be defined by a list and is synonymous with the number of
elements in the network. But network has a second attribute which
repertoire does not—the structure or relations of its parts. We know
little about subcultural differences in the use of this verbal network in
purely mediational, covert ways, because few experimental psychologists have been interested in individual differences, much less group
differences, among their subjects.

The work of Jensen, (1963*a*, 1963*b*, 1966) indicates important directions for such research. He reports an experiment (Jensen, 1963*a*) in

which gifted, average, and retarded junior high school students, predominantly middle-class, were presented with a multiple stimulus-response problem. On the first presentation of 200 trials, only students in the gifted and average groups gave evidence of learning. Students in the retarded group were given additional trials on subsequent days until their performance also rose above the chance level of correct response. Each day a new procedure was used: first verbal reinforcement by the experimenter, then stimulus naming by subject prior to responding, stimulus naming while learning, and last, enforced delay of response following reinforcement. All three groups were then tested on a similar but harder task. Here the groups still differed significantly, but the retarded group showed marked improvement. An unusual feature of the data was that the retarded group, while as homogeneous in I.Q. as the other two groups, was far more heterogeneous in learning ability. The Mexican-American children, who constituted one-third of the retarded group, were significantly lower than the rest of that group on the first test but then improved markedly.

In discussing these results, Jensen (1963*a*, p. 138) suggests:

> The normal and fast learners in the retarded group are not really retarded in a primary sense, but are children who, at some crucial period in their development, have failed to learn the kinds of behavior which are necessary as a basis for school learning. . . . The habit of making verbal responses, either overtly or covertly, to events in the environment seems to be one of the major ingredients of the kind of intelligence that shows itself in school achievement and on performance on intelligence tests. Without this habit, even a child with a perfectly normal nervous system in terms of fundamental learning ability will appear to be retarded, and indeed is retarded so long as he does not use verbal mediators in learning. Some of the fastest learners among our retarded group, for example, were those who showed no appreciable learning until they were required to make verbal responses to the stimuli.

Jensen (1963*b*) also reports an experiment by Jacqueline Rapier in which Mexican-American children who were taught verbal mediating links spontaneously used them to form new associations. He suggests that comparisons of the amount of gain in learning ability from such instruction can be used to separate retardation due to neurological causes from retardation due to a verbally impoverished environment. In addition, he gives (Jensen, 1966) extensive proposals for further research.

We do, however, know something about group differences in characteristics of the verbal network. Three studies are available on subcultural differences in word-association responses. In one dating back almost half a century, Mitchell, Rosanoff, and Rosanoff (1919) found that Negro children, ages 4–15, from New York City were less apt to give a common specific reaction (e.g., *chair* to the stimulus *table*) than white children of the same age, and correspondingly more apt to give idiosyncratic reactions. Since commonality of response increases with age, the authors concluded that the Negro children were developmentally immature. The other two studies, both current, deal with another trend in word-association responses. This developmental trend, related to increasing commonality, is the shift from syntagmatic responses (*deep . . . hole*) to paradigmatic responses (*deep . . . shallow*). In an all-Negro sample of first- and fifth-grade children, John (1963) found significant social-class differences only in the first-grade latency scores. Entwisle (1966) also found very slight social-class differences between high-status and low-status urban Maryland elementary school children, matched for I.Q., but some retardation for rural Maryland children at the lower I.Q. levels, and further retardation in an Amish group. Recent evidence thus shows that status differences are less dramatic for word-association measures than for other measures of verbal ability, and that those differences decrease, rather than increase, with age. The tendency to give common and paradigmatic responses reaches an asymptote during the age range being studied, and the initially retarded children do catch up.

Vocabulary tests indicate whether certain items are part of a person's verbal network and thereby provide estimates of its total size. They can, if the definitions are scaled, provide additional information on network structure. Carson and Rabin (1960) matched three groups of fourth- to sixth-graders—Northern White, Northern Negro, and Southern Negro (recent in-migrants)—on the Full Range Picture Vocabulary Test. They then administered the same test as a word vocabulary test and grouped the definition into six levels. For example, the six levels for *wagon* could be: (1) *a vehicle*—categorization; (2) *a cart*—synonym; (3) *a wooden thing with four wheels*—essential description; (4) *you ride in it out West*—essential function; (5) *it bumps into people*—vague description or function; and (6) complete error. Even though the groups were matched when the task required only finding a picture to match a word, the Northern White children gave significantly more definitions from levels 1–3 and the Southern Negro children least.

Spain (1962) analyzed definitions given by "deprived" and "non-deprived" elementary school children in central Tennessee. Ten stimulus words were carefully selected to insure that both the word and its superordinate (e.g., *bread* and *food*) were of high frequency and familiar to local first-graders. Definitions were categorized as generic (superordinate), descriptive, and functional. He found that functional definitions remained the predominant response for the deprived children at all age levels; descriptive definitions increased with age at a rate similar for both groups; and that generic definitions increased most sharply for the non-deprived, while the deprived group showed a 4-year lag in this mode of response by the end of elementary school.

The use of language in relation to cognition can also be tapped by categorizing tasks. In general, status differences on such measures increase with age (e.g., see John, 1963). But here the line between studies of language and studies of concept formation disappears, and the limitations of this paper preclude a proper review of such research.

Nevertheless, mention must be made of the large-scale project of Hess and his associates at the University of Chicago, reports of which are now beginning to appear in the published literature (Hess and Shipman, 1965*a*, 1965*b*). This is a particularly important study because it relates intra-individual and inter-individual modes of communication. It has been planned as a test of the Bernstein hypothesis of a relation between the child's cognitive development and the mother's verbal ability, maternal teaching style, and characteristic mode of family control. In all, 160 Negro mothers from four socio-economic levels were interviewed, tested, and brought to the university for a structured session of mother-child interaction. Each mother was taught three tasks—two sorting tasks and the use of an Etch-a-Sketch board—and then asked to teach those tasks to her four-year-old child. Her maternal teaching style was monitored and analyzed. The children were subsequently tested by being asked to sort new material and give a verbal explanation. (See Bing, 1963, for similar use of an experimental teaching situation to study mother-child interaction.)

Preliminary results indicate that, while there were no social-class differences in affective elements of the interaction or in persistence of the mothers or in cooperation of the children, on at least some of the performance measures social-class differences were in the direction expected. Hess and Shipman (1965*a*, p. 192) have reported:

> Children from middle-class homes ranked above children from the lower socio-economic levels in performance on these sorting tasks, particularly in offering verbal explanations as to the basis of sorting. These differences clearly paralleled the relative abilities and teaching skills of the mothers from the different groups.

Additional information on a subset of this sample is available in Stodolsky's (1965) doctoral research. One year after the original data had been collected, she administered the Peabody Picture Vocabulary Test and Kohlberg's Concept Sorting Test to 56 of the original 160 children from three of the four socio-economic groups. The children's scores were then correlated with a selected set of maternal variables from the previous year to find the best predictors. She found that there were significant social-class differences in the vocabulary scores of the children, and that a set of maternal variables predicted those scores with a multiple correlation of .68. The best single pair of maternal variables, in this respect, proved to be the mother's score on the vocabulary part of the W.A.I.S. and one of the indices of teaching style. The latter was the "discrimination index" that measures the extent to which the mother isolates task-specific qualities of the environment. While scores on the W.A.I.S. differentiated among the mothers on social-class lines, scores on the discrimination index did not. In other words, there is an interaction between characteristics that are class-linked and those that are not.

The entire Hess project is planned to continue until the children have completed four grades of school, with further data being collected on both the mothers and children. Hopefully, analysis of all the data will proceed beyond a test of the Bernstein hypothesis to provide a differentiated picture of how the maternal variables interact in affecting the verbal and cognitive behaviors of the child.

Summing Up

In conclusion, the relative space devoted to the three main divisions of this paper is a rough guide to the extent of our present knowledge. We know little about dialect differences as yet; but we should learn much, about urban Negro speech in particular, from the contrastive studies in progress. Relatively, we know the most about language development. Here the evidence of retardation among lower-class children is extensive, and future work will probably concentrate on more precise analysis of the process variables that mediate this relationship. We know very little about differences in language function. Basic research is needed in this area on ways of categorizing the functions that language serves in natural speech communities, and on ways of analyzing the mediational use of language as well.

At the present time, we cannot completely resolve the difference-deficiency issue on which this review has focused. Children who are socially disadvantaged on such objective criteria as income and educational level of their parents do tend to be deficient on many measures of verbal skills. But the concept of subcultural relativity is nevertheless relevant. We must be sure that developmental scales of language development do not distort our assessment of children who speak a nonstandard dialect. We must be equally sure that studies of language function do not simply reflect the predilection of the investigators. In short, subcultural relativity provides an essential perspective for objective analysis and for any program of planned change. Unfortunately, when pressure for change is great, the danger exists that such perspective may be discarded just when we need it most.

References

Anastasi, Anne, and Cruz De Jesús. 1953. Language development and non-verbal I.Q. of Puerto Rican children in New York City. *J. abnorm. soc. Psychol.*, 1953, **48**, pp. 357–366.

Ausubel, D. P. 1964. How reversible are the cognitive and motivational effects of cultural deprivation? Implications for teaching the culturally deprived child. *Urban Educ.*, **1**, pp. 16–38.

Bellugi, Ursula. 1966. A transformational analysis of the development of negation. In T. Bever and W. Weksel (eds.), *Psycholinguistic studies: experimental investigations of syntax* (New York: Holt, Rinehart and Winston, Inc.).

————, and R. Brown (eds.). 1964. The acquisition of language. *Monogr. Soc. Res. Child Develpm.*, **29**, No. 1, Serial No. 92.

Bernstein, B. 1962a. Linguistic codes, hesitation phenomena and intelligence. *Lang. & Speech*, **5**, pp. 31–46.

————. 1962b. Social class, linguistic codes and grammatical elements. *Lang. & Speech*, **5**, pp. 221–240.

————. 1961. Social class and linguistic development: a theory of social learning. In A. H. Halsey, Jean Floud, and C. A. Anderson (eds.), *Education, economy and society* (New York: The Free Press), pp. 288–314.

————. 1960. Language and social class. *Brit. J. Sociol.*, **11**, pp. 271–276.

————. 1959. A public language: some sociological implications of a linguistic form. *Brit. J. Sociol.*, **10**, pp. 311–326.

Bing, Elizabeth. 1963. Effect of child-rearing practices on the development of differential cognitive abilities. *Child Develpm.*, **34**, pp. 631–648.

Bloom, B. S. 1964. *Stability and change in human characteristics* (New York: John Wiley & Sons, Inc.).

————, A. Davis, and R. Hess. 1965. *Compensatory education for cultural deprivation* (New York: Holt, Rinehart and Winston, Inc.).

Bossard, J. H. S. 1954. *The sociology of child development*. Second ed. (New York: Harper & Row).

Brown, R., and Ursula Bellugi. 1964. Three processes in the child's acquisition of syntax. *Harvard educ. Rev.*, **34**, pp. 43–79.

————, and C. Fraser. 1964. The acquisition of syntax. In Ursula Bellugi and R. Brown (eds.), The acquisition of language. *Monogr. Soc. Res. Child Develpm.*, **29**, No. 1, Serial No. 92, pp. 43–79.

Carroll, J. B. 1964. *Language and thought* (Englewood Cliffs, N.J.: Prentice-Hall, Inc.).

————. 1961. Language development in children. In S. Saporta (ed.),

Psycholinguistics: a book of readings (New York: Holt, Rinehart and Winston, Inc.), pp. 331–345.

————. 1958. Some psychological effects of language structure. In P. Jock and J. Zubin (eds.), *Psychopathology of communication* (Boston: Ginn & Company), pp. 28–36.

————. 1939. Determining and numerating adjectives in children's speech. *Child Develpm.*, **10**, pp. 215–229.

Carson, A. S., and A. I. Rabin. 1960. Verbal comprehension and communication in Negro and white children. *J. educ. Psychol.*, **51**, pp. 47–51.

Cazden, Courtney B. 1965. *Environmental assistance to the child's acquisition of grammar* (Cambridge, Mass.: Harvard University). Unpublished doctoral dissertation.

Center for Applied Linguistics. 1965. *Urban language study: District of Columbia proposal* (Washington, D.C.: The Center).

Cherry, Estelle. 1965. Children's comprehension of teacher and peer speech. *Child Develpm.*, **36**, pp. 467–480.

Cofer, C. N., and Barbara Musgrave (eds.) 1963. *Verbal behavior and learning* (New York: McGraw-Hill, Inc.).

Cohn, W. 1959. On the language of lower-class children. *School Rev.*, **67**, pp. 435–440.

Cronbach, L. J. 1957. The two disciplines of scientific psychology. *Amer. Psychologist*, **12**, pp. 671–684.

Davé, R. H. 1963. *The identification and measurement of environmental process variables that are related to educational achievement.* (Chicago, Ill.: University of Chicago). Unpublished doctoral dissertation.

Davis, A. L., and R. I. McDavid, Jr. 1964. A description of the Chicago speech survey: communication barriers to the culturally deprived. *Project Literacy Reports*, No. 2 (Ithaca, N.Y.: Cornell University), pp. 23–25.

Deutsch, M. 1963. The disadvantaged child and the learning process. In A. H. Passow (ed.), *Education in depressed areas* (New York: Teachers College, Columbia University), pp. 163–179.

————, and B. Brown. 1964. Social influences in Negro-white intelligence differences. *J. soc. Issues*, **20**, pp. 67–84.

Eells, K., A. Davis, R. J. Havighurst, V. E. Herrick, and R. W. Tyler. 1951. *Intelligence and cultural differences* (Chicago, Ill.: University of Chicago Press).

Entwisle, Doris R. 1966. Developmental socio-linguistics: a comparative study in four subcultural settings. *Sociometry*, **29**, pp. 67–84.

Ervin-Tripp, Susan. 1964. An analysis of the interaction of language, topic and listener. In J. J. Gumperz and D. Hymes (eds.), *The* ethnography of communication. *Amer. Anthrop.*, **66**, No. 6, Part 2, pp. 86–102.

———. 1964. Imitation and structural change in children's language. In E. Lenneberg (ed.), *New directions in the study of language* (Cambridge, Mass.: M.I.T. Press), pp. 163–189.

———, and W. R. Miller. 1963. Language development. In H. W. Stevenson (ed.) Child psychology. *Yrbk. Nat. Soc. Study Educ.*, **62**, Part I, pp. 108–143.

Fiske, D. W., and S. R. Maddi. 1961. *Functions of varied experience* (Homewood, Ill.: Dorsey Press).

Fodor, J. A. (n.d.) *How to learn to talk: some simple ways.* Unpublished manuscript.

Frake, C. O. 1961. The diagnosis of disease among the Subanun of Mindanao. *Amer. Anthrop.*, **53**, pp. 113–132. In D. Hymes (ed.), *Language in culture and society* (New York: Harper & Row), pp. 193–211.

Fries, C. C. 1952. *The structure of English* (New York: Harcourt, Brace & World, Inc.).

———. 1940. *American English grammar* (New York: Appleton-Century-Crofts).

Goldman-Eisler, Frieda. 1958. Speech analysis and mental processes. *Lang. & Speech*, pp. 59–75.

Gray, Susan W., and R. A. Klaus. December 1964. *An experimental preschool program for culturally deprived children.* A paper read at the American Association for the Advancement of Science, Montreal.

Hess, R. D., and Virginia Shipman. 1965a. Early blocks to children's learning. *Children*, **12**, pp. 189–194.

———. 1965b. Early experience and socialization of cognitive modes in children. *Child Develpm.*, **36**, pp. 869–886.

Hockett, C. F. 1950. Age-grading and linguistic continuity. *Language*, **26**, pp. 449–457.

Hunt, J. McV. 1964. The psychological basis for using preschool enrichment as an antidote for cultural deprivation. *Merrill-Palmer Quart.*, **10**, pp. 209–248.

———. 1961. *Intelligence and experience* (New York: The Ronald Press Company).

Hymes, D. 1964a. Directions in (ethno-) linguistic theory. In A. K. Romney and R. G. D'Andrade (eds.), Transcultural studies in cognition. *Amer. Anthrop.*, **66**, No. 3, Part 2, pp. 6–56.

—. 1964b. Introduction: toward ethnographies of communication. In J. J. Gumperz and D. Hymes (eds.), The ethnography of communition. *Amer. Anthrop.*, **66**, No. 6, Part 2, pp. 1–34.

————. 1963. Notes toward a history of linguistic anthropology. *Anthrop. Linguistics*, **5**, pp. 59–103.

————. 1961. Functions of speech: an evolutionary approach. In F. C. Gruber (ed.) *Anthropology and education* (Philadelphia, Pa.: University of Pennsylvania Press), pp. 55–83.

Irwin, O. C. 1960. Infant speech: the effect of systematic reading of stories, *J. Sp. H. Res.*, **3**, pp. 187–190.

————. 1948*a*. Infant speech: the effect of family occupational status and of age on use of sound types. *J. Sp. H. Disord.*, **13**, pp. 224–226.

————. 1948*b*. Infant speech: the effect of family occupational status and of age on sound frequency. *J. Sp. H. Disord.*, **13**, pp. 320–323.

Jensen, A. R. (in press). Social class and verbal learning. In M. Deutsch, I. Katz, and A. R. Jensen (eds.), *Social class, race and psychological development* (New York: Holt, Rinehart and Winston, Inc.).

————. 1963*a*. Learning ability in retarded, average, and gifted children. *Merrill-Palmer Quart.*, **9**, pp. 123–140.

————. 1963*b*. Learning in the preschool years. *J. Nursery Educ.*, **18**, pp. 133–139.

Jespersen, O. 1964. *Mankind, nation, and individual from a linguistic point of view*. First ed., 1946 (Bloomington, Ind.: University of Indiana Press).

————. 1922. *Language: its nature, development and origin* (London: George Allen & Unwin, Ltd.).

John, Vera P. 1964. *Position paper on preschool programs*. Unpublished manuscript prepared for Commissioner Keppel (New York: Yeshiva University).

————. 1963. The intellectual development of slum children. *Amer. J. Orthopsychiat.*, **33**, pp. 813–822.

————, and L. S. Goldstein. 1964. The social context of language acquisition. *Merrill-Palmer Quart.*, **10**, pp. 265–275.

Katz, J. 1966. *The philosophy of language* (New York: Harper & Row).

Keller, Suzanne. 1963. The social word of the urban slum child: some early findings. *Amer. J. Orthopsychiat.*, **33**, pp. 823–831.

Klima, E. S. 1964. Relatedness between grammatical systems. *Language*, **40**, pp. 1–20.

Koch, Helen. 1954. The relation of "primary mental abilities" in five- and six-year-olds to sex of child and characteristics of his siblings. *Child Develpm.*, **25**, pp. 209–223.

Labov, W. 1965. Stages in the acquisition of Standard English. In R. W. Shuy (ed.), *Social dialects and language learning* (Champaign, Ill.: National Council of Teachers of English), pp. 77–103.

Lawton, D. 1964. Social class language differences in group discussions. *Lang. & Speech*, **7**, pp. 183–204.

Lee, Dorothy. 1960. Developing the drive to learn and the questioning mind. In A. Frazier (ed.), *Freeing capacity to learn* (Washington, D.C.: Association for Supervision and Curriculum Development), pp. 10–21.

Lenneberg, E. H. 1964. The capacity for language acquisition. In J. A. Fodor and J. J. Katz (eds.), *The structure of language: readings in the philosophy of language* (Englewood Cliffs, N.J.: Prentice-Hall, Inc.), pp. 579–603.

Lesser, G. S., G. Fifer, and D. H. Clark. 1965. Mental abilities of children in different social and cultural groups. *Monogr. Soc. Res. Child Develpm.*, **30**, No. 4, Serial No. 102.

Loban, W. D. 1963. *The language of elementary school children* (Champaign, Ill.: National Council of Teachers of English).

Lorge, I., and Jeanne Chall. 1963. Estimating the size of vocabularies of children and adults: an analysis of methodological issues. *J. exp. Educ.*, **32**, pp. 147–157.

McNeill, D. 1954. Developmental psycholinguistics. In G. Lindzey (ed.), *Handbook of social psychology* (Reading, Mass.: Addison-Wesley Publishing Company, Inc.).

Miller, W., and Susan Ervin-Tripp. 1964. The development of grammar in child language. In Ursula Bellugi and R. Brown (eds.), The acquisition of language. *Monogr. Soc. Res. Child Develpm.*, **29**, No. 1, Serial No. 92, pp. 9–34.

Milner, Esther. 1951. A study of the relationship between reading readiness in grade one school children and patterns of parent-child interaction. *Child Develpm.*, **22**, pp. 95–112.

Mitchell, I., Isabel R. Rosanoff, and A. J. Rosanoff. 1919. A study of association in Negro children. *Psychol. Rev.*, **26**, pp. 354–359.

Nida, E. A. 1958. Analysis of meaning and dictionary making. *Internat. J. Amer. Linguistics*, **24**, pp. 279–292.

Nisbet, J. 1961. Family environment and intelligence. In A. H. Halsey, Jean Floud, and C. A. Anderson (eds.), *Education, economy and society* (New York: The Free Press), pp. 273–287.

Pederson, L. A. 1964. Non-standard Negro speech in Chicago. In W. A. Stewart (ed.), *Non-standard speech and the teaching of English* (Washington, D.C.: Center for Applied Linguistics), pp. 16–23.

Provence, Sally, and Rose C. Lipton. 1962. *Infants in institutions* (New York: International Universities Press, Inc.).

Putnam, G. N. and Edna M. O'Hern. 1955. The status significance of an isolated urban dialect. Language dissertation No. 53, *Language*, **31**, No. 4, Whole Part 2.

Razran, G. 1961. The observable unconscious and the inferable conscious in current Soviet psychophysiology: interceptive conditioning, semantic conditioning, and the orienting reflex. *Psychol. Rev.*, **68**, pp. 81–147.

Rheingold, Harriet L. 1961. The effect of environmental stimulation upon social and exploratory behavior in the human infant. In B. M. Foss (ed.), *Determinants of infant behavior* (London: Methuen & Co., Ltd.), pp. 143–170.

———. 1960. The measurement of maternal care. *Child Develpm.*, **31**, pp. 565–575.

———, J. L. Gewirtz, and Helen W. Ross. 1959. Social conditioning of vocalizations in the infant. *J. comp. physiol. Psychol.*, **52**, pp. 68–73.

Rosenbaum, P. S. 1964. Prerequisites for linguistic studies on the effects of dialect differences on learning to read. *Project Literacy Reports*, No. 2 (Ithaca, N.Y.: Cornell University), pp. 26–30.

Schatzman, L., and A. Strauss. 1955. Social class and modes of communication. *Amer. J. Sociol.*, **60**, pp. 329–338.

Schoor, A. 1964. The nonculture of poverty. *Amer. J. Orthopsychiat.*, **34**, pp. 907–912.

Schramm, W., J. Lyle, and E. B. Parker. 1961. *Television in the lives of our children* (Stanford, Calif.: Stanford University Press).

Smith, Madora E. 1935. A study of some factors influencing the development of the sentence in preschool children. *J. genet. Psychol.*, **46**, pp. 182–212.

Spain, C. J. 1962. *Definition of familiar nouns by culturally deprived and non-deprived children of varying ages* (Nashville, Tenn.: George Peabody College for Teachers). Unpublished doctoral dissertation.

Staats, A. W., and Carolyn K. Staats. 1963. *Complex human behavior* (New York: Holt, Rinehart and Winston, Inc.).

Stewart, W. A. 1965. Urban Negro speech: socio-linguistic factors affecting English teaching. In R. W. Shuy (ed.), *Social dialects and language learning* (Champaign, Ill.: National Council of Teachers of English), pp. 10–18.

———. 1964. Foreign language teaching methods in quasi-foreign language situations. In W. A. Stewart (ed.), *Non-standard speech and the teaching of English* (Washington, D.C.: Center for Applied Linguistics), pp. 1–15.

Stodolsky, Susan. 1965. *Maternal behavior and language and concept formation in Negro pre-school children: an inquiry into process* (Chicago, Ill.: University of Chicago). Unpublished doctoral dissertation.

Strodtbeck, F. L. 1965. The hidden curriculum in the middle-class home. In J. D. Krumboltz (ed.), *Learning and the educational process* (Skokie, Ill.: Rand McNally & Company), pp. 91–112.

Templin, Mildred C. 1957. *Certain language skills in children: their development and interrelationships* (Minneapolis, Minn.: University of Minnesota Press).

Thomas, D. R. 1962. *Oral language, sentence structure, and vocabulary of kindergarten children living in low socio-economic urban areas* (Detroit, Mich.: Wayne State University). Unpublished doctoral dissertation.

Thomas, O. C. 1965. *Transformational grammar and the teacher of English* (New York: Holt, Rinehart and Winston, Inc.).

Weissberg, P. 1963. Social and non-social conditioning of infant vocalizations. *Child Develpm.*, **34**, pp. 377–388.

Wolf, R. M. 1964. *The identification and measurement of environmental process variables related to intelligence* (Chicago, Ill.: University of Chicago). Unpublished doctoral dissertation.

Wortis, H., J. L. Bardach, R. Cutler, R. Rue, and A. Freedman. 1963. Child-rearing practices in a low socio-economic group. *Pediatrics*, **32**, pp. 298–307.

40   A Socio-linguistic Approach to Social Learning*

BASIL BERNSTEIN, *Sociological Research Unit, University of London Institute of Education*

This paper is concerned with:

1. The neglect of the study of speech by sociologists;
2. The role of speech as a major aspect of culture and the means of its transmission;
3. The relations between forms of speech and forms of social relation;
4. The social and educational consequences of differential access to forms of speech.

The reader may well think that the early discussion bears little relation to education. It is important, however, although the argument is a complex one.

Perhaps one of the most important events that has taken place in scientific endeavour in the twentieth century is the convergence of both the natural and social sciences upon the study of linguistic aspects of

* *Social Science Survey*, **1965**. Reprinted by permission.

communication. The consequences of this convergence and the new relations between the disciplines which it has brought about may well be worthy of a chapter in the next book on the sociology of knowledge. Through the study of language the link between biological and socio-cultural orders is gradually being established. The clarification of this link and the resultant theories may well have consequences for control as exciting as the progress in our understanding of the genetic code. This is not the place to discuss the trends in separate disciplines which have led to this convergence, but a number of works may serve as guides for the reader.[1] What is a little odd is the negligible contribution of sociology to the study of language. The textbooks celebrate the fact of man's symbolic possibilities in chapters on culture and socialisation and then the consequences are systematically ignored. One might go as far as saying that the only time one is made aware that humans speak in the writings of contemporary sociologists is incidentally through the statistical relations induced from social-survey inquiries.[2] And here all that is required is that the subjects can read: speech confounds the later arithmetic. Even when what a person says is considered to be relevant, what is actually said is rarely, in itself, singled out as worthy of systematic study. The origins and consequences of forms of saying, linguistic forms, their conditions, formal patterning, regulative functions, their history and change are not included in the sociologist's analysis. And yet long ago both Durkheim and Weber drew attention to the social significance of language.

In its struggle for recognition, sociology has continuously insisted upon the fact that there exists an order of relations, arising out of the

[1] O. S. Akhmanova *et al.*, *Exact Methods in Linguistic Research*, University of California Press, 1963; C. Cherry, *Language and Human Communication*, McGraw-Hill, Inc., New York, 1957; M. Cohen, *Pour une sociologie de langage*, Albin-Michel, Paris, 1956; E. Gellner, *The Crisis in the Humanities and the Mainstream of Philosophy*, in J. H. Plumb (ed.), *Crisis in the Humanities*, Penguin Books, 1964; J. O. Hertzler, *Towards a Sociology of Language*, Social Forces, 32, 1953, pp. 109–119; D. H. Hymes, *Linguistic Aspects of Cross-Cultural Personality Study*, in B. Kaplan (ed.), *Studying Personality Cross-Culturally*, Row, Peterson & Company, Evanston, Ill., 1961; D. H. Hymes, *The Ethnography of Speaking*, in T. Gladwin and W. C. Sturtevant (eds.), *Anthropology and Human Behaviour*, Anthropological Society of Washington, D.C. (A.S.W. Smithsonian Institution), 1962; D. H. Hymes (ed.), The Ethnography of Communication, *American Anthropologist*, Special Issue (December), 1964; G. H. Mead, *Mind, Self and Society: From the standpoint of a social behaviorist*, University of Chicago Press, 1936; G. Miller, *Language and Human Communication*, McGraw-Hill, Inc., New York, 1951; S. Saporta (ed.), *Psycho-linguistics: A Book of Readings*, Holt Rinehart and Winston, Inc., New York, 1961.

[2] J. H. S. Bossard, Family Modes of Expression, *American Sociological Review*, 1945, pp. 226–237. There are, of course, exceptions; for example, L. Schatzman and A. L. Strauss, Social Class and Modes of Communication, *American Journal of Sociology*, 60, pp. 329–338, 1955.

inter-actions of members of a society, which constrains and directs behaviour independent of the unique characteristics of its members. Sociologists have been concerned to explain the nature of this order, in particular the processes making for its diversity and change, and to develop on a formal level a grammar or syntax which controls the conceptualising of this order. They have studied the major complexes of social forms which shape the social order, their inter-relations, and the factors responsible for their change. Language is seen as an integrating or divisive phenomenon; as the major process through which a culture is transmitted; the bearer of social genes. However, this has rarely given rise to a study of language as a social institution comparable to the analyses made of say the family, religion, etc. As far as speech is concerned this has been viewed as a datum, taken for granted, and not as an object of special inquiry. It is, of course, true that through the writings of George Mead the role of language, really the role of speech, has been explicitly recognised in the formation of a distinctly social self. And yet, in the study of socialisation, it is not possible to find an empirical study which systematically examines the role of speech as the process by which a child comes to acquire a specific *social* identity. In fact, in the numerous studies of child-rearing with the exception of very few, there is no account of the patterning of the linguistic environment.[3] Groups are studied, their formal ordering elegantly discussed, but the implications and consequences of *linguistic* aspects of their communications seem to be unworthy of sociological consideration. Graduates are trained to conduct surveys, to construct questionnaires, to interview, without, at least, in England, any explicit and systematic training in what Dell Hymes has called the ethnography of speech—although there is an intuitive or unsystematic recognition of differences in the patterning and consequences of speech events in various sub-cultures.

Sociologists, who focus upon social dynamics as these are expressed through changes in the major institutional forms, have thrown a shadow on problems implicit in the work of the great nineteenth century theorists. Weber, for example, discusses various types of rationality, and their associated institutional orders and forms of authority. Complex societies involve various forms of rationality which may be differentially distributed among their members. Weber's typology of rationality bears some resemblance to cultural themes which determine modes of action. How does an individual come to acquire a particular form of rationality? Weber's concept of rationality requires an explicit formulation of the inter-relations between institutional and cultural orders *and* of the process whereby individual experience manifests itself in special modes of social

[3] I am ignoring here the many studies limited to the development of speech in children.

action. Durkheim's analysis of the origins and consequences of mechanical and organic solidarity pre-suppose the same problem.[4] The concept of the individual in Durkheim is reduced to an unstable state of appetites—an instinct-system tending towards disintegration in conditions where the energies are not subordinate to a normative order of a particular kind. His formulation has the distinct merit of stating the problem of the relationship between biological and socio-cultural orders.

A major attempt to relate biological, institutional and cultural orders has been made with the use of the writings of Freud. Indeed, much work on socialisation, on the relation between culture and personality, both in anthropology and sociology, implicitly or explicitly attempts a solution of Durkheim's problem in these terms. However, this approach precludes the study of language and speech. As a result of working with the Freudian theory certain elements within the theory limited interest in linguistic phenomena. The gains of this approach are partly outweighed by the tendency to reduce the social to the psychological by means of a theory of unconscious motivation giving rise to an affective theory of learning. Although the ego in psychoanalytic theory is essentially a linguistically differentiated organisation, speech tends to be regarded epi-phenomenally as a process shaped by the patterning of the mechanisms of defence. It is, of course, true that in this theory reality-testing is accomplished essentially through verbal procedures, but the patterning of speech is accorded no independence in this theory nor in the behaviour which the theory illuminates.[5] As a result, anthropologists and sociologists who used Freudian theory in their attempts to understand the transformation of the psychic into the social paid little attention to either language or speech, and so carried over into their work the dichotomy between thought and feeling implicit in Freud. Further, the institutional and cultural order are often interpreted in terms of projections of unconscious formations within the individual.

It would seem then that sociologists, because of their emphasis on changes in the major institutional forms in industrial society, have tended to neglect until very recently the study of the transmission of culture. Where this has been attempted, for example in the study of socialisation, the influence of Freud has diverted attention from the linguistic environment. The influence of George Mead, who stressed the role of speech in the formation of a distinct social identity, assisted the rise of what has been called inter-action theory, but paradoxically not to any special study

[4] **Durkheim tends to leap from types of social integration to the quality of a series of individual acts.**

[5] **The major interest has been concerned with symbolism. It is important to note work done in the area of schizophrenic thought disorder and the stress on communication emphasised by the existential school.**

of the medium of inter-action, i.e., speech. The net effect of these movements has been to weaken the possibility of connexion between sociology and linguistics and the cross-fertilisation of theories and methods between the two disciplines.

This neglect of the study of language and speech in sociology has certainly not been typical of a school of anthropologists who have firmly and boldly stated a controversial relation between language and the interpretation of reality. William von Humboldt's statement in 1848 that "man lives with the world about him principally indeed . . . exclusively as language presents it" was echoed by Boas (1911) who claimed that a purely linguistic analysis "would provide the data for a thorough investigation of the psychology of the peoples of the world." However, it was with Sapir, a student of Boas, that a new elegance, clarity, subtlety, and originality was introduced into the discussion of the inter-relations between language, culture, and personality and which has deeply affected all work in this area. Language, according to Sapir (1933), "does not as a matter of fact stand apart from or run parallel to direct experience but completely interpenetrates it." Hoijer (1962) succinctly stated Sapir's thesis as follows: Peoples speaking different languages may be said to live in different "worlds of reality" in the sense that the languages they speak affect to a considerable degree both their sensory perceptions and their habitual modes of thought.

Sapir writes: Language is a guide to 'social reality.' Though language is not ordinarily thought of as of essential interest to the students of social science, it powerfully conditions all our thinking about social problems and processes. . . . It is quite an illusion to imagine that one adjusts to reality essentially without the use of language and that language is merely an incidental means of solving specific problems of communication or reflection. The fact of the matter is that the real world is to a large extent unconsciously built up on the language habits of the group. . . . We see and hear and otherwise experience very largely as we do because the language habits of our community predispose certain choices of interpretation (Sapir, 1929). Whorf (1941, 1956), a student of Sapir, went further and attempted to derive from the morphological syntactic and lexical features of Hopi the "habitual thought" or "thought world" of the people. The thought world is "the microcosm that each man carries about inside himself by which he measures and understands what he can of the macrocosm." Hoijer (1962), one of the major interpreters of Whorf, states that "the fashions of speaking peculiar to a people, like other aspects of their culture, are indicative of a view of life, a metaphysics of their culture, compounded of unquestioned and mainly unstated premises which define the nature of the universe and man's position within it."

This is not the place to follow the many twists and turns of the controversy these writings give rise to, or to examine the empirical support for the theory, but the reader will find a guide to this literature below.[6] This thesis had repercussions for psychology and has been an important factor in bringing about a relationship between linguistics and psychology. One of the many difficulties associated with it is that it focuses upon *universal* features of the formal patterning of language. Although Whorf (1941, 1956) insists that "the influence of language upon habitual thought and behaviour does not depend so much on *any one system* (e.g., tense or nouns) within the grammar as upon ways of analysing and reporting experience which have become fixed in the language as integrated 'fashions of speaking' which cut across the typical grammatical classifications, so that a 'fashion' may include lexical, morphological, syntactic, and otherwise systematically diverse means co-ordinated in a certain frame of consistency," these fashions of speaking the frames of consistency are not related to an institutional order, nor are they seen as emerging from the structure of social relations. On the contrary, they are seen as determiners of social relations through their role in shaping the culture. In Whorf's later writings, and in the writings of his followers, it is certain morphological and syntactic features of the *language* made psychologically active through the fashion of speaking which elicit habitual and characteristic behaviour in the speakers. In other words, the link between language, culture and habitual thought is *not* mediated through the social structure.

The view to be taken here is different in that it will be argued that a number of fashions of speaking, frames of consistency, are possible in any given language and that these fashions of speaking, linguistic forms, or codes, are themselves a function of the form social relations take. According to this view, the form of the social relation or more generally, the social structure generates distinct linguistic forms or codes and *these codes essentially transmit the culture and so constrain behaviour.*

This thesis is different from that of Whorf. It has more in common with some of the writings of Mead, Sapir, Malinowski, and Firth. Whorf's psychology was influenced by the writings of the Gestalt school of psychology whereas the thesis to be put forward here rests on the work of Vygotsky (1962) and Luria (1959, 1961). In a sense the Whorfian theory is more general and more challenging; although, perhaps, it is less open to

[6] Roger Brown, *Words and Things*, The Free Press, New York, 1958; J. A. Fishman, A Systematisation of the Whorfian Hypothesis, *Behavioral Science*, University of Michigan, 5, 1960, pp. 323–339; H. Hoijer (ed.), *Language in Culture*, American Anthropological Association Memoir, no. 79, 1954 (also published by University of Chicago Press); H. C. Triandis, The Influence of Culture on Cognitive Processes, in L. Berkowitz (ed.), *Advances in Experimental Social Psychology*, Academic Press, Inc., New York, 1964.

empirical confirmation, for it asserts that owing to the differential rates of change of culture and language *the latter determines the former*. The thesis to be developed here places the emphasis on changes in the social structure as major factors in shaping or changing a given culture through their effect on the consequences of fashions of speaking. It shares with Whorf the controlling influence on experience ascribed to "frames of consistency" involved in fashions of speaking. It differs and perhaps rela-tivizes Whorf, by asserting that, in the context of a common language in the sense of a general code, there will arise distinct linguistic forms, fashions of speaking, which induce in their speakers *different* ways of relating to objects and persons. It leaves open the question whether there are features of the *common culture* which all members of a society share which are determined by the specific nature of the general code or language at its *syntactic* and *morphological* levels. It is, finaly, more distinctly sociological in its emphasis on the system of social relations.

Elaborated and Restricted Codes

A general outline of the argument will be given first. This will be followed by a detailed analysis of two linguistic forms or codes and their variants. The discussion will be linked to the problem of educability as this is conceived in industrial societies.

Introduction

To begin with, a distinction must be made between language and speech. Dell Hymes (1961) writes: "Typically one refers not to the act or process of speech, but to the structure, pattern or system of language. Speech is a message, language is a code. Linguists have been preoccupied with inferring the constants of the language code."[7] The code which the linguist invents in order to explain speech events is capable of generating *n* number of speech codes, and there is no reason for believing that any one language or general code is in this respect better than another, whether it is English or whether it is Hopi. On this argument language is a set of rules to which all speech codes must comply, but which speech codes are generated is a function of the system of social relations.

The particular form a social relation takes acts selectively on what is said, when it is said, and how it is said. The form of the social relation regulates the options which speakers take up at both syntactic and lexical levels. For example, if an adult is talking to a child he or she will use a speech form in which both the syntax and the vocabulary is simple. Put

[7] **See footnote 1.**

in another way, the consequences of the form the social relation takes are often transmitted in terms of certain syntactic and lexical selections. In as much as a social relation does this, then it may establish for speakers principles of choice, so that a certain syntax and a certain lexical range is chosen rather than another. The specific principles of choice which regulate these selections entail from the point of view of both speaker and listener planning procedures which guide the speaker in the preparation of his speech and which also guide the listener in its reception.

Changes in the form of certain social relations, it is argued, act selectively upon the principles controlling the selection of both syntactic and lexical options. Changes in the form of the social relation affect the planning procedures used in the preparation of speech and the orientation of the listener. The speech used by members of an army combat unit on manoeuvres will be somewhat different from the same members' speech at a padre's evening. Different forms of social relations can generate quite different speech-systems or linguistic codes by affecting the planning procedures. These different speech-systems or codes create for their speakers different orders of relevance and relation. The experience of the speakers may then be transformed by what is made significant or relevant by the different speech-systems. This is a sociological argument, because the speech-system is taken as a consequence of the form of the social relation, or to put it more generally, is a quality of the social structure.

As the child learns his speech or, in the terms used here, learns specific codes which regulate his verbal acts, he learns the requirements of his social structure. The experience of the child is transformed by the learning which is generated by his own apparently voluntary acts of speech. The social structure becomes the sub-stratum of his experience essentially through the consequences of the linguistic process. From this point of view, every time the child speaks or listens the social structure of which he is a part is reinforced in him and his social identity is constrained. The social structure becomes the developing child's psychological reality by the shaping of his acts of speech. Underlying the general pattern of his speech are, it is held, critical sets of choices, preferences for some alternatives rather than others, which develop, and are stabilised through time and which eventually come to play an important role in the regulation of intellectual, social, and affective orientations.

The same process can be put rather more formally. Individuals come to learn their roles through the process of communication. A role from this point of view is a constellation of shared learned meanings, through which an individual is able to enter into persistent, consistent, and recognised forms of interaction with others. A role is thus a complex coding activity controlling the creation and organisation of specific meanings *and* the conditions for their transmission and reception. Now, if it is the case that the communication system which defines a given role behaviourally is essentially that of speech, it should be possible to distinguish critical roles in terms of the speech forms they regulate. The consequences of specific speech forms or codes will transform the environs into a matrix of particular meanings which becomes part of psychic reality through acts of speech. As a person learns to subordinate his behaviour to a linguistic code, which is the expression of the role, different orders of relation are made available to him. The complex of meanings which a role-system transmits reverberates developmentally in an individual to inform his general conduct. On this argument it is the linguistic transformation of the role which is the major bearer of meanings: it is through specific linguistic codes that relevance is created, experience given a particular form, and social identity constrained.

Children who have access to different speech-systems (i.e., learn different roles by virtue of their status position in a given social structure) may adopt quite different social and intellectual procedures despite a common potential.

Elaborated and Restricted Codes: Definitions and Brief Description

Two general types of code can be distinguished: *elaborated* and *restricted*. They can be defined, on a linguistic level, in terms of the probability of predicting for any one speaker which syntactic elements will be used to organise meaning across a representative range of speech. In the case of an elaborated code, the speaker will select from a relatively extensive range of alternatives and the probability of predicting the organising elements is considerably reduced. In the case of a restricted code the number of these alternatives is often severely limited and the probability of predicting the elements is greatly increased.

On a psychological level the codes may be distinguished by the extent to which each facilitates (elaborated code) or inhibits (restricted code) an orientation to symbolise intent in a verbally explicit form. Behaviour processed by these codes will, it is proposed, develop different modes of self-regulation and so different forms of orientation. The codes themselves are functions of a particular form of social relationship, or more generally, qualities of social structures.

A distinction will be made between verbal or linguistic, and extra-verbal or para-linguistic components of a communication. The linguistic or verbal component refers to messages where meaning is mediated by words: their selection, combination, and organisation. The para-linguistic or extra-verbal component refers to meanings mediated through expressive associates of words (rhythm, stress, pitch, etc.) or through gesture, physical set and facial modification.

Restricted Code (lexical prediction)

The pure form of a restricted code would be one where all the words and hence the organising structure irrespective of its degree of complexity are wholly predictable for speakers and listeners. Examples of this pure form would be ritualistic modes of communication: relationships regulated by protocol, types of religious services, cocktail-party routines, some story-telling situations. In these relations individual difference cannot be signalled through the verbal channel except in so far as the *choice* of sequence or routine exists. It is transmitted essentially through variations in extra-verbal signals.

Consider the case of a mother telling her child stories which they both know by heart. "And little Red Riding Hood went into the wood," (ritualistic pause). "And what do you think happened?" (rhetorical question). If the mother wishes to transmit her discrete experience, her uniqueness, she is unable to do this by varying her words. She can only do it by varying the signals transmitted through extra-verbal channels; through changes in intonation, pitch, speech rhythm, facial set, gesture, or even through changes in muscular tension, if she is holding the child. The code defines the channels through which new information (i.e., learning) can be made available. The discrete intents of mother and child, inter-personal aspects of the relation, can only be transmitted extra-verbally.

Given the selection of the sequence, new information will be made available through the extra-verbal channels, and these channels are likely to become the object of special perceptual activity. The code defines the form of the social relationship by restricting the *verbal* signalling of individual differences. Individuals relate to each other essentially through *the social position or status they are occupying*. Societies differ in terms of the use made of this code and the conditions which elicit it.

It is suggested that where there is an *exchange* of verbal message of maximal predictability, such as social routines, the context will be one where the participants have *low* predictability about each other's individual attributes. The code offers here the possibility of deferred commitment to the relationship. Decisions about its future form will be based upon the significance given to the exchange of extra-verbal messages.

Consider a cocktail party. Two people are introduced who have never met before. A social routine is likely to develop. This establishes mutual predictability and so the basis of a social relation. What is said is impersonal in that the verbal messages are all previously organised. The individuals will be highly sensitive to extra-verbal signals and so these signals are likely to become the object of special perceptual activity. How the social relation will develop initially depends upon the choice of social routine and the significance accorded to extra-verbal signals. Here, orientation is towards the extra-verbal channels: there is a minimal level of planning involved in the preparation of speech; the exchange of verbal sequences pre-supposes a shared cultural heritage which controls the verbal communications offered by the occupants of this cocktail-party status.

It is important to note that:

1. The status or positional aspect of the social relationship is important.

2. Orientation is likely to be towards the extra-verbal channels as new information will pass through these channels.

3. Specifically verbal planning is confined to choice of sequence, rather than involving the selection and organisation of the sequence.

4. The code restricts the verbal signalling of individual difference.

Restricted Code (syntactic prediction)

What is more often found in a restricted code, where prediction is only possible at the syntactic level.[8] The lexicon will vary from one case to another, but in all cases it is drawn from a narrow range. It is necessary to point out that because a lexicon is drawn from a narrow range this is no criterion for classifying the code as a restricted one. The most general condition for the emergence of this code is a social relationship based upon a common, extensive set of closely-shared identifications and expectations self-consciously held by the members.[9] It follows that the social relationship will be one of an inclusive kind. The speech is here refracted through a common cultural identity which reduces the need to verbalise intent so that it becomes explicit, with the consequence that the structure of the speech is simplified, and the lexicon will be drawn from a narrow range. The extra-verbal component of the communication will become a major channel for transmitting individual qualifications and so individual difference. The speech will tend to be impersonal in that it will not be specially prepared to fit a given referent. *How* things are said, *when* they are said, rather than what is said, becomes important. The intent of the listener is likely to be taken for granted. The meanings are likely to be concrete, descriptive or narrative rather than analytical or abstract. In certain areas meanings will be highly condensed. The speech in these social relations is likely to be fast and fluent, articulatory clues are reduced; some meanings are likely to be dislocated, condensed, and local; there will be a low level of vocabulary and syntactic selection; *the unique meaning of the individual is likely to be implicit.*

[8] Prediction here refers to an ability of a special observer, *not* of the speakers.

[9] Restricted codes will arise in prisons, combat units of the armed forces, in the peer group of children and adolescents, and so on.

Restricted codes are not necessarily linked to social class. They are used by all members of a society at some time. The major function of this code is to define and reinforce the form of the social relationship by restricting the verbal signalling of individual experience.[10]

Elaborated Code (low syntactic prediction)

An elaborated code, where prediction is much less possible at the syntactic level, is likely to arise in a social relationship which raises the tension in its members to select from their linguistic resources a *verbal* arrangement which closely fits specific referents. This situation will arise where the intent of the other person cannot be taken for granted, with the consequence that meanings will have to be expanded and raised to the level of *verbal* explicitness. The verbal planning here, unlike the case of a restricted code, promotes a higher level of syntactic organisation and lexical selection. The preparation and delivery of relatively explicit meaning is the major function of this code. This does not mean that these meanings are necessarily abstract, but abstraction inheres in the possibilities. The code will facilitate the *verbal* transmission and elaboration of the individual's unique experience. The condition of the listener, unlike that in the case of a restricted code, will *not* be taken for granted, as the speaker is likely to modify his speech in the light of the special conditions and attributes of the listener. This is not to say that such modifications will always occur, but that this possibility exists. If a restricted code facilitates the construction and exchange of communalised symbols, then an elaborated code facilitates the verbal construction and exchange of individualised or personal symbols. An elaborated code, through its regulation, induces in its speakers a sensitivity to the implications of separateness and differences and points to the possibilities inherent in a complex conceptual hierarchy for the organisation of experience.

An example at this point is necessary to show how these various codes control social relations. Imagine a man is at a party where he finds a large number of people whom he has never met before. He goes up to a girl. He will then use, initially, a restricted code (lexicon prediction), which will provide the basis for the social relation. He will attempt to improve upon his understanding of her specific attributes by the meaning he gives to her presence and extra-verbal transmissions. He is then likely to move towards an elaborated code (if he possesses one) so that they may both have a means for elaborating verbally their distinctive experience. The possibility of discovering common ground is in this way increased, and the man may then move into a restricted code (syntactic

---

[10] A restricted code does not necessarily affect the *amount* of speech, only its form.

prediction). The quality of the relationship at this point has shifted, and the girl may then regard this as slightly presumptuous and so force the man back to an elaborated code, or, if he is very unfortunate, to a restricted code (lexicon prediction). On the other hand she may accept the change in the social relation. The important points here are that the codes are induced by the social relation, are expressing it, *and* are regulating it. *The ability to switch codes controls the ability to switch roles.* This is a very simple example but it illustrates all the points made earlier.

Formal Sociological Conditions
for the Emergence of the Two Codes

It is possible to state the formal sociological conditions for the emergence of the two codes by distinguishing between the generality of the meanings controlled by the codes and the availability of the speech models from whom they are learned. To the extent that meanings are made explicit and are conventionalised through language, meanings may be called *universalistic* whilst if they are implicit and relatively less conventionalised through language, meanings can be called *particularistic*. Similarly, if the speech models are potentially generally available, such models can be called universalistic, whilst if the speech models are much less available they can be called particularistic.

Using these concepts, a restricted code is *particularistic* with reference to its meaning and so to the social structure which it presupposes. However, it is *universalistic* with reference to its models, as such models are generally available. It is important to note here that the concern is with the availability of a *special syntax*. An elaborated code is *universalistic* with reference to its meanings and so to the social structure which it presupposes. However, it is likely that the speech models for this code will be *particularistic*. This does not mean that the origin of this code is to be sought in the psychological qualities of the models but that the models are encumbants of specialised social positions located in the system of social stratification. In principle this is not necessary, but it is likely to be empirically the case.

Thus, because a restricted code is universalistic with reference to its models, all people have access to its special syntax and to various systems of local condensed meanings; but because an elaborated code is very likely to be particularistic with respect to its models, only some people will have access to its syntax and to the universalistic character of its meanings. Following this argument, the use of an elaborated code or an orientation to its use will depend *not* on the psychological properties of a speaker but upon access to specialised social positions, by virtue of which a particular type of speech model is made available. Normally, but not inevitably, such social positions will coincide with a stratum seeking or already possessing access to the major decision-making areas of the society.

In terms of learning the codes, the codes are different. The syntax of a restricted code may be learned informally and readily. The greater range of and selection from, the syntactic alternatives of an elaborated code normally requires a much longer period of formal and informal learning.

These distinctions are useful in isolating the general conditions for a special case of a restricted code (syntactic prediction). This is where the speech model is particularistic and the meaning is also particularistic. In this situation the individual is wholly constrained by the code. *He has access to no other.* The consequences of this are thought to be relevant to the problem of educability in developed or emergent industrialised societies. The sociological conditions may be summarised as follows:

Restricted Code (lexical prediction)

Ritualistic components of status or positional relationships

Restricted Code (high syntactic prediction)

1. Model : universalistic ; meaning : particularistic
2. Model : particularistic ; meaning : particularistic

Elaborated Code (low syntactic prediction)

Model : particularistic ; meaning : universalistic

Verbal Planning, Linguistic Codes, and Social Structures

The codes have now been defined, briefly described, and their formal sociological determinants specified. It is necessary to show how these codes may become established on a psychological level and this will be done by looking more closely at the process called verbal planning.

When one person talks to another it is suggested that the following processes at different levels occur in the listener before he is able to produce a sequential reply.

Orientation: The listener first scans the communication for a pattern of dominant signals. Not all the words and extra-verbal signals will carry the same value; some will carry greater significance than others for the listener.

Selection: There will be associations to the patterns of dominant signals which will control the selections the listener makes from his potential stock of words, sequences and extra-verbal signals.

Organisation: The listener will then have to fit the selected words and sequences into a grammatical frame and integrate them with the extra-verbal signals.

On a psychological level codes are generated by specific kinds of verbal planning. It follows that restricted and elaborated codes will establish different kinds of regulation which crystallize in the nature of verbal planning. The originating determinant of the kind of orientation, selection, and organisation, is the form of the social relation or, more generally, it is a quality of the social structure. The codes, linguistic translations of the meanings of the social structure, are nothing more than verbal planning activities at the psychological level and *only at this level can they be said to exist.*

The consequences of the form of the social relationship are transmitted and sustained by codes which at the individual level consist of verbal planning processes. Particular orders of relationship to objects and persons inhere in linguistic codes. These orders of relation are then spontaneously generated by the individual as the verbal planning processes become stabilised. Following this argument, changes in the social structure, in the organisation of forms of social relation, modify speech systems or linguistic codes. These in turn, by virtue of verbal planning procedures, change the order of significance which individuals spontaneously create as a consequence of their acts of speech and which in their creation transform them. Clearly not all aspects of social structure are translated into elements of the linguistic code, but it is considered that the major aspects are so translated.

The following diagram[11] might be helpful in distinguishing the levels of analysis.

Level I (Code Determining)

A	B	C
Social Structure	Forms of Social Relation	Linguistic Codes
(Complex of meanings)	(Specific orders of meaning)	

Level II (Code Generating)

Verbel Planning Functions   Created Order of Meaning   Speech Events

[11] I am grateful to Miss J. Cook, Sociological Research Unit, University of London Institute of Education, for her help in this formulation.

The arrows indicate reciprocal influence as it is possible for a verbal planning function to develop which creates novel orders of meaning and social relation.

Some Implications of Restricted[12] and Elaborated Codes

An elaborated code generated originally by the form of the social relation becomes a facility for transmitting individuated verbal responses. As far as any one speaker is concerned, he is not aware of a speech-system or code, but the planning procedures which he is using both in the preparation of his speech and in the receiving of speech creates one. These planning procedures promote a relatively higher level of syntactic organisation and lexical selection than does a restricted code. What is then made available for learning, by an elaborated code, is of a different order from that made available in the case of a restricted code. The learning generated by these speech systems is quite different. By learning, the reference is to what is significant, what is made relevant: socially, intellectually and emotionally. From a developmental perspective, an elaborated code user comes to perceive language as a set of theoretical possibilities available for the transmission of unique experience. The concept of self, unlike the concept of self of a speaker limited to a restricted code, will be verbally differentiated, so that it becomes in itself the object of special perceptual activity. In the case of a speaker limited to a restricted code, the concept of self will tend to be refracted through the implications of the status arrangements. Here there is no problem of self, *because the problem is not relevant.*

As a child learns an elaborated code he learns to scan a particular syntax, to receive and transmit a particular pattern of meaning, to develop a particular verbal planning process, and very early *learns to orient towards the verbal channel.* He learns to manage the role requirements necessary for the effective production of the code. He becomes aware of a certain order of relationships (intellectual, social, and emotional) in his environment, and his experience is transformed by these relations. As the code becomes established through its planning procedures, the developing child voluntarily, through his acts of speech, generates these relations. He comes to perceive language as a set of theoretical possibilities for the presentation of his discrete experience to others. An elaborated code, through its regulation, induces developmentally in its speakers an expecta-

[12] **The reference here and throughout is to a restricted code (high syntactic prediction).**

tion of separateness and difference from others. It points to the possibilities inherent in a complex conceptual hierarchy for the organisation of experience.

It is possible to distinguish two modes of an elaborated code. One mode facilitates the verbal elaboration of *inter-personal relations*, and the second facilitates the verbal elaboration of relations between *objects*. These two modes of an elaborated code would differentiate different ranges of experience and would presuppose learning to manage different role relations. The two modes possess the general features of an elaborated code. They both carry low syntactic prediction; they both serve as facilities for the verbal elaboration of discrete intent; they orient their users to the expectation of difference; they point to logically similar conceptual orders: *but the referents of the relationships are different.*

An individual going into the arts is likely to possess an elaborated code oriented to the person; whilst an individual going into the sciences, particularly the applied sciences, is likely to possess an elaborated code oriented to object relations. C. P. Snow's two cultures may be related to the experiences differentiated through these two modes of an elaborated code. To be able to switch from one mode to the other may involve a recognition of, and an ability to translate verbally, different orders of experience. It may also involve a *recognition* of and an *ability to manage* the different types of role relations which these modes of speech promote. Over and above genetic dispositions towards person or object relations, it may well be that certain kinds of family settings and schools can orient the child towards, and stabilise, the use of one or both of these two modes of an elaborated code. It is possible for an individual to be limited to an elaborated code and to the role relations of either of its two modes, or to possess both modes, or to possess all forms of elaborated and restricted codes. These alternatives may be subject to considerable environmental influence.

A child *limited* to a restricted code will tend to develop essentially through the regulation inherent in the code. For such a child, speech does not become the object of special perceptual activity, neither does a theoretical attitude develop towards the structural possibilities of sentence organisation. The speech is epitomised by a low-level and limiting syntactic organisation and there is little motivation or orientation towards increasing vocabulary.

There is a limited and often rigid use of qualifiers (adjectives, adverbs, etc.) and these function as social counters through which individual intent is transmitted. This drastically reduces the verbal elaboration of intent which instead tends to be given meaning through extra-verbal means. Words and speech sequences refer to broad classes of contents rather than to progressive differentiation within a class. The reverse of this is also possible; a range of items within a class may be listed without knowledge of the concept which summarises the class. The categories referred to tend not to be broken down systematically. This has critical implications if the reference is to a subjective state of the speaker. Although the speech possesses a warmth and vitality, it tends to be impersonal in the literal sense of that word. The original social relation between mother and child exerted little pressure on the child to make his experience relatively explicit in a verbally differentiated way. Speech is not perceived as a major means of presenting to the other inner states. The type of learning, the conditions of learning, and the dimensions of relevance initiated and sustained through a restricted code are radically different from learning induced through an elaborated code.

The rigid range of syntactic possibilities leads to difficulty in conveying linguistically logical sequence and stress. The verbal planning function is shortened, and this often creates in sustained speech sequences a large measure of dislocation or disjunction. The thoughts are often strung together like beads on a frame rather than following a planned sequence. A restriction in planning often creates a high degree of redundancy. This means that there may well be a great deal of repetition of information, through sequences which add little to what has already been given. The following passages may illustrate these points:

> It's all according like these youths and that if they get into these gangs and that they must have a bit of a lark around and say it goes wrong and that and they probably knock someone off I mean think they just do it to be big getting publicity here and there.

Boy, age 16. I.Q. verbal 104, non-verbal 100.

> Well it should do but it don't seem to nowadays, like there's still murders going on now, any minute now or something like that they get people don't care they might get away with it then they all try it and it might leak out one might tell his mates that he's killed someone it might leak out like it might get around he gets hung for it like that.

Boy, age 17. I.Q. verbal 99, non-verbal 126+

Role relations may be limited and code switching may be hampered by the regulative consequences of a restricted code. An individual limited to a restricted code will tend to mediate an elaborated code through the regulation of his own.

The structure and function of the speech of children and adults limited to a restricted code is of the *same general order* as the speech induced by social relations generating a restricted code outlined earlier. Some children have access to no other code; their only code is a restricted one. Clearly one code is not better than another; each possesses its own aesthetic, its own possibilities. Society, however, may place different values on the orders of experience elicited, maintained, and progressively strengthened through the different coding systems.

The orientation towards these codes, elaborated and restricted, may be independent of the psychology of the child, independent of his native ability, although the *level* at which a code is used will undoubtedly reflect purely psychological attributes. The orientation towards these codes may be governed entirely by the form of the social relation, or more generally by the quality of the social structure. The intellectual and social procedures by which individuals relate themselves to their environment may be very much a question of their speech models within the family and the codes these speech models use.

I should like to draw attention to the relations between social class and the two coding systems. The sub-cultural implications of social class give rise to different socialisation procedures. The different normative systems create different family-role systems operating with different modes of social control.[13] It is considered that the normative systems associated with the middle-class and associated strata are likely to give rise to the modes of an elaborated code whilst those associated with some sections of the working class are likely to create individuals limited to a restricted code.[14] Clearly social class is an extremely crude index for the codes and more specific conditions for their emergence have been given in this paper. Variations in behaviour found within groups who fall within a particular class (defined in terms of occupation and education) within a mobile society are often very great. It is possible to locate the two codes

[13] U. Bronfenbrenner, Socialisation and Social Class Through Time and Space, in E. E. Maccoby *et al.* (eds.), *Readings in Social Psychology*, Methuen & Co., Ltd., London; M. L. Kohn, Social Class and the Exercise of Parental Authority, *American Sociological Review*, 24, 1959, pp. 352–366; M. L. Kohn, Social Class and Parental Values, *American Journal of Sociology*, 64, 1959, pp. 337–351; D. R. Miller and G. E. Swanson, *Inner Conflict and Defence.* Holt, Rinehart and Winston, Inc., New York, 1959; J. Newson and E. Newson, *Infant Care in an Urban Community*, George Allen & Unwin Ltd., London, 1963; Penguin, 1965; F. Reissman, *The Culturally Deprived Child*, Harper & Row, New York, 1963.

[14] B. Bernstein, Language and Social Class, *British Journal of Sociology*, *11*, 1960, p. 271; B. Bernstein, Linguistic Codes, Hesitation Phenomena and Intelligence, *Language & Speech*, 5, 1962, pp. 31–46; B. Bernstein, Social Class, Linguistic Codes and Grammatical Elements, *Language & Speech*, 5, 1962, pp. 221–240; D. Lawton, Social Class Differences in Language Development: A study of some samples of written work, *Language & Speech*, 6, 1963, pp. 120–143; D. Lawton, Social Class Language Differences in Group Discussions, *Language & Speech*, 7, part 3, July–September, 1964; D. Lawton, *Social Class Language Differences in Individual Interviews* (private circulation), 1964; T. Ravenette, *Intelligence, Personality and Social Class: an investigation into the patterns of intelligence and personality of working-class secondary school children*, unpublished Ph.D. thesis, University of London Library, 1963.

and their modes more precisely by considering the orientation of the family-role system, the mode of social control, and the resultant linguistic relations (Bernstein, 1964). Variations in the orientation of the family-role system can be linked to the external social network of the family and to occupational roles. It is not possible to do more than mention the possibilities of these more sensitive indices.

Children socialised within middle-class and associated strata can be expected to possess *both* an elaborated and a restricted code whilst children socialised within some sections of the working-class strata, particularly the lower working-class, can be expected to be *limited* to a restricted code. If a child is to succeed as he progresses through school it becomes critical for him to possess, or at least to be oriented towards, an elaborated code.

The relative backwardness of lower working-class children may well be a form of culturally induced backwardness transmitted to the child through the implications of the linguistic process. The code the child brings to the school symbolises his social identity. It relates him to his kin and to his local social relations. The code orients the child progressively towards a pattern of relationships which constitute for the child his psychological reality, and this reality is reinforced every time he speaks.

Conclusion

Two general linguistic codes or speech-systems have been discussed, their social origins explored, and their regulative consequences briefly discussed. It is thought that the theory might throw some light on the social determinants of educability. Where a child is sensitive to an elaborated code the school experience for such a child is one of symbolic and social development; for the child limited to a restricted code the school experience is one of symbolic and social change. It is important to realise that a restricted code carries its own aesthetic. It will tend to develop a metaphoric range of considerable power, a simplicity and directness, a vitality and rhythm; it should not be disvalued. Psychologically, it unites the speaker to his kin and to his local community. A change of code involves changes in the *means* whereby social identity and reality are created. This argument means that educational institutions in a fluid society carry within themselves alienating tendencies. To say this is *not* to argue for the preservation of a pseudo-folk culture but is to argue for certain changes in the social structure of educational institutions; it is also to argue for increased sensitivity on the part of teachers towards both the cultural and cognitive requirements of the formal educational relationship. The problem goes deeper than this. It raises the question of a society which measures human worth, accords respect, grants significance by means of a scale of purely occupational achievement.

From a more academic point of view it is tentatively thought that the thesis might well have a more general application. Elaborated and restricted codes and their variants should be found in any society where their originating conditions exist. The definitions should, in principle, be capable of application to a wide range of languages (and to other symbolic forms, e.g., music), although in any one case elaboration and restriction will be relative. The theory might be seen as a part, but clearly not the whole, of the answer to the problem of how the psychic is transformed into the social. The theory is sociological and is limited by the nature of these assumptions. Individual differences in the use of a particular code cannot be dealt with except on an insensitive more-or-less basis. It is also clear that there is more to culture and communication than what might be revealed by a consideration of limited aspects of speech. Finally, it is thought imperative that sociologists recognise in their analyses the fact that man speaks.

References

Bernstein, B. 1964. *Family role systems, socialisation and communication.* A paper given at the Conference on Cross-Cultural Research into Childhood and Adolescence, University of Chicago.

Boas, F. 1911. *Handbook of American Indian languages,* Part I (Washington, D.C.: U.S. Government Printing Office).

Hoijer, J. 1962. The relation of language to culture. In S. Tax (ed.), *Anthropology today: selections* (Chicago, Ill.: University of Chicago Press, Phoenix Books).

Luria, A. R. 1961. *The role of speech in the regulation of normal and abnormal behaviour* (New York: Pergamon Press, Inc.).

———, and F. I. Yudovich. 1959. *Speech and the development of mental processes in the child* (London: Staples Press, Ltd.).

Sapir, E. 1933. *Encyclopedia of the social sciences,* vol. 9, pp. 155–169.

———. 1929. The status of linguistics as a science. In D. G. Mandelbaum (ed.), *Selected writings of Edward Sapir* (Berkeley, Calif.: University of California Press).

Vygotsky, L. S. 1962. *Thought and language* (New York: John Wiley & Sons, Inc.).

Whorf, B. L. 1941. The relation of habitual thought and behaviour to language. In L. Spier (ed.), *Language, culture and personality: essays in memory of Edward Sapir* (Menasha, Wisc.: Wisconsin Sapir

Memorial Publication Fund); also in J. B. Carroll (ed.), *Language, thought and reality: selected writings of Benjamin Lee Whorf* (New York: John Wiley & Sons, Inc., 1956).

41   Early Experience and the Socialization of Cognitive Modes in Children*

ROBERT D. HESS, *University of Chicago*
VIRGINIA C. SHIPMAN, *University of Chicago*

The Problem

One of the questions arising from the contemporary concern with the education of culturally disadvantaged children is how we should conceptualize the effects of such deprivation upon the cognitive faculties of the child. The outcome is well known: children from deprived backgrounds score well below middle-class children on standard individual and group measures of intelligence (a gap that increases with age); they come to school without the skills necessary for coping with first grade curricula; their language development, both written and spoken, is relatively poor; auditory and visual discrimination skills are not well developed; in scholastic achievement they are retarded an average of 2 years by grade 6 and almost 3 years by grade 8; they are more likely to drop out of school before completing a secondary education; and even when they have adequate ability are less likely to go to college (Deutsch, 1963; Deutsch and Brown, 1964; Eells, Davis, Havighurst, Herrick, and Tyler, 1951; John, 1963; Kennedy, Van de Riet, and White, 1963; Lesser, 1964).

For many years the central theoretical issues in this field dealt with the origin of these effects, argued in terms of the relative contribution of genetic as compared with environmental factors. Current interest in the

* *Child Development*, December 1965, vol. 36, no. 4. Reprinted with permission of The Society for Research in Child Development, Inc. Copyright 1965 by The Society for Research in Child Development, Inc. This research is supported by the Research Division of the Children's Bureau, Social Security Administration; Department of Health, Education, and Welfare; Ford Foundation for the Advancement of Learning; and grants-in-aid from the Social Science Research Committee of the Division of Social Sciences, University of Chicago. Project staff members who made specific contributions to the analysis of data are Jere Brophy, Dina Feitelson, Roberta Meyer, and Ellis Olim. Hess's address: Committee on Human Development, University of Chicago, Chicago, Ill. 60637.

effects of cultural deprivation ignores this classic debate; the more basic problem is to understand how cultural experience is translated into cognitive behavior and academic achievement (Bernstein, 1961; Hess, 1964).

The focus of concern is no longer upon the question of whether social and cultural disadvantage depress academic ability, but has shifted to a study of the mechanisms of exchange that mediate between the individual and his environment. The thrust of research and theory is toward conceptualizing social class as a discrete array of experiences and patterns of experience that can be examined in relation to the effects they have upon the emerging cognitive equipment of the young child. In short, the question this paper presents is this: what *is* cultural deprivation, and how does it act to shape and depress the resources of the human mind?

The arguments we wish to present here are these: first, that the behavior which leads to social, educational, and economic poverty is socialized in early childhood—that is, it is learned; second, that the central quality involved in the effects of cultural deprivation is a lack of cognitive meaning in the mother-child communication system; and, third, that the growth of cognitive processes is fostered in family control systems which offer and permit a wide range of alternatives of action and thought and that such growth is constricted by systems of control which offer predetermined solutions and few alternatives for consideration and choice.

In this paper we will argue that the structure of the social system and the structure of the family shape communication and language and that language shapes thought and cognitive styles of problem-solving. In the deprived-family context this means that the nature of the control system which relates parent to child restricts the number and kind of alternatives for action and thought that are opened to the child; such constriction precludes a tendency for the child to reflect, to consider and choose among alternatives for speech and action. It develops modes for dealing with stimuli and with problems which are impulsive rather than reflective, which deal with the immediate rather than the future, and which are disconnected rather than sequential.

This position draws from the work of Basil Bernstein (1961) of the University of London. In his view, language structures and conditions what the child learns and how he learns, setting limits within which future learning may take place. He identifies two forms of communication codes or styles of verbal behavior: *restricted* and *elaborated*. Restricted codes are stereotyped, limited, and condensed, lacking in specificity and the exactness needed for precise conceptualization and differentiation. Sentences are short, simple, often unfinished; there is little use of subordinate clauses for elaborating the content of the sentence; it is a language of implicit meaning, easily understood and commonly shared. It is the language form often used in impersonal situations when the intent is to promote solidarity or reduce tension. Restricted codes are nonspecific clichés, statements, or observations about events made in general terms that will be readily understood. The basic quality of this mode is to limit the range and detail of concept and information involved.

Elaborated codes, however, are those in which communication is individualized and the message is specific to a particular situation, topic, and person. It is more particular, more differentiated, and more precise. It permits expression of a wider and more complex range of thought, tending toward discrimination among cognitive and affective content.

The effects of early experience with these codes are not only upon the communication modes and cognitive structure—they also establish potential patterns of relation with the external world. It is one of the dynamic features of Bernstein's work that he views language as social behavior. As such, language is used by participants of a social network to elaborate and express social and other interpersonal relations and, in turn, is shaped and determined by these relations.

The interlacing of social interaction and language is illustrated by the distinction between two types of family control. One is oriented toward control by *status* appeal or ascribed role norms. The second is oriented toward *persons*. Families differ in the degree to which they utilize each of these types of regulatory appeal. In status- (position-) oriented families, behavior tends to be regulated in terms of role expectations. There is little opportunity for the unique characteristics of the child to influence the decision-making process or the interaction between parent and child. In these families, the internal or personal states of the children are not influential as a basis for decision. Norms of behavior are stressed with such imperatives as, "You must do this because I say so," or "Girls don't act like that," or other statements which rely on the status of the participants or a behavior norm for justification (Bernstein, 1964).

In the family, as in other social structures, control is exercised in part through status appeals. The feature that distinguishes among families is the extent to which the status-based control maneuvers are modified by orientation toward persons. In a person-oriented appeal system, the unique characteristics of the child modify status demands and are taken into account in interaction. The decisions of this type of family are individualized and less frequently related to status or role ascriptions. Behavior is justified in terms of feelings, preference, personal and unique reactions, and subjective states. This philosophy not only permits but demands an elaborated linguistic code and a wide range of linguistic and behavioral alternatives in interpersonal interaction. Status-oriented families may be regulated by less individuated commands, messages, and responses. Indeed, by its nature, the status-oriented family will rely more heavily on a restricted code. The verbal exchange is inherent in the structure—regulates it and is regulated by it.

These distinctions may be clarified by two examples of mother-child communication using these two types of codes. Assume that the emotional climate of two homes is approximately the same; the significant difference between them is in style of communication employed. A child is playing noisily in the kitchen with an assortment of pots and pans when the telephone rings. In one home the mother says, "Be quiet," or "Shut up," or issues any one of several other short, peremptory commands. In the other home the mother says, "Would you keep quiet a minute? I want to talk on the phone." The question our study poses is this: what inner response is elicited in the child, what is the effect upon his developing cognitive network of concepts and meaning in each of these two situations? In one instance the child is asked for a simple mental response. He is asked to attend to an uncomplicated message and to make a conditioned response (to comply); he is not called upon to reflect or to make mental discriminations. In the other example the child is required to follow two or three ideas. He is asked to relate his behavior to a time dimension; he must think of his behavior in relation to its effect upon another person. He must perform a more complicated task to follow the communication of his mother in that his relationship to her is mediated in part through concepts and shared ideas; his mind is stimulated or exercised (in an elementary fashion) by a more elaborate and complex verbal communication initiated by the mother. As objects of these two divergent communication styles, repeated in various ways, in similar situations and circumstances during the preschool years, these two imaginary children would be expected to develop significantly different verbal facility and cognitive equipment by the time they enter the public-school system.

A person-oriented family allows the child to achieve the behavior rules (role requirements) by presenting them in a specific context for the child and by emphasizing the consequences of alternative actions. Status-oriented families present the rules in an assigned manner, where compliance is the *only* rule-following possibility. In these situations the role of power in the interaction is more obvious, and indeed, coercion and defiance are likely interactional possibilities. From another perspective, status-oriented families use a more rigid learning and teaching model in which compliance, rather than rationale, is stressed.

A central dimension through which we look at maternal behavior is to inquire what responses are elicited and permitted by styles of communication and interaction. There are two axes of the child's behavior in which we have a particular interest. One of these is represented by an *assertive, initiatory* approach to learning, as contrasted with a *passive, compliant* mode of engagement; the other deals with the tendency to reach solutions impulsively or hastily as distinguished from a tendency to *reflect*, to compare alternatives, and to choose among available options.

These styles of cognitive behavior are related, in our hypotheses, to the dimensions of maternal linguistic codes and types of family control systems. A status-oriented statement, for example, tends to offer a set of regulations and rules for conduct and interaction that is based on arbitrary decisions rather than upon logical consequences which result from selection of one or another alternatives. Elaborated and person-oriented statements lend themselves more easily to styles of cognitive approach that involve reflection and reflective comparison. Status-oriented statements tend to be restrictive of thought. Take our simple example of the two children and the telephone. The verbal categoric command to "Be quiet" cuts off thought and offers little opportunity to relate the information conveyed in the command to the context in which it occurred. The more elaborated message, "Would you be quiet a minute? I want to talk on the phone" gives the child a rationale for relating his behavior to a wider set of considerations. In effect, he has been given a *why* for his mother's request and, by this example, possibly becomes more likely to *ask* why in another situation. It may be through this type of verbal interaction that the child learns to look for action sequences in his own and others' behavior. Perhaps through these more intent-oriented statements the child comes to see the world as others see it and learns to take the role of others in viewing himself and his actions. The child comes to see the world as a set of possibilities from which he can make a personal selection. He learns to role play with an element of personal flexibility, not by role-conforming rigidity.

Research Plan

For our project a research group of 163 Negro mothers and their 4-year-old children was selected from four different social status levels: Group A came from college-educated professional, executive, and managerial occupational levels; Group B came from skilled blue-collar occupational levels, with not more than high-school education; Group C came from unskilled or semiskilled occupational levels, with predominantly elementary-school education; Group D from unskilled or semiskilled occupational levels, with fathers absent and families supported by public assistance.

These mothers were interviewed twice in their homes and brought to the university for testing and for an interaction session between mother and child in which the mother was taught three simple tasks by the staff member and then asked to teach these tasks to the child.

One of these tasks was to sort or group a number of plastic toys by color and by function; a second task was to sort eight blocks by two characteristics simultaneously; the third task required the mother and child to work together to copy five designs on a toy called an Etch-a-Sketch. A description of various aspects of the project and some preliminary results have been presented in several papers (Brophy, Hess, and Shipman, 1965; Jackson, Hess, and Shipman, 1965; Meyer, Shipman, and Hess, 1964; Olim, Hess, and Shipman, 1965; Shipman and Hess, 1965).

Results

The data in this paper are organized to show social-status differences among the four groups in the dimensions of behavior described above to indicate something of the maternal teaching styles that are emerging and to offer examples of relations between maternal and child behavior that are congruent with the general lines of argument we have laid out.

Social-Status Differences

VERBAL CODES: RESTRICTED VERSUS ELABORATED. One of the most striking and obvious differences between the environments provided by the mothers of the research group was in their patterns of language use. In our testing sessions, the most obvious social-class variations were in the total amount of verbal output in response to questions and tasks asking for verbal response. For example, as Table 1 shows, mothers from the middle-class gave protocols that were consistently longer in language productivity than did mothers from the other three groups.

TABLE 1
Mean Number of Typed Lines in Three Data-Gathering Situations

	Upper Middle N = 40	Upper Lower N = 40	Lower Lower N = 36	ADC N = 36
School situations	34.68	22.80	18.86	18.64
Mastery situations	28.45	18.70	15.94	17.75
CAT card	18.72	9.62	12.39	12.24
Total	81.85	51.12	47.19	48.63

Taking three different types of questions that called for free response on the part of the mothers and counting the number of lines of typescript of the protocols, the tally for middle-class mothers was approximately 82 contrasted with an average of roughly 49 for mothers from the three other groups.

These differences in verbal products indicate the extent to which the maternal environments of children in different social-class groups tend to be mediated by verbal cue and thus offer (or fail to offer) opportunities for labeling, for identifying objects and feelings and adult models who can demonstrate the usefulness of language as a tool for dealing with inter-personal interaction and for ordering stimuli in the environment.

In addition to this gross disparity in verbal output there were differences in the quality of language used by mothers in the various status groups. One approach to the analysis of language used by these mothers was an examination of their responses to the following task: They were shown the Lion Card of the Children's Apperception Test and asked to tell their child a story relating to the card. This card is a picture of a lion sitting on a chair holding a pipe in his hand. Beside him is a cane. In the corner is a mouse peering out of a hole. The lion appears to be deep in thought. These protocols were the source of language samples which were summarized in nine scales (Table 2), two of which we wish to describe here.

The first scale dealt with the mother's tendency to use abstract words. The index derived was a proportion of abstract noun and verb types to total number of noun and verb types. Words were defined as abstract when the name of the object is thought of apart from the cases in which it is actually realized. For example, in the sentence, "The lion is an *animal*," "animal" is an abstract word. However, in the sentence, "This animal in the picture is sitting on his throne," "animal" is not an abstract noun.

In our research group, middle-class mothers achieved an abstraction score of 5.6; the score for skilled work levels was 4.9; the score for the unskilled group was 3.7; for recipients of Aid to Dependent Children (ADC), 1.8.

The second scale dealt with the mother's tendency to use complex syntactic structures such as coordinate and subordinate clauses, unusual infinitive phrases (e.g., "To drive well, you must be alert"), infinitive clauses (e.g., "What to do next was the lion's problem"), and participial phrases (e.g., "Continuing the story, the lion . . ."). The index of structural elaboration derived was a proportion of these complex syntactic structures, weighted in accordance with their complexity and with the degree to which they are strung together to form still more complicated structures (e.g., clauses within clauses), to the total number of sentences.

In the research group, mothers from the middle class had a structure

TABLE 2
Social Status Differences in Language Usage
(Scores are the Means for Each Group)

Scale	Social Status			
	Upper Middle N = 40	Upper Lower N = 42	Lower Lower N = 40	ADC N = 41
Mean sentence length[a]	11.39	8.74	9.66	8.23
Adjective range[b]	31.99	28.32	28.37	30.49
Adverb range[c]	11.14	9.40	8.70	8.20
Verb elaboration[d]	.59	.52	.47	.44
Complex verb preference[e]	63.25	59.12	50.85	51.73
Syntactic structure elaboration[f]	8.89	6.90	8.07	6.46
Stimulus utilization	5.82	4.81	4.87	5.36
Introduced content	3.75	2.62	2.45	2.34
Abstraction[g]	5.60	4.89	3.71	1.75

[a] Average number of words per sentence.

[b] Proportion of uncommon adjective types to total nouns, expressed as a percentage.

[c] Proportion of uncommon adverb types to total verbs, adjectives, and adverbs, expressed as a percentage.

[d] Average number of complex verb types per sentence.

[e] Proportion of complex verb types to all verb types, simple and complex.

[f] Average number of weighted complex syntactic structures per 100 words.

[g] Proportion of abstract nouns and verbs (excluding repetitions) to total nouns and verbs (excluding repetitions), expressed as a percentage.

elaboration index of 8.89; the score for ADC mothers was 6.46. The use of complex grammatical forms and elaboration of these forms into complex clauses and sentences provides a highly elaborated code with which to manipulate the environment symbolically. This type of code encourages the child to recognize the possibilities and subtleties inherent in language not only for communication but also for carrying on high-level cognitive procedures.

CONTROL SYSTEMS: PERSON VERSUS STATUS ORIENTATION. Our data on the mothers' use of status- as contrasted with person-oriented statements comes from maternal responses to questions inquiring what the mother would do in order to deal with several different hypothetical situations at school in which the child had broken the rules of the school, had failed to achieve, or had been wronged by a teacher or classmate. The results of this tally are shown in Table 3.

As is clear from these means, the greatest differences between status groups is in the tendency to utilize person-oriented statements. These differences are even greater if seen as a ratio of person-to-status type responses.

The orientation of the mothers to these different types of control is seen not only in prohibitive or reparative situations but in their instructions to their children in preparing them for new experiences. The data on this point come from answers to the question: "Suppose your child were starting to school tomorrow for the first time. What would you tell him? How would you prepare him for school?"

One mother, who was person-oriented and used elaborated verbal codes, replied as follows:

"First of all, I would remind her that she was going to school to learn, that her teacher would take my place, and that she would be expected to follow instructions. Also that her time was to be spent mostly in the classroom with other children, and that any questions or any problems that she might have she could consult with her teacher for assistance."

"Anything else?"

"No, anything else would probably be confusing for her at her particular age."

TABLE 3
Person-Oriented and Status-Oriented Units
on School Situation Protocols (Mothers)

	A. Mean Number				
Social Class	Person-Oriented		Status-Oriented		P/S Ratio	N
Upper middle	9.52	(1–19)	7.50	(0–19)	1.27	40
Upper lower	6.20	(0–20)	7.32	(2–17)	0.85	40
Lower lower	4.66	(0–15)	7.34	(2–17)	0.63	35
ADC	3.59	(0–16)	8.15	(3–29)	0.44	34

B. Mean Per Cent			
Social Class	Person-Oriented	Status-Oriented	N
Upper middle	36.92	27.78	40
Upper lower	31.65	36.92	40
Lower lower	26.43	40.69	35
ADC	20.85	51.09	34

In terms of promoting educability, what did this mother do in her response? First, she was informative; she presented the school situation as comparable to one already familiar to the child; second, she offered reassurance and support to help the child deal with anxiety; third, she described the school situation as one that involves a personal relationship between the child and the teacher; and, fourth, she presented the classroom situation as one in which the child was to learn.

A second mother responded as follows to this question:

"Well, John, it's time to go to school now. You must know how to behave. The first day at school you should be a good boy and should do just what the teacher tells you to do."

In contrast to the first mother, what did this mother do? First, she defined the role of the child as passive and compliant; second, the central issues she presented were those dealing with authority and the institution, rather than with learning; third, the relationship and roles she portrayed were sketched in terms of status and role expectations rather than in personal terms; and, fourth, her message was general, restricted, and vague, lacking information about how to deal with the problems of school except by passive compliance.

A more detailed analysis of the mothers' responses to this question grouped their statements as *imperative* or *instructive* (Table 4). An im-

TABLE 4
Information Mothers Would Give to Child
on His First Day at School

Social Status	Imperative	Instructive	Support	Preparation	Other	N
		% of Total Statements				
Upper middle	14.9	8.7	30.2	8.6	37.6	39
Upper lower	48.2	4.6	13.8	3.8	29.6	41
Lower lower	44.4	1.7	13.1	1.2	39.6	36
ADC	46.6	3.2	17.1	1.3	31.8	37
		% of Mothers Using Category				
Upper middle	48.7	38.5	76.9	33.3	87.2	..
Upper lower	85.4	17.1	39.0	19.5	70.7	..
Lower lower	75.0	5.6	36.1	8.3	77.8	..
ADC	86.5	16.2	43.2	8.1	86.5	..

perative statement was defined as an unqualified injunction or command, such as, "Mind the teacher and do what she tells you to do," or "The first thing you have to do is be on time," or "Be nice and do not fight." An instructive statement offers information or commands which carry a rationale or justification for the rule to be observed. Examples: "If you are tardy or if you stay away from school, your marks will go down"; or "I would tell him about the importance of minding the teacher. The teacher needs his full cooperation. She will have so many children that she won't be able to pamper any youngster."

STATUS DIFFERENCES IN CONCEPT UTILIZATION.   One of the measures of cognitive style used with both mothers and children in the research group was the S's mode of classificatory behavior. For the adult version, (Kagan, Moss and Sigel, 1963) S is required to make 12 consecutive sorts of MAPS figures placed in a prearranged random order on a large cardboard. After each sort she was asked to give her reason for putting certain figures together. This task was intended to reveal her typical or preferred manner of grouping stimuli and the level of abstraction that she uses in perceiving and ordering objects in the environment. Responses fell into four categories: descriptive part-whole, descriptive global, relational-contextual, and categorical-inferential. A descriptive response is a direct reference to physical attributes present in the stimuli, such as size, shape, or posture. Examples: "They're all children," or "They are all lying down," or "They are all men." The subject may also choose to use only a part of the figure—"They both have hats on." In a relational-contextual response, any one stimulus gets its meaning from a relation with other stimuli. Examples: "Doctor and nurse," or "Wife is cooking dinner for her husband," or "This guy looks like he shot this other guy." In categorical-inferential responses, sorts are based on nonobservable characteristics of the stimulus for which each stimulus is an independent representative of the total class. Examples: "All of these people work for a living" or "These are all handicapped people."

As may be seen in Table 5, relational responses were most frequently offered; categorical-inferential were next most common, and descriptive

TABLE 5
Mean Responses to Adult Sigel Sorting Task (Maps)

	Social Status			
Category	Upper Middle $N = 40$	Upper Lower $N = 42$	Lower Lower $N = 39$	ADC $N = 41$
Total descriptive	3.18	2.19	2.18	2.59
Descriptive part-whole	1.65	1.33	1.31	1.49
Descriptive global	1.52	0.86	0.87	1.10
Relational-contextual	5.52	6.79	7.38	6.73
Categorical-inferential	3.30	3.00	2.23	2.66

most infrequent. The distribution of responses of our status groups showed that the middle-class group was higher on descriptive and categorical; low-status groups were higher on relational. The greater use of relational categories by the working-class mothers is especially significant. Response times for relational sorts are usually shorter, indicating less reflection and evaluating of alternative hypotheses. Such responses also indicate relatively low attention to external stimuli details (Kagan, 1964). Relational responses are often subjective, reflecting a tendency to relate objects to personal concerns in contrast with the descriptive and categorical responses which tend to be objective and detached, more general, and more abstract. Categorical responses, in particular, represent thought processes that are more orderly and complex in organizing stimuli, suggesting more efficient strategies of information processing.

The most striking finding from the data obtained from the children's Sigel Sorting Task was the decreasing use of the cognitive style dimensions and increasing nonverbal responses with decrease in social-status level. As may be seen in the tables showing children's performance on the Sigel Sorting Task (Tables 6 and 7), although most upper middle-class children

TABLE 6
Children's Responses to Sigel Sorting Task (Means)

| | Social Status | | | |
Category	Upper Middle $N = 40$	Upper Lower $N = 42$	Lower Lower $N = 39$	ADC $N = 41$
Descriptive				
part-whole	2.25	0.71	0.20	0.34
Descriptive global	2.80	2.29	1.51	0.98
Relational-contextual	3.18	2.31	1.18	1.02
Categorical-inferential	2.02	1.36	1.18	0.61
Nonscorable				
verbal responses	5.75	6.31	6.64	7.24
Nonverbal	3.00	6.41	7.08	8.76
No sort	1.00	0.62	2.21	1.05

and a majority of the upper lower-class children use relational and descriptive global responses, there is no extensive use of any of the other cognitive style dimensions by the two lower lower-class groups. In looking at particular categories one may note the relative absence of descriptive part-whole responses for other than the middle-class group and the large rise in nonverbal responses below the middle-class level. These results would seem to reflect the relatively undeveloped verbal and conceptual

TABLE 7
Percentage of Four-Year-Old Children
Responding in Each of the Categories

Category	Social Status			
	Upper Middle $N = 40$	*Upper Lower* $N = 42$	*Lower Lower* $N = 39$	*ADC* $N = 41$
Descriptive				
part-whole	40.0	28.6	18.0	14.6
Descriptive global	70.0	54.8	53.8	31.7
Total descriptive	80.0	66.7	59.0	39.0
Relational-contextual	77.5	66.7	41.0	43.9
Categorical-inferential	52.5	45.2	30.8	24.4
Nonscorable verbal	85.0	88.1	92.3	85.4
Nonverbal	52.5	66.7	82.0	87.8
No sort	12.5	7.1	25.6	19.5

ability of children from homes with restricted range of verbal and conceptual content.

Relational and descriptive global responses have been considered the most immature and would be hypothesized to occur most frequently in preschool children. Relational responses are often subjective, using idiosyncratic and irrelevant cues; descriptive global responses, often referring to sex and occupational roles, are somewhat more dependent upon experience. On the other hand, descriptive part-whole responses have been shown to increase with age and would be expected to be used less frequently. However, these descriptive part-whole responses, which are correlated with favorable prognostic signs for educability (such as attentiveness, control and learning ability), were almost totally absent from all but the upper middle-class group. Kagan (1964) has described two fundamental cognitive dispositions involved in producing such analytic concepts: the tendency to reflect over alternative solutions that are simultaneously available and the tendency to analyze a visual stimulus into component parts. Both behaviors require a delayed discrimination response. One may describe the impairment noted for culturally disadvantaged children as arising from differences in opportunities for developing these reflective attitudes.

The mothers' use of relational responses was significantly correlated with their children's use of nonscorable and nonverbal responses on the Sigel task and with poor performance on the 8-Block and Etch-a-Sketch tasks. The mothers' inability or disinclination to take an abstract attitude on the Sigel task was correlated with ineffectual teaching on the 8-Block task and inability to plan and control the Etch-a-Sketch situation. Since relational responses have been found (Kagan, Moss, and Sigel, 1963) to be correlated with impulsivity, tendencies for nonverbal rather than verbal teaching, mother-domination, and limited sequencing and discrimination might be expected and would be predicted to result in limited categorizing ability and impaired verbal skills in the child.

Analysis of Maternal Teaching Styles

These differences among the status groups and among mothers within the groups appear in slightly different form in the teaching sessions in which the mothers and children engaged. There were large differences among the status groups in the ability of the mothers to teach and the children to learn. This is illustrated by the performance scores on the sorting tasks.

Let us describe the interaction between the mother and child in one of the structured teaching situations. The wide range of individual differences in linguistic and interactional styles of these mothers may be illustrated by excerpts from recordings. The task of the mother is to teach the child how to group or sort a small number of toys.

The first mother outlines the task for the child, gives sufficient help and explanation to permit the child to proceed on her own. She says:

"All right, Susan, this board is the place where we put the little toys; first of all you're supposed to learn how to place them according to color. Can you do that? The things that are all the same color you put in one section; in the second section you put another group of colors, and in the third section you put the last group of colors. Can you do that? Or would you like to see me do it first?"

Child: "I want to do it."

This mother has given explicit information about the task and what is expected of the child; she has offered support and help of various kinds; and she has made it clear that she impelled the child to perform.

A second mother's style offers less clarity and precision. She says in introducing the same task:

"Now, I'll take them all off the board; now you put them all back on the board. What are these?"

Child: "A truck."

"All right, just put them right here; put the other one right here; all right put the other one there."

This mother must rely more on nonverbal communication in her commands; she does not define the task for the child; the child is not provided with ideas or information that she can grasp in attempting to solve the problem; neither is she told what to expect or what the task is, even in general terms.

A third mother is even less explicit. She introduces the task as follows: "I've got some chairs and cars, do you want to play the game?" Child does not respond. Mother continues: "O.K. What's this?"

Child: "A wagon?"

Mother: "Hm?"

Child: "A wagon?"

Mother: "This is not a wagon. What's this?"

The conversation continues with this sort of exchange for several pages. Here again, the child is not provided with the essential information he needs to solve or to understand the problem. There is clearly some impelling on the part of the mother for the child to perform, but the child has not been told what he is to do. There were marked social-class differences in the ability of the children to learn from their mothers in the teaching sessions.

Each teaching session was concluded with an assessment by a staff member of the extent to which the child had learned the concepts taught by the mother. His achievement was scored in two ways: first, the ability to correctly place or sort the objects and, second, the ability to verbalize the principle on which the sorting or grouping was made.

Children from middle-class homes were well above children from working-class homes in performance on these sorting tasks, particularly in offering verbal explanations as to the basis for making the sort (Tables 8 and 9). Over 60 per cent of middle-class children placed the objects correctly on all tasks; the performance of working-class children ranged

TABLE 8
Differences among Status Groups in Children's Performance in Teaching Situations (Toy Sort Task)

Social Status	Placed Correctly (%)	Verbalized Correctly (%)		N
A. Identity sort (cars, spoons, chairs):				
Upper middle	61.5	28.2	45.8[a]	39
Upper lower	65.0	20.0	30.8	40
Lower lower	68.4	29.0	42.3	38
ADC	66.7	30.8	46.2	39
B. Color sort (red, green, yellow):				
Upper middle	69.2	28.2	40.7[a]	39
Upper lower	67.5	15.0	22.2	40
Lower lower	57.9	13.2	22.7	38
ADC	33.3	5.1	15.4	39

[a] Per cent of those who placed object correctly.

TABLE 9
Differences among Status Groups in Children's Performance in Teaching Situations (8-Block Task)

Social Status	Placed Correctly (%)	One-Dimension Verbalized (%)		Both Verbalized (%)		N
A. Short O:						
Upper middle	75.0	57.5	57.5[a]	25.0	33.3[a]	40
Upper lower	51.2	39.0	43.2	2.4	4.8	41
Lower lower	50.0	29.0	33.3	15.8	31.6	38
ADC	43.6	20.5	22.2	2.6	5.9	39
B. Tall X:						
Upper middle	60.0	62.5	64.1[a]	27.5	45.8[a]	40
Upper lower	48.8	39.0	42.1	17.1	35.0	41
Lower lower	34.2	23.7	26.5	7.9	23.1	38
ADC	28.2	18.0	20.0	0.0	0.0	39

[a] Per cent of those who placed object correctly.

as low as 29 per cent correct. Approximately 40 per cent of these middle-class children who were successful were able to verbalize the sorting principle; working-class children were less able to explain the sorting principle, ranging downward from the middle-class level to one task on which no child was able to verbalize correctly the basis of his sorting behavior. These differences clearly paralleled the relative abilities and teaching skills of the mothers from differing social-status groups.

The difference among the four status levels was apparent not only on these sorting and verbal skills but also in the mother's ability to regulate her own behavior and her child's in performing tasks which require planning or care rather than verbal or conceptual skill. These differences were revealed by the mother-child performance on the Etch-a-Sketch task. An Etch-a-Sketch toy is a small, flat box with a screen on which lines can be drawn by a device within the box. The marker is controlled by two knobs: one for horizontal movement, one for vertical. The mother is assigned one knob, the child the other. The mother is shown several designs which are to be reproduced. Together they attempt to copy the design models. The mother decides when their product is a satisfactory copy of the original. The products are scored by measuring deviations from the original designs.

These sessions were recorded, and the nonverbal interaction was described by an observer. Some of the most relevant results were these:

middle-class mothers and children performed better on the task (14.6 points) than mothers and children from the other groups (9.2; 8.3; 9.5; [Table 10]). Mothers of the three lower-status groups were relatively persistent, rejecting more complete figures than the middle-class mothers; mothers from the middle class praised the child's efforts more than did other mothers but gave just as much criticism; the child's cooperation as rated by the observer was as good or better in low-status groups as in middle-class pairs (Table 11), there was little difference between the groups in affect expressed to the child by the mother (Brophy et al., 1965).

TABLE 10
Performance on Etch-a-Sketch Task (Means)

| | Social Status | | | |
	Upper Middle N = 40	Upper Lower N = 42	Lower Lower N = 40	ADC N = 41
Total score (range 0–40)	14.6	9.2	8.3	9.5
Average number of attempts	12.7	17.2	12.2	15.1
Complete figures rejected	2.3	3.6	3.5	3.4
Child's total score	5.9	4.0	3.4	4.0
Child's contribution to total score (per cent)	40.4	43.5	41.0	42.1

TABLE 11 [a]
Mother-Child Interaction on Etch-a-Sketch Task (Means)

| | Social Status | | | |
	Upper Middle N = 40	Upper Lower N = 41	Lower Lower N = 39	ADC N = 39
Praises child	4.6	6.9	7.2	7.5
Criticizes child	6.4	5.5	6.4	5.9
Overall acceptance of child	2.2	3.2	3.4	3.6
Child's cooperation	5.6	5.3	4.5	5.1
Level of affection shown to child	4.8	5.4	5.2	5.8

[a] Ratings made by observer; low number indicates more of the quality rated.

In these data, as in other not presented here, the mothers of the four status groups differed relatively little, on the average, in the affective elements of their interaction with their children. The gross differences appeared in the verbal and cognitive environments that they presented.

Against this background I would like to return for a moment to the problem of the meaning, or, perhaps more correctly, the lack of meaning in cultural deprivation. One of the features of the behavior of the working-class mothers and children is a tendency to act without taking sufficient time for reflection and planning. In a sense one might call this impulsive behavior—not by acting out unconscious or forbidden impulses, but in a type of activity in which a particular act seems not to be related to the act that preceded it or to its consequences. In this sense it lacks meaning; it is not sufficiently related to the context in which it occurs, to the motivations of the participants, or to the goals of the task. This behavior may be verbal or motor; it shows itself in several ways. On the Etch-a-Sketch task, for example, the mother may silently watch a child make an error and then punish him. Another mother will anticipate the error, will warn the child that he is about to reach a decision point; she will prepare him by verbal and nonverbal cues to be careful, to look ahead, and to avoid the mistake. He is encouraged to reflect, to anticipate the consequences of his action, and in this way to avoid error. A problem-solving approach requires reflection and the ability to weigh decisions, to choose among alternatives. The effect of restricted speech and of status orientation is to foreclose the need for reflective weighing of alternatives and consequences; the use of an elaborated code, with its orientation to persons and to consequences (including future), tends to produce cognitive styles more easily adapted to problem-solving and reflection.

The objective of our study is to discover how teaching styles of the mothers induce and shape learning styles and information-processing strategies in the children. The picture that is beginning to emerge is that the meaning of deprivation is a deprivation of meaning—a cognitive environment in which behavior is controlled by status rules rather than by attention to the individual characteristics of a specific situation and one in which behavior is not mediated by verbal cues or by teaching that relates events to one another and the present to the future. This environment produces a child who relates to authority rather than to rationale, who, although often compliant, is not reflective in his behavior, and for whom the consequences of an act are largely considered in terms of immediate punishment or reward rather than future effects and long-range goals.

When the data are more complete, a more detailed analysis of the findings will enable us to examine the effect of maternal cognitive environments in terms of individual mother-child transactions, rather than in the

gross categories of social class. This analysis will not only help us to understand how social-class environment is mediated through the interaction
between mother and child but will give more precise information about
the effects of individual maternal environments on the cognitive growth
of the young child.

References

Bernstein, B. February 1964. *Family role systems, communication, and
socialization.* A paper presented at the Conference on the Development of Cross-National Research on the Education of Children and
Adolescents, University of Chicago.
———. 1961. Social class and linguistic development: a theory of social
learning. In A. H. Halsey, Jean Floud, and C. A. Anderson (eds.),
Education, economy, and society (New York: The Free Press).
Brophy, J., R. D. Hess, and Virginia Shipman. March 1965. *Effects of
social class and level of aspiration on performance in a structured
mother-child interaction.* A paper presented at the Biennial Meeting
of the Society for Research and Child Development, Minneapolis,
Minnesota.
Deutsch, M. 1963. The disadvantaged child and the learning process. In
A. H. Passow (ed.), *Education in depressed areas* (New York:
Teachers College, Columbia University), pp. 163–180.
———, and B. Brown. 1964. Social influences in Negro-white intelligence
differences. *J. soc. Issues*, **20**, 2, pp. 24–35.
Eells, K., Allison Davis, R. J. Havighurst, V. E. Herrick, and R. W. Tyler.
1951. *Intelligence and cultural differences* (Chicago, Ill.: University
of Chicago Press).
Hess, R. D. 1964. Educability and rehabilitation: the future of the welfare
class. *Marriage Fam. Lvg.*, **26**, pp. 422–429.
Jackson, J. D., R. D. Hess, and Virginia Shipman. February 1965. *Communication styles in teachers: an experiment.* A paper presented at
the American Educational and Research Association, Chicago.
John, Vera. 1963. The intellectual development of slum children: some
preliminary findings. *Amer. J. Orthopsychiat.*, **33**, pp. 813–822.
Kagan, J. 1964. Information processing in the child: significance of
analytic and reflective attitudes. *Psychol. Monogr.*, **78**, No. 1, Whole
No. 578.
———, and H. A. Moss, and I. E. Sigel. 1963. Psychological significance
of styles of conceptualization. *Monogr. Soc. Res. Child Develpm.*,
28, No. 2.

Kennedy, W. A., V. Van de Riet, and J. C. White, Jr. 1963. A normative sample of intelligence and achievement of Negro elementary school children in the southeastern United States. *Monogr. Soc. Res. Child Develpm.*, **28**, No. 6.

Lesser, G. 1964. *Mental abilities of children in different social and cultural groups.* Cooperative Research Project No. 1635, New York.

Meyer, Roberta, Virginia Shipman, and R. D. Hess. September 1964. *Family structure and social class in the socialization of curiosity in urban preschool children.* A paper presented at a meeting of the American Psychological Association, Los Angeles, California.

Olim, E. G., R. D. Hess, and Virginia Shipman. March 1965. *Relationship between mothers' language styles and cognitive styles of urban preschool children.* A paper presented at the Biennial Meeting of the Society for Research and Child Development, Minneapolis, Minnesota.

Shipman, Virginia, and R. D. Hess. April 1965. *Social class and sex differences in the utilization of language and the consequences for cognitive development.* A paper presented before the Midwest Psychological Association, Chicago.

PART **8** *What Should Be Taught in the Preschool?*

Two significant factors are having a far-reaching influence on programs for preschoolers: (1) the accumulating evidence pointing to the preschool years as an optimum period for rapid intellectual growth, and (2) the systematic failure of schools to compensate for the effects of early deprivation. These conclusions are suggesting to educators that they start educational experiences earlier and that they search diligently for more effective compensatory approaches for the disadvantaged.

Teachers who accept the inevitability of change, Helen Heffernan appropriately points out, find teaching a rewarding and satisfying task. Yet many preschools are taking on the characteristics of a formalized first-grade program with the accompanying rigid expectation. Now that children are five they should *all* learn to read because *some* fives have. This is no less a tragic error than the assumption that *all* six-year-olds *will* read. Such expectations as these are out of character with present understanding of the developmental process.

Heffernan directs our attention to the relevant issues. "Are we providing a program that has horizontal coherence and meaning at each age level and vertical continuity during the four-year-span?" In reply to the critics who say that children don't learn anything in the kindergarten she describes ways in which *content* and *method* are woven into programs. Throughout the usual kindergarten experience the child has experiences designed to develop competencies regarding human relations, his social and physical world, communication, problem solving, and creative expression.

Poverty is a relative newcomer to the preschool scene. The effects of its introduction have been bomb-like. Preordaining failure for most of its victims, poverty is currently education's number one problem. Maya Pines (*Harper's* January, 1967) described one experimental

487

compensatory effort for preschoolers. She gets off to a
shaky start by leaving the impression that Arnold Gesell's
contributions may be written off the books and continues
to erroneously suggest that early childhood educators are
unaware of educational implications arising from the
efforts of the "cognitive" school. Such verbalism, however, has had no small effect upon its readers. Educators
are analyzing Carl Bereiter and Siegfried Englemann's
program. Some are awaiting longitudinal results. Others
are experimenting with certain aspects of the program in
their own schools. Time has taught the futility of expecting quick or ready-made solutions to our concerns for
educating children.

Pines aptly called the program an "intellectual pressure cooker." A selection from *Phi Delta Kappan* draws
from her writing in describing this approach. Very close
in spirit to the kind of programs written for teaching
machines and computers, children are noisily drilled in
mathematics and language. It is a rigid, logical, efficient,
academically-oriented procedure. Three highly trained
teachers work with fifteen children. As many as 500
responses may be required of each child during a twenty-
minute period.

Bereiter and Englemann have not observed "extreme
anxiety, dread of school, or robot-like conformity" among
the children. They believe the results have been beneficial.
During a seven-month period the scores of 15 four-year-
olds on the Illinois Test of Psycholinguistic Abilities increased a year and a half to "approximately normal."
Their Stanford-Binet scores rose from the low 90's to
slightly over 100 (such I.Q. gains are expected for children during a summer Head Start program). The ultimate test of this and other experimental programs will
await answers to the queries of Maya Pines. Will the children's confidence collapse when they are denied the support of this close-knit group? Will it survive twelve years
in crowded slum schools? Have the children learned, deep
down, to parrot unquestionably whatever they are told
by people in authority?

Although lip service is being given to cognitive
learning processes, few have systematically analyzed
and programmed for the total situational-developmental

learning encounters of young children. William Fowler proposes a model that may be useful in conceiving programs. Beginning with a recommendation for psycho-cognitive diagnosis of each child, to be continued periodically, he outlines steps for a structural, functional, and analytical approach to program designing, with careful pacing of stimulation sequences. Such programming suggests a shift of focus to the changes required for helping teachers develop skills needed for facilitating cognitive developmental learning.

Richard R. Ellis carries the cognitive emphases further. The tendency of teachers of young children to support the child's natural inclinations by not imposing directions neglects stimulation of intellectual development. Such programs work quite well with most children who have had continuing stimulation since birth.

Teachers have learned to be quite defensive about a number of terms that have been equated with rigidity and poor teaching in our unsuccessful (for the disadvantaged) schools of the past. Now these same terms are needed to convey meanings about emerging programs for young children. *Structure* can mean rigidity or flexible guidelines. *Organize* can mean to disregard individuality or to analyze tasks appropriately for learners. *Teach* can mean to convey content indiscriminately or to base learning on antecedent conditions. We cannot proceed open-mindedly and flexibly toward program improvement unless we replace the custom of attaching meanings *to* situations with the practice of gleaning meaning *from* situations.

The work of Piaget, Hunt, Bruner, Jensen, Luria, Montessori, Deutsch, and others has influenced Ellis (and many others) to explore possibilities for structuring pre-school programs in a sequential progression involving considerations of step size, individual pacing and feedback. Global goals must be replaced by specific short-term and long-range goals analyzed in behavioral terms. Such precision in planning does indeed require greater skill than most teachers are presently demonstrating. And surprisingly, for some, greater precision in defining the elements of teaching-learning requires *greater*, not less, flexibility. Approximating a close relationship between the child's present conceptual level and the content to be learned in educational encounters is a highly individualized matter.

This section concludes with the contribution by Celia Stendler Lavatelli. The Piagetian current penetrating many of the selections in this book is placed in educational focus. A Piaget-derived preschool curriculum stressing actions upon classes and relations between classes rather than perceptual experiences is presented. Stendler's contribution represents a type of interpretative action sorely needed by curriculum developers faced with the complicated task of bridging the gaps between research, theory, and practice.

42   A Vital Curriculum
for Today's Young Child*

HELEN HEFFERNAN, *California State Department of Education*

Because education *is* dynamic, teachers at every level must be ever conscious of its movement. Movement can be backward as well as forward. Involving as education does vast numbers of human beings growing up in a changing world, it can never become fixed and static. The teacher can never do the same thing over and over day after day for group after group of young children, because the needs of individuals and groups change and the social needs of the time in which they are living change.

Teachers who accept the inevitability of change find living and working with children, with the mothers and fathers of the children they teach, and with their professional colleagues an exciting and satisfying adventure in lifelong learning. Teachers who want to settle into a fixed pattern which can be repeated again and again are probably doomed to feel very frustrated in a profession which must serve a world in which change is accelerating constantly.

But teachers of young children throughout the country are greatly disturbed because of the accusation that the educational program of the kindergarten and early grades "lacks content." The more extreme critics propose eliminating the kindergarten altogether because children "don't learn anything there." It is not enough to say that the critics do not know what they are talking about, that their opinions are not based on objective evidence, or that the critic has not bothered to visit a kindergarten to see what does go on there.

All of these responses to the criticisms may be true but as professional workers we must look at all sides of the issue. We must ask ourselves: What are appropriate educative experiences for five-, six-, seven- and eight-year-old children? Are we providing a program that has horizontal coherence and meaning at each age level and vertical continuity during the four-year span? Are we adapting content and method to the individual needs of each child so that we lose none of the promise, the undiscovered potential of each child?

Like Thoreau's companion "you may march to the beat of another drummer" but, I believe that the kindergarten-primary period must

* *The Journal of Education*, January 1966, no. 12. Reprinted by permission.

endeavor to provide opportunity for substantial growth and development in four significant directions. Throughout the entire period the child needs:

> 1. Experiences designed to maintain and improve his physical and mental health and guide him to increasingly more satisfying relationships with other children and adults.
> 2. Experiences designed to extend and deepen his understanding of his social and scientific world.
> 3. Experiences designed to develop his competence in the skills of communication, in mathematical understanding and in the use of mathematical vocabulary and symbols.
> 4. Experiences designed to open windows on life through music, the graphic arts, literature, drama, and rhythmic expression.

If we examine each of these areas of experience, it becomes evident that content and method are inextricably interwoven. How the teacher teaches and the quality of the educational transaction are what makes the difference. The school provides a multitude of experiences and services to promote and maintain the child's physical health and vigor: medical and dental examinations, vision and hearing testing, daily health inspection, school lunch and other nutrition periods, rest periods, provision for vigorous outdoor play and many others. But the effectiveness of these services depends largely on the teacher's guidance and the habituation of good health practices, such as washing hands before eating and after toileting, resting, safety in using equipment and in playing with other children and many others. But far more subtle are the techniques a teacher uses to promote sound mental health and bring about effective emotional adjustment to other children and adults.

Years of guidance by skillful teachers have certainly made a great contribution to the present longevity of our people and to the prediction that children now in our elementary schools have a life expectancy of 100 years!

Because reasonably good health habits are practised by many people in our culture, adults may think they come as standard equipment when a child is born. They are all *learned behaviors*, however, and are taught and slowly acquired (sometimes with considerable resistance) by every human being. Adults are too prone to brush off the significance of education in the area of health but its importance to the personality and success of the individual is too apparent to require much argument.

Learnings in the broad field of health continue to occupy a large portion of the child's school time during these early years with a *very large* allocation of time at the kindergarten level and lessening somewhat during succeeding years as sound routines are established and children grow in experience and ability to take care of themselves.

The real content of life is to be found in man's relationship to man and man's relationship to his physical environment. The experiences for which young children are eager and ready in social sciences and physical sciences are limitless. The neighborhood and community afford countless opportunities for children to acquire genuine understanding about how man has satisfied his basic human needs. Firsthand experiences are the best learning experiences and good schools everywhere provide opportunity for children to visit the supermarket, the bakery, the farm, the creamery, the fire station, the airport, the post office, the harbor, the zoo, the park, the museum and every place in the community where man works to satisfy his needs for food, clothing, shelter, transportation, communication, recreation, education, religious and aesthetic expression.

In the field of science, young children are interested in all living things—the plants and animals of their environment and with their interdependence. They are interested in the earth and in the celestial wonders of outer space, they are interested in power and energy, in the technological world of which they are a part. These four items constitute the basic content of all science.

At every age level, the major portion of the child's day should be devoted to experiences in the social sciences and in the physical sciences. Sometimes they are closely related and it is difficult (and unnecessary) for a child to find out where one stops and another begins. A careful analysis of a unit on the dairy farm which was the recommended content in a social studies program for second grade in a city course of study revealed that 90 per cent of the experiences suggested were really science experiences.

But our success in helping young children understand their social and scientific environment does not depend primarily on the content selected. The content is limitless and can be explored to any depth the children's interest and the teacher's knowledge takes them. The real success here comes as a result of the teacher's skill in arranging an environment which opens up new experiences for children, which impels them to question, to explore, to discover, to gain new ideas and feelings to express in words, in construction, in painting, in modelling, in dramatic play, in rhythmic expression; *This is really the time when the children acquire skills*. Where there is zest, meaning and depth in the social studies and science experiences, skills fall into their proper relations.

And now, our third significant area of the total curriculum—understanding the skills of communication and mathematics. These skills are involved in all the activities in which the children are engaged. The more zest and meaning and depth in these experiences, the more will children wish to express themselves about them and later read about them and develop understanding about the quantitative and qualitative relations inherent in them. But, I would like to return to this in another connection shortly in relation to the question: When to teach reading?

And finally to take a brief look at number four on our list of significant areas. The years of the kindergarten-primary span are not long enough to introduce children to all the beautiful music that is a part of their cultural heritage. Nor is it long enough to acquaint them with all the wonderful stories and poems that will be a never ending source of joy throughout their lives. The days are not long enough so everyone can work at finger painting and painting at the easels and modelling with clay.

But these are the beginnings of the arts and without opportunity to experiment freely in a hospitable climate where it is safe to express his honest self, how can a child ever discover his potential, how can he discover what has meaning for him, "sharp-pointed meaning" to use Robert Frost's words? These are the years for experimenting, for painting every day, modelling every day, singing every day, dancing every day, listening to poetry and learning certain favorite poems every day, dramatizing loved stories and recreating all adult life in dramatic play.

In discussing the four-fold nature of an educational program for young children, I hope I have made it clear that I have been describing the kind and quality of experience for *all* the fives to eights and I would go further to the twelves!

Unfortunately the high prestige value society places on the skills induces teachers to devote an inordinate amount of time to teaching the skills. Throughout this entire developmental period, children need great freedom for physical movement and activity, for choice in the selection and use of a wide variety of materials, for study trips into the out-of-school environment, for opportunity to collect and classify materials.

It is tragic to hear an occasional first grade teacher bemoan the fact that children learned to play in kindergarten and it is so hard "to settle them down" in the first grade. A good first grade is hard to distinguish from a good kindergarten except on the basis of physical size.

With all these possibilities, life for the young child should be full of joy and enthusiasm but again it all depends on the quality of the person who guides them in the classroom. Is she intellectually curious, loving, competent, self-confident, informed and responsible? Does she recognize the social significance of her life role? If so, all is well. It depends on the teacher.

Now, let us examine the question we reserved for later consideration: When should a child learn to read? Traditionally our children embark on the exciting adventure of learning to read when they enter the first grade around six. Many exceedingly well-informed authorities have questioned the wisdom of attempting to impose reading on all six year olds. A group of thirty first graders, all chronologically about six, may vary in mental age from four years to eight years. Traditionally, we have forced them all into the same "reading shoes" even though we know their "intellectual feet" are widely different in size. The experience of many frustrated first grade teachers attest to the fact that their best efforts are really unsuccessful with about 25 per cent of the children. The net result is not only children who have not learned to read but children who *have learned* to feel themselves to be inadequate and who reject the situation which produced these miserable feelings of fear, frustration and failure in them.

How long will we continue to operate on this invalidated and unwarranted assumption? No wonder such Procrustean methods continue to contribute to the increase in emotionally disturbed children and to those who become a statistic among the dropouts.

But now some parents and some teachers and some administrators believe the kindergarten program is not "challenging enough." They believe that children have had all these experiences in nursery school, or by watching television or by just living in this exciting space age. They mistake a superficial sophistication, imitation of some technical terms heard on television and a welter of secondhand experience as evidence of budding genius. Their recommendation for "challenging the children" is usually workbooks in reading and arithmetic and beginning a basic reading program.

Now let us look at it more closely. Can we teach kindergarten children to read? The answer is "yes" we can, some children and under some conditions. There are certain important questions we must answer before we arrive at a decision to teach reading. What are the visual hazards to the young child? He is normally far-sighted at age five. Reading forces attention on near and very small symbols. The opthamologists, to whom we have a right to turn for an answer to our question, have not yet produced evidence on the effect of close work on young eyes. However, they are agreed that the number of their patients in the early childhood group has increased astonishingly in recent years. Nationally known pediatricians point out that while children may seem to suffer no damage at the time, in two or three years the enrolment of patients in their psychological clinics who have a previous history of being taught reading early has definitely increased. A reasonably prudent parent or teacher would want to explore the evidence much further before consenting to premature reading instruction.

Eventually the evidence from opthamologists, pediatricians, psychologists and psychiatrists may answer the question with the same finality as the research on the causes of lung cancer has answered that question but in the meanwhile we must be willing to test this proposal against our own educational philosophy.

Obviously, learning to read is a sitting-down, physically passive task. While a child is so engaged he cannot be pedaling his trike vigorously, he cannot be exploring a park, or a pond or the seashore, he cannot be building with blocks, he cannot be planting and caring for a garden, he cannot be singing or listening to music, he cannot be creating bodily rhythms, he cannot be developing motor coordination walking the narrow edge of a board, he cannot be learning hand-eye coordination throwing a ball, he cannot be playing store or airplane pilot or postman or locomotive engineer as he strives to get inside experiences and see how they feel.

We may agree that some five-year-olds can learn to read but is this the best use to make of their fiveness? They will never be five again. The innate wisdom of the organism tells them to be gathering firsthand experiences and piling up personal experiences; it tells them to be physically active, to communicate with other human beings, to build with whatever is at hand the world they are trying to understand, to ask questions, to recreate all the adult activities of their environment in dramatic play, to experiment, to observe, to discover for themselves. Everything we know about children supports the belief that all this is necessary for the well-rounded development of the human organism.

Are we warping children to satisfy adult demands? Are we denying children their childhood by forcing formal language and reading on them at too early an age? There is a cultural pressure in our society to make every child learn to read in kindergarten or first grade. Children with a developmental lag in language maturation are extremely vulnerable in our society.

When children have difficulty in reading, parents blame the school and teachers blame the home for exerting undue pressure. But, probably neither is able to identify causes among the multiple factors which must be considered: (1) unrecognized dull normal intelligence, (2) unrecognized hearing defects, (3) unrecognized visual defects, (4) speech difficulties, (5) cultural factors including language, (6) inadequate nutrition, (7) inadequate rest, (8) frequent changes of school and home environment, (9) chronic illness, (10) physical handicaps, (11) maturity—physical and emotional, (12) unrecognized seizures, (13) emotional problems, (14) specific disability including minimal brain damage, mild cerebral dysfunction, defect in cerebral integrative mechanism without signs of gross brain damage.

Perhaps we need to enlist the cooperation of pediatricians in trying to reverse this cultural pressure on children for early reading. Unfortunately those who know least about it are usually most vociferous in their demands upon the school. Perhaps we need to seek the answer to the question: What does the professional person do in the face of these pressures?

Erik Erikson agrees with Freud that society is too autocratic in demanding impossible feats from her children. At the same time that society speaks out loud and sharp about teaching the skills, equally vigorous voices in our society say, "we need creative people." The imposition of skills and the release of creativity are utterly antithetical.

What can we say by way of advice to all teachers of young children? Let us study childhood, let us recognize the uniqueness of each child, let us provide a wealth of worthwhile experiences, let us de-emphasize the skills and put the emphasis on the rich content of our cultural heritage, let us be concerned about how the child feels about himself, let us be certain he thinks well of himself and sees shining possibilities as he looks ahead.

43 Instructional Planning in Early Compensatory Education*

CARL BEREITER, *University of Illinois*

The history of teaching shows cycles of vigorous times followed by periods of stultification and rigidity. During the vigorous times people are concerned with what children are learning. During the dull times people are concerned with putting children through the motions that, previously, had been more finely tuned to the production of learning. In our present haste to provide preschool programs for disadvantaged children, we are in danger of leaping directly to a blind concentration upon what children should do without going through the productive phase of considering what children should learn and devising methods that will bring this learning about. This is occurring, ironically, at a time when in other areas of education we are in a stage of vigorous growth, in which the question of what children should learn is being reexamined more deeply and in more detail than ever before and in which new methods are being developed with a clearer view to the attainment of learning objectives and less reliance upon pedagogical ritual.

But wait. Is there not a great deal of research going on to determine the needs of disadvantaged children and to test ways of meeting

* *Phi Delta Kappan*, March 1967, vol. 68, no. 7. Reprinted by permission.

these needs? To be sure. But this is not the same thing as instructional planning. It leaves out the essential step of converting "deficits," "needs," and "conditions" into specific learning objectives and then developing instructional methods to achieve these learning objectives, rather than trying to treat the deficits, needs, and conditions directly, which is something that education cannot hope to do except by a remarkable stroke of luck.

This kind of instructional planning is what Siegfried Engelmann and I have been trying to do in an experimental program at the University of Illinois. We have, for instance, tried to convert the general goal of improving language abilities into a series of specific concepts and language operations to be taught. These were arrived at in the same way that curriculum planners go about determining the content of science and mathematics courses—not by empirical means but by a consideration of what concepts and skills were necessary or most powerful in relation to future tasks. We have done the same kind of thing with reading and arithmetic. Although these latter subjects had already been worked over by curriculum planners, the analysis of tasks into their component concepts and skills has not been carried down to a low enough level to permit a clear specification of the first steps in learning for naive four-year-olds. Thus it was necessary to design "sub-zero" curricula, as it were, in reading and arithmetic; but we have tried to do this in as direct and specific a fashion as is done for higher-level mathematics instruction, rather than contenting ourselves with more indefinite kinds of "readiness" training.[1]

Curriculum planning for young disadvantaged children—that is, the specification of what should be taught and in what order—has been discouraged by a kind of medical orientation to disadvantaged children on the one hand and by strong anti-instructional biases on the other. The medical orientation has led to regarding cultural deprivation as an ailment or complex of ailments that need to be diagnosed and cured. For people who hold to this orientation, the important question to ask of any proposed curriculum is whether it will get to the heart of the ailments and cure them—and the answer has to be negative, because no curriculum ever cured anything. More generally, the medical orientation leads to a fruitless concern over whether a given curriculum is the "right one" for disadvantaged children. How do we know, for instance, that the particular language concepts and operations that we have elected to teach are the ones that disadvantaged children really need to learn?

---

[1] These curricula are described in detail in *Teaching Disadvantaged Children in the Preschool,* by Carl Bereiter and Siegfried Engelmann, Prentice-Hall, 1966.

This unanswerable question does not seem to come up when one is planning curricula for ordinary children. The planner of a junior high school biology course knows that there are many alternative choices of content and that there is plenty of room for argument against any particular selection, but he is under no illusion that there exists, somewhere in the unprobed psyches of his students, a key that would tell him which is the "right one." He simply tries to do the best he can with the knowledge and imagination at his disposal. If curriculum planners had to worry about finding a key to the "right one," curriculum innovation would remain at a standstill.

The anti-instructional bias is tied to a number of widely held convictions about not "forcing" young children, about the importance of play and free exploration, the primacy of social or nonverbal learning, and so on. There is no logical reason why these convictions should militate against the defining of instructional objectives, however, since specifying *what* children should learn does not in itself rule out or entail any particular ways of treating children. On the other hand, it can bring about a showdown, in which the advocates of a certain method must either demonstrate how their method can produce the designated learnings or else come up with some alternate set of learnings which their method can accomplish and which can be defended in open competition. This kind of showdown is badly needed, but it is not likely to occur so long as achievement objectives of any kind are met with hostility.

The second part of instructional planning is finding a practical way of getting all children to learn the specified content. It is on this point that our experimental program has aroused the most controversy. In fact, *all* of the controversy seems to have centered on this point, which is unfortunate. It is unfortunate because constructive debate on educational methods cannot really be carried on without a consideration of what one is trying to teach. Opponents should either claim that they can teach the same things in better ways or that other things should be taught. Simply arguing about teaching methods without reference to what the children are to learn is rather like arguing the merits of different means of transportation without reference to where one is going.

We have chosen to teach in the most direct manner possible, striving in each lesson to make it clear to the children what they are supposed to be learning, what the criteria of learning are, how what they are learning now relates to what they have learned previously, and what good it does them to learn it—that is, what they can do with what they have learned. With disadvantaged four-year-olds, very little of this can be communicated to them through explanation. They have to be shown through example, through the structure of the tasks themselves, and through careful control of the teacher's responses.[2] The methods we have developed are appropriate for a live teacher working with small and relatively homogeneous groups. Other methods of teaching the same content could be used. Individual tutorial methods, for example, would call for somewhat different procedures. With more heterogeneous groups one might make more use of modeling behavior and of children's helping one another. Some of the teaching could be automated, although this is difficult for teaching verbal responses. The use of television or other unresponsive media would create new problems but also new possibilities. A more potent system of contingent rewards might lessen the need for dramatizing the intrinsic value of what is being learned. It might also be possible, though it appears to us much more difficult and time-consuming, to make greater use of discovery methods. Given the same content to be learned, however, these alternate methods would have to be judged on economy and effectiveness.[3]

Debate over the "right" method of teaching is likely to be as unproductive as debate over the "right" content. The best method of teaching a given body of content is likely to be the one that is the most thoroughly developed at the time, although for the long haul one should probably put his money on the method that has the greatest potentiality for development. I would venture the guess, for instance, that in the first trials of our program we would have gotten better results with the same basic program by incorporating into it a "token reward economy" of the kind favored by behavioristic psychologists. Had we maintained a more consistently high level of motivation through inadequately designed parts of the program, children would have been more likely to learn in spite of defective methods of presentation and gaps in the sequence of learning steps. But to the extent that this occurred, we should have been unable to discern what the gaps and defects were. As it was, lagging motivation and halts in learning provided sensitive indicators of trouble spots in the curriculum, and as these weaknesses were remedied, the need for an ancillary reward system with its added burden and possible troublesome side effects has all but vanished. We could be wrong, however. There is room for the development

---

[2] See "Observations on the Use of Direct Instruction with Young Disadvantaged Children," by Carl Bereiter and Siegfried Engelmann, *Journal of School Psychology*, May 1966, pp. 55–62. For an outside observer's perceptions, see "A Pressure Cooker for Four-Year-Old Minds," by Maya Pines, *Harper's*, January 1967, pp. 55–61.

[3] Some developmental programs that do pursue definite instructional objectives, but by different means, are those of L. Gotkin at the Institute for Developmental Studies, New York University, and R. L. Spaulding at the Educational Improvement Project, Duke University.

of a variety of methods of teaching young disadvantaged children, and there is a good chance that any serious and extended effort at the development of such methods will yield results that are of benefit to the others.

The key word in the preceding sentence is "development." By circumventing the problem of defining explicit curriculum content and explicit methods for teaching it, early childhood educators cut themselves off from possibilities for program development. They may create a program that is pretty good, as judged by terminal or long-range measures, but they have no systematic way of making it better or even telling whether it can be made better. That is why the evaluations of Project Head Start are so difficult to get excited about. We are naturally curious to know what the Head Start programs have accomplished; but, on the premise that they must do some good while falling short of perfection, we cannot expect the results to tell us anything that would lead to substantive program changes. At best they may encourage people to keep up the good work or try harder.

A preschool program that is capable of true development rather than haphazard change must have instructional objectives and methods that are sufficiently well defined and closely wedded that it is at least possible to judge the effectiveness of individual activities and units. The smaller the units that can be evaluated, the greater the possibilities for development. Ideally, one should be able to evaluate single sentences and questions spoken by the teacher, particular examples and demonstrations, and the sequencing of items within small units. Data for such evaluations are not likely to be of very high quality, but for developmental purposes it seems preferable to have low quality data, even merely impressionistic data, on a minute-to-minute basis than to have very high quality psychometric data that can be obtained only after the program has run to completion.

It is worth noting, in this regard, that for the evaluation of preschool programs high quality data are not presently available at all. A few mental ability tests of high reliability, such as the Stanford-Binet Intelligence Test, are available, but it is not known whether changes on these measures have any validity. Their use as evaluative criteria is therefore questionable. There are no achievement tests on the market which are appropriate for preschool use. The Preschool Achievement Test, as well as the standard readiness tests, appear to be nothing more than general scholastic aptitude tests, and so their use as evaluative criteria is subject to the same reservations as the use of other aptitude tests. In our work we have made use of the Wide Range Achievement Test, which has norms extending down through the kindergarten level for reading, arithmetic, and spelling; but this test does not provide very precise measurement and covers only a very narrow range of content. The reason that there are no preschool achievement tests is that there have been no achievement objectives. It is getting the cart ahead of the horse to produce achievement tests before curricula with achievement objectives are in wide use, but in the present case it would not be a bad idea. My colleague, Siegfried Engelmann, has developed one such test, the Concept Inventory,[4] which assesses the kinds of language concepts and skills that we have built our language curriculum around. As far as I know, it is the only language test for young children that can properly be called an achievement rather than an aptitude test—a test, in other words, which could be used to assess how successfully a program had taught language operations rather than merely showing how capable the children are with verbal tasks.

In so far as we can judge from the crude achievement measures available, our program has been quite successful in fostering academic achievement in young disadvantaged children. Our first experimental class, which was composed of typically deprived urban Negro children, obtained mean grade level scores on the Wide-Range Achievement Test of 1.6 in reading, 2.6 in arithmetic, and 1.7 in spelling at the end of the kindergarten year, having completed two years of preschool training. By present indications the second group, which is now in the middle of its kindergarten year, should do considerably better than this in reading; and the third group, which is now in its first year of work, is progressing faster than earlier groups in all areas.

The long-range effects of preschool training are, of course, a matter of great social concern. For the planner of preschool programs, however, the matter is not a simple one of waiting for the pudding that brings the proof. On the one hand, the preschool educator cannot be responsible for the failures of the elementary schools to follow through on achievements made during the preschool period. He must be sure, however, that the achievements are genuine and not illusory. A preschool program might produce gains in I.Q. or other psychological indices, but if these gains disappear in later years and have no apparent effect on school performance, this is not necessarily the fault of the elementary schools. It may simply indicate that the gains did not reflect any significant learning or improvement in educability. Only when there is evidence of genuine learning can it be claimed that something has been accomplished which the schools should take account of.

On the other hand, the preschool educator has not only the responsibility of teaching disadvantaged children material relevant to the content of later instruction but also the responsibility of teaching the children skills and habits that will enable them to make use of this material under

---

[4] **Follett Publishing Company, 1967.**

the conditions of elementary school life, which usually include large classes, a considerable amount of independent seatwork, and frequently teaching of a not very skillful kind. As the children in our original experimental class now make their way through the first grade in a variety of different classroom situations, we are beginning to recognize some of the things that should have been included in our curriculum but weren't or were not emphasized enough. For instance, one of the requirements of many first-grade classes, for which our children (and, it would appear, children in most other heavily staffed preschool classes) were not adequately trained, is that of carrying out extended seatwork assignments with minimal supervision and help. Middle-class children may well learn the necessary habits and skills for this kind of activity through solitary play extended over a number of years. They gradually work their way up from activities that are immediately and continually rewarding to ones that yield dividends only after a considerable period of effort. A preschool program, however, lacks both the time and the appropriate conditions for establishing these habits through undirected play—and in any event it is questionable whether the result is worth the time it would take to achieve it through this means. But the necessary learnings can be formulated as instructional objectives and once this is done it should be possible to find more efficient means of teaching them. For instance, a schedule of increasingly spaced token rewards for solitary effort would seem to be an appropriate training procedure. The advantage of a well-defined instructional program for picking up loose ends such as these is that, when you know what children have learned, it is much easier to detect what they have not learned.

I have said practically nothing in this discussion about problems or methods unique to disadvantaged children. This is not to imply that preschool programs for disadvantaged children need to be no different from those for more privileged children. What is implied, however, when one approaches preschool education as an instructional problem, is that the same achievements are expected of all children, these achievements having been dictated not by empirical norms or the needs of individual children but by the requirements of future learning tasks. If disadvantaged children need special programs, it is because they are unable to meet some of the achievement criteria under the same conditions as other children. If, for instance, there are certain criteria of language mastery that middle-class children appear to meet through nothing more than informal language activities, but disadvantaged children do not, then there is an evident need for building into the educational program of disadvantaged children some special kinds of teaching to bring these achievements about. It may be presumed, however, that other kinds of children may also need the same special teaching. Why children might happen to be in a condition to need it is not a very relevant issue. It is unnecessary to treat the disadvantaged child as a stereotype possessed of certain characteristics by virtue of his social status. It is enough to know what required learnings a child lacks and to have available the means of producing them. A great deal of the agony over "defining the disadvantaged" and "meeting their needs" seems to be unnecessary and leads only to further agonizing over the issue of cultural differences versus cultural handicaps, and similar false dilemmas.

At the present time preschool education is largely restricted to children who either hardly need it at all or else need it so badly that practically anything that is done for them is of some help. This is not a very favorable condition for progress in instructional methodology. We would do better to look ahead to the time when preschool education will be available to all children. If at that time we have no clearer conception of achievement goals for early education and no more effective ways for reaching them than we have today, we will have a pretty poor bill of goods to offer the public. If, on the other hand, we are able to define a reasonable set of concepts, skills, and habits that can serve as a foundation upon which to build later school curricula, and if we have developed reliable and efficient means of teaching these things to children who lack them, then we shall be in a position to offer a variety of preschool programs to which children may be assigned on the basis of what they need to learn rather than on the basis of their skin color, aptitude test scores, or the incomes of their parents. The sooner we are in a position to do this, the sooner we shall be able to stop floundering and start moving toward the development of more effective programs for today's needy children.

INTELLECTUAL PRESSURE COOKER—A REPORT ON BEREITER'S SCHOOL

To Carl Bereiter, professor of special education at the University of Illinois' Institute for Research on Exceptional Children, "first grade is hurtling toward [the disadvantaged preschooler] like an express train . . . and the child's fate may well depend on what . . . a teacher is able to do and how quickly."

Acting on this sentiment, Bereiter, in November, 1964, and Siegfried Engelmann, author of the controversial *Give Your Child a Superior Mind*, opened an unusual preschool for the disadvantaged—what Maya Pines in the January, 1967, *Harper's* calls "A Pressure Cooker for Four-Year-Old-Minds." Miss Pines notes that the two are adherents of the "cognitive" school of psychology, which holds that "an individual's achievement in life depends very largely on what he has been helped to learn before the age of four" and that "millions of children are irreparably damaged because they do not learn enough during this crucial period."

She reports that Bereiter and Engelmann have, as a result, "totally rejected the standard, play-oriented nursery school, making no attempt to reproduce a middle-class environment for . . . youngsters. Instead they concentrate fiercely on a few areas and drill the children like Marines for two hours a day."

The school offers the basics—reading, spelling, and arithmetic. Free play is considered superfluous and time wasting. " 'Group experience' and 'playing with their peers' are the *least* of the kids' needs," says Bereiter. The atmosphere is tense and exciting, Miss Pines indicates, the theory being that "a little stress is good for children as long as it is not due to fear of failure, concern over pleasing the teacher, or sheer competitiveness, but caused by curiosity or a desire to achieve competence. The idea is to make the children feel they are succeeding at something very, very tough—when, in fact, the problems are carefully geared to their capabilities."

The program is designed to induce logical thinking and clear speaking and was written, Miss Pines notes, "very close in spirit to . . . those written for teaching machines and computers." The children, many of whom "could not utter or repeat a single statement when they arrived" are urged to speak out and often excitedly yell their answers. "It's an intensely physical kind of teaching," reports Miss Pines, "rhythmic movements, clapping of hands, cheers like those of a cheer leader, lots of concrete objects related to the matter at hand, arm and hand movements to illustrate points. The chants serve to remind the children how to proceed, attack problems, think."

Miss Pines described the following scene from an arithmetic class:

$1 + 1 = \square$ the teacher wrote on the board. Then each child came in turn to the blackboard, to point to and translate each symbol, "One plus one equal box." Then, together, all the children yelled, "Whenever you see a box, you have to figure-it-out" (in rising hexameter). The teacher said, "The problem tells you what to do: Start out with one (the children raise one finger), get *more*—one more! You end up with two! Count your fingers, one, two. So I can erase the box, and put in a two: $1 + 1 = 2$."

In a class of fifteen four-year-olds she heard:

"Spring is *after* winter. Summer is after spring." "Is fall *before* summer?" asks the teacher. "No," the children shout. One little boy keeps rocking sideways on his chair as if to ease the tension. "Fall is *after* summer!" he shouts, and then bursts out, "Me and Jimmy are doing a *good* job!"

Many early childhood authorities cringe at the school's regimen, but the children's morale is high and the results are startling. At the end of the year a group of eight five-year-olds

. . . placed at mid-second-grade level in arithmetic and mid-first-grade level in reading and spelling on the Wide-Range Achievement test. The four-year-olds had gained an average of seventeen points of I.Q. and scored at first-grade level in arithmetic, reading, and spelling. Both groups performed nearly on a par with gifted children of their age.

The program requires no special equipment, Miss Pines concludes, but has three specially trained teachers for 15 students, an unusually high ratio and far from inexpensive.

Nor does anyone know how effective it will be in the long run. Will the children's confidence collapse when they are denied the support of this close-knit group, with its extra attention and many rewards? Will it survive twelve years in crowded slum schools that are geared to turning out failures? From another point of view, have they learned, deep down, to parrot unquestioningly whatever they are told by people in authority?

The answers will not be in for many, many years to come. It is not even clear yet whether the project itself—with its highly charged atmosphere, its mystique, its sense of excitement—can survive alone, or whether it depends on the presence of its two creators.

—Quotations by permission of *Harper's*

44   Observations on the Use
          of Direct Instruction with Young
          Disadvantaged Children*

CARL BEREITER, *University of Illinois*
SIEGFRIED ENGELMANN, *University of Illinois*

Many experimental projects in early education of disadvantaged children are concerned with the *what* of compensatory education, the content; typically, however, these projects do not depart from the low-pressure, activity-centered methods of the traditional nursery school and kindergarten. The methods are often accepted as the part of the project that is "given." The writers believe that the *how* of educating disadvantaged children is as important as the *what* and that to fail in developing more effective teaching methods is perhaps to fail completely in equalizing the educational attainment of children from differing cultural backgrounds.

One of the major obstacles to experimentation with new teaching methods for preschool children is the widespread belief that any very demanding or rigorous teaching methods would be harmful to young children. The writers, in their work with preschool children, have made extensive use of teaching methods which, according to popular beliefs about early childhood education, should not have worked at all or should have encouraged extreme anxiety, dread of school, or robot-like conformity. These dire results did not emerge, however; in fact, the overall effect of the teaching methods on the children seems to have been beneficial.

This paper will describe the teaching methods employed and report observations and data on the feasibility, educational effectiveness, and apparent effects of these methods on children's attitudes, motivation, and personal adjustment. It is hoped that these observations will encourage other educators to experiment more freely in a search for

* *Journal of School Psychology*, Spring 1966, vol. 4, no. 3. Reprinted by permission.

improved methods of teaching young disadvantaged children and to question those popular beliefs that have served to restrain experimentation in the past.

Methods

The writers' preschool program for disadvantaged children is built around three daily 20-minute sessions of intensive direct instruction—one devoted to language learning, one to arithmetic, and one to reading. The distinctive characteristics of the instructional method are:

1. Fast pace. During a twenty-minute period as many as 500 responses may be required of each child. Usually five or more different kinds of tasks are presented during a single period.

2. Reduced task-irrelevant behavior. The teacher controls the session relying only incidentally on spontaneous exchanges to dictate the direction of instruction. Efforts of both teacher and children are focused on the tasks being studied.

3. Strong emphasis on verbal responses. These are often produced in unison, so that each child's total output can be maximized.

4. Carefully planned small-step instructional units with continual feedback. The teacher is not receptive to irrelevant exchanges but is very sensitive to possible areas of difficulty, possible ambiguities that arise from her presentation. She quickly corrects mistakes. She tries to anticipate and avert them.

5. Heavy work demands. Children are required to pay attention and to work hard. They are rewarded for thinking; half-hearted or careless performance is not tolerated.

Although the classes are conducted in a business-like manner, the atmosphere is usually friendly and pleasant, occasionally lightened by humor or playfulness. The following sketch of a typical language lesson will illustrate how the methods are put into practice. The children are disadvantaged four-year-olds who have been attending preschool for about three months. There are 15 children in the preschool, divided into groups of about five each. While one group is receiving language instruction, the other groups are receiving instruction from other teachers.

The lesson begins with review of a concept that has been studied previously. The children still have some difficulty with it. The teacher draws a circle and a square on the chalkboard, the square partly hidden by the circle. The children, who are seated in a row facing the chalkboard, talk freely among themselves and to the teacher until she has completed the drawing and turns toward them. They then quiet down and attend to the figures on the chalkboard.

Teacher: Is the circle in front of the square?

Children (in unison, rhythmically): Yes, the circle is in front of the square.

Teacher: How do you know?

Several children (ad lib): Cause you can't see the whole square . . . Cause it cover it up.

Teacher: Is the square in front of the circle?

Children (ad lib): No . . . In back . . . No, circle in front.

Teacher: All right, give me the whole statement. Is the square in front of the circle? No, the square is——"

Children (in unison): The square is *not* in front of the circle. The square is *in back of* the circle.

Teacher (to James, who has stumbled through the last statement): James, where is the square?

James: Back.

Teacher: That's right. You're getting it. Now try to say the whole thing. The square is *in back of* the circle.

After about four minutes devoted to elaborations of this task, the teacher switches to higher-order class concepts. First comes a quick review of a previously learned—and popular—class concept.

Teacher: Tell me something that is a weapon.

Children (ad lib): A gun . . . A rifle . . . A sword . . . Bow'n arrow . . .

Teacher: What's the rule? If you use it——"

Children (in unison): If you use it to hurt someone, it's a weapon.

Teacher: Can you use a stick to hurt somebody?

Children (ad lib): No . . . Yeah . . . You can hit 'em . . . You can throw it . . . If it's a big stick . . .

Teacher: If you use a stick to hit somebody, then what do you know about it?

Children (more or less in unison): It's a weapon.

Teacher: Tell me something that is *not* a weapon.

The review takes less than two minutes. The teacher then moves immediately into the presentation of a new concept—*part*.

Teacher (pointing): This is Tyrone. Now listen. (Holding up Tyrone's hand and speaking slowly and methodically in a way that the children have learned to recognize as a signal that something new is being presented.) This is a *part of* Tyrone. This part of Tyrone is a——

Children: Hand.

Teacher (pointing to Tyrone's nose): And this is a part of Tyrone. This part of Tyrone is a——

Children: Nose.

Several other parts of Tyrone are introduced in this way and then the teacher alters the presentation to require the children to provide more of the statement.

Teacher (pointing to Tyrone's ear): Is this a part of Tyrone?

Children: Yeah.

Teacher: Yes, this is a——

Children: Part of Tyrone.

Progressively the children are led to the point where they are supplying the entire pair of statements. Negative instances are introduced.

Teacher (pointing to Marie's nose): Is this a part of Tyrone?

Children: No, this is not a part of Tyrone.

Consideration is then shifted to parts of a chair and parts of an automobile (using a picture in a picture book). At the end of six minutes the children have achieved a tenuous mastery of the concept but have started to become restless and to make thoughtless errors. The teacher then shifts to a concept that had been introduced the day before— *vehicle*. She will return the next day to further work on the concept, *part*. During the closing minutes of the period, when some of the children are becoming inattentive, the teacher says, "Try real hard to get this, and then we'll have time to do some more jungle animals." This enticement serves to pull the group together for the final exercise on vehicles.

She then opens a picture book to a double-page spread of pictures of jungle animals which the children had become fascinated with during earlier work on the concept, *animal*. The last two minutes of the period are spent in a more informal exchange, with practice in identification, using the statement form, "This animal is a——," interspersed with casual commentary about the animals depicted. As the children leave the room, the teacher shakes the hand of each one and gives him a personal word of commendation, encouragement, or exhortation. "Marie, I want you to talk more. Talk, talk, talk."

Feasibility

A natural question to ask is whether children of four to six years of age can be brought to behave in such a highly disciplined and purposeful manner. Approximately 150 disadvantaged children in this age range have taken part in programs that included regular instruction of the kind indicated above. Teachers generally have reported no difficulties at all in getting children to participate enthusiastically in the intensive instruction sessions. No long breaking-in period is required. The pace and pattern are usually established the first day of school. The writers know of only one case where a teacher purportedly tried to establish such a teaching program and failed. The teacher was also unsuccessful in managing a traditional activity-type program with the children. The writers visited the class during its sixth week (when it was in a sorry state of chaos); they were nevertheless able to involve the children immediately in a lively and well-controlled instructional session, which suggested that the source of the difficulty was the teacher rather than the children or the method.

The same direct instructional method has been tried successfully with four-year-olds from more privileged homes. If anything, lower-class children seem to adapt to direct instruction somewhat more readily than middle-class children. Middle-class children are more likely to come to the preschool with preconceptions of what it should be like—a place to play—and are more likely to have become accustomed to a casual and somewhat haphazard kind of relationship with adults in "teaching" situations. By contrast, the disadvantaged child usually enters preschool with no preconceptions and no previous experience with such teaching situations.

As in any preschool, there are likely to be occasional shy, rebellious, or hyperactive children who have trouble adjusting to the school routine. The very clearly defined and consistent behavioral rules of the direct instruction sessions, however, tend to minimize such problems and to speed up adjustment. The short attention span that is sometimes attributed to disadvantaged children has presented no problem. For the first week or two of instruction, intensive teaching sessions are limited to 15 minutes rather than 20 and, as illustrated in the sample lesson, it has been found desirable to change tasks every five minutes or less.

Educational Effectiveness

The only group of children who have received direct instruction over a long enough period to permit objective assessment of educational gains is the original pilot case, which consisted of 15 four-year-old children, all Negroes, from a very low income area. The children were identified by public school teachers as coming from particularly deprived homes in which there were older siblings who were having school problems. According to scores on the Illinois Test of Psycholinguistic Abilities, the children selected were a year and a half below average in language abilities at the time they entered school. By the end of seven months their scores had risen to approximately normal—a gain of two years. In the same period of time their mean IQ on the Stanford-Binet rose from the low 90's to slightly over 100. By the end of nine months (shortly before they entered kindergarten), they scored at the second grade level on arithmetic and at the first grade level in reading on the Wide-Range Achievement Test. At this writing, after 14 months, all of the remaining 14 children are well into first grade reading work, are doing arithmetic at the upper primary level, and are progressing successfully in a science program that teaches concepts ordinarily reserved for the upper elementary grades.

It is not possible to separate the effects of teaching method from the effects of the curriculum, which also involved radical departures from tradition. However, it is important to recognize that the language, arithmetic, and reading curricula used in this experiment—as well as any other carefully organized and sequenced curriculum—could not be implemented with the indirect teaching methods generally employed in early childhood education. Some method would have to be used which ensured closer control over the children's attention and over relevant responses.

Attitudinal Effects of Direct Instruction

The major worry that teachers express about the use of more intensive or directive teaching methods with young children is that it may somehow harm the children or warp their development. Some of the worries merely reflect an unrealistic perspective. For instance, concern that direct instruction will deprive a child of needed time for play and interaction with his peers and "rob him of his youth" seems quite unrealistic if one is considering devoting only one hour a day to such instruction. The harm, if any, that might result from direct instruction would have to arise from what *does* happen during direct teaching and not from what the child misses as a result of devoting an hour a day to it. The folk-lore of education suggests a number of potential ill-effects, which we shall consider in the light of our experience.

EXCESSIVE STRESS AND ANXIETY. The mounting pressures on school children to compete and achieve are a just cause for concern. We have tried to minimize competition and emphasis on error avoidance, placing the emphasis instead on hard work, attention, and improvement. Exertion in itself—as shown by children at a playground or swimming pool—does not seem to be either harmful or unnatural. After a morning of spaced sessions of intense "mental" exertion, the children show many of the same characteristics as children who have spent the same length of time in intense physical play. They are tired but relaxed and cheerful.

Among the children whom we have observed most closely there have not been more than the usual number of anxiety symptoms. When an occasional child has shown signs of mounting disturbance in school, he was almost invariably attempting a task for which he was inadequately prepared; the disturbance generally abated as soon as the learning problem was taken care of, usually by some modification in the instructional program that proved to be of benefit to the other children as well.

If anything, the stable and work-oriented atmosphere of the school seems to have made it an island of security. The home lives of many of the children have been chaotic and filled with violence. During the early months of the school the behavior of the children clearly reflected the ebb and flow of crises in the home neighborhood. As time went on, however, their school behavior became more and more equable and independent of outside influences. Recently close relatives of three of the children in one class were involved in a sensational killing; yet, hardly a ripple of the turmoil invaded the classroom.

DISLIKE FOR SCHOOL AND LEARNING.   Starting children too young in academic work has often been blamed for school failures and the development of a chronic dislike for school. The writers fully acknowledge the dangers in presenting young children tasks for which they lack the prerequisite learning, and for this reason would urge that direct teaching not be attempted without a carefully worked out curriculum that starts with the abilities the children already have, building up from that point in a way that insures that the children can handle each new task that is presented.

However, our experience does not suggest, that early exposure to academic instruction *per se* develops negative attitudes toward schooling. What it does, rather, is build up attitudes toward school work that should provide a basis for better adjustment to school in later years. Direct instruction is not as much fun as some other kinds of nursery school activities, but we do not know of any responsible early childhood educators who use "maximizing fun" as a major criterion for designing a curriculum. Most children seem to enjoy direct instruction most of the time, so long as it is enabling them to make steady progress; but what is more important, they learn that it is worthwhile and that it will bring them benefits even when it is not great fun. Thus they develop a more mature kind of motivation toward learning that can sustain them through the inevitable ups and downs of school experience.

LACK OF SPONTANEITY, INDEPENDENCE, AND CREATIVITY.   Although the kind of instruction we have used is highly controlled and makes a great deal of use of repetition and patterned responses, the children have shown a general increase rather than decrease in the spontaneity with which they approach new tasks. Like many groups of disadvantaged children, the ones in the pilot experiment were initially rather stolid and self-effacing, lacking in curiosity and intellectual assertiveness. Over the months they have become bold, inquisitive, and argumentative, confident of their intellectual strengths.

The curriculum we have used includes a number of divergent thinking tasks—from thinking of things that are not weapons, inventing new verses for songs, devising possible uses for an unfamiliar object such as a tea strainer. The children approach these tasks with considerable alacrity. Training in divergent thinking does not occupy a major place in the program, but this is a curricular decision and is not dictated by the teaching method. From what little is known about methods of fostering creative thinking, it would seem that direct instruction in divergent thinking tasks should be a better means of promoting creative abilities than the conventional unstructured nursery school activities, which may provide a child with opportunities to think creatively but seldom challenge him to do so, or teach him much about how to do it.

As the preceding conclusions suggest, we have found direct instruction to be a thoroughly feasible and highly effective way of teaching needed academic skills to young disadvantaged children. Even though the teaching procedures are more rigorous than those found in many elementary schools, we have found the side effects to be beneficial rather than harmful. From the point of view of overall personality development, perhaps the most important side effect has been the children's development of a self-conscious pride and confidence in their own ability to learn and think. Indirect teaching, even if it is effective, tends to produce learning of which the children are only vaguely aware. They learn but do not know that they have learned, don't realize that they have accomplished something significant. Through direct instruction, on the other hand, children are fully aware of what they have learned and aware that they have learned it through their own effort, concentration, and intelligence. They come to think of themselves as being good at learning and thinking. They acquire the well-rounded and realistic self-confidence that one usually finds only in bright children from the most favorable home backgrounds, the kind of self-confidence that enables a child to excel rather than merely to adjust.

45   The Design of Early Developmental Learning Programs for Disadvantaged Young Children*

WILLIAM FOWLER, *Yeshiva University*

The concept of social disadvantage has served a useful purpose in capturing the popular imagination and energy in remedying social injustices to the poor. However, this concept can be used as no more than a crude

* *IRCD Bulletin Supplement,* vol. 3, 1A. Reprinted by permission.

guide in designing educational programs for the children of the poor. While there are a number of personality and intellectual problems that appear more frequently in children of the lower working class than in children of the more socially and economically advantaged classes, the problems appear in different combinations in different children. They are, moreover, not limited to this group of children. Personality traits such as apathy, withdrawal, hyperactivity and low impulse-control; and intellectual difficulties, including general and specific cognitive and language deficiencies; and perceptuo-cognitive diffuseness are to be found in nearly all populations of children. But it is not simply in the presence of this or that developmental deficiency, however severe, that the sole or even the major obstacle to designing effective learning programs for disadvantaged children lies. The main problem is the general lack of knowledge about how to define and implement an adequate learning situation.

In general, there are two ways of perceiving and explaining a child's behavior. We can attempt to explain his actions either by his past history or by his present social situation. In the former approach, attention is focused on the intellectual and personality characteristics a child is assumed to have developed from the interaction of biology with his past experience. The alternative orientation, developed by the late social psychologists Kurt Lewin (1935) and Harry S. Sullivan (1953), accounts for his actions not only in terms of his traits, but also by his current total social circumstances. In other words, it is assumed that a child behaves and learns as much according to how he is treated as he does by the personality he brings to a classroom. Following this orientation, it is the successive interactions between a child's personality and the set of conditions in a classroom under which stimulation is offered which determine the forms of a child's behavior in a learning situation. It is important, therefore, that the social and cultural contextual patterns of learning in the classroom be understood and controlled.

In a general way, many teachers already recognize the validity of what we may call the developmental ecology of the learning process. They realize that constant scolding may produce as much mischief-making as it eliminates, that praise for effort and accomplishment generally results in continued achievement. They are aware that a withdrawn child will often perform if given special attention or that an impulsive child whose energies are not channeled can disrupt an entire group. But these notions, even when applied by sensitive and understanding teachers between moments of harassment under the mass conditions of ghetto schools, do not begin to encompass the total social framework of the teaching-learning situation.

Similarly, research investigations on disadvantaged children at the early childhood level suggest that the potential power of this formulation is not widely understood. Results appear to be disappointing even in projects in which teaching conditions are a marked improvement over those prevailing in urban public schools—reduced class size, provision for guidance and professional personnel, and some definition of instructional aims. Even under such improved circumstances, the intellectual gains of disadvantaged children have not been large (Gray and Klaus, 1965; Long, 1966; Strodtbeck, 1964; Weikart, Kamii and Radin, 1964). While initially encouraging—e.g., I.Q. gains of 10–15 points (Gray and Klaus, 1965; Long, 1966; Strodbeck, 1964; Weikart, Kamii and Radin, 1964)—gains have often washed out (Long, 1966) and slipped back (Weikart *et al.*, 1964) later in the program. In one carefully controlled experiment, two years of special stimulation produced no significant improvements of trained children over their controls (Blatt and Garfunkel, 1965).

There are, of course, many interpretations which might be placed on these results which are, fortunately, preliminary. But, despite differences in certain details of their method, most current preschool programs for the disadvantaged do not have well-designed and systematic approaches to instruction. With the exception that today there is a greater awareness of the importance of concept learning, most programs either follow a traditional elementary school model or resemble a classical method of nursery school education. The approach tends to be either formal, mass-oriented, and bare of concepts, or diffuse and non-intellective, dominated by a social-emotional, and sensori-motor, free-activity framework that makes it difficult to gain consistent control of a child's attention. Although lip service is now widely given to cognitive learning processes, few programs have systematically analyzed the ecology of developmental learning; that is, the total situational-developmental learning circumstances of the young child. Yet a developmental learning approach appears useful for designing learning programs for disadvantaged children.

Developmental learning can be defined as the sequence of encounters between a child and the environmental stimulation he *cumulatively* experiences. It is concerned not only with the total present stimulation and social situation of a child but also with his past history. In both respects, developmental learning can be distinguished from traditional concepts of education.

To plan a program in which major sources of developmental cognitive learning are brought under control may not be as imposing a task as it might at first seem. There are, in fact, several evidential sources, some experimental, where a high degree of control over the forms and levels of stimulation has been exercised. And it is from these sources, as well as from empirical studies in longitudinal stimulation (Fowler,

1962*b*) that I have drawn in developing a model of the conditions central to the design of effective programs in developmental learning. These sources (Fowler, 1962*a*, 1967*a*, 1967*b*, 1967*c*) include certain classical longitudinal studies on infant and child learning (Ling, 1941; McGraw, 1935, 1939) and retrospective reports on the developmental circumstances in which precocious children have been reared (Cox, 1926). The accelerated cognitive development typical in these and my own investigations—both of which include studies on children from moderately disadvantaged backgrounds—is encouraging. It suggests that certain principles of program design, common in these studies, may prove useful in conceiving programs for all young children, regardless of biological potentials, particular personalities, social background, and individual cognitive styles and levels.

We may approach some of the principles involved in setting up a developmental learning program by describing them in the order in which we have found them to be most useful. We begin with a *psychocognitive diagnosis* of each child, a process which should be sustained on a continuing basis throughout the life of any program. At the introductory stage of program planning, however, the procedure takes a rather general form. It is assumed that, for all except the brightest preschool children, organized knowledge of any aspect of the world is limited. While young children have developed concepts, their concepts lack generality and abstraction and tend to be available principally in immediate situations of play and other activity. From this predominantly sensori-motor picture, described by Piaget (1952) and partially verified by developmental research (White, 1965), as well as by the ordinary experience of most nursery school teachers, stems much of the character of the identifiable learning conditions.

One of the most cogent principles is the importance of *order, and coherence in providing developmental stimulation*. It is valuable to *single out some content area* of reality, such as plants, sea-life, housing or transportation, and to analyze such an area in terms of its conceptual structure. By this we mean that it is useful to identify major objects in the defined category and their major parts (stimulus units), the network and hierarchy of their interrelations, and to determine how the units function in a system as well as ecologically in relationship to other systems. There are, for example, various forms of land, air, and water transportation vehicles, constructed with forms designed to serve different functions. In turn, the units themselves can be defined in terms of part-whole relations and mechanisms. The entire process may be described as a structural, functional, and analytic approach to program designing for imparting to a child an organized picture of the world.

This same technique may be utilized in preparing programs for learning language systems—mathematics, music, reading, and spoken, verbal language itself. The question of which of many reality content structures or language systems are selected for presentation is partly a matter of setting value priorities; it is partly resolved by another principle central to the concept of developmental learning. *The early incorporation of symbolic manipulation* has been shown to be a powerful agent for advancing cognitive development (Fowler, 1962*a*, 1967*a*, 1967*b*, 1967*c*). By anchoring language processes in perceptual object-action relationships a child is able to keep close to the visible, tangible world he knows, yet is also moved gradually towards more general and abstract systems, which are needed for logical types of thinking.

Seen in this context, the question of which content area ought to be "covered" becomes less important. For the young child, the value of intensively cultivating a few reality contexts is emphasized by the leverage for inductive generalization and abstractive construction that only thorough familiarity with concrete detail can provide.

Integral to the process of steering a child through the intricacies of reality structures is the necessity of *sequencing*. The notion of arranging curricula in some order of difficulty is as old as the idea of a curriculum itself. But what may be merely easier or more convenient for adults and older children is probably indispensable for the young child. Lacking logical systems and categories to mentally represent the external world, a young child is unable to sort out and conceptualize the relevant features of a given problem or situation. He is, for example, less likely to identify the rudders of boats and front wheels of land vehicles in terms of a general common function. He is more likely to see the direct but different relations these components have with their medium, as a consequence of *differences* in specific mechanisms (i.e., wheels track on land and rudders alter the directional flow of water). He is more likely to arrive at these essential generalizations if the number of stimulus units and sets of relationships are presented to him very gradually on a step-by-step basis.

If a child is eventually to make significant abstract constructions, *essential* perceptual features and functions must be selected out and isolated from less important ones. He must be presented with a sequence of selected and arranged stimulus units and patterns at a speed adapted to his learning rate. In short, stimulation sequences must be *paced*. If complex concepts are presented too rapidly, a child will either turn his attention to something else or may experience anxiety and a sense of failure as he tries unsuccessfully to comprehend. On the other hand, too much repetition of what is simple, familiar, or both causes boredom and a consequent reduction in motivation. There is, in fact, experimental evidence from the studies of Earl (1961), Dember (1965), and Thomas (1965) which indicates that children prefer and respond most readily to stimuli which are slightly more complex than the stimulus complexity levels with which they are most familiar and comfortable.

One of the most powerful secondary functions of stimulus pacing is the feedback it provides teachers; it furnishes them with a constant and running *psychocognitive assessment* of a child's developmental learning progress. By using as indices a child's task mastery and motivation, a teacher has a built-in method of deciding when to proceed to the next phase, when to review certain components, and even which components to review. Moreover, this assessment enables teachers to search for, observe, and become aware of learning paralysis at a given level.

Implicit in the orientation to learning as essentially a developmental problem is the utility of designing stimulation programs which fit all the important developmental characteristics of a child's early years. Learning tasks for young children should involve a child in *active, physical manipulation of materials* and should be set up as *play-activity* situations. Exposure to perceptual attributes and arrangements is best done not only through observation, but also through furnishing a child with *discrimination, sorting, and construction tasks* by means of which he comes to grips with the dimensions of conceptual structures. By finding all the "things with wheels" or "the vehicles which carry things (instead of people)," a child can learn concepts through physically defined problem-solving tasks. If, then, the tasks are presented as forms of play—suggesting that "he drive all the vehicles that make their own tracks to the repair shop"— the scene is set for a world of play in which the child becomes an actor.

It is, of course, not always necessary to define the play according to clear functional definitions. Especially when the process is complex (e.g., operation of a rudder), concern over whether a boat actually carries passengers or elephants is misplaced. Boundaries of meaning can extend rather widely and a child's interest can be greatly enhanced by assigning fanciful roles. A boat can be a fish or a sea monster or a ship full of gold. One fantasy leads to another. The process can in this manner become a form of *incidental learning*, with the restriction that the stimulus focus is, from time to time, defined in terms of relevance to a conceptual learning purpose intended by the program.

There are, of course, other important conditions to be considered in designing developmental learning programs, but they are too numerous to more than touch on here. Given the characteristics which a disadvantaged child may often bring to a classroom situation, however, one additional set of conditions—the *social psychological setting*—may assume particular importance. Teaching attitudes and techniques which define social relations, not only between teacher and child but also between child and child, on a *cooperative* basis seem especially significant. To this end, it is effective to set up *small group learning situations*. Repeated demonstrations, in novel and dramatic forms, have proven far more valuable than verbal corrections of error. This method of learning through observing models (imitation) and experimenting with tasks is preferable to explaining with words alone, where problems of resistance to authority often arise. Groups should be small enough to permit sustained individualization of program pacing, yet large enough to permit benefit to be reaped from the interest aroused through a child's identifying and interacting with a peer *reference group*. Tasks can be arranged in ways which require collaboration for solution in order to develop cooperative rather than competitive styles among the children.

Given the present teacher shortage and the urgency of the need, it is an interesting question whether so complex a set of skills can be found or developed in many teachers. There are two considerations which suggest that the problem may not be insuperable. The first of these suggests a shift of focus to the school principal. The principal needs to become the intellectual as well as the administrative leader of the school. The second suggests that under the supervision of a master teacher, individuals with little formal education may be able to facilitate cognitive developmental learning in the early years of life. There is growing evidence to support this view. In a series of investigations at the University of Chicago Laboratory Nursery School, teachers with varying backgrounds in elementary and nursery school education were, with few exceptions, able to learn and apply the essential principles of developmental learning outlined in this article (Fowler, 1965a, 1965b, 1967c). Programs were conducted with children from both advantaged and disadvantaged backgrounds. Several of the teachers who were most successful in teaching three- and four-year-olds had never acquired a college degree.

Similarly, observations which I have made recently of child care and nursery school facilities for children of working mothers in Warsaw, Poland, indicate that stimulating programs can be implemented on a widespread basis with minimally trained teachers. The central ingredient in both programs is the continuing function of highly educated teacher-guides—developmental or education psychologists—who know principles of developmental learning and provide written guides and frequent demonstrations for and discussions with teachers. The economics of expanding or supplementing the limited administrative functions now applied to the role of the principal suggest a potentially powerful vehicle to gain more control over the developmental learning ecology of disadvantaged preschool children.

References

Blatt, B., and F. Garfunkel. 1965. *A field demonstration of the effects of non-automated responsive environments on the intellectual and social competence of educable mentally retarded children.* Cooperative Research No. D-014, Boston University (Washington, D.C.: Office of Education, Department of Health, Education and Welfare). Mimeographed.

Cox, C. M. 1926. *The early mental traits of three hundred geniuses. Genetic studies of genius,* vol. II (Stanford, Calif.: Stanford University Press).

Dember, W. N. 1965. The new look in motivation. *Amer. Scient.,* **53,** pp. 409–427.

Earl, R. W. September 1961. *A theory of stimulus selection.* Special document SD–132 (Fullerton, Calif.: Hughes Aircraft Company Ground System).

Fowler, W. 1967a. Dimensions for environmental control over developmental learning. *Psychologia Wychowawcza.*

———. 1967b. Infant stimulation and the etiology of cognitive processes. In Jeanne L. Rivoire and Aline H. Kidd (eds.), *Behavioral development in infants.*

———. 1967c. Longitudinal study of early stimulation in the emergence of cognitive processes. In Robert D. Hess (ed.), *Early education: current theory, research and practice* (Chicago, Ill.: Aldine).

———. 1965a. A study of process and method in three-year-old twins and triplets learning to read. *Genet. Psychol. Monogr.,* **72,** pp. 3–89.

———. 1965b. Concept learning in early childhood. *Young Children,* **21,** pp. 81–91.

———. 1962a. Cognitive learning in infancy and early childhood. *Psychol. Bull.,* **59,** pp. 116–152.

———. 1962b. Teaching a two-year-old to read: an experiment in early childhood learning. *Genet. Psychol. Monogr.,* **66,** pp. 181–283.

———, and A. Burnett. 1967. Models for learning in an integrated preschool. *Elem. Sch. J.,* **67,** pp. 428–441.

Gray, Susan W., and R. A. Klaus. 1965. An experimental preschool program for culturally deprived children. *Child Develpm.,* **36,** pp. 887–898.

Lewin, Kurt. 1935. *A dynamic theory of personality* (New York: McGraw-Hill, Inc.).

Ling, B. 1941. Form discrimination as a learning cue in infants (*Comp. Psychol. Monogr.*, **17,** Whole No. 86, pp. 1–66.

Long, E. R., Jr. 1966. *The effect of programmed instruction in special skills during the preschool period on later ability patterns and academic achievement.* Cooperative Research Project No. D–104, University of North Carolina (Washington, D.C.: Office of Education, U. S. Department of Health, Education, and Welfare). Mimeographed.

McGraw, Myrtle B. 1939. Later development of children specially trained during infancy; Johnny and Jimmy at school age. *Child Develpm.*, **10,** pp. 1–19.

————. 1935. *Growth: a study of Johnny and Jimmy* (New York: Appleton-Century-Crofts).

Piaget, J. 1952. *The origins of intelligence in children* (New York: International Universities Press, Inc.).

Strodtbeck, F. L. 1964. *The reading readiness nursery: short-term social intervention technique.* Offset progress report (Chicago, Ill.: University of Chicago).

Sullivan, H. S. 1953. *The interpersonal theory of psychiatry.* Helen S. Perry and Mary L. Gawel (eds.) (New York: W. W. Norton & Company, Inc.).

Thomas, H. 1965. Visual-fixation responses of infants to stimuli of varying complexity. *Child Develpm.*, **36,** pp. 629–638.

Weikart, D. P., Constance K. Kamii, and Norma L. Radin. 1964. *Perry preschool project.* Offset progress report (Ypsilanti, Mich.: Michigan Public Schools).

White, S. H. 1965. Evidence for a hierarchial arrangement of learning processes. In L. Lipsitt and C. C. Spiker (eds.), *Advances in child development and behavior*, vol. II (New York: Academic Press, Inc.).

General References

Anastasi, Anne. 1958. *Differential psychology.* Third ed. (New York: The Macmillan Company).

Goodenough, F. L., and K. Maurer. 1940. The relative potency of the nursery school and the statistical laboratory in boosting IQ. *J. educ. Psychol.*, **31,** pp. 541–549.

Wellman, B. L. 1942. IQ changes of preschool and nonpreschool groups during the preschool years: a summary of the literature. *J. Psychol.*, **20,** pp. 347–368.

46   Educational Programming for Preschool Children*

RICHARD R. ELLIS, *New York University*

Only a few years ago the title of this paper would have evoked, at best, cries of disdain or horror. These expressions would have come from educators in general, but the greatest voice would have been the nursery school group. Educational programming for preschool children! No matter which word or words you emphasized, the whole phrase was anathema.

Within the past few years a continually growing body of information that points toward the importance of our topic has become available. This information comes to us from economists, statisticians, political scientists, and behavioral scientists. From these sources we hear that our schools stand indicted for failure to meet adequately the needs of our children. Even though the schools allude to recognizing individual differences, the allusion is frequently a misleading illusion. We know more about the economics, politics, and sociology of poverty than we did a few years ago. We are learning more about the effects upon human beings of life in socially and economically disadvantaged circumstances. We understand more about the weaknesses and untruths related to notions of racial superiority, fixed intelligence, and minority stereotypes. Furthermore, evidence from research (see suggested readings) indicates that it is during the early years of human life that a large part of perceptual and intellectual development occurs. Bloom points out that there are probably optimal times for stimulation toward development of characteristics, and that these optimal times usually occur during the early years. The timing of stimulation is important, and so too are the quality and quantity of stimuli.

Today there appears to be less patent resistance to the idea of providing educational experiences for young children. The United States federal government is making available hundreds of thousands of dollars for preschool education in communities all across the nation. Nursery school educators enjoy more visibility now than ever before. But all of this does not mean that today there is general acceptance of educational programming for preschool children. There is, unfortunately, considerable resistance to this notion by many educators. We suggest that the differences between the pros and the cons exist partially because of differing philosophies about fostering development of children, but, partially, also because of lack of a common understanding of the terminology used.

Philosophy upon which nursery school activities have been based

* *Child Study*, Summer 1967, vol. 28, no. 2(109). Reprinted by permission.

traditionally comes from Rousseau. In essence, this philosophy sees the development of a child as an unfolding process. The teacher's role is to support the child's natural inclinations by not imposing directions external to the child. The basic ingredients she supplies are warmth and affection. As Hunt points out, this encourages a neglect of stimulation for intellectual development because, if development proceeds from a predetermined nature, then there is no need to cultivate it.

Traditionally, in the United States, the nursery school enrolls toddlers through age four or five. These are "preschool" children in that some of our elementary schools include five-year-olds in kindergarten, while others have no kindergartens and begin with six-year-olds in first grade. The report that many elementary schools are now including four-year-olds in itself represents quite an innovation.

Most nursery schools are private and are supported by parents who recognize the need for such institutions. It follows, of course, that those families who feel the need and can afford it, send their children to nursery school. Most of the nursery school teachers have backgrounds similar to these families. For these advantaged children, the school programme based on the philosophy of Rousseau works quite well. And well it should: the advantaged child lives in an environment rich in varieties of experiences; available to the child are adults who have had enriched experiences and who wish to share them with the child; a large amount of stimulation and teaching of the child continues from the time he is born—a continuous situation that is tutorial in nature; both teachers and parents hold the same expectations of the child; the culture of the child is continuous with and contiguous to the culture of the school. The advantaged child brings with him on his first day of school a wide range of basic knowledge and skills.

Teachers who see themselves as guardians of the child's natural unfolding tend to see threats to the unfolding process when such words as *structure, organize,* or even *teach* are directed toward their classrooms. Structure could be equated with rigidity, imposed direction, and unrelated intervention; structure could also mean a flexible framework, a support, a guide, and a goal. To organize could be to disregard individual and group differences of the moment in favour of a prepared plan; to organize could also be to define long-range and short-term goals for individuals and the group; to define the task; to analyze learning; to prepare. To teach could be to operate as a conveyor of content with little regard for learning processes or interests of the learner; to teach could also be to accept responsibility for providing for each learner the best possible learning experiences based on his antecedent learning. Structuring, organizing, and teaching are rather global terms but their meaning becomes important and perhaps more clear as we plan for young disadvantaged children.

Underlying our planning of educational experiences for disadvantaged preschool children are several basic assumptions. These assumptions draw upon the findings of scientists such as Piaget, Hunt, Bruner, Jensen, Luria, and Montessori, and upon the work of the Institute for Developmental Studies, New York University. Deutsch and Deutsch of this Institute made a concise statement of the theory underlying early childhood enrichment programmes at the recent Social Science Research Council Conference on Early Childhood Education, Chicago, 1966.

One assumption is that environment plays a major role in the development of cognitive skills and intellectual functioning. Environment can either facilitate or inhibit the development of sensory-perceptual abilities and the development of intellectual skill, influencing both process and content. Lower class and slum environments appear to provide fewer facilitating stimuli than do middle and upper class environments.

Another assumption is that a given aspect of the environment exerts a different influence on the development of a function at different times. There are probably optimal times for the stimulation of a function, and there are probably certain kinds of stimuli that provide more advantageously for this development.

We assume, borrowing from Piaget, that in learning there is a developmental progression, a sequence including three stages or levels of learning and development, (1) the sensory-motor level, in which perceptual discriminations are facilitated through the child's actual contact with materials and his learning of the correct labelling and mediational responses; (2) the perceptual level, in which discriminations are facilitated through the presentation of contrasting stimuli (different colours, shapes, sizes, and sounds) and the coordination of those stimuli with differentiated verbal levels; and (3) the ideational-representational level, in which situations are presented verbally and conceptually with a minimum of concrete perceptual support.

These three levels seem to be related to the three modes of representation stated by Bruner. In stressing the processing of events and of experience, he identifies these three successive modes of representation: the enactive, the iconic, and the symbolic. The first level is enactive representation, which results from motor response. Riding a bicycle, for example, is learned through appropriate motor response. The second level is iconic representation, which includes images of visual, tactile, and auditory perceptions. Images stand for events. The third level is symbolic representation, which involves the ability to use natural or formal languages.

Our assumption that stages of cognitive development exist is not to imply that the final definitions of stages are available. At present there are conflicting views, and only more effort in research will bring us closer to a consensus.

In establishing operational programmes we find that techniques employed in the development of programmed materials are immediately applicable to the development of curriculum. The programming of a curriculum element or a series of elements involves considerations of sequence, step size, individual pacing, and feedback.

The preferred sequence is from simple to complex, both within an element and from element to element. We would have the child learn to recognize and label one shade of one colour, for example, blue, before we would ask him to identify everything in the room that is blue. A simple sequence in colour learning might begin, for example, by giving a child a number of identical objects all of which are coloured the same shade of blue. He is told the proper label, and uses this label as he handles the objects. A second set of objects identical to the first but of a different, single shade of colour is given to the child. Again, he is given the proper label and he handles the objects. The sequence continues by having the child sort a mixture of the two sets into the two classifications of colour.

Steps within each sequence must be small enough for the child to cope with. After he has learned to sort correctly two different colours, perhaps he is ready for the introduction of a third colour. The total number of objects comprising the three colours, however, might require a reduction if we are not to overwhelm him. What to us might seem to be tiny steps are usually giant strides to the disadvantaged child.

After the child has had several colour learning experiences and parallel shape learning experiences, we can ask questions of him commensurate with these experiences. The question, "Are you holding a blue circle or a yellow circle?" varies only one element, colour. Sequentially this question would precede the more complex task presented in "Are you holding a blue circle or a yellow rectangle?" Here, both elements vary. Further along the sequence we might ask, "What are you doing?" Whatever the required response is, it must not be beyond the child's ability.

In another example we might require the child to identify the blue circle from among several stimuli. A lower level task would offer a choice between a blue circle and a single totally different object. Complexity of task increases with the addition of more objects. When more objects are present there can also be an increased need for finer discriminations. An even higher level of task would be to select the blue circle from a variety of rounded shapes, e.g., ellipses or ovals, whose colours are violet, purple, and so on.

Proper pacing allows the child to proceed from element to element at the rate most comfortable for him. As he works his way through a sequence, he may be capable of rapidly devouring some steps, or he may require relatively greater amounts of time with other steps. Pacing is an individual matter, and, if this matter is sacrificed by the teacher for reasons of expediency, then the child may be pushed ahead while "soft spots" or incomplete notions may remain to plague him. For the disadvantaged child this can be especially disastrous. His environment may not provide him with means to fill in the gaps. It is the teacher's responsibility to insure his learning of basic skills and information at each step of the way.

Feedback, the response from the materials or teacher that gives the child confirming or corrective information, is a vital consideration. Through feedback the child learns which track he is on, which stimuli he should focus upon. He receives reinforcement of prior learning; he receives affirmative or corrective response to his applications of learnings. The more immediate the feedback to his response, the more impact on learning can the feedback have.

A problem of feedback arises in group teaching situations. Group response prevents the teacher from recognizing individual problems; the teacher, therefore, cannot be certain that her feedback to the group is adequate for each individual. The problem is manifest when the teacher responds to the most verbal or loudest children in the group. In responding to these children, she may miss completely a major portion of the children. The problem is compounded when we teach young children, because they are quite limited in the varieties of responses they can offer to a given situation. Feedback problems in group situations suggest that a more individualized approach to the teaching-learning experience may be more profitable for certain kinds of learnings.

The individual child isn't the only one who profits from feedback. He provides feedback to the teacher, and she learns how the child perceives his task, at what level he is operating, at what speed he is moving, and how effective her teaching is.

An issue here is the way in which teachers structure questions. With young children we have found a specific type of question to be useful; this type might be described as the "dichotomous question." The child is given a choice: "Are you holding a blue circle or a yellow circle?" "Are you holding a blue circle or a blue rectangle?" Through such questions the teacher limits the problem and provides the language; the child chooses the response. In other words, the structure of a teacher's question sets the level of the task required of the child. Suppose, for example, that the child is holding a blue circle, and the teacher asks him, "What are you doing?" The variety of responses possible and correct is enormous. For a four-year-old child correctly to tell her in response to the question that he is holding a blue circle can be a mammoth achievement. He has categorized an object simultaneously along two dimensions; he has supplied both labels; and, perhaps even more difficult, he has supplied the appropriate verb. In her question she is requiring him to select a narrow band from a wide range of possibilities, and to select a specific response from the narrow band. Her question is not of much help to him; it is neither dichotomous nor specific. He could wonder if she were asking whether he was sitting or standing, or looking at Joey, or playing a naming game, or holding a paper, or any number of other questions. Perhaps deciding on a response is beyond his ability. The child may not arrive at a decision. And what has the teacher found out? In his wondering the child used a great deal of language, involving different concepts. But did the teacher's question tap this language? Does she conclude from his non-response that he does not recognize a circle, or the colour blue, or that he does not realize that he is holding a blue circle?

Ideally, the teacher gives the child varieties of opportunities to demonstrate his knowledge of concepts if she is to know that he knows. Then, what are the implications of this ideal situation for concept development? It is easy to say that the teacher should provide varieties of opportunities for the child to demonstrate his knowledge of a concept. To ask a child with a blue circle what he is holding, she must be confident that he has had opportunity to learn the concept of blue and the concept of circle. If she employed the dichotomous questions, mentioned earlier, she would be presenting to the child a task of a lower order than is inherent in the question, "What are you holding?" However, she could ask, "Are you holding a blue circle or a yellow rectangle?" (Traditionally we have taught circle, triangle, and square. Triangle is a general classification. Square is a specific kind of rectangle. It would seem to be more consistent if we first taught rectangle and then square.) To provide him with more variety of opportunity to demonstrate his knowledge of blue circle, she could ask him to select the blue circle from among several different stimuli. The point here is that the structure of the teacher's questions can provide varieties of experiences at a given level of task, and can also change drastically the level of the task.

Much of what children learn depends upon or is accompanied by language. We have discussed some of the problems arising from sentence structure. At work here are other aspects of language that can be considered quantitatively and qualitatively. Quantity relates to number of words used per utterance, sentence length, number of ideas expressed, varieties of patterns, and so on. Quality includes grammar, syntax, speech production, affect, and effectiveness of communication.

The disadvantaged child frequently has and uses language that is rich in many respects, but, typically, is not sufficiently congruent to the tasks of school learning. Generally, the young child has not learned that things, persons, and ideas have names; that adults can be a source of information; that he must focus and listen for meaning.

The teacher's language, the language of instruction, requires careful consideration. Unfortunately for disadvantaged children, exposition by the teacher is a usual technique. This is unfortunate if the language used is beyond the mastery of the children; if the teacher uses patterns too lengthy or complex for the children to grasp; if her exposition is too long for their attention; or if the content is irrelevant to their experience.

Also, without careful consideration, the teacher may use certain concepts in ambiguous ways. The meaning of the concepts may be clear to her, but confusing to the children. For example, the teacher gives each child a piece of paper and holds her paper up (vertically) in front of her. She points to the top of her paper and says, "Print your name at the top; hold on to the bottom." Top and bottom, as used here, are vertical concepts. But confusion can exist because the children's papers are in a flat or horizontal position.

A related issue is that of the teacher's ability to handle children's responses. Children can give responses that are correct, but are not what the teacher expects. For example, suppose that she draws a picture of a ball, provides a child with the label, and asks him what shape it is. If he replies, "a circle," is he not correct?

When children do give a correct response the teacher can *not* safely assume that they "know" the concept involved. She may have taught, and they may have learned the appropriate response to a given stimulus, but they may not be able to hold the concept, to apply it to other situations, to generalize. Take our example of the child who is holding a blue circle. He may have learned that this specific object has one name, *bluecircle*. His cue may be the handle on the back, or a smudge on the front, or something that is not necessarily related to colour or to shape.

An interesting example of how children apply prior learnings to new situations occurred recently. Earlier this school year the children learned that they each had a *body* and they learned to name various parts. They also learned *suitcase* and that we put things in it and take it on trips. Last month a discussion about death came up. One child asked if anyone knew the name of the thing that the dead person was carried in. One little girl said, "A body suitcase." The point of this example is that experiences, such as the discussion, must be appropriate to the developmental level and past experience of the child. "A body suitcase" is a beautiful application by the little girl of her earlier learnings. If the teacher wanted to inject another term, she could say, "Yes that's a good name for it, Lillian. Other names that we use for it are a coffin or a casket."

Thus far we have briefly discussed some of the assumptions and principles we believe to be essential to programming educational experiences for the disadvantaged preschool child. From the work of researchers at the Institute for Developmental Studies and elsewhere we have identified major areas of the curriculum that should receive emphasis in plan-

ning for disadvantaged children. These areas are: (a) language development, (b) sensory-perceptual development, including auditory and visual
discrimination, (c) cognitive development, and (d) the development of
a positive self-concept. Not one of these appears to develop independently
of the others. Separation is made only for purposes of discussion. In
addition to the areas of curriculum, considerable effort at this Institute
goes into programmes for the parents. The overriding purpose of all
programmatic efforts is the stimulation of the development of the child.

Perhaps one of the strongest points to make in regard to our topic is
one that has been implied all through our discussion. That is, all of the
best philosophy, theory, and programming in the world (and there is some
trial and error) has little value in the classroom without a good teacher.
What is a good teacher? We don't really know.

It is becoming more apparent, though, that in order for her to work
effectively with young disadvantaged children, she must analyze the
experiences she provides much more carefully than is her custom. She
must learn to set goals for each child and the group. There are long-range
and short-term goals that she must state in behavioural terms. She needs a
means by which to evaluate her work constantly.

The kind of programming we advocate requires thoughtful analysis,
preparation, flexibility, evaluation, and professional thoroughness. This
kind of programming requires the efforts not only of teachers or pro-
grammers, but also of administrators, supervisors, classroom aides, and
parents. The proper task of our educational system is to provide the
learning experiences that all of our children require.

References

Bloom, B. 1964. *Stability and change in human characteristics* (New York:
John Wiley & Sons, Inc.).

Bruner, J. S. 1964. The course of cognitive growth. *Amer. Psychol.*, **19**,
pp. 1–15.

Deutsch, Cynthia P. 1964. Auditory discrimination and learning: social
factors. In Selected papers from the Institute for Developmental
Studies, Arden House Conference on pre-school enrichment of
socially disadvantaged children. *Merrill-Palmer Quart.*, **10**, 3, pp.
277–295.

————, and M. Deutsch. February 1966. *Brief reflections on the theory
of early childhood nrichment programs*. A paper prepared for the
Social Science Res⸱arch Council Conference on Early Childhood
Education, Chicago.

Deutsch, M. 1964. Facilitating development in the pre-school child: social and psychological perspectives. In Selected papers from the Institute for Developmental Studies, Arden House Conference on pre-school enrichment of socially disadvantaged children. *Merrill-Palmer Quart.*, **10**, 3, pp. 249–163.

———. 1963. Nursery education: the influence of social programming on early development. *J. Nursery Educ.*, **19**, 3, pp. 191–197.

———, and R. Ellis. (in press). *Curriculum guidelines for use with the disadvantaged pre-school child* (Boston: Houghton Mifflin Company).

Flavell, J. H. 1963. *The developmental psychology of Jean Piaget* (Princeton, N.J.: D. Van Nostrand Company, Inc.).

Gotkin, L. G. 1963. Cognitive development and the issue of individual differences. *J. progr. Instruc.*, **3**, 1, p. 1.

Hunt, J. McV. 1961. *Intelligence and experience* (New York: The Ronald Press Company).

Jensen, A. R. 1963. Learning in the pre-school years. *J. Nursery Educ.*, **18**, 2, pp. 133–138.

Luria, A. R. *The role of speech in the regulation of normal and abnormal behavior* (New York: Liveright Publishing Corporation).

Piaget, J. 1932. *The language and thought of the child.* Second ed. (London: Routledge & Kegan Paul Ltd.).

Whiteman, M. 1964. Intelligence and learning. In Selected papers from the Institute for Developmental Studies, Arden House Conference on pre-school enrichment of socially disadvantaged children. *Merrill-Palmer Quart.*, **10**, 3, pp. 297–309.

47 A Piaget-Derived Model for Compensatory Pre-school Education*

CELIA STENDLER LAVATELLI, *University of Illinois*

Today in America we are witnessing a sudden concern for the culturally-disadvantaged child, evidenced in the mushrooming growth of programs

* A paper delivered at a colloquium at the Institute of Human Development, University of California, Berkeley, Spring 1966. The point of view developed in this paper formed the foundation for a project in Compensatory Education financed by the Graduate College Research Board, University of Illinois, under the direction of Celia Stendler Lavatelli and Queenie Mills. The writer wishes to express appreciation to the teachers, Jeanne Morris, Head Teacher, Constance Solberg and Laurel Hertig for their creative efforts in developing and trying out activities.

of compensatory education, particularly at the pre-school level. While the poor, unfortunately, have always been with us, and while the learning problems of children of the poor have long been recognized, it is only recently that concern over these problems has resulted in so much action. Part of the reason for the change is undoubtedly the awakened conscience of Americans, but part is due, also, to a change in viewpoint with respect to early experience and intelligence. That the learning potential of the child can only in part be attributed to the genes has long been recognized, but emphasis upon the development of mental structures as an outcome of transactions that the young child carries on upon objects and events in the environment is more recent (Piaget, 1950). According to this latter viewpoint, stimulation via sensory-motor systems early in life is essential to intellective development (Hunt, 1961). In the same way that the eye will not develop normally unless it is stimulated by light, so cortical cells will not develop without electro-chemical stimulation received via sensory channels. Stimulation leads to action and from the actions develop mental structures or schemes for dealing with other stimuli seen as similar. Thus, the capacity of the child at any age to benefit from instruction hinges upon mental structures previously developed, and their development is the outcome of earlier experiences.

In several years of testing Champaign-Urbana children, aged 6 to 12 years, on the Piaget tasks, it became readily apparent that the culturally disadvantaged were retarded in logical development, sometimes by as much as 5 years. We found 11-year-olds who were still preoperational and who would assert, for example, that amount of a liquid changed when poured from a standard beaker to a tall narrow cylinder. These children, were, of course, severely retarded in school learning. Proper development of mental structures, of logical intelligence, is essential to the acquisition of knowledge, and where development is retarded, the child is unable to profit from school instruction. He cannot learn to read, to learn math new or old or to master the subject-matter the school tries to teach him because the ways of using his mind essential for such learning are not sufficiently developed. How does a child know that $5 = 5$? Only when he can do a one-one correspondence between each and every object in the sets of five, and when he knows it doesn't matter in what order he takes each number, so long as each is accounted for only once. How does he know whether to call a duck a bird? Only when he can compose the class of birds out of separate elements, and then do a one-one correspondence between each of those elements and the characteristics of the duck. The child in elementary school is called upon throughout the day to perform operations upon classes and operations upon relations between classes in order to learn what the school is trying to teach, but the school starts at a level of instruction requiring mental operations at a higher level than the culturally disadvantaged child is capable of; hence his difficulties in school learning. As Piaget points out, one cannot teach higher mathematics to a five-year-old because he does not yet have logical structures which enable him to understand. In the same way, one cannot teach the typical first-grade curriculum to the disadvantaged child because he has not yet developed ways of using his mind that make learning at that level possible.

The present viewpoint with respect to intellective development stems largely from the work of J. Piaget and his colleagues in Geneva. No attempt will be made here to review the broad outlines of Piaget's psychology of intelligence; translations of the earlier "standard" works on this subject have been available for some time (Piaget, 1950, 1952*a* and 1952*b*, 1954; Piaget and Inhelder, 1956; Piaget, Inhelder and Szeminska, 1960; Inhelder and Piaget, 1958), while two recent additions to the literature in English have the added advantage of having been translated so as to be more easily comprehended by the reader (Inhelder and Piaget, 1964; Ripple and Rockcastle (eds.), 1964). Suffice to say for this paper that Piaget conceives of intelligence as a special form of biological adaptation, characterized by a striving for equilibrium in mental processes. Beginning at birth, intelligence develops as the child carries on interactions with objects and events in the environment. The first adaptations are sensory-motor in nature; the infant performs actions that build a sensory-motor representation of phenomena. He comes to "know" that an object has permanence because of displacements made upon that object; it can be moved from place to place and even disappear from sight, but it continues to have an existence. He builds other schemas, and then he combines and coordinates schemas to come up with fresh solutions to problems. Toward the end of the period (18 months), he develops the capacity to represent actions rather than only to carry them out in the motor system, and thought becomes preoperational in character.

Thought is "preoperational" because such logical operations as reversibility, associativity, identity and combinativity are not yet part of the child's repertoire. Rather the child is perceptual in his thinking: his perception centers on one variable in a problem and he fails to take into consideration or to coordinate other variables. Thought is rigid and irreversible. It is not until six or seven years of age, on the average, that the child begins to use logical operations in his thinking.

The extent to which the intellective development of the child from a culturally-disadvantaged home may be retarded because he has been exposed to a minimum stimulation from the environment is difficult to appreciate without a realization of the extent of deprivation in the lower-lower class home. One such home in a midwestern ghetto consists of three basement rooms. There are no pencils, books, crayons, pictures, or writing paper in this house. There are beds lining every wall, a few chairs, a few utensils and a T.V. set. Three women and seven young children share the three rooms. The youngest baby, carried about by his mother, has no toys to grasp, mobiles to look at, cradle gym to manipulate. The mother does not play pat-a-cake with him, nor teach him "bye-bye" and "peek-a-boo." She does not omit this kind of play deliberately, but simply because she has not seen mothers behaving in this fashion with babies. There are no opportunities for the infant to carry on transactions that build notions of space, matter and causality out of which intelligence develops. And when language begins, deficit is piled upon deficit, so that the child at school entrance is severely handicapped in learning what the school wants to teach him.

The case for preschool education to counteract the deficit has been cogently argued by Hunt (1964), and, indeed, there is evidence from both early (Wellman, 1945) and more recent investigations (Gray, 1963) of dramatic changes in IQ as a result of improved environment. Deutsch (1964) cites evaluations of teachers who report improved performance of disadvantaged children who have had preschool training. In every project cited in literature where children of the poor have attended nursery school gains have been noted. It is interesting that improvement occurs regardless of the type of preschool program offered. Conceivably all of the schools offered more stimulation than the normal home environment.

There are not available at present data on what kind of pre-school curriculum will most efficiently compensate for early deficit. Some would argue that the good nursery school with its standard equipment to encourage dramatic play, creative activity, interest in stories and music and social interaction provides the setting in which intellective as well as social development flourishes. By enriching the traditional program with experiences available in culturally-privileged homes—trips to the zoo and other community facilities, caring for animals and plants and the like—and emphasizing language, the resulting enriched curriculum takes care of the problem of matching experiences to deficit. Head Start programs in operation in the summer of 1965 were based upon the enrichment principle.

There are others, however, who would argue that the traditional nursery school, even with enrichment experiences, by virtue of its unplanned nature, leaves too much to chance. Those of this school of thought favor planned intervention in the way of a structured curriculum geared to what they view as the special cognitive needs of the disadvantaged. Perhaps all of the compensatory programs that are university-research-centered would fall into this category, but the degree and kind of intervention vary considerably. Some support a curriculum to teach the 3 R's in preschool; they look with favor upon Fowler's (1962) success in teaching young children to read and reason,that, since reading is a major stumbling block for the culturally-deprived child, early instruction in this skill is necessary. While it has been repeatedly demonstrated that young children *can* learn to read, there is a question as to whether or not this is the most desirable emphasis to include in preschool education. Fowler, himself reports that his daughter Velia at age 8.5 was only 2–3 grades above reading level despite a "planned, broad program of intensive cognitive stimulation (30 minutes per day of reading instruction for 9 months beginning at age 2); yet it is rare to find a child with an IQ in the 150–170 range who does not read several grades above the norm and *without* special training. Fowler also believes that the intensive cognitive stimulation was a major factor in developing Velia's high IQ; yet again we must observe that IQ's above 150 are not exceptionally rare among faculty children who have not been taught to read in their preschool years. The fact that there was no phenomenal intellectual development may be due to the fact that learning to decipher written symbols and to tell the difference between the words "Dick" and "Jane" may not constitute a very exciting intellectual task, and so its stimulus value may be limited. In short, there is no evidence from Fowler's own report that the kind of stimulation he provided will make a significant contribution to cognitive development. In fact, one might ask whether early cognitive training heavily weighted in verbal structures might not so channel cognition as actually to interfere with the development of a broad spectrum of cognitions, unless other kinds of special training are included. For example, the logical structures necessary to learn non-verbal subjects like science and math are not likely to be constructed unless the preschool child engages in activities involving space, time, matter, causality, and number (Stendler, 1961, 1962).

Still another approach involving planned intervention emphasizes perceptual training. Compensatory programs using this approach provide the child with many experiences in finding similarities and differences in pictured objects, geometric figures and abstract symbols, in sounds and textures, and in perceiving more than one property of an object. Supporters of this approach argue that the culturally-disadvantaged child has lacked experiences that sharpen perceptions and make one a good observer, and that to match training to deficit, a curriculum for the culturally disadvantaged should emphasize perceptual training.

For Piaget, the answer to the question of whether a perceptual emphasis will aid the development of logical intelligence is an emphatic "No." In *Les Mécanismes Perceptifs* (Piaget, 1961) and *The Early Growth of Logic in the Child* (Inhelder and Piaget, 1964), Piaget has analyzed the relations between perception and intelligence. He has considered these hypotheses: Is there a direct line from primary perception to operative structures, through the intermediary of perceptual activities? Is knowledge of objects and events *first* perceptual, and then operational, with the perceptual being simply a more elementary form? Or, as an alternate hypothesis, is intelligence an autonomous development, deriving out of the actions of the subject? To accept or reject these hypotheses, Piaget conducted a searching analysis of the structures of perception and those of intelligence and directed a series of studies, using the genetic method upon classical optical-geometric illusions. His investigations (Piaget, 1961) led him to the conclusion that there are certain fundamental differences between perception and intelligence:

1. Perception is dependent upon the presence of the object, and perceptual knowledge is limited to certain physical characteristics. Perception of a rectangle, for example, is limited to the shape, dimensions and size of the particular rectangle being perceived. Operative structures (intelligence), on the other hand, can evoke the object even in its absence, and in its presence can interpret the rectangle as a particular case of rectangles, or even of quadrilateral figures in general.

2. Perception is bounded by limits of space and time. In viewing a full moon, one can only perceive at the same time its quarter by evoking memory or an operative structure. Intelligence, on the other hand, can consider any element independent of space-time, and can equally as well dissociate neighboring objects and reason about them in complete independence.

3. Perception is essentially egocentric; what is perceived is special to the point of view of a particular person. Furthermore, it is subject to systematic deformations through centration effects (an overvaluation of those elements upon which perception centers). The intelligence of operations, on the other hand, makes possible knowledge of an object apart from self, and from the particular point of view of an individual. Operational structures enable one to view objects or events from viewpoints other than the narrow, restricted one afforded by the perceptual.

4. Perception is limited to that which is cognizable by the senses. In perceiving a box which is closed, for example, one sees only a box in three dimensions with a particular volume and an interior, but other mechanisms are necessary to decide about the contents of the box. Intelligence, on the other hand, can go beyond sensory data and make a deductive guess about what the box contains.

5. Perceptual structures ignore abstractions; they cannot restrict themselves to certain elements of an object or event while making an abstraction of others. It is the province of intelligence to choose which data are necessary to resolve a particular problem and to pass up other data.

A Piaget-derived preschool curriculum would not, then, emphasize perceptual training. For Piaget, the complex structures of operational thought are founded, not upon increasing sophistication of perceptual structures, but upon simpler operational structures growing out of actions upon classes and relations between classes. Through the coordination of the actions of combining, dissociating, ordering and setting up correspondences, the structures of intelligence are built during the sensori-motor and preoperational stages and rebuilt during the operational. Operational thought is not the result of a cumulative stockpiling of perceptual data previously accumulated; the child comes to view phenomena in a completely different way when he can break the whole into its parts, compare parts, associate parts in different ways and reverse actions.

From the foregoing analyses, it would seem that a compensatory preschool curriculum derived from Piaget's developmental theory should have the following characteristics:

1. It should program activities to facilitate development of mental structures from the simple to the complex. If it is true that the culturally disadvantaged child lacks the cognitive structures to deal with the school curriculum, then every effort should be made in the preschool to ensure development of the more elementary structures upon which the logical operations of reversibility, associativity, combinativity and identity are founded. Activities in which the child combines objects, takes groups apart, orders objects, sets objects in one-one correspondence, considers two properties of an object at a time and carries on simple conservation tasks are basic to such development.

2. Emphasis should be placed upon *transactional* experiences rather than perceptual. Activities should require children to *operate* upon the data to which they are exposed and not merely to note likenesses and differences or changes as a result of actions. A young child thinks that he has more bubble gum when he pulls it out in a long string than when the gum is in a ball; he will say that the string is longer and that it is also skinnier, but if he denies conservation, it is because he fails to see how a change in one dimension *is compensated for* by a change in another—an awareness that requires that one operate on the data and not merely perceive them.

3. Rather than attempting to teach specific responses through reinforcement techniques, teachers should set the stage for concept acquisition through equilibration, acting only to call children's attention to dissonant information and to ask children to justify their responses. Given sufficiently interesting activities graded in difficulty, children would not perform the activities in routine, thoughtless fashion, but would attend to what they were doing and to the consequences of their transactions.

4. Since the middle-class child is more advanced in logical develop-

ment than the culturally disadvantaged, the latter needs concentrated instruction in small groups devoted to the type of structure-inducing activities that the advantaged child has been carrying on in the course of daily living for several years. There must be planned intervention in the way of scheduled periods for cognitive training to compensate for the deficit.

5. Special periods devoted to cognitive training are not sufficient to compensate for the deficit of the disadvantaged. Such periods should be part of the daily schedule of a conventional nursery school, but the conventional nursery school day offers countless opportunities for reinforcement of the cognitive training that would be given in special periods. To provide maximum opportunity for generalization, teachers should look for incidental opportunities for combining, ordering, conserving, etc., as children engage in block or doll play, art and motor activities, cooking, setting the table, and the like. Thus a child might have special practice in one-one correspondence during the period for training, and then have the concept reinforced as he sets the table for juice, putting out one paper cup and napkin for each person at the table.

6. Since there is a relationship between thought and language, so ably traced by Vygotsky, a compensatory program must include language training. Such training should, of course, permeate the whole school day, but in the special periods devoted to cognitive activities, teachers must take special care to verbalize each child's transactions, and to encourage him to put into words what is happening.

7. Intellective and affective development are interrelated. As children come to deal more competently with their environment, they develop self-confidence and a better self-image. Conversely, some young children have difficulty in concept acquisition because of a high anxiety level or flightiness. The good, conventional nursery school has always emphasized social and emotional adjustment, another reason for putting special cognitive training within such a framework.

8. The cooperation of the family must be obtained so that there can be additional intellective stimulation beyond the short nursery school day. The extended family of which the disadvantaged child is often a part needs to be informed as to what the school is doing and why, and how the family can help. Even an illiterate mother can carry on conversations with her child, rather than merely giving commands, and can talk about the story in picture books with him.

At the University of Illinois, special training activities to foster acquisition of schemas in disadvantaged four-year-old children were developed and tried out for six months. There have been additional trials in some of the Oakland (California) Children's Centers. At Illinois, the activities were carried on in three regularly scheduled, ten-minute periods each day, interspersed with conventional nursery school activities. As the children's attention span lengthened, there were two fifteen-minute periods each day in place of the three shorter ones. The class of 15 children was divided into three groups for the special training, with a trained teacher in charge of each group of five.

Following are the activities listed roughly in the order in which they were presented. These activities were begun after the children had had some training on names of colors and geometric shapes.

One-One Correspondence

The ability to match one-for-one develops as a basic mental operation that lays the foundation for the more complex. We establish the equality of two sets and put two systems in equilibrium by making a comparison, one-to-one, of each of the parts. We decide whether or not an object is a member of a particular class by making a one-one comparison of the properties that define that class and the properties of the object in question.

To foster development of one-one correspondence, children were exposed to a series of exercises beginning with establishing correspondence between objects arranged in linear and then circular order. The exercises included:

Linear Order
1. Matching up to four objects for number, all objects identical in shape, size and color. Ex.: Teacher strings two, three or four round blue beads in a straight line; children copy.
2. Matching objects for color and number. Ex.: Teacher strings two red, round and two blue, round beads in a straight line; children copy. Gradually more beads and colors are introduced. Teacher demonstrates how to put one's string under the model and check off each bead on it against the model one by one.
3. Matching objects for shape and number. Ex.: Teacher strings one red round, two red cubed, and one red round beads in a straight line; children copy. Gradually more beads and more shapes are added.
4. Matching objects for color, shape and number. Same procedure as above, but with color added as an additional variable.

Circular Order
Instead of stringing beads in a straight line, the string is made into a circle and the same sequence as for linear order is followed.

There are, of course, countless variations of the above exercises, using materials like M & M's, blocks, cardboard cut-outs, pictured objects, etc.; size can be added as a variable in addition to shape and color. It should be noted, however, that these exercises require little in the way of mental operations, relying more upon perceptual solutions. However, they do provide training for multiplicative classification by forcing the child to keep more than one property in mind as he matches objects. Also, the exercises in circular order, which are much more difficult to master than linear, may be helpful in developing the concept that two sets are equal if each member in one set can be matched with a member in the other, and if every member in each set is accounted for and accounted for only once, and that equality persists regardless of the change in configuration.

One-One Correspondence: Conservation of Number

The object of exercises of this kind is to foster development of the concept of conservation of number: that number of objects in a set is conserved even when the amount of space occupied by the objects is changed. These exercises take the child beyond the merely perceptual, for in order to solve the task at hand, he must think about the transformation upon the data confronting him, reversing the transformation or performing an identity operation. In each case he builds one-one correspondence through motor action first.

Conservation of Number: Sensorimotor Exercises

The first exercise is the simple one used at Geneva, in which a child drops a bead into a glass with one hand and at the same time drops a bead into another glass with the other hand. From time to time he is asked if there is the same number of beads in each glass. The young child will look at the level of beads in each glass before answering, but if one of the glasses has a cover with a slit in the top so that a bead can be dropped in but bead-level hidden, he is at a loss for an answer. Eventually, however, he comes to see that the number is the same "Because every time I put one here, I put one there." Again there are many variations of this exercise that can be worked out, where a child performs an action of one for one and is denied access to perceptual data that interfere with the conservation concept.

One-One Correspondence after Physical
Correspondence Is Destroyed

In these exercises the child begins by placing objects in physical correspondence with objects laid out by the teacher. For example, the teacher may put out a row of miniature nursing bottles, each one of which is to be purchased for one penny by the child. He is given more pennies than there are bottles, and lays out enough pennies, one for each bottle. Then physical correspondence is destroyed, first by bunching pennies together and then the bottles, and the child is asked whether there is now the same number of each. If he denies equality, he is asked to add or subtract to achieve equality, and then he restores physical correspondence. Putting out napkins and cups for juice, one for each child at a table, is another variation of this exercise.

Relativity of Perspective

Exercises of this kind are designed to help the child see something from another vantage point. The exercises involve making first a 90° and then a 180° transformation upon a given scene. To begin, the teacher makes a simple place setting—plate, knife, fork and cup—on a place mat on one side of a table. The children are to set up an identical place setting on the opposite side, so that the knife would be closest to the same hand as the teacher's, the same with the fork, etc. At first children go back and forth from side to side of the table, devising their own system of "remembering" where the fork went (clenching the left, or fork-fist, for example). Gradually more sophisticated solutions develop, as the children break down the whole setting into its parts and begin to do a one-one correspondence between the objects on the mat (knife tip to cup, for example).

Conservation of Continuous Quantities

Experiences to foster development of conservation of continuous quantities like water, sand and clay begin with free play. Children are given a 12 oz. juice can filled with water and an empty 12 oz. coke bottle and are asked to predict water level in the bottle after pouring from the can (a funnel is necessary). Or children might be asked to indicate a preference for a 12 oz. can of juice or two 6 oz. cans before pouring from the large can into the small and back again. A wide variety of shapes and sizes of containers can be used for pouring activities, with the teacher asking for predictions as to water level, or whether there would be "more juice, not as much juice, or just as much juice" after pouring.

Seriation Activities

Seriation activities are to be carried on simultaneously with the experiences described above. Nesting cans, nesting dolls, and cylinders graduated in height and diameter are examples of the many materials that can be used to induce schemas essential to seriation.

Seriation involves operations upon relations between classes; to order objects or events with respect to one property the child must identify the extreme of that property and consider relationships of each succeeding object or event in terms of being more than the preceding and less than what is to follow, and to the same degree. Seriation may be said to be operational when the child can follow both directions of the series at the same time, and can *anticipate* where a new element belongs in a series, without having to resort to trial-and-error. Eventually the concept of transitivity emerges: that if A is greater than B, and B is greater than C, then A is greater than C.

Seriation schema contribute to the formation of more difficult systems of compensations. The "inching" that we sometimes do in putting a system in equilibrium (e.g., short-cuts in subtracting 46 from 91 by inching up to 50 and inching down to 90 and then taking into account the inching process; adding a little to one side of a balance and subtracting a bit from the other) results from seriation schema, and represents an important concrete operation before we can advance to formal thinking.

Classification Activities

All programs for disadvantaged children stress so-called classification activities, but many of these are actually perceptual rather than operational in character. That is, the activities provide training in visual or tactile perception, but they do not demand that the child make transformations upon the data. To ask a child to put all objects that are the same color in one pile and all objects that are different in color in another pile simply requires that he make a visual discrimination between two colors. To ask a child, however, to separate geometric shapes that are squares and circles, pink and blue, large and small, into *two* piles, putting the shapes that are alike in some way in one pile and those alike in some other way in another pile, requires that *he* abstract from the shapes the property that will form the basis for the dichotomy, and, further, that he then abstract a second and still a third property when asked to do so. Dichotomizing activities of this type were the first step in the U.I. Project in building operational classification.

To carry through a dichotomizing activity to a successful conclusion requires that the child have both hindsight and anticipation. He must have available to him a retroactive process by which he remembers the way in which he started to put things together, as well as a process for foreseeing what is to come that enables him to make a choice of what constitutes the class he is forming. Only then can the child achieve coherence between what he has already done and what he still must· do.

Abstracting a common property is essential to classification, but in the dichotomy activity, it is performed as a simple operation. At a more complex level, the child is required to extend the class to all objects having the common property and to classify *all* the elements. Extending the class is not difficult to do in the case of geometric shapes; once the property of the class has been abstracted, perceptual cues permit completion of the task. However, given a collection of miniature objects—people, other animals, household utensils, buildings—and four boxes into which to place objects alike in some way, and required, furthermore, *to use all the objects,·* the child must do more than abstract a property and then let perception take over. Now he must keep the property in mind and *discover it in each object* he puts into a particular class, and the four classes that he sets up must be such that *all the objects can be classified*. As Piaget points out, the young child making perceptually-based graphic collections does not feel compelled to use all of the objects; he may choose objects on the basis of "belonging"—cups and saucers belong with people because people drink out of them—and thus have objects left over that are unclassed.

In the University of Illinois project, the next step in building operational classification after dichotomizing activities was to plan activities where the child was required to extend the class, and to classify all the elements on the basis of a property that was not available to the child on the basis of perception alone. Miniature objects, or pictures of objects, and boxes for each class of objects were available to each child to separate into a specified number of piles according to which ones were alike in some way. The teacher made the rules of the game clear and asked each child from time to time to explain why he was separating the objects in a particular way—what he had in mind when he started, and where he was going.

A still more difficult step in the development of classification involves the notion of a hierarchy: that a particular class is included in every higher ranking class which contains all its elements. Such class-inclusion has several implications: that sub-classes can be combined into a supra-class; that the supra-class is always larger than the sub-class; that *all* members of the sub-class are contained in the supra-class, while only *some* members of the supra-class are members of the sub-class. Lessons with a collection of real fruit were worked out, where vocabulary was first developed (most of the children in the project knew only "banana" and "apple" by names), and where children also discovered that fruit is the edible part of a plant that develops from a flower. Then followed exercises where, after a child handed the teacher an orange, apple, cherry, or whatever she requested, he was asked, "Do I have any oranges?" "Do I have any fruit?," and after several pieces of fruit were in front of the teacher, "Do I have more fruit or more oranges?" There were many such lessons with other classes of objects, all designed to foster class-inclusion structures.

Evaluation of projects for disadvantaged children presents many difficulties. The 11 children in the Illinois group for whom Binet scores were available both at school entrance and after 10 weeks of school gained approximately 6 IQ points—and this in a very short period of time. It is not hard to raise scores on IQ tests; when children have had little in the way of stimulation, just being in a school environment with more to see, hear and do is bound to have an accelerating effect. What we need for evaluation in depth are longitudinal studies, comparing the effects of different treatments upon comparable populations, and including assessment over a wide range of areas of development. Only then can we make decisions about the nature and degree of curricular intervention to produce maximum results.

References

Deutsch, M. 1964. Facilitating development in the pre-school child: social and psychological perspectives. *Merrill-Palmer Quart.*, **10**, pp. 249–263.

Fowler, W. 1962. Cognitive learning in infancy and early childhood. *Psychol. Bull.*, **59**, pp. 116–152.

Gray, S., and R. Klaus. 1965. An experimental preschool program for culturally deprived children. *Child Develpm.*, **36**, pp. 887–898.

Hunt, J. McV. 1964. The psychological basis for using pre-school enrichment as an antidote for cultural deprivation. *Merrill-Palmer Quart.*, **10**, pp. 209–248.

———. 1961. *Intelligence and experience* (New York: The Ronald Press Company).

Inhelder, B., and J. Piaget. 1964. *The early growth of logic in the child* (New York: Harper & Row).

———. 1958. *The growth of logical thinking from childhood to adolescence: an essay on the construction of formal operational structures* (New York: Basic Books, Inc.).

Piaget, J. 1961. *Les Mécanismes perceptifs* (Paris: Presses Univer. France).

———. 1954. *The construction of reality in the child* (New York: Basic Books, Inc.).

———. 1952a. *The child's conception of number* (London: Routledge & Kegan Paul Ltd.).

————. 1952*b*. *The origins of intelligence in children* (New York: International Universities Press, Inc.).

————. 1950. *The psychology of intelligence* (London: Routledge & Kegan Paul Ltd.).

————, and B. Inhelder. 1956. *The child's conception of space* (London: Routledge & Kegan Paul Ltd.).

————, and A. Szeminska. 1960. *The child's conception of geometry* (New York: Basic Books, Inc.).

Ripple, R., and V. Rockcastle (eds.). 1964. *Piaget rediscovered: a report of the conference on cognitive studies and curriculum development* (Ithaca, N.Y.: School of Education, Cornell University).

Stendler, C. 1962. Elementary teaching and Piagetian theory. *Sci. Teach.*, **29**, 5.

————. 1961. Cognitive development in children and readiness for high school physics. *Amer. J. Physics*, **12**, pp. 832–835.

Wellman, B., and E. Pagram. 1944. Binet IQ changes of orphanage preschool children. *J. genet. Psychol.*, **65**, pp. 239–263.

Attuned to the unprecedented expansion of preschool facilities educators are meeting unfamiliar problems of planning for young children. In keeping with the spirit of Head Start and good nursery schools and kindergarten programs of the past, a greater degree of program flexibility than is common in public schools is demanded of planners. And consistent with the experimentation of the present, greater attention to program structure is essential.

Anticipating requests for planning assistance, the Office of Education held a three-day conference of experts in child development, school administration, architecture, school-building planning, and teacher education to establish planning guidelines for early childhood education. Minnie P. Berson and William W. Chase present this synthesis of ideas, beginning with recommendations for establishing objectives, elaborating upon the nature of desirable physical facilities, pupil-teacher ratio, daily routines, activity space, equipment, and other educational program requirements. Space relationship diagrams are included for clarity.

Additional suggestions for developing good preschool programs are the available, already established projects in widely separated geographical areas. Brief overviews of programs in Michigan, New York, Oregon, Iowa, New Mexico, Florida, Texas, Ohio, and California emphasize such factors as language development, parent involvement, use of aides, physical facilities, provision of food, and instructional programs. Support through federal funds appears to be recognized as a key factor in renewed interest in such programs.

Materials for enhancing the exploratory tendencies of young children during free play and teacher-directed activities are available in the good preschool. A comprehensive list is provided by Anna Marie Evans. This may serve as a guide for equipment selection. Individual needs

545

will obviously dictate additions, deletions, and substitutions.

Administrators and school boards charged with the responsibility for making decisions about the establishment of new programs often raise legal questions. Lee O. Garber, school law consultant to *Nation's Schools*, states his opinions on typical questions:

1. May the state legislature make provisions for preschool programs if they are not specifically mentioned in its constitution?

2. May a school board establish preschool facilities in the absence of legislative authority to do so?

3. Are established programs for preschool-age children outside the scope of legislative control?

4. What is the legal status of the pupil in preschool classes?

48   Planning Preschool Facilities*

MINNIE P. BERSON, *U.S. Office of Education*
WILLIAM W. CHASE, *U.S. Office of Education*

All over America this year, tens of thousands of children are being enrolled in newly formed nursery and kindergarten programs. A few—very few—are having their first school experiences in delightful classrooms and play areas especially designed and equipped to make the most of the young child's blotter-like capacity for learning. Many preschoolers, however, are in makeshift quarters.

Communities that never before offered public preschool classes are now able to do so with funds provided under the Elementary and Secondary Education Act of 1965. The Congress, convinced that the learning process must begin much earlier than the first grade, has included many benefits for preschool education under the act. Provisions for teacher training, remodeling of facilities, hiring of teachers in areas with concentrations of low-income families, use of research and demonstration centers, and supplementary centers and services can all benefit nursery school education.

Now that funds are available, however, most communities have not yet had time to provide—or even to plan for—appropriate space for preschool classes.

Anticipating requests from many school districts for information and guidance on planning good preschool facilities, the Office of Education held a three-day conference. Experts in child development, school administration, architecture, school-building planning, and teacher education from various parts of the United States came together to share their knowledge and experience.

No attempt was made to lay down rigid rules or specifications. The conference did, however, produce a blend of information which can serve as a guide to any community in planning good facilities for their littlest scholars. The cardinal word at the conference was *planning*: intelligent planning on the basis of carefully gathered information.

The conferees agreed that any community preparing to build a nursery or kindergarten should begin with a wisely selected cooperative planning group. Such a group should represent varied skills and backgrounds. It might include a member of the board of education, the superintendent of schools, the principal of the community's elementary school,

* *American Education*, December 1965–January 1966, vol. 2, no. 1. Reprinted by permission.

and several teachers. Some members would be lay citizens of the community at large who would contribute to the planning but would also help interpret the plans to the community. An educational consultant might add some specialized knowledge. He would conduct local surveys, develop educational specifications, and then interpret those specifications to the architect chosen to work with the group.

At the outset, the planners should identify every element in the whole preschool program. They should first outline the characteristics, aims, objectives, and purposes of the program, then determine exactly how many pupils, teachers, aides, parents, and others will be accommodated. They need to know the types of equipment to be used. From these elements they can determine the space relationships within the school and the school's relation to its surroundings.

After identifying the teaching and learning activities required and the groups to be accommodated, the planners' next step is to determine the kinds of physical facilities that are necessary to the smooth, efficient functioning of the program.

In terms of the general location, the nursery-kindergarten should, of course, be placed on an easily accessible site. The site should be large enough to provide safe access to the building and separate play spaces for individual and group activities. If the nursery-kindergarten program is included in a larger educational complex, it is important that this area be located in a separate wing of the building with its own entrance, play space, toilet area, learning spaces, and auxiliary areas.

Planners need to be aware of certain characteristics of preschool activities. For instance, they can expect the occupants of the nursery or kindergarten to be endlessly active. Children of nursery school age are not ready to sit quietly for any length of time. They learn through doing, touching and trying things out.

Everything the preschooler does is part of his learning process. His most pleasurable learning—and the kind that makes the most indelible impression on him—comes through play. The planned activities of the day, the school building, and the materials and equipment used can all capitalize on this and foster the growth of the child from a dependent to an increasingly self-reliant person.

Nursery schools usually serve children aged three, four, and five, while kindergartens enroll late four-, five-, and early six-year-olds. This overlap in age and development calls for facilities that are flexible and easily adaptable.

Classes in any nursery or kindergarten should be small. The younger the children, the smaller the group because of small children's great need for individual guidance and attention. The following group sizes and child-adult ratios have been suggested by experts in the field:

—for *three-year-olds*, a maximum of 15 children to a group is recommended, with a ratio of one adult to five three-year-olds;
—for *four-year-olds*, a maximum of 18 children to a group is recommended, with a ratio of two adults to fifteen children;
—for *five-year-olds*, a maximum of 20 children is recommended for a group, with one teacher and one assistant.

An important prerequisite to planning for a nursery or kindergarten is a knowledge of the typical daily routine of such a school. It is useful to know, for instance, that a nursery school or kindergarten session lasts from two and one-half to three hours. A kindergarten child can do quite a bit for himself and is beginning to show some readiness for group participation. The nursery school child, on the other hand, needs more time to do a given task, more adult assistance and individual attention, and more active, firsthand experiences.

It is desirable for both nursery school and kindergarten children to have a three-hour session in order that individual children and the group as a whole may move from routine to routine and activity to activity with a minimum of pressure. It takes time to provide rich, relaxed daily experiences that will have cumulative value and meaning.

For the purposes of planning facilities, planners can divide the day's activities into several main categories: arrival, indoor activities, outdoor activities, clean-up, and departure.

The first half hour is usually a free-for-all of arrivals. The nursery school child comes with an adult either by carpool, public transportation, or on foot, and needs a flexible arrival time. The child is first checked by either teacher or nurse, for symptoms of illness or infection and given the necessary assistance with wraps. Then he joins a play group. The kindergartner usually walks to school with an older child and enters with the opening bell. He removes his own wraps, submits to a health check, and then usually sits down with the teacher and the class to talk and plan the day's activities.

With all this daily traffic, the main entrance should have flooring that will permit easy maintenance. Plenty of storage space should be available for little coats and hats.

The classrooms are usually arranged in interest centers that offer children opportunities to move about easily and make choices. There are usually areas for building with blocks; a household center for make believe; a carpentry bench and tools for construction; records, books, rhythm instruments; gadgets for "science"; pegs, beads, numerals for "math"; crayons, scissors, paste, paint, finger paint, clay and other artistic media; pets and plants to watch and care for; and other materials and pieces of equipment to manipulate, take apart, put together, and use in one's own way.

Nursery school children need many opportunities to be loners, to get off by themselves and work on some project. They need the opportunity to try out a variety of equipment and materials. And they need to experiment in social relationships. Their play and work in groups seldom goes beyond two or three companions. They are not ready to be in large groups, all working on the same activity.

Kindergarten children also need individual freedom to move about and to make choices. They are apt to play and work in groups which include about five or six and are ready for whole class activity which may last for about 15 or 20 minutes for "lessons" in literature, science, music making and interpretation, or dramatics.

Both nursery school and kindergarten children are ready for such projects as making valentines, baking cookies, churning cream, and other activities combining enjoyment and learning. It is important, however, to recognize that the rule of thumb is respect for the individual child, allowance for individual behavior patterns, and a program which enables each child to be comfortable and productive within a flexible framework.

The large instructional space should be entirely unlike a typical elementary classroom. It should have no partitions and should be equipped with furniture and cabinets that are easily moveable for a variety of activities. The large space should have both hard and soft floor coverings, depending upon the activities involved. The reading and browsing areas should have rugs. In the housekeeping, science, and water-play areas, hard surfaces should be used for ease of maintenance.

Varied floor levels and ceiling heights relieve monotony in a large area. Lowered ceilings tend to create a friendly atmosphere, but some areas need to have higher ceilings so that such play apparatus and equipment as slides, climbing devices, and wheeled toys may be set up.

After a period indoors, youngsters need to get outside if weather permits. An hour out of doors offers much more than an opportunity to let off steam. It is a time for learning to get along with others as well as a

Adapted from architects' notebooks, various interpretations of the planning process from doodling stage through finished concept. Top, space relationships; center above, learning areas clustered around a core; below, a rough floor plan followed by architect's sculptural sketch.

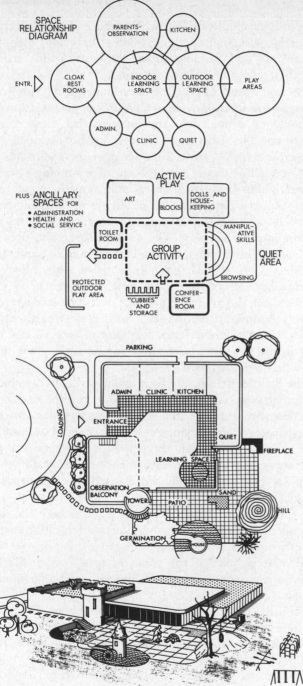

SPACE RELATIONSHIP DIAGRAM

ENTR.

PARENTS-OBSERVATION

KITCHEN

CLOAK REST ROOMS

INDOOR LEARNING SPACE

OUTDOOR LEARNING SPACE

PLAY AREAS

ADMIN.

CLINIC

QUIET

PLUS **ANCILLARY SPACES** FOR
- ADMINISTRATION
- HEALTH AND
- SOCIAL SERVICE

ACTIVE PLAY

ART

BLOCKS

DOLLS AND HOUSE-KEEPING

TOILET ROOM

GROUP ACTIVITY

MANIPUL-ATIVE SKILLS

QUIET AREA

BROWSING

PROTECTED OUTDOOR PLAY AREA

"CUBBIES" AND STORAGE

CONFER-ENCE ROOM

PARKING

ADMIN   CLINIC   KITCHEN

LOADING

ENTRANCE

QUIET

FIREPLACE

LEARNING SPACE

OBSERVATION BALCONY

TOWER

SAND

PATIO

HILL

GERMINATION

HOUSE

time for physical development. Their little bodies are constantly improved through running, jumping, climbing, sliding, crawling, digging, pulling, pushing, reaching, and bending in an outdoor facility that has been arranged with freedom and safety in mind.

The exterior space of the nursery-kindergarten program is just as important as the interior rooms. Continuous access from indoors to outdoors should be provided in such a way that close supervision of both areas is possible. Important features to be included are a hard surfaced area for wheeled toys, a gardening area, a dirt hill for sliding and digging, a sandbox, water in the form of a running stream or series of pools with pump-circulated water, animal pens, apparatus areas, a treehouse, trees, large conduits, and other objects for climbing.

Social skills are developed through meeting and resolving conflicts that arise in vigorous play. The outdoor scene also provides countless environmental lessons in how vehicles look and sound, how people travel, how leaves are shaped, how snow flakes melt, how water runs, how dirt feels, how insects live, how birds build nests.

Youngsters can learn a great many valuable lessons from water, sand, sunlight, shadows, rainbows, the smell of wet earth, the sound of wind, the texture of earth surfaces, the hum of insects, and other wonderments that are new and fascinating to the little child, who is free to perceive them from his own viewpoint.

In all the daily activities, the little child gradually assumes responsibility for putting away equipment if a good storage place is conveniently located. He learns to care for himself if toilet facilities are easily accessible; he participates in the serving of a snack if serving utensils and food are suitable. And he learns that there is a proper time for resting and relaxing if proper cots or other equipment are ready for use and easy to put away. In these routines the nursery school child needs more help than the kindergartner.

While the nursery school child usually "helps" the teacher put away the tools of work and play, the kindergarten child seems ready to become a team worker. The fickle, transient three-year-old who played only a small part in putting the room in order eventually emerges as the self-assured, competent five-year-old who can be counted on to get the job done.

The secret of helping children take responsibility for indoor cleanup of equipment and materials is well planned storage space, good organization, and easy-to-clean surfaces that are suitable for assorted activities. These features are especially necessary in order that the child may know where to go when he needs certain materials to carry out a plan. He learns the value of orderliness. Are the brushes clean and in place? Is the paper easy to reach? Are the blocks of similar shapes stacked together? Are puzzles in the rack, pegs in a box, peg boards together?

When going-home time comes, the nursery school children leave one by one or in small carpool groups. The kindergartner who, at the beginning of the school year, came with an older escort, eventually leaves the schoolroom with the whole group and either walks home alone or meets his escort at the designated exit.

In terms of space requirements for nursery-kindergarten pupils, the conferees agreed that there should be a minimum of 35 square feet of clear space per pupil but that each large instructional room should contain a minimum of 1,000 square feet of floor space exclusive of storage, toilets, and built-in equipment.

Heating and ventilation, lighting, acoustical treatment, and color treatment of floors, walls, and ceilings should meet all recommended standards.

Safety factors include avoidance of sharp corners and edges and the provision of non-skid surface and space areas which provide children with a sense of security and freedom. At the same time, they should be protected from their own immaturity and enabled to live and learn in a school environment that is both functional and beautiful.

The children are not the only ones to be considered, however. A nursery or kindergarten must accommodate a number of grown-ups. The professional teaching staff is often supplemented by part-time consultants in such fields as speech therapy, psychology, medicine, nursing, and social service.

Assistant teachers carry out some teaching responsibilities under the supervision of the teacher and sometimes assume responsibility for a group of children. Teacher aides assist in such activities as preparing paints, clay, and other materials, assisting in the preparation of snacks and meals, and setting up cots and other equipment for rest and naps. Parents, other community members, and older children with skills or interest in the program serve as volunteer teacher aides.

Observation space should be provided so that parents, teachers, and others can see into the large instructional area and also out into the exterior play and work areas. This space should be elevated above the main floor level and should have one-way glass so that the pupils will not be aware of observers. This observation space can be used as an area where parents may gather, a conference space, and an informal teacher lounge where light lunches can be served.

Secretarial services and clerical services for correspondence, record keeping, and other office functions depend on the size of the program. Service workers including a cook, custodian, bus driver, and other nonprofessional staff are employed whenever necessary.

There should be administrative office space for the director who is usually responsible for operating the program and who serves as liaison between the staff and the policy-making officers.

It is apparent from the number of persons involved in the nursery school and kindergarten programs that a variety of spaces is needed. There are a number of different kinds of spaces to be considered and the relationship of one area to another is extremely important in terms of pupil traffic, educational program requirements, and a free flow of activity.

It is extremely useful for planners to work with a diagram of these general space relationships. The focal points which should be included are the entry with cloak and rest room, indoor and outdoor learning space, and the play areas. Any diagram of these areas, to be fully useful to a planning group, should suggest various possibilities for room relationships including multiple uses of spaces.

The following is a checklist of major areas needed for teaching and learning (indoors and outdoors) which have implications for the planning of nursery-kindergarten facilities: creative activities—work with clay, paints, wood, puzzles, beads, simple tools; block building; library and browsing corner; water and sand play; housekeeping; discussion, story-telling, and reading; storage for educational materials, wraps, furniture, and equipment; display space; snacking; resting; observation (for parents); health; lavatory; administration teacher preparation; and storage space.

These recommendations, drawn from the OE-sponsored conference, are, of course, designed as a guide to the elements that make up an ideal learning atmosphere for preschoolers. Facilities can be as simple or as complex as local initiative and budget limitations may dictate.

In the midst of careful planning for adequate, flexible, and safe facilities, the planners must remember that the building and grounds should be a source of delight to the children. The experiences a child has in nursery school or kindergarten may form habits, attitudes, and impressions that will be reflected throughout the remainder of his school years.

The little child views the world and its people with curiosity and wonder. He takes in the environment about him through his senses and through continuous activity—looking, listening, smelling, tasting, touching, manipulating, and interacting. He communicates the freshness of his discoveries and explorations to the children and adults close by. Sometimes he dashes off for new experiences. At other times he pursues one activity for days.

The child's first school contact must nurture his endless curiosity and desire to probe. It must provide an environment that stimulates learning. The school must say "yes" to the child's natural inclination to work for self-enhancement. Present joys and fulfillment must promise future aspiration and attainment.

Needless to say, preschool teaching can be done in far from ideal facilities. Conscientious parents have struggled for years to provide early training for their youngsters through cooperative nursery schools in whatever quarters were available.

Children from disadvantaged homes and low-income neighborhoods, perhaps more than any others, need the advantages of good preschool education. As the funds and time become available, those responsible for preschool education should take into consideration the added benefits that can come to children from having their first school experiences in appropriate surroundings.

49   What Schools Are Doing To Get Their Preprimary Projects Going*

Detroit Program Focuses on Language Development

Preschool education is a year-round activity in Detroit. A program funded by the Office of Economic Opportunity enrolls 400 inner-city disadvantaged 3 and 4 year olds during the regular school year. In summer months, approximately 6,000 students attend Head Start classes.

Head Start teachers are recruited from the primary teaching staffs of inner-city schools. They staff 120 centers.

The school-year program funded by O.E.O. is being expanded under E.S.E.A.; and by September 1966, 1,000 children will attend preschools in 25 centers.

Although both programs are within the district's department of early childhood education and have the same basic approach, they differ in length of time a child may participate: two years in the regular school year program; one summer in Head Start.

Eight specific emphases contribute to the quality of our total preschool program:

* Reprinted, with permission, from *Nation's Schools*, June 1966, vol. 77, no. 6. Copyright 1966, McGraw-Hill, Inc., Chicago. All rights reserved.

CITYWIDE ADVISORY COMMITTEES. Committees of professional and lay personnel help to guide the preschool programs. Representation includes: citizens from the areas of the city served by the program, school administrators and teachers, city social service and health agencies, the Michigan State Department of Public Instruction, the local Community Action Program, and several universities.

LANGUAGE DEVELOPMENT. The core of the daily program revolves around a stress on language development. Many kinds of material such as songs, poems, stories and so forth, offer an opportunity to develop listening skills. Pegboards, matching games, and picture story sequence activities develop eye discrimination. Role playing and the use of puppets help shy children express themselves more fluently. Many shared experiences such as trips to the children's zoo where they may feed and touch animals, local parks, and fire stations enrich backgrounds and facilitate interpupil discussion.

A preschool language education specialist has prepared a teacher guide entitled "First Steps in Language Experiences for Preschool Children." In addition, specific lesson plans designed to promote language development have been written. These special lesson plans are used with small groups of children whose achievement on a language screening was very poor.

PARENT INVOLVEMENT. One day each week is set aside for planned parent meetings. These may take many directions: simple discussions of mutual problems, assistance from nutritionists and homemaking experts, trips to enrich backgrounds, films on child development, and so forth. A major goal of the adult program is the strengthening of parent self-image by offering self-help ideas in a friendly cooperative atmosphere. In addition to the regular weekly meetings, parents are encouraged to personally bring their children to school and to become involved in the ongoing activities.

HEALTH EXAMINATIONS. All children in the preschool program receive health examinations, and follow-up where needed is carefully pursued. The health examination reports assist in program development and other planning. For example, when medical reports indicated the prevalence of vitamin C deficiency, fruit juices were added to the children's daily snack. In another instance, the Department of Public Health checked all of the preschool children for lead poisoning, a condition found more frequently in inner-city children. Where this condition existed, follow-up was carried on by the department to correct unhealthful conditions in the child's environment which caused the condition; and medical treatment was given to the child.

COOPERATION WITH SOCIAL SERVICE AGENCIES. When children and

families are in need of specific kinds of help, the teachers and administrators call upon a close working relationship with many social service agencies, public and private, available in the city. Care is taken to make certain that the matter is handled properly and that families are not only made aware of the fact that community help is available, but are assisted in reaching the source of help.

TESTING. The preschool project is developing an experimental test battery to assess the level of development of each child and, more important, for use as a diagnostic tool for adjusting the program to the individual needs of the children. School psychologists do the individual testing, and the test situation is carefully controlled so that valid program judgments may be made.

USE OF COMMUNITY AIDS. Each preschool center employs persons who live in the community. They serve the program in many ways, but are especially important in developing and maintaining contact with parents who have often had poor relations with the official world and are hesitant about participating in the activities of the preschool center.

INSERVICE EDUCATION OF TEACHERS. Regular biweekly, full-day teacher workshops for all the teachers in the program develop and expand the teacher skills necessary to make the program a success. Experts in many areas lead discussions, and teachers have an opportunity to plan together for program improvement.—ARTHUR M. ENZMANN, *director, department of early childhood development, Detroit Public Schools.*

Mt. Vernon, N.Y., Mixes Mothers and Montessori

Mount Vernon's preschool program for 4 year olds mixes Montessori and mothers in a store-front child center located in the disadvantaged neighborhood it serves.

The physical layout of the center, a renovated brick building which served the city in the 1890s as a police lockup, might be called a "nurserymat." From its store-front entrance at street level, the mothers enter a small reception area equipped with a sofa, chairs, a table of popular magazines, and an abundance of ash trays which invite them to relax and be neighborly. A large L-shaped room serves as the school proper. A door from this room leads to a rather large one utilized as the teachers' workshop.

A great deal of work went into selecting and orienting the mothers whose children would be in the initial project. They were told that the center would not be a place where they could park their children for an hour while they did some shopping. Nor was it to be a social-welfare type of educational center.

They were told they would have a role as vital as the teachers have.

The pilot project started on a small scale with only 24 children and was conducted for five months. In fall 1965 the board appropriated $90,000 to expand the program to include 120 children. There are two shifts of teachers: one for the morning session and one for the afternoon. The children come at specific times, for one-hour sessions, from 9 to 3. These sessions concentrate on Montessori "didactic" materials to develop expressive language use. One of the most sophisticated versions of this "didactic" material used in the center is an instrument popularly called "the talking typewriter." Each class of 12 children has a teacher, an assistant, and two mothers who work with the teachers and children and make periodic home visits. The instructors are certified conventional teachers drawn from a pool of 45 kindergarten teachers who took a 30 hour Montessori inservice course. The teaching assistants and mothers are trained on the job and after school.

The board has requested funds under Title I of the Elementary and Secondary Education Act of 1965 to expand the program even further. If funds are granted, the center will operate for 12 months a year, providing for 240 pupils in two terms of six months each.

For school systems contemplating a similar children's center, Mount Vernon superintendent, John H. Martin, and center director, Nancy Rambusch, prepared these suggestions:

1. The creation of a new educational institution must not look or function like the conventional school. It cannot be attached to a rigid public school program.

2. The sponsors and all concerned must believe in a highly democratic approach. It cannot be a line and staff operation but must be a participating democracy in which mothers must be partners.

3. The mothers must *not* be lectured to about what their children's aspirations should be, but helped to learn what they are and then to work actively to assist them in achieving them.

4. A great deal of preliminary work must be done with the mothers before launching the program. The mothers must clearly understand that the center is a school and not either a "baby sitting" project or another social service agency to minister to their physical needs.

5. The sponsors must be satisfied with slow initial growth. The mothers served by the center will eventually communicate with others in the neighborhood and generate enthusiasm for the center and its purpose.

6. Teachers must be trained in Montessori. If it is adopted on a large scale and inserted in the center and kindergartens without the insights and

teaching processes necessary to make it effective in helping children to learn, the results will be barren and there will be only manipulated children.

7. The early introduction of standard "reading readiness" materials designed for conventional teaching in the first grade must not be used with 4 year olds.

8. Records of each child's progress must go to the kindergarten teacher as the child leaves the center. Otherwise, the teacher will be wasting the child's time awaiting evidences of readiness to manifest themselves while the child is able and eager to proceed.

9. A center should stress multisensory materials directly related to verbal symbols in a concentrated approach toward language and reading development.—ALFRED M. FRANKO, *director of school community relations, Mount Vernon Schools, Mount Vernon, N.Y.*

Lebanon, Ore., Brings in Parochial School Pupils

Although public school personnel assumed leadership and responsibility, all parochial schools (Catholic, Episcopal, Adventist) and private kindergarten operators were brought into preschool project planning at Lebanon, Ore. Once feasibility was established, school board approval and initial community communications were started; and the project application was developed.

Lebanon's program is small: 107 five year olds. Classrooms are located in each elementary school building, and pupils attend two and one-half hour half-day sessions. Bus transportation is provided in accord with district regulations.

Called "Sure Start," the program represents a downward extension of Lebanon's ungraded progress program to include 5 year olds. The project also calls for a follow-up of 6 and 7 year olds who continue to have difficulty. Lebanon officials deliberately decided not to call the Title I program preschool or kindergarten—feeling these terms often are associated with nonschool activities and wishing to integrate the project closely with the existing primary school curriculum.

The teaching staff was selected on the basis of special academic preparation for primary and kindergarten teaching and special talent in art and music. A week of inservice training was provided prior to the program's start, and continuing inservice activities are planned through the school year. Inservice activities for parents have also been developed. —GEORGE M. HENDERSON, *assistant superintendent, Lebanon, Ore.*

Woodward, Iowa, Takes Head Start
Home to Parents

It's Home Start not Head Start in Woodward, Iowa. Home Start is the name of the Title I E.S.E.A. project now operating in the Woodward-Granger district.

Rather than take preschool children to school to strengthen their educational foundation, Woodward's project attempts to strengthen it in the home. By reinforcing the home educationally, all of the children within the family will benefit and parents will have the satisfaction of being a part of this process.

Individual as well as group contacts are being made with the homes to become more aware of the needs within each family. To help in carrying out the project, a child development specialist has been added to the faculty.

One of the project's main objectives is parent education. Small groups of mothers of preschool children attend meetings on a variety of topics, such as discipline, nutrition, activities and materials for readiness, behavior patterns, and so forth. The mothers are also given a chance to discuss some of their own problems and profit from the experiences of the group.

In addition to parent education, Home Start is also providing a means of early identification and correction of speech and hearing defects. The child development specialist visits the homes of all preschool children; during these visits she has an opportunity to talk with the child and can gain some insight into problems which may hinder him later when he enters school. All information gained is transferred to the kindergarten teachers so that they can better evaluate the child and be more aware of home situations.

A spring screening session of one week is held for all children eligible for kindergarten in the fall. During this period they will be observed carefully to identify and eliminate those too immature to profit from kindergarten. It has been shown in Greene County that a screening program such as this can be effective in preventing retentions at a later grade level.

Cost of the program is low. Operating the program for four and one-half months for 60 families will cost $5,453. For the 1966–67 school year, the total will be approximately $9,500, amounting to $158 per family. But an average of three children from each family will bring the cost per child down to about $53.—D. H. FEAZELL, *superintendent, Woodward-Granger Community School District, Woodward, Iowa.*

These Preschool Problems Trouble Schoolmen

Hatch, N.M.: Federal Timing Gives Us a Budget Headache

Although providing all-important operating revenue, federal funds have complicated budget planning at Hatch, N.M. Teacher contracts are issued in mid-April, but federal funds are not appropriated until late summer. This time gap requires Hatch to maintain local cash reserves to guarantee contract fulfillment should federal funds be reduced or late in distribution.

Hatch's preschool project is an English Language Program for 5 and 6 year old children from Spanish-speaking families. Speaking no English when they enroll, the children participate in an entirely oral program, and learn English by repeating sentences and words until they know the meaning of what they are saying.

A large primary classroom with appropriate language supplies and equipment is adequate for the 30 pupils involved. The teacher has a background of training and experience in English and Spanish and has taught language at both the primary and high school level.

The project has been made part of Hatch's regular school program. The teacher is on the same salary schedule as regular certified employes, and federal funds are deposited to the credit of the school district's operation fund rather than carried as a separate account. Cost of the project approximates the per student cost of regular instruction.—M. E. LINTON, *superintendent, Hatch, N.M.*

Bartow, Fla.: We're Seeking Space, Staff, and Teamwork

Space, staff and administrative coordination have been the biggest problems for "Operation Retrieve" in Polk County, Fla.

Finding adequate housing for the three centers in our plan has been difficult. With no space available in existing school buildings, the program has been operating in rented facilities and makeshift quarters. We are in the process of purchasing several portable classrooms—which should help.

Recruitment of competent teachers and other needed employes has also posed problems, but we have been surprised at the number of talented and competent people willing to work on the project. In planning, we purposefully provided for some half-time positions; and this has helped attract some well-trained housewives not available otherwise.

Our biggest problem has been establishing this program as a component part of our entire operation. There is a great temptation to set up a Title I program as a separate entity in its financial operation, administration and supervision. We *have* employed a full-time supervisor of special projects, but have been insistent that regular channels be followed in employment practices (salaries conform to regular salary schedules), purchasing procedures, budgetary operation, and educational supervision. Our insistence on this approach has required hours of conferences, but we feel it is necessary if the program is to have any real value.—A. R. ADAMS, *assistant superintendent for instructional affairs, Polk County Public Schools, Bartow, Fla.*

Jacksonville, Fla.: We Didn't Have Time To Do All We Should Have

While thorough planning of pre-school programs is vital, there may not be time to do it.

In Duval County, Fla., the Kindergarten Project started last January 17, but administrative delays made it a hurried start. It definitely was a crash program because the guidelines from the federal and state education offices arrived later than expected.

Thirty-eight units in 17 centers were established; and 38 teachers, 38 project teacher aides, 20 project utility workers, and 17 clerk typists were employed. The enrollment exceeds 800 kindergarten-age children. The preschool program was developed for this age because there are presently no public kindergartens in Duval County.

Because of the speed with which the centers were opened, no materials or equipment were available during the first six weeks, and teachers were thrown on their own to carry on adequate programs.

The influx of personnel into all federal projects, which began on approximately the same date, also caused payroll problems. The overwhelmed payroll department was unable to release initial pay checks on time, causing hardships to some personnel.

Finding teachers with degrees and regular certificates was difficult; in cases where it was impossible, substitute teachers were employed. But hiring teachers for the project in no way weakened the regular school program. Only three teachers were released from regular classrooms; and in these cases, principals felt the teachers were exceptionally fitted to work in early childhood education because of their qualifications and experience.—PATRICIA COLEMAN, *coordinator of Kindergarten Project, Duval County Schools, Jacksonville, Fla.*

San Antonio, Tex., Models Title I on Head Start

Head Start not only enrolled 2,600 students last summer in San Antonio but served as a model for the Title I preschool program operated by the district during the 1965–66 school year.

The Title I program serves approximately 2,000 children in 112 classrooms, located in 28 target area schools and staffed by 56 teachers. Program costs totaled $529,916. Expense breakdown: salaries, $364,916; equipment, $30,000; materials and supplies, $45,000; medical supplies and follow-up, $14,000; repairs to equipment, $7,000, and snacks (milk and cookies), $69,000.

Nearly 45 per cent of students in San Antonio schools come from homes in which Spanish is the only language spoken. Another 13 per cent are Negro children. From these two ethnic groups come nearly all the disadvantaged children for which San Antonio's preschool program was developed.

Staffing was not easy. Although San Antonio was among the first school districts in the country to have its Title I program approved, federal appropriations were not forthcoming until after the regular school program was in progress, making it difficult to obtain teachers. The preschool teachers have all benefits of professional staff members, including teacher retirement, social security, and so forth.

Preschool classrooms are located in 28 schools in the target areas. At the outset, plans were made to construct two-room buildings for placement as needed. But this required time; and, in some cases, classes were delayed in opening.

To reach parents of disadvantaged children, newspapers, radio and TV were used to publicize opening dates and locations of the classes. Public school officials worked jointly with nonpublic school officials in the disadvantaged areas to contact as many parents as possible.

Developing the list of needed teaching materials and equipment was facilitated by the district's experience in Head Start. Materials purchased with Head Start funds were authorized for use in the regular program. Audiovisual equipment, normally available in each elementary school, such as film, slide and overhead projectors and tape recorders, and primary playground equipment are shared with the preschool classes.

Inservice training, included in most Title I preschool programs, was planned in cooperation with the University of Texas. Ten meetings for preschool teachers and principals of schools in which preschool classes were located were offered. Stretching from late January to mid-May, the courses covered:

1. Characteristics of disadvantaged children;
2. Problems of the disadvantaged child in the middle-class American school;
3. English language for the Spanish-speaking child;
4. Structuring the learning environment for young children;
5. How children learn;
6. Furnishing the classroom as a learning laboratory;
7. Music for preschool children;

8. Health appraisal;
9. Early learning experiences as preparation for success in language skills;
10. Evaluating the learning process.

The district also prepared a 28 page guide for teaching disadvantaged preschoolers, containing model program schedules, curriculum outlines, and an extensive list of suggested activities.—RAYMOND W. ARNOLD, *assistant superintendent of schools, San Antonio, Tex.*

How Cleveland Uses Food in Its Preschool Programs

While food in most preschool programs provides nourishment to overcome poor home diets and eating habits, it has added functions in Cleveland's preschool curriculum. Lunches there feature new foods, and food itself is an intensive object of study. Purpose of Cleveland's emphasis: to use common objects to contribute to the broadening experience of preschool activities.

Cleveland's preschool program operates year round, enrolling nearly 5,500 inner-city 4 and 5 year olds.

To introduce children to new foods, weekly "taste tests" are offered during the regular school year. Although the children receive fruit, juice, milk and graham crackers daily, these weekly tests provide special foods which many of the children have never seen, tasted or touched. Class discussions precede the tests, and the children do the buying and preparing themselves.

A special curriculum unit in summer Head Start classes is devoted to food. Called the "nutrition unit," its objectives are:

1. Acquaint children with new foods;
2. Develop a food vocabulary;
3. Demonstrate that meal time is a pleasant time;
4. Create good eating habits and table manners;
5. Promote understanding of good nutrition.

The basic types of food are presented to the preschoolers in weekly study units. The first week is spent discussing vegetables; the second, dairy products; the third, meat and other protein food; the fourth, fruits. To initiate discussion, appropriate foods are displayed in the classroom; and the children set up play kitchens with proper food models. Teaching aids, films, stories, poems, games and slides illustrate and supplement the presentation.

Enhancing discussions by participation, preschoolers plant vegetables, visit farm animals at the zoo, peel oranges, and visit a bakery. During the first week of the 1965 Head Start program, a live cow was brought into the schools for a milking demonstration.

Head Start lunches are planned to provide a wide range of food experiences. (See sample menu below.)

WHAT CLEVELAND FEEDS ITS PRESCHOOLERS

Monday—July 12
Sliced Spiced Ham Sandwich
Crisp Carrot Pieces
Homemade Cookie
3   Canned Stewed Prunes
3 oz.   Juice

Tuesday—July 13
Sliced Cheese Sandwich
Sweet Pickle Chips
Brownie
Fresh Apricot
3 oz.   Juice

Wednesday—July 14
Minced Ham Sandwich
¼ cup   Calico Salad
Fruit Torte
¼ cup   Apple Sauce
3 oz.   Juice

Thursday—July 15
Peanut Butter & Jelly Sandwich
¼ cup   Shredded Lettuce
Home Made Cookie
California Grapes
3 oz.   Juice

Friday—July 16
Egg Salad Sandwich
2   Celery Curls
Raisin Spice Bar
1   Fresh Peach
3 oz.   Juice

Realizing that a successful program depends on parent response, school officials send menus home with the children each week. Nutrition bulletins, pamphlets and booklets obtained from local agencies are given out at parents' meeting and on home visits by social workers and nurses.

A weekly television series, "Parent Education," occasionally schedules food programs. In summer 1965, for example, the series included two demonstrations by nutrition specialists from the community.

Schools found community organizations anxious to help. The National Dairy Council arranged for the cow's visit and donated pictures, posters, flannelgram foods, exhibits, filmstrips and take-home materials. The state agricultural extension service and city health department provided materials, consultants and home visitation services; and the Nutrition Association of Greater Cleveland provided speakers, bulletins and TV demonstrations—CHRISTINE BRANCHE, *supervisor, preschool programs, Cleveland.*

California Program Relies on a Four-way Partnership

California got a headstart on Head Start with its statewide system of children's centers. First approved in 1943 by the state legislature to free mothers of preschool children for wartime defense work, the centers began in remodeled basements of large older homes or temporary war housing projects. Today, the newest centers occupy bright, modern buildings and provide instruction and educational supervision for children ages 2 through 13, whose parents are forced to work through financial necessity and require supervision of their children.

California's children's centers operate on a four-way partnership. Individual cities provide the sites and buildings—usually on the grounds of existing elementary schools. Staff and supervision are provided by the state department of education, and the centers operate under jurisdiction of the local school district. Parents contribute one-third of the operational costs; the state, two-thirds. Eligibility of parents is determined by a state "means" test.

The staff at each children's center includes a head teacher and supervising teachers, who have the specific responsibility of carrying out the program of instruction and supervision. The cook and kitchen-helper are responsible, under the direction of the head teacher, for preparing and serving food for the children and the staff. A housekeeper and part-time custodian see that facility and grounds are cared for.

50   How to Equip and Supply Your Prekindergarten Classrooms*

ANNE MARIE EVANS, *Cincinnati Public Schools*

This list of suggested equipment and supplies for a prekindergarten class is compiled from items that appeared on similar lists available from the Association for Childhood Education and Project Head Start. The list is comprehensive; schools organizing prekindergarten classes should consider classroom space and budget in preparing orders.

For each 20 children you will need:

CLASSROOM FURNITURE

1	Teacher desk
2	Adult chairs
1	Adult rocker
1	Bookcase, 34½" wide, 30" high, 12" deep; or 36" wide, 55" high
2	Bulletin boards (portable, if wall not available)
1	Filing cabinet, two-drawer
1	Metal storage cabinet
1	Mobile cart, for lunch supplies, audio-visual materials
1	Piano
1	Refrigerator
2–3	Shelves, low open; for toys, books and blocks
20	Pupil chairs, colored, fiberglas, stack chairs, 10"-11" high
5	Tables, trapezoidal 2-20"; 3-21" laminated plastic top, colored
1	Table, round, 36" diameter 20" high
2	Chairs, small rocker

Storage for 20 pupils: either individual lockers 45" high, 10' wide, 10" deep, 2 shelves 9" from top; or 2 movable coat racks with shelf for rubbers at bottom.

CLASSROOM EQUIPMENT

1	Double easel (if space permits, 2 double easels)
2	Movable pegboard screens

* Reprinted, with permission, from *Nation's Schools*, June 1966, vol. 77, no. 6. Copyright 1966, McGraw-Hill, Inc., Chicago. All rights reserved.

1	Paper cutter 18″ blade
1	Sandbox, movable, 24″ high × 32″ square × 8″ deep
1	Water play table with top
1	Carpenter's workbench with 3″ or 5″ C-clamps; or 3 sturdy wooden tables on casters, with C-clamps or workhorses
1	Phonograph (3 speed) with plug for listening posts
15–20	Records: games, songs, literature
1	Tape recorder
1	Filmstrip projector
1	Camera
1	35mm. camera
1	16mm. movie projector
1	Screen
1	Set listening post (12 units)
1	8mm. Loop projector

ART SUPPLIES

2	balls Cord: 3 oz. macrame (red, white)
12	Brushes, paint, camel hair or bristle, ½″ to 1″ thick, long handle (artist brush is recommended)
12	Brushes, paste, short handle, ½″; or, 12 paste sticks
25	lbs. Clay, dry or mixed
5	Clay boards 9″ × 12″
16	Containers, ½ pint or pint, plastic or metal, with covers, for paint
1	Garbage can, plastic, with cover, for clay; or 2 gal. clay jar with lid
1	box Chalk, poster, ¼″ boxes, 36 assorted colors
1	box Dressmaker pins (½ lb.)
8	doz. Crayons (wax); 1 doz. red, orange, yellow, green, blue, purple, black, brown; large size
6	hanks Yarn, bright colors
2	Markers, felt tip, black ink, red ink
10	pints Paste, library
17	lbs. Paint, powder, cold water; 3 lbs. each red, yellow, blue, white; 2 lbs. each, black, green, brown, orange, purple
11	jars Paint, finger, ½ pint; 2 each red, yellow, green, blue; 1 each brown, purple (wheat paste and powder paint can be substituted)
2	pkg. Paper, cutting, black, 18″ × 24″

8   pkg. Paper, construction, 12″ × 18″, assorted colors
5   pkg. Paper, finger painting, 16″ × 22″, or glazed shelf
12   pkg. Paper, folding, 4″ × 6″, assorted colors
4   pkg. Paper, manila, 12″ × 18″, 500 sheets to pkg.
6   pkg. Paper, unprinted news, 24″ × 36″, 100 sheets to pkg. (newspaper may be substituted)
3   pkg. Paper, unprinted news, 18″ × 24″
6   pkg. Paper, tissue, green, red, blue, pink, white, yellow
1   roll White wrapping paper, 36″ wide
12   pkg. Paper, unprinted news, assorted colors
10   lbs. Wheat paste powder (for finger paint)
1   doz. Scissors, blunt
6   Scissors, left-handed, blunt
1   Scissors, storage block
4   Aprons, old shirts, or smocks

Miscellaneous
     Orange juice cans
     Baby food jars
     Corn starch, laundry starch
     Drying rack
     Florist wire
     Flour and salt for play dough
     Pipe cleaners
     Armature wire
     Colored toothpicks
     Transparent colored paper
     Wallpaper books

CRAFT/WOODWORKING

4   Hammers, claw, 6 oz. to 10 oz. weight
5   lbs. Nails, large heads, assorted sizes
     Sandpaper, fine
1   Saw, 12″, crosscut
     Wood, scraps, soft, mill ends

Miscellaneous
     Buttons
     Washers
     Corks
     Wire
     Nuts
     Hooks and eyes
     Spools
     Bottle caps

HOUSEKEEPING

2   Brooms, small size
1   Broom, small push
2   Brushes, floor, long handle, 16" and 18"
12   yds. Cheesecloth
1   Clothes rack
1   Dish pan
2   Draining racks
2   Dustpans, long handle
1   Dustpan, long handle, child size
1   Mop, cone
1   Mop, cone, child size
2   Pails, different sizes, 1 cone pail
4   Sponges
6   yds. Oilcloth, red, yellow, white
12   pkg. Cleanser
1   Container for paper towels
1   First-aid cabinet, filled at recommendation of school physician
1   Mirror
2   Mops, wet
         Soap, cake, granules
         Tissues
         Toilet paper
18   pkg. Towels, paper (250 to pkg.)
         Vases, various sizes

LANGUAGE ARTS

         Flannel board with story characters
         Large alphabet blocks
         Hand puppets
3   sets Play story characters, wooden, firm base (The Three Pigs, Goldilocks and the Three Bears, Gingerbread Boy)
3   Puzzles, SeeQuees (Humpty Dumpty, Hey Diddle Diddle, This Little Pig)
2   sets Letters of the alphabet (large 2" lower case and capitals)
Miscellaneous
         Photographs of children or places visited

Posters and pictures from various travel agencies
Paper bags, potatoes, old gloves for making puppets

LITERATURE

30   Story and picture books, carefully selected on the basis
        of age levels, and including a wide variety of subjects
        to assist children in learning and understanding the
        world about them (Consult local librarian for selection)
4–6   sets Large pictures that give accurate information and
        stimulate children's discussion and story telling

LUNCH/HALF-DAY SESSIONS

20   boxes Straws, single (100 to box)
4   Baskets for serving cookies
30   pkg. Cups, small, paper, 100 to pkg. for tomato juice,
        water
4   yds. Oilcloth or plastic, for mats
4   pkg. Napkins, paper, 1,000 to pkg.
4   Pitchers, small, easy pour, good handles
6   Trays, small

FOOD SERVICES/FULL-DAY SESSIONS

*(All utensils used for cooking and eating should be made of
materials which can be sterilized.)*

4   doz. Bibs, self-help, if possible
20   Bowls, shallow, low sides, unbreakable
20   Cups, or small glasses, unbreakable
30   pkg. Cups, small, paper, 100 to pkg. for tomato juice,
        water
20   Dishes, dessert, unbreakable
20   Forks, salad size
6   Forks, for teachers
6   Glasses, large
        Mats, paper
6   Knives, for teachers
8   pkg. Napkins, paper, 1,000 to pkg.
2   yds. Oilcloth or plastic, for mats
4   Pitchers, quart, easy pour, good handles
4   Pitchers, small, easy pour, good handles
24   Plates, breakfast size, unbreakable
1   Table, 18″ × 36″, on casters

12   Tablespoons
24   Teaspoons, straight handle
20   boxes Straws, single
4   Baskets for serving cookies
2   Trays, large, aluminum
6   Trays, small

MUSIC

1   set Rhythm instruments (24 piece) to include drum, triangle, tamborine, cymbals, maracas, tone blocks, rhythm sticks, song bells, shakers
1   Autoharp (12 bar)
3   pr. Bells, jingle (wrist)
4–6   Dancing scarves 5′ × 3′
1   Chromatic pitch pipe
2   Tom-toms (Chinese skin)

Miscellaneous

Large can and rubber inner tube
Chopping bowl and circular piece of drumhead skin
Dowel sticks ½″ diameter, 12″ long
Small boxes
Pebbles, stones, beans, cherry pits
Paper plates and bottle caps

MISCELLANEOUS

1   box Adhesive tape
4   boxes Fasteners, round head, 100 to box; 1 box ¾″, 2 boxes 1″, 1 box 1½″ or 2″
2   boxes Labels, gummed
4   boxes Paper clips, large
2   boxes Rubber bands
5   boxes Thumb tacks No. 2, ⅜″, 100 to box
1   Flag, United States
1   Punch, large eyelet
2   boxes Eyelets (500 to box)
12   rolls Tape, masking, ¾″ × 25′
12   rolls Tape, cellophane, ¾″ × 25′
1   Stapling machine, ¼″ staples
3   boxes Staples, ¼″ (500 to box)
        Silencers for chairs and tables
        Vinyl or nap mats, throw rugs for resting program
3   Wastebaskets

1   Window stick
1   Yardstick

SCIENCE

1   Aquarium, large
1   Bird feeding shelf and suet feeder
1   Cage for visiting pets, removable bottom
1   Cage for insects
        Flower boxes
2   Magnets, bar, U, horseshoe
1   Magnifying glass (hand)
1   Magnifying glass (tripod)
2   Prism glass
        Preserving fluid
        Pulleys, with buckets
        Seeds and bulbs
1   Terrarium
1   Thermometer, play
2   Thermometers, indoor, outdoor
        Vases, various sizes, frogs
2   Watering cans, plastic, long spout
Miscellaneous
        Large jars for terrarium
        Rock collections, seeds
        Pets
        Collections of materials of various types and textures

PLAY EQUIPMENT

1   Climbing structure, or ladder box, or nesting sets
        Gardening tools, such as rakes, shovels, watering cans and hose, jr. size
3   Ladders (steel or wood, light enough for children to drag around, sturdy enough to withstand rough usage) with cleats or hooks on each end, sizes $3' \times 14''$, $4' \times 14''$, $5' \times 14''$
2–3   Kegs, for rolling (painted)
3–4   Packing boxes, large wooden
6–8   Planks, $6' \times 10'$, with cleats at end to hold place on climbing structure, boxes
1   Platform and steps, step $6'' \times 11\frac{3}{4}'' \times 3''$, landing $4' \times 6'$. If space permits, have seat $9''$ wide.
1   Punching bag, floor model

4	Sawhorses, 2-18" high, 12" to 24" wide; 1-18" high, 18" wide; 1-4' high, 6' wide with side strips for climbing steps
1	Slide
2	Walking beams or boards, 12' long, clear grain wood, beveled edges and corners, heights varied to meet age need
1	Rocking board

BUILDING BLOCKS

	Block attachments, steering wheels
8	Boards, 6" × 3'
1	set of Unit type solid building blocks, including straight cut as well as circular and arched blocks (500 approximately)
1	set Giant grooved domino blocks
36	Hollow blocks, 12" × 12" × 6", with hand holes or rope handles
12	Hollow blocks, 24" × 6"
12	Hollow blocks, half units, triangles

WHEEL TOYS

1	Engine, large enough to ride on
1	Kiddie Kar, with pedals, different sizes
1	Dump truck, large enough to ride on
2	Tricycles, 16", 20"
1	Wagon, medium
1	Wagon, 34" × 15¾"
1	Wheelbarrow

PLAY SUPPLIES

Apparatus
5	Balls 2–8½" rubber, 2–5" rubber, 1–14" plastic
6	Bean bags
3	Brushes, house painters, for water play
	Egg beaters, funnels, pitchers for water play
	Plastic dishpans, cans, cups, bottles, bowls for water play
6	Jump ropes, 10' long
1	Ringtoss game and rings
	Sand

Sand toys such as spades, shovels, pails, large spools, small dishes, cans
Soap, flakes, granules

PLAYHOUSE

1	Chest, for doll clothes
4	yds. Cloth for doll clothes
6	yds. Cloth for doll covers
10	Cooking utensils, toy, assorted, aluminum
1	Dish cupboard
2	Dishpans
1	Doll, rubber, baby
2	Dolls, 16", unbreakable, white, Negro
1	Doll bed, big enough for children to curl up in
1	Doll carriage
1	set Doll dishes, regular size, unbreakable
2	Housekeeping sets, small size, including broom, dustpan, dust mop
1	Laundry set
1	Mirror, full length 12" × 48"
1	Rocking chair, 11"
1	Sink
1	Stove, toy, wooden, 24" high
1	set Doll table and 2 chairs
	Assortment of artificial fruit and vegetables
2	Telephones, toy
1	Wooden ironing board and wooden iron

Miscellaneous
jewelry, shoes, handbags, hats, coats, dresses for play

PUZZLES

1	Puzzle frame for storage, wooden or steel
12–15	Puzzles, wooden, jigsaw, simple, 7–17 pieces, locked in frame

TOYS

12	Animals, hard rubber or vinyl
1	set Animals, wooden, firm base and scaled to correct proportional sizes
2	boxes Beads, 1" wooden, colored, for stringing (500 to box); shoe strings
1	set Blocks, wood nested

1	set Blocks, parquetry
1	set Blocks, wooden, holed, with wheels and dowels
1	Color cone
1	Lacing boot
1	set Play people, wooden, firm base and scaled to correct proportional sizes: community helpers and family
3–4	Pounding pegboards
5	Pegboards
5	boxes Pegs (100 per box)
2	Pegboards, landscape
6	Push and pull toys
7	Transportation toys, large size, sturdy, wood or metal
	Bus
	Car
	Tractor
	Trains (3) interlocking wooden, flat bottom
	Truck, pickup
	Truck, transfer
	Station wagon
12	Transportation toys, small, sturdy, rubber or wood
	Airplanes
	Boats
	Cars
	Fire engines
	Tractors
	Train and track (2 sets)
	Trucks

51   How the Courts View Preprimary Programs*

LEE O. GARBER, *The University of Pennsylvania*

Establishing educational facilities for the preschool child appears to pose no new legal problems for states or school districts; nevertheless, some administrators and board members raise questions about the authority needed to operate and maintain these programs. Some typical questions:

* Reprinted, with permission, from *Nation's Schools*, June 1966, vol. 77, no. 6. Copyright 1966, McGraw-Hill, Inc., Chicago. All rights reserved.

1. *May the state legislature make provisions for preschool programs if they are not specifically mentioned in its constitution?*

Emphatically, Yes. The legislature does not look to the constitution for a specific grant of authority—only for restraints upon its authority. Unless the constitution prohibits establishment of such schools, and apparently none does, the legislature may provide for them.

2. *May a school board establish preschool facilities in the absence of legislative authority to do so?*

The answer to this question is not clear. Usually the local school district has no inherent authority and must look to the legislature and the constitution for specific grants of power. But there are two exceptions: In addition to those powers specifically granted to it, a local district or school board has (1) all other powers which are necessarily and fairly implied within those specifically granted, and (2) those essential to carry out required duties.

The question then becomes: "Is the authority to maintain facilities for preschool children implied within a general grant of authority to 'maintain schools for the education of children'?" It isn't easy to answer this question because of the difficulty in determining which powers are implied and which are essential. Only the courts can decide, but it's safe to say that few, if any, of our higher courts today would deny a school board the right to maintain preschool facilities. Even in the past, when far less emphasis was placed on social change and its implications, carefully reasoned court decisions upheld the right of a school board to establish and maintain kindergartens in the absence of specific legislative authority.

3. *Are established programs for preschool-age children outside the scope of legislative control?*

Again the answer is emphatic—but this time it is No. While there is little litigation in this area to establish precedent, it seems clear that if a school board sees fit to establish classes for the preschool child—or for out-of-school youth—such classes become a part of the school system and are subject to all legislative enactments that affect the system as a whole. The board, in administering such classes, must observe all statutory provisions for such matters as employment of teachers and so forth.

4. *What is the legal status of the pupil in preschool classes?*

Again, if the board decides to make provisions for such classes, they become a part of the system; and the pupils enrolled take on the status of public school pupils. This means they are subject to the board's rules and regulations for regular pupils.

This appears to be the law as it relates to programs that are purely and clearly educational in character. If, however, such programs have other primary objectives, such as public or individual welfare, it is possible that some courts might hold them illegal, even though they have educational implications. Example: In 1958, the supreme court of Pennsylvania ruled that the school district of Philadelphia was without authority to spend or contribute funds, services, materials or facilities in carrying out an agreement to assist the city in support of a youth conservation commission designed to curb juvenile delinquency.* The court's reasoning:

* **Barth *v*. School District of Philadelphia, 393 Pa. 357, 143 A. (2d) 909 (1958).**

"A program to curb juvenile delinquency, and to control gangs, and to coordinate programs of various agencies of and throughout the city for the purpose of reducing juvenile delinquency and to organize sensitive areas in the city on a block-to-block basis in an effort to improve living conditions—these are not and never have been a part of the function, power or duty of a school or a school district. . . . They are not and never have been a part of or embraced within 'education' as that term has always been understood. . . ."

This is important since it represents one point of view. The other point of view—one which some other courts might accept—is illustrated by the opinion of Justice Musmanno, who wrote a strong dissenting opinion. He said, in part:

"Of what use is education, if instead of inculcating into youth the principles of honesty, morality, patriotism and discipline, it turns out hoodlums, miscreants, ruffians, wrong-doers and criminals?"

Name Index

Subject Index

Adoption, effects of, 237–241
American nursery schools (*see* Nursery schools)

Baltimore Early School Admissions Project, 292
Behavior, human, motivations for, 106
Bell-Magendie law, 188

Child
    behavior, approaches to, 514
    concept formation of, 32–34
    creative development of, 35–36
    curiosity of, inhibited, 85
    disturbed, 51
    dreams of, 213–221, *tables* 214, 219
    early experiences, permanence of, 56–58
    emotional development of, 55–56
    and environmental factors, 340–342
    intelligence, nature of, 16–17
    language development of, 34–35
    mentally retarded, adoption and, 238–239
    misbehavior, dealing with, 337–338
    modeling for, 17–18
    motor-development techniques for, 17–18
    peer groups and, 335
    personal limitations, treatment of, 340
    physical maturity affects self-concept of, 159
    as reactive, 13
    reality-concept of, 221–223, *table* 223
    rediscovery of, 11–12
    self-concept of, 31–32, 159
    self-image of, 333–336
    self-understanding of, 336–344
    social development of, 55–56, 333–334, 338–340
    stimuli and, 18–19

See also Disadvantaged child; Infant; related entries
Codes for future learning, 41–42
Cognition, defined, 265–266
Cognitive development (*see* specific entries)
Cognitive experience versus emotional experience, 190–191
Cognitive skills, overview of, 266–272
Communication, modes of, 429–438
Compensatory education
    codes for future learning in, 41–42
    discontinuity and, 38
    effectiveness of, 45–46
    environment and, 39
    failure and, 42–43
    inadequacies of, 515
    middle-class values and, 46–48
    need for, 48
    programs, nature of, 43–44
    results of, 514–515
    studies measuring, 93–94
    timing of learning experience in, 39–40
Compensatory education, curriculum planning, 497–506
    anti-instructional bias and, 499
    development, role of, 500–501
    evaluation methods, 501–502
    example of, 504–506
    goals of, 498
    medical orientation to, 498–499
    preparation for elementary school and, 502–503
    preschools distinct from, 503–504
    teaching methods, 499–501
Compensatory education, developmental learning approach, 513–521
    principal, role of, 519–520
    psycho-cognitive child diagnosis in, 516
    sequence of stimulation in, 516–518
    social psychological setting in, 519